WE WANT TO HEAR FROM YOU!!

By sharing your opinions about this book, you will help us ensure that you are getting the most value for your textbook dollars. After you've used the book for awhile, please fill out this form fold, tape and drop it in the mail.

Course Title:______________________ Text Title & Author: ______________________

1. Are you a major in this subject? ❒ yes ❒ no ❒ undecided
Were you required to purchase this text? ❒ yes ❒ no

2. Did you purchase this book: ❒ for yourself? ❒ for yourself and at least one other student?
Was a copy available when you needed one? ❒ yes ❒ no

3. Was a study guide available for purchase? ❒ yes ❒ no ❒ don't know
If yes, did you purchase it? ❒ yes ❒ no
Might you purchase it in the future? ❒ yes ❒ no

Fold | Here

4. Were any other supplements to the text available (for example, software, a workbook, etc.)?
❒ yes ❒ no If yes, what? ______________________
Did you purchase any other supplement? ❒ yes ❒ no

5. How far along in the course are you? ❒ only starting ❒ less than midway
❒ more than midway ❒ completed

6. How much have you used this text? ❒ only skimmed it ❒ read/studied a few chapters
❒ read/studied most chapters ❒ read/studied entire text

7. Have you read the introductory material (such as the preface)? ❒ yes ❒ no
Do you feel you know how to effectively use this book? ❒ yes ❒ no

8. Even if you've only skimmed the text, please rate your perception of it in terms of the following:

a) Value as a reference	❒ highly valuable	❒ somewhat valuable	❒ not valuable
b) Readability	❒ consistently clear	❒ sometimes clear	❒ generally unclear
c) Illustrations/photos	❒ very effective	❒ somewhat effective	❒ ineffective
d) Design/use of color	❒ very effective	❒ somewhat effective	❒ ineffective
e) Study help in the text	❒ very effective	❒ somewhat effective	❒ ineffective
f) Level	❒ too difficult	❒ appropriate	❒ too easy/not challenging
g) Problems	❒ too difficult	❒ appropriate	❒ too easy/not challenging
h) OVERALL PERCEPTION:	❒ better than average	❒ average	❒ less than average

Fold | Here

9. Do you find the examples in the text relevant to you? ❒ yes ❒ no
Note any that you find particularly relevant ______________________

10. By looking at the text, do you think it treats the subject as interestingly as possible?
❒ yes ❒ no ❒ hard to tell

11. What do you like most about this book? ______________________
What *don't* you like about this book? ______________________

12. At the end of the semester, what do you intend to do with this text?
❒ keep for future reference ❒ sell back to bookstore or other students ❒ unsure

WILEY

THANK YOU FOR YOUR HELP!

Student Comments

May we quote you?   ☐ Yes   ☐ No

Name _____

School _____

Applied Data Communications
A Business-Oriented Approach

APPLIED DATA COMMUNICATIONS
A BUSINESS-ORIENTED APPROACH

JAMES E. GOLDMAN
Purdue University

John Wiley & Sons, Inc.

New York □ **Chichester** □ **Brisbane** □ **Toronto** □ **Singapore**

ACQUISITIONS EDITOR: Beth Lang Golub
PRODUCTION MANAGER: Linda Muriello
MARKETING MANAGER: Debra Riegert
SENIOR PRODUCTION EDITOR: Marjorie Shustak
SENIOR DESIGNER: Ann Marie Renzi
MANUFACTURING MANAGER: Lori Bulwin
ILLUSTRATION COORDINATORS: Anna Melhorn/Rosa Bryant
ILLUSTRATIONS: Boris Starosta/Nick Nichols
COVER: Photograph by Michael Simpson/FPG
        Designed by David Levy

This book was set in Palatino by ATLIS Graphics & Design, Inc. and printed and bound by R. R. Donnelley (Willard). The cover was printed by Phoenix Color Corp.

Library of Congress Cataloging-in-Publication Data

Goldman, James E.
    Applied data communications : a business-oriented
approach / James E. Goldman.
        p.   cm.
    Includes bibliographical references and index.
    ISBN 0-471-59217-X (acid-free paper)
    1. Electronic data interchange.   2. Business—Communication
systems.   3. Computer networks—Planning.   I. Title.
HF5548.33.G65   1995
658′.0546—dc20   94-9354
                                                                                   CIP

Printed in the United States of America
10 9 8 7 6 5 4 3 2 1

To Susan, Eric, and Grant

Preface

THE GROWING IMPORTANCE OF DATA COMMUNICATIONS

As the business climate of the 1990s continues to evolve, many of the outcomes of this evolution point to an increasingly strategic role for data communications and networking. Increased emphasis on productivity, the dawn of the mobile professional, the flattening of managerial hierarchies, and the downsizing of corporate information systems all depend on well-designed corporate networks to varying degrees. As a result, there has been a corresponding increase in the demand for data communications professionals fluent in both the language of business as well as the language of data communications technology.

THE NEED FOR THIS BOOK

Although several business data communications books have been written, none have placed an on-going emphasis on business orientation as concepts and technology change. None have equipped the student with thinking models through which data communications can be viewed objectively as technology inevitably changes in the future. That is where this book succeeds.

By equipping students first with the analytical models with which to organize data communications and networking requirements as well as the functionality of currently available technology to meet those requirements, this text teaches students how to *do* data communications analysis and design from a business-oriented perspective rather than merely telling students about data communications concepts and technology.

UNIQUE FEATURES OF THE BOOK

Business Orientation

This book starts by familiarizing the student with the forces at work shaping the data communications industry, allowing the student to become an informed player, rather than a victim, of this technology-dominated industry. Realizing that the data communications industry itself is a product of interacting business forces is but a first step toward an awareness of the business orientation of data communications and networking analysis and design.

Thinking Models

Second, the text introduces students to key thinking models such as the top-down model and the Input-Processing-Output model that will be used throughout the text as tools for effective data communications and networking analysis and design. As introduced in Chapter 1, the top-down model forces data communications and networking systems to be viewed from the perspective of the information systems and business objectives which those networks are required to support. Business objectives are discussed first, and final systems designs are always evaluated in terms of their ability to meet stated business objectives. As new data communications concepts and technology are introduced throughout the text, they are continually evaluated as to their proper application through the use of the top-down model.

Business Cases

A real-world, practical approach to the industry is supported by the inclusion of business cases from professional periodicals in the text. Students are required to take real-world examples of implemented networking solutions and apply the facts of the case to the top-down model. In doing so, students are able to evaluate delivered networking functionality in terms of the implemented system's ability to deliver on stated business objectives. Additional questions are asked of the students as a means of gaining insight into objective evaluation of real-world networking solutions. In this way, students gain familiarity with the current trends in business data communications with the assurance of explanations and supporting conceptual material supplied by the text.

Abundant Diagrams

The text is generously endowed with over 360 diagrams illustrating real-world implementations and effective application of networking technology. The diagrams clearly illustrate how business problems are solved in real-world applications with the proper deployment of technology.

Process-Oriented Writing Style

The writing style of the text lends itself well to familiarizing the student with a process-oriented approach to data communications analysis and design. Problems or obstacles to implementation are clearly identified and then investigated and addressed in a logical manner. In this way, students are able to build problem-solving skills and practical thought processes by following the problem-solving logic I have mapped out. The book is easy to read while still serving as a comprehensive technical reference.

ORGANIZATION

Data communications means many different things to different people. As a result, course content of data communications courses varies widely among institutions due to instructor background, department philosophy, laboratory and technology availability, and other factors. This text contains an abundance of material for a first course in data communications regardless of course orientation. The book has been designed so that you can choose the chapters that best fit your course outline. Remaining chapters may prove to be interesting supplementary reading for students, or may even support a different course in data communications. It is my hope that the book will serve as a desk reference for data communications professionals, providing at least a starting point for solving a wide variety of data communications opportunities with a top-down, business oriented approach.

SUPPLEMENTS

Instructor's Manual

The instructor's manual for this text has been specially prepared to offer additional background information for instructors who may not possess a great deal of industry experience in data communications. Teaching tips and annotations on diagrams included in the text offer suggested structure for lectures.

Technology Review sections for most chapters offer practical information on real-world data communications and networking technology associated with concepts covered in each chapter. Specific page number cross references to data communications technology catalogs such as Glasgal Communications' *Network Products Directory* and Black Box Corporation's *Black Box Catalog* are included in all Technology Review sections.

Articles reprinted from professional periodicals such as *Network World* and *LAN Times* are also included as supplementary material in the Instructor's Manual. These articles represent concrete examples of "tools of the trade" for the data communications professional. These articles can be shared with students or be used as background material for preparation of lectures. Suggested additional references for background information are also included for each chapter.

Suggested answers to end-of-chapter review questions and business case study questions are included in the instructor's manual as well.

Computerized Test Bank

In addition to the over 700 review questions included in the text, a computerized test bank with over 700 additional questions is available. Question styles are varied, including multiple choice, true/false, fill-in-the-blank, and short answer.

Multimedia Technology Supplement

A multimedia supplement that explains and illustrates key concepts and technology associated with each chapter is available on 3.5" diskettes. This supplement is especially useful for data communications courses that lack a laboratory equipped with actual technology to be examined. For example, after the concepts of modulation and demodulation are illustrated, modems and their proper implementation are illustrated in detail.

☐ ACKNOWLEDGMENTS

I am indebted to a number of people for their assistance in this undertaking.

For assistance with industry insight early in the development process of the book I'd like to acknowledge Dick Curry of UNUM, Dan Breton of New England Telephone, and last but never least, Jim Palmieri of NYNEX.

For development of original illustrations for the text, as well as supplying insightful suggestions and never wavering support, special thanks go to Curt Snyder of Purdue University.

For his untiring efforts to develop a useful and high quality instructor's manual, as well as his ability to simplify the complex, I thank Dr. Mark Smith of the Computer Technology Department at Purdue University.

For all of their probing questions, youthful energy, and shared excitement over our data communications successes in the networking lab, I'd especially like to thank my students at Purdue University, West Lafayette, Indiana. Your quest for knowledge and your high expectations are the inspiration and energy source for my teaching.

I owe a special debt of gratitude to the dedicated and talented individuals who agreed to serve on the review team for this book. I appreciated your suggestions and guidance as we navigated previously uncharted territory in data communications and networking education. Special thanks to: Dave F. Allen, San Antonio College; Warren W. Benson, University of Nebraska–Omaha; James S. Cross,

Longwood College; Alan Dennis, University of Georgia; Frances Giodzinsky, Sacred Heart University; Akhil Kumar, Cornell University; J. David Naumann, University of Minnesota; Robert O'Brien, City University of New York–Baruch; Tapie Rohm, California State University–San Bernadino; Darcy Running, Hennepin Technical College; Satya Prakash Saraswat, Bentley College; Judith Scheeren, Westmoreland Community College; Jeane A. Schildberg, Chaffey Community College; James Van Speybroeck, St. Ambrose University; Scott Turner, Oklahoma State University; Margaret Whyte, University of Georgia, Robert Wilson, California State University–San Bernadino.

For their help and guidance in helping to transform fresh ideas into a finished product, I would like to thank all of my associates at John Wiley & Sons, especially Beth Lang Golub, Editor, David Kear, Editorial Assistant, and Marjorie Shustak, Production Editor.

Contents

| CHAPTER 7 | **BASIC PRINCIPLES OF WIDE AREA NETWORKING** | **303** |

| CHAPTER 8 | **EMERGING WIDE AREA NETWORKING SERVICES & TECHNOLOGY** | **344** |

Applied Data Communications

A Business-Oriented Approach

Introduction

☐ WHAT IS DATA COMMUNICATIONS?

Data communications is most often defined as the transmission of encoded data via electrical or optical means from one location to another. That probably doesn't mean a whole lot to you at this point, nor should it.

To my way of thinking this definition is far too narrow in scope and, as a result, misses out on the excitement of data communications. Data communications is no longer focused only on the transmission of data.

Today, data communications is an entire field of study unto itself. It is a unique combination of elements of business, information systems, and network engineering. This hybrid area of study is sometimes referred to as "Business Data Communications." The field of data communications is really a complex system of interactive forces in a state of rapidly accelerating change. In Chapter 1, the current state of data communications as well as the skills required to cope with this rapidly changing environment will be explored in detail.

☐ THE BEST WAY TO APPROACH DATA COMMUNICATIONS

If this field is in such a state of constant change—some refer to it as chaos—how can one study data communications and still keep one's sanity?

The primary points to remember are the first two of Goldman's Laws of Data Communications. (For a full listing, see Appendix A.)

Law 1: You will never know all there is to know about data communications.
Law 2: Be honest with yourself concerning what you don't know.

If you can accept these facts, you will be well on your way to survival in this most exciting field.

What, then, can you expect to master in a one-semester course in data communications based around this textbook? After successful mastery of the material contained in this text, you should be able to:

1. Hold an intelligent conversation on a variety of data communications topics.
2. Analyze networking requirements, evaluate networking options, ask proper networking questions, and know where to seek answers to those questions.

Understand, however, that you will not have all the answers. You will not necessarily be qualified to design networks. You will possess enough information to ask essential questions and keep yourself from getting in over your "networking" head.

Data communications can be viewed as a foreign language. Just as the mastery of any foreign language requires practice in speaking and writing that language, so it is with data communications as well. I would encourage you to speak the language as often as possible. Don't be afraid of making mistakes. Form informal study groups if possible and review key concepts by "speaking" data communications. You will be pleasantly surprised at the speed with which you become comfortable with this new language.

☐ ABOUT THE BOOK

General Organization

In order to remain true to the title of this book as a practical, business-oriented text, I have organized the structure of the individual chapters as follows:

1. Each chapter begins with:
   a. An outline of objectives for the chapter
   b. A listing of those concepts being reviewed
   c. A listing of those concepts being introduced
   d. An introduction

2. Within each chapter will be multiple sections entitled "In Sharper Focus." These sections either introduce related additional topics or provide more in-depth coverage of previously introduced concepts. The "In Sharper Focus" sections may or may not be assigned at the discretion of individual instructors.

3. Management Perspective sections are highlighted throughout the text to indicate business-oriented outlooks on a variety of data communications topics.

4. To reinforce the business implications of data communications, business case studies will be presented whenever possible and appropriate. These case studies are, in most cases, based on real industry applications of data communications. These business analysis activities will allow the student to apply technological solutions to business opportunities.

5. Charts and diagrams will summarize key concepts in all chapters. It is my hope that this text will be useful to you as a practicing data communications professional long after you have completed this course.

6. Each chapter will close with review questions as well as activities to apply studied concepts, references for further reading, key terms, key points to remember, and key questions to ask or things to watch out for when dealing with the technology or concepts covered in each chapter.

Chapter Synopsis

As mentioned previously, Chapter 1 introduces the data communications industry, its players, and those skills necessary to actively participate in this industry successfully. Perhaps more importantly, Chapter 1 begins to explain what is meant by the *business* implications of *business data communications*. Chapter 1 also introduces several models or frameworks in which to organize one's analysis of the dynamic field of data communications. The focus of the chapter is to supply the reader with a set of thinking tools or models which will enable the reader to develop dynamic thinking processes with which to make sense of this often confusing industry.

Once we understand the environment in which we must function, Chapter 2 equips us with the basic concepts and jargon needed in order to "talk" data communications.

Chapter 3 starts our tour of networking technology options. PC connectivity refers to all those ways we can communicate to and from a standalone PC *other than* a local area network (LAN).

In Chapter 4, we will look at the proper business application of available local area networking technology from a functional or logical standpoint. This process is known as logical network design.

In Chapter 5, we examine currently available Local Area Networking technology in order to complete our physical network design. This portion of the network design entails choosing the correct networking components for integration into our physical network implementation.

The next logical progression following individual LAN implementation would naturally be to link these LANs. Chapter 6 introduces the fast-paced world of Internetworking which addresses the challenge of linking LANs of various topologies, operating systems and geographic locations.

Wide area networking and its relationship to the telecommunications industry and its services are addressed in Chapter 7 and Chapter 8. The relationship between end-user business demand, phone companies' profitability and wide area networking services offered by the phone companies will be explored in depth. Chapter 7 discusses principles of wide area networking such as switching and transmission architectures while Chapter 8 explores emerging WAN services and technologies such as ISDN, frame relay, SONET, SMDS, and ATM.

Once we understand local area networks, Internetworking, and wide area networks, Chapter 9 takes an in-depth look at all that is involved with enterprise networks and client–server architectures which, in many cases, employ a combination of these three networking categories. We will examine both the business motivation and technological implementation issues which account for the current popularity of this architecture.

The unique requirements and options of voice transmission and the integration of data and voice transmission will be addressed in Chapter 10. Business impact of the proper use of voice transmission options will be detailed.

The networking aspects of videoconferencing, imaging, and multimedia and the financial implications and break-even analysis of these technologies will be analyzed in Chapter 11.

Chapter 12 will provide insight into the "how-to" of network analysis and design. The need to begin any such analysis with a thorough understanding of business needs and constraints will be stressed.

Having mastered the vocabulary, technology, business implications and analytical skills of data communications, Chapter 13 attempts to take another look at the data communications industry with an eye towards the future. Future technologies, network services, and their implication for the data communications professional are explored.

CHAPTER · 1

The Current State of the Data Communications Industry

Concepts Reinforced

What Is Data Communications?

Concepts Introduced

Data Communications as a System
    Major Systems Components:

Technology	Manufacturers
Regulatory	Standards
Carriers	Vendors/consultants
Research	Business users
Users	Political/legislative

Deregulation and Divestiture
Top-Down Model
Input-Processing-Output Model (IPO)
OSI Reference Model
Data Communications Careers and Required Skills

OBJECTIVES

Upon successful completion of this chapter, you should be able to:

1. Understand today's data communications industry as a system of interacting components.

2. Understand the driving forces at work within the data communications industry.

3. Understand the current state of the data communications industry as well as the major issues facing each of the industry's constituent components.

4. Given the current status and driving forces, understand the likely future scenarios for various data communications industry constituencies.

5. Understand the structure and importance of the top-down model.

6. Understand the relationship of network analysis and design to information systems analysis and design.

INTRODUCTION

Data communications is a field of study and industry in a most rapid state of change. The overall objective of this chapter is to introduce the reader to a series of models or thinking frameworks into which one can organize thoughts, facts, requirements, solutions, and technology. By mastering these thinking models, the reader will be developing a business-oriented, technology-independent process for the analysis and design of data communications systems.

☐ DATA COMMUNICATIONS AS A SYSTEM

The classic definition of data communications as stated earlier in the introduction as "the encoded transmission of data via electrical or optical means" is really just the goal or outcome of a much larger process collectively known as Data Communications.

The field of data communications is so vast and changing so rapidly that it is necessary to break it down into a series of more manageable components. These components can then be studied individually and analyzed as to how they interact with other components of the data communications industry.

Figure 1-1 shows one way of breaking the complex world of data communications into a group of interacting components.

In order to understand the entire system known as data communications, its constituent components must first be understood. Each component will be examined in detail, exploring the present state of each in the diagram as well as some history related to how each segment of the data communications industry reached its present state. Most of the discussion of the future trends of each of these industry segments will be postponed until Chapter 13, "Where Do We Go From Here? Trends to Watch."

As can be seen from the diagram, data communications is the sum total of the interacting components outlined. There is no distinct beginning nor end. No one component is more important than another. Therefore, it is really rather arbitrary where to start a detailed analysis of the system components.

No better example can probably be found in this diagram of two components so tightly dependent upon each other and in as constant and on-going state of change than **regulatory agencies** and **carriers**. At this early stage in the study of data communications, it is sufficient to define regulatory agencies as state and federal agencies charged with regulating telecommunications, and carriers as what are commonly referred to as phone companies.

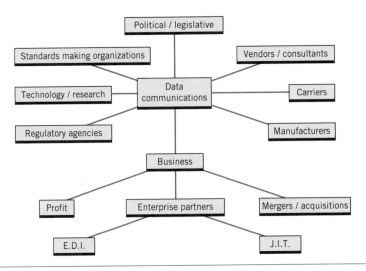

Figure 1-1 Today's data communication environment.

☐ REGULATORY AND CARRIERS

In order to fully understand these two important components of today's data communications environment, their interaction, those forces that join them and influence their present status, must be focused on. This interaction is a rather formal process of a series of proposals from the carriers to the state and federal regulatory agencies and the issuance of rulings and approvals in return. This relationship is illustrated in Figure 1-2.

Divestiture and Deregulation

Today's competitive telecommunications industry in the United States is largely the result of rulings by the Justice Department in the early 1980s. These rulings are generally referred to as **deregulation** and **divestiture**. These two terms are related but not synonymous.

Prior to deregulation and divestiture, America's telecommunications needs (data and voice hardware and services) were all supplied, with few exceptions, by one vendor: AT&T—American Telephone and Telegraph. At that time, homeowners were not allowed to purchase and install their own phones, something taken for granted today.

Local Bell operating companies provided local service but were still a part of AT&T. All telephone service, local as well as long-distance, was coordinated through one telecommunications organization. Most indoor wiring was also the responsibility of AT&T, not the owner of the building in which the wiring existed.

This top-to-bottom control of the telecommunications industry was seen as a monopoly, especially by other telecommunications vendors wishing to compete in the industry.

As a result, the two previously mentioned rulings, *deregulation* and *divestiture* were enacted in the late 1970s and early 1980s. Rulings concerning deregulation and divestiture continue to be handed down today through interpretation of a ruling known as the **Modified Final Judgement**, or **MFJ**, as issued by Federal Judge Harold Greene in 1982.

During the summer of 1991, a ruling was issued which allowed telecommunications companies to sell information services over their own networks. This ruling is being challenged by potential competitors in the information services arena such as newspaper publishers and cable TV operators. More about the possible outcomes of this situation will be analyzed in Chapter 13 when a look at possible future scenarios in the telecommunications industry is taken.

Divestiture broke up the network services of AT&T into separate long-distance and local service companies. AT&T would retain the right to offer long-distance services while the former local Bell operating companies were grouped into new **regional bell operating companies (RBOCs)** to offer local telecommunications service. See Figure 1-3 for a listing of RBOCs and their constituent former Bell operating companies.

Deregulation, on the other hand, addressed an entirely different aspect of the telecommunications industry in the United States: the ability of "phone compa-

Figure 1-2 Systems relationship of regulatory and carriers.

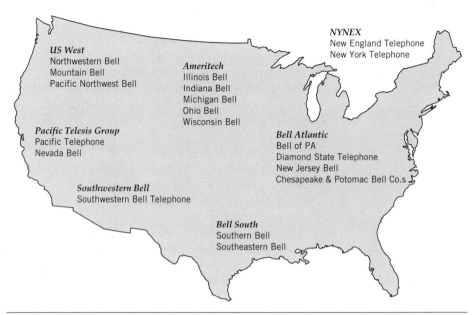

Figure 1-3 22 BOCs become 7 RBOCs.

nies" in America to compete in an unrestricted manner in other industries such as the computer and information systems fields.

Prior to deregulation, phone companies were either banned from doing business in other industries or were subject to having their profits and/or rates monitored or "regulated" in a similar fashion to the way in which their rates for phone service were regulated.

As a result of deregulation, both AT&T and the RBOCs were allowed to enter into other industries by forming additional subsidiaries. For the first time, phone companies were competing in a market-driven, customer-dictated economy. A common misconception about deregulation is that phone companies became totally deregulated and can basically charge whatever the market will bear for phone services. This is not the case.

Phone companies today have both regulated and deregulated portions of their business, often segregated into separate companies. See Figure 1-4 for an example

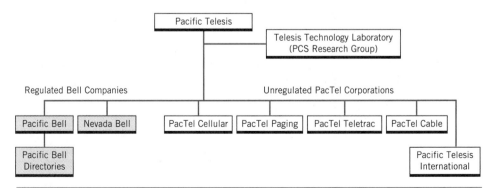

Figure 1-4 Pacific Telesis Group organization chart.

of the regulated and deregulated segments of Pacific Telesis (PACTEL), one of the post-divestiture RBOCs.

Network services offered by phone companies are still regulated. New rate proposals from phone companies are filed as tariffs with state or federal regulatory authorities. Local service rate changes are filed on the state level with a particular state's Public Utilities Commission and on a federal level with the Federal Communications Commission for interstate service proposals and rate change requests.

These commissions must balance objectives which are sometimes contradictory:

1. Basic phone service must remain affordable enough that all residents of a state can afford it. This guarantee is sometimes known as "universal service" or "universal access."
2. Phone companies must remain profitable in order to be able to afford to constantly reinvest in upgrading their physical resources (hardware, cables, buildings) as well as educating and training their human resources.

☐ THE BUSINESS OF DEREGULATION AND DIVESTITURE

There were, and continue to be, three main parties affected by deregulation and divestiture. The first two parties involved should be obvious:

1. The former AT&T, which is now AT&T plus the RBOCs.
2. The competitors to AT&T, which had been excluded from the telecommunications industry.

Each of these had something to gain, and perhaps lose, through the processes of deregulation and divestiture. The third party involved in the process who have truthfully been more recipients, but some would say victims, of the process rather than active participants are:

3. The telecommunications users of the United States.

Figure 1-5 illustrates these parties and summarizes the effects, both positive and negative, of deregulation and divestiture on each.

As Figure 1-5 is analyzed, a few points are worth noting. AT&T's big gain was permission to compete in the lucrative computer industry. There was talk at the time that AT&T with its vast financial resources and imbedded customer base would rival IBM for market share. In fact, that never happened. After a largely unsuccessful and costly venture into the field, AT&T acquired computer and information systems industry expertise by merging with NCR Corporation of Dayton, Ohio in 1991.

Another very important adjustment on the part of AT&T and the RBOCs was the realization that competing in a customer-oriented, market-driven industry such as the divested telecommunications industry would require a significant change in corporate culture and attitudes. Some members of the former monopoly have done better than others at working with both residential and business customers to deliver outstanding customer service.

From a telecommunications user's standpoint, one nice thing about having only one phone company was that it was easy to know who to call for new service or a repair problem. Installation and maintenance of hardware, as well as long-distance and local service for voice or data were all coordinated through one company.

BEFORE

Players	Status Quo	Pros	Cons
AT&T/RBOCs	Totally regulated environment Market not customer driven Noncompetition environment	No competition Effective monopoly	Barred from other nonregulated industries
Users	One telecommunications vendor	No finger-pointing among telecom vendors "One-stop shopping" Total coordination	Occasional "take it or leave it" attitude on part of phone company
Other telecom companies	Largely barred from market entry	?	"Out in the cold"

AFTER

Players	Status Quo	Pros	Cons
AT&T/RBOCs	Divestiture Deregulation	Branched into unregulated industries	Unfamiliar with customer driven markets
Users	Many competing telecom vendors	More competitive pricing in some cases	Much finger-pointing among competing vendors Coordination nightmare
Other telecom companies	Equal access to local switches	Free to compete on level playing field in multi-billion-dollar industry	?

Figure 1-5 Deregulation and divestiture players: winners and losers?

It is this loss of coordinated installation and troubleshooting which is perhaps the biggest loss to telecommunications users as a result of deregulation and divestiture. Service problems often result in finger-pointing between hardware vendors, local service carriers, and long-distance carriers. The telecommunications users are left rather helplessly in the middle. Believe it or not, it is actually illegal in most cases for the three aforementioned vendors to get together to solve a service problem unless specifically and officially requested to do so by the customer. This request is not immediately met, however. Schedules must be coordinated and the entire coordination process must be carefully monitored and documented so as not to undercut the initial purpose of divestiture, namely, the fostering of competition in the telecommunications industry.

Competing long-distance carriers such as MCI and U.S. Sprint are now allowed to sell long-distance services on a level playing field with AT&T thanks to a result of divestiture known as **equal access**. This means that AT&T must be treated like any other long-distance carrier by the local BOCs in terms of access to the local carrier switching equipment, and ultimately to their customers. Ironically, this equal treatment was carried to an extreme in some cases when, immediately after divestiture, some AT&T sales offices had difficulty getting phones installed for local service because the local carriers were treating AT&T like any other new business without a credit history.

While examining Figure 1-5, consider the gains and losses of each of the major deregulation and divestiture players. Were there clear winners and losers?

In September 1992, the FCC enacted additional rulings that enabled competition in the *local loop*. Prior to these rulings, only the RBOCs were allowed to transport calls from a residence or business to the local *CO* (central office) and ultimately to the point of presence (POP) of any of the long-distance carriers. The local loop represented the last remnants of the former telecommunications monopoly.

In addition, local area alternate carriers such as MFS (Metropolitan Fiber Systems) were only allowed to transport calls from buildings which were attached directly to MFS's own fiber equipment, in an arrangement known as metropolitan area networks.

A *central office* is a facility belonging to the local phone company in which calls are switched to their proper destination. If that destination is considered a long-distance call, then the call is switched to a long-distance company's switching facility, which is known as a *point of presence*. The particular long-distance company's point of presence to which the call is transferred is determined by the user's choice of long-distance carrier.

Through a mandated process known as **co-location**, RBOCs must allow alternate carriers, such as MFS, to install their equipment in the RBOC's central office in order to gain equal access to the *private* or *leased line* traffic from the CO to the POP. The rulings opened only the leased line market immediately, while proposing opening competition in the *switched* traffic market at a later date.

Obviously, the RBOCs are not going to allow co-location of alternate carrier's equipment for free. In addition, having analyzed the gains and losses of the players involved in the original AT&T divestiture and deregulation, it should be clear that the RBOCs must have gained something in the deal. What the RBOCs gained was pricing flexibility in what they are allowed to charge for *access charges* for co-location of the alternate carrier's equipment in their COs.

Perhaps the most significant change from the end-user's perspective is the ability for end-users to also co-locate networking equipment in the RBOC's CO. Businesses can now build their own virtual private networks by co-locating their own networking equipment in local phone company central offices. Remembering that this ruling only affects leased line traffic, only those businesses which have a need for point to point or multipoint leased lines, usually for data transmission, are likely to benefit from the more competitive pricing and additional service offerings likely to materialize as a result of this ruling. The average consumer using only switched services is not likely to benefit from this ruling unless the divestiture is extended fully into the switched traffic arena.

☐ POLITICS AND THE LEGISLATIVE AND JUDICIAL PROCESSES

It is important to note that the initial divestiture and deregulation of the telecommunications industry was *not* the result of a purely regulatory process. This enormously important event was primarily a judicial process fought out in the courtrooms, largely fostered by one man, Bill McGowan, former president of MCI.

Although the FCC, a federal regulatory agency, initially ruled in 1971 that MCI could compete with AT&T for long-distance service, it was McGowan's 1974 lawsuit that got the Justice Department involved and led to the actual breakup of the telecommunications monopoly in America. The Justice Department, primarily U.S. District Court Judge Harold Greene, continues to monitor the telecommunications industry and issue directives regulating the industry through a judicial, rather than regulatory process.

Another interesting alternative form of regulation of the telecommunications industry can emerge from the political or legislative arena. If and when the regulatory or judicial branches of government allow the telecommunications industry to function in a manner that may not please certain special interest groups, an enormous lobbying effort can be launched. The result of this lobbying campaign may be the introduction by politicians of legislation seeking to control the telecommunications industry in a manner favorable to the special interest group.

For example, in 1991 the Bell operating companies were given permission to offer information services over their networks to consumers as a value-added service. Other industries, such as the publishing and newspaper industry who were seeking to offer their own on-line information systems at the time, felt that letting the phone companies offer information service over their own networks gave them an unfair advantage.

As a result, numerous bills were introduced in Congress to either ban outright or restrict the Bell companies' abilities to offer information services over their own networks. Political discussions and legislation on this issue as well as other telecommunications issues will undoubtedly continue in the future. The Justice Department will also likely play an ongoing role in the telecommunications industry as well.

☐ ROLE OF STANDARDS-MAKING AGENCIES IN DATA COMMUNICATIONS

Why Are Standards Important?

A careful examination of Figure 1-1 may have pointed out the relationship between the *standards* component and the *manufacturers* component of the data communications environment.

Standards are very important to users of data communications technology. For example:

1. Standards allow users to *physically* connect cables and equipment manufactured by different vendors with some assurance or predictability of operation. For instance, the RS-232 interface, illustrated in Figure 1-6, describes a physical standard for the common 25-pin data connector known as a DB-25. The meaning of the presence or absence of an electrical signal on any one of the 25 pins is understood by all who either manufacture or interface to the connector. Utter chaos would exist without such a standard. The RS-232 standard will be explained in detail in Chapter 2.

2. Other standards are more concerned with the internal *operational* specifications of data communications equipment. For example, operational standards for Token Ring Networks, which will be introduced in Chapter 4, have been developed so that hardware and software manufactured by different vendors can all work together.

☐ HOW DOES THE STANDARDS MAKING PROCESS WORK?

Standards Making Organizations

There are several national as well as international organizations whose work is significant to the data communications industry. Figure 1-7 summarizes information regarding some of these key standards-making organizations.

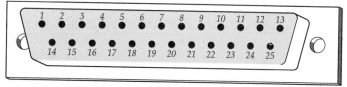

Pin Number	Signal Designation	Pin Number	Signal Designation
1	Protective ground	14	Secondary transmit data
2	Transmit data	15	Transmit clock (DCE)
3	Receive data	16	Secondary receive data
4	Request to send	17	Receive clock
5	Clear to send	18	Local loop back
6	Data set ready	19	Secondary request to send
7	Signal ground	20	Data terminal ready
8	Carrier detect	21	Signal quality detector
9	Positive DC test voltage	22	Ring indicator
10	Negative DC test voltage	23	Data signal rate selector
11	Unassigned	24	Transmit clock (DTE)
12	Secondary carrier detect	25	Busy
13	Secondary clear to send		

Figure 1-6 RS-232 interface, a physical standard.

The contributions of each of these organizations in the area of standards development will be outlined in subsequent chapters of the text.

The OSI Seven-Layer Model

One contribution of the International Standards Organization (ISO) is of such importance that it should be introduced here and will be referred to continually throughout the text.

As an introduction, the OSI (open systems interconnection) Model will be described in general terms, leaving specifics and reinforcing examples of the use of

Full Name	Abbreviation	Authority/Charter	Mission/Major Contributions
International Standards Organization	ISO	International; voluntary	OSI 7-layer model
Comité Consultatif International Télégraphique et Téléphonique	CCITT	International; U.N.-chartered	Telecommunications standards
International Telecommunications Union	ITU-T	International; U.N.-chartered	Parent organization and successor to CCITT
American National Standards Institute	ANSI	U.S. government representative to ISO	Information systems standards
Institute of Electrical and Electronics Engineers	IEEE	Industrial professional society	Local area network standards

Figure 1-7 Standards making organizations.

the model for later chapters. One of the most important things to remember about the OSI Model is that *it is not a standard, nor a collection of standards.*

The OSI model, as illustrated in Figure 1-8, is a framework or an architecture in which standards can be developed, compared, and understood. The OSI Model allows data communications technology developers as well as standards developers to talk about the interconnection of two networks or computers in common terms without dealing in proprietary vendor jargon.

These "common terms" are the result of the layered architecture of the **OSI seven-layer model.** The architecture breaks the task of two computers communicating into separate but interrelated tasks, each represented by its own layer. As can be seen in Figure 1-8, the top layer (Layer 7) represents the application program running on each computer and is therefore aptly named the *application layer.* The bottom layer (Layer 1) is concerned with the actual physical connection of the two computers or networks and is therefore named the *physical layer.* The remaining layers (2 through 6) may not be as obvious but, none the less, represent a sufficiently distinct logical group of functions required to connect two computers as to justify a separate layer.

Perhaps the best analogy for the OSI Reference Model, which illustrates its architectural or framework purpose, is that of a blueprint for a large office building or skyscraper. The various subcontractors on the job may only be concerned with the "layer" of the plans that outlines their specific job specifications. However, each specific subcontractor needs to be able to depend on the work of the "lower" layer subcontractors just as the subcontractors of the "upper" layers depend on these subcontractors performing their function to specification.

Similarly, each layer of the OSI Model operates independently of all other layers, while depending upon neighboring layers to perform according to specification while cooperating in the attainment of the overall task of communication between two computers or networks.

The OSI Reference Model has its weaknesses, which will be pointed out later in the text. However, its value as a common starting point from which any data com-

Layer	Major Functionality	Blueprint
7: Application	Layer where application programs reside; layer that the user interfaces with	*Furnishings:* chairs, couches, tables, paintings
6: Presentation	Assures reliable session transmission between applications; takes care of differences; data representation	*Interior Carpentry:* cabinets, shelves, mouldings
5: Session	Enables two applications to communicate across the network	*Electrical:* connection between light switch and light wiring
4: Transport	Assures reliable transmission from end-to-end, usually across multiple nodes	*Heating/Cooling/Plumbing:* furnace, A/C, ductwork
3: Network	This layer sets up the pathways, or end-to-end connections usually across a long distance, or multiple nodes	*Structural:* studs, dry wall
2: Data Link	Puts messages together, attaches proper headers to be sent out or received, assures messages are delivered between two points	*Foundation:* concrete support upon which entire structure is built
1: Physical	Layer that is concerned with transmitting bits of data over a physical medium	*Excavation:* site preparation to allow other phases (layers) to proceed according to plans

Figure 1-8 The OSI reference model.

munications user or vendor can start a conversation regarding data communications functions or standards cannot be minimized.

Significant use of the OSI Model will be made in Chapters 5 and 6 during the study of local area networks and internetworking. At that time, and in subsequent chapters, the functional characteristics of each of the seven layers of the OSI model will be explained further. Numerous examples of protocols specific to each layer of the OSI model will be supplied as well.

The Standards Making Process

Although the charter of each standards making organization dictates the exact procedure for standards development, the process can be generalized as follows:

1. *Recognition* of the need for a standard.
2. *Formation* of some type of committee or task force.
3. *Information/recommendation gathering* phase.
4. *Tentative/alternative standards* issued.
5. *Feedback* on tentative/alternative standards.
6. *Final standards* issued.
7. *Compliance* with final standards.

☐ WHAT DO MANUFACTURERS HAVE TO GAIN/LOSE FROM STANDARDIZATION?

Development Precedes Standardization

The standards making process is very important to manufacturers and one which they monitor closely and participate in actively. It is important to understand that the development of new technology most often precedes the standardization of that new technology. The development process is often carried out at a significant expense by either individual or groups of manufacturers as part of research and development work. Competing manufacturers may propose differing technological solutions to a given opportunity. It is often only after these competing technologies are about to come to market that the need for standardization prompts the formation of a standards committee. It should be obvious that competing manufacturers have a strong desire to get their own technology declared as "the standard." Make no mistake about it, standards making can be a very political process.

Furthermore, by the time standards are actually adopted for a given technology, the next generation of that technology is sometimes ready to be introduced to the market. Figure 1-9 attempts to illustrate this time lag between technological development and standards resolution.

It should be noted, however, that in some cases standards are actually developed *before* the introduction of related technology. For example, standards for metropolitan area networks (MANs) were completed by the IEEE 802.6 committee before major development of MAN technology. MANs will be studied further in Chapter 8.

The Economic Power of Standards

At times, nonofficial or defacto standards are developed. An example will illustrate the clear economic power of standards. Prior to the widespread distribution of the IBM PC there were two major microcomputer operating systems: MS-DOS and CPM. IBM chose MS-DOS as their operating system of choice and the rest is history. When is the last time you heard of CPM?

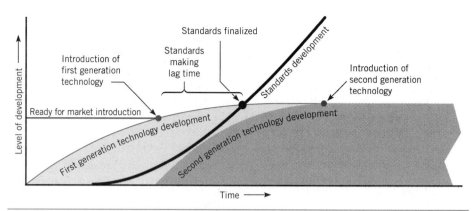

Figure 1-9 Technology and standards development.

Another example of the economic power of standards is the issuance by the U.S. government of **GOSIP** or government OSI procurement guidelines. These are not the typical standards developed through a formal process as outlined above, followed by the compliance of manufacturers. Rather, these standards are issued by a single customer, in this case the U.S. government, which in effect says, "If you want to sell computer or data communications equipment to us, that equipment must meet these standards." Given the buying power of the U.S. government, such a non-negotiated standard carries significant clout.

WHAT SHOULD USERS BE AWARE OF REGARDING STANDARDS?

In general, standards work to the advantage of the data communications consumer as they provide assurance as to the interoperability of equipment manufactured by a variety of vendors.

However, users should be aware of at least two standards-related issues that can cause confusion and potentially lead to bad purchase decisions and operational nightmares.

Standards "Extensions"

Recalling the potentially competitive nature of the standards making process, it should come as no surprise that final standards are sometimes "least common denominator" implementations of competing proposals. Although we will discuss network management in detail later in the text, the standards setting process for multivendor network management provides an excellent example of the danger of the "least common denominator" standards setting approach.

Multivendor network management systems store information about the operation of the network in something called a management information base (MIB). Competing vendors each had their own idea about how information should be stored in the MIB and a compromise MIB definition was reached. That's the good news.

The bad news is that vendors then proceeded to build "extensions" to the "standard" MIB definition for their systems. Naturally, one vendor's "extensions" do not necessarily match all the other vendors' "extensions." It should be pointed out that in some cases, one vendor's network management software may, in fact, support another vendor's MIB extensions.

Users must be careful to ensure not only that a particular vendor's equipment meets industry standards, but *how* the equipment meets the standard and whether or not the vendor has implemented extensions to the standard.

The Jargon Jungle

As noted above, standards usually revolve around the *physical*, sometimes called *interface*, or *operational* characteristics of data communications equipment. Unfortunately, standards do not apply to the vocabulary used by sales people and marketing agencies to describe that equipment.

As a result, the data communications user is trapped in a situation sometimes referred to as the "jargon jungle." Competing manufacturers often call similar features or operational characteristics by different names, leaving it to the data communications consumer to sort out the differences. In other words, although there may be technical definitions to words like "bridge" and "router," there is nothing to prevent sales people from using these words as they wish in addition to coining new phrases such as "brouter" or "bridging router." There is no standards making body that regulates data communications vocabulary and its use.

Put another way:

Law 3: There are no data communications police.

The best way to prevent being lost in the jargon jungle is to ask questions, lots of questions. Be prepared to determine functionality of equipment based on operational characteristics rather than on package labels.

In order to stay abreast of current activity in the standards making arena, following the "Standards Watch" section that appears in each month's issue of *Data Communications* magazine, or other data communications related publications, may be beneficial.

DATA COMMUNICATIONS IS BUSINESS

Just as the Regulatory and Carriers components of the data communications environment were grouped together based upon their respective interactions, the remaining component entities portrayed in Figure 1-1 can be legitimately grouped together based upon their most important interactive force: *business.*

Unlike the formal interactions of proposals and rulings that join regulatory and carrier components, the interacting forces which join the remaining components as well as carriers are supply and demand, basic economic concepts. That's right, *data communications is business.*

Figure 1-10 attempts to illustrate graphically the complex relationship between these many data communications environment components. The present status and near-term trends of any particular component are directly related to the net effect of the supply and demand forces of all other components combined.

As an example, business and users may *demand* faster transfer of data. However, if research has not *supplied* the technology to accomplish these faster transfers, then manufacturers cannot produce and *supply* (sell) these products to business and users while vendors and consultants cannot distribute and recommend their use. (This relationship between user demand and vendors' ability to meet that demand is clearly described in Stan Levine's article, "The Tactics Behind Strategic Relationships and Alliances" in this chapter's featured references section in the text supplement.)

Figure 1-10 will continue to be an effective analysis tool for determining what

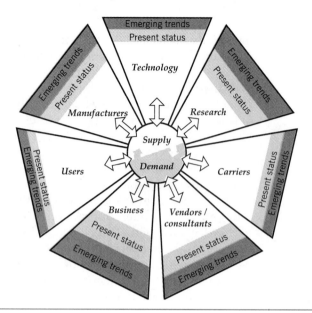

Figure 1-10 Supply and demand in data communications.

forces are really at work behind current data communications-related business strategies and announcements. Like many of the models introduced in this text, the strength of Figure 1-10 comes from its overall organization or framework architecture in which the current status or detailed information can change over time without diminishing the effectiveness of the overall model.

☐ TECHNOLOGY AS AN ENABLER

As indicated by both the "Supply & Demand" model illustrated in Figure 1-10 and the "Today's Data Communications Environment" diagram illustrated in Figure 1-1, the current sophistication level of basic technology dictates the eventual sophistication of data communications equipment. Before examining some of these enabling technologies further, it is first necessary to gain a more thorough understanding of data communications processing in general.

In its most basic form, data communications is nothing more than "getting bits and pieces of data from here to there" (wherever there is). Dovetailing on this slight oversimplification, it would follow that business data communications must be "getting bits and pieces of data from here to there as cheaply as possible."

Given these two definitions, two overriding trends in the development of data communications technology today are, as illustrated in Figure 1-11:

1. Get the bits and pieces of data delivered *faster*.
2. Get the bits and pieces of data delivered *cheaper*.

Figure 1-11 Overriding trends in data communications.

Additional overriding trends of business data communications will become evident throughout the remainder of the book.

In general, the process that nearly any piece of data communications hardware goes through as it attempts to deliver these bits and pieces of data might be simply summarized as illustrated in Figure 1-12.

THE I-P-O MODEL

Later in the text, as various pieces of data communications technology are analyzed, the steps outlined in Figure 1-12 will be kept in mind. The analysis of data communications equipment could actually be simplified even further by summarizing the overall process into just three steps.

1. The data comes *in*.
2. The data gets *processed*.
3. The data goes *out*.

In order to understand the basic function of any piece of data communications equipment, one really need only understand the differences between the characteristics of the data that came *in* and the data that went *out*. Those differences identified were *processed* by the data communications equipment being analyzed.

This *input–processing–output* or **I-P-O model** is another key model which will be used throughout the textbook in order to analyze a wide variety of data communications equipment and opportunities. The I-P-O model is more formally introduced in Chapter 2.

Figure 1-13 outlines the state-of-the-art enabling technologies that underlie the achievement of today's data communications environment's overriding objectives of "faster" and "cheaper" delivery of data from here to there. Particular enabling technologies are associated with individual steps of the data communications processing as outlined previously in Figure 1-12.

A detailed discussion of these technologies is inappropriate at this early stage of the text or, in some cases, at all in a text of this level. However, some explanation is appropriate in order to understand the impact of enabling technologies on manufactured data communications equipment.

VLSI stands for very large scale integration, a process through which very powerful, and fast, computer chips are made very small. As larger numbers of these tiny, powerful CPU chips are manufactured, economies of scale contribute to a lower per chip price. The result is that these relatively cheap, powerful chips are included in various pieces of data communications hardware delivering the two primary trends in hardware development—faster and cheaper.

Another way in which data communications equipment can function faster is by temporarily storing bits and pieces of data which are either waiting to be examined and processed or waiting to be sent on their way to their proper destination. High-density memory chips capable of storing millions of characters of data can

1. *Receive* the bits and pieces of data.
2. *Examine* the bits and pieces of data.
3. *Decide* how to *Process* the data.
4. *Send* the data to its proper destination.

Figure 1-12 Major data communication processes.

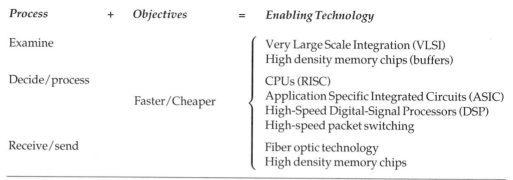

Figure 1-13 Major data communication processes/technology.

now be included at a reasonable cost in many different pieces of data communications equipment. These memory chips are gathered together to form *memory buffers*, which temporarily hold data in order to speed the overall processing of the piece of data communications equipment.

Examination and processing of data can be accomplished more quickly using application specific integrated circuits (ASIC). These chips are designed for only a single processing purpose and instructions are often included right in the chip. This "permanent software" is sometimes referred to as "firmware."

The actual handling and passing of the bits and pieces of data has increased in speed thanks to developments in digital signal processors and high-speed packet switching equipment. These parts of a piece of data communications equipment are charged with seeing to it that the bits and pieces of data get sent to the proper destination, in the proper format, at the proper time.

Finally, the speed with which these bits and pieces can be sent from one point to another has been increased significantly thanks to advances in fiber optic technology. Fiber optic technology will be studied in several later chapters. However, it is important to note at this time that data transmission capacities in the range of billions of characters per second are a real possibility thanks to fiber optic technology.

Although the enabling technologies outlined in Figure 1-13 will most certainly evolve and change, the basic processes of data communications as well as the overall objectives of "faster and cheaper" should remain fairly constant.

Therefore, as an informed participant in the data communications industry, you should be able to add new enabling technologies to Figure 1-13, and anticipate their impact on newly developed data communications equipment, which may utilize these new enabling technologies.

☐ BUSINESS DEMAND + AVAILABLE TECHNOLOGY = EMERGING NETWORK SERVICES

This same enabling or available technology plays a key role in the relationship between business and carriers. Understanding that:

1. The phone companies (carriers) are in business to make a profit.
2. The phone companies (carriers) need to sell the network services which business is willing to buy at a price business is willing to pay.

It therefore should follow that these enabling technologies tie the business demand for network services to the carrier's supply of network services. Stated another way, a carrier cannot provide the network services that businesses demand without the proper technology in place. Carriers can only afford to invest in new technology through profitable operations.

Figure 1-14 provides some examples of the relationship between business demand, available technology, and emerging network services. Network services are included at this point only to illustrate the relationship between the three data communications industry components. Both the technology and network services listed in Figure 1-14 will be discussed in depth later in the text.

As the various business demands in Figure 1-14 are analyzed, similarities in the data communication characteristics and the network requirements to deliver these demands are highlighted in the column labeled "Overall Characteristics of Enabling Data Communications Applications."

Videoconferencing, Full Motion Video, Imaging, CAD (computer-assisted design), CAM (computer-assisted manufacturing), CAE (computer-assisted engineering), and LAN (local area network) interconnection all send large amounts of data which need to be sent very quickly. Most of these aforementioned applications are screen-oriented and need that entire screen's worth of data delivered all together, instantaneously.

Bandwidth

Large amounts of data requiring very fast transmission require large amounts of what is known as *bandwidth*. Although bandwidth will be discussed in more detail later, for now, an analogy may help. Think of these data delivery requirements as water delivery requirements. A single family home has smaller water delivery requirements than a factory that uses water in its manufacturing operations. The single family home will have a smaller diameter inlet pipe (less bandwidth), while the factory will have a much larger diameter inlet pipe (greater bandwidth).

On an application-oriented basis, videoconferencing or multimedia applications require a great deal more bandwidth than local area network interconnec-

Business Opportunities for Improvement	Business Solutions	Business Demand (Data Comm Applications)	Overall Characteristics of Enabling Data Comm Applications	Technologies	Network Services
Profitability	Reduce expenses Reduce inventory Reduce travel Enterprise Partnerships Increase sales Mergers Acquisitions Telecommuting	Video Conferencing E.D.I. LAN interconnections High speed CAD/CAM/CASE FAX Imaging Full motion video E-mail	Fast Switching Delivery of intelligent services Bandwidth on demand	Fiber optics VLSI ASIC High-speed DSP High speed packet switching	ISDN B-ISDN MANs SONET SMDS Switched 56K Switched 128K Switched 384K ATM
Productivity	Increase worker productivity				Frame relay Cell relay Global LAN Interconnect

Figure 1-14 Business demand + available technology = emerging network services.

tion, which, in turn, requires a great deal more bandwidth than terminal to mainframe traffic or a simple voice call.

Bandwidth is measured as a range of frequencies between the lowest and highest frequency that can be transmitted on any given circuit. A dial-up voice grade circuit used to make a normal phone call can transmit frequencies from about 300 Hz (1 Hertz = 1 cycle/second) to about 3300 Hz. These frequencies correspond roughly to the range of frequencies detectable by human hearing. The bandwidth of a voice grade circuit is therefore 3000 Hz (3300 Hz.–300 Hz.). The relationship between bandwidth and the actual number of bits per second which can be transmitted over a given circuit will be explained in Chapter 2 as terms such as bandwidth, baud rate, and bps (bits per second) are differentiated.

One other characteristic that many of the business demands listed in Figure 1-14 share is that their need for this large bandwidth is not constant, 24 hours a day, 7 days a week. This requirement of large amounts of bandwidth needed only at certain unpredictable times is commonly referred to as **bandwidth on demand**. Simply stated from a customer's perspective, bandwidth on demand means, "I want all the bandwidth I need, only when I want it, at a price I want to pay." If this sounds like a customer-oriented, market driven product definition, it should.

Many of the network services listed in Figure 1-14 attempt to deliver bandwidth on demand in different ways.

The remaining business demands listed, EDI (electronic data interchange), FAX, and E-mail also have some similar data communication characteristics. In general, each of these business demands is sending some kind of relatively short message to a particular destination or destinations. These destinations will change over time. Requirements to effectively provide these types of services might include fast transmission as well as sophisticated addressing and switching equipment that will get these messages to their proper destination in a timely manner. Additional user services might include the ability to send one message to multiple locations, or to locations on various lists, message confirmation, and delivery to users on different networks. Network services that deliver these requirements are often different in design and intent than those delivering bandwidth-on-demand type services.

Having highlighted the relationship between business demands, enabling technologies and network services, it may be enlightening to examine the business motivation behind the data communications-related business demands listed in Figure 1-14.

In the first column, *profitability* and *productivity* are listed as "Business Opportunities for Improvement," while the second column represents possible business solutions to solve each of the first column's "Business Opportunities for Improvement." Tracing a business opportunity through business solutions to data communications-related business demands should highlight the relationships at work within Figure 1-14.

One way to increase profitability is to reduce expenses. One area of expense reduction is inventory reduction. This process of closely managed inventory ordering, receipt, and usage is called **JIT** or "just in time," referring to the fact that the inventory is received just in time to use in manufacturing, thus reducing warehousing expense and inventory carrying charges.

JIT requires firm agreements with suppliers, and sometimes with customers as to the reliability of shipping and receipt of goods on short notice. Paperwork cannot get lost or delayed, so how is the accurate and timely delivery of inventory data among these "enterprise partners" assured?

This is a perfect example of how *data communications solutions are business solutions*. **EDI**, electronic data interchange, electronically sends purchase orders, acknowledgments, packing slips, invoices and payments among these JIT enterprise partners. EDI will be studied further in later chapters.

Other examples of data communications solutions fulfilling business opportunities for improvement can be found in Figure 1-14 in a similar manner. Again, this chart should be kept up to date as the entries in any of the columns change. Although the entries within individual columns will undoubtedly change, the basic relationship of data communications solutions fulfilling business opportunities by utilizing carrier network services enabled through available technology will remain constant.

TOP-DOWN APPROACH

The fact that the analysis of Figure 1-14 started with a *business* analysis is indeed significant. Although data communications needs analysis will be dealt with in detail in Chapter 12—"The Network Development Life Cycle"—the process illustrated in Figure 1-14 in which business level concerns were matched with available network services, is central to a thorough understanding of business data communications.

Known as the *top-down approach*, this process is key to assuring that implemented data communications solutions will actually solve business problems and not merely throw some technology at them.

The Top-Down Model

Figures 1-15 and 1-16 graphically illustrate the top-down approach to business data communications analysis. This top-down approach requires students to understand business constraints and objectives as well as information systems applications and the data on which those applications run, before considering data communications and networking options.

Notice where the network layer occurs in the top-down approach model. It is no accident that data communications and networking form the foundation of today's sophisticated information systems. A properly designed network supports flexible delivery of data to distributed application programs allowing businesses to respond quickly to customer needs and rapidly changing market conditions.

The *network model* and the *technology model* of the top-down model are differentiated with the terms logical network design versus physical network design. The network layer of the model represents the logical network design and is concerned with network functionality: *What* are we asking our network to do for us?

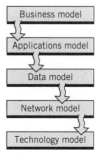

Figure 1-15 Top-down design approach, business data communications analysis.

Overall Architecture	Overall Process
Information Systems Architecture	**Strategic Information Systems Planning**
Business model	Strategic business planning
	Identify major business functions
	Identify business processes
	Identify business opportunities
Applications model	Applications development
	Systems analysis & design
	Identify information needs
	Relate information to business processes and opportunities
Data model	Database analysis & design
	Data modeling
	Data distribution analysis
	Relate data collection & distribution to information and business needs
	Client-server architecture design
	Distributed database design
Network model	Network analysis & design
	Network implementation
	Network performance monitoring
	Relate network architecture to data distribution analysis results
	Input–processing–output & logical network design
Technology model	Technology analysis grids
	Hardware–software–media analysis
	Physical network design

Figure 1-16 Network analysis and design environment, an integrated top-down approach.

The technology layer represents the currently available networking technology and will probably change rapidly as new products are announced. Configuring the available data communications devices or technology into a functioning network represents physical network design and is concerned with network implementation and operation: *How* are we accomplishing the *what* of our logical network design?

Although the physical implementation of a network may change frequently as new technology is introduced on the technology layer, the required functionality (logical design) represented on the network layer won't change until requirements from upper layers (business, applications, data) dictate a need for additional network functionality.

A rigid, poorly designed network will stifle distribution of data on a timely basis, preventing operation of distributed information systems and thereby failing to support business decision makers in an effective manner.

Although this top-down approach may seem to be only common sense, the fact is that, traditionally, a "bottom-up" approach has often been used in data communications analysis and design in which networks have been configured without adequate knowledge of the business objectives and information systems applications which these networks were supposed to support.

This top-down approach will be stressed throughout the text and covered extensively in Chapter 12. This top-down approach can also be considered a frame of reference when evaluating new technology. It has at times been called a "so-what attitude" frame of reference. In other words, if a new piece of technology does not solve a particular business problem at a reasonable cost, what good is it?

What are the possible consequences of blindly investing in technology for technology's sake while ignoring its impact (or lack thereof) on worker productivity or other business layer opportunities for improvement?

☐ TECHNOLOGY INVESTMENT VERSUS WORKER PRODUCTIVITY

Figure 1-17 clearly shows the less-than-impressive results, in terms of impact on worker productivity, resulting from technology expenditures in the U.S. service sector during the past decade.

The technology investment referenced in Figure 1-17 included technology of all types. Applying the results of this study more specifically to data communications and networking technology, it might be safe to say that:

> **Law 4:** If the network doesn't make good business sense, it probably makes no sense.

Insisting that a top-down approach to network analysis and design is undertaken should assure that the network design implemented will meet the business needs and objectives which motivated the design in the first place.

☐ OVERALL INFORMATION SYSTEMS ARCHITECTURE

But how is this top-down approach to data communications analysis and design actually implemented in today's corporations? What is the overall information systems structure into which this top-down approach fits? Figure 1-18 illustrates one way in which a top-down approach could be implemented within the overall framework of an information systems architecture.

Several key points illustrated in the diagram are worth noting. Predictably, the entire information systems development process begins with the business analysis process. What is important to note, however, is that *all* major sections of the top-down approach model, business, applications, data, network, and technology take part in the business analysis process.

In some cases, a separate technology assessment group exists within a corporation and partakes in the business analysis phase of the information systems development process. In so doing, each layer of the top-down model is represented by trained individuals and complementary processes in the top-down approach to information systems development.

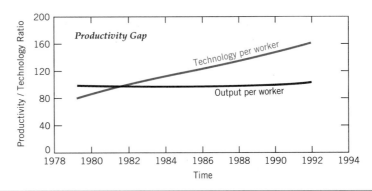

Figure 1-17 Technology investment versus worker productivity.

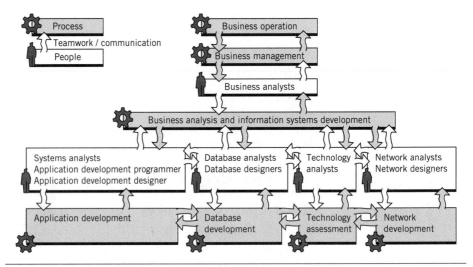

Figure 1-18 The top-down approach to information systems development.

This initial participation of all segments of the information systems development team in the business analysis of the process provides assurance that the system as implemented will adequately support the business functions for which it is intended.

☐ THE ROLE OF THE DATA COMMUNICATIONS PROFESSIONAL

After this initial participation of all segments of the team in the business analysis phase, each segment develops their portion of the information system. However, merely knowing the business needs that an information system is trying to meet is an insufficient guarantee of a successful implementation. It is essential that during the development process, the applications, database, network, and technology development teams communicate continually in order to assure that their finished subsystems will communicate effectively to support those business needs initially identified.

This critical communication between subsystems as well as between the individuals who develop these subsystems is illustrated in Figure 1-18.

☐ TRAINING FOR DATA COMMUNICATIONS PROFESSIONALS

The accomplishment of this communication between business, application, database, and network analysts should not be taken for granted. These analysts must be able to speak each other's languages and jargon in order to communicate effectively. This need to understand all aspects of the information systems architecture has major implications for the proper training of data communications and networking professionals.

James Carlini states, "A good pracademics [practical-academics] program would teach a mix of managerial, technical, marketing, entrepreneurial and interpersonal skills—the proverbial big picture." Unless one understands the "big picture" of the entire top-down model, one cannot effectively design and implement the data communications and networking foundation which must support this same big picture.

The pracademic orientation to which Carlini refers is a major influence on this textbook. Data communications cannot be studied in a vacuum. The study of data communications and networking must be approached from "the big picture" perspective, ever-mindful of the tremendous potential and far-reaching effect which data communications and networking decisions can have.

☐ JOB OPPORTUNITIES FOR THE DATA COMMUNICATIONS PROFESSIONAL

In order to understand where opportunities for well-educated data communications professionals might lie, it is necessary to understand the major trends currently exhibited by the three dominant elements of today's data communications environment:

> Business
> Technology
> Carriers

Figure 1-19 lists a few of the current major trends for these three elements. In the future, changes in trends specific to any of these could be analyzed in order to deduce future opportunities in data communications which would complement these emerging trends.

☐ CRITICAL SKILLS FOR DATA COMMUNICATIONS PROFESSIONALS

So what do the current trends in data communications indicate for employment opportunities? Given the recognition by business of the importance of networks and given the complicated nature of both the data communications technology as well as the integration of that technology to carrier-provided network services, it would seem that job opportunities should be ideal for data communications professionals who:

1. Understand and can speak "business."
2. Understand and can evaluate technology with a critical eye as to the cost/benefit of that technology.
3. Understand comparative value and proper application of available network services and can work effectively with carriers to see that implementations are completed properly and cost effectively.

Business	Technology	Carriers
Recognition of information as a corporate asset	Rapidly changing technology	Overwhelming abundance of emerging network services
Recognition of the timely delivery of information as a competitive advantage	Confusion over vendor claims and inconsistent use of technical jargon	No more "one-stop" shopping
Reliance on data communication networks as corporate nervous system for maximization of business opportunities		Focus on selling services, not necessarily properly integrating these services consistently with overall company business goals and directions

Figure 1-19 Opportunity analysis: summary of actual state of the data communications industry.

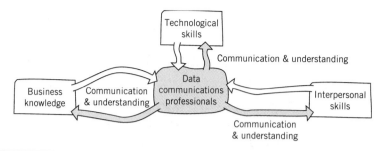

Figure 1-20 Critical skills analysis for data communication professionals.

4. Can communicate effectively with technically oriented people as well as with business management personnel.

The multitalented nature of these data communications professionals is illustrated in Figure 1-20.

The following are a few quotes from human resource experts regarding the opportunities for data communications professionals:

"I would say categorically, that [data communication professionals] are in the right place, at the right time, doing the right job. They are placed for an explosion and scarcity for folks with their skills. Companies are looking for individuals that have business, interpersonal, and technological skills." *Richard Wonder, National Director, IS Division, Robert Half International*

"They are in the area where there is the greatest amount of growth. They are in the heart of a company's computing system today. Information doesn't mean anything unless it is networked." *Jeff Kaplan, Director, Dataquest/Ledgeway*

These quotes are from a special report from *LAN Times* included in the featured references section of this chapter. For a more humorous view of pursuing a career in data communications, see "10 Top Reasons to be in Data Communications" in Appendix B.

To say that these are exciting times in the field of data communications is an understatement of untold proportions. The opportunities are indeed significant for those individuals properly prepared.

I invite you to enter the exciting world of data communications with me. I am confident that it is a journey you will not soon forget.

CHAPTER SUMMARY

Today's data communications industry is characterized by an environment consisting of a group of interacting components such as: business, technology and research, standards making organizations, regulatory agencies, and common carriers. The state of the overall industry at any point in time is the product of the interaction of these components. In order to be an effective participant in the data communications field, one must be aware of the forces at work which are shaping the industry.

Data communications and networking are integral parts of an overall information systems architecture. The ultimate success of an implemented information system depends largely on the design of the network which forms the foundation of that system. This high degree of integration between networking and other information system architecture components is graphically illustrated in a model known as the top-down model.

The top-down model implies that any information

system design must begin with a thorough understanding of business requirements before subsequent issues such as applications, data, networking, and technology are addressed.

The integrated nature of the network layer of an information systems architecture is mirrored in the skills required of today's data communications professionals. The demand is high for individuals well versed in a combination of business analysis, information systems, and networking design.

KEY TERMS

bandwidth on demand	equal access	OSI Seven Layer Model
carriers	GOSIP	RBOC
co-location	I-P-O Model	regulatory agencies
data communications	JIT	standards
deregulation	MFJ	telecommunications
divestiture	Modified final judgment	top-down model
EDI		

REVIEW QUESTIONS

1. What are the major interacting components that comprise today's data communications industry?
2. What are the specific interaction scenarios between the following components?

   Manufacturers and standards making organizations
   Business and manufacturers
   Carriers and regulatory agencies
   Carriers and political/judicial/legislative/organizations

3. Where do data communications and networking fit in an overall information systems architecture?
4. What is the role of business requirements analysis in network analysis and design?
5. What is the top-down model and how is it employed in network analysis and design?
6. What are the business demands that are affecting carrier services offerings?
7. What are the enabling technologies that are supporting these recent carrier offerings?
8. What skills are required of today's data communications professional?
9. What is divestiture and how does it differ from deregulation?
10. What is an RBOC?
11. Why is the data communications industry in such a state of change?
12. What is the modified final judgment and why is it important?
13. What are the key events which led up to divestiture and deregulation?
14. Who were the big winners and losers as a result of divestiture?

15. From a data communications user's perspective, what have been the most important impacts of divestiture and deregulation?
16. Explain how carriers can engage in both regulated and unregulated business ventures.
17. What is the OSI Model and why is it important?
18. Why is the standards making process so politically charged at times?
19. Why do standards often lag behind technological development?
20. Do standards always lag behind technological development? If not, give an example.
21. What are the possible business impacts of standards on a manufacturer of data communications equipment?
22. How do the laws of supply and demand apply to the data communications industry? Give examples.
23. What are some of the overriding trends in data communications and why are they important?
24. What is the I-P-O Model and of what value is it?
25. What are the major processes performed by most data communications equipment?
26. What is buffer memory and what role does it play in data communications equipment?
27. What is bandwidth on demand?
28. What is meant by the statement,"Data communications solutions are business solutions"?
29. What is EDI?
30. What is JIT?
31. How are EDI and JIT related?
32. What are the major differences between logical network design and physical network design?
33. Explain how the processes associated with each lay-

er of the top-down model contribute to effective information systems development.

34. How can one avoid wasting money on technology that does not improve productivity?

35. What kinds of opportunities are available in the data communications industry for properly trained graduates?

36. What does pracademics mean to you?

37. What would be some of the characteristics of a data communications book or course which professed a pracademic orientation?

38. How can models such as "Business Demands + Available Technology = Emerging Network Services" remain useful to you in the future?

ACTIVITIES

1. Contact the local provider of telecommunications services to your home or business. Inquire as to how long-distance calls are passed along to user-specified long-distance carriers.

2. If your local telecommunications provider is not one of the 7 RBOCs, inquire as to:
   a. The history of this company's providing telecommunication service in this area.
   b. Why one of the RBOCs doesn't supply local telecommunications service in this area.

3. Contact your state public utilities commission. Inquire as to the current state of intra-LATA (local carrier) competition in your state. Is it currently allowed? Are proposals pending?

4. Inquire of your public utilities commission regarding the regulations in your state for shutting off one's phone service due to nonpayment. Is phone service seen more as a right or privilege in your state?

5. Ask your local telecommunications carrier or RBOC which aspects of its business are regulated versus unregulated. Draw a diagram similar to Fig. 1-4.

6. Are any of your local carrier's unregulated activities being considered for regulation?

7. Invite a telecommunications professional who was in the business at the time of divestiture to speak to your class regarding life before and after divestiture. Try to get speakers representing both the user's as well as the carrier's perspective.

8. Gather job postings for networking related careers. Put together a scrapbook or bulletin board display. What types of technical and nontechnical skills are required? What are the salary ranges? Do all jobs require experience?

9. What types of professional certifications, if any, are currently available to people in the field of data communications and networking? How are such certifications viewed by companies hiring networking professionals?

10. Which agencies are responsible for regulation of carriers on both a state and federal level?

11. Who is the current director of the FCC and what are his/her qualifications?

12. Find out who are the Public Utility Commissioners in your home state. What are their qualifications for the position?

13. Which committees in the House of Representatives and Senate consider legislation related to telecommunications?

14. Which representatives/senators currently serve on those committees?

15. What telecommunications related legislation is currently being considered by Congress?

16. Find out which operations of AT&T are unregulated and which are regulated.

Featured References

Eckerson, Wayne. "IS Spending Fails to Increase Productivity," *Network World*, vol. 9, no. 21 (May 25, 1992), p. 29.

Dosters, Michelle. "Wanted: LAN Personnel," *LAN Times*, vol. 8, no. 6 (March 18, 1991), p. 53.

"Where the Money Goes: A Typical Operating Budget," *Data Communications*, vol. 20, no. 14 (October 1991), p. 26.

"What Will the RBOCs Do with Their New Freedom?" *Data Communications*, vol. 20, no. 11 (September 1991), p. 22.

Stephenson, Peter. "Beyond the Server: Good Network Administrators Require Good Training," *LAN Times*, vol. 8, no. 14 (August 5, 1991), p. 37.

Carlini, James. "Net Managers Need Instruction in Many Disciplines," *Network World*, vol. 9, no. 3 (January 27, 1992), p. 37.

Stephenson, Peter. "Standardize the Process of Standardizing Standards," *LAN Times*, vol. 8, no. 6 (March 18, 1991), p. 45.

St. Clair, Melanie. "Special Report: Network Managers," *LAN Times*, vol. 9, no. 10 (June 8, 1992), p. 51.

Rose, Marshall. *The Open Book: A Practical Perspective on OSI* (Englewood Cliffs, NJ: Prentice Hall), 1990.

Zimmerman, H. *IEEE Transactions on Communications*, "OSI Reference Model—The ISO Model of Architecture for Open Systems Interconnection," COM-28, no. 4 (April 1980).

C H A P T E R ▪ 2

Introductory Concepts

Concepts Reinforced

Importance of Standards and Standards-Making Organizations
Importance of the OSI Reference Model
I-P-O Model
Top-down Model

Concepts Introduced

Basic Vocabulary

Encoding	ASCII
EBCDIC	RS-232
Analog	Digital
Synchronous	Asynchronous
Full-duplex	Half-duplex
Two wire	Four wire
Serial	Parallel
bps	Baud rate
Leased line	Dial-up/switched line
Modulation	

I-P-O Frame of Reference to Technology Analysis
Modularity of Design in Technology
Hardware/Software/Media Model (HSM)
Public Phone Network: Operation, Structure, and Services

OBJECTIVES

Upon successful completion of this chapter, you should be able to:

1. Distinguish between the following related concepts and understand the proper application of each.

analog	digital
synchronous	asynchronous
full-duplex	half-duplex
two wire	four wire
serial	parallel
bps	baud rate
leased line	dial-up/switched line

2. Understand the importance of standards to the field of data communications, in general, and the RS-232 standard in particular.

3. Understand on both a conceptual as well as a practical level the basic three components of any data communications system: hardware, software, media .

4. Apply the I-P-O frame of reference to technology (hardware) analysis.

5. Understand the concept of modularity of design as it applies to both currently available and yet-to-be-designed data communications hardware.

6. Illustrate the use of the OSI model as a frame of reference or architecture, which can be used as an analysis tool to compare network source and destination characteristics.

7. Understand the basic structure and operation of the public phone network, as well as its impact on data transmission.

8. Understand the impact and limitations of various modulation techniques.

☐ INTRODUCTION

As new vocabulary and concepts are introduced in this chapter, it's important to understand that these words and concepts will be used throughout your study of data communications. Future concepts will be built upon the foundation of a thorough understanding of the vocabulary in this chapter.

This is the time to begin to speak in this foreign language that is called data communications. Don't be timid. Try to get together with other data communications students or professionals outside of class and practice this new vocabulary.

The potential for the productivity impact of applied technology was a concept introduced in Chapter 1. In this chapter, techniques will be introduced for use in the analysis of technology from a potential business benefit perspective. The OSI reference model will also be used in this chapter for technology analysis.

Building on the basic objective of data communications introduced in Chapter 1, "to get the bits and pieces of data from here to there," the *how* of the transmission of data will be covered in-depth. Ever-mindful of the impact of data communication decisions, the implications of various alternative ways of *how* we get the data from here to there will be outlined. Discussions of specific technology will be kept to a minimum in this chapter, concentrating instead on the conceptual aspects of *how* data is transmitted. Although **modems** will be mentioned in this chapter, the in-depth study of technology, including its business impact, will begin in Chapter 3.

Critical thinking will be stressed in this chapter and throughout the book. Remember this is *business* data communications. The development of analytical, business-oriented thinking skills must accompany the introduction of vocabulary and concepts which form the basis of understanding the field of data communications.

☐ GETTING THE BITS AND PIECES OF DATA FROM HERE TO THERE

When the term "data" is used these days, it is no longer referring merely to alphanumeric characters. As will be explained further in later chapters, voice and video transmissions can now be transformed in such a way as to enable them to be homogeneously transmitted with the more traditional definition of data.

In order to get data "from here to there," it must be transformed from its humanly understandable form (letters, numbers, voices, images) to an electronically-based, machine-understandable form.

Remember the basic steps of data communication introduced in Chapter 1:

1. *Receive* the bits and pieces of data.
2. *Examine* the bits and pieces of data.
3. *Decide* how to *process* the data.
4. *Send* the data to its proper destination.

The major focus in this chapter is the introduction of the transmission-related concepts which deliver these basic steps of data communications. Topics beyond the scope of this chapter will be identified with references to later chapters. These chapter references can be referred to now or at a later time according to reader preference.

The transmission-related data communications concepts to be introduced in this chapter are illustrated in Figure 2-1.

Figure 2-1 illustrates:

Column 1. The various major transmission-related processes required for serial transmission of data from one PC to another over a phone line.

Column 2. Follow-up chapters in which either the concepts or technology listed are covered in greater depth.

Column 3. Concepts to be covered at each stage of the overall process. In some cases, these concepts may represent decision points or call for explanation of alternatives. (asynchronous vs. synchronous, full-duplex vs. half-duplex, etc.).

Column 4. Technology related to each stage of the transmission process. This technology will be featured and analyzed either in this or later chapters.

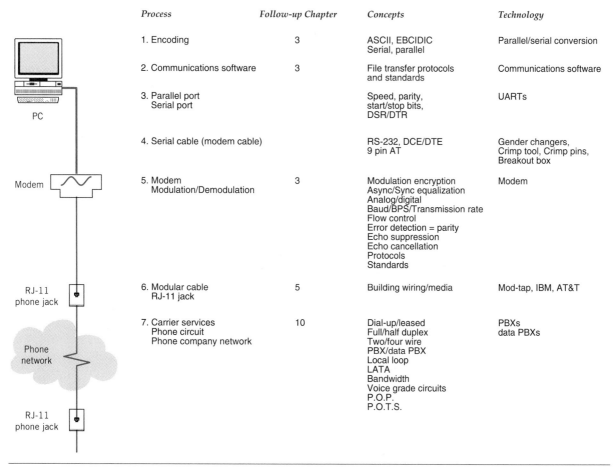

Process	Follow-up Chapter	Concepts	Technology
1. Encoding	3	ASCII, EBCIDIC Serial, parallel	Parallel/serial conversion
2. Communications software	3	File transfer protocols and standards	Communications software
3. Parallel port Serial port		Speed, parity, start/stop bits, DSR/DTR	UARTs
4. Serial cable (modem cable)		RS-232, DCE/DTE 9 pin AT	Gender changers, Crimp tool, Crimp pins, Breakout box
5. Modem Modulation/Demodulation	3	Modulation encryption Async/Sync equalization Analog/digital Baud/BPS/Transmission rate Flow control Error detection = parity Echo suppression Echo cancellation Protocols Standards	Modem
6. Modular cable RJ-11 jack	5	Building wiring/media	Mod-tap, IBM, AT&T
7. Carrier services Phone circuit Phone company network	10	Dial-up/leased Full/half duplex Two/four wire PBX/data PBX Local loop LATA Bandwidth Voice grade circuits P.O.P. P.O.T.S.	PBXs data PBXs

PC

Modem

RJ-11 phone jack

Phone network

RJ-11 phone jack

Figure 2-1 Basic data transmission concepts and technology.

☐ **ENCODING**

In order for the data communications equipment to examine and decide how to process the data it receives, that data must be in some type of electrically-based format that the data communications equipment can interpret.

This transformation of humanly-readable characters into machine-readable characters is known as **encoding**. Voice and video transmissions have their own unique encoding techniques which will be covered in their respective chapters.

Several data encoding standards have been developed over the years. The two most widely used schemes today are commonly known as **EBCDIC** (Extended Binary Coded Decimal Interchange Code) and **ASCII** (American Standard Code for Information Interchange). Recalling our discussion of the politics of the standards-making process from Chapter 1, why do you think there is more than one widely used encoding scheme today?

Using ASCII or EBCDIC coding tables, characters are turned into a series of 1's and 0's. Why 1's and 0's? The 1 and 0 represent two discrete states, much like a light switch being on or off. These discrete states can be easily represented electrically by discrete voltages of electricity.

These discrete voltages of electricity represent coded characters that can then be easily transmitted, received, and examined by data communications equipment. See Figure 2-2.

For example:

The letter "A" in humanly readable form	A
Transformed into ASCII	1000001
Transformed into EBCDIC	11000001

The 1's and 0's that constitute the character "A" are known as **bits**. The entire encoded letter "A" (1000001 or 11000001) is known as a **byte**. These 1's and 0's, or digits, represented by discrete voltages of electricity are in **digital** format and known as **digital data**.

Now that the humanly-readable character is in machine-readable form, it (these bits) can now be *transmitted* in a process generally known as *data communications*.

☐ **SERIAL VERSUS PARALLEL**

These bits that represent humanly-readable characters can be transmitted in either of two basic transmission methodologies. They can be transmitted either simulta-

Character encoding is humanly readable
characters transformed into ASCII:

A	1000001
B	1000010
C	1000011
D	1000100
E	1000101

or EBCDIC:

A	11000001
B	11000010
C	11000011
D	11000100
E	11000101

Figure 2-2 Character encoding.

neously (**parallel**) or in single file, one after the other (**serial**). The advantages, limitations, and typical applications of each transmission methodology are summarized in Figure 2-3.

As can be seen from Figure 2-3, parallel transmission is primarily limited to transmission of data within a computer and between a computer's parallel port and a parallel printer. In the technology section of this chapter, parallel transmission related technology such as parallel-to-serial converters and parallel interface extenders will be investigated.

Serial transmission is the basis of most data communications between computers and, therefore, deserves further investigation. The transmission of data between two PCs via modems as illustrated in Figure 2-1 is an example of serial transmission.

☐ COMMUNICATIONS SOFTWARE

Following the overall transmission process as outlined in Figure 2-1, it should be noted that the data has been encoded into machine-readable form and is now ready for further transmission from within the local PC out through its serial port to begin the journey to a distant PC.

This process of getting the data out of the local PC's **serial port**, through a serial (modem) cable, into a local modem, onto a phone line, through another PC's modem and serial port and finally into the remote PC must be set-up and managed properly in order to guarantee reliable transmission. **Communications software** is specially written to perform this function. A comparative study of the features and prices of communications software will be presented in Chapter 3.

Generally speaking, communications software can store phone numbers and automatically dial and answer the phone. It can initiate, monitor, resume and terminate the transfer of files between two PCs. It can make a PC appear to be a termi-

	Serial	Parallel
Transmission Description	One bit after another one at a time	All bits transmitted simultaneously
Comparative Speed	Slower	Faster
Distance Limitation	Farther	Shorter
Application	Between two computers	Within the computer
	To lower speed printers	To "parallel" high-speed printers
	To data transmission equipment	
Cable	All bits travel down one wire one bit at a time	Each bit travels down its own wire simultaneously

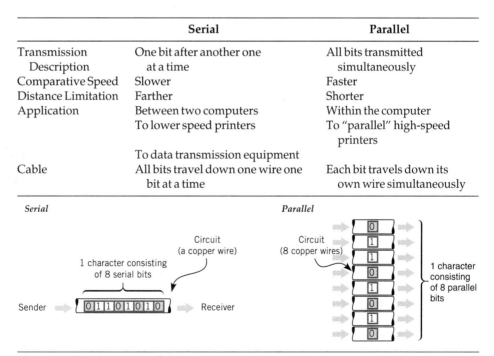

Figure 2-3 Serial versus parallel.

nal hooked directly to a mainframe or minicomputer through a process known as **terminal emulation**, and can call on-line information services like Prodigy or Compuserve.

Typical interaction with communications software might resemble the following steps:

1. Run the communications software on the local PC by either choosing the software selection from a menu or by typing in an appropriate command to begin communications software execution.

The communication software would:

2. Make sure it could "talk to" the modem, which in Figure 2-1 is an external or stand-alone modem hooked to the PC's serial port by means of a **modem cable**, before proceeding with other commands which may be given to the software. In the transmission example illustrated in Figure 2-1, the most likely first command would be to dial the phone number of the location of the remote PC with which the local PC wishes to communicate.

☐ PARALLEL TO SERIAL

Remember that data travels via parallel transmission within a PC over the PC's main data highway, known as a *bus*. Busses will be discussed further in Chapter 5. The data emerging from the serial port and out into a modem must be in serial format however. Therefore, somewhere inside the PC a parallel-to-serial conversion must be taking place. A specialized computer chip known as a **UART (**Universal Asynchronous Receiver Transmitter**)** acts as the interface between the parallel transmission of the CPU and the serial transmission of the serial port. UARTs and their impact on data transmission performance will be studied in Chapter 3. Some high speed modems do connect to PCs via their parallel ports. These "V. FAST" modems will be studied in chapter 3.

☐ SERIAL PORT

Before proceeding further with discussions of modems and their operation, it would be wise to gain an understanding of this thing called a serial port. Figure 2-4 illustrates a typical 25-pin serial port and a 9-pin serial port most often found on PC-ATs. The 25-pin and 9-pin connectors themselves are sometimes referred to as **DB-25** and **DB-9**, respectively.

The presence or absence of an electrical charge on each of these 25 pins has been designated as having a specific meaning in data communications. These standard definitions are officially known as **RS-232-C**, were issued by the Electronics Industries Association (EIA), and are listed in Figure 2-4.

Although all 25 pins are defined, in most cases, 10 or fewer of the pins are actually used. On some PCs, such as PC-ATs and compatibles as well as many notebook and laptop computers, the serial port has only 9 pins and is configured as in Figure 2-4.

☐ SERIAL CABLE OR MODEM CABLE

So how do we transport these meaningful electrical signals from the serial port on the local PC to a similar looking port, or interface on the local modem? The answer is: Either buy or make a data cable in a configuration known as a modem cable.

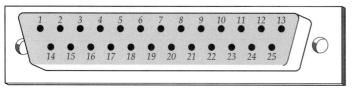

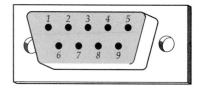

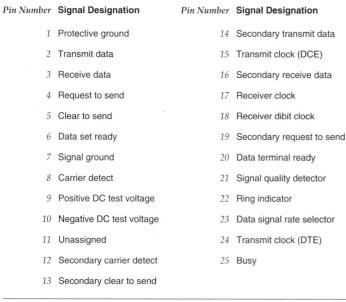

Pin Number	Signal Designation	Pin Number	Signal Designation	Pin Number	Signal Designation
1	Protective ground	14	Secondary transmit data	1	Carrier detect
2	Transmit data	15	Transmit clock (DCE)	2	Receive data
3	Receive data	16	Secondary receive data	3	Transmit data
4	Request to send	17	Receiver clock	4	Data terminal ready
5	Clear to send	18	Receiver dibit clock	5	Protective ground
6	Data set ready	19	Secondary request to send	6	Data set ready
7	Signal ground	20	Data terminal ready	7	Request to send
8	Carrier detect	21	Signal quality detector	8	Clear to send
9	Positive DC test voltage	22	Ring indicator	9	Ring indicator
10	Negative DC test voltage	23	Data signal rate selector		
11	Unassigned	24	Transmit clock (DTE)		
12	Secondary carrier detect	25	Busy		
13	Secondary clear to send				

Figure 2-4 25-pin serial port and PC-AT 9-pin serial port.

The cable has several small insulated wires within an outer jacket. These cables come with different numbers of "inner" wires depending on how many signals need to be transferred from one serial port to another. Each signal to be carried requires its own individual inner wire.

The next question is: Which of the possible 25 signals are meaningful, and therefore worth transferring over the modem cable in this example? Figure 2-5 summarizes the 12 pins most commonly included in modem cables.

DTE/DCE

In addition to being able to identify certain signals according to their pin numbers, it is necessary to also be able to identify which end of the cable goes to the PC and which goes to the modem.

The PC and the modem in our example are given generic designations of **DTE** (data terminal equipment) and **DCE** (data communications equipment) respectively.

These designations are important as RS-232 and cable construction are studied further. Many of the RS-232 pins and signals have a directionality to them. In other words, either the terminal is informing the modem of something by raising or lowering electrical voltages to a certain pin, or the modem is informing the terminal of something by the same means. Figure 2-5 outlines the directionality of the signals of commonly used RS-232 pins in the columns labeled "from" and "to."

RS-232 Communication between PC and Modem

To reinforce what has been learned thus far, let's initiate a conversation between a local PC and a remote PC and "watch" the conversation take place via RS-232 sig-

DB-9 Pin#	DB-25 Pin #	Name	Abbr.	From	To
5	1	Protective ground	PG		
3	2	Transmit Data	TXD	DTE	DCE
2	3	Receive Data	RXD	DCE	DTE
7	4	Request to Send	RTS	DTE	DCE
8	5	Clear to Send	CTS	DCE	DTE
6	6	Data Set Ready	DSR	DCE	DTE
5	7	Signal Ground	SG		
1	8	Carrier Detect	CD	DCE	DTE
	15	Transmit Clock	TC	DTE	DCE
	17	Receive Clock	RC	DCE	DTE
4	20	Data Terminal Ready	DTR	DTE	DCE
9	22	Ring Indicator	RI	DCE	DTE

Figure 2-5 Commonly used RS-232 pins on modem cables.

nals. The modem cables will have 12 data leads or inner wires, one for each of the commonly used RS-232 pins outlined in Figure 2-5. The wires will be pinned "straight-through," in other words, the wire from pin #2 on the DTE (PC) end will go "straight through" to pin #2 on the DCE (modem) end, and so on with the remaining pins. Cable arrangements other than "straight through" will be discussed in Chapter 3.

Discussions in the remainder of this chapter will focus on modem operation, including terms like carrier wave, and interfacing to various types of phone lines. The purpose of Figures 2-6 and 2-7 is to outline the use of varying RS-232 signals in data communications. This example is for illustrative purposes only. The exact occurrence of RS-232 signals can vary according to modem, communications software and type of phone line accessed. Figure 2-6 illustrates a representative physical configuration of PC to PC communications while Figure 2-7 details the possible RS-232 signalling which might take place.

Monitoring RS-232 Signals
The way these electrical signals on the various RS-232 pins are detected is by using a piece of technology called a *breakout box*. The breakout box illuminates an LED for each RS-232 signal which passes through it.

☐ MODEM
So exactly what does a modem do? In order to analyze what any piece of data communications equipment does, the input-processing-output or **I-P-O** analysis model, introduced in Chapter 1, is employed.

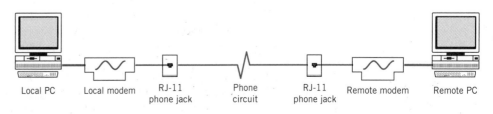

Local PC   Local modem   RJ-11 phone jack   Phone circuit   RJ-11 phone jack   Remote modem   Remote PC

Figure 2-6 RS-232 signalling: local PC to remote PC.

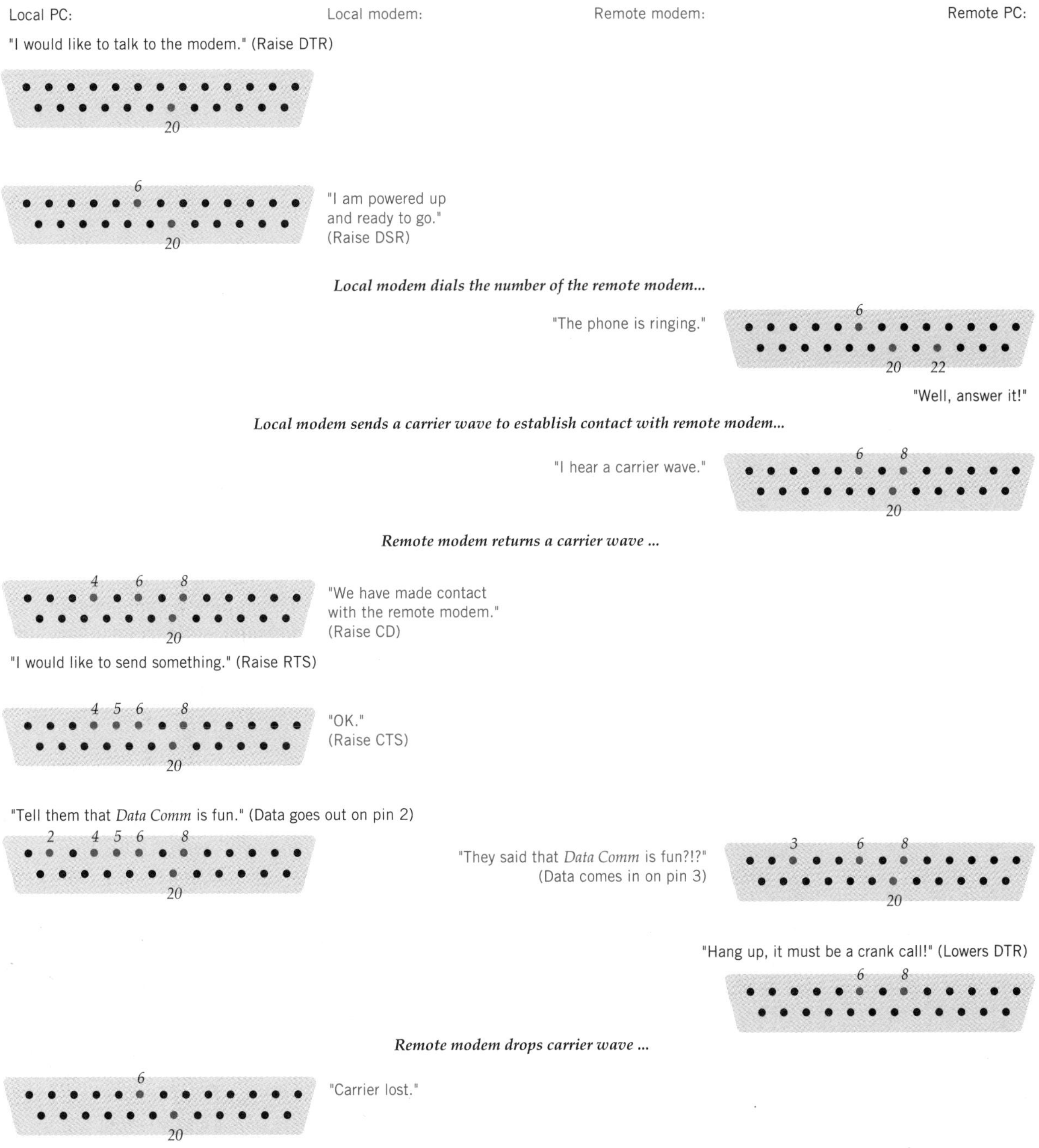
Local PC:
Local modem:
Remote modem:
Remote PC:
"I would like to talk to the modem." (Raise DTR)
20
6
20
"I am powered up and ready to go." (Raise DSR)
Local modem dials the number of the remote modem...
"The phone is ringing."
6
20 22
"Well, answer it!"
Local modem sends a carrier wave to establish contact with remote modem...
"I hear a carrier wave."
6 8
20
Remote modem returns a carrier wave ...
4 6 8
20
"We have made contact with the remote modem." (Raise CD)
"I would like to send something." (Raise RTS)
4 5 6 8
20
"OK." (Raise CTS)
"Tell them that Data Comm is fun." (Data goes out on pin 2)
2 4 5 6 8
20
"They said that Data Comm is fun?!?" (Data comes in on pin 3)
3 6 8
20
"Hang up, it must be a crank call!" (Lowers DTR)
6 8
Remote modem drops carrier wave ...
6
20
"Carrier lost."

Figure 2-7 A conversation between a local and a remote modem.

The I-P-O model provides a framework in which to focus on the difference between the data that came into the modem (*I*) and the data that came out of the modem (*O*). By defining this difference, we have defined how the modem processed the data (*P*).

In general terms, based upon what we have learned thus far, we could say:

Input Data (I): From the PC: A series of 1's and 0's representing characters and transmitted as discrete voltages of electricity in *digital* format.

Output Data (O): To the public phone network on a normal phone line.

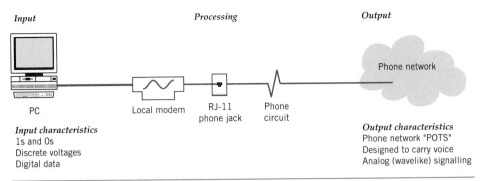

Figure 2-8 Role of the I-P-O model analysis.

Figure 2-8 summarizes what we know about the characteristics of the input data (I) and the output data (O).

It should be obvious that in order to better understand the processing (*P*) which goes on in a modem, it is first necessary to have a better understanding of output (*O*) data transmission over a "normal" or dial-up phone line.

☐ DATA TRANSMISSION OVER A DIAL-UP PHONE LINE

A **switched** or **dial-up line i**s the type of phone line you typically have installed in your home or place of business. To place a call, you pick up the receiver or handset, wait for a dial-tone, and dial the number of the location you wish to call. This ordinary type of phone service is sometimes called *POTS* or *Plain Old Telephone Service*.

A large switch in a telephone company building called a *central office* or **CO**, connects your phone equipment to the phone equipment of the party you wish to call by finding an available **circuit** or path to your desired destination. It is important to understand at this point that the **CO switch** tries to find a path as quickly as possible to your destination. The actual circuits it chooses represent the best path available at that time. The particular circuits or path chosen may vary from one occasion to another, even for calls to the same location. Calls placed over dial-up lines through CO switches which have connections built from available circuits are called *circuit-switched connections.*

The greater the distance of the call, the more likely that different paths will be taken through a larger number of different switches for subsequent calls to the same number. Factors such as time of day, day of the week, and equipment failures can have a large impact on circuit availability from which to build the connection for your requested call. This unpredictability of equipment through which your call is routed leads to an unpredictability of the quality of the connection. Figure 2-9 illustrates the possible circuit-switched connection of two calls placed to the same number.

☐ ANALOG TRANSMISSION

The next important characteristic related to transmitting data over a dial-up phone line has to do with how the data is represented on that phone line. First, it is important to realize that today's dial up phone network was originally designed to carry voice conversations efficiently and with reasonable sound quality.

This "efficiency of design with reasonable sound quality" meant reproducing

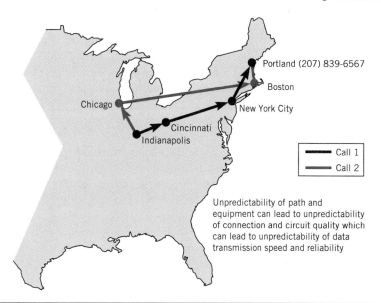

Figure 2-9 Dial-up connection: circuit switched.

a range of the frequencies of human speech and hearing *just* wide enough to produce reasonable sound quality. That range of frequencies, or **bandwidth**, as it is more commonly called, is 3000 Hz (from 300 Hz to 3300 Hz), and is the standard bandwidth of today's voice-grade dial-up circuits (phone lines).

This 3000 Hz is all the bandwidth with which the modem operating over a dial-up circuit has to work. Remember also that because today's dial-up phone network was designed to be able to mimic the constantly varying tones or frequencies that characterize human speech, only these continuous, wave-like tones or frequencies can travel over the dial-up phone network in this limited bandwidth.

The challenge, then, is to represent the *discrete*, *digitized* 1's and 0's from the input (PC) side of the modem in a continuous or **analog** form within a limited bandwidth so that the data may be transmitted over the dial-up network. Figure 2-10 summarizes the transformation requirements of a modem under the processing section of the I-P-O Model.

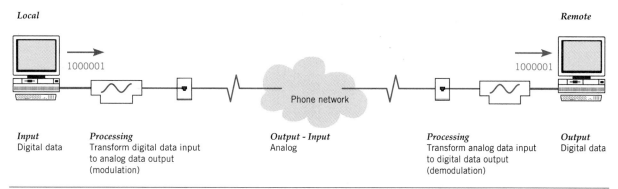

Figure 2-10 Role of the I-P-O model analysis.

☐ I-P-O: A LOGICAL MODEL

The use of the I-P-O model in Figure 2-10 can be extended beyond its use in the analysis at only the local end of the transmission circuit. A similar I-P-O model would be constructed for the remote end of the transmission circuit. In order to assure successful transmission of data from the local PC and modem to the remote PC and modem, the details contained within their respective I-P-O models must be complementary. Stated another way, the local and remote I-P-O models must be "balanced" if successful end-to-end transmission is to occur.

A logical model such as the I-P-O model is concerned with the *process* or "*what*" needs to be accomplished by a given data communications device.

"*How*" such processes are accomplished in a *physical* sense can also be modeled using either the **H-S-M** (hardware-software-media) model which will be introduced shortly or the OSI Model which will be employed throughout the text. Regardless of which model is used to document the physical characteristics of the nodes, or ends, of a circuit, the contents of the models must be complementary if successful transmission is to occur.

☐ MODULATION/DEMODULATION

After examining Figure 2-10, it should be clear that a modem's job must be to convert digital data into analog data for transmission over the dial-up phone network and to convert analog data received from the dial-up network into digital data for the terminal or PC. The proper names for these processes are **modulation** and **demodulation** as illustrated in Figure 2-11. In fact, the name modem is actually a contraction for *mod*ulator/*dem*odulator.

Modulation Techniques

Now that we know *what* a modem does (modulation/demodulation), we should really gain a better understanding of *how* the modem modulates/demodulates. Some of the modulation techniques used in today's sophisticated, high-speed modem are beyond the scope of this book. Suitable references for such technical information are included in the Featured References section of this chapter.

It is important, however, to understand the basics of modulation/demodulation in order to understand the limitations any modem faces regardless of the sophistication of its implemented modulation technique.

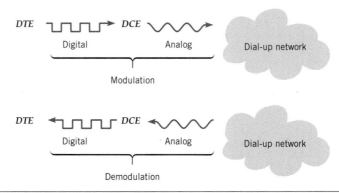

Figure 2-11 Modulation and demodulation.

Carrier Wave

In order to represent the discrete-state 1's and 0's or bits of digitized data on a dial-up phone line, an analog wave must be able to be changed between at least two different states. This implies that a "normal" or "neutral" wave must exist to start with, which can be changed to represent these 1's and 0's.

This "normal" or "neutral" wave is called a **carrier wave**. The RS-232 pin #8–carrier detect refers to this carrier or reference wave. Modems generate carrier waves which are then altered (modulated) to represent bits of data as 1's and 0's. Figure 2-12 illustrates a simple carrier wave.

There are only three physical characteristics of this wave that can be altered or modulated: *amplitude, frequency,* and *phase.* In some modulation schemes more than one of these characteristics are altered at a time.

Amplitude Modulation

Figure 2-13 illustrates the **amplitude modulation** of a carrier wave. Notice how only the amplitude changes, while frequency and phase remain constant. The portions of the wave with increased height (altered amplitude) represent 1's and the lower wave amplitude represent 0's. Together, this portion of the wave would represent the letter "A" using the ASCII-7 encoding scheme.

Frequency Modulation

Figure 2-14 represents the **frequency modulation** of a carrier wave. The frequency can be thought of as how frequently the same spot on two subsequent waves pass a given point. Waves with a higher frequency will take less time to pass while waves with a lower frequency will take a greater time to pass.

The distance between the same spots on two subsequent waves is called the **wavelength**. The longer the wavelength, the lower the frequency and the shorter the wavelength, the greater the frequency. Notice in Figure 2-14 how the higher frequency (shorter wavelength) part of the wave represents a 1 and the lower frequency (longer wavelength) part of the wave represents a 0, while amplitude and phase remain constant. Again, the entire *bit stream* represents the letter "A" in ASCII-7 .

Phase Modulation

Figure 2-15 illustrates an example of **phase modulation**. Notice how the frequency and amplitude remain constant in the diagram. Phase modulation or *phase shifting*, as it is sometimes called, can be thought of as a shift or departure from the "normal" continuous pattern of the wave. Notice in Figure 2-15 how we would expect the pat-

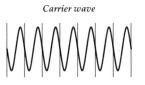

Carrier wave

Figure 2-12 Carrier wave.

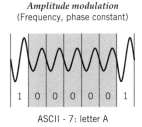

Amplitude modulation
(Frequency, phase constant)

1　0　0　0　0　1

ASCII - 7: letter A

Figure 2-13 Amplitude modulation (frequency, phase constant).

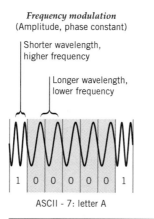

Frequency modulation
(Amplitude, phase constant)

Shorter wavelength,
higher frequency

Longer wavelength,
lower frequency

| 1 | 0 | 0 | 0 | 0 | 0 | 1 |

ASCII - 7: letter A

Figure 2-14 Frequency modulation (amplitude, phase constant).

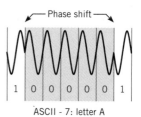

Phase shift

| 1 | 0 | 0 | 0 | 0 | 0 | 1 |

ASCII - 7: letter A

Figure 2-15 Phase modulation (frequency, amplitude constant).

tern of the wave to follow the broken line, but suddenly the phase *shifts* and heads off in another direction. This phase shift of 180 degrees is a *detectable event* with each change in phase representing a change in state from 0 to 1 or 1 to 0 in this example.

BAUD RATE VERSUS BPS

This notion of a detectable event mentioned in the previous paragraph is key to an understanding of the speed of modem transmissions. Notice in Figures 2-13, 2-14, and 2-15 that each of the modulations or changes to the carrier wave represented either a 1 or a 0. These modulations are sometimes called **detectable events** or *signalling events*. A signalling event represents a period of time in which a carrier wave can either be manipulated or left alone by a transmitting modem, and is also known as a **baud**. From the receiving modem's perspective a signalling event is the period of time in which the modem "listens" to the carrier wave, determines whether or not the carrier wave has been changed, and concludes whether the condition of the wave at that split second in time represents a 1 or a 0.

It should stand to reason that: The more signalling events per second that a modem can perform, the more data that can be transmitted per second.

These *signalling events per second* are known as the **baud rate**. Although baud rate and **bps** (bits per second) are often used interchangeably, the two terms are in fact related, but not identical. In Figures 2-13, 2-14, and 2-15 only one bit was interpreted at each signalling event (one bit/baud), therefore, in these cases the baud rate was equal to the bps (bits per second).

More sophisticated modulation techniques are able to interpret more than one bit per baud. In these cases, the bps is greater than the baud rate. For example, if the baud rate of a modem was 2400 signalling events per second and the modem was able to interpret 2 bits per signalling event, then the transmission speed would be 4800 bps.

ASYNCHRONOUS VERSUS SYNCHRONOUS TRANSMISSION

These *detectable events* must be produced on one modem, transmitted over the public phone network, and detected reliably on a remote modem. In a modem with a baud rate of 2400 baud (samples) per second, the remote modem has exactly 0.416 milliseconds (1 divided by 2400) to accurately detect and interpret the incoming data.

Obviously, the modems must have a reliable way to know exactly when to sample the line for data. Somehow, the modems must establish and maintain some type of timing between them so that these detectable events are produced, transmitted, and detected accurately.

There are two main alternatives to establishing and maintaining this timing of detectable events. These two timing alternatives are known as:

> **Asynchronous** transmission
> **Synchronous** transmission

Figure 2-16 summarizes some important characteristics about asynchronous and synchronous transmission methods. The most noticeable difference is that the synchronization, or detectable event timing, itself is re-established with the transmission of *each character* in asynchronous transmission via the use of **start** and **stop** bits and with *each block of characters* in synchronous transmission. In asynchronous transmission, there may be 1, 1.5, or 2 stop bits. The timing in the case of synchronous transmission is supplied by a clock, which may be supplied by either the remote or local modem, or by the carrier.

Secondly, when comparing idle time activity, synchronization is maintained, thanks to the ever-present clocking signal, in synchronous transmission and dropped in asynchronous transmission while no characters are being transmitted. The effect of these characteristics on transmission efficiency is illustrated in Figure 2-16.

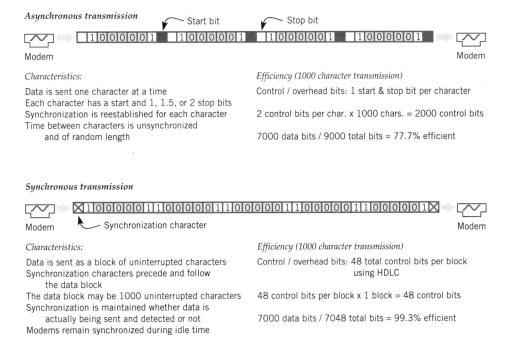

Asynchronous transmission

Start bit   Stop bit

Modem   Modem

Characteristics:

Data is sent one character at a time
Each character has a start and 1, 1.5, or 2 stop bits
Synchronization is reestablished for each character
Time between characters is unsynchronized
    and of random length

Efficiency (1000 character transmission)

Control / overhead bits: 1 start & stop bit per character

2 control bits per char. x 1000 chars. = 2000 control bits

7000 data bits / 9000 total bits = 77.7% efficient

Synchronous transmission

Modem   Synchronization character   Modem

Characteristics:

Data is sent as a block of uninterrupted characters
Synchronization characters precede and follow
    the data block
The data block may be 1000 uninterrupted characters
Synchronization is maintained whether data is
    actually being sent and detected or not
Modems remain synchronized during idle time

Efficiency (1000 character transmission)

Control / overhead bits: 48 total control bits per block
                    using HDLC

48 control bits per block x 1 block = 48 control bits

7000 data bits / 7048 total bits = 99.3% efficient

Figure 2-16 Asynchronous/synchronous transmission.

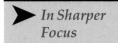

MORE THAN ONE BIT PER BAUD

There are really only two ways in which a modem can transmit data faster:

1. As mentioned previously, increase the signalling events per second, or baud rate.
2. Find a way for the modem to interpret more than one bit per baud, or signalling event.

By modifying a phase modulation technique such as that illustrated in Figure 2-15, a modem can detect, interpret, and transmit more than one bit per baud. In Figure 2-15 each phase shift was 180 degrees. What if the modem could shift the phase of the carrier wave at angles other than just 180 degrees?

For example, what if the modem could produce and detect phase shifts of 90 degrees, 180 degrees, 270 degrees, and 0 or 360 degrees which is really no shift at all. Remembering that all digitized data has only two states, 1 and 0, it should stand to reason that with four distinct detectable events (four different phase angles listed above), the modem should be able to interpret two bits/baud.

The mathematical proof is as follows:

Bits/Baud
Number of states = Number of different detectable events

Number of states = 2 (Data is either a 1 or 0)
Number of detectable events = 4 different phase angles in this example

To solve:

2 (the number of states) raised to what power equals
4 (the number of different detectable events)?

The answer is 2, meaning that 2 bits/baud can be interpreted at a time. Two bits at a time are known as a **dibit**. The following dibits could be assigned to the 4 phase-angle shifts which were suggested for this example:

Phase Shift	Dibit
90	01
180	11
270	10
360	00

Such a four phase shift modulation technique is known as *quadrature phase shift keying*.

By extending the mathematical proof above, it should be obvious that:

Number of Detectable Events	Bits/Baud
8	3 = **tribit**
16	4 = **quadbit**

How far can we go with increasing the number of phase shift angles or detectable events ? One limiting factor to increasing the bits/baud in phase shift modulation is: Given that the modem is being used on a dial-up line of unpredictable quality, how small (least number of degrees) a phase shift can be *reliably* detected?

Sixteen different phase shifts would require reliable detection of phase shifts of as little as 22.5 degrees.

QAM—Quadrature Amplitude Modulation

Remembering that phase is not the only wave characteristic that can be varied, 16 different detectable events can also be produced using:

> 8 different phase angles for each of 2 different amplitudes = 16 different detectable events

This would allow 4 bits/baud or quadbits to be produced or detected per signalling event. In this case the transmission rate in bps would be 4 times the baud rate.

Many of today's high-speed modems use quadrature amplitude modulation. For example, the CCITT V.29 Standard is for a 9600 bps modem using **QAM**. Knowing that QAM uses quadbits or 4 bits/baud, what is the baud rate of a V.29 9600 bps modem?

> 9600 bits/second divided by 4 bits/baud = 2400 baud.

TCM—Trellis Coded Modulation

Another modulation scheme frequently employed in today's most sophisticated modems is called Trellis Coded Modulation. **TCM** adds a calculated fifth bit to the quadbit of QAM. This fifth calculated bit is used by the decoding modem to help it more accurately decipher which quadbit was actually sent. This extra "hint" improves modem performance, especially on "noisy" phone lines.

TCM will be discussed further in Chapter 3 in the discussion of error correction.

☐ MODEM STANDARDS

The particular modulation scheme as well as the frequency or tone of the carrier wave used in a particular modem are defined by modem standards. Frequency is measured in hertz (Hz) or cycles. Modem standards will be discussed in detail in Chapter 3.

At this point, you should have a general understanding of how *digital* data, understood by PCs, can be transmitted successfully over an *analog* dial-up phone network. The approach in this chapter has been primarily logical, employing the I-P-O model as a frame of reference.

☐ HARDWARE-SOFTWARE-MEDIA ANALYSIS METHODOLOGY

The **I-P-O** analysis methodology is process-oriented, or logical, in that it focuses on the processing necessary to convert the characteristics of the input data to the requirements of the output data.

Another analysis methodology for data communications is more component-oriented, or physical, and is known as the **H-S-M** or hardware-software-media data communications analysis methodology. Recognizing that any data communications system must have these three components, the H-S-M model can be employed to analyze the PC to PC data communication via the dial-up network that has been used as an example of a simple data communications task in this chapter.

The H-S-M methodology is used to separately analyze *each* node, or processing location, on a data communications system. By analyzing the hardware, software, and media of each location separately in this manner, differences in **interfaces** (hardware), **protocols** (software), or **circuits** (media) will become evident and can be resolved. Exactly how these differences can be resolved is the topic of the remainder of the book. Figure 2-17 summarizes some of the categories requiring investigation for the PC to PC data communications system using the H-S-M methodology.

Figure 2-17 introduces several new concepts and leaves a few unanswered questions. The new vocabulary will be covered in the next section on carrier services while the modem and hardware related new concepts will be covered in Chapter 3.

As to the unanswered questions, one of the most important uses of such an analysis grid is to point out *what you don't know*. A second important benefit is to highlight possible incompatibilities between nodes on either a hardware, software, or media level. This simple tool, when completely filled in with the technical details of each node can assure proper network performance. To leave blanks in such a grid of technical details, thereby dismissing the significance of what you don't know, increases the likelihood of network failure dramatically. In network analysis and design, always remember:

Law 5: Technical details are important!
Technical details are important!
Technical details are important!

Characteristics/Questions		Node 1	Compatibility Issues with Other Nodes
Hardware	Modem:		
	Manufacturer:		
	Baud rate:		
	bps:		
	Interface:		
	Error detection standard:		
	Error correction standard:		
	Data compression standard:		
	Fallback speed:		
	PC:		
	Operating system:		
	Operating system version:		
Software	Communication Software:		
	File transfer protocol:		
	Error detection standard:		
	Error correction standard:		
Media	Phone Network:		
	Switched or leased line:		
	Analog to digital:		
	2-wire or 4-wire:		
	Async or sync transmission:		
	Half of full duplex:		
	Modem cable from PC to modem:		

Figure 2-17 Hardware-software-media (H-S-M) network analysis model.

☐ IMPORTANCE OF STANDARDS

Another observation of Figure 2-17 is the frequency with which the words "standard" or "protocol" appear in the software section of the analysis grid. One major category of standards affecting modem operation is the "V" series of modem standards as recommended by the CCITT. The second major set of standards are **defacto standards** in that they are widely accepted as industry standards but have not been recommended by a chartered standards making organization such as the CCITT.

The defacto standards to which we are referring are the MNP (Microcom Networking Protocol) series of data communications protocols which assure error-free transmission using modems over dial-up circuits.

It is important that communicating modems share similar standards and protocols in order to assure proper operation. This assurance of matching standards and protocols may be done by a network analyst by completing a H-S-M chart. An alternative to protocol matching is to let the modems agree on common protocols themselves. For instance, Microcom currently has at least 10 classes or levels of MNP protocols which are implemented on many manufacturers' modems. Many modems possess the ability to "introduce" themselves to each other and negotiate as to the highest common level of modem standards at which to communicate.

☐ CARRIER STRUCTURE, OPERATION, AND SERVICES

Following the overall process roadmap as illustrated in Figure 2-1, a more specific understanding of the structure, operation, and available services of local and long-distance phone carriers is now in order.

As will soon become evident, different carrier services require different data communications equipment characteristics and have different business applications. The I-P-O chart for data communications systems analysis will be employed to sort out the relationship between carrier services and data communications equipment.

As additional available carrier network services (O) are analyzed or input data characteristics (I) are changed, the interface processes (P) which must be accomplished will be deduced and the required data communications equipment which offers those processes will be analyzed.

☐ LONG-DISTANCE CARRIER OPERATION AND SERVICES

To start with, merely increasing the distance between the communicating PCs will introduce a variety of new topics. Using either the I-P-O or H-S-M analysis tools to enter this change in the network design should probably not cause any Input or Processing changes in the case of the I-P-O analysis, nor any Hardware or Software changes in the case of the H-S-M analysis.

Practically speaking, all that the longer distance connection will require is dialing a longer phone number. However, behind the scenes in the public phone network, there is a great deal of difference caused by the longer call.

This characteristic of network design, wherein the required changes in the operation of the phone network to deliver the long-distance call are invisible and of no concern to the rest of the network design, is known as **transparency**.

☐ REENFORCEMENT OF OSI MODEL CONCEPTS

Transparency is one of the key underlying concepts of the OSI model, which was introduced in Chapter 1. The implementation of transparency in this example illustrates another underlying design characteristic of the OSI Model as well. In the current network design, all that is required to access the phone network (OSI physical layer 1) is to make sure that the phone plug, known as an RJ-11, fits into the phone jack. This phone jack is sometimes called an **interface**.

Just as it is not necessary to worry about anything that happens on the phone company side of the interface, upper OSI layers don't have to worry about operation or protocols on any of the lower OSI layers. Upper OSI layer protocols are merely concerned with "connecting" properly to the interface with lower OSI layers.

Even though the operation of the phone network to handle the long-distance call has no effect on the simple PC to PC network design, it would still be worthwhile to examine the operation, structure, and services of the long-distance network as they apply to data communications.

☐ DIAL-UP LONG DISTANCE SERVICES

Figure 2-18 illustrates the major components of the public switched network (PSN) necessary to support long distance dial-up service for data communications. The acronym **LATA** in Figure 2-18 stands for *Local Access and Transport Areas* which were established as a result of divestiture. A **LATA** is often, but not always, equivalent to the area covered by a given area code. There can be several LATAs per area code. LATAs can cross state boundaries but area codes cannot. All local phone traffic within a LATA, known as **intra-LATA** traffic, is handled by the local phone company, most often one of the RBOCs listed in Chapter 1. The circuits between a residence or business and the local CO (Central Office) are known as **local loops**, while the circuits between POPs (Point of Presence) are known as interexchange circuits.

Any phone traffic destined for locations outside of the local LATA, known as **inter-LATA** traffic, must be handed off to the long-distance or **Interexchange carrier** of the customer's choice. Competing long-distance carriers wishing to do business in a given LATA maintain a switching office in that LATA known as a **POP** or *point of presence*. This POP handles billing information and routes the call over the long-distance carrier's switched network to its POP in the destination's LATA. The circuit between the POPs may be via satellite, microwave, fiber optical cable, traditional wiring or some combination of these media. Depending on traffic levels, the long distance carrier's network calls may be routed through any combination of switches before reaching their final destination.

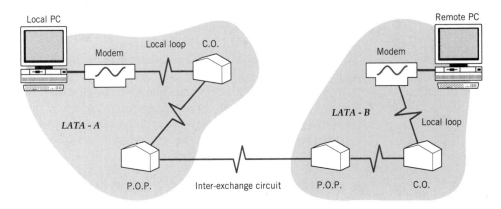

Figure 2-18 Long-distance dial-up call.

Therefore, just as was noted with local dial-up calls, long-distance dial-up calls are *circuit-switched* calls which may vary in quality from one instance to another thereby having an impact on the possible speed of data communications.

☐ VOICE-GRADE LEASED LINES

One alternative to "taking one's chances" with a circuit-switched voice grade connection is to lease a **voice-grade leased line** from a local or long-distance carrier. Characteristics of voice-grade leased lines as well as other carrier network service are summarized in Figure 2-19. Figure 2-19 is not a complete listing of all possible carrier services. Many other services will be introduced in later chapters.

A voice-grade *leased* line is a normal voice-grade line that bypasses the carrier's switching equipment. When the service is ordered, you must name the two or more locations that are to be connected. A new circuit is installed into these locations with a new RJ-11 jack interface added at each circuit location. There is no dial-tone on this new line because it does not go through any switching equipment. With only two locations connected, the circuit is called *point-to-point*, with more than two locations, the circuit is called *multipoint*.

For leased lines, charges include both an installation charge as well as a flat monthly charge. The installation charge may be significant, especially if the circuit crosses LATAs. The flat monthly fee does not vary by usage, unlike the dial-up voice-grade circuits. The circuit is exclusively yours to use, 24 hours per day, 7 days per week.

Service Name	Dial-up/ Leased	Analog/ Digital	Async/ Sync	2-wire/ 4-wire	Rates: Flat or Usage	Transmission Rate
Analog P.O.T.S.	D	A	Depends	2	U	14.4 Kbps w/ V.32bis 28.8 Kbps w/ V.Fast
Voice Grade Leased	L	A	S	4	F	14.4 Kbps w/ V.32bis 28.8 Kbps w/ V.Fast
Narrowband Digital DDS	L	D	S	4	F	9.6 Kbps 19.2 Kbps 56 Kbps
DS-0	L	D	S	4	F	64 Kpbs
Wideband/Broadband Digital T-1	L	D	S	4	F	1.544 Mbps
T-3	L	D	S	Fiber	F	44.836 Mbps
Digital Dial-up ISDN	D	D	S	4	U	144 Kbps
SWITCHED 56K	D	D	S	4	U	56 Kpbs

Figure 2-19 Carrier services summary, partial listing.

☐ TWO-WIRE VERSUS FOUR-WIRE

Another difference between dial-up and leased voice grade lines is that dial-up lines are usually **two-wire** circuits while leased lines are most often **four-wire** circuits. The technical differences between the two circuit types are not as important as the impact that they have on data transmission capacity.

Implication of Two-versus Four-Wire: Full- versus Half-Duplex

The two-wire, dial-up circuit typically only supported **half-duplex**, or one direction at a time transmission. Modems that interfaced to a dial-up circuit had to support this half-duplex transmission method. What this meant was that once the two modems completed initial **handshaking**, one modem would agree to transmit while the other received. In order for the modems to reverse roles, the initially transmitting DTE (terminal or computer) drops its RTS (request to send) RS-232 Pin #4 , the transmitting DCE (modem) drops its CTS (clear to send) RS-232 Pin #5, and perhaps its carrier wave. Next, the initially receiving DTE must raise RTS, the initially receiving DCE (modem) must generate a carrier wave and raise CTS, and the role reversal is complete.

This role reversal is known as **turnaround time** and can take two-tenths of a second or longer. This may not seem like a very long time, but if this role-reversal is needed to be done several thousand times over a long-distance circuit, charged by usage time, it may have a large dollar impact. The monetary impact of various circuit and modem choices will be presented in Chapter 3.

Not all modems are limited to half-duplex transmission over two-wire circuits. Modems manufactured to the CCITT's V.32 standard can transmit at 9600 bps in **full-duplex** transmission, thereby receiving and transmitting simultaneously over dial-up two-wire circuits. These modems use sophisticated **echo cancellation** techniques and are significantly more expensive than slower, half-duplex modems. Echo cancellation as well as the cost/benefit analysis of V.32 Modems will be explored in Chapter 3. Half-duplex and full-duplex transmission methodologies are illustrated in Figure 2-20.

Until the advent of the V.32 9600 bps full-duplex modem, the only way to get full-duplex transmission was to lease a four-wire circuit. Two wires were for transmitting data and two wires were for receiving data. There was no "role reversal" necessary and therefore, no modem turnaround time delays.

☐ NARROWBAND DIGITAL SERVICES

As can be seen in Figure 2-19, the next major category of carrier network services after analog services such as POTS and voice-grade leased lines are digital services. Unlike the analog services which were originally designed to carry voice, digital services imply an all digital transmission thereby eliminating the need for digital-to-analog conversion as performed by modems.

DDS or *digital data service*, available from most carriers, offers leased lines that can be purchased for local or long-distance, point-to-point or multipoint, all digital transmission. No digital to analog modulation is necessary. Rather than terminating the circuit with a modem, a **CSU/DSU** (*customer service unit/data service unit*) is employed. These devices will be explored further in Chapter 3. When ordering a digital circuit the speed of that circuit must be specified. Typical choices are: 2400, 4800, 9600, 19.2K, and 56K bps. This "declaring your speed" brings up a key difference in operation of analog and digital circuits.

When an analog circuit, dial-up or leased, degrades or has some kind of trans-

Half-duplex: Modems transmit in both directions, only one direction at a time

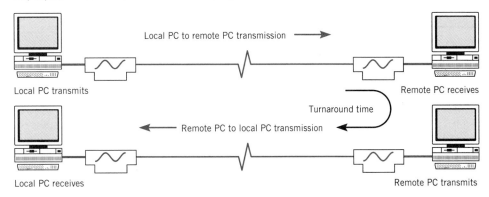

Full-duplex: Modems transmit in both directions simultaneously

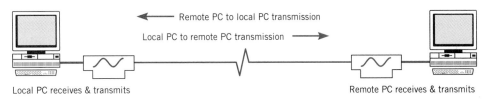

Figure 2-20 Half-duplex versus full-duplex.

mission impairment, many modems use **fallback** or lower speeds automatically and continue with data transmissions. With a digital circuit, the speed of the circuit is set at the CO, the CSU/DSUs are set to the speed of the circuit, and if there is a problem with the line, the data transmission ceases. It should be pointed out that digital circuits tend to be more error free than analog circuits. Causes and cures of errors in data transmission will be covered in Chapter 3.

Simply stated, the key determining factor in the transmission speed of an analog circuit is the modem, while the key determining factor in the case of a digital circuit is the configured speed of the circuit itself.

☐ BROADBAND DIGITAL SERVICES

Higher capacity digital services are also available. Services such as T-1 (1.544 Megabits/sec) and ISDN (integrated services digital network) as well as several other emerging carrier services will be outlined in several later chapters. These digital services may be of a switched or leased variety. Key facts about many such services are summarized in Figure 2-19. As will be seen in later chapters, emerging network services are moving toward the basic user requirement of "bandwidth on demand."

CHAPTER SUMMARY

Using the transmission of data from one PC to another via a dial-up phone line as an example of a simple data communications opportunity, many key concepts were introduced in this chapter. Communications software plays an important role in bridging the gap between the data within the PC and the modem that prepares data for transmission over the dial-up network.

Because the dial-up phone network was initially designed for voice or analog traffic only, the modem's major task is to transform digital data to analog and vice-versa (modulation/demodulation). Modems can accomplish this modulation by any combination of amplitude, frequency, or phase modulation. The greater the number of bits that can be interpreted per baud, or signalling event, the greater the overall transmission rate of bits as measured in bits per second (bps).

The timing of signalling events between distant modems is crucial to successful data transmission. Asynchronous transmission uses start and stop bits surrounding each character to achieve this inter-modem timing, while synchronous transmission uses a constant clocking signal to keep modems constantly synchronized.

Once the parallel data of the PC have been modulated into serial format onto the phone network, it may reach its remote destination using a variety of available network services. Circuits may be switched, more commonly known as dial-up, or may be leased, in which case a customer would have access to these lines 24 hours a day, 7 days a week. Charges would be based on the length of this permanent circuit rather than on circuit usage time, as is the case with dial-up lines.

Digital network services are also available, in which case a CSU/DSU rather than a modem is employed, since there is no need for analog to digital conversion on an all-digital link.

Data communications devices such as modems and CSU/DSUs combine with available network services to provide end-to-end transmission between computers. The complicated interaction between hardware, software, and network services is transparent to the end-user. In analyzing and designing such a network, data communications professionals concentrate on how changes in one aspect of a design affect other aspects of a design. For example, changing from analog to digital leased lines would have a major impact on the type of data communications devices employed.

Using network analysis models such as the I-P-O (Input-Processing-Output) and H-S-M (Hardware-Software-Media) models provides a framework in which to plan network connections from a simple modem to modem transmission to a complex transcontinental wide-area network.

KEY TERMS

amplitude modulation	DCE	H-S-M	RS-232-C
analog	DDS	interexchange carrier	serial
ASCII	de facto standard	interface	serial port
asynchronous	demodulation	inter-LATA	start bit
bandwidth	detectable event	intra-LATA	stop bit
baud	dial-up line	I-P-O	switched line
baud rate	dibit	LATA	synchronous
bit	digital	leased line	TCM
bps	DTE	local loop	terminal emulation
byte	EBCDIC	modem	transparency
carrier wave	echo cancellation	modem cable	tribit
circuit	encoding	modulation	turnaround time
CO	fallback	parallel	two-wire
CO switch	four-wire	phase modulation	UART
communication software	frequency modulation	POP	voice-grade leased line
CSU/DSU	full-duplex	protocol	wavelength
DB-9	half-duplex	quadbit	
DB-25	handshaking	QAM	

REVIEW QUESTIONS

1. What is the difference between analog transmission and digital transmission?
2. What is the difference between asynchronous transmission and synchronous transmission? Which is more efficient?
3. What is a carrier wave?
4. What three characteristics of a carrier wave can be varied?
5. How are the number of detectable events related to the baud rate and bits per second (bps)?
6. Why do high speed modems vary more than one characteristic of a carrier wave?
7. What is the difference between full-duplex and half-duplex data transmission?
8. What is the difference between bps and baud rate?
9. What is the difference between a leased line and a dial-up line?
10. What is a LATA?
11. What are the four basic steps of any data communications process?
12. What is encoding and why is it necessary?
13. What are the two major encoding standards?
14. Why isn't there a single encoding standard?
15. What is a bit and how is it represented within a computer?
16. How must bits be represented on a voice-grade dial-up line?
17. What are the primary differences between serial and parallel transmission?
18. Which type of transmission (serial or parallel) is most often used in data communications and why?
19. What is the role of communications software in the overall process of getting data from a local PC to a remote PC?
20. What is a UART and what role does it play in the overall process of getting data from a local PC to a remote PC?
21. List the 10 most commonly used RS-232 pins including name, abbreviation, and DCE/DTE orientation.
22. What is the name of the device employed to monitor and manipulate RS-232 signals?
23. What is the purpose of the I-P-O model and how can it be used to model both ends of given circuit?
24. How does the purpose of the H-S-M model differ from that of the I-P-O model?
25. Explain in simple terms how a circuit-switched or dial-up call is established.
26. Compare the differences in call set-up between a local dial-up call and a long-distance dial-up call.
27. What is the bandwidth of a dial-up circuit?

28. What is the significance of the range of frequencies of a dial-up circuit?
29. What are some of the shortcomings of a dial-up circuit in terms of data communications?
30. Modem is actually a contraction of which two words?
31. Complete an I-P-O chart illustrating the required functionality of a modem.
32. What role does a carrier wave play in data transmission over a dial-up line?
33. How is the fact that different modems can use carrier waves with different frequencies resolved?
34. How is the fact that different modems can use different modulation schemes resolved?
35. What does MNP stand for?
36. What is the difference between MNP standards and "V" series standards?
37. What is the relationship between wavelength and frequency?
38. What is a signalling event?
39. How long (in seconds) is a signalling event on a 1200 baud modem?
40. How long (in seconds) is a signalling event on a 2400 baud modem?
41. Which transmission methodology requires an external clocking source? Why?
42. What are the two ways in which modems can be modified to transmit data faster?
43. What are the primary benefits of using a model such as the H-S-M model to a network analyst?
44. What is a defacto standard?
45. What are the advantages and disadvantages of defacto standards?
46. What is transparency and why is it a key requirement of data communications design?
47. Give an example of transparency from the network design developed in Chapter 2.
48. What is the purpose of a LATA?
49. What is the relationship of a LATA to the following: area codes, state boundaries, long-distance carriers, local carriers?
50. How are two-wire and four-wire circuits related to full-duplex and half-duplex transmission?
51. How are handshaking and turnaround time related to full-duplex and half-duplex transmission?
52. What is a CSU/DSU and how does it differ from a modem?
53. What are the differences in functionality between a modem and a CSU/DSU when encountering line problems?

ACTIVITIES

1. Gather advertisements or product specifications for modems of various types. What are the price ranges of these modems? What are the various modulation techniques employed by these modems?

2. Contact your local phone service provider. Inquire as to how many of the services listed in Figure 2-19 are available in your area. Are there other services available which are not listed? Are there any current plans to provide additional services?

3. Inquire of your local phone company how the decision is made whether or not to provide a particular data service in a given area.

4. Inquire of your local phone company the approximate time it takes to "roll out" a new service from conception, through regulatory approval, to actual deployment.

5. Contact the electrical engineering or electrical engineering technology department at your school. Ask about the availability of a guest speaker who might be able to bring an oscilloscope to class to demonstrate the wave characteristics described in Chapter 2.

6. Inquire of your local phone company whether most local loops supplied to homes in your area are two- or four-wire.

7. Ask about the difference between ground start and loop start subscriber trunks (local loops).

8. How many LATAs are in your home state? Construct a map showing the relationship between LATA boundaries, area code boundaries, and state boundaries. How are LATAs identified?

Featured References

Briere, Daniel. "Buyer's Guide to Digital Private Line Services," *Network World*, vol. 9, no. 24 (June 15, 1992), p. 47.

Newton, Harry. *Newton's Telecom Dictionary* (New York: Telecom Library, 1992).

Seyer, Martin. *RS-232 Made Easy* (Englewood Cliffs, NJ: Prentice Hall, 1984).

Bartee, Thomas ed. *Data Communications, Networks, and Systems* (Indianapolis: SAMS, 1987).

McNamara, John. *Technical Aspects of Data Communications* (Digital Press, 1982).

Personal Computer Connectivity

Concepts Reinforced

Top-Down Approach to Business Data Communications
I-P-O Analysis Methodology for Network Modeling
H-S-M Analysis Methodology for Network Implementation
Modems and Modulation
Modem Standards

Concepts Introduced

Modem Comparative Features
Error Prevention, Detection, and Correction
Data Compression
Phone Line Conditioning
Communications Software
Non-LAN PC Connectivity

OBJECTIVES

After having successfully mastered the material in this chapter, you should be able to:

1. Understand the many alternatives available to connect two or more personal computers and/or peripherals that do not involve the installation of a local area network (LAN).

2. Understand the features, limitations, and proper business applications of these non-LAN connectivity alternatives.

3. Understand modem operation, comparative modem features, the importance of modem standards, as well as the cost/benefit analysis of various modem purchases.

4. Understand the comparative features and proper business application of communications software.

5. Understand the implications in terms of technology and cost/benefit of the use of digital rather than analog carrier services.

INTRODUCTION

Having introduced PC-to-PC communications via **modems** in Chapter 2 as a means of explaining many introductory concepts, the operation and comparative features of modems will be studied in detail in this chapter. The role of communications software in the establishment, maintenance, and termination of reliable data communications will also be explored. An introduction to the world of digital carrier services will include studies of the required technology as well as the cost/benefit analysis of employing such services.

PC-to-PC communications via modems falls into the data communications technology category of non-LAN PC connectivity. In addition to connecting PCs via modems, there are many other such non-LAN PC connectivity alternatives as well.

In the second part of Chapter 3 the often overlooked world of non-LAN PC connectivity solutions will be explored. This exploration will provide the perfect opportunity to employ the top-down model of network design. By thoroughly understanding business needs first, the most appropriate connectivity solution at the least possible cost will be more effectively chosen. This business analysis of data communications technology alternatives is the essence of business data communications.

☐ MODEM OPERATION AND COMPARATIVE FEATURES

Business Motivation Behind Modem Design: The Top-Down Model

In Chapter 1 Figure 1-11, "Overriding Trends in Data Communications Technology," two demands of the user community which could be included in the business model layer of the top-down model for data communications analysis were identified. To these two demands of *faster* and *cheaper*, Figure 3-1 adds the need for business data communications to also be more *reliable* and *secure*.

To these four business layer demands, data model layer concepts have been added as they relate to modem technology in Figure 3-1 as well.

☐ FUTURE VALUE OF THE TOP-DOWN MODEL

It is more important at this point to understand the structure of the top-down model and its on-going viability for future use, rather than to merely memorize its

Business Model	**Faster** **Cheaper** **More reliable** **More secure**

Data Model	*Faster*
	    New modem standards
	    Data compression
	    Digital transmission
	Cheaper
	    Modem sharing
	    Compatibility with older modems
	Reliable
	    Error prevention
	    Error detection
	    Error correction
	    Backup for leased line failure
	Secure
	    Unauthorized access prevention
	    Encryption

Figure 3-1 Overriding trends in data communications modem operations and comparative features.

present contents. As a next step, the *network model* layer of the top-down model will be outlined. The equipment and standards listed will represent today's enabling technology of modem operation and comparative features. The study of the concepts, standards, and equipment listed in the network model layer will constitute the first part of this chapter.

As new technologies are introduced in the future, their business value can be judged using such a model with the following questions:

1. Does the new technology fit into one of the listed *data model* concept categories?
2. If not, does it represent a new category or does it not meet any currently perceived business need?
3. Does the new technology identify a new as yet unlisted business data communications need?
4a. If so, add it to your *business model* layer.
4b. If not, then perhaps the newly evaluated technology is either ahead of its time or not currently cost justifiable.

The entries listed on each model layer are based upon the author's experience and observations in business data communications. If your experience yields different results, then change the entries in the model. If you use *your* top-down model as a frame of reference for data communications technology evaluation, it will assist you in making sense of the current explosion of technology while maintaining an objective "so-what attitude" toward that technology.

Current Enabling Technology and Concepts: The Network Model

Figure 3-2 takes each of the data model layer attributes identified in Figure 3-1 and associates network model layer attributes, characteristics, and abilities with each. In this way, network model layer characteristics deliver on data model layer requirements, which in turn, deliver on business model layer requirements. This is the essence of the top-down approach, in which lower-layer solutions meet upper-layer requirements.

Figure 3-2 constitutes a roadmap of concepts to be covered in the remainder of this section of Chapter 3. Each of the major business layer requirements (faster, cheaper, reliable, secure) will be examined in order according to the outline presented in Figure 3-2.

☐ FASTER

New Modem Standards: V.32

Modems complying with the CCITT **V.32** standard provide:

A worldwide standard for full-duplex transmission over dial-up lines or leased lines at 9600 bps transmission rate with a fallback rate of 4800 bps.

The V.32 standard accomplishes this by employing two advanced technology techniques:

Trellis Coded Modulation
Echo Cancellation

Business Model	Data and Network Models
Faster	*New Modem Standards* V.Fast V.32 V.32 bis Fast retrain Echo cancellation *Data Compression* V.42 bis *Digital Transmission* DDS services CSU/DSU
Cheaper	*Modem Sharing* Line bridges Modem & port sharing devices Line sharers & splitters *Compatibility with Older Modems* Handshaking Fallback compatibility Hayes AT command set
Reliable	*Error Prevention* Line conditioning Adaptive protocols *Error Detection* Parity Checksums LRC CRC *Error Correction* ACK/NAK ARQ Sliding window protocols Forward error correction *Backup for Leased Line Failure* Auto dial backup Auto restoral Standalone & integral
Secure	*Unauthorized Access Prevention* Password protection Callback security Standalone & integral *Enryption* Standards Stand-alone or integral

Figure 3-2 Network layer-entries deliver data and business layer requirements.

> *In Sharper*
> *Focus*

TRELLIS CODED MODULATION AND MODEM CONSTELLATIONS

Trellis Coded Modulation was first introduced in Chapter 2. Reviewing briefly, **Trellis Coded Modulation** adds a redundant fifth bit to each quadbit of data transmitted in order to help the receiving modem determine the correct detectable event by predicting the most likely occurrence of each detectable event.

In a V.32 modem, each detectable event is comprised of both an amplitude value and a phase-shift value. The phase-shift component of each detectable event can be assigned values from 0 degrees to 360 degrees and plotted around the center point of a two-axis graph. The amplitude can be assigned values as a varying distance from the intersection of the two axes.

The combination of possible values of phase shift and amplitude represent possible detectable events. These possible detectable events can be plotted as points, with the resultant graph resembling a constellation. Hence, these individual detectable events are sometimes called **constellation points**. A V.32 constellation has 2 to the 5th (for 5 bits/baud) power or 32 constellation points. Four of the five bits represent data, yielding the fact that V.32 defines a modem operating at 2400 baud $\times$ 4 bits/baud = 9600 bps. Figure 3-3 illustrates a V.32 constellation. Although it is not important to understand all of the intricacies of a modem constellation, it is important to understand what a modem constellation represents.

32 possible points
(4 data bits and 1 trellis coded modulation value represented by each point)

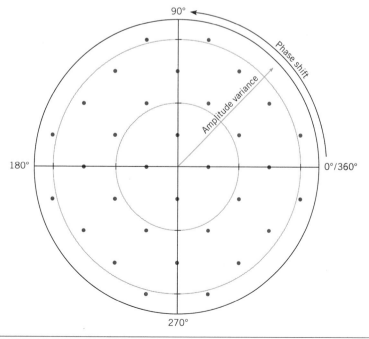

Figure 3-3 V.32 Modem constellation.

Echo Cancellation

Echo cancellation is a sophisticated technique which allows for the *simultaneous* use of the full bandwidth of a two-wire, dial-up circuit by each modem. How can both modems be using all of the circuit's bandwidth at the same time? First, the modem "learns" the echo characteristics of the particular circuit employed. Next, by remembering exactly what electrical signals a modem transmitted and then subtracting the *exact echo* of that transmission from the full received signal, the remaining signal is what the remote modem meant for the local modem to receive.

How can all this remembering and subtracting take place at such high speeds? Once again the relationship between enabling technologies and manufactured datacomm equipment is evident. High speed DSPs or Digital Signal Processors allow V.32 modems to be manufactured and sold at a price which the data communications consumer is willing to pay.

Without the technological advances underlying high speed, affordable DSPs, this would not be the case. It should also be pointed out that this echo cancellation is *adaptive*, in that as the phone line's echo characteristics change, the receiving modem will adapt the subtracted echo of its own transmitted data accordingly.

V.32bis

The **V.32bis** standard is an extension to the V.32 standard. "bis" refers to the second version of the V.32 standard. The constellation consists of 128 points or detectable events rather than the 32 constellation points of the V.32 standard. Seven bits are interpreted (2 to the 7th = 128) for each baud, with one bit reserved for Trellis coding and the remaining six bits for data. 2400 baud $\times$ 6 bits/baud = 14,400 bps. Remember, this is on a voice-grade dial-up phone line.

Fast Retrain

The other major difference between V.32 and V.32bis is the ability for two V.32bis modems to retrain or adjust data rates on the fly quickly. Depending on the quality of the dial-up circuit accessed, V.32bis modems can switch speeds up or down (4800, 7200, 9600, 12000, or 14400 bps) within a matter of milliseconds and continue data transmissions. **Fast retrain** is sometimes known as rapid rate renegotiation.

V.Fast

The CCITT (ITU-T) is currently working on a new standard called **V.Fast** which will extend the V.32bis standard by:

Delivering a maximum data rate of 24000 bps over dial-up voice-grade lines.

The significance of this standard is enhanced when one considers the combination of this 24000 bps transmission rate with **V.42bis data compression** (explained below) which will optimally produce data rates of nearly 100,000 bps. Remember, this is over a regular, analog, dial-up circuit. When finalized, the V.Fast standard will be known as V.34. Many currently available V. Fast modems are capable of transmission speeds of 28,800 bps.

Beating the Standards to Market

The market penetration implications of being the first manufacturer to offer modems compliant with new standards have become so important that manufacturers have now introduced products before standards are even finalized and announced.

For instance, Motorola Codex has introduced a V.Fast modem capable of

115.2Kbps (115,200 bps) even though the V.Fast standard has not been announced. Motorola states that they will provide a free upgrade to the future CCITT V.Fast standard. Hayes and Microcom are also actively marketing V. Fast modems with upgrade promises.

Such a promise requires technological planning to back up this market planning. Contingencies for easy software upgrades had to be included in the initial design of the device. Remember the equation introduced in Chapter 1: Business Demand + Enabling Technologies = Today's Data Communications Equipment.

An alternate solution to the delay in a V.Fast standard has been a proposal for a third version of the V.32 standard known as V.32ter, or more commonly as V.32terbo. This standard seeks to upgrade the 14.4Kbps of V.32bis to 19.2Kbps.

Why V.32 and V.32bis Are Important to Business

Remember the business analysis from Chapter 1 which highlighted *bandwidth on demand* as a major demand of data communications consumers? The fact that V.32bis modems can deliver up to 57.6Kbps over a dial-up line goes a long way toward supplying that demand. V.32 and V.32 bis modems are selling for around $300.00 to $400.00 with prices dropping steadily due to intense competition in the high-speed modem market.

Investment in a V.32 or V.32bis modem will support use on both dial-up and leased lines if the modems are fully standard compliant. Previous CCITT standards were for one or the other. The phrase "fully standard compliant" is significant. I have purchased a V.32 modem whose manual simply stated that it did not support the leased-line operation feature.

The international nature of the CCITT standard assures worldwide compatibility. Fast retrain available with V.32bis assures that the maximum data rate possible on any given line at any given time will be delivered *without operator intervention*.

V.42bis and MNP Class 5 Data Compression

A major contributor to high levels of throughput over dial-up lines is a standard for data compression known as CCITT V.42bis. Data compression can now be included as a standard modem feature. In the past, data compression was often done by a stand-alone device using a proprietary algorithm.

V.42bis is not the first nor the only integrated modem data compression standard. **MNP Class 5** yields data compression ratios in the range of between 1.3:1 and 2:1. V.42bis meanwhile, can yield data compression ratios of from 3.5:1 to 4:1. This means that a V.32 modem with transmission rate of 9600 bps can increase that transmission rate nearly fourfold to 38,400 bps. MNP stands for Microcom Networking Protocol. Ten classes of such protocols have been defined to date.

It is important to understand how data compression works and the fact that all of the 38,400 bits per second do not actually travel across the circuit. It is equally important to understand that V.42bis data compression only works if *both* of the modems on the circuit support V.42bis. Data compressed by the sending modem must be *uncompressed* by the receiving modem using an identical algorithm or methodology.

How Data Compression Works

The data compression software examines the data, looking for repetitive patterns of characters, before it sends the data onto the circuit. Having spotted a repetitive pattern of up to 32 characters, the two V.42bis modems store this pattern, along with a code or key, in a constantly updated library. The next time this pattern of data comes along to be sent, the sending modem just sends a character or characters which represent the pattern's code or key, rather than the entire data stream itself. The receiving modem, then consults its library to see which "uncompressed" pattern is represented by the code character(s) received.

Obviously, the more "repetitive patterns" that V.42bis can find in the data, the higher the compression ratio that can be expected. Thus, some data is more compressible than others and would yield a higher data compression ratio.

Given the transmission of compressed data in which a single character may "uncompress" into many characters, the importance of error prevention, detection, and correction should be obvious. An erroneously transmitted character could be referenced in the receiving modem's library of repetitive patterns and incorrectly "uncompressed" into the wrong data stream.

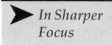

In Sharper Focus

DIGITAL TRANSMISSION AND DDS SERVICES: A BUSINESS ANALYSIS

The availability of high-speed, high-quality modems for dial-up analog circuits has had, and continues to have, a dramatic effect on the leased line services offered by carriers. This should come as no surprise remembering the interrelationships of the components of the data communications industry as illustrated in Figure 1-1. The market responses by the carriers to the increasing speeds of dial-up modems over the past 15 to 20 years are summarized in Figure 3-4 and the subsequent paragraphs. Recent articles found in the featured references section of the chapter bear out this trend as well.

Carrier Services Market Response to Advancing Dial-up Modem Technology

As recently as the early 1980s, 1200 bps was the highest transmission rate one could reliably expect from a voice-grade dial-up line. As a result, carriers offered, and data communications consumers leased, a great number of *conditioned leased analog* circuits. Remember that a leased line implies a fixed connection between two or more points. Points or locations to be connected by the carrier must be declared before installation. The *conditioning* aspect of the line reduces the noise or interference on the line and allows data transmission at rates higher than the normal 1200

	Dial-up Speed	Services Offered/Purchased
Late 1970s Early 1980s	1200	Conditioned analog leased (9600)
Mid-1980s	2400	Digital leased (DDS) 2400, 4800, 9600, 19.2K, 56K
Late 1980s	9600	High bandwidth, digital leased 64K DS-0, 1.54 MT-1, 45M T-3
Early 1990s	14.4K	Switched digital 56K, 128K, 384K
Mid-1990s	100+ Kbps (V.Fast)	?

Figure 3-4 Carriers market response to advancing dial-up modem technology (or, "If I can do it on a dial-up, why should I lease it from you?")

bps of the typical dial-up circuit. Transmission rates of 9600 bps over these conditioned leased analog lines were typical.

As 9600 bps dial-up modems came into the mainstream, carriers emphasized the sale of **DDS** or *digital data service* which were four-wire digital leased lines, point-to-point or multipoint, with declared transmission rates of 2400, 4800, 9600, 19.2K, and 56Kbps. These leased lines often had installation charges of thousands of dollars and significant monthly charges based on the mileage between the points on the leased line. On the positive side, the digital transmission aspects of the line offered greater bandwidth, and therefore faster potential transmission rates, than analog leased lines and, in most cases, fewer errors and line problems.

CSU/DSUs

Modems are not used to interface to digital leased lines since there is no modulation/demodulation to be accomplished. Rather, a device called a **CSU/DSU** (*customer service unit/data service unit*) is employed. CSU/DSUs cost between $700 and $900 dollars.

CSU/DSUs and Line Troubleshooting

One of the major functions of the CSU/DSU is to perform diagnostic tests to determine the cause of service interruption. *A word of warning*—If you buy your own CSU/DSUs rather than renting or buying them from the provider of the DDS service, you run the risk of being stuck between the proverbial rock and a hard place during service interruptions when:

1. The DDS leased line provider says the problem is in your CSU/DSU.
2. The CSU/DSU provider says the problem is in your DDS service.

Many DDS providers also rent or sell the CSU/DSUs. In my experience, there was no significant difference in price between buying CSU/DSUs from the carriers or from a data communications equipment distributor. By buying CSU/DSUs from the DDS provider, I was able to make them totally responsible for the delivery of the service through their DCEs to my DTEs and avoided any possible finger-pointing.

DDS Pricing Trends

As digital switching equipment has steadily replaced analog equipment in the carriers' central offices, the price of DDS services has declined steadily. As an incentive to switch from analog to digital leased lines, carriers began offering digital leased lines services at a lower monthly rate than analog leased line services of corresponding bandwidths.

As dial-up transmission rates continue to climb thanks to V.32 and V.32bis modem standards and V.42bis data compression, consumers find themselves asking the carriers, "Why should I lease this line from you when I can dial-up the same rate myself?" As a result, the carriers are offering *high bandwidth digital leased lines* such as the 64kbps DS-0, 1.544Mbps T-1 (that's 1.544 *million* bits per second) and the 45Mbps T-3. These high bandwidth digital leased lines will be discussed in more detail including their proper business application in Chapter 7—Wide Area Networks.

The mid-1990s will see an increase in the demand for *switched digital services*. Unlike the significant difference in line quality and performance of switched analog versus **conditioned leased analog lines**, switched digital versus **leased digital lines** offer virtually the same quality and performance. Now data communications consumers are asking, "Why should I lease this 56K digital line from you 24 hours per day when I only use it 4 hours per day? I want to dial-up the 56K digital bandwidth when I want for only as long as I need it!"

These switched digital circuits are ideal for connecting LANs, otherwise known as *internetworking*, over long distances. This application of **switched 56K** services will be examined in later discussions of internetworking. Switched 56K circuits are also being used for *backup* and *disaster recovery* for failed leased 56K circuits. CSU/DSUs which automatically access switched 56K services upon failure of leased 56K circuits are featured in the technology section of this chapter.

Another rapidly growing use of switched 56K services is *videoconferencing*. A specialized device known as an *inverse multiplexer* uses multiple switched 56K circuits to quickly and easily set up and transmit video conferences. Videoconferencing and its associated hardware and carrier services will be studied further in Chapter 11.

If this is beginning to sound like *bandwidth on demand*, that is exactly where carrier services are headed. Future trends of carrier services will be explored in more depth in Chapter 13, "Where Do We Go From Here? Trends to Watch."

☐ CHEAPER

Having completed the analysis of the ways in which data transmission can be accomplished *faster*, how data transmission can be accomplished more economically or *cheaper* will now be explored. Figures 3-1 and 3-2 serve as roadmaps to the concepts covered in Chapter 3.

Modem Sharing

Simply stated, it takes modems and circuits to complete remote data transmission. If a way can be found to effectively use either fewer modems or fewer circuits without sacrificing performance, money could potentially be saved.

Figure 3-5a graphically illustrates one way of transmitting data more economically known as **modem sharing**. Modem sharing only makes sense from a data communications standpoint, if it also makes good *business* sense.

The top-down model will be employed to analyze the proper use and implementation of modem sharing. I-P-O and H-S-M analysis will be used for logical and physical design, respectively.

Business Model: Six local terminals occasionally need dial-up access to a remote computer. Rarely, if ever, would more than one terminal need to be on-line to the remote computer simultaneously.

Data Model: Find a way for all six terminals to share one modem and one dial-up line at a reasonable cost.

Network Model: I-P-O Analysis

　　Input: Six terminals

　　Process: Share the modem without special prioritization for particular ports or any need for special processing

　　Output: One modem and one dial-up phone line

　　H-S-M Analysis

　　Hardware: Terminals—Asynchronous, 9600bps, RS-232/DB-25

　　　　Modem—V.32 w/ V.42bis, RS-232/DB-25, RJ-11 jack for phone line

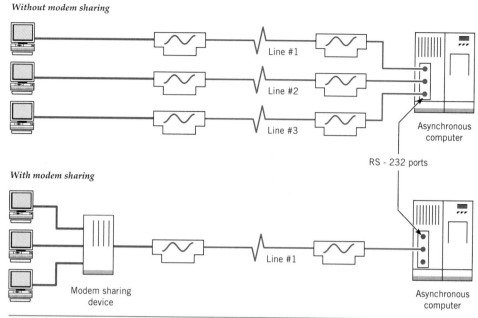

Figure 3-5a Basic modem sharing.

Software: None. We want the modem sharing device to pass data transparently from the terminal to the modem.

Media: RS-232/DB-25 modem cable from each terminal serial port to modem sharing device

RS-232/DB-25 modem cable from modem sharing device to modem

RJ-11 modular phone cable from modem line output jack to RJ-11 jack

One dial-up analog voice-grade phone circuit

Technology Model: What currently available technology will deliver required functionality as identified in the I-P-O analysis and interface with the physical constraints of the current components as identified in the H-S-M analysis?

The most important thing to remember about this example is that when a terminal is using the modem and the phone line, it has 100 percent use of these resources. Multiple terminals *cannot* use the modem and phone circuit simultaneously. Simultaneous sharing of phone circuits by multiple terminals is known as **multiplexing** and will be studied in Chapter 7.

	Savings	Costs
4 modems (2 each, lines 2 & 3) × $200 each	= $800	
2 lines (@ approximately $40/month plus long distance charges) at least	=$180/month	
2 computer ports available	= $?	
Costs of modem sharer		= $99

If using this modem sharing device delivers required levels of service, then the cost justification should be obvious.

Figure 3-5b Cost savings via modem sharing.

If the terminals needed simultaneous access to resources, that fact should appear in the business model with accommodations for that business requirement reflected in subsequent analysis layers.

Variations on modem sharing devices such as: modem splitters, port sharing devices, and programmable sharing devices will be reviewed in the technology section of this chapter.

In conclusion, this example shows that in those cases in which *business needs* have been carefully and reliably defined, modem sharing can yield significant financial savings.

Compatibility with Older Modems

Compatibility with older modems has been included as an economic issue because the lack of such compatibility would cause a data communications consumer to replace *all* existing modems with the introduction of each new modem performance standard—a rather costly venture.

It should also be obvious that a network manager cannot control the sophistication of the equipment of enterprise partners with whom data communications may be required. To summarize, the introduction of new performance standards or technology, must not render all previous technology useless. New technology must be able to interact successfully with existing technology. This existing or older technology is sometimes referred to as **legacy technology**.

Handshaking

The enabling of this interoperability between new and existing technologies takes place in a formal, standardized initial interaction between two modems commonly known as **handshaking**. During this handshaking, the two pieces of data communications equipment get to know each other and establish the greatest common operating characteristics between themselves. Standards governing this ritual include MNP Class 6 (Microcom Network Protocol), otherwise known as Universal Link Negotiation and MNP Class 9, Enhanced Universal Link Negotiation.

Hayes AT Command Set

Another important compatibility feature to consider when the need for communicating with modems of older or unknown sophistication exists, is the support of the **Hayes AT Command Set**. Originally designed by Hayes for its Smartmodems, the Hayes AT Command Set has become a de facto standard operating system for modems attached to personal computers. Most communications software packages for the PC implement the Hayes AT Command Set, perhaps in addition to other proprietary command sets. The Hayes AT Command Set is nothing more than a series of commands that allow the PC to control the set-up and performance of the modem.

☐ **RELIABLE**

Improving the reliability of the data transmission link between two modems will ultimately make that data transmission *faster* and *cheaper*. Fewer retransmissions due to data errors will increase the throughput of information bits, thus reducing the time necessary to transmit a given message, thereby minimizing the cost of the data transmission.

The goal of *reliable* transmission is to reduce the error rate of a data transmission session as close as possible to zero errors. The first category of methodologies which will be covered strive to *prevent* errors from happening in the first place by optimizing the condition of the transmission link (**error prevention**). Should errors still occur, it is essential that these errors are accurately *detected* (**error detection**). Once detected, the errors must be reliably *corrected* (**error correction**).

Error Prevention

Line Conditioning   As mentioned earlier in this chapter, **line conditioning** is a value-added service available from the phone company from whom one leases analog leased lines. Various levels of conditioning are available at prices that increase proportionally to the level of conditioning, or noise reduction, requested. Conditioning represents a promise from the phone company as to levels of noise or interference which will occur on a given analog leased line. In order to deliver on this promise, the phone company may have to install additional equipment to guarantee signal quality.

Repeaters and Amplifiers   A **repeater** is often used by a phone company to assure signal quality over the entire length of a circuit. As a signal travels through a medium such as copper wire, it loses some of its strength due to the resistance of the wire. This loss of signal strength or volume is known as *attenuation*.

A repeater on an *analog* circuit, sometimes called an **amplifier**, strengthens and repeats or retransmits the signal. Unfortunately, on analog circuits, the amplifier cannot distinguish between the voice or data and the background noise on the circuit and, as a result, also strengthens, repeats and retransmits the noise of the circuit.

In contrast, repeaters on *digital* circuits are able to actually regenerate digital signals (remembering that digital signals are discrete voltages—Chapter 2) before repeating and retransmitting them. Thus a digital signal, including digitized voice, transmitted over a digital circuit will more reliably arrive at its destination without the need for line conditioning. The repeaters in this application are primarily used only by the phone company and should not be confused with local area network repeaters, which will be covered in Chapter 5.

As analog leased lines give way to digital leased and dial-up services, the purchase of line conditioning will become a non-issue in the error prevention arena. In fact, the use of DDS or digital leased lines could be seen as an error prevention technique.

Adaptive Protocols   Another way in which errors can be prevented during data transmission is through the use of **adaptive protocols** which are able to adjust transmission session parameters in response to varying line conditions. The MNP classes of networking protocols offer several examples of such adaptive protocols.

Adaptive Size Packet Assembly is an MNP Class 4 protocol which can increase or decrease the amount of data sent in each *packet* according to the current condition of the transmission circuit. A packet that includes data and overhead information is analogous to a handwritten message (the data) plus a sealed, addressed envelope (the overhead).

This protocol tries to optimize the amount of data per packet by building packets containing the greatest amount of data which can be transmitted reliably and, therefore, not require retransmission.

Optimization may be a moving target as line conditions change. Each packet must be processed individually, which takes time. Therefore, it stands to reason that it would be advantageous to get as much data as possible into each packet. Returning to the previous analogy, it would be advantageous to write as long a letter as possible for each envelope. Too little data per packet and time is wasted processing overhead (i.e., opening envelopes in the analogy).

However, if too much data is put into each packet, retransmissions will be required, thereby consuming significant amounts of transmission time. By enclosing too much data per packet, time is wasted retransmitting packets received in error, (receiving back, rewriting and remailing letters for insufficient postage in our analogy).

Adaptive Size Packet Assembly solves the data per packet dilemma by adapting the amount of data included in each packet according to varying line conditions.

Dynamic Speed Shifts is an MNP Class 10 adaptive protocol which allows two modems to change speeds up or down (faster or slower) in the midst of their data transmission in response to varying line conditions. The adaptive nature of this protocol assures that the highest practical transmission speed will be used at all times, dependent upon current line conditions. This adaptive protocol is especially useful in cellular phone environments in which line quality can vary significantly over short periods of time.

Dynamic Speed Shifts can be a double-edged sword, however. In the event of degraded line quality, MNP 10 modems may automatically downgrade their transmission speeds. Unless a personnel procedure is in place to take note of the lower transmission speed, the problem may go undetected and unreported to the carrier for an extended period of time.

Error Detection

Once everything possible to *prevent* errors has been done, the next task is to *reliably detect* those errors that do occur. Several error detection techniques of varying degrees of complexity have been developed. The following error detection techniques will be briefly introduced:

> Parity
> Checksums and Longitudinal Redundancy Checks (LRC)
> Cyclic Redundancy Checks (CRC)

Remembering that transmitted data, on the most elementary level, is merely a stream of 1's and 0's, the role of error detection can be defined as providing the assurance that the receiving modem receives the same 1's and 0's in the exact sequence as transmitted by the transmitting modem.

This assurance is achieved through the cooperative efforts of the transmitting and receiving modem. In addition to transmitting the actual data, the transmitting modem must also transmit some type of verifiable bit or character, which the receiving modem can use to decide whether the transmitted data was received correctly or not. All of the error detection techniques listed above adhere to this general principle of operation.

Parity   **Parity** is the simplest of the error detection techniques. Remembering that the ASCII 7-bit code for the letter "A" is: 1000001, a parity bit is added as the eighth bit. Whether this bit should be a 0 or a 1 depends on whether odd or even parity has been defined or agreed upon in advance by the PCs or terminals and computer ports involved in the data transmission. These devices can also agree to data transmission with no parity. Examples of the letter "A" with odd and even parity are illustrated in Figure 3-6.

Letter "A" with odd and even parity

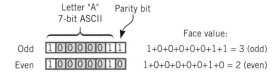

Figure 3-6 Parity.

When the letter "A" is transmitted with odd parity, the parity bit is set to 1 so that the sum of the face values of all of the bits in the character will be odd. Conversely, when even parity is chosen by both ends of the data transmission circuit, the parity bit is set to 0 so that the face value of the transmitted data is even.

If the *even* parity is chosen and the receiving computer adds up the face values of the bits in a character and finds that the sum is *odd*, then it knows that it has detected a transmission error.

Parity checking has a limitation however. Figure 3-7 illustrates parity checking's inability to detect multiple bit errors within the same character. As can be seen in Figure 3-7, the received character has an even face value so that the receiving computer would think everything was fine, however in fact, a letter "Q" was received even though the letter "A" was transmitted.

Longitudinal Redundancy Checks Longitudinal Redundancy Checks (**LRC**) seek to overcome the weakness of simple bit-oriented, one directional parity checking, sometimes called Vertical Redundancy Checking or VRC. One can think of LRC as adding a second dimension to VRC. Figure 3-8 illustrates Longitudinal Redundancy Checking with even parity in two dimensions.

In this illustration, both the parity bits of individual characters (VRC) as well as the parity bits of the Longitudinal Redundancy Check character would be checked to be sure that even parity existed in both directions.

Checksums Checksums seek to correct the weakness in single dimension parity checking (VRC) in a slightly different manner. A checksum adds up the ASCII decimal face values of several characters (128 for instance), rather than just one character, and appends an entire character, rather than just a bit, to a message block. This transmitted appended character represents a checksum, which is a mathematical derivative of the total face value of all the characters in a message block and is verifiable by the receiving computer. The sophistication of this "mathematical derivative" of the transmitted data bits varies among different error detection techniques.

Even parity chosen

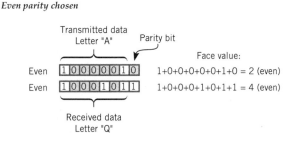

Figure 3-7 Parity checking limitation: the inability to detect multiple bit errors.

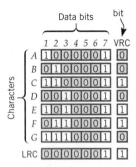

Figure 3-8 LRC and VRC. This example is based on even parity.

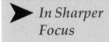 *In Sharper Focus*

CHECKSUM CALCULATION: AN IN-DEPTH LOOK

The Formula
The formula for calculating a checksum, in this example as part of the XMODEM file transfer protocol, is as follows:

1. Add the ASCII decimal face value (see next paragraph) of each of the 128 characters in the block.
2. Divide this number by 255.
3. The remainder of this answer is the checksum character to be transmitted to and verified by the receiving modem.

The ASCII Table
In order to understand the inner workings of this formula, it is necessary to further understand the ASCII table. Every value in the ASCII table has a decimal equivalent computed by transforming the 1's and 0's of any character, into their Base 2 column values and adding the decimal values of those Base 2 columns in which 1's appear.

Example:
Capital letter A 7-bit ASCII code is 1000001
Now assign Base 2 place values to each column

Power of 2	7	6	5	4	3	2	1	0
Decimal value	128	64	32	16	8	4	2	1
Letter "A" code		1	0	0	0	0	0	1

There is a "1" in the "64" column and a "1" in the "1" column. Adding these place values, yields 64 + 1 or 65 (Base 10) or decimal 65. Therefore the ASCII decimal face value of the capital letter "A" is 65.

Transmit a Block of 128 Characters
If 128 capital "A"s were transferred, the total ASCII face value of the block would be $128 \times 65 = 8320$. Divide the total ASCII face value by 255 yields $8320/255 = 32$ r 160. So the remainder is 160.

Represent the Remainder as a Single Checksum Character
Recalling the place values of the powers of 2, compute the Base 2 value of decimal 160.

Power of 2	7	6	5	4	3	2	1	0
Decimal value	128	64	32	16	8	4	2	1
Binary representation of decimal 160	1	0	1	0	0	0	0	0

Thus, the transmitted checksum character would be 10100000.

Worst Case Remainder—254

When dividing our total ASCII face value by 255, the highest remainder possible would be 254. Decimal 254 would be represented in binary and transmitted in a single checksum character (8 bits) as follows:

Power of 2	7	6	5	4	3	2	1	0
Decimal value	128	64	32	16	8	4	2	1
Binary representation of decimal 254	1	1	1	1	1	1	1	0

Cyclic Redundancy Checks or CRC

Cyclic Redundancy checks seek to improve on the error detection capability of checksums and LRCs. A Cyclic Redundancy Check is really a more sophisticated form of a checksum, calculating and transmitting this checksum or Block Check Character to the receiving modem for recalculation and verification. CRC-16 or CRC-32 may be seen in modem product descriptions—this stands for 16 bit or 32 bit Cyclic Redundancy Checking.

CRC-16 and CRC-32

In order to understand CRC-16 and CRC-32, binary division is required. In cyclic redundancy checking, the entire message block of 1's and 0's, even if it is 1000 bits long, is treated as a single, gigantic binary number.

This gigantic string of 1's and 0's is divided by a predetermined prime binary number (a 17-bit divisor for CRC-16 and a 33-bit divisor for CRC-32). Remembering that these divisors are prime (only divisible by 1 and themselves) they will produce a 16-bit and 32-bit remainder respectively.

This remainder is then attached to the actual data message (the original string of 1's and 0's to be transmitted) and transmitted to the receiving modem where the data string is again divided by the same 16-bit or 32-bit divisor. The remainder calculated at the receiving modem is compared to the recently received remainder calculated at the transmitting modem.

Using this technique, a CRC-16 modem can detect error bursts of up to 15 bits 100 percent of the time, while a CRC-32 modem can detect error bursts of up to 31 bits 100 percent of the time.

The CRC-16 modem can detect error bursts larger than 16 bits 100–1/2 to the 16th percent of the time and a CRC-32 modem can detect error bursts of larger than 32 bits 100–1/2 to the 32nd percent of the time.

Computing the percentage for CRC-16 yields an error detection rate of 99.999984742 percent!

◄

Checksums and cyclic redundancy checks are often used to assure error-free transmission of file transfers between computers. Checksums will be explored further in the communications software section of this chapter. For now, it is sufficient to know that:

1. Both transmitting and receiving computers must agree on how the checksum is to be calculated.
2. The transmitting computer calculates and transmits the checksum along with the transmitted data.
3. The receiving computer recalculates the checksum based on the received data and compares its calculated checksum to the checksum that was calculated and transmitted by the transmitting computer.
4. If the two checksums match, everything is fine. If the receiving computer's calculated checksum does not match the transmitted checksum, an error has been detected.

Error Correction

Now that it is understood how data transmission errors can be *detected*, the numerous ways in which these errors can be *corrected* will be explored. In simple terms, error correction amounts to:

1. The receiving modem *detecting* an error and *requesting retransmission*.
2. The transmitting modem *retransmitting* the incorrect data.

The differences in sophistication between the various error correcting protocols which will be explored are centered around:

1. How is the retransmission requested?
2. How much data must be retransmitted?
3. How is retransmission time minimized?

Error correction could easily have been included in the *cheaper* section of the business model layer. Retransmissions take time and, in business, time is money.

ARQ—Automatic Retransmission Request   ARQ or Automatic Retransmission Request is a general term that really describes the overall process of error detection using one of the previously described methods as well as the subsequent *automatic request for retransmission* of that data. As noted above, the actual request for retransmission can occur in different ways. These varieties of ARQ could be categorized as:

Discrete ARQ
Continuous ARQ

Discrete ARQ—ACK/NAK   Discrete ARQ is sometimes also known as "stop and wait" ARQ. In a protocol using Discrete ARQ or **ACK/NAK**, the transmitting device sends a block of data and *waits* until the remote receiving device does the following:

1. Receives the data.
2. Tests for errors using either parity, LRC, checksum or CRC.
3a. Sends an *acknowledgement (ACK)* character back to the transmitting device if the transmitted data was error free.
    or
3b. Sends a *negative acknowledgement (NAK)* character if the data was not successfully received.

After waiting for this ACK/NAK, the transmitting device does the following:

1a. Sends the next block of data if an ACK was received.

or

1b. Retransmits the original block of data if a NAK was received.

This entire process repeats itself until the conclusion of the data transmission session.

Obviously, the transmitting device spends a significant amount of time idly waiting for either an ACK or NAK to be sent by the receiving device. As may have been suspected, there is an ARQ methodology that takes a different, more efficient approach to error detection and correction.

Continuous ARQ—Sliding Window Protocols   A variation of ARQ known as **Continuous ARQ**, eliminates the requirement for the transmitting device to wait for an ACK or NAK after transmitting each block before transmitting the next block of data. This obviously eliminates a great deal of idle time and increases overall data throughput.

With Continuous ARQ, sometimes known as a **sliding window protocol** when implemented in a communications software package, a **block sequence number** is appended to each block of data transmitted. The transmitting device continuously transmits blocks of data *without* waiting for ACK or NAK from the receiving device after each block of data sent. However, there is often a sliding window block limit to prevent a modem from transmitting indefinitely without having received either an ACK or NAK.

The receiving device still checks each block of data for errors just as it did with Discrete ARQ. However, when the receiving device detects an error in a block of data, it sends the block sequence number along with the NAK back to the transmitting device.

The transmitting device now knows which particular block of data was received in error and can retransmit that block. As will be seen later in this chapter in the study of communications software, some variations of Continuous ARQ can retransmit *only* those blocks of data received in error, in a process known as *selective ARQ*, while other implementations must retransmit *all* blocks of data from the NAK block forward.

How does the transmitting device remember what data was in which block? Obviously, the data must be stored and saved somewhere in the block sequence order in which it was transmitted. That somewhere is in **buffer memory**. The addition of this buffer memory as well as the sophisticated programming necessary to manage the flow of data into and out of this memory adds additional costs to these devices. The benefits of increased data throughput and resultant reduced phone circuit usage must be weighed against the increased cost of this more sophisticated technology when making informed business decisions on technology acquisition.

The ability to properly use buffer memory can be a function of the communications software that one may purchase to control data communications sessions. As will be seen in the study of communications software packages later in this chapter, some software does a better job than others when it comes to buffer utilization.

Flow Control   The constant storage and retrieval of blocks of data from this finite amount of buffer memory necessitates some type of management of the use of this memory. That management is commonly known as **flow control**. Simply stated flow control controls the flow of data into and out of the buffer memory in order to avoid any loss of data.

The flow control management software must constantly monitor the amount of free space available in buffer memory and tell the sending device to stop sending data when there is insufficient storage space. That signal to stop sending data, and the subsequent signal to resume sending data, may be either *hardware* or *software* based.

Hardware Flow Control—RTS/CTS Hardware flow control was actually introduced in Chapter 2 in the section of RS-232. Pin 4, request to send (**RTS**) and pin 5, clear to send (**CTS**) are the essential elements of hardware flow control. A transmitting device will only send data into buffer memory as long as pin 5, clear to send, continues to be "held high" or carry an appropriate voltage. As soon as clear to send is "dropped," or the appropriate voltage ceases on pin 5, the transmitting device immediately ceases transmitting data.

Software Flow Control—XON/XOFF Rather than controlling flow through pins 4 and 5, actual characters could be transmitted on pin 2 and received on pin 3, which would mean either "stop sending data" or "resume sending data." When a device cannot receive data any longer, it sends an **XOFF** character to the transmitting device. The more familiar keyboard representation of XOFF is the keystroke combination of CTRL-S.

The transmitting device would not resume data transmission until it received an **XON** character, CTRL-Q on the keyboard.

It has been my experience that hardware flow control is more reliable and probably faster than software flow control. Remember that software flow control is nothing more than transmitted characters susceptible to the same transmission problems as normal data. Occasionally, an XOFF may be transmitted in error and stop a data transmission session for no apparent reason. Secondly, because XON and XOFF are characters, they are received in on pin 3 along with all the "normal" data and must be differentiated from that data. This process takes time and is subject to error.

Forward Error Correction All of the error correction techniques examined thus far have one thing in common: They all depended on a retransmission of the data as the basis of their error correction. Sophisticated error correction techniques exist that send sufficient redundant data to the receiving modem to enable it to not only *detect* but also *correct* data transmission errors in some cases, *without the need for retransmission*.

Beware, however. In data communications, as in life, you can't get something for nothing. In order to give the receiving modem sufficient redundant data to be able to correct its own detected errors, the overall throughput of informational data on the circuit is reduced.

This process, known as **forward error correction**, tries to favorably balance how much redundant data can be sent "up front," thereby avoiding costly retransmissions, in order to maximize overall throughput on the circuit. It's a bit of a gamble, really:

Don't send enough redundant data, and the overall throughput is reduced due to retransmissions.

Send too much redundant data, and the overall throughput is reduced because the redundant data is taking up space that could be occupied by "new," nonredundant, informational data.

Trellis Coded Modulation, discussed briefly at the beginning of this chapter, is an example of a forward error correction technique. Other examples of forward error correction techniques include: Hamming Code, Hagelbarger Code, and Bose-Chaudhuri Code.

The detailed explanations of these codes are beyond the scope of this book. Forward error correction is a very sophisticated technique that may add substantial cost to a modem. Be sure that the incremental performance benefits justify any incremental cost increases.

Error Control Standards Summary　As modems are examined in the technology section of this chapter, error control standards supported by any given modem will be noted.

MNP Standards　MNP standards for error control implemented by both Microcom modems as well as modems of other manufacturers include MNP classes 2, 3 and 4. These error control standards optimize the full-duplex transmission of data over dial-up lines through Adaptive Size Packet Assembly (described earlier) and the elimination of redundant or overhead information from transmissions.

CCITT Standard—V.42　V.42, not to be confused with the CCITT V.42bis standard for data compression, actually incorporates MNP class 4 error control as the first of two possible error control protocols. In addition, a second error control protocol known as *link access protocol* for modems, or **LAP-M**, will add selective ARQ to the capabilities of MNP class 4 error control protocol. Selective ARQ, described earlier, only requires retransmission of specific blocks received in error rather than all blocks subsequent to the block in which the error was detected.

V.42 also provides for negotiation during modem handshaking to allow two modems to decide whether they will implement MNP 4 or LAP-M as an error control protocol for their data transmission.

Hardware Error Control　It is important to note at this time that MNP 4 and V.42 are error control protocols implemented within modems. Using these protocols, the modems themselves assure error-free transmission. There is no need for additional error control protocols that can be supplied by communications software packages running as an application program on a PC. When communications software packages are studied later in this chapter, it will be important to note whether or not the modems to be used with the communications software supply hardware-based error control through such protocols as MNP 4 or V.42.

Backup for Leased Line Failure

Leasing either an analog or digital dedicated circuit (leased line) from a phone company can provide high bandwidth data transmission of guaranteed quality. That's the good news.

The bad news is that, despite what the phone company sales representative may say, *leased lines do fail*. It should stand to reason that the more complicated the circuit, the more likely it is to fail. It has been my experience that multipoint lines are more likely to fail than point-to-point leased lines.

Coping with leased-line failure requires a business decision. The technology is available to backup failed leased lines by automatically establishing connections via dial-up lines between points on the failed circuit. However, there are at least two incremental costs involved in this *automatic backup*. First, there is the cost of the additional technology necessary to detect the leased line failure and establish the dial-up connection. Secondly, dial-up circuits must be available for the auto **dial backup unit** to utilize in the event of a leased line failure. These dial up circuits would incur both installation and monthly charges whether they are used or not. In addition, if the established dial backup connection is long distance, then per minute usage charges for the dial-up lines could amount to a significant incremental cost.

The other side of the cost–benefit equation would require the following question to be asked, "What is the cost of the business lost during the time that the leased line is down?" If that lost business can be translated into lost sales dollars in excess of the incremental cost of establishing and maintaining the dial-up backup for the failed leased line, then the acquisition of the equipment and phone lines to enable automatic backup would constitute a prudent business decision.

Some leased line modems possess sufficient technology to be able to monitor the failed leased line after establishing the dial-up backup, sense when service on the leased line has been repaired and has stabilized, and automatically restore the data transmission back onto the leased line in a process known as **auto restoral**.

Sometimes this automatic backup and/or restoral capability is built into the modem (analog) or CSU/DSU (digital). These built-in features are known as integral whereas the dedicated devices designed to only do automatic backup and/or restoral are known as standalone devices. In this way, the automatic backup and restoral capability can be added after the initial modem or CSU/DSU purchase, if required.

CSU/DSUs used on digital leased lines can offer an additional backup option as compared with analog modems. Automatic backup and restoral features on a CSU/DSU have a choice as to which available switched or dial-up services to access when establishing the backup connection. Some digital CSU/DSUs access *analog* dial-up lines from the Public Switched Telephone Network (PSTN) for backup, while other CSU/DSUs access Switched 56K dial-up *digital* services in the event of a digital leased line failure.

☐ SECURE

In addition to the need for *reliable* data communications, there exists an increasing business need for *security* of both the transmitted data as well as *controlled access* to the corporate network over which that data is transmitted.

Modem technology has been developed which provides solutions to both of these security-related issues. Remembering the premise introduced in Chapter 2, *"modularity of design,"* it should come as no surprise that these security features are integrated into certain modems, while also being available as stand-alone, add-on units. The concepts behind the solutions to these security issues will be examined here, while specific technological implementations of these solutions will be reviewed in the technology review section of this chapter.

Access Control
Granting dial-up network access to only those individuals properly authorized is most often accomplished through either one or both of the following techniques:

> Password protection
> Dial-back security

Password Protection
Password protection may already be familiar as a means of controlling access to a local area network, minicomputer, or mainframe. However, it is important to understand that, in this case, it is an *additional* layer of password protection which is offered by certain modems. Typically, a modem would answer an incoming call

and require a password to allow the calling party access to the network. Failure to enter a valid password in a limited amount of time will cause the answering modem to terminate the call.

Dial-Back Security

Some modems add an additional layer of security beyond password protection. Once a valid password (and sometimes user I.D. also) has been entered, the answering modem:

1. Terminates the call.
2. Looks up the user ID and/or password in a directory.
3. Finds the phone number of the valid user in the directory.
4. *Dials back* the valid user and establishes the communication session.

Do not confuse this **dial-back** unit with the *dial backup* unit employed for leased line failure recovery.

The advantages of a dial-back system include:

1. Assurance that only valid users can gain access to the network.
2. Easy maintenance of valid users in one central directory. By merely eliminating terminated employees from the directory, one can prevent unauthorized network access. Of course, this assumes that users do not tell each other their passwords, either purposefully or accidentally.
3. Users can also have network access restricted according to time of day or day of the week. This information would also be stored in the central directory.
4. Some dial-back units save and report usage information such as: user ID, date and time, length of session, resources accessed, etc.

The disadvantages of a dial-back system include:

1. By always dialing back valid users, the central location of the dial-back unit always incurs any long-distance phone charges.
2. The fixed dial-back phone number for each valid user does not work well for traveling users. This process is known as **fixed callback**. To overcome this problem, some dial-back units feature **variable callback**, wherein valid users enter both a password as well as a phone number to which the dial-back unit should return the call.

Network Security Begins with User Integrity

It should be clear from this example that the overall integrity of the network security offered by the dial-back unit depends heavily on the secrecy of the passwords and the integrity of the valid users. Ideally, passwords should be changed frequently (once or twice per month) and should never be shared, written down, or taped to monitors.

Encryption

Encryption involves the changing of data into an unreadable or unmeaningful form prior to transmission. In this way, even if the transmitted data is somehow intercepted, it cannot be interpreted. The changed, unmeaningful data is known as *ciphertext*. Encryption must be accompanied by decryption, or changing the unreadable text back into its original form. Figure 3-9 illustrates a typical installation of encryption devices.

The decrypting device must use the same algorithm or method to decode or

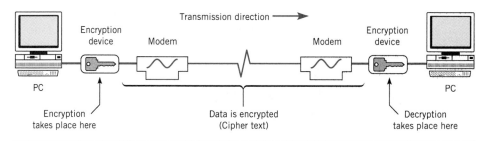

Figure 3-9 Encryption devices.

decrypt the data as the encrypting device used to encrypt the data. Although proprietary standards do exist, a standard known as **DES** (data encryption standard), originally approved by the National Institute of Standards and Technology (NIST) in 1977, is often used, allowing encryption devices manufactured by different manufacturers to interoperate successfully. The DES encryption standard actually has two parts that serve to offer greater overall security. In addition to the standard *algorithm* or method of encrypting data 64 bits at a time, the DES standard also uses a 64 bit *key*.

The encryption key customizes the commonly known algorithm to prevent anyone without this **private key** from possibly decrypting the document. This private key must be known by both the sending and receiving encryption devices and allows so many unique combinations (nearly 2 to the 64th power), that unauthorized decryption is nearly impossible. The safe and reliable distribution of these private keys among numerous encryption devices can be difficult. If this private key is somehow intercepted, the integrity of the encryption system is compromised.

As an alternative to the DES private key standard, *public key encryption* can be utilized. Public key encryption could perhaps more accurately be named public/private key encryption as the process actually combines use of both public and private keys. In public key encryption, the sending encryption device encrypts a document using the intended recipient's public key. This **public key** is readily available in a public directory. However, in order to decrypt the document, the receiving encryption device must be programmed with the recipient's private key.

In this method, only the receiving party needs to know the private key and the need for transmission of private keys between sending and receiving parties is eliminated.

As an added security measure, **digital signature encryption** uses this public key encryption methodology in reverse as an electronic means of guaranteeing authenticity of the sending party and assurance that encrypted documents have not been tampered with during transmission. The digital signature has been compared to the wax seals of old which (supposedly) guaranteed tamper-evident delivery of documents.

With digital signature encryption, a document's digital signature is created by the sender using a private key and the encrypted document. To validate the authenticity of the received document, the recipient uses a public key associated with the apparent sender to decode the transmitted digital signature. This decoded transmitted signature is then compared by the recipient to a digital signature produced by the recipient using the public key and the received document. If the two digital signatures match, the document is authentic.

Encryption devices can be standalone or integrated into other devices.

Encryption devices that can be installed in a PC as an expansion card and store data in encrypted form on local or remote disks are also available.

Encryption standards are in a state of development and evolution. The recent articles referred to in the Featured References section of this chapter not only explain some of the emerging encryption standards, but raise some rather disturbing possibilities of the interaction between the political and regulatory components of the data communications industry.

☐ COMMUNICATIONS SOFTWARE

Having completed the study of modem operation and comparative features, the role of software in modem-based data communications will be explored. The successful accomplishment of data transmission involves more than just data communications hardware.

Role of Data Communications Software

Picture yourself sitting in front of a PC in which you have just installed an integral modem card, or perhaps a stand-alone modem hooked via a modem cable to the PC's serial port. You power up the modem, hook a phone line to it and . . . nothing happens.

Somehow, communication with this modem through the local PC must be established in order to tell it what to do.

It is the communications software that interprets the business data communications needs into a language that the data communications hardware can understand. Communications software is the interface between data communications desires and the data communications hardware. Figure 3-10 graphically illustrates where communications software fits in an end-to-end diagram of a PC-based data communications session.

Communications software is an application program that should offer easy to understand screens from which users can initiate, maintain, and terminate data communications sessions. Commands entered or menu items selected in the communications software are passed along to the operating system of the PC in question which, in turn, interfaces directly to the PC's hardware such as an integral modem card or serial port. Figure 3-11 shows an example of a sample screen of a communications software package.

Communications Software Features and Uses

The comparative features and operation of communications software will be examined in order to allow the purchase of the software component of the data communications equation which best meets business requirements and needs.

This comparative analysis will start with the same top-down approach used to examine the hardware side of modem communications. Figure 3-12 summarizes the business uses, operational features, and technical issues of communications software.

The Top-Down Approach to Communications Software Analysis

Business Perspectives   The first concerns in the needs analysis are the business related needs. In Figure 3-12, the business layer model has been divided into two distinct segments, namely, Business Perspectives and Business Activities. Business perspectives are those overriding business needs that underlie business activities. These business perspectives are key assumptions that must be documented before

HARDWARE
Personal computer with data to be transmitted (sent) or received
  Necessary Components
    v.32 modern
    Async
    Serial port (in PC)
    RJ-11 jack (outside PC)

SOFTWARE
Personal computer with an operating system (DOS)
  Necessary Components
    Operating system
    Communications software

MEDIA
Personal computer to modem:
  RS-232 modern cable; pins 2 and 3 perform straight through communication

Modem to phone jack:
  Modular cable with RJ-11 plugs on both ends

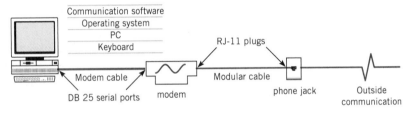

Figure 3-10 The role of communications software in data transmission.

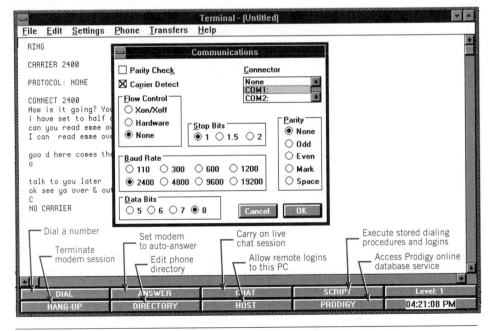

Figure 3-11 Sample screens of a communications software package.

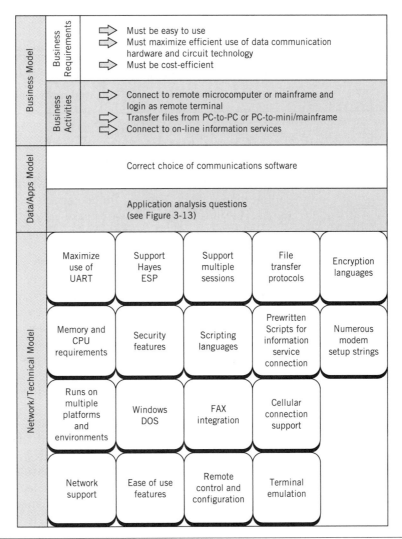

Figure 3-12 Business uses, operational features, and technical issues of communications software.

business activity analysis begins. In Figure 3-12, the following as business perspectives are listed:

Key Business Perspectives

1. Communications software must be easy to use.
2. Communications software must maximize the efficient use of available hardware and circuit technology.
3. Purchase of communications software must be cost effective. (Prices can range from free to $400 or more.)

These themes of: ease of use, maximum efficiency, and cost-effectiveness will be further evaluated as to implementation by software packages and evaluated by users in the Network Model section of the communications software analysis.

It is important to note that other non-listed Business perspectives as dictated by yourself or your business should be added to this model at this layer and evaluated through subsequent layers.

Business Activities   Broadly speaking, the following items summarize typical business uses of communications software. Again, you should add your own unlisted business uses of communications software, if any.

Business Uses of Communications Software

1. Connect to a remote minicomputer or mainframe and log in as a remote terminal.
2. Transfer files from PC to PC, or from PC to Mini/Mainframe.
3. Connect to value-added information services such as Compuserve, Prodigy, Dow-Jones, etc.

Although these three general statements summarize the most popular uses of communications software, additional analysis is necessary in order to determine the *best* communications software package for an individual or company based on their particular required activities and perspectives.

Choosing the Best Communications Software for Your Use

Notice the placement of the "Correct Choice of Communications Software" in the top-down analysis model (Figure 3-12). It bridges the gap between the business perspectives and activities of the upper layer and the myriad of technical features found in different communications software packages as listed in the network model or technology layer.

Figure 3-13 summarizes some key analysis questions used to assist in determining the best communications software package for a particular individual or business, as well as the options and implications of those questions. Again, add to the list of questions as you see fit.

As the implications of each of the questions listed in Figure 3-13 are explored, each of the technical features listed in the network/technical model layer of Figure 3-12 will be explained. Few, if any communications software packages contain all of these features. Furthermore, few, if any, businesses *need* all of these features. The real challenge is to determine which of these technical features are truly necessary in order to support business activities and then to find the best-priced communications software package which offers those features.

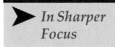

In Sharper Focus

NETWORK MODEL—TECHNICAL FEATURES

Windows

Windows is a graphical user interface (GUI) which runs over the DOS operating system and allows users to run multiple applications concurrently in various sized "windows." Most application programs, such as communications software, must be written especially to run in the Windows environment. Do not assume a communications package can run in Windows unless specifically stated.

Any operating system, like DOS, or user interface, like Windows, must contain a piece of software known as a communications driver which actually controls the PC's serial port and devices such as modems attached to that serial port. These communications drivers are like a link in chain, in that they are one of the controlling or limiting factors of an end-to-end data transmission. The overall end-to-end performance of a data transmission system can be no faster or more sophisticated than the communications driver controlling the serial ports of the PCs.

Windows Version 3.0 contains a communications driver that limits data transmission speeds to 19.2Kbps. It doesn't matter if you are using modems with a

Question	Implication/Options
Will you be accessing this communication software through Windows? If so, which version of Windows?	Cannot assume every communications package works with Windows. Windows 3.0 driver is limited to 19.2 Kbps. Does not support buffered UART.
Which minicomputer or mainframe do you wish to log into?	Must be sure that the proper terminal emulation is included and that it works effectively.
Do you wish to transfer files to or from a minicomputer or mainframe?	Requires compatible version of the communications software. It *must* also run on the minicomputer or mainframe in question.
Is the modem hooked directly to your PC, or will you be accessing your modem through a network? Which network?	Communications software must have ability to access the modem via the network. This is *not* always the case.
Do you want to log on to Information Services? If so, which ones?	Software packages vary in the number of prewritten automatic log-in scripts for various information services.
How much RAM is available for your PC?	Some communications software takes as much as 512K RAM.
Will other PCs be dialing into this PC? If so, what level of security is required?	Some communications software packages offer password security and call logging.
Are the modems you have been using capable of error detection and correction?	If not, you will need file transfer protocols supplied with communication software which provide for error detection and correction.
Will you need to control or configure the PC remotely?	Some communications software packages offer remote control functions.
Will you be using the cellular phone network for data transmission?	Some communications software packages include feature to enable successful data transfer over cellular facilities.
Will you be sending faxes through the modem?	Some software packages include the ability to communicate with a fax machine.
Are you likely to be using modems of many different manufacturers?	Communications software must send a "setup string" to a modem before it can fully communicate with that modem. These "setup strings" can vary between modems. Some communications software packages come with many more pre-defined "setup strings" for many more modems than others.
Will you need to conduct more than one communication session at a time?	Some software packages offer support for management of multiple, simultaneous communication sessions.

Figure 3-13 Choosing the best communications software for your use.

higher speed capability; with Windows 3.0, 19.2Kbps is the maximum transmission speed. A chain is only as strong as its weakest link. A data transmission system is only as fast as its slowest segment. Windows Version 3.1 is not limited to 19.2 Kbps thanks to modifications to the Version 3.1 communications driver.

UART Support

Another hardware-related issue that should be considered when analyzing communications software needs has to do with a hardware component on the serial port PC board known as the *universal asynchronous receiver transmitter* or *UART* chip.

A UART chip is the piece of hardware that actually does the parallel-to-serial and serial-to-parallel conversion of data between the PC and its serial port. Parallel-to-serial conversion is performed from the PC to the serial port (and then out to a modem and phone line) and serial-to-parallel conversion is performed from the serial port to the PC itself.

Besides its conversion duties, the UART also acts as a mediator between the serial port and the CPU (central processing unit) of the PC. In this role, the UART must interrupt the CPU when data arrives in through the serial port so that the CPU may process the data and forward it to the proper destination in the PC's memory. All of these interruptions could be a nuisance, especially in today's more powerful multitasking CPUs. A multitasking CPU may be juggling several jobs and/or users at a time; it cannot dedicate 100 percent of its time to the UART's interruptions and its data.

A new UART chip, known as the 16550AFN, has solved the constant interruption problem. A 16-byte on-board buffer memory allows the UART chip to store data before interrupting the CPU. This leads to fewer CPU interrupts and a smoother and faster overall data flow. All of this sounds great except that there's a catch—the communications software must enable this buffer memory and be able to use it properly. If high speed (9600 bps or faster) data transmission is a requirement assurances should be made that:

1. The serial port board has a 16550AFN UART chip
2. The communications software can enable and use the buffer memory on the UART

The ability to enable and fully utilize the UART chip would support the upper-level business perspective to *maximize the effective use of hardware* as articulated in the top-down model analysis of Figure 3-12.

Hayes ESP Board Support

And speaking of maximizing the effective use of hardware: what could possibly be better than *one* UART chip and *one* serial port? Why, *two* UART chips and *two* serial ports, of course! This is essentially the contents of the enhanced serial port (ESP) board manufactured by Hayes Microcomputer Products.

The two serial ports and two UARTs contained on the ESP board do more than simply double the transmission capacity, however. As described in the previous paragraph on UARTs, the interruption of the CPU by the UART is followed by the CPU storing the data received from the UART in memory. The Hayes ESP board doesn't interrupt the CPU at all, but rather transfers the received data directly to memory by itself in a process known as *direct memory access* or **DMA**. In addition, the Hayes ESP board has a larger 1K (approximately 1000 characters) buffer memory of its own to maximize overall transmission speed.

Remember, however, that the Hayes ESP board is a piece of hardware, and like the new UART chip, must be enabled and managed by communications software in order to deliver its capabilities. If high speed (9600 bps or faster) data transmission using V.32bis or V.Fast modems and a Hayes ESP board are a requirement, make sure that the communications software package purchased supports the ESP board.

Terminal Emulation

One of the most common uses of communications software is to support the remote connection to minicomputers or mainframes. In this role, the communications software must make the PC "emulate" or pretend to be a dedicated terminal of the type usually connected to these computers. Physically, however, the PC's keyboard is often different than the keyboard of the terminal that the PC is attempting to emulate.

Many times these minicomputer and mainframe keyboards have additional function and editing keys not found on PC keyboards. This problem is overcome by the communications software in a process known as **keyboard mapping**. Keystrokes from the "real" terminals are simulated or "mapped" by various keystrokes on the PC keyboard. How effectively and easily this keyboard mapping is accomplished is a differentiating factor among communications software packages. Some packages map the majority of keys on the "real" terminal and allow the users to define their own keystroke combinations as well.

Besides keyboard mapping, another key criterion in evaluating the **terminal emulation** capability of a communications software package is assuring that the particular terminal that you require is indeed emulated by a given communications software package. Among the most popular terminals emulated are DEC VT 52, DEC VT 100, DEC VT 220, and IBM 3101. Two generic terminal types commonly known as ANSI and TTY are also popular. The DEC VT 320 is a graphics terminal emulated by some communication software packages. Numbers of different terminals emulated by various communications software packages range from just two or three to over 30. Make sure the terminal emulation needed is included in the list of supported terminals before buying the software.

Multiple Platform File Transfers

In order to transfer files between two PCs, compatible software to initiate, manage and terminate that file transfer must exist on both PCs. This file transfer software must work according to similar "rules" if the transfer is to be well managed and successful. These "rules" are commonly known as *protocols*. File transfer protocols will be discussed in detail a bit later on. Most PC-based communications software packages support numerous **file transfer protocols**. As a result, a PC-to-PC file transfer is relatively straightforward.

However, if rather than transferring files to/from another PC, transferring files to/from a *minicomputer* or *mainframe* is a requirement, the software search can be a bit of a challenge. Just as similar file transfer protocols are required on both PCs to accomplish PC-to-PC file transfer, similar file transfer protocols on the PC and the mini/mainframe are required in order to accomplish PC-to-mini/mainframe file transfer. Some PC-based communications software packages are also available in versions that run on certain minicomputers or mainframes.

If PC to mini/mainframe file transfer is a business requirement, make sure that the selected communications software package also runs on the required mini/mainframe. File transfer software that runs on a number of different computers, both PCs as well as minicomputers and/or mainframes, is known as multi or multiple platform software. The **Kermit** file transfer protocol, discussed later, is an example of a multiple platform file transfer protocol.

Modem Access Via a Network

With the great proliferation of LANs (local area networks), many times a user will not have a dedicated modem connected directly to the serial port on their PC. Instead, a modem or multiple modems are shared, and accessed via the network to which a user's PC is attached. Sharing modems in this way can be a very cost-effective alternative to all users having their own dedicated modems. The shared modem is hooked to a PC known as a server. In some cases, the sole job of this server is to manage modem access and other data communications related tasks, in which case it is known as a *communications server* or *remote access server*.

Even though a user's PC is hooked to a network, the communications software is still running on that individual user's PC. The difficulty arises in that the modem is not hanging off the serial port of the user's PC where the communications software would normally expect to find it. In order to access the modem attached to the network's communication server, the communications software must send instructions and data out through the PC's **network interface card** rather than the PC's serial port. A network interface card is a board that plugs into a PC and allows the network's cabling to attach this particular PC to other PCs on the same network. Network interface cards will be studied in detail in Chapter 5.

Some, but not all, communications software packages will support modem access via networks. If modems are to be accessed over a network, make sure that the particular network operating system is supported before purchasing the software. See the list of featured references at the end of this chapter for articles that review communications software in greater depth.

Information Service Access

If a required business activity was to access information services such as Compuserve, MCIMail, Dow-Jones, etc., then a feature offered by some communication software packages known as prewritten or "canned" scripts may add significantly to the software's *ease of use*. Canned scripts are executable files which are custom written to automatically access a given information service. All the user has to do is execute the desired "canned" script, in most cases by merely choosing it from a menu.

Some communications software packages come with more information service prewritten scripts than others. Typical packages come with as few as none and as many as 12 prewritten login scripts.

Scripting Language Capabilities

Beyond the prewritten scripts delivered with some packages, the ability for users to write, save, and recall their own customized scripts are a significant point of differentiation among communications software packages. Using a **scripting language,** a powerful and perhaps lengthy series of commands could be written, saved, and then rerun at will or automatically at preset times.

A popular application for such a customized script is the polling of individual retail stores by a regional office or corporate headquarters. By utilizing the prewritten script, the calling can all be done automatically, unattended, most often at night to take advantage of lower dial-up rates.

Differences in scripting language capability tend to center around how many different commands are available in the scripting language and whether or not the scripting language offers a feature known alternatively as: **logging, scroll-back buffering,** or **autolearning**.

What all of these descriptions refer to is the ability of the communications software to store and record in a file, commands entered and responses received during a "live" communications session. This command file can then be recalled and edited with additional scripting language commands if desired, and subsequently executed on an as-needed basis. If repetitive calling to multiple locations is among the business uses planned for the communications software, a comparative analysis of scripting language capabilities should be a part of the communications software search.

Memory and CPU Requirements

In general, as the sophistication of the communications software grows, so does the amount of RAM (random access memory) required to store and run the communications software. Before purchasing a particular communications software package, be sure that sufficient RAM memory is available to run the package. Some communications software packages can ease the burden on RAM memory and CPU requirements by one or both of the following options:

1. The communications software can exist as a *terminate-and-stay-resident* **(TSR)** program.
2. The communications software can use extended and/or expanded memory. In the case of DOS, **expanded memory** is memory between the base 640K memory and 1 megabyte of memory while **extended memory** is RAM memory greater than 1 megabyte.

A TSR program is loaded into memory and is always *ready* to run, but not actually consuming CPU time. These TSR programs can be "recalled" and activated usually by a designated keystroke combination, often referred to as a "hot-key." By only requiring CPU time when activated, the TSR program frees up the CPU to work on other tasks.

By allowing program storage in extended/expanded memory, the communications software package frees the primary 640K of DOS's addressable memory for other programs.

Security Features

If allowing dial-in access to the PC on which this communications software is installed is a requirement, consider security requirements before purchase of the communications software. Remember from the discussion of modem features earlier in this chapter that security features are often supplied by the modem itself. These same modem security features are also sometimes available as communications software features as well. The two most popular security features described earlier are:

Password security
Dial-back security

Another security feature known as **call logging** records important information about each call handled by the modem or communications software. Call logging is sometimes a feature of security modems (hardware). If this security feature is required but not supplied by the modem, then look for a communications software package with appropriate security features.

File Transfer Protocols

As identified on the business activities layer of our top-down model, the establishment, management, and termination of file transfers is one of the most common uses of communications software. Obviously, these file transfers must be free of errors. In some cases, the necessary error control is supplied as a function of the modems employed in the data transmission. MNP Class 4 and V.42, discussed earlier in this chapter, are two of the most common modem-based error control protocols.

File transfer protocols, part of a communications software package, can also offer error control capabilities. As many as 15 or more file transfer protocols may be included in a given communications software package. If the modems to be used for data transmission do not supply their own error control, then be sure to purchase communications software which includes sufficient file transfer protocols with error control. Remember, in order for modems to furnish error control capabilities over a data transmission circuit, *both* modems must support the same error control protocol.

Figure 3-14 summarizes the characteristics of popular file transfer protocols, including their error control capabilities.

To simplify the information presented in Figure 3-14 regarding the most popular file transfer protocols, the criteria by which these protocols differ from one another have been identified. This list of differentiating criteria will also serve as a means to evaluate the applicability of future file transfer protocols.

Differentiating Factors Among File Transfer Protocols

1. Error checking technique: checksum, CRC, CRC-16, CRC-32
2. Request for retransmit: stop and wait ACK/NAK, sliding window, none (streaming)
3. Block size in bytes: 128, 1K , variable depending on line quality
4. Others: batch capability, multiple platforms, auto-recovery

As can be seen by these differentiating factors, although there may exist an overwhelming list of file transfer protocols from which to choose, these protocols actually differ according to a relatively few criteria.

Error checking techniques were explained earlier in the chapter and are listed in increasing order of error detection ability. Choose the appropriate file transfer protocol that incorporates the percentage of error detection required for a given business application.

Request for retransmission, also discussed earlier in the chapter, can have a great impact on the overall throughput of a data transmission session. File transfer protocols with the suffix of "G" (XMODEM-G, YMODEM-G) are known as **streaming protocols** because they do not stop transmitting a file until they reach an end of file indicator. These file transfer protocols are an appropriate choice if error control is being handled by the modems using MNP Class 4 or V.42 error control protocols. In these cases, whereas the error control is being handled by the hardware, there is no need for the communications software to add additional error control and its associated overhead.

Block size may be of a fixed length of either 128 or 1K bytes, or it may vary according to the quality of the data transmission circuit. The adaptive packet length protocols will usually produce the greatest throughput on circuits of varying quality.

Fire Transfer Protocol	Summary	Differentiating Features	Block Size	Error Control	Application Notes
X modem— checksum			128 bytes of data per block	ACK/NAK, stop and wait ARQ. Checksum error control	Public Domain, widely used. Stop and wait takes time
X modem— CRC		CRC improves error detection			
X modem—1K (sometimes called Y modem)		1024 characters of data per block	1K/128 fallback— sometimes		Also uses CRC. May have batch capability
X modem—G	G → streaming No error correction here	Y modem → CRC-16 16 error control		CRC-16	
Y modem— batch		Batch capability allows transfer to be controlled by separate batch executable files. Multiple transfers at set time			
Z modem	Dynamically adjusts packet size A/LA MNP 4	Automatic recovery from aborted file transfers		CRC-32 sliding window	Widely used by BBS users
Kermit		Multiple platform availability		ACK/NAK stop and wait ARQ	Great for micro to mainframe file - transfers. Not very fast
Sliding Window Kermit		Adds sliding window		Sliding window	Faster, may not be available on all platforms Kermit is available on

Figure 3-14 Comparative features of file transfer protocols.

Other features that may be important depending on the detailed business activities as analyzed in the top-down analysis might include:

Batch capability, which would allow multiple file transfers to take place sequentially without user intervention.

Multiple platform capability, which is essential for those users or businesses who wish to conduct PC to minicomputer or mainframe file transfers. Kermit is an excellent example of a multiplatform file transfer protocol.

Finally, **ZMODEM** offers a rather unique feature which has become especially popular with BBS (bulletin board service) users who pay by the minute for connection to on-line bulletin boards. An auto-recovery feature allows an aborted file transfer to resume at the point where the transfer aborted rather than starting the transfer over at the beginning of the file. Amazingly, it also doesn't matter when you resume the transfer, assuming both files still exist.

Proprietary File Transfer Protocols

Some communications software vendors also include *proprietary file transfer protocols*, which have been optimized for error control and overall throughput. The only thing to remember about these proprietary protocols is that they must be installed on the PC or computer on *each* end of the data transmission circuit. If this is not a problem, then improved performance from a proprietary protocol, as compared to one of the public domain file transfer protocols listed in Figure 3-14, may well be the outcome.

Matching Hardware and Software: The Modem Setup String

Communication software and the modem "talk" via the RS-232 pins of the serial port and the modem. Voltages, or lack thereof, on these pins control the entire data transmission process. Users communicate with the communications software running on the PC which, in turn, communicates with the modem via the RS-232 interface.

In order to communicate effectively with the modem, the communications software must first set up some "ground rules" with the modem. These "ground rules" take the form of a string, or series, of commands which tell the modem how to set itself up in order to communicate properly with the communications software. The series of commands is commonly known as a **setup string** and can vary according to the particular modem and communications software package involved.

The Hayes AT command set is a series of commands understood by most modems and communications software packages which can be used to construct and send setup strings. The "AT" is itself a command that stands for "attention," a command sent from the communications software to the modem to gain its attention. Modems that understand commands from the AT command set are known as "Hayes compatible."

These setup strings are not always straightforward or easily written by novices to the field of data communications. For this reason, it is important that the communications software package purchased includes a setup string for the modem or modems which are to be used. If many different modems from many different manufacturers are to be used, it is essential to purchase a communications software package with numerous setup strings. Numbers of included setup strings may vary from none to several hundred.

Special Use Considerations

Some communications software packages include provisions for special business applications. Among these are:

1. *Support of multiple simultaneous communications sessions.* Multiple communications sessions assumes that the necessary hardware to conduct these sessions is present. For instance, these sessions may involve more than one serial port and modem, or an additional session conducted through a network interface card to a modem connected to a communications server. The user could initiate these multiple communications sessions and then either toggle between the screens monitoring the ses-

sions or fit them all on a single screen if the communications software was running in a Windows environment.

2. *Support of data transmission over cellular network.* Transmission of data over the cellular phone network poses several unique challenges especially in the area of error control. Cellular technology will be discussed in subsequent chapters. For now, realize that if the communications software is to be used to manage data transmissions over the cellular network, then it must be a communications software package which explicitly states support for such transmission. MNP 10 consists of several adverse channel enhancements (ACE) written especially for modem operation in a cellular environment.

3. *Support of remote control and/or remote configuration.* Being able to remotely control another PC can be very convenient. It also requires a fair amount of security to preclude abuse and unauthorized access. A popular use of the remote control of a PC is the ability to dial in from one's home and control the PC in one's place of business. There are specialized remote control or remote access packages written for this use which will be studied in detail in Chapter 6—Internetworking. However, some communications software packages also include remote control and configuration capabilities.

4. *Support of FAX transmission.* The ability to communicate with fax machines is frequently incorporated into a hardware device known as a *faxmodem.* Alternatively, a "normal" modem can be used when combined with the special faxing software feature included with some communications software packages. Faxing directly from a PC eliminates the need to print out documents and feed them into a fax machine. Documents are sent directly from the disk of the PC out onto the phone circuit through the faxmodem and into the remote fax machine. Specially written FAX software packages are also available for both Windows and non-Windows environments.

Ease of Use General Features

Several features which fall under the general category of "ease of use" are now included in virtually every communications software package available. The following list includes a brief explanation of most of the features which could be reasonably expected to be included:

Drop-down menus. Communications software, like most other applications, has become more user friendly. Commands no longer need to be memorized. Drop-down menus and on-line help make getting around the software considerably easier.

Keyboard dialing. Keyboard dialing allows the user to enter phone numbers to be dialed from their PC keyboard rather than having to dial the phone manually.

Autoredial. The software can now remember previously dialed numbers and redial them at given time intervals without intervention, if desired.

Stored number directories. Phone numbers as well as setup parameters can be stored and easily recalled from within the communications software. Setup parameters might include items such as baud rate, parity, terminal emulation type, etc.

Auto answer. The software manages incoming calls, tells the modem to answer, handles password security, if any, and may log the call as well.

Technical support. One final feature on which to compare communications software packages and on which to base a purchasing decision is the technical support of a given package. What is the availability of technical support for the software? What hours are technical support available? Is there a toll-free number? Is there a cost for the technical support?

◄

☐ FURTHER RESEARCH AND THE IMPACT OF CHANGING TECHNOLOGY

After having answered the business analysis questions outlined in Figure 3-13, and having studied the subsequent explanation of the features typically found in today's communications software packages, the result should be a better understanding of which features are required in the communications software package that will meet these outlined business needs.

By remaining focused on these predetermined business needs as a variety of technological alternatives—in this case communications software packages—are being evaluated, one can avoid being distracted by clever marketing techniques or "gee-whiz" features. By maintaining a business-oriented frame of reference throughout the technology analysis, one can be assured of acquiring technology that will meet stated business requirements.

Many communications software "Buyer's Guide" articles appear annually in numerous computer or data communications related periodicals. Several such references are listed in the featured references section of this chapter.

Communications software technology will undoubtedly change and new features will be introduced. These new features should be added to the network/technical layer of the top-down model for communications software (Figure 3-12). Evaluate this new technology in terms of listed business activities and perspectives.

Likewise, as business requirements change, and they will, new business perspectives and activities can be listed on the business model layer of Figure 3-12. Examine the network/technology layer for features that meet these new business needs. If they don't yet exist, a new market demand has been identified. The dynamic or changing nature of the top-down model should help to articulate the importance to business objectives of missing software features and will hopefully hasten the introduction of new enabling technology which will deliver those features.

Having concluded the study of the hardware and software technology required to complete a PC-to-PC connection via modems, other non-LAN (local area network) PC connectivity alternatives will be explored in the next section.

☐ NON-LAN PC CONNECTIVITY

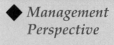
◆ *Management Perspective*

Perhaps one of the most overlooked areas of data communications, non-LAN PC connectivity can offer data communications solutions with potentially significant financial savings. Sometimes referred to as **peripheral sharing devices**, these connectivity alternatives are often ignored as uninformed users and aggressive salespeople see local area networks (LANs) as the sole answer to PC connectivity questions. Cost per connected PC can be as low as $150 for peripheral sharing devices and as high as $1000 for a sophisticated local area network. Additional costs such as the need for hiring technically-oriented personnel to manage local area networks add to the overall impact of PC connectivity decision-making.

The same top-down analysis approach will be taken with non-LAN PC connectivity as was taken with communications software. This top-down analysis can be mapped as follows:

1. An analysis of potential business uses and requirements (Figure 3-15).
2. An outline of key questions necessary to assist in choosing the proper solution (Figure 3-16).

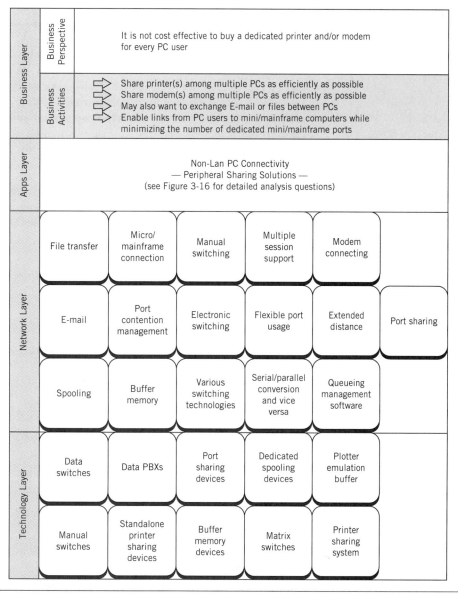

Figure 3-15 Business activities and technical possibilities of non-LAN PC connectivity.

3. An analysis of existing technology in this category of data communications devices in order to find the device which meets the requirements identified in steps 1 and 2 (Figure 3-17).

Chapters 4 and 5, "Local Area Networks" and "Local Area Network Technology," will offer a continuation of this study of connectivity alternatives as they explore typical "full-blown" LANs such as Novell, Banyan, and LANManager. Among the additional LAN alternatives that will be studied are: file transfer software, printer sharing networks, zero slot LANs, and DOS-based or peer-to-peer LANs.

Figure 3-15 summarizes the business activities and technical possibilities of Non-LAN PC connectivity.

Business Perspective of Peripheral Sharing

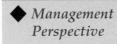

Management Perspective

The business motivation that usually brings one into the world of non-LAN PC connectivity is the recognition of the large expense involved in equipping individual PC users with their own dedicated printers and/or modems. All PC users need *access* to a printer, not necessarily an individual printer of their own.

However, granting this access to shared printers while still maximizing the productivity of PC-based workers is the key challenge of PC connectivity analysis. The trick is to find the best connectivity solution for a given situation. An incorrectly analyzed situation may yield unsatisfactory results. Two typical scenarios representing less than optimal solutions follow:

Scenario 1: Too many users are forced to share too few printers linked via simple manual switches resulting in long periods of time in which users are unable to work because they are waiting for their turn to use the printer.

Financial expenditure: Low   Productivity: Low

Scenario 2: A full-blown local area network is installed. All users can get printout immediately.

Financial Expenditure: High   Productivity: High

Ideally, then, what is sought is the best possible user productivity for the least possible financial expenditure.

Business Activities of Peripheral Sharing

The *primary* specific business activities involved with peripheral sharing are relatively straightforward:

1. Users may wish to share one or more printers among numerous PCs.
2. Users may wish to share one or more modems among numerous PCs. Sharing numerous modems is known as accessing a **modem pool**.

Additional *secondary* peripheral sharing business activities may include:

3. Users may also wish to send E-mail or files to one another.
4. Users may wish to occasionally log onto a minicomputer or mainframe. Given the occasional nature of this use, it is important to minimize the number of minicomputer/mainframe ports dedicated to this purpose.

Business Analysis Questions Yield Technical Requirements

Given the above four general business uses of peripheral sharing, a more thorough analysis of peripheral sharing needs must be undertaken in order to assist in the analysis of currently available peripheral sharing technology. Figure 3-16 outlines a series of questions that will yield a more specific set of technical requirements.

Technology Analysis Grid Maps Requirements to Solutions

These resultant technical requirements can then be compared to the non-LAN PC connectivity technology analysis grid (Figure 3-17) for initial possible technology solutions. The technology analysis grid maps peripheral sharing functionality on the vertical axis against available technology alternatives on the horizontal axis. Intersections indicate whether a given feature or function is standard or occasionally included in a given device.

The functionality (logical design) entries can also be found in the network layer of the non-LAN PC connectivity top-down model (Figure 3-15). Likewise, the Peripheral Sharing Devices can also be found in the technology layer (physical design) of Figure 3-15. Recall that a logical design dictates *what* is required in terms of functionality and a physical design dictates *how* that functionality is to be delivered.

As each of these devices are described below, refer to the non-LAN PC connectivity technology analysis grid to assist in differentiating the features of one device from another.

Finally, any possible technology solutions identified from the technology analysis grid can be researched in more depth by studying the individual detailed product descriptions in articles listed in the featured references section of this chapter.

---

1. How many PCs will be involved in this peripheral sharing arrangement?
2. How many printers will be involved in this peripheral sharing arrangement?
3. Are the printers parallel or serial?
4. Will you be linking the PCs through their parallel or serial ports?
5. Will you need serial-to-parallel or parallel-to-serial conversion?
6. Will any of the printers be laser printers?
7. What is the nature of the print jobs sent to these printers? Mostly large jobs? Mostly numerous small jobs?
8. Will users tolerate "Printers Busy" messages or must a printer always be available?
9. Is the number of PCs or printers in your peripheral sharing arrangement likely to change either totally or relatively (PC to printer ratio)?
10. Will you need to print out at more than one location simultaneously?
11. Will any printers be at a greater distance than 100 feet from a PC?
12. Will users wish to exchange files and E-mail?
13. Will users be sending graphics data to plotters or printers?
14. Will users be sharing modems and/or fax machines?
15. Will some printers or PCs be transmitting at different speeds than others?
16. Will PC users need occasional access to minicomputers or mainframes?
17. Will Apple Macintosh computers be sharing peripherals as well?
18. Will any users need the ability to maintain multiple communications sessions simultaneously?
19. Will any printers be dedicated to particular forms (for example: letterhead, envelopes, multipart invoices, packing slips?)

Figure 3-16 Business analysis questions for non-LAN PC connectivity.

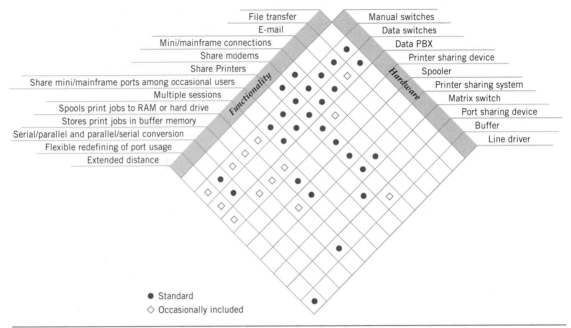

Figure 3-17 Non-LAN PC connectivity. Technology Analysis Grid.

TECHNICAL FEATURES VERSUS CURRENT TECHNOLOGY

As the implications of each of the business analysis questions listed in Figure 3-16 are analyzed, it will not necessarily be possible to jump to a conclusion as to which peripheral sharing device is best in any given situation. Rather, which *technical features* are important in support of given business situations must first be discerned.

The technology itself is in a constant state of change. Furthermore, as discussed earlier, there are no industry standards for naming peripheral sharing devices. What one manufacturer calls a *data switch* may be called a *multiport spooler* or *data pbx* by another manufacturer. For this reason, it is more appropriate to focus on available technical features and their proper application. In studying currently available technology in this chapter, the focus will again be on which technical features are delivered by a given device, rather than on the label that the manufacturer has chosen to assign to that device.

When features or functionality of data communications devices must be evaluated objectively, the I-P-O model is ideal. Accordingly, each of the peripheral sharing devices listed on the technology analysis grid (Figure 3-17) will be analyzed using the I-P-O Model (Figures 3-18*a* to 3-18*i*).

Technical Issues

Simple Switching   Several of the questions in Figure 3-16 revolve around the issues of numbers of PCs and printers and whether each will be communicating via serial or parallel ports. The simplest printer sharing device is a **manual switch**, sometimes also known as a mechanical switch or an A/B switch. Up to six PCs can share a single printer in such an arrangement. The switch must be physically set to give each user access to the printer. If the printer is busy, all other users must wait.

Close physical proximity of all users to the shared printer is the key to the success of such a setup. All users should ideally be within sight or talking distance to one another in order to more efficiently coordinate the switching of the printer access from one user to another. Manual switches are most often manufactured with a fixed number of serial and/or parallel ports. Input (PC) and output (printer) ports are most often of a fixed number and not interchangeable. See Figure 3-18*a*.

Manual versus Electronic Switching

An important incremental improvement on the manual switch is the simple **electronic switch**. This device is especially important if a laser printer is among the printers to be shared. The small voltage spike which can be generated during the physical switching of a manual switch can be potentially damaging to the circuit boards of the laser printer. Electronic switches are often manufactured with built-in software that scans attached PCs for waiting print jobs.

User intervention is not necessary with these scanning type electronic switches. Users either have immediate access to the printer or receive a "printer busy" message. As soon as the printer is again free, the electronic switch automatically connects a waiting PC with the available printer. Buffered and non-buffered printer sharers, data switches, and data PBXs all utilize electronic switching. See Figure 3-18*b*.

Serial-to-Parallel Conversion

If serial-to-parallel or parallel-to-serial conversion is required, then a more expensive device, commonly known as a **data switch** is a possible solution. Serial-to-parallel and parallel-to-serial conversion is also available in standalone conversion devices.

Data switches also offer greater overall capacity in terms of both expandability and total numbers of PCs and printers that can be attached, as well as more advanced features which will be discussed shortly.

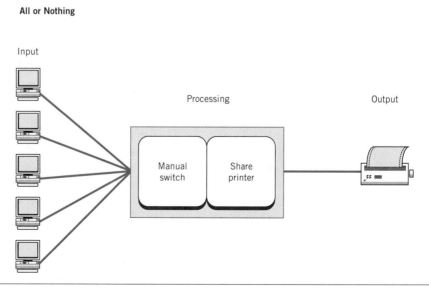

Figure 3-18a Manual switch functionality.

All or Nothing

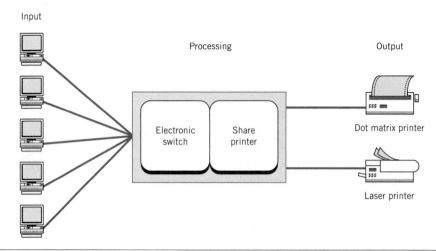

Figure 3-18b Electronic switch functionality.

Buffer Memory, Spooling, and Queueing   When a printer is busy print-ing, any other user will be unable to use that same printer and will have to wait until that printer is available. Depending on the peripheral sharing device in use, users may get some sort of "printer busy" message.

Buffer memory, spooling software, and queueing software are either added to existing peripheral sharing devices or built into standalone devices (**buffers** and **spoolers**) to overcome this "printer busy" message, thereby increasing worker productivity.

Buffer memory allows print jobs to be off-loaded from a PC immediately, whether or not a printer is available, allowing the PC user to return to work. When an appropriate printer becomes available, the print job is downloaded from the buffer memory to the printer. This buffer memory may be in a standalone device called a buffer or may be integrated into a data switch or printer sharing device. Additional buffer memory can usually be added to existing devices in the form of buffer memory upgrades. Specialized buffers prepare graphical data for plotters or graphics printers. These graphics buffers, sometimes called *plotter emulation buffers*, allow PCs running graphics software to download graphics output quick-ly, thereby freeing the PC for more productive uses. See Figure 3-18c.

Spooling software works in a slightly different way to keep PCs from waiting for available printers. Rather than store copies of print jobs in buffer memory, spooling software "spools" a copy of the print job either into the PC's RAM (ran-dom access memory) or onto its hard drive. Spooling software also has the ability to send multiple copies of a given print job to multiple printers simultaneously, if this happens to be a required peripheral sharing business activity. Standalone spoolers store copies of print jobs in their own buffer memory. See Figure 3-18d.

What then, is the difference between a standalone spooler and a standalone buffer? In general, a buffer connects one, or perhaps two, PCs to a single printer whereas a spooler may connect numerous (10 or 12) PCs to three or four printers. These distinctions are by no means guaranteed and a careful analysis of any peripheral sharing device will reveal the futility of trying to state concrete distinc-

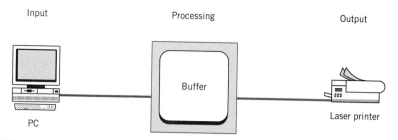

Figure 3-18c Buffer functionality.

tions between these devices. Again, the important analysis technique is to focus on operational features rather than manufacturer's labels.

Devices that send printout to multiple printers often include **queue management** software. This software manages and monitors the distribution of print jobs to various printers. It also allows printers to be enabled or disabled, or assigned to different PCs. If business requirements dictate the need for several printers serving numerous PCs, it may be wise to look into the sophistication of the included queue management software of a given peripheral sharing device.

Buffered and Non-Buffered Printer Sharing Devices A non-buffered printer sharer is essentially an electronic switching device. These devices are often expandable allowing users to start with as few as two PCs sharing a single printer and expand to 20 PCs sharing several printers. Without buffering, however, printer access is still an all-or-nothing proposition. Users either have access to the printer or they wait.

For this reason, many printer sharers are buffered, allowing requested print jobs to be sent immediately to the printer sharing device where they are held until a printer becomes available. This buffer memory allows PCs requesting printing ser-

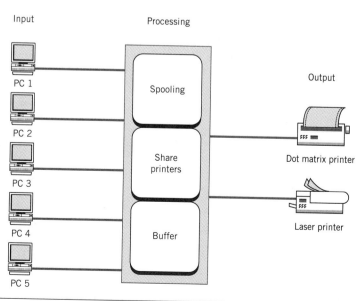

Figure 3-18d Spooler functionality.

vices to be free to continue working immediately after "spooling" their print job to the buffered printer sharer. See Figure 3-18*e*.

Expandability and Port Characteristic Definition Because manual switches, electronic switches, and buffered printer sharers are usually manufactured with a fixed number of serial and parallel ports, which are in turn defined as either input (PC) or output (printer) ports, it is important to know both: how many PCs and printers are likely to be in the printer sharing arrangement, as well as whether they communicate via serial or parallel ports, before making a purchase decision.

Some printer sharers are expandable while others are not. Therefore, it is important to know the likelihood of a need for expanded peripheral sharing before making a purchase decision.

The customary difference between buffered printer sharers and data switches, as outlined in Figure 3-17, is the ability of data switches to redefine ports from input (PC) to output (printer) and vice-versa. In other words, data switches are more flexible, allowing port characteristics to be changed as peripheral sharing needs change. These port characteristics include port speed, which can vary widely, especially among printers.

Sophisticated data switches are also able to send E-mail and transfer files between attached PCs. Some data switches also have the ability to allow connection to minicomputers, mainframes and modem pools. When users wish printout, the data switch's buffer memory and spooling software allow users to continue working, even if the requested printer is busy. In summary, the most sophisticated data switches are like "networks in a box," delivering both flexible connectivity as well as buffering and spooling ability. See Figure 3-18*f*.

A type of data switch known as a **matrix switch** allows all possible combinations of connections among attached input and output devices. Figure 3-18*g* illustrates how easily any PC could be attached to any printer, modem, or plotter connected to the matrix switch. See Figure 3-18*g*.

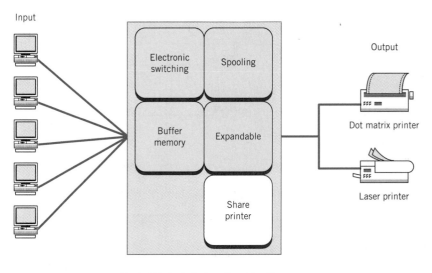

Shaded blocks indicate optional functions

Figure 3-18e Printer sharer functionality.

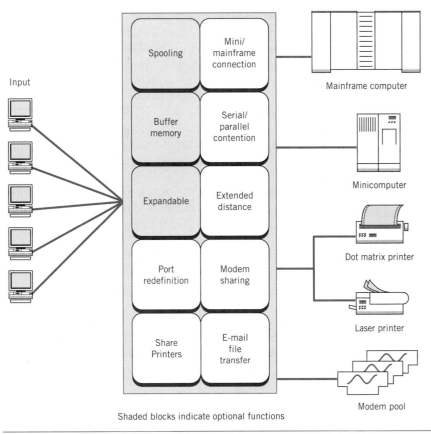

Shaded blocks indicate optional functions

Figure 3-18f Data switch functionality.

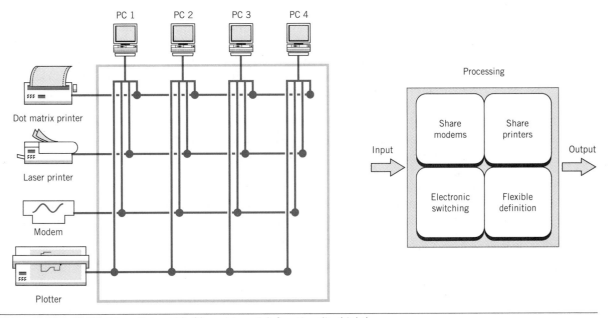

Figure 3-18g 4 2 4 Matrix switch grid (left); matrix switch functionality (right).

Advanced Peripheral Sharing and Switching More sophisticated user-business requirements cause a significant increase in peripheral sharing device sophistication as well as an inevitable increase in acquisition cost. As identified in Figure 3-15, users occasionally need access from their PCs to more than just printers. For example, access to modems, fax machines, minicomputers, or mainframes are fairly common PC connectivity requirements.

Occasionally, Apple Macintosh computers or "dumb" asynchronous terminals may need to be part of the peripheral sharing arrangement. With the need for access to these sophisticated devices comes a need to arbitrate what is known as *port contention*. Whereas it would not be cost effective to allow each one of these occasional users to be assigned a permanent port and connection to the minicomputer or mainframe, *port sharing* is a peripheral sharing feature which orchestrates the sharing of a limited number of ports among many PC users. This port sharing feature may be incorporated into a standalone device usually known as a *port sharing device* or may be integrated into a sophisticated peripheral sharing device known as a data PBX. As mentioned above, some data switches also offer minicomputer and mainframe connections as well as port sharing abilities.

Data PBXs allow flexible interconnection of PCs, Macs, printers, modems, fax machines, asynchronous terminals, minicomputers, and mainframes. They provide port sharing ability and allow for the transfer of E-mail and files among connected devices provided that appropriate E-mail or file transfer software has been installed on the communicating PCs or computers. Data PBXs can also allow multiple sessions or multiple connections between a given PC and other available connected services.

Data PBXs do not store print jobs by either buffering or spooling. A data PBX's job, just like a voice PBX, is to establish, maintain, and terminate connections between devices as requested. If the requested printer is busy, a "busy message" of some type is generated from the data PBX.

This is the major difference between data switches and data PBXs. Data PBXs are really only concerned with creating connections between attached devices, whereas data switches provide additional buffering, spooling, and queue management capabilities. A functional diagram of a data PBX is illustrated in Figure 3-18*h*.

It should be noted that the **file transfer** mentioned above is distinct from **file sharing**. File transfer is just sending a copy of a file from one device to another, while file sharing implies two users having access to a file simultaneously. File sharing as a business requirement falls into the realm of local area networking and exceeds the capabilities of simple peripheral sharing devices and this study of non-LAN PC connectivity.

Printer Sharing System—A Package Deal

Occasionally, an entire printer sharing system including buffered printer sharing device, spooling, and queue management software, cables, and adapters to connect the cables to the PCs and printers is all put together and sold as one product. This all-in-one approach takes the worry out of buying the correct cables in order to properly connect a standalone printer sharing device to all of its associated PCs and printers. A functional diagram of a printer sharing system is illustrated in Figure 3-18*i*.

Cost is another factor when considering cable purchases. Depending on the requirements of the peripheral sharing device in question, a 10 ft. cable could cost anywhere from less than $5.00 to more than $40.00. To have all appropriate cables

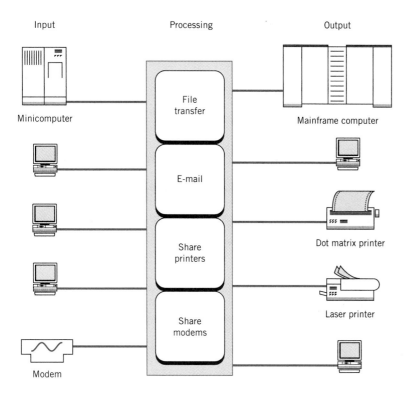

Data PBX's are connection oriented; about the only
thing it doesn't do is spool or buffer print jobs

Figure 3-18h Data PBX functionality.

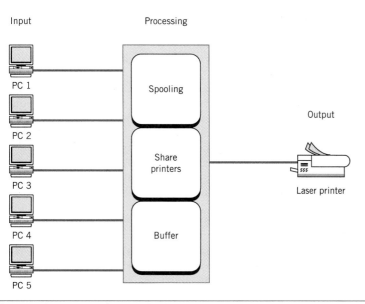

Figure 3-18i Printer sharing system functionality. (All cables and connections included.)

included in a reasonably priced printer sharing system could save a substantial amount of money as well as worry.

Extended Distance Printing

When distances between a PC and printer exceed 100 feet, a **line driver**, sometimes called a distance extender or short haul modem, must be employed. This may be a standalone device or may be integrated into another peripheral sharing device. Specially made, and more expensive, cables may also allow extended distance transmission precluding the need for line drivers. **Short haul modems** also have additional applications in the micro to mainframe and internetworking connectivity arenas and will be further studied in Chapter 6—Internetworking.

SUMMARY

By employing the top-down model in the analysis of currently available modem technology, any modem functionality should deliver on at least one of the following business communication requirements:

Faster
Cheaper
More secure
More reliable

By focusing on how data communications devices of any type deliver on predetermined business requirements and objectives, one can avoid purchasing technology that may be appealing or cleverly marketed, but which lacks the ability to deliver a positive impact on business objectives.

Current modulation standards such as V.32 (9600 bps) and V.32 bis (14,400bps) can deliver even more throughput over dial-up lines when compression standards such as MNP 5 or V.42bis are applied. The V.Fast (V.34) standard promises transmission rates approaching 24,000 bps.

As this increasing sophistication in dial-up modems has yielded ever-faster transmission speeds over dial-up lines, the types of network services carriers have offered have evolved in a parallel manner. As bandwidth-on-demand has increasingly become the stated need of network services consumers, carriers have had to offer increasing amounts of digital network services, in general, and switched digital services such as Switched 56K, in particular.

The relationship between data communications devices and network services is illustrated by the fact that a change from analog to digital network services would necessitate a change from modems to CSU/DSUs.

Reliability of data transmissions is assured by the net effect of three related methodologies: error prevention, error detection, and error correction. Error prevention can be accomplished via forward error correction techniques such as TCM or through adaptive protocols that adjust transmission characteristics in response to changing line conditions. Error detection is accomplished through a variety of techniques in which the transmitting and receiving modems transmit and verify some sort of error check bit or character in addition to the transmitted data itself. Techniques such as parity, LRC, checksums, CRC-16, and CRC-32 vary in both the level of complexity of their error checking routines and their ability to detect bursts of multiple bit errors.

Error correction is accomplished in general through retransmission of those characters received in error. Techniques such as Discrete ARQ, Continuous ARQ, and Selective ARQ vary in how efficiently this retransmission is accomplished.

Security is provided by a variety of techniques that can be supplied by modems including password protection, dial-back access, and encryption. Encryption between trading partners relies on standards such as DES and Digital Signature Encryption, which assure interoperability while maintaining integrity of individual corporation's security.

Communications software is a key component in linking a user's communications requirements to the modems and network services that deliver on those desires. Communications software varies widely in capabilities and price. As a result, a careful business-oriented analysis is required using a technology analysis guide, such as those supplied in this chapter, in order to compare the many technological alternatives in a structured and objective manner.

PCs can be linked together by a category of technology known as non-LAN PC connectivity. This category of technology is particularly important because it is often overlooked in favor of the installation of LANs. By careful analysis of available non-LAN PC connectivity technology by using technology analysis grids, such as

the one supplied in this chapter, analysts can assure that they are recommending the most cost-effective solution to business networking requirements.

KEY TERMS

ACK/NAK
adaptive protocols
adaptive size packet assembly
adverse channel enhancements
amplifier
analog leased line
ARQ
auto-learning
auto-restoral
block sequence number
buffer
buffer memory
call logging
checksums
constellation points
continuous ARQ
CRC
CRC-16
CRC-32
CSU/DSU
data compression
data pbx
data switch

DDS
DES
dial back unit
dial backup unit
digital leased line
digital signature encryption
discrete ARQ
DMA
dynamic speed shifts
echo cancellation
electronic switch
encryption
error correction
error detection
error prevention
expanded memory
extended memory
fast retrain
fiber-optic line driver
file sharing
file transfer
file transfer protocol
fixed callback
flow control

forward error correction
handshaking
Hayes AT command set
Kermit
keyboard mapping
LAP-M
line conditioning
line driver
LRC
manual switch
matrix switch
MNP 5
modem
modem eliminator
modem pool
modem sharer
modem sharing
network interface card
null modem
parity
peripheral sharing devices
printer sharing device
printer sharing system
private key
public key

queue management
repeater
RTS/CTS
scripting language
scroll-back buffering
setup string
short-haul modem
sliding window protocols
spooler
streaming protocol
switched 56K
terminal emulation
trellis coded modulation
TSR
UART
V.32
V.32bis
V.42
V.42bis
variable callback
V.Fast
XMODEM
XON/XOFF
ZMODEM

REVIEW QUESTIONS

1. What is the primary difference between a data PBX and a data switch?
2. How is a technology analysis grid employed in a business networking requirements analysis and design?
3. How does one determine which non-LAN PC connectivity alternative is appropriate for a given situation?
4. What is the difference between discrete ARQ and continuous ARQ?
5. What inefficiency is inherent in a data transmission session utilizing discrete ARQ over a full-duplex circuit?
6. Which modulation technique is employed in a V.32bis modem?
7. How many bits per baud are interpreted in a V.32 modem?
8. What is the baud rate of a V.32 modem? What is the transmission rate of the same modem?
9. What is the potential throughput of a V.32bis modem with V.42bis data compression?
10. Why are standards important when it comes to data compression?
11. What four overriding trends or user demands were introduced as the framework for related data, network, and technology concepts? Can you think of others?
12. How can the top-down model remain useful given the rate of rapidly changing technology?
13. Explain in your own words what a "so-what" attitude toward data communication technology entails.
14. What is a constellation point and how is it interpreted?

15. How many constellation points are in a V.32 constellation?
16. How many constellation points are in a V.32bis constellation?
17. What is the relationship between the number of points in a constellation and the number of data bits interpreted per detectable event?
18. What effect does trellis coded modulation have on the number of constellation points and the number of data bits interpreted per detectable event?
19. What technology enables sophisticated echo cancellation to be included in many modems?
20. What is meant by an adaptive protocol? Give at least two examples.
21. How does echo cancellation work and what benefits does it offer?
22. What are the key differences between V.32 and V.32bis?
23. What does "bis" stand for?
24. What is fast retrain and why is it important?
25. What is V.Fast?
26. How does V.32terbo differ from V.32 bis and V.FAST?
27. Explain the significance of the phrase "fully standard compliant" in terms of modem standards.
28. How does data compression work?
29. Why can't a 4:1 compression ratio always be achieved with V.42bis?
30. What is the difference between V.42 and V.42bis?
31. Why is error-free transmission so important to successful data compression?
32. How have carrier services responded to the advances in dial-up modem technology?
33. What has happened to the market for conditioned analog leased lines?
34. In general what are the advantages of DDS over analog leased lines?
35. How can one avoid being caught in the middle of fingerpointing when purchasing a CSU/DSU?
36. Why is a CSU/DSU different in function than a modem?
37. What are some of the most common uses of switched digital services?
38. What is modem sharing and when does it make sense?
39. What are some of the analysis questions that should be answered before installing a modem sharing arrangement?
40. What is handshaking and what does it have to do with modem interoperability?
41. What is the Hayes AT Command Set and why is it significant?
42. Elaborate on the relationship between error prevention, error detection, and error correction.
43. What are the major differences between repeaters and amplifiers?
44. Explain how multiple bit errors can remain undetected using simple parity checking.
45. Explain how LRC overcomes parity checking's inability to detect multiple bit errors.
46. Explain in simple terms how checksums and CRCs detect transmission errors.
47. What is meant by a sliding window protocol?
48. What is selective ARQ?
49. How are block sequence numbers related to sliding window protocols?
50. What role does buffer memory play in the implementation of sliding window protocols?
51. Explain the differences between hardware and software flow control.
52. Explain why hardware or software flow control may be more reliable.
53. What is forward error correction and what is the trade-off involved in such a protocol?
54. What is the difference between a dial-back unit and a dial backup unit?
55. What is variable callback and when might it be required?
56. What are the potential security risks in variable callback?
57. What are the important nontechnological issues related to computer and network security?
58. What is ciphertext?
59. What are the important issues to bear in mind when investigating encryption equipment?
60. How does a digital signature encryption offer added security above just encrypting data transmissions?
61. What are the important issues to consider when purchasing communications software?
62. What are the issues when modems are to be accessed via a LAN rather than directly attached to a PC?
63. What is a UART and how does it relate to communications software choices?
64. What is DMA and how does it relate to communications software choices?
65. What business application of communications software would require a quality integrated scripting language?
66. What is a TSR and how does it conserve computer resources?
67. What is the difference between extended and expanded memory?
68. What are the key differentiating factors between file transfer protocols?
69. What are the primary and secondary activities of peripheral sharing? Can you think of others?
70. What are some of the key business analysis questions that help identify proper non-LAN PC connectivity solutions?
71. What is the difference between buffering and spooling?

72. What are the differences between a null modem and a modem eliminator?
73. What are the differences between a line driver and a short haul modem?
74. What is important to remember when purchasing fiber optic line drivers?

ACTIVITIES

1. Compare the cost of installing a printer sharing device capable of sharing at least two printers among six PCs with a similar setup using a LAN such as NetWare Lite or LANtastic. What are the other differentiating factors besides cost between the two alternatives?
2. Install a modem and asssociated communications software. Document your installation procedure as well as any problems encountered and problem-solving techniques employed.
3. Using a modem advertisement of your choice or one chosen by your instructor, write a technical memo to a nontechnically oriented manager explaining the features of the modem in terms of business layer impact. Prepare a cost/benefit analysis and make a recommendation as to whether or not the modem in question should be purchased.
4. Investigate and report on the difference between modem standards and Fax modem standards. Which organizations set Fax standards? Does communications software interact with the Fax part of the modem or is other software required?
5. Write to your Congressional representative regarding any current or pending legislation involving encryption and/or authentication of data communications transmisssions.
6. Write an essay on the need/right of the government to monitor encrypted data transmissions versus the rights of individuals and corporations to transmit data freely without fear of such invasion of privacy.
7. Prepare a comparative budget for a long-distance data transmission between two cities of your choice. Compare the cost of such a transmission for each of the following two scenarios.
   a. V.Fast modems, dial-up lines
   b. CSU/DSUs, Switched 56K lines
8. Investigate the current status of the standardization process for the V.Fast standard. Are other modem standards in progress?
9. Prepare a comparative analysis of how different modem manufacturers are attempting to beat new modem standards such as V.Fast to market, and how they propose to upgrade such modems to standards compliance at a later date.
10. Using file transfer or communications software, prepare a graph showing the results of the transfer of various sized files using different file transfer protocols as outlined in Figure 3-14. Record any error messages received as well as transfer time and file size. Abort and restart the transfer midway using different file transfer protocols and record results.

Featured References

Carrier Services

Briere, Duncan. "Buyers Guide: Digital Private Line Services," *Network World*, vol. 9, no. 24 (June 15, 1992), p. 47.

Johnson, Johna Till. "Switched 56K Service Takes off," *Data Communications*, vol. 22, no. 6 (April 1993), p. 93.

Communications Software

Derfler, Frank. "GUI Comm Software: Simple or Simplistic?" *PC Magazine*, vol. 12, no. 8 (April 27, 1993), p. 239.

Modems

Pickholtz, Raymond. "Modems, Multiplexers, and Concentrators" *Data Communications, Networks, and Systems* (Indianapolis: Howard W. Sams & Co., 1987) p. 63.

Held, Gilbert. *Data Communications Networking Devices*, 2nd ed. (New York: John Wiley & Sons, 1990).

McNamara, John. *Technical Aspects of Data Communication*, 2nd ed. (Bedford, MA: Digital Press, 1982).

Derfler, Frank. "Portable and Fast: Sizzling Modems to Go," *PC Magazine*, vol. 11, no. 14 (August 1992), p. 371.

Stone, M. David. "14,400 bps Modems: Life in the Fast Lane," *PC Magazine*, vol. 12, no. 12 (June 29, 1993), p. 241.

Ayre, Rick. "Negotiating the FAX Modem Jungle," *PC Magazine*, vol. 11, no. 21 (December 8, 1992), p. 343.

Standards

Black, Ulysses. "A User's Guide to the CCITT's V-series Modem Recommendations," *Data Communications*, vol. 18, no. 7 (June 1989), p. 109.

Saunders, Stephen. "V.32bis: The Modem in the Middle," *Data Communications*, vol. 21, no. 3 (February 1992), p. 87.

Johnson, Johna Till. "Modem in the Middle: Sizing up V.32terbo," *Data Communications*, vol. 22, no. 6 (April 1993), p. 57.

Weiss, Jeffrey and Schremp, Doug. "Putting Data on a Diet," *IEEE Spectrum*, vol. 30, no. 8 (August 1993), p. 36.

C A S E   S T U D Y

Coldwell Banker Upgrades LAN-WAN Links

Since its formation after the 1906 San Francisco earthquake, Coldwell Banker, the third-ranking residential real estate franchise in the United States, has built a solid foundation. During 1991 Coldwell listed more than 437,000 residential properties and transacted more than $44.5 billion in home sales.

In the past, communicating information to more than 1900 real estate offices with nearly 40,000 sales associates was a formidable task for the real estate giant. Particularly daunting was the task of economically integrating remote sales offices into the information flow of the company's central-site, IBM Token-Ring LAN located in Mission Viejo, Calif. More often than not, Coldwell Banker reverted to "sneaker net" and courier service.

To further complicate the task, as a member of the Sears Financial Network, Coldwell also had to report the same information, after it had been analyzed by Coldwell Banker headquarters staff, to the corporation's IBM mainframe in Dallas.

For a real estate company, information exchange is crucial. Yet, even though Coldwell's brokerage offices already had DOS-based, IBM PS/2 computers, personnel used to manually fill out forms that would then be sent to a metropolitan or regional office where data would in turn be keyed into a 3270 host data entry terminal. The large metropolitan and regional offices used leased lines to communicate with the Texas-based mainframe. Delays were inherent due to courier and keyboarding time; mistakes were introduced during keying; and the leased lines and mainframe processing were expensive.

Jason Shane, director of distrib-

uted services for Coldwell Banker, and his staff started an exhaustive, two-year search for a wide-area communication system that would tie together all the isolated LANs and other computing resources, be economically viable, and provide an automatic and streamlined system that could be easily used by a multitude of non-technical personnel. They finally settled on Xcelle-Net Inc.'s Remote-Ware Communications Management System, a set of software tools, providing manageable connections on low-cost telecommunications across both WANs and LANs.

"This may seem obvious, but there are two ways to increase profitability: generate more revenue and decrease overhead costs," said Shane. "Although I can't directly affect a specific sale, I can provide our agents the automation to do a more effective job, and then we can drive down the costs of communications. It is difficult for me to compare our new dial-up network with our previous mainframe data entry methods with its limited communications options. Our new system has opened a door that wasn't available previously because all the options were literally multimillion-dollar choices."

Remote PCs to a Central LAN

"Our initial plan was to provide remote communications to our 500 company-owned brokerage offices with subsequent roll-out to our 1,400 franchised locations," explained Shane. "Dedicated leased lines, which can be economical if you are moving large amounts of data on a continuing basis, just didn't make sense for our remote offices because—although we were

transferring mission-critical information such as number, value, and expiration of real estate listings—that data exchange needed to occur only intermittently."

In 1990 Shane began installing RemoteWare to send and receive information over standard dial-up telephone lines. In this case, Coldwell Banker uses industry-standard 9600bps V.32bis dial-up modems. This combination of RemoteWare and dial-up connections for a "network on demand" is a critical element in helping the firm keep costs in line.

The software at the 500 brokerage offices automatically calls the central site each week. The central-site server consists of an IBM PS/2 running OS/2 with 16 communications ports. Two additional servers are dedicated for communications with Coldwell's franchised locations and its Relocation Services division. All three central-site servers are connected to the Mission Viejo IBM Token Ring, which also supports about 250 PCs for corporate personnel. The final link is a 3174 Token-Ring gateway to the IBM mainframes in Dallas.

When he began providing electronic communications to the 1900 remote offices, Shane had three primary reasons, in addition to cost savings, for moving to the RemoteWare dial-up system. First, with predominantly non-technical staff members at the remotely-located sites, an automatic, one-step communication process was a necessity. "We've made communications transparent to our users," said Shane. "They simply fill out an online form and press a single key to automatically transmit the information to Mission Viejo. But, in addition to our initial 500 corporate-owned installations, we have to provide the 1400 independent franchises a simple communications method that they can make ready use of."

Second, with so many remote locations, Coldwell Banker needed a network that was easy to support from the central site. "We've transferred the setup and day-to-day support of the Remote-Ware system from the information systems staff to our customer service representatives. With very basic training, they are able to add remote nodes, reconfigure telephone numbers, and deploy new definition files. Occasionally they can't complete some of the very technical tasks, and we supply backup support. By using the customer support staff that already has daily contact with our remote offices, we are able to support and maintain a large network that wouldn't have been possible with our limited technical staff."

Coldwell Banker has also found the system to be highly reliable—with automatic error recovery that restarts at the specific packet where the communication was interrupted—even for longer sessions. "Several large offices are transferring nearly 20 megabytes every night in less than two hours," said Shane. "Because of the data compression algorithms in RemoteWare, we are getting an actual data rate of nearly 25Kbps, which is almost double the rated capacity of the 14.4Kbps modems used at these large offices."

"This solution has been so successful that new projects continue to come in at an increasing rate from divisions such as the brokerage finance group. This group wants to electronically communicate its budget spreadsheets across the country, have the remote sites enter data, and then send them back to Mission Viejo for consolidation," continued Shane. "It's a

relief to know that we have a one-button solution that's easy to use and won't be a nightmare for us to support," he said.

Third, with so many independent locations, Coldwell Banker needed a system that could flexibly support a variety of computing resources including DOS, Windows, OS/2, Macintosh, Unix, and others. "Even if an office has a minicomputer, if they can hang a PC from the LAN, we can still give them cost-effective central-site connectivity. We had to have the most versatile connections for the diverse environments of our franchised offices."

Advanced Applications

Coldwell Banker is beginning to look at the Remote Ware system for a variety of new advanced applications. For example, a new project being considered by the company is the further automation of relocation services, especially for Fortune 500 companies that are clients of Coldwell Banker Relocation Services Inc. In order to achieve instant access to information such as current expenses or whether a transferee's house has been sold, the human resources departments of these companies expect to communicate electronically with the real estate companies handling their employees' relocations. If that information were resident only on the Sears Financial Network mainframe and Systems Network Architecture (SNA) network, some clients who are not SNA-based could encounter cumbersome and difficult procedures to access such data.

"We are now in the position to easily make our relocation clients nodes on our RemoteWare network, regardless of their computing resources," said Shane. "At virtually no incremental cost to us, we can provide them one-button

access to their data. This will provide a marketing advantage to Coldwell Banker as we are able to provide value-added services that will allow our clients to continuously track and manage their relocation expenses."

Several layers of security ensure that clients cannot access one another's information. For example, with the RemoteWare software at both Coldwell Banker's central site and on the client's PCs, a "hand-shake" comparison of registration numbers and encoded passwords makes access to anyone's information except a client's own, impossible.

Shane also considers the RemoteWare network a "retaining tool" for both independent franchises and agents. "This isn't just a one-way road of information into the corporation," said Shane. "Simply put, we've built a data freeway to our field offices and personnel. Everything we do is designed to keep the agents away from administrative overhead and give them access to data that will help them sell."

Also, his staff is planning how to integrate the laptop computers of 50 Coldwell Banker consultants who travel around the country to work with local offices. And, by having the remote offices, which are the revenue-generating entities, call in rather than having the central site placing calls this particular cost of doing business is distributed among profit centers, rather than shouldered solely as a corporate expense.

"Whatever we put out to the field offices, our first consideration is the communications themselves, and secondly how we can support the process," said Shane. "We're convinced we have the most accurate, efficient, and low-cost system available, and it is a strategic element of our ability to compete."

Source: "Coldwell-Banker Interconnects 1900 Offices," *LAN Times*, Vol. 9, Num. 13, July 20, 1992, p. 41. Reprinted with Permission of McGraw-Hill, *LAN Times*.

Business Case Study Questions

Business

1. Business perspectives: Find quotes within the case study that reflect the importance of networking to the strategic mission of the business.
2. What was the financial motivation for the initial investigation?
3. What size business was involved? Approximate yearly sales? Number of locations? Why would size and number of locations matter?
4. What three specific evaluation criteria were established during the search for a solution to this data communications opportunity?
5. What have been some of the business level benefits of the new network installation?
6. Give specific examples of how this network provides market differentiation or competitive advantage for Coldwell-Banker.

Application

1. What types of applications are being run at the various corporate locations?
2. Was the remote link primarily for nightly batch jobs or on-line transaction entry?
3. How might the answer to question 2 affect networking decisions?
4. What new applications are being considered for this network?

5. Will these new applications be easily handled? Why or why not?

Data

1. What different types of PCs, workstations, mainframes, and minicomputers are needed to be able to communicate?
2. What were the shortcomings of the current way in which information was "shared" between these various platforms?

Network

1. What were the company's feelings regarding leased lines versus dial-up services?
2. What were some of the security issues addressed in the network design?

Technology

1. Which communications software was chosen and why?
2. How were the remote offices integrated with the other types of corporate computers previously identified in the data section?
3. What type of modems were used in this network? Do you feel that this was a good choice?

CHAPTER · 4

Local Area Networks (LANs) and LAN Look-alikes

Concepts Reinforced

Top-Down Model

Concepts Introduced

Distributed Database Access
File Server versus Database Server Databases
Network Applications
Printer Sharing Networks

File Transfer Software
Zero Slot LANs
DOS-Based LANs
Fully-Integrated LANs

OBJECTIVES

After mastering the material in this chapter, you should be able to:

1. Ask key questions concerning PC connectivity (business layer) needs in order to determine the most appropriate hardware/software local area networking (LAN) solution.

2. Understand the major characteristics, advantages, and limitations of each of the following major connectivity categories:

Printer sharing network
File transfer software
Zero slot LANS
DOS-based LANS or peer-to-peer LANs
Non-DOS based LANS or LANS with self-contained operating systems
Fully-integrated LANS

3. Understand the major differences, advantages, and limitations of the following major LAN operating systems:

Appletalk
Novell Netware
Microsoft LAN Manager
Banyan Vines
OS/2 LAN Server
Digital Pathworks

4. Understand the major characteristics of the following zero-slot and DOS-based LANS.

Artisoft LANtastic-Z
Artisoft LANtastic
Netware Lite
PowerLAN

5. Understand the role of network application analysis and data distribution analysis in logical network analysis and design.

☐ AN OVERALL ROADMAP TO NETWORKING IN CHAPTERS 3–9

In order to better understand "the big picture" of networking design and technology, Figure 4-1 offers a roadmap of sorts showing how Chapters 3–9 complement each other to form a cohesive body of networking knowledge.

In Chapter 3, "Personal Computer Connectivity" solutions, which were primarily hardware oriented and non-LAN in nature, were investigated. Examples included programmable data switches, manual and electronic switches, data PBXs, and printer sharing devices. In Chapter 4, because of more complex business layer demands, software-oriented and combined hardware/software-oriented PC connectivity solutions will be investigated.

Among these solutions will be the hardware and software combination commonly known as **local area networks** or **LANs**. It may come as a surprise to discover how many ways there are to link PCs other than the typical "full-blown" local area network. Some of the vocabulary surrounding these typical full-featured and fairly expensive local area networks such as Novell Netware, Microsoft LanManager, Banyan Vines, Token Ring, and Ethernet may be familiar. The many alternatives to these "full-blown" LANs are referred to as *LAN look-alikes*.

Chapter 4 covers "LANs and LAN Look-alikes" from a decision-making perspective. Figure 4-2 summarizes some of the choices available among networking and applications options in the design of LANs and LAN Look-alikes. The sheer number of options is indeed overwhelming. The entire decision-making process is

Chapter 3	Non-LAN PC connectivity Modems	
Chapter 4	Local area network Logical design LAN lookalikes	
Chapter 5	Local area network Physical design LAN technology	Chapter 9 *Enterprise Networking* Combining elements studied in Chapters 3–8 into a cohesive, efficient information system
Chapter 6	Internetworking Protocol conversion Multiplatform design	
Chapter 7	Wide area networking Basic principles Switching and transmission	
Chapter 8	Wide area networking Emerging services ISDN, SONET, Frame relay, SMDS, ATM	

Figure 4-1 An overall roadmap to networking in Chapters 3–9.

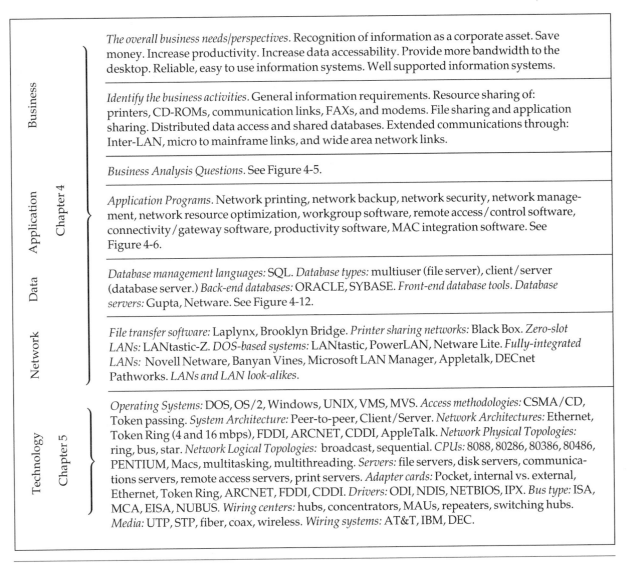

Business		*The overall business needs/perspectives.* Recognition of information as a corporate asset. Save money. Increase productivity. Increase data accessability. Provide more bandwidth to the desktop. Reliable, easy to use information systems. Well supported information systems.
		Identify the business activities. General information requirements. Resource sharing of: printers, CD-ROMs, communication links, FAXs, and modems. File sharing and application sharing. Distributed data access and shared databases. Extended communications through: Inter-LAN, micro to mainframe links, and wide area network links.
Application	Chapter 4	*Business Analysis Questions.* See Figure 4-5.
		Application Programs. Network printing, network backup, network security, network management, network resource optimization, workgroup software, remote access/control software, connectivity/gateway software, productivity software, MAC integration software. See Figure 4-6.
Data		*Database management languages:* SQL. *Database types:* multiuser (file server), client/server (database server.) *Back-end databases:* ORACLE, SYBASE. *Front-end database tools. Database servers:* Gupta, Netware. See Figure 4-12.
Network		*File transfer software:* Laplynx, Brooklyn Bridge. *Printer sharing networks:* Black Box. *Zero-slot LANs:* LANtastic-Z. *DOS-based systems:* LANtastic, PowerLAN, Netware Lite. *Fully-integrated LANs:* Novell Netware, Banyan Vines, Microsoft LAN Manager, Appletalk, DECnet Pathworks. *LANs and LAN look-alikes.*
Technology	Chapter 5	*Operating Systems:* DOS, OS/2, Windows, UNIX, VMS, MVS. *Access methodologies:* CSMA/CD, Token passing. *System Architecture:* Peer-to-peer, Client/Server. *Network Architectures:* Ethernet, Token Ring (4 and 16 mbps), FDDI, ARCNET, CDDI, AppleTalk. *Network Physical Topologies:* ring, bus, star. *Network Logical Topologies:* broadcast, sequential. *CPUs:* 8088, 80286, 80386, 80486, PENTIUM, Macs, multitasking, multithreading. *Servers:* file servers, disk servers, communications servers, remote access servers, print servers. *Adapter cards:* Pocket, internal vs. external, Ethernet, Token Ring, ARCNET, FDDI, CDDI. *Drivers:* ODI, NDIS, NETBIOS, IPX. *Bus type:* ISA, MCA, EISA, NUBUS. *Wiring centers:* hubs, concentrators, MAUs, repeaters, switching hubs. *Media:* UTP, STP, fiber, coax, wireless. *Wiring systems:* AT&T, IBM, DEC.

Figure 4-2 Decisions, decisions, decisions . . .

complicated by the fact that the choice of a particular option on any given layer may restrict options on other layers. For example, choosing a particular network topology may restrict adapter card and media choices.

Furthermore, technological innovation or changes on one layer may have an impact on options in other layers. As will be seen, the new more powerful CPU chips have had a direct impact on the features now available in DOS-based LANs.

The overall mission in this chapter is to work through this top-down model (Figure 4-2) of local area networking business requirements and design options, understanding both the possibilities available at any given layer as well as the relationship between options across layers. The major focus of Chapter 4 will be to *gain experience with the analysis and decision making process* down through the network layer in Figure 4-2. This decision making and network design process is sometimes known as **logical network design** because no particular hardware components have been chosen at this point.

In other words, the logical network design will yield *what* the network needs to do, but not *how*, or with what particular technology, these network requirements will be accomplished.

Chapter 5, "Local Area Networking Technology," examines all of the options found in Figure 4-2 in the technology layer. This layer represents the currently available networking technology in many different categories. Choosing among these various components and combining them in an actual network structure that will support the logical network design is sometimes called **physical network design**. In this phase of network design, actual, touchable hardware and software components are being combined to deliver required network functionality.

Chapter 6, "Internetworking," delves into the intricacies of connecting LANs to each other as well as to minicomputer and mainframe platforms of various types. Protocol conversion as well as internetworking hardware devices such as bridges, routers, and gateways are explored in depth.

Chapter 7, "Basic Principles of Wide Area Networking," will explore such wide area networking topics as the basic principles of conventional switching and transmission architectures while Chapter 8, "Emerging WAN Services and Technology," will explore such services as ISDN, Frame Relay, SONET, SMDS, and ATM.

Finally, Chapter 9, "Enterprise Networking and Client/Server Architectures," ties it all together by exploring how elements of LANs, Internetworks, and WANs can be combined across entire enterprises to deliver distributed information in a manner that supports strategic business objectives.

☐ BUSINESS NEEDS—THE UNDERLYING MOTIVATION

Business needs as articulated by management are not inherently local area networking business needs, nor do they necessarily imply local area networks as a business solution. Only by working one's way down through the top-down model, analyzing business activities and asking business analysis questions, will it be determined whether or not a local area networking solution is appropriate.

Business needs or perspectives provide the motivation for further business network analysis and design. By clearly understanding management's perspectives before beginning any technical analysis, an easier time will be had selling eventual proposals to management after having completed technical analysis, to assure that this proposal will meet management's business objectives. These business needs and perspectives provide the network analyst with a frame of reference within which to conduct research and evaluate options. Figure 4-3 lists a few typical business needs and perspectives which may lead to local area networking solutions.

The previously listed high-level business needs and perspectives are representative examples, typical of the kinds of upper-level management priorities that have been articulated to me during my consulting engagements. There are many other possible business needs or perspectives which could have been listed. Business needs and perspectives are dynamic, changing in response to changing economic and competitive climates, and management teams and philosophies.

In order to make this model more effective, add business needs and perspectives that have been articulated to you by management. Management's business needs and perspectives should be clearly documented and understood before beginning network analysis and design. These same needs and perspectives should be referred to on a continuing basis as a means of testing the feasibility of various technical networking options.

Recognition of information as a corporate asset
Increase data accessibility
Improve customer service
Save money, reduce expenses
Increase productivity
More bandwidth to the desktop for faster data accessibility
Information systems must be:
    Reliable
    Easy to install and use
    Well supported
Information systems must minimize the need for large staffs of highly trained
and high salaried technically-oriented individuals

Figure 4-3 Business needs and perspectives that may lead to local area networking solutions.

☐ BUSINESS ACTIVITIES SHOULD SUPPORT BUSINESS NEEDS

Having identified strategic business needs and perspectives, the next step in a top-down approach to network analysis is to identify those network-related business activities that may support the strategic business needs listed in Figure 4-3. Some possible examples of such information system or networking-related business activities are listed in Figures 4-2 and 4-4.

It is important to point out that the business activities listed in Figure 4-4 are strictly networking-related. Obviously, if overall strategic business goals are to be achieved, all corporate departments such as sales, accounting, research and devel-

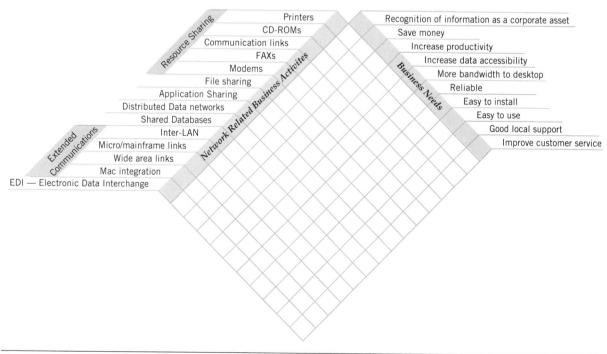

Figure 4-4 Network-related business activities should support business needs.

opment, and inventory control must define their own key business activities consistent with corporate business objectives.

In order to ensure consistency within the top-down business model and compliance of business activities with stated business needs, a grid such as Figure 4-4 can be used. For each network-related activity that must be supported in the eventual network design, check off which strategic business perspective is being satisfied. Any proposed network activities that do not support a strategic business need or perspective should be reevaluated. Modify the grid as necessary, substituting your own business needs and/or activities, and evaluating them accordingly.

The reason for the assurance at this point that possible network-related business activities fulfill specific, stated business needs is to avoid seeking technical local area networking options or features which either do not support or, even worse, contradict stated overall business needs.

Once the initial merit of the business activities has been assured by completing an evaluation grid such as that found in Figure 4-4, substantially more detailed data regarding these network-related business activities must be gathered before proceeding with the investigation of technical options. These technical options include the various entries in the LANs and LAN look-alikes category.

☐ ROLE OF THE NETWORK ANALYST AS INTERMEDIARY

These information systems-related business activities are often expressed by nontechnical business management people either directly or through interviews. It is important to understand that these listed activities are general in nature, rather than technically specific. Don't expect business management to be able to articulate technical specifications.

Armed with these general business needs, the network analyst prepares a series of business analysis questions to learn more about the information system-related business activities in order to assure that the eventual networking proposal will adequately support the required business activities.

Subsequent analysis by the network analyst of available technology through interaction with vendors and technical specialists creates a role as intermediary for the network analyst. On the one hand, the network analyst must be able to clearly understand the business needs and activities of an organization, while at the same time, understanding the technical specifications of the networking hardware and software which will ideally meet the organization's business needs.

☐ BUSINESS ANALYSIS QUESTIONS DIG DEEPER

Possible business analysis questions for local area networking solutions are listed in Figure 4-5. Notice that these questions "dig deeper" into the more general previously listed business activities. These questions would be directed toward end users and business management and are centered around *what* the network must eventually do, rather than *how* it will do it. The *how* questions will be more technical in nature and will be dealt with further down this trip through the top-down model.

This list of business analysis questions is not meant to be exhaustive or all-encompassing. The questions listed are a direct result of the business activities and needs from the top-down model used in this chapter as an example. Add, modify, delete questions from this list as necessary. Two important things to remember about any list of business analysis questions are:

	Current	2–3 Years	5 Years
User Issues How many users? What are their business activities? What is the budgeted cost/user? Comprehensive cost of ownership? What are the security needs? (password protection levels, supervisor privileges) What are the support issues?			
Local Communication Required speed?			

Resource Sharing
How many CD-ROMs, printers, modems, and FAXs
    are to be shared?
What is the greatest distance from the server to each
    service?			

File Sharing Is printer/queue management required? How many simultaneous users?			
Application Sharing What is the number and type of required applications? Are E-mail services required?			
Distributed Data Access Where will shared data files be stored?			
LAN Management/administration Will training be required to manage the network? How easy is the network to use?			

Extended Communication
How many MACs will be part of the network?
How many mini/mainframe connections are needed?
    (and what type, IBM, DEC, UNIX based?)
Will this be an Inter-LAN network? (LAN-LAN concerns.
    Which NOS? Must other protocols be considered?
    Are the connections local or remote (long-distance)?)			

Figure 4-5 LAN and LAN look-alikes: business analysis questions.

1. The questions should dig deeper into the required information systems-related business activities.
2. The answers to these questions should provide sufficient insight to enable the investigation of possible technical solutions.

Each of the business analysis questions' categories is explained briefly below:

User Issues

User satisfaction is the key to any successful network implementation. In order to satisfy users, their needs must be first thoroughly understood. Beyond the obvious questions "How many users must the network support?" are these more probing questions dealing with specific business activities of individual users.

Do users process many short transactions throughout the day?
Do users require large file transfers at certain times of day?
Are there certain activities that absolutely must be done at certain times of the day or within a certain amount of elapsed time?

These questions are important in order to establish the amount of network communication required by individual users. Required levels of security also should be addressed.

Are payroll files going to be accessed via the network?
Who should have access to these files and what security measures will assure authorized access?
What is the overall technical ability of the users?
Will technical staff need to be hired?
Can support be obtained locally from an outside organization?

Budget Reality

The most comprehensive, well-documented, and researched networking proposal is of little value if its costs are beyond the means of the funding organization or business. As will be seen in Chapter 12, "The Network Development Life Cycle," initial research into possible networking solutions is often followed by feasibility option reports that outline possible network designs of varying price ranges. Senior management then dictates which options deserve further study based upon financial availability.

In some cases, senior management may have an approximate project budget in mind which could be shared with network analysts. This acceptable financial range, sometimes expressed as budgeted cost per user, serves as a frame of reference for analysts as technical options are explored. In this sense, budgetary constraints are just another overall, high-level business need or perspective which helps to shape eventual networking proposals.

Local Communication

Remembering that these are business analysis questions and not technical analysis questions, users really can't be asked how fast their network connections must be. Bits per second or megabits per second have little or no meaning for most users. If users have business activities such as CAD/CAM (computer aided design/computer aided manufacturing) or other 3-D modeling or graphics software, which will be accessing the network, the network analyst should be aware that these are large consumers of network bandwidth.

Bandwidth requirements analysis as well as the bandwidth offered by various networking alternatives will be explored later in this chapter. It is sufficient at this point to document those information system-related business activities which may be large consumers of networking bandwidth.

Resource Sharing

The resource sharing business analysis questions for LANs are similar to the business analysis questions for non-LAN PC connectivity as outlined in Chapter 3. It is important to identify which resources and how many are to be shared: printers, modems, faxes, CD-ROMs; and the preferred locations of these shared resources. The required distance between shared resources and users can have a bearing on acceptable technical options.

File Sharing: Application Sharing

Which programs or software packages are users going to need to perform their jobs?

Which programs are they currently using?

Which new products must be purchased?

In many cases, network versions of software packages cost less than multiple, individual licenses of the same software package for individual PCs. The network analyst is really trying, at this point, to compile a listing of all applications programs that will be shared by users. Not all PC-based software packages are available in network versions and not all PC-based software packages allow simultaneous access by multiple users.

Once a complete list of required shared application programs has been completed, it is important to investigate both the availability and capability of the network versions of these programs in order to assure happy, productive users and the successful attainment of business needs.

Distributed Data Access

Although users cannot be expected to be database analysts, sufficient questions must be asked in order to determine which data is to be shared by whom, and where these users are located. This process is known as data distribution analysis and will be studied in greater depth in Chapter 12. The major objective of data distribution analysis is to determine the best location on the network for the storage of various data files. That best location is usually the one closest to the greatest number of active users of that data.

Some data files that are typically shared, especially in regionalized or multilocation companies, include customer files, employee files, and inventory files. Distributed data access is even more of a concern when the users sharing the data are beyond the reach of a local area network and must share the data via wide area networking solutions.

A good starting point for the network analyst might be to ask:

Has anyone done a comparison of the forms that are used in the various regional and branch offices to determine which data need to be sent across the network?

Extended Communications

The ability of certain local area networking solutions to communicate beyond the local area network remains a key differentiating factor among local area networking alternatives. Users should be able to articulate connectivity requirements beyond the LAN. The accomplishment of these requirements is the job of the network analyst.

Some possible examples of extended communications might include communications to another LAN. If this is the case, the network analyst must investigate all of the technical specifications of this target LAN in order to determine compatibility with the local LAN. An example of such a compatibility issue would be the need to connect an Apple Macintosh network to a PC-based network. The target LAN may be local (within the same building) or remote (across town or around the world). LAN-to-LAN connection is known as *internetworking* and will be studied in depth in Chapter 6.

Other examples of extended communications may be the necessity for LAN users to gain access to minicomputers or mainframes, either locally or remotely. Again, users are only asked *what* they need connections to, and *where* those connections must occur. It is the network analyst's job to figure out *how* to make those connections function.

LAN Management and Administration

Another key differentiating factor among LAN alternatives is the level of sophistication required to manage and administer the network. If the LAN requires a full-time, highly-trained manager, then that manager's salary should be considered as part of the purchase cost as well as the operational cost of the proposed LAN.

Secondly, the users may have requirements for certain management or administration features which must be present. Examples might be user-ID creation or management, or control of access to files or user directories.

Accurate and Complete Budgets Are a Must

Detailed and accurate cost projection is a very important skill for network analysts. Management does not like surprises due to unanticipated costs. In Chapter 12 the "Comprehensive Systems and Networking Budget Model" will be studied as a method of assuring that all possible costs are identified at the time of proposal.

In order to assure that all necessary costs have been determined, it is essential that all user needs (the cost generators) have been identified. Thorough user needs identification is the goal of the business analysis questions phase of the top-down model.

Anticipated Growth Is Key

User needs are not always immediate in nature. These needs can vary dramatically over time. In order to design networking solutions that will not become obsolete in the near future, it is essential to gain a sense of what the anticipated growth in user demands might be. Imagine the chagrin of the network analyst who must explain to management that the network which was installed last year cannot be expanded and must be replaced due to the unanticipated growth of network demand.

One method of gaining the necessary insight into future networking requirements, illustrated in Figure 4-5, is to ask users the same set of business analysis questions with projected time horizons of two to three years and five years. Incredible as it seems, five years is about the maximum projected lifetime for a given network architecture or design. Of course, there are exceptions. End users may not have the information or knowledge necessary to make these projections. Management can be very helpful in the area of projected growth and informational needs, especially if the company has engaged in any sort of formalized strategic planning methodology.

☐ NETWORK APPLICATIONS: WHAT CAN A LAN DO FOR YOU?

Beyond merely being able to share the same application software packages (spreadsheets, word processing, databases) that ran on individuals' PCs before they were networked together over a LAN or LAN lookalike, networking PCs together provide some unique opportunities to run additional networked applications that can significantly increase worker productivity and/or decrease costs.

Figure 4-6 summarizes the attributes, issues, and availability of some of the most popular uses of a LAN or LAN look-alike. It should be noted that the uses, features, and issues described below apply only to the listed applications functioning on a *local* area network. Many of these same functions become much more complicated when running across multiple LANs (internetworking) or over long-dis-

Network Application	Issues	Availability				
		File transfer software	Printer sharing networks	Zero-slot LANs	DOS-based LANs	Fully-integrated LANs
Network Printing	Printers shared print requests, buffered and spooled. Second generation network printers faster/smarter. Queue/device management, multiple operating system print servers, multiple print formats		■	■	■	■
Network Backup	Match hardware and software to your needs and network. Check out restore features. Scheduling unattended back-ups. Generation of LOG reports. Hardware dependencies and capacities				■	■
Network Security	Virus control. Additional user ID/password protection. Encryption. User authentication. Automatic logout of inactive terminals				■	■
Network Management	Network monitors. Diagnostic and analysis tools, which may be separate depending upon cable and network type. Administration concerns. Software often in NOS for simple LANs			■	■	■
Network Resource Optimization Configuration mgmt. Inventory mgmt.	Hardware and software inventory database. Reporting and query capabilities. Planning and network configuration tools. Monitoring and network alarm capabilities					■
Remote Access/ control Software Connectivity/Gateway software Mac Integration software	Included in many fully-integrated LANs. Needs analysis listings to be studied further in Chapter 6, "Internet-working"					■
Groupware	Workflow automation. Interactive work document review. Information sharing. Group schedules. Enhanced E-mail					■

Figure 4-6 LANs and LAN look-alikes: network applications analysis.

tance WANs (wide area networks). The internetworking and wide area networking implications of these applications will be analyzed in their respective chapters: "Internetworking," Chapter 6; "Wide Area Networking," Chapters 7 and 8.

A short description of each of these LAN applications follows.

Network Printing

Perhaps the single greatest motivating factor for installation of a LAN or LAN lookalike, network printing continues to evolve as user demands change and technology changes to meet those demands. Since much of the functionality of shared printing was discussed in Chapter 3, it should come as no surprise that the evolution of network printing begins with devices discussed there.

Network Printing Grows in Demand and Sophistication

Non-LAN Solutions

Stage 1: Manual or electronic switches
Stage 2: Buffered printer sharing devices
      Data switches
      Data PBXs
      Printer sharing systems

LAN-Based Solutions

Stage 3: Access to printers through serial or parallel ports of PCs attached to a "real" LAN.
Stage 4: Special purpose, dedicated PCs acting as print servers, with attached printers.
Stage 5: Printers themselves are nodes on network via their own network interface cards.

When a standalone or non-networked PC requests printing services, it sends the document to be printed directly to an attached printer through either the PC's serial or parallel port.

On a typical LAN, a networked PC would send a request for printing out onto the network through a network interface card. The networked request for printing services would be accepted by a device in charge of organizing the print requests for a networked printer. Depending on the LAN implementation configuration, that device may be a PC with attached printer, a specialized print server with attached printers, or a directly networked printer.

Some type of software must manage all of this requesting, spooling, buffering, queueing, and printing. The required software may be part of an overall network operating system or may be written specifically for network printer management.

The so-called "network attached" (stage 5) printers combine many of the formerly distributed features of other network printing alternatives. This combination of features puts the network interface card, the necessary networking and printer management software, as well as buffer memory, into the printer itself in another excellent example of the modularity of design methodology so prevalent in data communications. Advanced features of networked printers required when several LANs of varying varieties are linked together will be studied in Chapter 6, "Internetworking." Figure 4-7 illustrates three common methods of printing via a LAN.

Network Backup

Backing up data and application files on a network is essential to overall network security and the ability to recover from the inevitable data-destroying disaster. Although the process and overall components are relatively simple, the implementation can be anything but simple.

Basically there are only two components to a network backup system:

1. The software that manages the backup.
2. The hardware device that captures the backed-up files.

Method 1: Through the Serial or Parallel Port of a LAN Attached PC

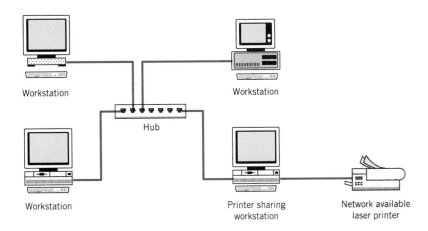

Method 2: Dedicated Print Server

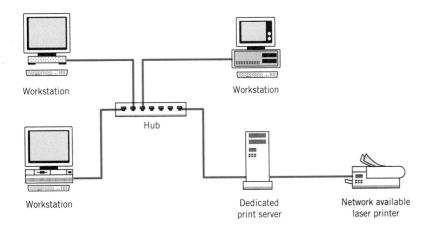

Method 3: LAN Attached Printer

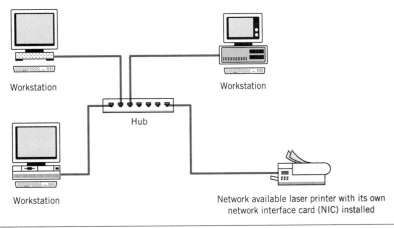

Figure 4-7 Printing on the LAN.

Device Type	Capacity	Transfer Rate
Tape cartridge	250 MB	6 MB/minute
	525 MB	12 MB/minute
	1 GB	18–36 MB/minute
Digital audio tape	2 GB	18–36 MB/minute
8mm video tape	5 GB	30 MB/minute
Removable drives	40 MB–80 MB	240 MB/minute

Figure 4-8 LANs and LAN look-alikes: network backup devices.

It is important that each of these components meet both the business as well as technical requirements of the network. Some network backup software and hardware work with only certain network operating systems. Other network backup software will work with only the hardware device with which it is sold. The interaction between hardware devices and software such as operating systems or network operating systems is often controlled by specialized software programs known as *drivers*. Drivers will be studied in more detail in Chapter 5. It is essential to ensure that the necessary drivers are supplied by either the tape backup device vendor or software vendor in order to ensure the operability of the tape backup device.

Hardware devices may be various types of tape subsystems, diskette drives, or optical drives. Various types of common backup hardware devices are listed in Figure 4-8. Key differences among hardware devices include:

1. *How much?* What is the storage capacity of the backup device?
2. *How fast?* How quickly can data be transferred from a PC or server to the backup device? This attribute is important if you are backing up large capacity disk drives.
3. *How compressed?* Can data be stored on the backup device in compressed form? If so, it may save a lot of room on the backup media.

Remember: Backup is not necessarily a one-way process. *Restoral* of backed-up files, and the ease with which that restoral can be accomplished, is a major purchasing consideration. Being able to schedule unattended backups or restorals, as well as the ability to spool or print log reports of **backup/restoral** activity, are also important to network managers.

Once network backup hardware and software have been chosen, another decision must be faced. Should the backup device be installed on a client PC on the network or in the server itself? Figure 4-9 illustrates the two installation options for backup devices.

More detailed backup hardware and software attributes concerning selective backup and restoral according to a number of different criteria are included in most product reviews and buyer's guides.

Backup Device Installed on a Network Client

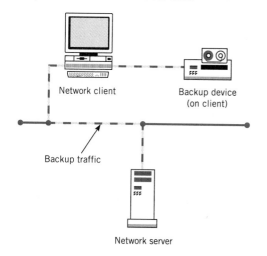

Network client

Backup device
(on client)

Backup traffic

Network server

Pro: Client PC manages backup, leaves server CPU alone

Con: All backup traffic goes across the network

Backup Device Installed on a Network Server

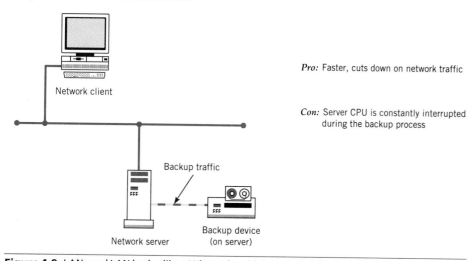

Network client

Backup traffic

Network server

Backup device
(on server)

Pro: Faster, cuts down on network traffic

Con: Server CPU is constantly interrupted during the backup process

Figure 4-9 LANs and LAN look-alikes: Where should the network backup device be installed?

Network Management

LAN Monitoring   The overall task of network management is usually broken down into at least three distinct areas of operation. First, networks must be *monitored*. Therefore, one of the foremost jobs of network management software is to monitor the LAN to detect any irregular activity such as malfunctioning network adapter cards, or an unusually high data transmission rate monopolizing the available network bandwidth to be shared among all attached workstations.

Sophisticated **LAN monitoring** programs can display maps of the network on graphics terminals. Operators can zoom-in on a particular node or workstation for more information or performance statistics. Some monitoring programs also have the ability to compare current network activity to preset acceptable parameters and to set off *alarms* on network monitor terminals, perhaps by turning a node symbol bright red on the screen, when activity goes beyond acceptable limits.

Monitoring software is also written specifically for monitoring file servers on a LAN. Besides monitoring server performance and setting off alarms, some monitoring packages have the ability to dial and set off pagers belonging to network managers who may be away from the network console. By integrating additional existing technologies such as digitized voice, voice recognition, and touch-tone response units, servers will be calling managers at home, discussing their problems, and agreeing on a mutual plan of action.

LAN Problem Analysis and Diagnosis   Once a problem has been monitored and identified, it must be *analyzed* and *diagnosed*. This is the second major task of network management software. Diagnosis is often done by a class of devices known as protocol analyzers or by the more common name—**sniffers**. These devices are attached to the LAN and watch, measure, and in some cases, record every bit of data that passes their way. By using multiple sniffers at various points on a LAN, otherwise known as *distributed sniffers*, bottlenecks can be identified and performance degradation factors can be pinpointed. LAN testing devices, or **LAN analyzers**, must be able to test and isolate the three major segments of any LAN:

1. The wire or cable of the network.
2. The network adapter cards that interface between the cable and the workstation.
3. The workstation or PC that generates the network activity.

LAN Administration   Having diagnosed the cause of the networking problem, corrective action must be taken against that problem. Perhaps a misbehaving network interface card must be disabled or an application on a workstation which is monopolizing network resources must be logged out. The power to do these things is sometimes called **LAN administration** or management. In this case, the term "administration" is preferable in order to provide a contrast to the previous more general use of the term network management.

To summarize then, network management, regardless of the size of the network, requires hardware and/or software tools to provide:

Monitoring
Analysis/diagnosis
Administration

These three major areas of network management are also part of the larger network development life cycle to be covered in detail in Chapter 12. Figure 4-10 summarizes the key concepts and technology associated with the various aspects of network management.

Remembering that the discussion of network management in this chapter is only concerned with self-contained LANS, most often the required network management software to manage such a relatively simple LAN is included in the network operating system itself. As typical LAN and LAN lookalike operating systems such as Netware, Vines, LANManager and LANtastic are reviewed in this chapter, their respective network management capabilities will be analyzed and compared.

LAN monitoring software and other specialized network management functions are available as add-on products for most network operating systems. When these add-on products are manufactured by a company other than the original net-

Major Functional Area	Concepts and Functions	Technology
Monitor	Monitor operation of the LAN and evaluate performance in relation to defined acceptable parameters. Trigger alarms when performance is outside of acceptable parameters. Graphical displays	Protocol analyzers LAN analyzers Sniffers Software-only solutions
Analyze Diagnose	Use LAN analyzers to trap and analyze transmitted LAN traffic packets or to generate LAN traffic packets in order to detect LAN bottlenecks. Filters allow analyzers to detect, trap, and analyze only certain types of LAN traffic	Protocol analyzers LAN analyzers Sniffers
Administration	Take corrective action against network problems. Disable or suspend applications or workstations. Also user-ID administration, directory control, overall LAN security, and virus control	Most often software-only solutions included with network operating system or available as third-third party add-ons. For: Security Virus control Resource management

Figure 4-10 LAN management concepts and technology.

work operating system vendor, they are known as **third-party products**. These third-party enhancements are often of high quality but should be purchased with caution. Compatibility with associated software or future releases of the network operating system are not necessarily guaranteed.

As more complicated internetworks and wide area networks are built, it would stand to reason that more sophisticated network management tools will be required. These more sophisticated tools will be reviewed in their respective chapters.

Network Security

In addition to the typical security features such as password protection and directory access control supplied with most network operating systems, more sophisticated network security software is available for LANs. Some LAN security systems require a hardware add-in board as well.

Access Control and Encryption For instance, security software may be added to workstations and or servers which will:

1. Require user I.D. and valid password to be entered before the PC can even be booted (powered up).
2. Encrypt important data or application files to prevent tampering.
3. Automatically logout inactive terminals to prevent unauthorized access to system resources.
4. Allow certain users to run only certain applications.
5. Require verification of user authenticity by security verifiers or signature cards.

If a high level of security was identified as a business level need, applications solutions exist to meet that need.

Virus Control   Another area of network security that is receiving a lot of attention regards viruses. Virus control software is sometimes included in network security packages. Virus control is really a three-step process, implying that effective virus control software should address at least the following three areas:

Virus protection: User access to systems is sufficiently controlled as to prevent an unauthorized user from "infecting" the LAN.

Virus detection: Sophisticated software to find viruses regardless of how cleverly they may be disguised.

Virus eradication: Sometimes called "antibiotic programs," this software eliminates all traces of the virus.

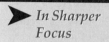
In Sharper Focus

OTHER NETWORK APPLICATIONS

Network Resource Optimization; Network Configuration Management; Network Inventory Management

As LANs continue to grow, it becomes increasingly impossible to keep track of all network components attached to a LAN. These three categories of software: network resource optimization software, network configuration software, and network inventory management software, all keep track of network resources in similar fashion. Many of these programs also *monitor* LANs, which provides some overlap with network management software.

Once these programs are initialized with the data describing LAN hardware and software components on client PCs as well as servers, they continue to run on the clients and servers in order to verify that no changes to the hardware or software configurations are taking place. All of this configuration data is kept in a database where inquiries or reports can be easily run. Imagine how much easier it would be for a network administrator to ask the following questions of a database rather than having to personally inspect hundreds of PCs.

Sample Questions:

How many PCs on our LAN have less than 2MB ram memory?
How many mice are attached to PCs on the LAN?
How many PCs have the new 16MB token ring network interface cards?
How many copies of Lotus 1-2-3 version 2.01 are installed?

Some of these network inventory software packages will work across multiple LANs such as Netware, Vines, LANManager or Macintosh , or even over wide area networks. Some of the packages that also provide monitoring capability will page or send E-mail to a designated network administrator if some preset parameter has been exceeded.

Network changes such as the removal or addition of hardware or software can be detected and reported as well. LAN usage statistics can be used as a basis for billing or charge-back systems.

These tools can be used for planning purposes as well. By gathering statistics on current usage and configurations, network administrators can more easily plan and budget for network upgrades and changes.

If any of the previously mentioned capabilities appeared on the list of business needs, look into this relatively new but rapidly developing area of network application software.

Groupware

Groupware is the name of a category of software that seeks to take advantage of the fact that workers are networked together electronically in order to maximize worker productivity. If maximizing or increasing worker productivity was one of the top layer business needs of the top-down model, then groupware may be of some interest.

Groupware is a general term that describes all or some of the following software categories:

Workflow automation
Interactive work
Group scheduling
Document review
Information sharing
Enhanced electronic mail

Lotus Notes is probably the best known of the currently available groupware offerings.

Workflow Automation   **Workflow automation** allows geographically dispersed coworkers to work together on project teams. As project assignments change, there is no need for moving offices or workstations. The work from the new project simply flows to the current worker location thanks to workflow automation.

A second aspect of workflow automation tracks time spent on given projects by individuals in order to simplify client charge-back and billing for professional or consulting organizations.

Interactive Work   Some **interactive work** software offers opportunities for workers to interact electronically. Brainstorming or idea generation sessions are conducted via the network and managed by the groupware software package. Ideas can be generated on "private" screens and then shared with the group. Meetings can be held electronically, and thereby anonymously, allowing more honest interaction not subject to the political pressures of many face-to-face meetings.

Ideas can be prioritized, consensus can be reached, action items can be established, and meeting minutes can be electronically recorded, edited, and approved.

Group Scheduling   **Group scheduling** or calendaring packages can be an efficient way to schedule electronic or face-to-face meetings or conferences. By simply listing those with whom one wishes to meet, a meeting could be scheduled without making a single phone call. Some scheduling software even has the ability to work over internetworks or wide area networks, allowing meetings to be scheduled with people across the country or around the world.

Although this electronic scheduling process may sound simple, be forewarned! Implementation of group scheduling software can fail miserably due to people factors, not software bugs. If *everyone* in a given organization does not make a firm commitment to keep their electronic schedule and calendar accurate and up-to-date, then the product simply cannot work. Also, inevitably, controls must be put into place as to who has the authority to add commitments to someone else's schedule. The politics of group scheduling can turn out to be much more complicated than the software.

Document Review and Information Sharing Specialized groupware is written for contract or proposal review by appropriate individuals within an organization. The software keeps track of who must review a given document, and in which order the given document is to be reviewed by whom. This "electronic routing slip" also suits the publishing industry well as manuscripts are reviewed by various reviewers, editors, publishers, and production directors.

Enhanced E-Mail E-mail enhancements allow network users to customize their E-mail systems with personal mailing lists, mass mailing capability, delivery confirmation, and mail forwarding. Some enhanced E-mail systems are integrated with voice mail systems using add-in PC voice boards to allow network users to leave voice messages for other network users.

Connectivity/Gateway Software; Remote Access/Control Software; MAC Integration Software

This category of software allows extended communication beyond self-contained LANs. Each of these software categories will be dealt with in detail in Chapter 6, "Internetworking." They are listed here because of their frequent inclusion in the list of business requirements or needs gathered during network analysis.

Just as simultaneous file access by multiple users was the differentiating factor between simple PC connectivity (Chapter 3) and LANs and LAN lookalikes (Chapter 4), this need for extended and/or heterogeneous connectivity beyond the self-contained LAN is the differentiating factor between the study of LANs and LAN lookalikes in Chapter 4 and the study of Internetworking in Chapter 6.

In other words, the non-LAN connectivity devices studied in Chapter 3 could do nearly anything a LAN could do except handle multiple users sharing files, applications, or data. Those more advanced file-handling capabilities were reserved for the LANs which were studied in Chapter 4. In Chapter 4, however, LANs are studied only from a self-contained perspective. When connectivity to other LANs, mainframes, and minicomputers becomes an issue, those topics will be covered in Chapter 6, "Internetworking."

☐ NETWORK DATABASE CONSIDERATIONS

Having completed a thorough analysis of the *applications* layer considerations and opportunities of the top-down model, (Figures 4-2 and 4-6), an analysis of *data* layer requirements and opportunities should be considered.

It is important to understand that asking data-related questions does not make one a database analyst. It is also important to understand that it is not inappropriate for network analysts to ask data-related questions or for database issues to be included in a data communications textbook. As the top-down model indicates, without a thorough understanding of data layer issues and requirements, a network analyst would be hard-pressed to design an effective network that will meet data, applications, and business requirements.

Below are just a sample of the kinds of questions which should be asked in order to gain an understanding of data layer issues as they affect overall network design.

Data Layer Analysis Questions

What data must be shared by whom?
Where are these individuals located?

What kind of speed requirements for database inquiry or transaction entry are realistic?

Are there certain data files which will be read from and written to simultaneously by many users?

Will end users need to be able to perform ad hoc inquiries and develop their own database reports?

How critical are the transactions being entered?

What would happen if power was lost in the middle of a transaction?

The sophistication of the data sharing requirements will have a direct bearing on the selection of a particular LAN or LAN lookalike alternative. Only a brief overview of the issues involved with database analysis will be covered at this point. In large network analysis and information systems analysis projects, specially trained database analysts would assist with the database design and data distribution analysis.

File Server Databases versus Database Server Databases

Data distribution analysis and the design of data distribution networks incorporating minicomputers and mainframes will be studied in more detail in Chapter 9, "Enterprise Networking and Client/Server Architectures." For now, it will suffice to distinguish between the two major classes of databases available for local area networks: **file server databases**, also known as multiuser databases, and **database server databases**, also known as client server databases.

Although there are several differences between the two types of databases in terms of both expense and capabilities, the key functional difference lies in how much data gets sent across the network from the server where the database is stored to the workstation PC requesting the data. Another way of looking at this same characteristic would be to say that the key difference between the two database types lies in the server's behavior upon receipt of a request for data.

The Language of Database Requests

Figure 4-11 illustrates both a file server installation and a database server installation receiving the same request for data from a workstation PC. As can be seen, a file server or multiuser database sends the *entire file* across the network to the requesting PC where record selection and list generation will occur. Conversely, the database server of the client/server database processes the record selection request itself, using the server-based software referred to as the **database back-end** or database engine, and then sends only *selected records* across the network.

Some poetic license has been taken with the actual conversation between the two devices. The actual data-requesting language that PCs and servers use is very structured and may vary from one database to another. In some cases, the data requesting language, or **query language** may be proprietary. In other cases, it may be a language which databases from a number of different vendors understand and which may be controlled by a standards making organization such as ANSI (American National Standards Institute).

If a data layer need exists to share data not only within a LAN but also with databases on other LANs, minicomputers and mainframes, a database which uses the **SQL** (*Structured Query Language*) database request language would be worth investigating. "SQL" is pronounced like the word "sequel." SQL, as well as a related device known as a **database gateway** and their importance to sharing data between PCs, minicomputers, and mainframes will be covered further as part of the study of client–server architectures in Chapter 9.

File Server Databases vs. Client/Server Databases

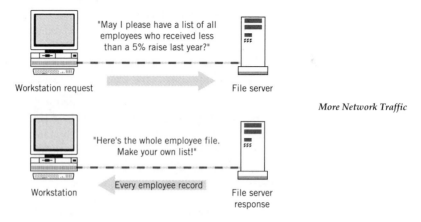

File Server Installation (Often Called Multi-user)

More Network Traffic

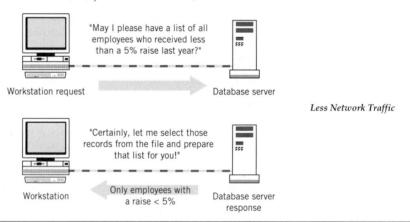

Database Server Installation (Often Called Client/Server)

Less Network Traffic

Figure 4-11 LANs and LAN look-alikes: database layer decisions.

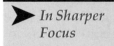

KEY DATABASE ATTRIBUTES

Beyond the major functional difference between file server and database server databases illustrated in Figure 4-11, several other key attributes can serve as a point of comparison between the two database types. These additional differences as well as examples of each type of database are summarized in Figure 4-12. Business needs and requirements should be recalled for possible impact on a database type decision and resultant LAN type decision as the comparative capabilities of the two database types are read.

Major Difference in Price

The attribute evaluations for each of the two database types in Figure 4-12 obviously are vague. Given the range of products and their associated capabilities within each of the two database types, this is inevitable. In general, it is safe to say that database server (client server) databases are more expensive, sophisticated,

	Multi-user Databases	Client/Server Databases
Installed on:	File server	Database server
Usually originated on: (heritage)	Standalone PCs	Minicomputer/mainframe
Data integrity and security	Usually less secure	Usually more secure
Sophisticated automatic record and file locking	Not usually	Usually
Price	Less expensive	10–100 times more expensive
Front-end application development environment included	Usually	Not usually
Transaction entry protection	Not usually	Usually
Portability	Runs on multiple platforms	Usually available
Connectivity	Can talk to other databases	Usually available
Programming abilities	Usually less sophisticated	Usually more sophisticated
On-line backup	Not usually	Usually
Examples:	Microsoft Access Paradox R:Base SuperBase Advanced Revelation Dataease Knowledgeman FoxPro	Ingres Microsoft SQL Server Oracle Netware SQL Gupta SQLBase Server Sybase SQL Server

Figure 4-12 LANs and LAN look-alikes: database layer decisions.

and powerful than file server (multiuser databases). It should be pointed out that, in fact, SQL client/server databases can be 10 or 100 times more expensive! Therefore, the prudent business-oriented network or database analyst will not jump too quickly to the database server conclusion without clear business requirements and cost/benefit analysis in mind.

Heritage

Most of the multiuser databases have been developed from earlier versions of the product which ran on standalone PCs. DBase IV, FoxPro and R:Base all had, and still have, standalone PC versions of their software prior to the introduction of their multiuser offering. Obviously, file sharing and record locking were not key issues when the database was limited to single user access. It is this security and integrity during multiple simultaneous database access which had to be added to these former single-user products.

Conversely, many of the client–server databases were first developed for the multiuser minicomputer and mainframe market, and therefore required and included the sophisticated file sharing security and record locking integrity from the outset.

Data Integrity and Security

Data integrity and security in a database environment goes beyond simply locking a record so that more than one person cannot be trying to change information on that same record at the same instant. A database consists of a number of different files, many of which are related by common pieces of information, or fields. Databases that contain multiple files related by common fields are known as **relational databases**.

Figure 4-13 illustrates an example of a relationship between two fields in different files. In this example, on a customer master database record for a particular customer, there would probably be a field containing the total amount of money which that customer owed to the company. Obviously, there would also be a need for detailed information to tell all of the detailed transactions whose sum total rolled up into the total printed in the single "total customer balance" field on the customer master record. The grand total of all of the "transaction amount owed" fields on the individual transaction records must be identical to the "total amount owed" field on the customer master record in order to preserve an important characteristic of relational databases known as **data integrity**. Figure 4-13 illustrates data integrity.

Preserving data integrity is really nothing more than being able to trust that the data in a database is accurate and dependable. Database packages vary in their overall ability and approach to data integrity. Again, in general, database server databases include more sophisticated automatic data integrity guarantees.

Security in databases is really a matter of the amount of data which is being locked or denied access from certain users. For instance, some users may be locked

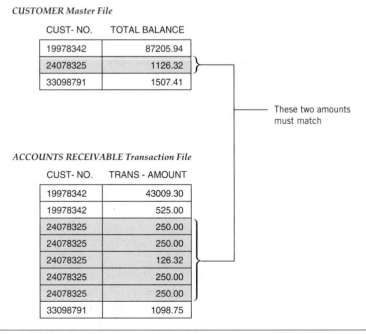

CUSTOMER Master File

CUST- NO.	TOTAL BALANCE
19978342	87205.94
24078325	1126.32
33098791	1507.41

These two amounts must match

ACCOUNTS RECEIVABLE Transaction File

CUST- NO.	TRANS - AMOUNT
19978342	43009.30
19978342	525.00
24078325	250.00
24078325	250.00
24078325	126.32
24078325	250.00
24078325	250.00
33098791	1098.75

Figure 4-13 Database integrity in relational databases.

out of individual fields of data or customer records only if someone else is writing to those fields or records. Other users may be totally locked out of entire files, such as payroll files, to which access must be tightly controlled.

This regulation of the amount or scope of "locked" information is known as **lock granularity**. In other words, how large a "granule" of information is being locked (an individual field or record? multiple records? entire files?)?

A by-product of record locking and database security is whether the database package's locking mechanism is sophisticated enough to allow **on-line backups** to tape, disk, or other media while users are going about their business accessing the database. Hiring a night operator to run system backups can be an expensive proposition. Also, increasingly, database systems must run 24 hours a day in support of customer service or public safety applications. In circumstances such as this, the ability for a database to support on-line backup is essential.

Transaction Entry Protection

Another data integrity related feature included in the more sophisticated, and more expensive, databases has to do with protection of data integrity during transaction entry. Most transactions update several databases simultaneously.

As an example transaction, let's use the purchase of an appliance, perhaps a large-screen TV, to be paid by a credit card. Listed below are only some of the databases that might have to be updated for this one transaction:

> Customer master database
> Accounts receivable transaction database
> Accounts receivable control database
> Inventory master database
> Inventory transaction database
> Sales history database
> Salesperson commission database
> Purchase order database
>
> and so on . . . and so on. . . .

In addition, databases on other systems such as those belonging to suppliers or manufacturers may need to be updated either directly or via EDI (electronic data interchange).

What if the system crashed or lost power in the middle of these databases being updated with this transaction? Would it be acceptable for this transaction to post only partially or not at all? Certainly not!

One form of transaction entry protection is known as **database rollback** or **transaction rollback**. If this transaction were to only partially post due to a power failure, or a network problem of some type, some database systems would automatically *rollback* all of the effected databases to their initial state before this transaction posting began. How can a database system remember all that information and restore these databases with guaranteed integrity? This added sophistication comes at a premium price. Most client–server databases have some type of transaction entry protection while few of the significantly less expensive multiuser databases offer this level of data integrity.

Although we won't go into detail here about all of the ways in which transaction protection can be provided, be aware of this potential threat to data integrity when reviewing and prioritizing business needs and requirements. Transaction entry protection may be a feature that your business can't afford to be without.

Database Front-Ends and User Programming Environments

A database is only useful to a business if the business decision makers can access the information stored in that database easily in order to get questions answered and reports generated without needing a dedicated programmer or MIS (Management Information Systems) staff at their beck and call.

Asking a database one-time questions is known as doing an **ad hoc query**. Some databases come with easy-to-use *query languages* that allow nontechnical people to access databases at will. The ease of use and power of these query languages can vary significantly by product.

Beyond the "quick answer"-type queries, business decision makers often need flexible report generation capability in order to spot trends or isolate performances above or below expected values. **Report generators** are included with many database packages which allow users to create and save reports of their own design. Just as with query languages, the ease of use and sophistication of these report generators can vary widely.

Unlike the query languages and report generators that are often designed for nontechnical end-users, program development environments or languages are included for trained programming staff to more quickly and easily write application programs which will interact with the database system.

These database front-ends offer many features or productivity aids that allow programmers to produce application programs with fewer mistakes or bugs. For instance, the programmer might pick a database field to be updated from a listing of all database fields supplied by the programming environment or by verifying valid database field names as the programmer types them in. Without this verification of valid database names and characteristics during program development, the programmer wouldn't know the program had a problem until much later when the program was compiled and run.

Screen generators allow programmers to set up an input or inquiry screen quickly thanks to a technology known as **"WYSIWYG"** (What You See Is What You Get) programming. These programming environments are sometimes known as **fourth-generation languages** or **database front-ends**. They are not always available for multiuser databases and are often not included in the base price of the more expensive **client–server** databases.

Internetworked Databases—The Client–Server Architecture

Once beyond the self-contained LAN, numerous additional database related decisions are faced. Many of these will be addressed in Chapter 9, "Enterprise Networking and Client–Server Architectures." However, a few distributed database-related issues merit introduction at this time.

If business requirements or needs dictate that data will need to be shared in any of the following ways:

> Across multiple LANS
> From a LAN to a database on a minicomputer or mainframe
> From a LAN over a wide area network to another LAN, minicomputer, or mainframe

then you will need to seek a database that has been designed to function in multiple environments. Perhaps surprisingly, this need for sharing data across multiple environments does not necessarily require purchase of the more expensive client–server type databases.

Two different attributes of databases relate to this distribution of data.

Portability refers to the ability of a given database package to run on multiple computers of various sizes made by various manufacturers. Obviously, data sharing is simplified among identical database packages, even if they are running on different types of computers.

The second attribute is that of *connectivity*. Connectivity is the ability of one vendor's database to talk to a different database package, which may also be installed on a different LAN, minicomputer, or mainframe. Getting two different database packages to share data requires the two databases to be able to speak a common data sharing language. That common data sharing language is most often *SQL*, mentioned earlier in this chapter. If SQL is not the "native" language of the database package, then a *database gateway* may be available, usually at an added cost, which will "translate" the data sharing requests between the two different database computer combinations.

However, be forewarned! This database sharing language translation can take a significant amount of processing. As a result, the database gateway can easily become the bottleneck (slowest component) of the network. Secondly, most database gateways are manufactured to translate from one particular database/computer combination to another specific database/computer combination.

An analogy would be that you could hire a translator to be your "gateway" from English to French, but you couldn't expect that same "gateway" to translate from English to Japanese or from Russian to German.

Database portability, connectivity, database gateways, distributed access and much more will be explored in Chapter 9. For now, compare business needs and requirements to the database attributes just outlined. Spend some time researching particular database packages to discover options and features. The level of data sharing sophistication required will have a direct bearing on the local area network or alternative which will ultimately be chosen.

☐ LANS AND LAN LOOK-ALIKES

Having decided the following:

1. Which business application programs must be available to end-users in order to meet stated business needs
2. The level of sophistication required in the database layer in order to support those applications and users

it is now time to examine available alternatives for local area networking (logical network design) which will, in turn, support the required data and application program distribution.

In this section, the capabilities, similarities, and differences of the following local area networking alternatives will be compared.

Printer sharing networks
File transfer
Zero-slot LANS (hardware and software)
DOS-based, low cost, alternate, or peer-to-peer LANs
Fully-integrated LANS or non-DOS based

Figure 4-14, the "LANS and LAN Look-alikes Technology Analysis Grid" summarizes and compares the attributes of the aforementioned local area networking alternatives. In many cases, it is difficult to form either:

Figure 4-14 LANs and LAN look-alikes: technology analysis grid.

	Number of users	Price/User	Windows integration	Speed	File transfer	E-Mail	File sharing	Printer sharing	CD-ROM sharing	Distributed database	Application sharing	Linked via adapter cable	Linked via serial/parallel ports	Software loaded on client	Software loaded on server	External adapters	Dedicated server	Peer-to-peer architecture	Client/server	Workgroup software	UNIX	ISDN	Naming services	MAC support	Runs in background	Runs in foreground	Resources appear local	Separate PC for client/server	Print queue and spooling	Security	Administration
	Functions																		**Extended Communications**												
Fully-integrated LAN (server based)	>50					■		■		■	■	■							■	■	■		■	■	■		■	■	■	■	■
DOS-based LAN (peer-to-peer)	>50		■		■	■	■	■			■	■						■							■		■		■	■	■
Zero-slot LAN	2				■	■							■												■						
File transfer software	2				■	■							■									■				■					
Printer sharing network		$200			■	■		■				■																			
Data switch		$150			■	■		■																							

1. generalizations within a local area networking category, or
2. distinctions between categories.

The information presented in the grid is expanded on below with each of the sections describing a particular local area networking alternative, outlining currently available products in these categories as well as some examples of proper utilization of these products. The detailed descriptions start with printer sharing networks at the bottom of the grid and work their way up to the full-featured LANs at the top of the grid.

As offerings in each of these product categories mature, additional functionality will no doubt become available. These changes in features should be added to the technology analysis grid in order to keep it up to date.

☐ PRINTER SHARING NETWORKS

Printer sharing networks are discussed in this chapter rather than in Chapter 3, "PC Connectivity," due to one key distinction. Unlike the printer sharing devices highlighted in Chapter 3, a printer sharing network requires the installation of some type of adapter card in an expansion slot of the PC. In most cases they also require printer sharing software to be loaded into each PC on the printer sharing network. This software can then "pop up" on a user's screen to allow for printer management as well as other printer sharing network capabilities such as E-mail and file transfer.

It is important to note that these E-mail and file transfer capabilities are local only. The networking software on such a network is proprietary and does not include any of the sophisticated gateway and connectivity capabilities of other local area networking alternatives which would allow attached PCs to communicate with other LANs or minicomputers/mainframes.

These printer sharing networks can handle more networked users than most of the data switches and buffered printer sharers featured in Chapter 3. Thirty or more printer sharing network users can share a similar number of printers, plotters, or modems while most data switches are limited to less than 20 users. The per user cost on a printer sharing network is about $200 compared to about $150 per user attached to a data switch.

The business decision of whether or not a printer sharing network is the correct local area networking alternative comes down to a few simple points:

1. If the per user cost is appealing and...
2. If the printer sharing network offers the required functionality to meet business application needs...
3. Then the key issue comes down to expansion capabilities of the printer sharing network.

If the business's networking requirements are likely to expand in either:

1. Numbers of users

or

2. Required applications (database sharing for instance)

then a printer sharing network using proprietary software is probably not a wise investment. Figure 4-15 highlights the differences between printer sharing networks and the printer sharing devices featured in Chapter 3.

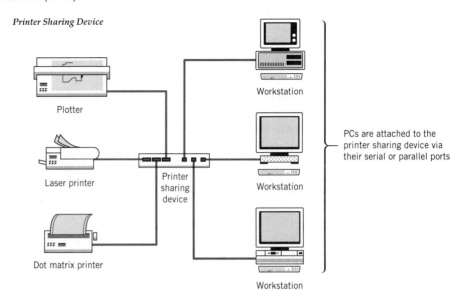

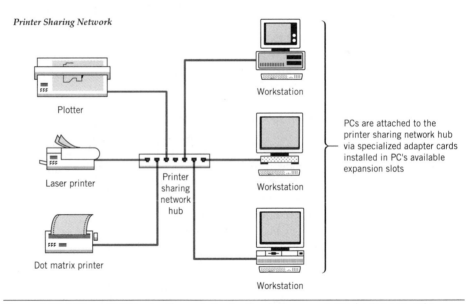

Figure 4-15 LANs and LAN look-alikes: printer sharing devices vs. printer sharing networks.

☐ FILE TRANSFER SOFTWARE

Not all networking needs are of a permanent nature. Not all PCs sit on the same desk or worktable all day long. Recognizing both the proliferation of portable/notebook computers and the need for occasional or temporary networking of PCs, a powerful and easy to use category of networking software known as **file transfer software** has developed.

Figure 4-16 summarizes the possible business applications, currently available functionality, and technical requirements and characteristics of file transfer software. The available functionality blocks listed are not likely to all be found in a sin-

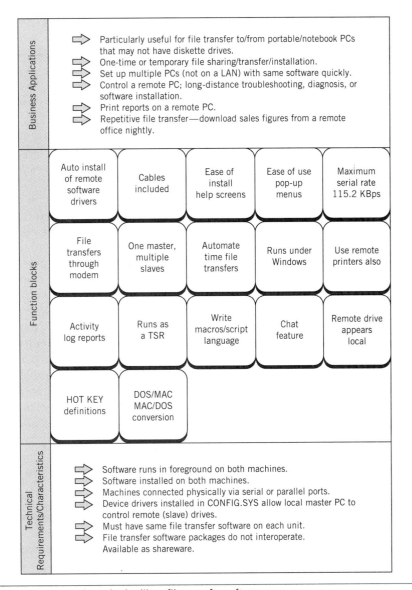

Figure 4-16 LANs and LAN look-alikes: file transfer software.

gle file transfer software package. They are listed in order to enable a decision as to which of these function blocks are important in support of business applications.

Having identified required functionality, possible purchase options can be objectively reviewed by consulting a recent product comparative review, or manufacturers' literature. Among the current products available in this category are LapLink Pro 4.0 and FastLynx 2.0. Both are available for about $100 and come complete with color-coded cables—to connect PCs via serial or parallel ports—as well as all necessary software.

The key operational characteristic of all file transfer software is that it runs in the **foreground** on linked PCs. The file transfer software *is* the application program running over DOS or, is some cases, within Windows. No other applications programs (word processing, spreadsheets, database) can run while the file transfer software is running.

This need to run in the foreground limits file transfer software's business uses to temporary networking requirements such as occasional file transfer, remote file access, or remote printer access. The ability to control a remote PC is included in some file transfer software packages as well as in an entire category of software known as **remote control** or *remote access* software which will be reviewed in Chapter 6, "Internetworking." The Norton pcAnywhere 4.5 is an example of remote control software and sells for around $100.

Another important operational feature is that only one of the two linked PCs is really in control of the file transfer session. This active PC, commonly known as the "master" PC, can transfer files to/from the passive or "slave" PC, and can access files or printers on the slave PC, or on the network to which the slave PC may be attached. The passive PC merely runs the file transfer software during the file transfer session and accepts commands from the active or master PC.

File transfer software is popular among information systems professionals responsible for maintenance and troubleshooting of personal computers as well as among auditors and other field service personnel. When PCs are not connected to LANS, updating software or diagnosing problems can be very time consuming. With the aid of file transfer software, a PC support person can load a software upgrade on a portable PC equipped with file transfer software and move from one PC to another updating all necessary files with a single key stroke thanks to the script language and transfer automation capabilities of the file transfer software.

In some cases, portable or notebook PCs may not have a diskette drive at all, or the drive may be a different size or incompatible density as compared to another PC with which it must transfer data files. File transfer software is an ideal solution to this problem as the transfer of data actually takes place via the PC's serial or parallel ports. In the name of ease of use and installation, some file transfer software packages also include the necessary cables to physically link the two PCs. Some file transfer software such as Mac-in-DOS provides conversion between Macintosh and DOS or Windows file formats in addition to traditional file transfer capabilities.

> *In Sharper Focus*

DEVICE DRIVERS AND VIRTUAL DRIVES

Thanks to a piece of software known as a **device driver**, the slave PC's disk drives, and the files contained therein, appear as local or **virtual drives** on the master PC. They are called virtual drives because although they are not *actually* contained in the master PC, through the magic of device drivers and file transfer software, they appear to be attached locally. A device driver is a piece of software that tells the operating system how to control peripheral devices like disk drives, printers, and network interface cards.

The name and location of the device driver is added as a line in a file called CONFIG.SYS. This system configuration file gets read and executed when a DOS-based PC first gets powered up or booted. These device drivers are loaded into memory "fooling" the local (master) PC into thinking that the remote (slave) PCs disk drives are really attached directly to, and locally accessible by, the local master PC.

◀

As the functionality and possible business applications of file transfer software is reviewed, keep in mind its affordable price: generally around $100. Although no replacement for a full-function network, file transfer software can be a real time saver, and as the saying goes: Time is money.

ZERO-SLOT LANS

The terms data switch, file transfer software, software-based zero-slot LANs and hardware-based zero-slot LANs represent technologies offering similar functionality with slightly different operational characteristics. As a result, the terms are often confusing and sometimes misapplied. Remembering that there are no data communications police enforcing what manufacturers call their data comm devices adds to the confusion.

Similarity among the Four Related Technologies

Figure 4-17 summarizes the key operational characteristics of these four similar technologies. A key similarity among all four of these technologies is that they utilize existing serial or parallel ports for communication, thereby helping to contribute to their relatively low per user cost.

Software Zero-Slot LANs versus File Transfer Software

The key difference between the file transfer software examined in the previous section and **software-based zero-slot LANs** is that file transfer software runs in the foreground on connected PCs and the software-based zero-slot LAN software runs in the **background** allowing other application software to run in the foreground. The two technologies share similar benefits: local access to virtual drives from the remote PC, file transfer, and remote printing capabilities.

Technology Analysis						
	Shares a central specialized hardware switching device	Requires special software loaded on each PC	Software runs in foreground	Software runs in background	Links via existing serial/parallel ports	Links via adapter cards
Data switches	■	□	■	□	■	
File transfer software		■	■		■	
Hardware-based Zero-slot LANs	■	■		■	■	
Software-based Zero-slot LANs		■		■	■	
DOS-based LANs		■		■		■

■ Standard item with this component
□ Optional item with this component

Figure 4-17 LANs and LAN look-alikes: zero-slot LANs and related technologies.

Hardware Zero-Slot LANs versus Data Switches

A **hardware-based zero-slot LAN** is centered around a central data switch with attached PCs connected usually via their serial or parallel ports. The data switch provides the physical connections which allow any attached device to communicate with any other attached device. The only difference between the capabilities of the hardware-based zero-slot LAN and a standalone data switch is the level of sophistication and location of execution of the software associated with the central data switch.

Data switches typically offer software to handle printer management and peripheral sharing only. This software usually runs in the foreground. When a user wants to print a document or manage printers, a hot key combination usually brings up a pop-up menu with all printer management options listed. Once the printer management operations have been completed, the pop-up menu disappears and the user resumes the previous application.

Hardware-based zero-slot LANs usually include software to be loaded onto each connected PC offering more sophisticated capabilities such as E-mail, file transfer, and perhaps virtual drive access. In addition, the software portion of these zero-slot LANs usually runs in the background, transparent to the user.

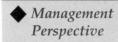
♦ *Management Perspective*

Although distinguishing characteristics between these four similar technologies have been outlined, these distinctions should not be construed as hard and fast rules. For example, devices labeled as data switches may possess all of the capabilities listed above under hardware-based zero-slot LANs. This label confusion is the "name game" of data communications and is a market reality that will not soon disappear.

The key to survival in the name game is to develop the skills necessary to avoid being misled by the labels given to data communications devices. The following three-step process for coping with the name game will allow comparisons based on data communication device functionality and cost/benefit rather than labels.

1. Identify the function blocks.
2. Calculate the price per user.
3. Determine the capability and cost for expansion.

Regardless of the name of the device, list its function blocks. What does the device actually do? This will yield an objective list of the device's benefits.

Next, compute the cost per user of the device for the number of users that will be connected initially. This will yield an initial cost–benefit comparison for each alternative device evaluated.

Finally, determine objectively the need for possible future expanded use of this device as compared to both the capability and cost of the expanded use of the device.

By following these three simple steps in the comparative evaluation of data communications equipment, victimization by the data communications name game can be avoided.   ♦

Zero-Slot LANs—Applications, Capabilities, Limitations

The term "zero-slot" refers to the fact that these networking arrangements connect via serial or parallel ports rather than via network adapter cards. Because no network adapter cards are required, "zero slots" (no expansion slots) within the PC are required. This networking alternative could just as correctly be called "adapterless" LANs, but somehow that name just doesn't have the same ring to it.

Linking computers via serial or parallel ports rather than adapter cards has a significant impact on the speed or available bandwidth of the communications link between PCs. Maximum realistic throughput for a serial-to-serial connection is about 80Kbps while a parallel-to-parallel connection can yield about 130Kbps. This is probably fine for linking two PCs. However, compared to Token Ring communications of 4 and 16Mbps and Ethernet communications of 10Mbps, it should be obvious that the savings offered by the avoidance of a network adapter card in a zero-slot LAN comes at the price of a substantial reduction in communications bandwidth.

Additionally, the duty of network adapter cards to prepare data for transmission onto the network medium and conversely receive data from the network medium must fall to some other computer component in a zero-slot LAN. This added duty falls to the CPU itself, with additional interruptions executed for data transmission and receipt via the serial or parallel port at the cost of reduced available CPU time for processing other programs or applications.

Zero-slot LANs are the ideal networking solution for the two- or three-person office. Figure 4-18 summarizes some of the business applications, function blocks, and technical requirements and characteristics of zero-slot LANs. No currently available zero-slot LAN package offers all of the function blocks listed. Lantastic-Z from Artisoft is perhaps the best known zero-slot LAN.

At a per user cost of about $100, offering the ability to share printers, send E-mail, and share files, zero-slot LANs are hard to beat when it comes to cost/benefit analysis.

Two or three coworkers sharing project responsibilities could easily and affordably be set up on a zero-slot mininetwork, which would allow them to access each others files transparently through the use of virtual drives.

A zero-slot LAN can also be used to piggyback a PC onto a full-featured or media-sharing LAN, such as Ethernet or Token Ring, by connecting it via serial or parallel ports to the PC connected to the network backbone via a network adapter card. Network drives available to the network-attached PC are now also available to the "piggybacked" zero-slot LAN attached PC. Figure 4-19 illustrates such a piggyback arrangement.

As possible function blocks of zero-slot LANs are compared with those of file transfer software, many similarities will be found. Remember, the key difference between the two networking alternatives is the zero-slot LANs' ability to run in the background.

Another key criterion for comparison among zero-slot LANs is their expandability. For instance, Artisoft's LANtastic-Z is a two- or three-user zero-slot LAN that can be easily upgraded to Artisoft's very popular DOS-based LAN named LANtastic, which can easily support over 100 users! LANtastic will be discussed in more detail in the DOS-based LAN section of this chapter.

A second option for expandability of a zero-slot LAN is offered by LANLink 5X, from The Software Link. With LANLink 5X, up to 16 users can be linked via serial or parallel port connections. As may have been suspected, there is a key difference in network architecture which allows 16 users to be connected to this zero-slot LAN while most others maintain a maximum of two or three users. This option also yields an increase in both price per user as well as sophistication and the inherent complication of network installation.

Client–Server versus Peer-to-Peer

The LANLink 5X network requires one PC on the network to be designated as a *server*, which contains all the resources (disk drives, files, printers, modems) to be

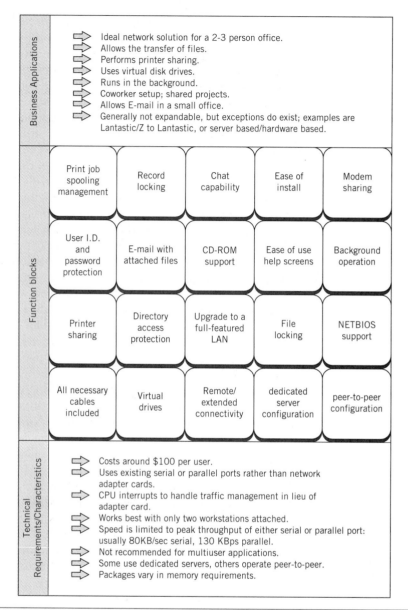

Figure 4-18 LANs and LAN look-alikes: zero-slot LANs.

shared. This server PC runs special software which allows its resources to be shared by the other PCs connected to it. Each of these other *client* PCs on the network run a different piece of software which allows them to make requests to the server to share its resources. This network setup is sometimes called a **client/server architecture**. The irony of this particular setup is that most true client/server LANs are connected via high-speed network adapter cards rather than serial or parallel ports as is the case with LANLink 5X. Thus, LANLink 5X offers the added capability and complication of a dedicated server without the typical client–server benefit of high-speed network communications.

A version of the client–server architecture known as **dedicated server** implies that the server cannot be also used as a workstation to run applications or request network services. Client–server architectures can be very complicated and can imply

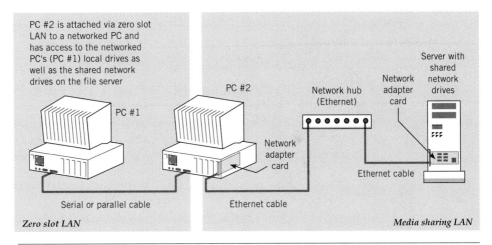

Figure 4-19 LANs and LAN look-alikes: zero-slot LAN application—LAN piggyback.

a great deal more networking and database distribution sophistication as will be seen in Chapter 9—"Enterprise Networking and Client–Server Architectures."

Most zero-slot LANs are networked together using an architecture known as **peer-to-peer**. Peer-to-peer networks allow any PC on the network to *offer* resources to be shared by other networked PCs as well as *request* to share resources attached to or contained within other PCs on the network. This implies that, unlike the client–server architecture, in a peer-to-peer architecture, all networked PCs run the same piece of networking software. In a sense, on a peer-to-peer network, every PC is both a client *and* a server.

The next LAN alternative to be studied, **DOS-based LANs**, frequently use a peer-to-peer architecture with 50 or more users. As will be seen, the key difference between zero-slot and DOS-based LANs, which allows support of these larger numbers of users, is the fact that DOS-based LANs communicate through higher speed network adapter cards rather than serial or parallel ports.

☐ DOS-BASED LANS: ALSO KNOWN AS PEER-TO-PEER LANS, LOW COST LANS, ALTERNATE LANS

As the newer, more powerful CPU chips (80386,80486 PENTIUM) have been introduced and as DOS 5.0 has allowed use of memory above the former 640K limit, the two major limiting factors to the performance and features offered by DOS-based LANs have disappeared. As a result, many of the differences in available functionality between DOS-based LANs and the so-called full-featured, **non-DOS-based** or **fully-integrated** LANs (Netware, Vines, LANManager) have disappeared.

One thing that has not disappeared, however, is the price discrepancy between DOS-based LANs and non-DOS-based LANs. While the price per user of DOS-based LANs averages around $350 to $400 per user, the non-DOS-based price ranges from $500 to $1000 per user. These facts give DOS-based LANs a very favorable price/performance ratio and have led many users to choose DOS-based LANs as their networking platform.

Examples of peer-to-peer LANs include:

LANtastic
Netware Lite
Invisible LAN

Windows for Workgroups
10NET
SilverNET
WEB for Windows and DOS

As specific features of DOS-based LANs are examined below, it should become obvious why such a LAN could admirably meet the networking requirements of most any business. Bear business and application requirements in mind as the capabilities of DOS-based LANs are reviewed. In the next, and final, section of this chapter, the fully-integrated LANs (Netware, Vines, LANManager) will be

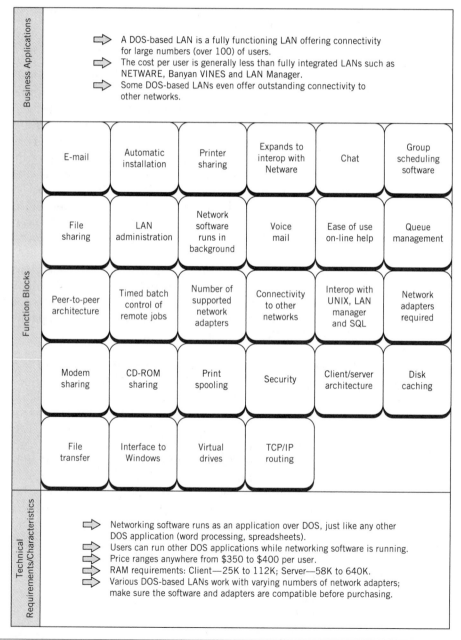

Figure 4-20 LANs and LAN look-alikes: DOS-based LANs (also known as low-cost LANs, and peer-to-peer LANs).

examined and those instances where these more expensive LAN alternatives outperform their DOS-based counterparts will be highlighted.

For now, choose the DOS-based LAN function blocks from Figure 4-20 that meet stated business needs. The sum total of all chosen function blocks yields a logical network design. The physical network design and hardware alternative decisions required to implement any of these logical network designs will be explored in the next chapter on local area network technology.

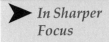

In Sharper Focus

EXPANDABILITY/UPGRADABILITY

The fact that some of these DOS-based LANs support as many as 300 users alleviates the expandability concerns of many network decision makers. Linking additional users can be as simple as loading the client software into the new PC and hooking the network adapter card interface to the network. Most DOS-based LANs offer an unlimited user license option to simplify adding users to large networks.

If a 300-user LAN is not sufficient, then segmentation of users into more than one local area network probably should be considered. Although linking multiple LANs falls into the realm of internetworking, a few points will be briefly explored here. Some DOS-based LANs have a specific user limit per LAN while others have no user limit.

The first step to linking multiple LANs is to divide users in some logical fashion, by department, project, etc., so as to minimize the amount of network traffic which must pass between these multiple LANS. Put another way, users should be arranged to maximize local (within the LAN) traffic. These multiple LANs, running another copy of the same DOS-based LAN operating system, can then be linked using a device known as a **bridge**, which will allow non-local traffic to travel between the multiple LANS. Figure 4-21 illustrates how such a network configuration might work. Internetworking will be explored in detail in Chapter 6.

Connectivity/Interoperability

Connectivity of LANs via bridges is offered by some DOS-based LANs. In general, sophisticated connectivity and interoperability are the domain of the more expensive full-featured LANs. However, if connectivity needs are clearly analyzed and documented, a DOS-based LAN that will meet those connectivity needs may be available.

Beyond connectivity of multiple DOS-based LANs running the same networking software, other possible connectivity needs might include:

1. Connectivity to popular full-featured LANs such as Netware, Vines, or LANManager.
2. Connectivity to Unix machines such as SUN Workstations.
3. Connectivity to minicomputers or mainframes by using the TCP/IP internetworking protocol.
4. Connectivity to database servers by using SQL Data Query Language.

Solutions to connectivity or interoperability needs such as those listed may be offered by the more sophisticated DOS-based LANs. For instance, LANtastic 5.0 offers gateways to Netware and Macintoshes, as well as TCP/IP hosts.

Device Sharing

Device sharing is one of the primary reasons for investigating network alternatives in the first place. DOS-based LANs can share printers, modems, and CD-Roms.

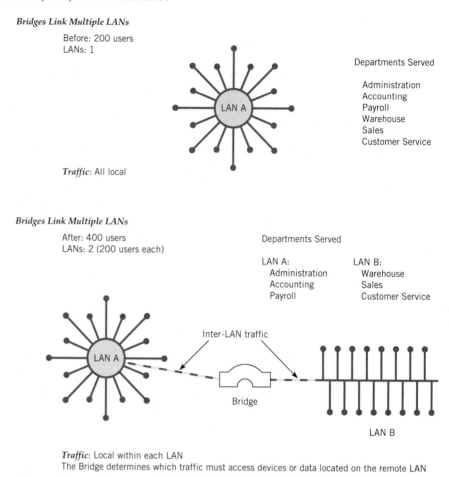

Bridges Link Multiple LANs

Before: 200 users
LANs: 1

Departments Served

Administration
Accounting
Payroll
Warehouse
Sales
Customer Service

Traffic: All local

Bridges Link Multiple LANs

After: 400 users
LANs: 2 (200 users each)

Departments Served

LAN A:
  Administration
  Accounting
  Payroll

LAN B:
  Warehouse
  Sales
  Customer Service

Inter-LAN traffic

Bridge

LAN B

Traffic: Local within each LAN
The Bridge determines which traffic must access devices or data located on the remote LAN

Figure 4-21 LANs and LAN look-alikes: Bridges link multiple LANs.

Printer sharing can be especially sophisticated including printer spooling, printer control, and queue management. Some specific features include the ability to include customized "banner" pages in between print jobs, the ability to notify users when print jobs have been completed, and the ability to direct certain print jobs to certain printers.

Some DOS-based LAN network operating systems are also sophisticated enough to interact with another very important device known as a UPS or uninterruptable power source. Should the normal electrical service fail, the UPS automatically turns on within a billionth of a second of a significant electrical failure, thereby signalling to the network server that there has been a power interruption and prompting the server to shut the network down in an orderly fashion.

Another important power failure related feature included in some DOS-based LANs is the ability to automatically re-boot all client PCs remotely once the network server has resumed normal operation. In this way, a network manager would not have to go around personally to see that each client PC has been re-booted, a potentially significant time savings.

File and Data Sharing
File and data sharing is probably the second most popular use of networks. On a properly functioning DOS-based network, a user on a client PC should be able to

access files and applications transparently. In other words, if a network version of an applications program like word processing or spreadsheet is installed on the server, a user at a client PC should be able to easily run these programs from their own workstation.

Furthermore, once these programs are running, a user should be able to work on a document or spreadsheet file located on another PC by accessing that document from a locally appearing virtual drive. The word "transparency" refers to the fact that the actual physical location of the desired document doesn't matter because the virtual drive makes it appear as a locally accessible resource. The fact that the document may actually be physically stored on a disk drive far from the user matters not, making the actual retrieval of the remote document "transparent" to the local user.

A feature included in some DOS-based LANs that can have a significant impact on data sharing performance is known as **disk caching**. When users request information from databases, the most time consuming part of that inquiry is often the physical retrieval of the data off of the mechanically operated disk drive. Although disk drives usually access data in a matter of milliseconds, the fact remains that the mechanical positioning of the disk's read/write heads over the proper data location is the slowest portion of the overall data retrieval process.

Disk caching seeks to minimize this seek time by storing in memory portions of the data files that users are accessing. The transfer time from memory to a user's PC is significantly less than the full data access sequence involving the disk drives spinning to find the location of data. Now that DOS 5.0 offers the ability to use megabytes of memory over the former 640K limit, disk caching is easily implemented and immediately appreciated.

Another form of disk caching stores various requests for data from multiple users and then mechanically moves the read/write heads of the disk drive in the most efficient pattern while retrieving data, rather than a first-come, first-served access pattern. An analogy could be made with mail delivery. Requests for data delivery (letters) are cached and optimized for the most efficient operation (are gathered and sorted by route and street address for efficient delivery) by the read/write heads (by the mail carriers). Imagine a first-come, first-served delivery pattern of letters received by the post office for delivery.

LANtastic by Artisoft offers another data sharing enhancement known as **delayed record locking**. Realizing that multiple users may occasionally need access to the same record, LANtastic "saves" a user's request for a particular record if another user currently has that record locked. Once the record in question is unlocked, LANtastic forwards the "saved" record request. Without this feature, a dialogue of repeated requests and denials will go on between the server and the requesting PC.

Worker-to-Worker Communications

E-mail, Enhanced E-Mail and Chat capabilities are available on most DOS-based LANs and have all been discussed earlier in previous local area network alternatives sections. One unique worker-to-worker communications option available with the DOS-based LAN LANtastic is the ability to send voice-mail over the network.

This rather interesting application requires the addition of an add-on expansion card installed in each PC designated to use the voice-mail feature. The card consists of a combination of hardware and software to digitize the voice (remembering that voice is analog) of the user. Voice digitization is discussed further in

Chapter 10. Attached to each card is an ordinary phone handset (receiver/transmitter or earphone/microphone).

The digitized voice messages of a user can be sent over the network like an ordinary data file to any other PC on the network and stored on remote disks. The recipient of the voice-mail then receives the voice message when the voice card in their PC turns the stored digitized voice message back into an analog voice signal, which is sent through the phone handset for the recipient to hear.

LAN Administration and Security

In combination with the more advanced connectivity and interoperability features offered, the greater sophistication of available LAN administration and security features from fully-integrated LANs are the two most common business networking requirements, which force users to seek networking solutions from the more expensive alternatives to DOS-based LANs.

Nonetheless, DOS-based LANs still offer some fairly impressive features in the LAN administration and security area beyond the normal user-management type options. Among these are:

1. The ability to log and report network usage statistics by user for the purpose of network monitoring or charge-backs.
2. The ability to form user groups with similar network privileges.
3. The ability to assign expiration dates to both user I.D.s and passwords.
4. The ability to restrict network access to certain physical locations (PCs) and/or certain days, times.
5. The ability to run network management or security software from any networked PC with proper password protection.

If specific LAN administration and/or security needs exist, they should be outlined specifically and compared carefully to features listed in product comparisons.

Hardware Issues: Network Adapter Cards

Remembering that the key increase in sophistication of DOS-based LANs over zero-slot LANs was the former's use of network adapter cards for network communications, compatibility between the chosen network operating system and the employed network adapter cards must be assured.

The simplest solution to this compatibility pitfall is to buy the adapter cards from the company that sells the DOS-based LAN network operating systems. Many companies have responded to this market demand and offer "LAN Starter Kits" or "LAN-in-a-CAN," which include network operating system software, compatible adapter cards, correct cabling, and instructions.

If for some reason this is not a viable option, then you must review the DOS-based LAN's product literature to assure that the adapter cards that you will be using are compatible with the network operating system software. Network adapter cards can vary in many ways including:

Supported network architecture (Ethernet, Token Ring)
Network drivers supported (and supplied!)
Media interfaces
Computer bus interfaces

Consider both the number of network adapter cards supported by a particular peer-to-peer LAN and the associated number of drivers included for those supported adapter cards.

All of these variables, as well as numerous other networking technology alternatives will be thoroughly explained in Chapter 5, "Local Area Networking Technology."

FULLY-INTEGRATED LANS

The role that DOS played in DOS-based LANs was primarily that of managing the disk drives and files according to the instructions passed to it by the DOS-based network operating system such as LANtastic, Powerlan, or 10Net. However, it is important to note that DOS could only execute one of these instructions at a time (although very quickly). As more users are added to a DOS-based LAN, more instructions are sent more quickly to the "one task at a time" DOS processor, and overall performance eventually degrades.

In order to overcome this performance degradation with 50 or more users, the limitations of DOS's "one task at a time" processing must be overcome. DOS itself must be replaced with some other operating system which will process multiple requests quickly for data access from disk drives, print requests to printers, and network management requests to keep track of network activity and report any problems. What is needed is a **multitasking** environment in which more than one request for service can be processed concurrently. **UNIX** is a multitasking operating system and is the basis, in some cases hidden or altered, for many of the so-called full-featured or non-DOS-based LANs.

These LANs are called **fully-integrated LANs** because the operating system which handles the processing and device management is fully integrated into the networking software with which the users and their application programs interface. This integration of the operating system with the networking software is unlike the DOS-based LAN arrangement in which the networking software ran as an application over an unaltered DOS, just like any other application. DOS was not integrated into the networking software. It was still possible to access DOS directly.

Novell Netware, Microsoft LAN Manager, and Banyan Vines are the most popular fully-integrated LAN packages accounting for over 80 percent of all LAN installations among them. Over 60 percent of all LAN installations are Novell Netware installations. The comparative features of these three LANs will be discussed in the technology review section of this chapter.

Discussion of networks that include minicomputers and mainframes such as IBM's SNA and Digital's DECnet will be introduced in Chapter 6, "Internetworking."

Applications, Functionality, Characteristics

Business requirements, constraints, and needs have been examined in comparison with the offered functionality of local area networking alternatives throughout this chapter. Each of the alternatives analyzed has become progressively more expensive, more sophisticated, and more complex.

Only those business needs or requirements which could not be satisfied by DOS-based LANs, the most recent LAN alternative examined, could have lead to the conclusion that the incremental functionality offered by these fully-integrated LANs was the answer to meeting business networking requirements. The power and sophistication of the most recent versions of DOS-based LANs makes the list of these incremental function blocks both predictable and rather short. Figure 4-22 summarizes the business applications, unique functionality, and general characteristics of fully-integrated LANs.

To summarize the added functionality offered by fully-integrated LANs, the list might be shortened to:

1. Complex connectivity and interoperability.
2. Fast, reliable performance with large numbers of (100+) users.
3. Sophisticated LAN administration and security on a par with that found on minicomputers and mainframes.

Impressive Interoperability

Local area networks, once considered departmental computing resources, have developed to the point where they can now support not just entire company-wide networks, but enterprise networks including wide area links to customers, suppli-

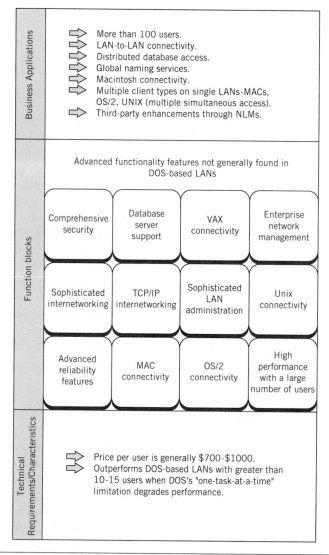

Figure 4-22 LANs and LAN look-alikes: fully-integrated LANs (also known as non-DOS-based LANs, dedicated server LANs, or full featured LANs).

ers, and other enterprise partners. This ability for a local area network to not just merely connect to nearly any type or size of computer, but to share data and interoperate with these varied platforms transparently to the user, is the essence of the burgeoning field of internetworking, or **interoperability** to be studied in Chapter 6. Each connectivity related functionality block listed in Figure 4-22 will be explored in detail.

Fast, Reliable Performance

Avoiding degradation of performance with 100 or more active users is primarily due to the multitasking ability of the operating system portion of these fully-integrated LANs. Many network operating systems have specially written versions to run on high-powered **multiprocessor** servers featuring more than one CPU. Disk caching, explained under DOS-based LANs also has a positive impact.

Additional reliability is available with some fully-integrated LANs in the form of at least two related methodologies known as **disk mirroring** and **disk duplexing**. Disk mirroring keeps identical data stored on two different disks attached to the same disk controller. All updates are done simultaneously to each disk. Should one disk fail, the "mirrored" disk takes over, transparent to the user.

Disk duplexing goes one step further than disk mirroring by having the two disks attached to two different controllers rather than the same single controller used with disk mirroring. In this scheme, even the disk controller can fail (not unheard of) and the "duplexed" disk will take over automatically.

If all of this sounds too good to be true, it probably is. First of all, one must assume the added expense for additional disks and disk controllers. Secondly, the software to manage these reliability processes is highly complex and usually sold at additional cost to the LAN operating system. Finally, the reliability of performance of this reliability software (no pun intended) has received mixed reviews. A well-managed backup program with preventive maintenance on disks may be a prudent path to follow while this industry niche matures.

LAN Administration and Security

The kinds of LAN administration and security offered by some of the fully-integrated LANs rival that of the more established multiuser operating systems that have been running on minicomputers and mainframes for years. Sophisticated password protection schemes, flexible definition of user groups and control of their inherent rights, and system monitoring, logging, and alarm notification capabilities are among the possibilities in this area.

Also, the enterprise networks built thanks to the connectivity and interoperability functionality mentioned above, must also be monitored and managed. This is no small feat remembering that an enterprise network often consists of computers from numerous manufacturers running numerous different operating systems. Several different standards have emerged which allow network status and performance information to be passed from these heterogeneous computers back to a central network management workstation. These networks and standards will be examined in detail in Chapter 6, "Internetworking," and in Chapter 9, "Enterprise Networking and Client/Server Architectures." For now, remember that if integration with enterprise networks is a business layer requirement, it would be wise to choose a fully-integrated LAN, which supports the current enterprise network management information systems and standards.

Before deciding that a fully-integrated LAN should be purchased solely for advanced administration and security functions, examine functional requirements carefully. Are there operational controls or physical security measures which could be instituted to accomplish the same goals? Are the security risks real or perceived?

Remember, some DOS-based LANs offer significant functionality in LAN administration and security. If a DOS-based LAN meets connectivity and performance needs, see if there isn't some way to live with or enhance its administration and security functionality. The potential savings of a DOS-based LAN as opposed to a fully-integrated LAN can be significant. Of course, don't forget to consider growth prospects and expandability requirements in any business needs analysis.

Relationship of Physical Network Design to Logical Network Design

At this point, a local area networking alternative should have been found to meet at least some of the business networking requirements identified in the top-down model. Internetworking and wide area networking extensions to this local area network *logical design* are remaining options yet to be explored.

Because issues such as cables, adapter cards, and network topologies have not been covered yet, only the *logical* or *functional* aspects of network design have been dealt with thus far.

All of the numerous hardware considerations will be explored in Chapter 5. As each set of technology alternatives are explored, additional decisions will be made that will eventually lead to a **physical network design**. This is the actual hardware that gets installed and connected and through which the data physically flows.

As physical network design is explored, the business requirements will be referenced less frequently. If the overall philosophy of the top-down model has been adhered to, the now complete logical network design should assure achievement of the business requirements. It should follow then, as Figure 4-23 illustrates, that as long as the physical network design supports the logical network design, then the final implemented network should support the business requirements—the ultimate goal.

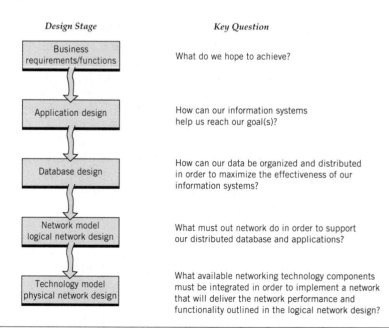

Design Stage	Key Question
Business requirements/functions	What do we hope to achieve?
Application design	How can our information systems help us reach our goal(s)?
Database design	How can our data be organized and distributed in order to maximize the effectiveness of our information systems?
Network model logical network design	What must out network do in order to support our distributed database and applications?
Technology model physical network design	What available networking technology components must be integrated in order to implement a network that will deliver the network performance and functionality outlined in the logical network design?

Figure 4-23 LANs and LAN look-alikes: Physical and logical network designs support business requirements.

CHAPTER SUMMARY

Logical network design defines required network functionality in detail. This functionality is based on the requirements defined in the business, application, and data layers of the top-down model. Only by thoroughly examining the requirements of the business, application, and data layers can one be assured that networking requirements have been properly defined.

Strategic business objectives are mapped to networking-related business activities such as resource sharing, file sharing, and extended communications to begin the top-down approach to logical network design.

Having determined which networking related business activities will meet strategic business objectives, the next step is to examine possible network applications to determine which of those may or may not deliver on the required business activities. Some network applications such as network printing, backup, and security are important resource sharing related applications. *Groupware* refers to a broadly-defined category of software that seeks to leverage the fact that workers are networked together to increase worker productivity through such applications as workflow automation and interactive work.

With a better understanding of which applications will deliver required business activities, data layer con-siderations must be taken into account. Although trained database analysts will be required to perform detailed data needs analysis, the network analyst must be aware of those data management issues with a large potential impact on network design and performance. Decisions related to file server versus data base server architectures, database distribution, inter-database communication, and database gateways are all examples of data layer decisions with large network layer implications.

Among the network solutions available to deliver on data and application layer requirements are alternatives that vary in price, functionality, and ease of use. Careful consideration must be given to each alternative in order to choose the one that delivers all required functionality at the best price. From least sophisticated to most sophisticated and, not coincidentally, from least expensive to most expensive, these networking alternatives are: file transfer software, zero slot LANs, DOS-based LANs, and fully integrated LANs. As PCs have become more powerful from both a hardware and operating systems perspective, the functional differences between DOS-based LANs such as LANtastic and fully integrated LANs such as NetWare, Vines and LAN Manager have been minimized.

KEY TERMS

ad hoc query
background
backup/restoral
bridge
client/server architecture
data integrity
database back-end
database front-end
database gateway
database server database
dedicated server
delayed record locking
device driver
disk caching
disk duplexing
disk mirroring
DOS-based LANS
file server database
file transfer software

foreground
fourth generation
  languages
fully-integrated LAN
group scheduling
groupware
hardware-based zero-slot
  LANs
interactive work
interoperability
LAN administration
LAN analyzers
LAN monitoring
local area network
lock granularity
logical network design
multiprocessor
multitasking
non-DOS based LAN

on-line backup
peer-to-peer
physical network design
printer sharing networks
query language
relational databases
remote-control software
report generators
screen generators
sniffers
software-based zero-slot
  LANs
SQL
third-party products
transaction rollback
UNIX
virtual drive
workflow automation
WYSIWYG

REVIEW QUESTIONS

1. What is the difference between a peer-to-peer network and a client–server network?
2. What is the difference between logical network design and physical network design?
3. How might groupware, as a networked application, deliver a business competitive advantage?
4. What are some of the key issues involved with data distribution analysis?
5. What are virtual drives and how might they be used?
6. What is the major difference between a software-based zero-slot LAN and file transfer software?
7. What is the major difference between a DOS-based LAN and a software-based zero-slot LAN?
8. Why is transaction rollback important in a database with shared simultaneous access to data?
9. What is meant by a database front-end and for whom is such an entity intended?
10. What is Banyan Vines key positive differentiating factor as compared to Novell Netware or Microsoft LAN Manager?
11. Which layer of the top-down model corresponds most closely to logical network design?
12. Which layer of the top-down model corresponds most closely to physical network design?
13. What are some of the typical business needs or perspectives that can lead to local area networking solutions?
14. How can one assure that proposed business activities to be supported by a network design actually meet stated business objectives?
15. What is the purpose of asking business analysis questions as part of an overall network design project?
16. What are some typical network-related business analysis questions?
17. What are some of the typical user issues which must be investigated during network analysis and design?
18. What are some of the ways in which network analysts can avoid losing their sense of budget reality?
19. What are some of the most popular business activities which are likely to be served by local area networking solutions?
20. Why is gaining a sense of anticipated growth so important to network analysis?
21. Where does a network analyst look for information concerning anticipated growth?
22. Name a few of the network applications a local area network can support and explain the significance of each. (See Figure 4-6).
23. Which network applications can be fulfilled only in a network environment?
24. Which network applications have the potential to increase worker productivity?
25. What are the three LAN-based network printing solutions? Draw a diagram of each highlighting differences between the three.
26. What are some of the key issues to keep in mind concerning LAN backup?
27. What are device drivers and what do they have to do with hardware/software compatibility?
28. Distinguish between the following segments of LAN management: monitoring, analysis/diagnosis, administration.
29. What technology, software or hardware, is available to fulfill the needs of each of the aforementioned areas of LAN management?
30. What is a third-party product and what are the potential dangers of getting involved with one?
31. What are the two major areas of network security and what technology is available for each of those areas?
32. What is the purpose of Network resource optimization software? What kinds of questions could such software answer, or what kinds of problems could it solve?
33. What are some of the subcategories of groupware and how might each of these contribute to improved worker productivity?
34. What are the potential weaknesses of groupware?
35. Do you think groupware is the wave of the future or a passing fancy? Defend your answer.
36. Why should a network analyst worry about database considerations?
37. What are some typical data analysis questions and what insight might the answers to these questions offer?
38. What are the major differences from a networking perspective between a file server database and a database server database?
39. What is SQL and why is it important?
40. What is a database gateway and what are the possible network impacts of such devices?
41. Name five database attributes with which the network analyst should be concerned and the possible impact of each.
42. What types of networking requirements would force a network analyst to look at full-featured LANs?
43. What are the major limitations of today's DOS-based or peer-to-peer LANs?
44. What type of professional people are likely to make frequent use of file transfer software? For what purpose?
45. What is the key limitation of a zero-slot LAN?
46. What are some strategies for coping with the "name game"?
47. What is the "name game" as it applies to data communications?
48. What is LAN piggybacking and what might be an appropriate application of such a network set-up?

49. What impact has the growth of laptop and portable computing had on alternative LAN technology?
50. Which of the alternative LAN technologies studied in this chapter is likely to benefit most from the growth of laptop and portable computing? Defend your answer.
51. What is a key limitation of Netware Lite as compared to Lantastic?
52. What is the best way to insure compatibility between a given network operating system and the network adapter cards over which it will run?
53. What is the difference between multitasking and multiprocessing?
54. Why is UNIX a preferable operating system to DOS for networks with 100 or more users?

ACTIVITIES

1. Find a comparative review of groupware software in a recent trade publication. Familiarize yourself with costs and functionality. Conduct a survey of local businesses to determine the current rate of usage of groupware products. For those companies currently using groupware, determine the following:
   a. Functions which are actually performed by the majority of users via groupware.
   b. Impact on productivity or other business layer objectives.
2. How is network backup performed on the network with which you interact at your school or business? Is it relatively uncomplicated to restore "lost" files?
3. Draw a simple network diagram illustrating the network printing set-up on your network. Be sure to illustrate numbers of printers, numbers of user workstations, and whether or not printer servers are dedicated.
4. List all of the network applications performed on your network. How many could have been performed by some alternative means such as a data switch or printer sharing device?
5. What are the minicomputer/mainframe connectivity requirements for your network? Approximately what percentage of network traffic remains on the local network and what percentage has remote destinations?
6. Choose particular examples of zero-slot, DOS-based, and fully-integrated LANs and obtain detailed product literature on these LAN products. Prepare a technology analysis grid detailing and comparing all of the available features of these three LAN alternatives.
7. Obtain recent trade publications that compare the functionality of the latest versions of NetWare, LAN Manager, Vines, and Windows NT. List the strengths and weaknesses of each LAN network operating system and predict the future market direction of each.
8. Find LAN managers or systems administrators who are responsible for NetWare, Vines, LAN Manager, or Windows NT LANs. Invite them to present guest lectures in your class or interview them individually and report on your findings.
9. Choose a multiuser database and a relational database from among those listed on Figure 4-12. Obtain recent reviews or articles about these products and prepare a report specifying differences in functionality, price, and platforms on which these databases run.

Featured References

Databases

Anderson, Ron. "SQL Databases: High Powered, High-Priced," *PC Magazine*, vol. 11, no. 15 (September 15, 1992), p. 369.

Venditto, Gus. "Nine Multiuser Databases: Robust and Ready to Share," *PC Magazine*, vol. 11, no. 6 (March 31, 1992), p.289.

Browning, Dave. "New Blood, New Power," *PC Magazine*, vol. 12, no. 9 (May 11, 1993), p. 108.

DOS-Based LANs

Derfler, Frank. "Peer-to-Peer LANs: Teamwork Without Trauma," *PC Magazine*, vol. 12, no. 10 (May 25, 1993), p. 203.

Derfler, Frank. "DOS Based LANS Grow up," *PC Magazine*, vol. 10, no. 12 (June 25, 1991), p. 167.

Derfler, Frank. "Low-Cost LANs Grow in Features and Performance," *PC Magazine*, vol. 11, no. 7 (April 14, 1992), p. 299.

"LAN Times Tests Alternative NOSes," *LAN Times*, vol. 9, no. 5 (March 23, 1992), p. 43.

Harrison, Gary. "Case Study: Simply Planning Ahead Can Result in 'Kink-Free' Network," *LAN Times*, vol. 9, no. 19 (October 12, 1992), p. 77 (10Net DOS-based LAN—Large Implementation).

File Transfer Software

Derfler, Frank. "File-Transfer Software," *PC Magazine*, vol. 10, no. 5 (March 12, 1991), p. 321.

Full-Featured LANs

Grieves, Michael. "LAN Manager: Stuck in Tomorrowland," *Data Communications*, vol. 20, no. 2 (February 1991), p. 97.

Derfler, Frank. "Network Operating Systems Go

Corporate," *PC Magazine*, vol. 11, no. 11 (June 16, 1992), p. 301.

Wylie, Margie. "Banyan Takes a New Tack in LAN Fight," *LAN Times*, vol. 9, no. 24 (June 15, 1992), p. 1.

Breidenbach, Susan. "Novell Takes a Piece of DOS Pie," *LAN Times*, vol. 8, no. 14 (August 5, 1991), p. 1.

Brandel, William. "Banyan Beats Novell to the Punch," *LAN Times*, vol. 9, no. 15 (August 10, 1992), p. 1.

Neff, Ken. "Three Hot Network Operating Systems," *LAN Times*, vol. 8, no. 4 (February 18, 1991), p. 53.

Didio, Laura. "Novell, DEC Marry Technologies," *LAN Times*, vol. 9 no. 3 (February 24, 1992), p. 1.

Salamone, Sylvester. "Test Shows Which NOS Performs Best for You," *Network World*, vol. 9, no. 3 (January 20, 1992), p. 1.

General Networking and Design

Derfler, Frank. "Connectivity Simplified: An Introduction to the Ways of Networking," *PC Magazine*, vol. 11, no. 6 (March 31, 1992), p. 251.

Groupware

Breidenbach, Susan. "1991 a Real Banner Year for Groupware Product Releases," *LAN Times*, vol. 8, no. 18 (September 16, 1991), p. 31.

Stevenson, Ted. "Best of a New Breed: Groupware—Are We Ready?" *PC Magazine*, vol. 12, no. 11 (June 15, 1993), p. 267.

LAN Add-on Software and Applications

Ellison, Carol. "LAN Inventory Software: Optimizing Network Resources," *PC Magazine*, vol. 11, no. 12 (June 30, 1992), p. 297.

Ubois, Jeff. "Buyers Guide: LAN Backup Programs Get Smart," *Network World*, vol. 9, no. 28 (July 13, 1992), p. 33.

Day, Mike. "Network Printing: The Second Gener-ation," *LAN Times*, vol. 9, no. 15 (August 10, 1992), p. 45.

Greenfield, David. "Novell Hub Management: How Big a Boost?" *Data Communications*, vol. 21, no. 1 (January 1992), p. 39.

LAN Analyzers and Monitors

Koontz, Charles. "LAN Times Lab Compares Analyzers," *LAN Times*, vol. 9, no. 1 (January 20, 1992), p. 53.

Derfler, Frank. "Server Monitoring Software: Getting Inside Your File Server," *PC Magazine*, vol. 11, no. 15 (September 15, 1992), p. 277.

Derfler, Frank. "Low-Cost Analyzers: An Eye into the LAN," *PC Magazine*, vol. 12, no. 1 (January 12, 1993), p. 277.

Jander, Mary. "Proactive LAN Management: Tools That Look for Trouble to Keep LANs out of Danger," *Data Communications*, vol. 22, no. 5 (March 21, 1993), p. 48.

Tolly, Kevin, et. al. "What's Missing From Your LAN Analyzer?" *Data Communications*, vol. 22, no. 2 (January 21, 1993), p. 40.

LAN Security and Virus Control

Stephenson, Peter. "The Age of the Secure LAN Has Arrived," *LAN Times*, vol. 8, no. 11 (June 3, 1991), p. 67.

Didio, Laura. "Special Report: Network Security," *LAN Times*, vol. 8, no. 23 (December 9, 1991), p. 58.

Raskin, Robin and M. E. Kabay. "Antivirus Software: Keeping up Your Guard," *PC Magazine*, vol. 12, no. 5 (March 16, 1993), p. 209.

Zero Slot LANs

Maxwell, Kimberly, and Patricia McGovern. "Zero Slot LANs," *PC Magazine*, vol. 9, no. 8 (April 24, 1990), p. 187.

C A S E   S T U D Y

EDMS Leads List-Management Market

Direct mail is one of the most common marketing methods employed by corporate America today. And there's a reason for that—the process has been fine-tuned to produce optimum results.

An insurance company or department store doesn't simply send special offers to every household in the United States. Rather, companies contact a management company and purchase names based upon selected criteria.

Expert Database Marketing Systems Inc. (EDMS), located in Irvine, Calif., is one of the most successful list-management companies in the nation. EDMS builds and maintains customer databases used by banks, insurance companies, and retailers for mailings and frequent-shopper programs.

EDMS has taken a unique approach to list management, which has allowed it to become a leader in its industry.

The company has developed its own proprietary address cleaning, standardizing, and householding software, which can be custom-tailored to process any customer list into a marketing database.

Since every client file represents a unique situation, EDMS has tailored the filtering process so that selected names will more closely match given models. This process involves a large volume of files.

"When building databases, we process very large files from multiple sources," said Juho Arens, president of EDMS. "We also process the client's customer files, whether they're bank account holders, frequent store purchasers, or insurance policyholders. We do this nationally so the total volume of files processed is around 300GB to

400GB per year."

Until 1990, the company used tape transfer or fast parallel port transfer to process the data. Company personnel would take a job and split it among separate workstations that had 2GB hard disks. Each workstation would then chug along for approximately two days, compiling the files. The data would then be merged back together again by transferring it across the parallel port or to streaming tape.

It was a loosely coupled parallel processing system, but there was no way of tying things together in an integrated manner.

In spite of the cumbersome way data was processed, EDMS initially resisted LAN technology, because the company was still fine-tuning its software to improve speed, accuracy, and precision.

"We didn't want to hassle putting in a LAN," said Arens. "Plus, two to three years ago, I don't think LANs were an answer for us. Most LANs were targeted toward having one fairly capable machine with two to three paltry XTs attached to it. If you did word processing off the server, that was terrific. We were looking for gigabytes of data transfer."

But 14 months ago, EDMS decided the timing was right to install a LAN, and it contacted American Digital Technologies (ADT), a systems integrator specializing in client/server technology that had also done a lot of work with relational databases.

EDMS was looking for a solution that would speed up its ability to process data and asked ADT to evaluate several network scenarios.

"When we were ready for a LAN, everything fell into place from a technology perspective," said Arens. "There was good hardware of the Tricord variety, and there was good operating system software. OS/2 had finally become fairly stable, and token-ring technology had finally stabilized the 16Mbps token-ring chip."

So, when all the technology finally came together about 14–15 months ago, EDMS went ahead and made the commitment. The company needed a lot of processing power, and it told ADT the network needed to be dependable and fast. The strategy was to build on the Intel architecture, because EDMS's software was all written in C and running under MS-DOS.

After a series of tests, EDMS decided LAN Manager could move the data at the quickest rate. The company implemented LAN Manager 2.0, running it over token-ring hardware supplied by Madge Networks Inc.

"In laying out our requirements, we thought token ring would perform better than other alternatives," said Arens. "We are running 16Mbps token ring over unshielded twisted-pair cable, and we have not had any problems at all."

The LAN includes three PC servers: two 50Mhz 486 systems from Dell and one Compaq SystemPro with a disk array and SCSI drives. The LAN also includes an enterprise server from Tricord: a 33Mhz 486 PowerFrame with 16MB of RAM, three network interface cards, and 10 1.3GB SCSI drives.

"Because of the separate I/O processor, the Tricord performs better under heavy load conditions," said Ken Charlton, ADT president.

Arens agreed. "The Power-Frame is the fastest machine here when running more than five jobs simultaneously," he said.

The LAN is employed primarily for data processing. EDMS uses a distributed processing system where jobs are divided into smaller chunks and distributed across the LAN. A mixture of workstations are actively working off a central server disk, and there are workstations that will access several hundred megabytes of information, take it to a local drive, and then operate locally for approximately 10 hours.

The processing power comes from an assortment of 486s from AST, Dell, and Compaq. According to Arens, a 386 or even a "slow 486" just won't cut it. The minimum PC configuration at EDMS is a 33Mhz 486 with plenty of internal cache memory.

Since installing the LAN, EDMS has seen tremendous improvements in productivity. Without it, Arens said, the company simply couldn't do many of the things it currently is doing.

"If we look at productivity as a straightforward processing job, then it's an order of magnitude. We're probably 10 times more productive and efficient."

That translates into a leadership position and increased accuracy, according to Arens. He said most other service bureaus can only dream of achieving what EDMS has in terms of processing data and cleaning it up.

"Most service bureaus hit 90 percent accuracy in terms of names and address ranges," Arens said.

"We hit about 95 percent accuracy. To get that extra 5 percent involves two to three times more processing, so there's a real hit in terms of the load you include."

The LAN also has allowed EDMS to achieve an impressive growth rate. Initially, EDMS was pretty much restricted to offering its services in Florida, but its clients were interested in mailing information on a national basis.

"While Florida is fairly populous, with 5 million households and 12 million individuals, that was pretty well the limit of what could be done on separate workstations without the LAN," Arens said. "With the LAN in place, we expanded first to the entire Southeast, and now we've expanded to include the entire country."

And this translates into a much larger revenue potential.

Source: Sherri Walkenhorst, "EDMS Leads List-Management Market," *LAN Times*, vol. 9, no. 16 (August 24, 1992), p. 47. Reprinted with permission of McGraw-Hill, *LAN Times*.

Business Case Study Questions

Activities

1. Complete a top-down model for this business case by gleaning facts from the case and placing them in the proper layer of the top-down model and by answering the layer specific questions below. After having completed your top-down model, analyze and detail those instances where requirements were clearly passed down from upper layers to lower layers of the model and where solutions to those requirements were passed up from lower layers to upper layers of the model.
2. Detail any questions about the case that may occur to you for which answers are not clearly stated in the article.

Business

1. How might differences in business requirements, such as the competitive environment, have affected requirements on other layers of the top-down model?
2. What is at the heart of EDMS' competitive advantage?
3. How vulnerable is this competitive advantage?
4. What kinds of productivity gains were realized as a result of this network design and implementation?

5. What is one method by which EDMS' competitive advantage is measured?
6. What is the impact on information systems and networks of keeping this competitive advantage?
7. What effect has the implementation had on market penetration?
8. Given the initial impact, what kinds of growth projections would you hypothesize on all layers of the top-down model for this project?

Application

1. What were the unique features of EDMS' applications and what requirements did these applications place on data and network models?
2. How long do applications generally run on workstations?
3. What kinds of reliability issues are involved on the application and data model layers?

Data

1. What were the size of the data files that EDMS was processing?
2. What constraints did the data characteristics put on the network design?

Network

1. What were some of the reasons that a LAN was not initially seen as a viable networking solution?
2. What happened that made a LAN-based solution viable?

Technology

1. What types of technology advances enabled the final physical network design that could deliver delineated business requirements?

2. Which network topology was chosen and why?
3. Requirements articulated in which layer of the top-down model do you think had the greatest influence on the choice of network topology?
4. Which network operating system was chosen and why?
5. Do you think that performance on a single criterion, such as processing speed, is a valid method for choosing a network operating system? Why or why not?

C H A P T E R · 5

Local Area Networking Technology

Concepts Reinforced

Top-Down Model
Technology Analysis Grids
I-P-O Analysis

Modularity of Design
OSI Model
Logical Network Design

Concepts Introduced

Interdependence of Networking
  Technology Decisions
Function of Protocols and
  Protocol Stacks
Physical versus Logical
  Topologies

Access Methodologies
Network Architectures
  Ethernet
  Token ring
  FDDI
  CDDI

OBJECTIVES

After mastering the material in this chapter, you should be able to:

1. Understand the underlying concepts of local area networks such as:
  Access methodologies
  Logical topologies
  Physical topologies
  Network configurations

2. Understand media options and their independence from network operating systems.

3. Understand the function of and differences between various protocols and protocol stacks.

4. Understand why UNIX/XENIX have become more popular as multiuser operating systems for the PC environment.

5. Understand the current technology, future trends, and implication on network decision making of the following:
  Hubs and concentrators
  Network adapter cards and drivers
  Media and cabling
  Building wiring systems

6. Understand the role of specialized servers in LANs.

7. Understand the role of the OSI model as a framework in which to conduct network analysis and design.

INTRODUCTION

The focus of Chapter 4 was logical network design, concerned primarily with ensuring that implemented network functionality would meet or exceed business networking requirements. Chapter 4 identified the *what*, or functionality, of the network design. In Chapter 5, the *how* of the network design will be identified as alternatives in networking technology are explored which, when physically connected, will constitute the data highway or backbone over which this network functionality will be delivered.

This networking technology that comprises the physical network is changing rapidly. Therefore, a comparative approach to technology analysis will be taken, ever mindful of cost/benefit ratios and the possible impact of specific emerging trends in networking technology.

A REVIEW OF THE TOP-DOWN MODEL'S ROLE IN TECHNOLOGY ANALYSIS

As the bottom and final layer of the top-down model is about to be explored, it is important to remember the analysis that has taken place previously on the upper layers of the model. A thorough examination of *business* needs was followed by an analysis of which information systems related activities and *applications* could best support those business needs. An examination of the distribution of the required *data* and processes to support those applications led to a definition of required network functions. These required *network* functions were used as a shopping list while comparing various available LAN and LAN look-alike logical networking alternatives. The examination of currently available network *technology* alternatives provides the bridge from logical network design to physical network design.

If valid decisions have been made at each layer based on meeting the requirements of the previous layers, the decisions made on the final layer, *technology*, should support the requirements of the initial layer, *business*. This proper application of networking technology to meet business requirements is a key to success in network and analysis and design, and a central theme of this text.

THE TECHNOLOGY LAYER

Having decided upon a LAN or LAN lookalike solution that meets the business, application, and data layer needs as articulated in the top-down model, the technology alternatives as outlined in Figure 5-1 are now ready to be examined.

Most of the technology categories that will be studied in this chapter will only be of interest if either of the two more sophisticated LAN options, namely DOS-based or fully-integrated LANs, were the result of the logical network design. The other categories, file transfer software, printer sharing networks, and zero-slot LANs, are fully configured solutions requiring no further decisions as to operating systems, network architectures, adapter cards and drivers, or media choices.

HOW DO ALL THESE CHOICES FIT TOGETHER?

As can be seen from Figure 5-1, numerous options exist in each of the many categories comprising the network technology layer. As has been stated before, a given choice in one option category may limit choices in other option categories. Figure 5-2 attempts to graphically portray the relationship or interaction between these

Business	*Chapter 4*	*The overall business needs/perspectives.* Recognition of information as a corporate asset. Save money. Increase productivity. Increase data accessability. Provide more bandwidth to the desktop. Reliable, easy to use information systems. Well supported information systems.
		Identify the business activities. General information requirements. *Resource sharing* of: printers, CD-ROMs, communication links, FAXs, and modems. *File sharing* and application sharing. *Distributed data access* and shared databases. *Extended communications* through: Inter-LAN, micro to mainframe links, and wide area network links.
		Business Analysis Questions. See Figure 4-5.
Application		*Application Programs.* Network printing, network backup, network security, network management, network resource optimization, workgroup software, remote access/control software, connectivity/gateway software, productivity software, MAC integration software. See Figure 4-6.
Data		*Database management languages:* SQL. *Database types:* multiuser (file server), client/server (database server.) *Back-end databases:* ORACLE, SYBASE. *Front-end database tools. Database servers:* Gupta, Netware. See Figure 4-10.
Network		*File transfer software:* Laplynx, Brooklyn Bridge. *Printer sharing networks:* Black Box. *Zero-slot LANs:* LANtastic-Z. *DOS-based systems:* LANtastic, PowerLAN, Netware Lite. *Fully-integrated LANs:* Novell Netware, Banyan Vines, Microsoft LAN Manager, Appletalk, DECnet Pathworks. *LANs and LAN look-alikes.*
Technology	*Chapter 5*	*Operating Systems:* DOS, OS/2, Windows, UNIX, VMS, MVS. *Access methodologies:* CSMA/CD, Token passing. *System Architecture:* Peer-to-peer, Client/Server. *Network Architectures:* Ethernet, Token Ring (4 and 16 mbps), FDDI, ARCNET, CDDI, AppleTalk. *Network Physical Topologies:* ring, bus, star. *Network Logical Topologies:* broadcast, sequential. *CPUs:* 8088, 80286, 80386, 80486, PENTIUM, Macs, multitasking, multithreading. *Servers:* file servers, disk servers, communications servers, remote access servers, print servers. *Adapter cards:* Pocket, internal vs. external, Ethernet, Token Ring, ARCNET, FDDI, CDDI. *Drivers:* ODI, NDIS, NETBIOS, IPX. *Bus type:* ISA, MCA, EISA, NUBUS. *Wiring centers:* hubs, concentrators, MAUs, repeaters, switching hubs. *Media:* UTP, STP, fiber, coax, wireless. *Wiring systems:* AT&T, IBM, DEC.

Figure 5-1 Decisions, decisions, decisions . . .

various networking technology choice categories. Arrows between choice blocks indicate possible influences among choice categories.

☐ A ROADMAP OF LOCAL AREA NETWORK TECHNOLOGY CHOICES

Black arrows form a roadmap of local area network technology choices down through the layers of Figure 5-2, from architectures, through operating systems, and down to media. This roadmap will be followed throughout Chapter 5, comparing alternative decisions along each step of the way. After having examined the numerous possibilities, these various pieces of network technology decision making will be assembled into several different existing network architectures using the *OSI 7-Layer Reference Model* as a framework and basis for comparison.

As options within categories are examined more closely, specific implications

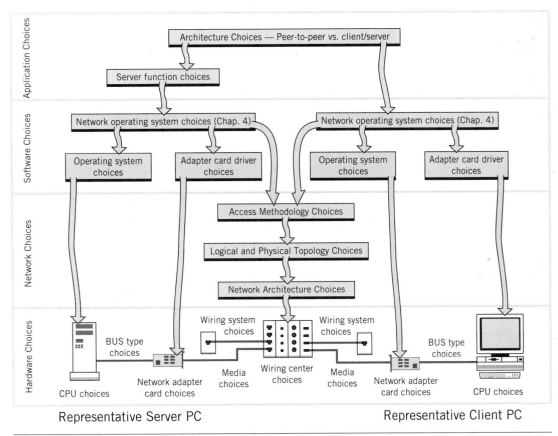

Figure 5-2 The technology layer: How do all these choices fit together?

of given choices in one category on subsequent choices in other categories will be pointed out. By referring back to the roadmap (Figure 5-2) as these implications of various choices are outlined, the effect of a given decision should be traceable throughout the entire networking technology layer.

☐ A NETWORKING TECHNOLOGY ANALYSIS MODEL

Notice how the diagram in Figure 5-2 has been divided into four main *choice* layers: *Hardware, Network, Software,* and *Application.* These four layers constitute a model. The fact that this model has not been adopted by an international standards making organization makes it no less useful or valuable in this situation. Choices within a layer have influences on other choices within that layer as well as choices in lower layers.

Additional influences and/or restrictions may be found among choices not currently included in Figure 5-2. If so, by all means, add them to Figure 5-2 in order to make it a more accurate reflection of currently available networking technology.

The four-layer model in Figure 5-2 is not unlike the OSI 7-layer model in some respects. Functionally, similar elements are grouped together in layers. The choices made in any given layer affect the interaction between layers. When networking technology choices are plotted in the OSI 7-layer model later in this chapter, it should become evident that the relative position of the Figure 5-2 choice elements in the 7-layer OSI model remains consistent with their position in this simple four-layer model. Hopefully, this model will help answer the question, "How do all these choices fit together?"

☐ APPLICATION CHOICES

Architecture Choice Revisited: Peer-to-Peer versus Client to Server

Although the model may imply a top-down, step-by-step linear approach to the decision-making involved with all of the listed choices, this is not necessarily always the case. Most often, a particular network operating system (Netware, Vines, LAN Manager) will first be chosen, hopefully because of its ability to fulfill the business networking requirements identified in earlier analysis. The characteristics of this network operating system may dictate the architecture choice listed on the applications choice layer: peer-to-peer versus client to server.

First introduced in Chapter 4 in the discussion of DOS-based LANs, a peer-to-peer network implies that each PC or workstation on the network has the ability to both:

1. Offer its resources (files, disk drives, printers) for sharing among other network attached PCs.
2. Request to share resources belonging to other PCs attached to the network.

Remember, however, that a DOS-based LAN does not necessarily imply a peer-to-peer network. Even zero-slot LANs such as Lantastic Z can be set up as either peer-to-peer or client to server networks. In a peer-to-peer arrangement DOS will always be asked to do two things at once. In the foreground, DOS will be running local applications programs, while in the background DOS will be fulfilling requests from other network-attached PC users who wish to share resources on the local PC. Whereas DOS is not inherently a **multitasking** operating system, the performance of the local PC while attached to a peer-to-peer network may not be satisfactory. In order to make DOS appear to accomplish more than one task simultaneously in a peer-to-peer arrangement, network operating systems add software to DOS which enable **task switching,** also known as time slicing. The DOS operating system then switches between its server tasks and its local application tasks quickly and "appears" to be doing two things at the same time. This is not the same as true multitasking, which is an inherent feature of other operating systems. Operating system implications will be discussed a bit later in this chapter.

As can be seen from Figure 5-2, choices of CPU chips can have an obvious impact on performance. PCs with 80386 or 80486 or the new Pentium CPU chips will probably deliver satisfactory performance while fulfilling both the client and server roles in a peer-to-peer network. Common sense would dictate, however, that the same PCs given only one role to perform, either client *or* server, would deliver greater performance.

The key difference between a peer-to-peer and a client to server (or client/server) network is that the networked PC on a client/server network does not serve dual roles. That is to say, in a client/server network, an attached PC is either a *resource offerer* (the server) or a *resource requester* (the client).

As stated earlier, the final decision on peer-to-peer versus client/server architectures may be dictated by the network operating system chosen. If not, overall superior network performance will be realized by allowing certain PCs to perform only server functions.

Servers Come in Many Flavors

In most cases, choosing a client/server architecture implies that the PCs assigned as servers will perform only as servers and will not be available as workstations on which to run local applications. In other words, server performance is the full-time job of these PCs, known as **dedicated servers**. Microsoft LAN Manager does have the ability to allow servers to also be used as workstations. Realize, however, that even though LAN Manager runs over true multitasking operating systems, the processing resources available for fulfilling server requests are reduced when local applications are run on that server in a workstation mode.

As has been seen, a server's job is to manage the sharing of networked resources among client PCs. Depending on the number of client PCs and the extent of the shared resources, it may be necessary to have multiple servers and/or to specialize some servers to the type of resources they manage.

If servers are to be specialized, then shared resources should be grouped in some logical fashion to optimize the server performance for managing the sharing of a particular type of resource. A list of potentially shared network resources would probably include:

Files
Application programs
Databases
Printers
Modems
Faxes
CD-ROMs
Access to minicomputer/mainframes
Access to other LANs (local)
Access to other LANs (remote)
Access to information services
Access to this LAN from remote PCs

As this list is examined, a logical differentiation may split the shared resource servers into three major categories:

File servers
Printer servers
Communications servers

Depending on the network operating system chosen, the software to manage one of these specialized servers may be included as part of the network operating system, may be available as a network operating system upgrade from the original vendor, or may be available from a third-party software vendor who has written add-on software for a network operating system.

Remember that one of the key features of Novell Netware is the existence of NLMs (NetWare loadable modules) often written by third-party software vendors to offer increased capabilities to Netware.

Communications servers and the shared resources they manage will be discussed further in Chapter 6, "Internetworking."

The typical LAN is likely to begin server specialization by splitting the tasks of managing the sharing of *files* and *printers*.

File Servers   A **file server** obviously manages the sharing of files. However, in fact, a file server does much more. First, the file server doesn't let just any user have access to any file. *Security files* and **access rights tables** are maintained and consulted by the file server first. Some network operating systems also have the file server maintain a **file audit database** that records information about which users accessed which files as well as when the files were accessed. Secondly, remembering that there are multiple users on this network, the file server arbitrates among multiple requests for the same data.

Some file servers go beyond merely managing the sharing of files among client PCs and actually take requests for specific data meeting certain criteria, process the database request or query, and send only data meeting the requested characteristics to the client PC. Servers running this more sophisticated software are known as *database servers* and were discussed in Chapter 4.

Equally as important as a powerful CPU to overall server performance is a fast, efficient, hard-disk drive, or better still, *several* fast, efficient hard-disk drives.

Printer Servers   **Printer servers** are often the first to be given a specialized role on a network. An older or unused PC can often perform well as a dedicated printer server, and most network operating systems come with the software to set up dedicated printer servers. The job of the printer server is fairly simple:

1. Available printers are attached directly to the printer server through either serial or parallel ports.
2. Requests for printer services from networked client PCs are fulfilled.
3. If requested printers are unavailable, the printer server PC either *buffers* the print job in memory or *spools* the print job onto its local disk drive until the requested printer becomes available.
4. The printer server may also perform some management functions such as notifying client PCs when print jobs have finished, keeping statistics of printer usage, managing the attached printers, and the queues to which they are attached. A **queue** is an imaginary waiting line in which print jobs wait until they can be shipped out either a serial or parallel port of the printer server PC and into the waiting printer attached to that port.

Another reason for installing printer servers on LANs is for proximity to users. By using multiple printer servers, clusters of printers can be installed within short distances from the users who request their printer services.

Perhaps the best advice on segregating file servers and printer servers is: If it ain't broke don't fix it. However, if a "spare" PC is available and if the network operating system supplies software to allow printer sharing services to be run on a separate server, improved performance will be gained in both file sharing and printer sharing by splitting the two functions.

Non-PC-Based Servers: Network Ready Servers   From a physical standpoint, a printer server does not necessarily have to be a "normal" PC with installed printer server software defining its functionality. If a "spare" PC is not available, there are **network ready servers** available that can offer printer sharing as well as modem sharing services.

These network ready servers, also called special function servers, often come fully pre-configured with network interface cards and server software already installed. Just attach the built-in network interface to your network, connect your printers or modems to be shared, and configure the pre-installed software. A word of caution regarding this pre-configuration however: Certain network ready servers may operate with only certain network operating systems, architectures, or media. For instance, a given network ready server may operate only with Netware, over thin-wire Ethernet. (Ethernet and media options will be covered later in this chapter.) On the other hand, for a bit more money, another network ready server may offer multiple network interfaces from which to choose.

Still other network ready servers take the form of add-on cards or featurepaks which are inserted directly into a given printer. This method of constructing network-ready printers is especially popular with laser printers.

☐ SOFTWARE CHOICES

Operating Systems and Network Operating Systems

Assuming that a network operating system has already been chosen due to the fact that its functionality delivered the business networking requirements identified in the top-down analysis, the choices of an *operating system* over which to run that network operating system may be somewhat limited.

In this section, a list of analysis questions to help determine which operating system might be the best choice will be presented. Secondly, the key characteristics of the three major PC-based operating systems: DOS, OS/2, and UNIX will be explored. Currently available implementations of the major network operating systems over these various operating system platforms as well as Windows, MACs, and VMS will be delineated. The various network operating system/PC-operating system combinations available for both client and server PCs will lead nicely into the internetworking discussions in Chapter 6.

Operating System Analysis Questions

1. *Heritage:* Was the operating system initially designed with multiuser networks in mind?
2. *Basic design:* How, if at all, does this operating system support the following environments: multiuser, multitasking, multithreaded (more than one simultaneous message per application program to CPU)?
3. *Hardware requirements:* Does the operating system require a particular CPU chip? What are the memory and disk requirements for operating system installation?
4. *Networkability:* Which networking features are included as part of the operating system? What networking functionality must be added by the network operating system? How available are network operating systems that run over this operating system as clients? as servers? What is the approximate cost per user of network operating systems that run over this operating system?
5. *Interoperability:* On how many different vendors' machines will this operating system run? Will this operating system run on MACs, high-powered workstations and minicomputers/mainframes?
6. *Applications:* How available are applications programs that run over this operating system? How easy are applications programs to develop for this operating system? Are applications development tools available for this operating system? Can this operating system run application programs written for other operating systems?
7. *Ease of use:* Consider the ease of use and level of expertise required in the following categories:

   System installation
   System configuration
   System management

System use
System monitoring
System troubleshooting and diagnosis

Are GUIs (graphical user interfaces) available for this operating system?

8. *Future potential:* What might the future hold for this operating system? Is it in the twilight or sunrise of its product life cycle? Is it the center of controversy among industry giants? Is it governed by domestic or international standards organizations? Is there a definite need for this operating system in the client server, open systems, distributed computing world of tomorrow?

DOS—A Single User Heritage

DOS, an acronym for disk operating system, has gone through an evolution in order to survive in the era of networks. Originally designed to work on standalone, single-user PCs, DOS introduced multiuser networking capabilities such as record and file locking with the release of Version 3.1. Network operating systems (NOS) are able to call these DOS commands transparently to the networking operating system users.

Network operating systems that run over DOS and rely on it for file management and record locking are known as DOS-based LANs and were reviewed in detail in Chapter 4. Lantastic by Artisoft is probably the best-known DOS-based LAN. As was seen in the Chapter 4 review, just because a NOS is DOS-based does not mean it cannot support many users or offer numerous sophisticated features.

DOS 5.0, which was released in the summer of 1991, added the ability to load programs and files of various types, including device drivers, in the PC's memory above the former 640K ceiling. Programs stored in this extended memory are often stored as **TSR**s, or terminate and stay resident, programs. Terminate and stay resident programs do not utilize any CPU processing time until they are reactivated. Many networking and interoperability software products are stored in expanded memory. How extended memory can be used to enable multiple protocol stacks to be loaded onto a single PC will be explained when internetworking is studied in the next chapter.

DOS 5.0 also included another important piece of networking support software known as the **redirector**. The redirector is like a bridge-keeper filtering file requests on the local client PC and deciding whether the requested service or file can be obtained locally or whether the request should be sent out over the network to the server via the network adapter card. How the redirector software interacts with the network operating system, the operating system, and the network adapter card driver software will be explained in the forthcoming section entitled, "Tracing Software Communications from Client to Server."

OS/2—Multitasking from the Start

OS/2, which stands for operating system 2, was jointly developed by Microsoft and IBM. OS/2 presents what is known as a graphical user interface or GUI. A GUI is a user-friendly interface with numerous click-on icons and a mouse for handling the majority of interaction with the user.

Microsoft left the OS/2 development partnership and now has a competing product, Windows, which runs as an application over DOS. To load and run either Windows or OS/2 usually requires at least a 80386 CPU, 40 megabytes of disk space and 4MB of RAM memory, although twice the RAM and disk space would improve performance. Ease of use and point-and-click icons do not come cheaply in terms of hardware requirements.

OS/2 is a true multitasking operating system. To be exact, it is a **preemptive multitasking** operating system, meaning that OS/2 deals out time slices to applications requesting processing from the CPU. A given application program can make more than one request for processing power through a process known as **multitasking threads**. Windows is *nonpreemptive,* meaning that once an application gets the CPUs attention, it can monopolize the CPU to the detriment of other applications. On the other hand, those tasks that should not be interrupted by the preemptive multitasking of OS/2, can run to completion uninterrupted under Windows.

IBM put significant resources into the development of OS/2 Version 2.0. It would be hard to believe that IBM would not do everything in its power to assure its success as the operating system and GUI of choice for PC-based computing. However, Microsoft, producers of the popular LAN Manager Network Operating System, would like to control the operating system and GUI markets also.

Microsoft has released *Windows NT* (new technology), which will include peer-to-peer networking capabilities within the operating system itself. Windows NT should run on both PCs using the popular Intel CPU chips (80386, 80486) as well as RISC (reduced instruction set computing) chips. Windows NT will be discussed further in Chapter 13, "Where Do We Go From Here? Trends to Watch."

UNIX—Its Multiuser Minicomputer Heritage Shows

UNIX's heritage of open systems and multiplatform operation has enabled many networking features to be included in the operating system itself, precluding the need to buy an additional networking operating system to run over UNIX. Perhaps best known of these features is the Internet Suite of Protocols, more commonly known as TCP/IP and associated protocols. TCP/IP, NFS (network file system) and other UNIX networking features will be studied in detail in Chapter 6 on internetworking.

Both Netware and Banyan Vines use either UNIX or a UNIX derivative as their underlying operating and file management system. UNIX's popularity in departmental LANs has increased significantly with advances in PC hardware and CPU capability. Intel 80386 and 80486 chips in a single PC-running UNIX can support a multiuser environment through UNIX terminals (not PCs) on the desktop. As the prices of RISC-based workstations has dropped, the popularity of UNIX in the business community has risen. Database management systems and fourth generation language application development environments now available on UNIX machines have added to the trend of bringing UNIX machines into the mainstream of corporate information systems.

Scalability or *multiplatform operation* has given UNIX a lot of attention in this era of information system downsizing and application rightsizing. Because UNIX runs not only on PCs, but also on numerous minicomputers and larger platforms, applications written for and installed on larger UNIX machines can be "downsized" to smaller client–server environments. Conversely, applications can be developed on less expensive personal work stations, yet installed and executed on larger, more powerful computers.

UNIX also offers *multiprocessing* (sometimes called **symmetrical multiprocessing**) capability, which goes beyond multitasking, in which a single CPU is shared, to splitting users' requests for processing power across multiple CPUs. UNIX has become increasingly popular as the operating system of choice for LAN servers. Many software packages have been developed to allow PC-based clients to communicate easily and effectively with UNIX-based servers. While some of the combinations of UNIX and non-UNIX clients and servers are described below, the PC to UNIX connectivity products that enable this networking combination will be explored in the chapter on internetworking.

On the negative side, it should be pointed out that all UNIX is not created equal. There are two main versions of UNIX: AT&T UNIX System V and Berkeley (University of California at Berkeley) UNIX, more commonly known as BSD, Berkeley Software Distribution. On PC platforms, SCO (Santa Cruz Operation) UNIX is very popular. Programs written to run on one of these versions of UNIX will not necessarily run on others.

Operating System/Network Operating System Options

Figure 5-3 summarizes the combinations of network operating systems available on various operating system platforms as either clients or servers while Figure 5-4 highlights whether or not the underlying operating system is available to the user on a command level basis. New versions of the listed network operating systems will undoubtedly be released that will render some of the information in these two figures inaccurate. Update these figures according to the characteristics of the latest version of each listed network operating system. Add or delete network operating systems as appropriate.

In graphic form, Figures 5-5, 5-6 and 5-7 outline the client and server network operating system/operating system combinations for the three most popular net-

Clients Operating Systems							Servers Operating Systems					
DOS	OS/2	Windows	UNIX	MAC	VMS		DOS	OS/2	Windows	UNIX	MAC	VMS
■	■	■	■	■		Novell Netware[a]	■	■	■	■		■
■	■	■	■	■		Banyan Vines			■	■		
■	■	■	■	■		Microsoft LAN Manager		■	■	■		
	■					IBM LAN Server		■				
■		■				NCR Star Group (LANmanager)			■	■		
■	■	■	■	■	■	DEC Pathworks		■	■	■		■

[a]Novell Netware 3.x boots from DOS; previous versions of Novell use its own proprietary system loader.

Figure 5-3 Network operating systems availability over popular operating systems: clients and servers.

Network Operating Systems

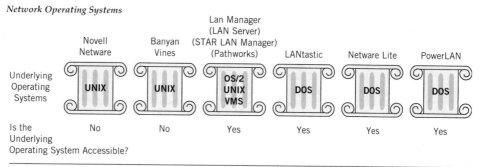

Figure 5-4 Network Operating Systems: operating system accessibility.

work operating systems: Netware, Vines, and LAN Manager. It is important to note that if the underlying operating system of the client and server are not identical, then some mediating software program must interpret between the two. This notion of mediating between different systems is central to a process known as **protocol conversion**.

These layers of operating systems software and associated network operating system software on either clients or servers are known as **protocol stacks.** The particular combination of software layers in this protocol stack define the personality of the computer as well as the required software necessary to converse between this computer and any other computer's protocol stack. Some computers have the ability to load and run multiple protocol stacks.

These **multiprotocol computers** have "split personalities" which allow them to communicate with other computers matching either of their protocol stacks without the need for **protocol conversion** software. The layers of the protocol stack can be delineated and compared between computers. These protocol stack layers correspond to the layers of the OSI Model that will be employed as different protocol stacks and their associated protocol conversion utilities are examined.

NETBIOS, the Redirector and the SMB Server

One thing that should have become clear as Figures 5-5, 5-6, and 5-7 were examined is the enormous number of potential combinations of client and server network operating systems and operating systems. How could it be possible for a client PC to request services from a server PC which may not even be running the same operating system or network operating system software?

What is needed is a way for applications programs, like word processing for instance, to request services of a server without having to worry about which operating system or network operating system the server may be running. In other words, the word processing program must be able to make its service requests, or interface, *transparently* to the other layers of software in the protocol stack.

A type of software known as an **API** (applications program interface) allows requests for services from application programs to be passed along to the networked servers that provide these services. **NETBIOS** (network basic input/output system) is an API which has become the de facto standard of network APIs for PC-based networks.

Technically speaking, NETBIOS, or any API for that matter, is a specification outlining a software interrupt to the network operating system in order to request network services for transportation of data across the network. In practice, an API such as NETBIOS allows a person running a word processing program on a client

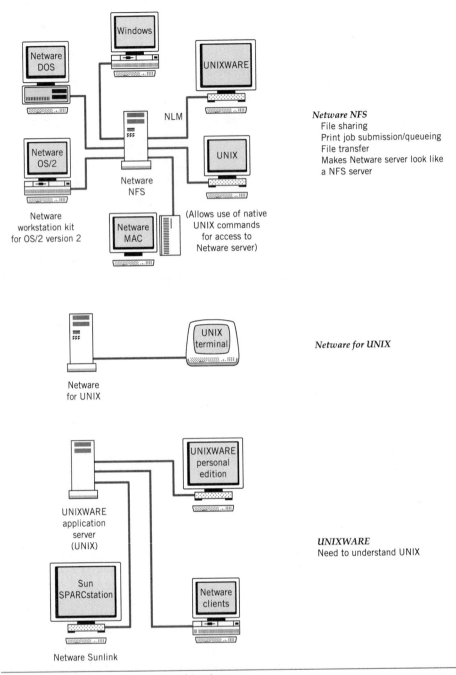

Figure 5-5 Netware: client/server combinations.

PC to ask to retrieve a document located on a disk drive that is physically attached to a server PC. For instance, all the user knows is that the document is located on a drive known as H:, and that once he or she requests that document, it appears on the screen of the client PC ready to be edited. All of the interpretation of requests between the various software layers of the client PC and server PC is of no concern to the user.

A standardized API, such as NETBIOS, allows applications programs to be

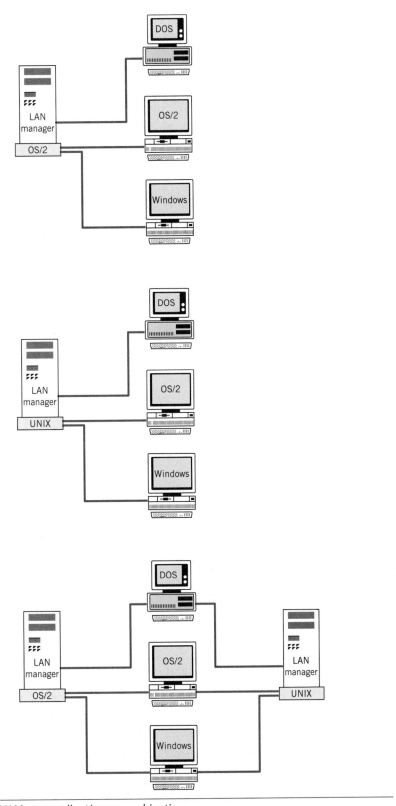

Figure 5-6 LAN Manager: client/server combinations.

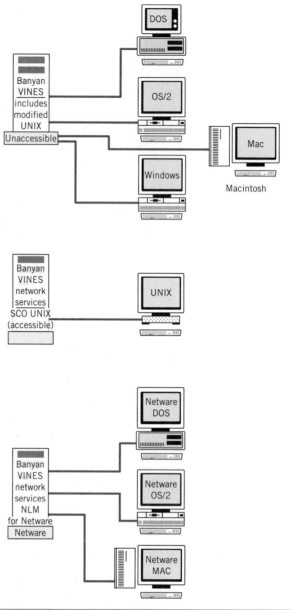

Figure 5-7 Banyan VINES: client/server combinations.

written without concern for which network operating system the application may run over as long as that network operating system understands NETBIOS requests. Likewise, a network operating system can run transparently underneath any application program, secure in the knowledge that it will be able to understand any requests for network services. This requesting and granting of services over the network is known as *program-to-program* or *peer-to-peer* communication.

NETBIOS is, by definition, a system that interprets requests submitted to it in proper format from the application program and passes these requests along to a network communications program. *NETBIOS application programs,* otherwise known as NETBIOS Protocols, which interface with the NETBIOS API, have been developed to perform specialized tasks on client and server PCs in order to enable this client/server communication. Two of the most famous of these NETBIOS application programs or protocols are the **redirector,** on the client, and the **SMB** (Server Message Block), on the server.

➤ *In Sharper Focus*

TRACING SOFTWARE COMMUNICATIONS FROM CLIENT TO SERVER

Figure 5-8 illustrates the interaction of a word processing application program, the redirector, NETBIOS API, the SMB server, and the network operating system. The details of the interaction between the network operating system and lower layer protocols handling the transportation of messages through the network adapter cards and out over the network media will be dealt with in more detail shortly.

The word processing program sends out a request for a particular document on a certain disk drive not knowing whether that disk drive is on the local client PC or on the remote server PC. This request is in an agreed-upon format or syntax known as *NCB* or *network control block.* This network control block is received by

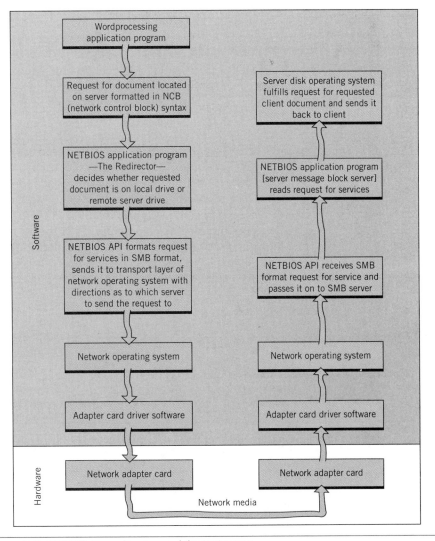

Figure 5-8 NETBIOS, the redirector, and the SMB server.

the redirector and evaluated as to whether the request should be handled by the local PC and passed to the local PC's operating system, or whether it should be sent on to the NETBIOS API for interfacing with the network operating system running on this client PC.

If the requested document is on a *remote* server, the NETBIOS API tells the network operating system which server the requested document resides on by preparing a server message block for transmission. The network operating system forwards the server message block to the proper remote server via the local network adapter card and network media of choice.

Once the server message block is received by the remote server, it is passed by the NETBIOS API to the server message block server, which passes requests for particular files or documents on to the disk operating system of the server PC. Once the server message block receives the requested document, it sends it back over to the client PC in a similar manner but opposite direction of how it received the request for service in the first place.

Notice how a particular network operating system was not referenced in Figure 5-8. Therein lies the importance of NETBIOS. It is an application program-to-application program communications protocol which is understood by and incorporated into most network operating systems. Different versions of NETBIOS have been developed to run over different operating systems. These varieties of NETBIOS are summarized in Figure 5-9.

NETBIOS is not the only API ever invented, however. Several other APIs have been implemented in various network operating systems as outlined in Figure 5-10. In many cases, these APIs have additional commands and features not found in NETBIOS. However, even in the network operating systems that use *non-NETBIOS APIs,* such as Netware or Vines, a NETBIOS emulator is often included in order to ensure compatibility across varied network operating systems.

NETBIOS or some other API are at the heart of client/server communication. Without this transparent layer of software keeping track of the location of shared resources and managing the requests for sharing those resources, there can be no client/server computing. In order to link client and server PCs of various network or disk operating systems, compatibility of the APIs must be ensured. NETBIOS and its derivatives are the most widely installed and supported API. Beware, however—not even all varieties of NETBIOS are fully compatible with each other.

NETBIOS protocol	RFC 1001/1002 (request for comment)	TOP (technical office protocol)	NETBEUI (NETBIOS extended user interface)	NETBIOS/IX
Communications Network Operating System	TCP/IP	OSI	LAN Manager LAN Server	UNIX

Figure 5-9 NETBIOS protocol varieties for various network types.

API (Application Program Interface)	APPC (Advanced Program to Program Communication)	Named pipes	SPX/IPX (Sequenced Packet Exchange/ Internet Packet Exchange)	Streams	Sockets	VIPC (VINES Interprocess Communications Protocol)
Network Operating System	IBM SNA	Microsoft LAN Manager	Novell Netware	AT&T UNIX System V	Berkeley UNIX	Banyan VINES

Figure 5-10 APIs other than NETBIOS and their network operating systems.

Adapter Card Driver Choices

In examining Figures 5-2 and 5-8, it should be obvious that the last piece of software to choose is the **driver** software for the network adapter card. Remember that the network adapter card plugs into the PC bus and offers a connection (interface) to whatever media (unshielded twisted pair, shielded twisted pair, coax, fiber, wireless, etc.) may be chosen (ugh, another choice!).

Noticing the relative position of the "Adapter Card Driver Software" blocks in Figure 5-8 should give a hint as to compatibility issues which must be taken into account in choosing a driver. Any driver software must obviously be compatible with the hardware card itself, which is why many adapter card manufacturers ship numerous drivers from which to choose with their adapter cards. But why would they have to ship *multiple* drivers? The answer lies in the block above "Adapter Card Driver Software" in Figure 5-8.

A given network adapter card may be required to be compatible with a number of different network operating systems. The network operating systems use the adapter card drivers to communicate with the adapter cards and the network beyond. Without the proper adapter card drivers, there can be no communication out through the adapter card and, as a result, there is no network.

Figure 5-11 summarizes the currently popular network adapter card drivers and the networking operating systems that require one or another. It is in adapter card manufacturers' best interests to include as many drivers as possible with their adapter cards in order to assure that they will work with as many network operating systems as possible. However, before purchasing any adapter card, be sure that proven software drivers compatible with the installed or chosen network operating system(s) are included with the purchase of the adapter cards.

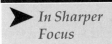 *In Sharper Focus*

OPEN STANDARDS FOR NETWORK ADAPTER CARD DRIVERS

As can be seen in Figure 5-11, an evolution has occurred in the specification and design of adapter card drivers. Initially, drivers were written for specific combinations; that is, a particular adapter card and a particular version of a network operating system. Examples of included drivers on such an adapter card might be: LANtastic, LANManager, Netware Version 2.2, Netware Version 3.1, Vines or any number of other specific network operating systems.

Driver Name or Specification	NDIS (Network Driver Interface Specification)	ODI (Open Data Link Interface)	IPX (Internet Packet Exchange)	NETBIOS	TCP/IP	Drivers written for specific adapter card/ Network Operating System combinations	APPLETALK Phase 2
Network Operating System	Microsoft LAN Manager and variations Banyan VINES	Novell Netware Lite	Novell Netware	Any network operating system that understands NETBIOS	Any network operating system that understands TCP/IP. (i.e., SUN OS, SCO UNIX AT&T UNIX)	LANtastic, Netware 2.2, Netware 3.11, Banyan VINES	MAC System 7, APPLETALK

Figure 5-11 Network adapter card drivers.

A more generic approach to the problem was for adapter card manufacturers to supply drivers that could interact successfully with either NETBIOS or TCP/IP. The reasoning in this case is that most network operating systems, in turn, communicate with either NETBIOS (PC environment) or TCP/IP (UNIX environment). These drivers were generally successful except for the occasional aforementioned incompatibilities among NETBIOS versions.

A third approach to adapter card standardization was undertaken by Microsoft, producers of LANManager and 3Com, a major adapter card manufacturer. **NDIS** (network driver interface specification) has become a standard driver now shipped with most adapter cards. Not to be outdone, Novell, producers of Netware, came out with their own specification: **ODI** (open data-link interface). Some, but not most, adapter cards are now also shipped with ODI drivers. The significant operational difference that these two drivers, NDIS and ODI, offer is that they are able to support *multiple protocol stacks* over a single adapter card. For example, a network adapter card with an NDIS driver installed could support communications to both a LAN Manager server as well as TCP/IP hosts.

In today's competitive networking market, the one way to insure that one's driver specification will gain attention is to distribute a popular networking operating system that only supports the adapter card driver specification which one is trying to promote. This is exactly what Novell has done with the release of their DOS-based LAN—Netware Lite. Netware Lite runs only over the ODI driver specification.

NETWORK CHOICES

Access Methodology Choices

Now that it is understood, at least from a software standpoint, how to get a request for data onto the network and get the requested data returned back over the network, an examination of the networking and hardware components of this system is in order.

Realizing that more than one user is sending requests onto the shared network media at any one time, the need for some way to control which users get to put their messages onto the network and when should be obvious. If the media is to be shared by numerous PC users, then there must be some way to control access to that media. "Sharing the media" is an important concept to local area networks, with fully-integrated LANs sometimes being called *media sharing LANs*.

If the LANs are to operate and interoperate efficiently, it is important for these **access methodologies** to be standardized and widely available, or open, as opposed to closed or proprietary with every LAN vendor implementing a different access control method. Luckily, the IEEE (Institute of Electrical and Electronic Engineers) saw the need for LAN standardization and issued (and continues to issue) the **IEEE 802** series of LAN standards, which will be elaborated on shortly.

Two Flavors of Access Control: CSMA/CD and Token Passing

Logically speaking, there are really only two philosophies for controlling access to a shared media. An analogy of access to a crowded freeway can provide a vivid illustration of access control choices.

CSMA/CD   One philosophy says, "Let's just let everyone onto the media whenever they want and if two users access the media at the exact same split second, we'll work it out somehow." (Or, the analogy "Who needs stop lights? If we have a few collisions, we'll work it out later!")

The access methodology based on this model is known as carrier sense multiple access with collision detection or **CSMA/CD** for short. A clearer understanding of how this access methodology works can be achieved if its name is examined one phrase at a time.

Carrier sense: the PC wishing to put data onto the shared media listens to the network to see if any other users are "on the line." If not, *multiple access* allows anyone onto the media without further permission required. Finally, if two user PCs should both sense a free line and access the media at the same instant, *collision detection* lets the user PCs know that their data was not delivered and controls retransmission in such a way as to avoid further data collisions. Each device involved in the data collision is preset to wait a different amount of time before retransmitting, thus reducing the likelihood of recurring collisions.

CSMA/CD is obviously most efficient with relatively little contention for network resources. The ability to allow user PCs to access the network easily without a lot of permission requesting and granting reduces overhead and increases performance at lower network usage rates. As usage increases, however, the increased number of data collisions and retransmissions can negatively affect overall network performance.

Token Passing   The second philosophy of access methodology is much more controlling. It says, "Don't you dare access the media until it's your turn. You must first ask permission, and only if I give you the magic token may you put your data onto the shared media." The highway analogy would be the controlled access ramps to freeways in which a driver must wait at a stop light and somehow immediately get to 60 mph in order to merge with the traffic.

Token passing assures that each PC User has 100 percent of the network channel available for their data requests and transfers by insisting that no PC accesses the network without first possessing a specific packet of data known as a *token*. The token is generated in the first place by a designated PC and passed among PCs until one PC would like to access the network.

At that point, the requesting PC seizes the token, puts its data onto the network, and doesn't release the token until it is assured that its data was delivered successfully. After the sending PC releases the token, it is passed along to the next PC, which may either grab the "free" token or pass it along. The software and protocols that actually handle the token passing and token regeneration, in the case of a lost token, are usually located in the chips on the network adapter card.

Token passing's overhead of waiting for the token before transmitting inhibits overall performance at lower network usage rates. However, because all PC users on a token passing access control network are well behaved and always have the magic token before accessing the network, there are, by definition, no collisions, making token passing a more efficient access methodology at higher network utilization rates.

The MAC Sublayer and the OSI Reference Model

In an attempt to use the OSI Model as a framework in which to organize networking concepts and protocols as they are encountered, the two access methodologies just introduced find a home in Layer 2—the "data link layer." To be precise, the data link layer has been divided into two sublayers:

The Logical Link Control Sublayer or **LLC**
and the
Media Access Control Sublayer or **MAC**

What better place to put access methodology protocols than on a sublayer named media access control? Figure 5-12 illustrates the proper placement of the access methodology protocols in the OSI reference model.

The purpose of the logical link layer is to provide transparent service or interface to the network layer, allowing the particular access methodology on the **MAC sublayer** to vary independently from the upper layers without compromising overall network performance. This ability for changes to take place in one layer of the OSI model without affecting protocols in other layers is one of the key underlying themes of the OSI reference model.

Access Methodology + Network Topologies = Network Architectures

As will be seen shortly, by adding additional specifications outlining logical and physical topologies to these access methodologies, various alternative network architectures can be defined, many of which have been issued as standards by domestic or international standards making organizations.

Logical and Physical Topology Choices

Logical Topologies   **Logical topologies** are concerned with how do data messages reach their proper destination. An analogy used to describe logical topologies has to do with how best to put out a fire in a PC user's wastebasket.

Layer Number	Layer Name	Examples of Protocols or Standards
7	Application	
6	Presentation	
5	Session	
4	Transport	
3	Network	
2	Data Link	
	Logical link control sublayer	
	Media access control sublayer	CSMA/CD, token passing
1	Physical	

Figure 5-12 The MAC sublayer of the OSI model.

The first logical topology or method of delivering data is known as **sequential**. In a sequential logical topology, also known as a *ring* logical topology, data is passed from one PC (or node) to another. Each node examines the destination address of the data packet to determine if this particular packet is meant for it. If the data was not meant to be delivered at this node, the data is passed along to the next node in the logical ring.

This is the *bucket brigade* logical topology method of putting out a fire in a PC user's wastebasket. A bucket of water is filled by one PC user and passed to the neighboring PC User. That user determines if his/her wastebasket is on fire. If it is, the user douses the flames with the bucket of water. Otherwise, the user passes the bucket along to the next user in the logical ring.

The second logical topology or method of delivering data is known as **broadcast.** In a broadcast logical topology, a data message is sent simultaneously to all nodes on the network. Each node decides individually if the data message was directed toward it. If not, the message is simply ignored. There is no need to pass the message along to a neighboring node. They've already gotten the same message.

This is the *sprinkler system* logical topology method of putting out a fire in a PC user's wastebasket. Rather than worry about passing a bucket of water around a logical ring until it finally reaches the engulfed wastebasket, the water is just broadcast over the entire network with the result being that the wastebasket that was on fire will know that the water was meant for it.

Physical Topologies   **Physical topologies** refer to the way in which PCs are physically hooked together on a network. The names of these physical topologies are derived from the geometric shape of the configured networks. The three most common physical topologies are:

Bus
Star
Ring

The truth of the matter is that the majority of networks today are configured using the **star topology** for reasons which will soon be seen. Figure 5-13 illustrates each of the aforementioned physical topologies.

Network reliability is a key factor when evaluating which physical topology one should employ in their network architecture. The bus topology and the ring topology can each suffer from reliability problems that have made the star topology the network configuration of choice. As will be seen, the chosen physical topology does not necessarily dictate other network choices such as network architecture or network operating system.

The **bus topology** is a linear arrangement with terminators on either end and devices connected to the "bus" via connectors and/or transceivers. The weak link in the bus physical topology is that a break or loose connection anywhere along the entire bus, will bring the whole network down.

The **ring topology** suffers from a similar Achilles heel. Each PC connected via a ring topology is actually an active part of the ring, passing data packets in a sequential pattern around the ring. If one of the PCs dies, or a network adapter card malfunctions, the "sequence" is broken, the token is lost, and the network is down.

The Shining Star   The star physical topology avoids these two aforementioned potential pitfalls by employing some type of central management device.

Bus topology

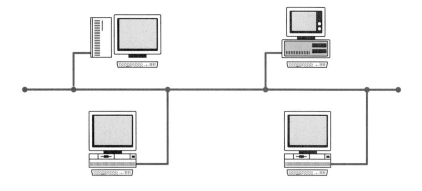

Star topology

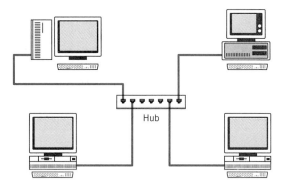

Hub

Ring topology

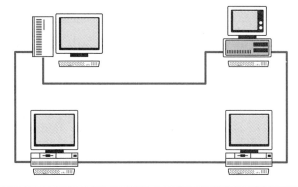

Figure 5-13 Local Area Network physical topologies.

Depending on the network architecture and sophistication of the device, it may be called a **hub**, a **wiring center,** a **concentrator,** a **MAU** (multiple access unit), a **repeater,** or a **switching hub.** All of these devices will be studied later in this chapter. By isolating each PC or node on its own leg or segment of the network, any node failure only affects that leg, while the remainder of the network continues to function normally.

Media

	Speed	Access Methodology	Physical Topology (configuration)	Maximum Stations	Maximum Cable Length	Packet Size	UTP	STP	COAX	FIBER	IBM Mainframe	Wireless	Logical Topology	Extended Communication
Token Ring	16 mbps 4 mbps	token passing	STAR	96 per STP	150 ft		■	■	■	■	■	■	Sequential	IEEE 802.5
Ethernet	10 mbps	CSMA/CD	STAR BUS	100 per segment	1000 ft		■	■	■	■	□	■	Broadcast	IEEE 802.3
FDDI	100 mbps	modified token passing	DUAL RING		200 km					■			Sequential	ANSI X3T9.5
CDDI	100 mbps	modified token passing	DUAL RING		200 km		■	■					Sequential	ANSI X3T9.5
ArcNET	2.5 mbps	token passing	BUS STAR				■	■	■				Broadcast	
TCNS	100 mbps	token passing	STAR					■	■	■				Uses ArcNET drivers, proprietary Thomas Conrad Corporation
MAN	1 mbps-200 mbps	DQDB	DUAL BUS							■				IEEE 802.6 ANSI X3T9.5
MAP		token passing CSMA/CD	BUS						■				Sequential	IEEE 802.4 IEEE 802.3
AppleTALK	230.4 kbps	CSMA/CD	STAR BUS				■						Broadcast	
ArcNET Plus	20 mbps	token passing	BUS STAR				■	■	■				Broadcast	
StarLAN	1 mbps	CSMA/CD	STAR				■						Broadcast	
StarLAN 10	10 mbps	CSMA/CD	STAR				■						Broadcast	Equivalent to Ethernet IEEE 802.3

Figure 5-14 Network architecture topology choices.

Since all network data in a star topology is going through this one central location, it makes a marvelous spot to add system monitoring, security, or management capabilities. The other side of the coin is that since all network data is going through this one central location, it makes a marvelous networking no-no known as a *single point of failure*. The good news is: any node can be lost and the network will be fine. The bad news is: lose the hub and the whole network goes down.

As will be seen shortly in the study of hubs, vendors have risen to the occasion offering such reliability extras as redundant power supplies, dual buses, and "hot swappable" interface cards.

Network Architecture Choices

Now that familiarity has been gained with the available choices of access methodologies, logical topologies, and physical topologies, they can be put together in various ways, and after letting the experts add additional specifications, these combinations of choices will yield a variety of **network architectures**. Figure 5-14 summarizes some popular network architectures and their key characteristics.

The Impact of Network Architecture Choice

As Figure 5-2 indicated, the choice of a particular network architecture will have a definite bearing on the choice of network adapter cards and less of an impact on the choice of media or network operating system. For instance, an **Ethernet** network architecture requires Ethernet adapter cards. As will soon be seen, it is the adapter card that holds the key, or *MAC layer protocol* to be more precise, which determines whether a network is Ethernet or **token ring.**

However, as can be seen in Figure 5-14, Ethernet runs over thick or thin coaxial cable, shielded or unshielded twisted pair, fiber or wireless—clearly a wide choice of media options. Also, Netware, Vines, and LAN Manager, as well as most other network operating systems, run over Ethernet or token ring, while Netware and many DOS-based LANs run over **Arcnet** as well. Another good example of the independence of network operating systems and network architectures is the fact that **Appletalk** (a NOS) runs just fine over 10Mbps Ethernet, which is often the network architecture of choice when compared to Apple's **Localtalk** network architecture, which transmits at 230.4 Kbps.

So how is one to choose among all these network architectures? In the next few paragraphs, the key characteristics, positive and negative, of each network architecture listed in Figure 5-14 will be outlined.

The Big Two: Ethernet and Token Ring

Ethernet   Ethernet, adhering to the **IEEE 802.3** standard, is a CSMA/CD-based network architecture traditionally installed in a bus configuration, but most often installed recently in a hub-based star topology. Every device, most often network adapter cards, attached to an Ethernet network has a unique hardware address assigned to it at the time of manufacture. As new devices are added to an Ethernet network, their addresses become new possible destinations for all other attached Ethernet devices.

The media access layer protocol elements of Ethernet form data packets for transmission over the shared media according to a standardized format. This Ethernet packet format is nearly equivalent to the IEEE 802.3 standard, and the two terms are often used interchangeably.

The potential for collisions and retransmission on an Ethernet network, thanks to its CSMA/CD access methodology, has already been mentioned. In some cases,

Ethernet networks with between 100 and 200 users barely use the 10Mbps capacity of the network. However, the nature of the data transmitted is the key to determining potential network capacity problems. Character based transmissions, such as typical data entry in which a few characters at a time are typed and sent over the network, are much less likely to cause network capacity problems than the transfer of GUI (graphical user interface) screen-oriented transmission such as Windows-based applications. CAD/CAM images are even more bandwidth intensive.

Simultaneous requests for full screen Windows-based transfers by 30 or more workstations can cause collision and network capacity problems on an Ethernet network. As with any data comm problem, there are always solutions or workarounds to these problems. The point in relaying these examples is to provide some assurance that although Ethernet is not unlimited in its network capacity, in most cases, it provides more than enough bandwidth.

Price is another factor in Ethernet's favor. Depending on a number of features outlined in the forthcoming study of network adapter cards, an Ethernet card can sell for as little as $150 while the least expensive token ring card would probably sell for twice that amount.

Ethernet can run over numerous media types. The unshielded twisted pair employed in an Ethernet standard known as **10BaseT** sells for as little as 6 cents per foot. The "10" in 10BaseT refers to 10Mbps capacity, the "Base" refers to **baseband transmission**, meaning that the entire bandwidth of the media is devoted to one data channel, and the "T" stands for twisted pair, the media. Another important distinction of 10BaseT is that it specifies the use of a star topology with all Ethernet LAN segments connected to a centralized wiring hub. Other Ethernet standards and associated media are listed in Figure 5-15.

Popular Name	Standard Name	Speed	Media	Maximum Segment Length
Orange Hose Ethernet	10Base5	10 Mbps	Thick COAX	500 meters
CheaperNET ThinNET	10Base2	10 Mbps	Thin COAX (Like cable TV cable)	185 meters
10BaseT	10BaseT	10 Mbps	Unshielded Twisted Pair	100 meters
Fiber Ethernet	10BaseF	10 Mbps	Fiber-Optic Cable	2 km
StarLAN	1Base5	1 Mbps	Unshielded Twisted Pair	500 meters
StarLAN10	10BaseT	10 Mbps	Unshielded Twisted Pair	100 meters

Figure 5-15 Ethernet (and close relatives) standards.

Token Ring IBM's **Token Ring** network architecture, adhering to the **IEEE 802.5** standard, utilizes a star configuration, sequential message delivery, and a token-passing access methodology scheme.

Remembering that the sequential logical topology is equivalent to passing messages from neighbor to neighbor around a ring, the token ring network architecture is sometimes referred to as: *logical ring, physical star.*

The token ring's use of the token-passing access methodology furnishes one of the key positive attributes of this network architecture. The guarantee of no data collisions with assured data delivery afforded by the token passing access methodology is a key selling point in some environments where immediate, guaranteed delivery is essential.

The second attribute in Token Ring's favor is the backing of a computer company of the magnitude of IBM. For those businesses facing integration of PCs with existing IBM mainframes and minicomputers, IBM's token ring network architecture offers assurance of the possibility of such an integration. As will be seen in the next chapter when SNA, IBM's overall system network architecture, is discussed, Token Ring is playing a more central role in IBM's overall networking strategy, in contrast to its onetime "low-end" stigma.

Although Token Ring is IBM's PC networking architecture, it is neither a closed system nor a monopoly. Third-party suppliers offer choices in the network adapter card and wiring hub (multiple access unit) markets, while numerous network operating systems run over the token ring architecture. Competition encourages research and development of new technology and can eventually drive prices down. Price is an important point about Token Ring. Network adapter cards for a Token Ring network tend to cost between one-and-one-half and two times as much as Ethernet network adapter cards.

> *In Sharper Focus*

ACTIVE MAUS

The wiring hub in a token ring network architecture is known as a **MAU** or multiple access unit. A designation of MAUs known as **active MAUs** or active management MAUs play a key role in the reliability of a token ring network. Remembering that the token ring's access methodology depends on the "bucket brigade" passing of the "free" token in sequential order around the ring from one workstation to the next, the potential for a "lost" token due to a network adapter card failure in one of the PCs in the ring should be evident.

If a token gets "lost," no workstations can access the network. Remember, a token ring network is a well-mannered network. No workstations speak (access the network media with their messages) without permission (without the free token). A lost token brings the token ring network to an absolute standstill. This is where the active MAU comes in. First, in a preventative role, it possesses the active management software necessary to detect misbehaving adapter boards and force the connected workstations off the ring. Secondly, should a token get lost (trapped in a bad adapter board), the active MAU has the ability to regenerate a new token, and the network activity continues.

Beware, however, not all MAUs are active MAUs possessing this ability to detect and detach bad adapter boards and regenerate tokens. Shop for MAUs, and any data comm device, by analyzing delivered functionality rather than by taking manufacturers' device names and labels at face value.

Two Flavors of Tokens

As has been previously stated, the token is really a specially formatted packet of data. In fact, there are two flavors of tokens. There is the "free" token variety, which can be grabbed by any workstation through which it passes on its sequential trip around the ring. Should a workstation wish to use the network media, the adapter card "grabs" the free token and puts its data message out onto the media along with a transformed "busy" token. When the busy token and the original data message make a complete trip around the ring back to the originating workstation, the busy token is transformed back into a free token and passed sequentially around the ring for another workstation to grab, if need be.

Token Ring's Future Prospects

The introduction of 16Mbps Token Ring over a variety of media, including unshielded twisted pair, bodes well for the future vitality of the Token Ring network architecture. Increased bandwidth combined with decreased media costs could bring Token Ring's popularity on a par with Ethernet. Running 16Mbps token ring over unshielded twisted-pair cable has some limitations and potential pitfalls. Before attempting such an installation, carefully read the articles on this topic in any current data communications professional periodical.

FDDI and CDDI: The Future?

In order to understand all the fuss about FDDI and CDDI, it is necessary to first understand why 10Mbps Ethernet and 16Mbps Token Ring may not contain sufficient bandwidth for the bandwidth-hungry applications of the not too distant future. What are some of these bandwidth drivers?

Bandwidth Drivers Build Demand for FDDI   The major bandwidth drivers fall into two major categories:

1. Network architecture trends
2. Network application trends

As far as trends in network architecture go, as more and more users are attached to LANS, the demand for overall network bandwidth increases. LANs are increasing both in size and overall complexity. Internetworking of LANs of various protocols via bridges and routers means more overall LAN traffic.

Network applications are driving the demand for increased bandwidth as well. The concepts of distributed computing, data distribution, and client/server computing, which will be studied in Chapter 9, all rely on a network architecture foundation of high bandwidth and high reliability. Imaging, Multimedia, and data/voice integration all require high amounts of bandwidth in order to transport and display these various data formats in "real" time.

In other words, if full-motion video is to be transported across the LAN as part of a multimedia program, there should be sufficient bandwidth available on that LAN for the video to run at full speed and not in slow motion. Likewise, digitized voice transmission should sound "normal" when transported across a LAN of sufficient bandwidth.

FDDI's Appeal (and a Few Negatives)   FDDI (fiber distributed data interface) supplies not only a great deal (100 Mbps) of bandwidth, but also a high degree of reliability and security while adhering to standards-based protocols not associated with or promoted by any particular vendor.

FDDI's reliability comes not only from the fiber itself, which as we know, is immune to both **EMI** (electro magnetic interference) and **RFI** (radio frequency interference). An additional degree of reliability is achieved through the design of the physical topology of FDDI.

FDDI's physical topology is comprised of not one, but two, separate rings around which data moves simultaneously in opposite directions. One ring is the primary data ring while the other is a secondary or backup data ring to be used only in the case of the failure of the primary ring. Whereas, both rings are attached to a single hub or concentrator, a single point of failure remains in the hub while achieving redundancy in the network media. Figure 5-16 outlines some of the key features of the FDDI physical topology.

In addition to speed and reliability, distance is another key feature of an FDDI LAN. The total media can stretch for up to 20 kilometers (12 miles) if repeaters are used at least every two kilometers. This increased distance capability makes FDDI

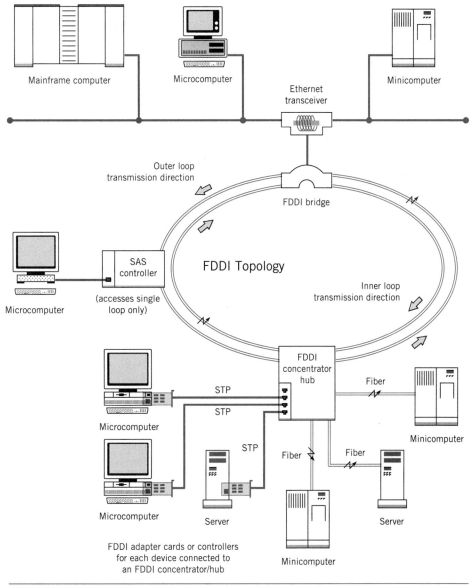

Figure 5-16 FDDI physical topology: dual, counter rotating rings, primary/backup for reliability.

an excellent choice as a high-speed backbone network for campus environments. As a matter of fact, our campus-wide backbone network here at Purdue is FDDI based.

Modified Token Passing Methodology   FDDI uses a modified token passing access methodology. The word "modified" is used here because it is different from the IEEE 802.5 token-ring type token passing in at least two key respects. First, due to the great potential distances on an FDDI LAN, it was impractical to turn "free" tokens into "busy" tokens and let a single station monopolize that token until it had received confirmation of successful delivery of its data. Instead, FDDI plays a sort of "flag football" in which a free token is dangled behind a data message of the PC who last grabbed the token. This dangling free token flag can then be grabbed by any station on the network.

Collisions are still avoided as only one station can have the free token at a time, and stations cannot put data messages onto the network without a token. A second token passing modification in FDDI is that numerous messages may be sent by a single PC before relinquishing the token, as opposed to the "one message per token per customer" philosophy of the IEEE 802.5 token-passing access methodology.

FDDI to Ethernet Interoperability   Another positive attribute of FDDI, illustrated in Figure 5-16, is its ability to interoperate easily with IEEE 802.3 10 Mbps Ethernet networks. In this way, a business does not have to scrap its entire existing network in order to upgrade a piece of it to 100Mbps FDDI. An FDDI to Ethernet bridge is the specific technology employed in such a setup. Although we will study bridges in depth in Chapter 6, we'll talk a bit more about FDDI–Ethernet Bridges shortly.

FDDI Negatives   After all these positive things to say about FDDI, surely there must be something negative about this LAN network architecture. Chief among the negatives is price, although how long price will be a negative remains to be seen. As with any other shared media network architecture, in order for a PC to access an FDDI LAN, it must be equipped with an FDDI network adapter card. These cards range from $1500 to $7500 with the "lower" priced FDDI network adapter cards able to attach to and use only one of the two FDDI data rings. Compare these prices with the average Ethernet card at $150 to $200 and the average Token Ring card at roughly twice that price.

As FDDI gains in popularity and competition increases in the FDDI technology market, prices will undoubtedly fall, although it is doubtful that they will ever reach Ethernet price levels. The fiber media itself is seen as a negative factor by some as well. Although fiber is light weight and can be packed more densely than copper wire, it is made of glass and can break. Also, connecting, terminating, and splicing fiber optic cables requires special tools and training. These obstacles can be overcome and, at least in some cases, the "fear of fiber" may be nothing more than the fear of the unknown.

Single Ring   Another way in which some network managers cut down on FDDI's cost while still benefitting from the 100Mbps bandwidth is to only connect to one of FDDI's two fiber rings. This type of connection is sometimes called **SAS**, or single access system, as opposed to **DAS**, or dual access system, in which both FDDI rings are accessed. Obviously, if a device is only attached to one FDDI ring, it forgoes the reliability offered by the redundant secondary data ring.

CDDI

One way of coping with the fear of fiber is to run FDDI over copper wiring, either shielded or unshielded twisted pair as used in Ethernet and Token Ring installations. Because running a fiber based architecture over copper sounds a little strange, this variation of FDDI has been dubbed **CDDI** or copper distributed data interface. While it will still support 100Mbps, distance is limited as compared with the fiber-based FDDI. Figure 5-17 summarizes the media choices and distance impact of various FDDI implementations.

The Standards Game CDDI requires its own standards for transmission over copper, rather than fiber media. The process involved in determining this standard is a classic example of the high stakes and politics of the standards game. Two rival proposals were put forth to ANSI for copper-based FDDI. One proposal, backed by IBM, was called SDDI and sought to have the copper-based FDDI run only over shielded twisted pair wiring. A rival proposal by AT&T, Apple, Cabletron and others sought to have the standard defined for both shielded and unshielded twisted pair wiring. ANSI has recommended the development of a FDDI standard for both shielded and unshielded twisted pair wiring to be known as CDDI.

Not all fiber-based, 100 Mbps network architectures are standardized, open systems. Some vendor-specific proprietary solutions do exist, perhaps the most notable being the TCNS network architecture from Thomas Conrad Corporation. Having been an ARCNET network adapter card and hub manufacturer, Thomas Conrad set out to provide an easy and affordable upgrade for existing ARCNET networks. And what an upgrade it was—from 2.5 Mbps to 100Mbps! Although less expensive than FDDI standards compliant technology, it is a proprietary-based technology and interoperability may present a problem.

FDDI Technology The technology involved with FDDI network architectures is similar in function to that of other network architectures, and is illustrated in Figure 5-16. PCs, workstations, minicomputers, or mainframes that wish to access the FDDI LAN must be equipped with either internal FDDI network adapter cards or external FDDI controllers.

At the heart of the FDDI LAN is the FDDI concentrator or hub. The design of these hubs is often modular, with backbone connections to both FDDI rings, management modules, and device attachment modules in various media varieties available for customized design and ease of installation.

Name Media	Segment Length (distance between repeaters)	Architectur (acronym)
Fiber	2 km	FDDI
Shielded		SDDI[a]
Twisted Pair	100 m	-or-
(STP)		CDDI[b]
Unshielded		
Twisted Pair	50 m	CDDI[b]

[a]SDDI, Shielded Distributed Data Interface
[b]CDDI, Copper Distributed Data Interface

Figure 5-17 FDDI media alternatives and impact on distance.

The third key piece of FDDI technology is the FDDI to Ethernet bridge, which allows 10Mbps Ethernet LANS to interface with the 100Mbps FDDI LANs. The Ethernet LANs are very often department-based networks, while the FDDI is more likely to be a campus-wide backbone. Bridges may be able to connect either a single Ethernet or several Ethernets to the FDDI LAN.

FDDI Applications   The uses of the FDDI network architecture seem to fall into three categories.

1. *Campus backbone.* Not necessarily implying a college campus, this implementation is used for connecting LANs located throughout a series of closely situated buildings. Remember that the total ring length can equal 20 kilometers and multiple FDDI LANs are a possibility also. Building backbones would fall into this category as well with perhaps a 100Mbps FDDI building backbone going between floors connecting numerous 10 Mbps Ethernet LANS located on the various floors.

2. *High-bandwidth workgroups.* This application category uses the FDDI LAN as a truly *local* area network, connecting a few (less than 20) PCs or workstations which require high-bandwidth communication with each other. Multimedia workstations, engineering workstations, or CAD/CAM workstations are all good examples of high-bandwidth workstations. As "power users" turn increasingly toward graphical user interfaces (GUI), such as Windows and OS/2, this constituency's bandwidth requirements will rise as well.

3. *High-bandwidth subworkgroup connections.* In some cases, only two or three devices, perhaps three servers, need high bandwidth requirements. As distributed computing and data distribution increase as part of the downsizing and applications rightsizing trends sweeping the information systems industry, an increasing demand for high-speed server-to-server data transfer will be seen.

☐ HARDWARE CHOICES

Network Adapter Card Choices

Network adapter cards, also known as network interface cards or **NIC**s, are the physical link between a client or server PC and the shared media of the network. Providing this interface between the network and the PC or workstation requires that the network adapter card have the ability to adhere to the access methodology (CSMA/CD or Token Passing) of the network architecture (Ethernet, Token Ring, Arcnet, FDDI/CDDI, etc.) to which it is attached. These software rules, implemented by the network adapter card, which control the access to the shared network media are known as media access control (MAC) protocols and are represented on the MAC sublayer of the data link layer (layer 2) of the OSI 7-layer reference model.

Keepers of the MAC-Layer Protocol

Since these are MAC-layer interface cards, and are therefore the keepers of the MAC-layer interface protocol, it's fair to say that it is the adapter cards themselves which determine network architecture and its constituent protocols more than any other component. Take an Ethernet adapter card out of the expansion slot of a PC and replace it with a Token Ring adapter card and you have a Token Ring workstation, simple as that. In this same scenario, the media may not even need to be changed since Ethernet, Token Ring, Arcnet, and FDDI/CDDI often work over the same media.

A network adapter card is a bit like a mediator or translator. On one side it has the demands of the client or server PC for network services, while on the other side it has the network architecture with its rules for accessing the shared network media. The network adapter card's job is to get the PC all of the network services it desires while adhering to the rules (MAC Layer Protocols) of the network architecture. Figure 5-18, "Network Adapter Card Technology Analysis Grid," summarizes many of the key characteristics of currently available network adapter cards. Most of the differentiating characteristics listed in the grid are explained in the following "In Sharper Focus" section. Not all characteristics of all network adapter cards have been entered on the technology analysis grid. As network adapter card technology evolves, add available characteristics to this grid.

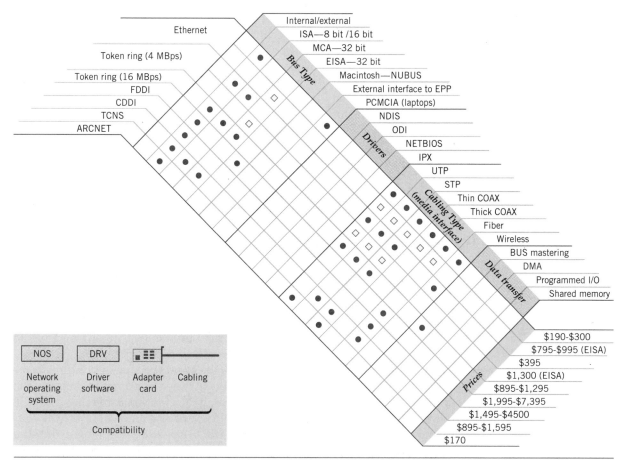

Figure 5-18 Network adapter card: technology analysis grid.

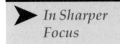

WHAT ARE THE DIFFERENTIATING FACTORS BETWEEN ADAPTER CARDS?

Now that the logical functionality of the network adapter card and where it fits in the overall networking scheme of things are understood, how network adapter cards can differ, and how these differences can affect overall performance will be investigated. Following are some of the key differences in adapter design and features which will be investigated in greater detail:

Bus Type Choices
 ISA (8 or 16 bit)
 EISA (16 or 32 bit)
 MCA
 NuBus
On-Board Processor Capabilities
Amount of On-Board Memory
Data Transfer Techniques
 Bus mastering DMA
 DMA
 Shared memory
 Programmed I/O
Media Interfaces
System Memory Requirements
Internal Adapters versus External Adapters
Network Architecture(s) Supported

Don't Miss the Bus

The **bus** into which a network adapter card is attached is known alternatively as the data bus, the I/O (Input/Output) bus, or the expansion bus. Whatever it may be called, this bus allows many different types of add-in cards to be attached to this data transfer pipeline leading to the CPU and RAM memory. The expansion bus in a PC is a lot like a straight line of empty parking spaces waiting to be filled by PC expansion cards of one type or another. These expansion cards draw electricity from and transfer data to/from other system components such as the CPU or memory through the expansion bus.

The speed and efficiency of the data transfer from expansion cards such as a network adapter card to RAM memory has a lot to do with the "width" of this data bus. In other words, how many bits can be read or travel down the bus simultaneously? This bus "width" and the nature of the system in which the data bus resides are the key differences between the four bus types listed above.

The **ISA** (industry standard architecture) bus comes in both 8-bit and 16-bit varieties, meaning it can read and transfer either 8 or 16 bits at a time, depending on how many bits at a time the expansion card can put onto the bus. Likewise, the **EISA** (extended industry standard architecture) bus can recognize either 16 or 32 bits at a time. The **MCA** (microchannel architecture) bus is another type of bus, first developed by IBM for its PS/2 line of computers, but now used by numerous manufacturers. Among the interesting capabilities concerning expansion cards that the MCA bus offers is the ability to detect newly installed cards and auto-configure the communications parameters to those cards. The **NUBUS** is specific to Apple Macintoshes.

Although data transfer issues will be explored shortly, the key point to remember about buses is that the "wider" the bus, the more data can be transferred simultaneously.

The important choice related to bus architecture is that a network adapter card is chosen that not only "fits" the installed bus, but more importantly, takes full advantage of whatever data transfer capability that given bus may afford.

The Network Adapter's Main Job: Transfer the Data

As stated earlier, the key job of the network adapter is to transfer data between the local PC and the shared network media. Ideally, this should be done as quickly as possible with a minimum of interruption of the PC's main CPU. By minimizing the interruption of the system CPU, it will be allowed to service other applications more effectively.

Two hardware-related network adapter characteristics that can have a bearing on **data transfer** efficiency are the amount of on-board memory and the processing power of the on-board CPU contained on the network adapter card. As will be seen below, when the four most popular data transfer techniques are compared, amount of on-board RAM and processing power play a key role in the more sophisticated data transfer techniques.

Figure 5-19 summarizes four network adapter card-to-PC memory data transfer techniques. Network adapter cards may support more than one of these techniques. Some of these data transfer techniques are only possible on the more sophisticated buses such as EISA and MCA. Others are most often implemented with adapter cards of a particular network architecture such as Token Ring. Some may require a CPU of a minimum level of sophistication and power, 80286 or 80386, for example. After reading the description of each of the data transfer techniques below, review product literature for network adapter cards in any number of professional publications. Compare the bus, CPU, and sometimes RAM requirements listed for the network adapter cards in question with the resources available on the PC into which they are to be installed.

To further explain the illustrations in Figure 5-19: Remembering that one of the objectives of network-to-PC data transfer was to minimize the number of interruptions of the system CPU, it can be seen in Figure 5-19 that only the **bus mastering DMA** (Direct Memory Access) data transfer technique leaves the system CPU alone to process other applications. In bus mastering DMA, the CPU on the network adapter card manages the movement of data directly into the PC's RAM memory, without interruption of the system CPU, by taking control of the PC's expansion bus.

Bus mastering DMA as a feature on adapter cards requires the expansion bus in the PC to support being "mastered" by the CPU on the network adapter card. Some buses are more sophisticated (MCA and EISA) when it comes to bus mastering by maintaining more control and management over how the mastering of the expansion bus by the network adapter card CPU is handled. Also, the CPU and operating system must have the capability to relinquish control of the expansion bus in order for bus mastering network adapter cards to function correctly. Bus mastering network adapter cards are more prevalent for the Token Ring architecture, than for Ethernet, FDDI, or Arcnet.

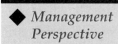
◆ *Management Perspective*

When it comes to data transfer via network adapter cards, how fast is fast enough? The answer may vary if the network adapter card is being purchased for a client PC or a server PC. Some network operating systems are able to operate over multiple (as many as four) adapters installed in a single server PC as a means of optimizing network communication between the client and server PCs. It stands to reason that

Programmed I/O

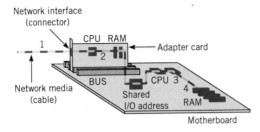

Steps
1. Data enters network interface card through the network media and connector
2. Adapter card CPU loads network data into a specific I/O address on the motherboard
3. Main CPU checks I/O area for data
4. If data exists, it is transferred to main memory, RAM, by main CPU

Keynote
The motherboard's CPU has the ultimate responsibility of data transfer into RAM

DMA (Direct Memory Access)

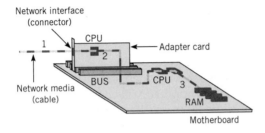

Steps
1. Data enters network interface card through the network media and connector
2. Adapter card CPU interrupts the motherboard CPU
3. Main CPU stops other processing and transfers data to RAM

Keynote
The motherboard's CPU has the ultimate responsibility of data transfer into RAM

Shared Memory

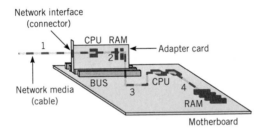

Steps
1. Data enters network interface card through the network media and connector
2. Adapter card CPU stores data on its RAM
3. Adapter card CPU interrupts the motherboard CPU
4. Main CPU stops other processing and transfers data to RAM

Keynote
The motherboard's CPU has the ultimate responsibility of data transfer into RAM

Bus Mastering DMA

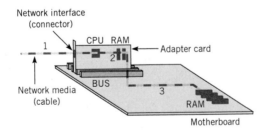

Steps
1. Data enters network interface card through the network media and connector
2. Adapter card CPU temporarily stores data on its RAM
3. Adapter card CPU sends data directly to motherboard RAM when network transfer completes (it does Not interrupt the main CPU)

Keynote
The adapter card's CPU has the ultimate responsibility of data transfer into RAM

Figure 5-19 Network adapter cards: data transfer techniques.

a server's adapter cards will be much busier than a client's adapter card, in general.

Therefore, it is usually wise to spend a little extra money and buy the faster, more sophisticated network adapter cards supporting more sophisticated data transfer techniques for the servers; less expensive models will often suffice for client PCs. It follows therefore, that server PCs should probably contain more powerful CPUs and higher capacity buses than client PCs as well.

Media Interfaces

A network adapter card must worry about hardware compatibility in two directions. First, the card must be compatible with the expansion bus into which it will be inserted. Secondly, it must be compatible with the chosen media of a particular network architecture implementation. Recall Figure 5-18, "The Network Adapter Technology Analysis Grid," and compare the media alternatives available for different network adapter cards listed there with Figure 5-14, and the different media options associated with different network architectures listed therein.

Several network adapter cards come with interfaces for more than one media type with "jumpers" or switches enabling one media type or another. Ethernet adapter cards with interfaces for both 10BaseT (RJ45 or 8-pin Telco plug) and thin coax connections known as a BNC connector, or with both thick and thin coax connections, are quite common. Thick coax connectors are also called AUI connectors.

The Role of Adapter Card Drivers

Being sure that the purchased adapter card interfaces successfully to both the bus of the CPU as well as the chosen media of the network architecture, will assure hardware connectivity. Full interoperability, however, depends on numerous software compatibilities discussed earlier in the section on network adapter card drivers. And speaking of drivers, it might be wise to note how much system memory is required to load the drivers supplied with network adapter cards. Remember that drivers for various cards are often supplied with the installed networking operating system as well. One of these drivers may be more efficient in terms of operation or required memory than another.

Internal versus External

All of the discussion thus far regarding installation of network adapter cards has assumed that the adapters are internal or connected directly to the system expansion bus. Alternatively, network adapters can be connected *externally* to a PC via the PC's parallel port. This niche market has grown considerably with the proliferation of laptop or notebook computers lacking internal expansion capability. In these cases, external adapters, as small as a pack of cigarettes, are interfaced between the PC's parallel port and the network media.

External adapters, also called *pocket adapters* (because they can usually fit in a shirt pocket) exist for Token Ring, Ethernet, and Arcnet network architectures. External adapters cannot draw electricity from the expansion bus like internal adapters and therefore require a power source of their own in most cases.

A chain is only as strong as its weakest link and a network is only as fast as its slowest segment. In the case of external network adapters, that slowest link is the parallel port to which it is connected. Throughput on existing parallel ports hovers around 130Kbps while a newer *high-performance parallel port,* also known as *EPP* or *enhanced parallel port,* delivers a throughput of up to 2 Mbps. Remember that the parallel port is a component of the laptop PC, not the external adapter.

PCMCIA

Some laptops actually have an external port that allows direct connection to the PC's system bus. This interface is standardized by a specification known as **PCM-CIA,** which stands for Personal Computer Memory Card International Association. The term memory card refers to the fact that the PCMCIA slot was originally to be used for removable flash memory cards, about the size of a credit card. Modems and network adapter cards of various types now interface to the

PCMCIA slot. Wireless PCMCIA Ethernet adapters have brought new meaning to the term *portable computing*.

Understandably, external adapters designed to interface to this PCMCIA external bus connector provide significantly higher throughput than those adapters connected via parallel ports.

Network Architecture

Although seemingly self-evident, a given network adapter card will only support the network architecture for which it was intended. A Token Ring card will not work on an Ethernet network. As crazy as it sounds, whereas both networks can run over similar media, such as coax, it would be possible to physically install the network adapter card and interface it to the shared media even though it is the wrong network architecture.

Remember that the network adapter card is, in fact, the keeper of the network architecture in the form of its media access control (MAC) sublayer protocols. Some features appear only on network adapter cards of a particular network architecture. For instance, Token Ring NICs have the ability to interface to the network at either 4Mbps or 16Mbps.

Future Trends in Network Adapter Cards

More Powerful, Multiprotocol Chips At least two companies, Texas Instruments and Chips and Technology, Inc., have produced a chip set that supports both Ethernet and Token Ring MAC-layer protocols on a single adapter card. This would likely allow preinstallation of such cards into PCs as the adapter would be capable of supporting the two most popular network architectures.

These more powerful and sophisticated chips will have sufficient power to improve performance in other ways as well. For instance, the processor on the adapter board can actually process the MAC-layer protocols for Token Ring or Ethernet rather than merely transferring the data for the system CPU to process. This adapter processor could also run network-oriented applications programs such as SNMP network management agents or 3270 terminal emulation.

The Positive and Negative Aspects of Network Monitoring

Both SNMP network management and 3270 terminal emulation will be studied in the next chapter, but, in a nutshell: **SNMP** stands for simple network management protocol and represents a group of rules or standards concerning the monitoring and gathering of performance (or lack thereof) statistics for a variety of networking hardware, including network adapter cards. The reference to SNMP in the previous paragraph implies that this performance monitoring could take place right on the adapter card by the adapter card's own CPU.

The monitoring capabilities afforded by the network adapter card CPU can go beyond acting as an SNMP agent. With the proper software loaded, these network-to-CPU interfaces can "peer" into the CPU and decipher what applications software, networking software, and operating system are running on the PC in which it is installed. All of this important status information can then be transported out of the adapter card, onto the network, and into a central monitoring facility or computer.

A few challenges remain to make this network manager's dream become a reality. The first challenge is to find a way for this monitoring software to be able to function regardless of installed operating system. A standards-based API (applications program interface) known as the desktop management interface **(DMI)** has been proposed. As will be seen in the next chapter on internetworking, sophisticated devices such as hubs, bridges, and routers are currently monitored successfully using SNMP agents. Individual PCs or workstations and their adapter cards are not included in this management and monitoring scheme at present. Support of the DMI API by operating system, network operating system, and NIC vendors would go a long way to make this dream a reality. That's the good news.

The bad news is that all of this wonderful monitoring and management information has to somehow travel from all of these (potentially hundreds) of workstations back to some central management PC or workstation *over the network*. That's right, this monitoring data will be contending for the same network bandwidth as applications programs' requests for data transfers, and adding additional network traffic overhead.

Terminal Emulation on the NIC Chip

The IBM 3270 is the standard synchronous terminal connected to IBM mainframes. Rather than purchase PCs *and* 3270 terminals, it makes better business sense to buy PCs that can disguise themselves as 3270 terminals. The process of terminal emulation makes a PC "appear to be" a 3270 terminal. Terminal emulation was discussed in the section on communications software in Chapter 3. The significance of the reference in the preceding paragraph is that rather than buying additional terminal emulation software and/or hardware and interrupting the system CPU for execution of the software, the more powerful CPU on the network adapter card can run the included terminal emulation software directly.

Another benefit of the more powerful network adapter card CPUs is performance, especially in the handling of small data packets (64 bytes/characters or less). Many of the confirmation of delivered messages and other "overhead" type messages on a network are 64 characters or fewer. The newest adapter chips have implemented programming and processing improvements to handle these smaller data packets more quickly and efficiently.

LAN-Ready PCs

LAN-ready PCs are also known as LAN adapters on the motherboard. The main circuit board in a PC which contains the CPU among other things, is known as the **motherboard**. One of the advantages of putting one of the aforementioned powerful new multiprotocol network adapter chipsets on the motherboard is the performance increase realized due to the fact that communication or data transfer between the network adapter and the system CPU will be along the system bus, rather than through the expansion or I/O bus.

A negative or unresolved issue is which media interface(s) to include. Even if the adapter chip can support either Ethernet or Token Ring, that still leaves at least four media options: UTP, STP, Coax, and Fiber.

Token Ring Connectivity to UNIX

Ethernet has traditionally been the network architecture of choice for the UNIX community. However, new higher performance Token Ring network adapter cards are now more ably suited to handle UNIX-based machines, especially those that possess the more powerful RISC (reduced instruction set) hardware architecture.

Remember that it takes more than just the adapter card to establish network communications to a PC. The network adapter card's chips and instruction sets must be able to communicate with the network operating system and operating system, such as UNIX, via drivers. These drivers may be especially written for each particular adapter card, networking operating system combination. Conversely, they may be written to standards such as NETBIOS, NDIS, or ODI, which are supported by most network operating systems and operating systems. These three driver standards were discussed earlier in this chapter.

Wiring Center Choices

As was mentioned earlier in the section on physical topologies, the heart of the popular star topology is the wiring center, alternatively known as a hub, a concentrator, a repeater or a MAU (multistation access unit). In this section, the role of the wiring center, currently available technology and comparative features, and future trends in hub development will be examined.

The Changing Role of the Wiring Center

Figure 5-20 summarizes some of the distinguishing features of various types of wiring centers. The chart is roughly arranged in ascending order by price and performance. In other words, a repeater is both the simplest and least expensive of the wiring center options. Features listed are limited to those features considered key to differentiating between the various wiring center technologies. A more complete listing of comparative features will be included in the wiring center technology analysis table (Figure 5-22).

	Repeats Digital Data Received	Ethernet	Token Ring	FDDI	Stand Alone	Chassis Rack	Provides Switched LAN Segment Connectors	Includes Internetworkign Devices (bridges, routers, etc.)	Includes Network Management	Includes ATM Switch	Includes Wide Area Network Links	LAN/WAN Analyzer
Repeaters	■	■	■		■							
Hubs	■	■		■	■				■			
MAUS	■		■		■				■			
Concentrators	■	■	■	■		■		■	■		■	
Switching Hubs	■	■	■			■	■		■			
Dense Switching HUBS/ LAN Superbox	■	■	■	■		■	■	■	■	■	■	■

Figure 5-20 The changing role of the wiring center.

Repeaters   A repeater, as its name implies, merely "repeats" each bit of digital data that it receives. This repeating action actually "cleans up" the digital signals by retiming and regenerating them before passing this repeated data from one attached device or LAN segment to the next.

Hubs   The terms "hub" and "concentrator" or "intelligent concentrator" are often used interchangeably. Distinctions can be made however between these two broad classes of wiring centers, although there is nothing to stop manufacturers from using the terms as they wish.

A hub is often the term reserved for describing a standalone device with a fixed number of ports which offers features beyond that of a simple repeater. The type of media connections and network architecture offered by the hub is determined at the time of manufacture as well. For example, a 10BaseT Ethernet hub will offer a fixed number of RJ-45 twisted-pair connections for an Ethernet network. Additional types of media or network architectures are not usually supported.

MAUs   A MAU or multistation access unit is IBM's name for a Token Ring hub. Discussed earlier in the section on Token Ring network architecture, a MAU is manufactured with a fixed number of ports and connections for unshielded or shielded twisted pair. IBM uses special connectors for Token Ring over shielded twisted-pair (STP) connections to a MAU. MAU's offer varying degrees of management capability. As previously discussed, MAUs possessing the ability to regenerate lost tokens are known as active management MAUs, while those lacking this ability are known as passive management MAUs.

Concentrators   The term **concentrator** or intelligent concentrator (or smart hub) is often reserved for a device characterized by its flexibility and expandability. A concentrator starts with a fairly empty, box-like device often called a chassis. This chassis contains one or more power supplies and a "built-in" network backbone. This backbone might be Ethernet, Token Ring, FDDI, ARCNET or Appletalk, or some combination of the above. Into this "backplane," individual cards or modules are inserted.

For instance, an 8- or 16-port twisted pair Ethernet module can be purchased and slid into place in the concentrator chassis. A network management module supporting the SNMP network management protocol can then be purchased and slid into the chassis next to the previously installed 10BaseT port module. In this "mix and match" scenario, additional cards can be added for connection of PCs with token-ring adapters, PCs or workstations with FDDI adapters, or "dumb" asynchronous terminals.

This "network in a box" is now ready for workstations to be hooked into it through twisted-pair connections to the media interfaces on the network interface cards of the PCs or workstations. Allowing different media types to be intermixed in the concentrator was one of its first major selling points. Remember that Ethernet can run over UTP, STP, thick and thin coax, as well as fiber optic cable.

Additional modules available for some, but not all, concentrators may allow data traffic from this "network in box" to travel to other local LANs via bridge or router add-on modules. Bridges and routers will be discussed in the next chapter on internetworking. These combination concentrators are sometimes called *internetworking hubs*. Communication to remote LANs or workstations may be available through the addition of other specialized cards, or modules, designed to provide access to wide area network services purchased from common carriers such as the phone company. These numerous available wide area network services will be studied in Chapter 7, "Wide Area Networks."

Switching Hubs   The "network in a box" or "backbone in a box" offered by concentrators and hubs shrinks the length of the network backbone, but doesn't change the architectural characteristics of a particular network backbone. For instance, in an Ethernet concentrator, multiple workstations may access the built-in Ethernet backbone via a variety of media, but the basic rules of Ethernet such as CSMA/CD access methodology at 10Mbps still control performance on this Ethernet in a box. Only one workstation at a time can broadcast its message onto the shared 10 Mbps backbone.

A **switching hub** seeks to overcome this "one-at-a-time" broadcast scheme, which can potentially lead to data collisions, retransmissions, and reduced throughput between high-bandwidth demanding devices such as engineering workstations or server-to- server communications. By adding the basic design of a data PBX to the modular designed concentrator, certain manufacturers such as Kalpana and Synoptics have delivered "switched" Ethernet connections at 10Mbps to multiple users simultaneously through a process known as parallel networking.

The Ethernet switch is actually able to create connections, or switch, between any two attached Ethernet devices on a packet-by- packet basis in as little as 40 milliseconds. The "one-at-a-time" broadcast limitation previously associated with Ethernet is overcome with an Ethernet switch. Figure 5-21 attempts to illustrate the basic functionality of an Ethernet switch. Note how the Ethernet switch module contains its own multiple 10Mbps switchable connections and doesn't use the backbone (or backplane) Ethernet.

Dense Switching Hubs—The LAN Superbox   What else can be added to the network in a box? A device sometimes called a LAN superbox, or **Dense switching hub,** includes all of the cumulative capabilities of the devices examined thus far plus additional switching and monitoring capability.

A high-speed switching methodology known as **ATM**, which stands for *asynchronous transfer mode* (not any time money) will be included in these LAN superboxes to transmit data between superbox components as well as between linked superboxes. ATM transmits at speeds from 155Megabits per second to several gigabits per second between the various LAN segments, backbones, bridges, routers, and wide-area links contained within such a LAN Superbox. ATM, bridges and routers will be studied further in future chapters.

Special monitoring software to analyze LAN and WAN performance will also be included in the LAN superbox. This is truly "one stop shopping" for LAN managers. Everything related to LAN performance and management is housed and controlled from a single location. Future possible additions to the LAN superbox might include modular file servers, database servers, and print servers. These modules just slide into an empty slot in the chassis just like any other module in this "plug and play" technology.

Wiring Centers Technology Analysis

Some of the major technical features to be used for comparative analysis are listed in Figure 5-22. Before purchasing a hub of any type, consider the implications of these various possible features from Figure 5-22. To summarize, the following major criteria should be thoroughly considered before a hub or concentrator purchase:

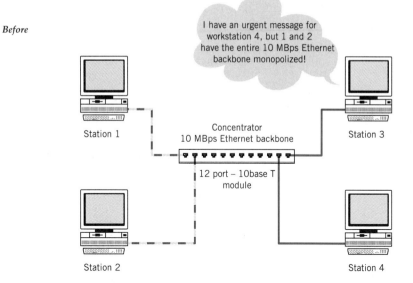

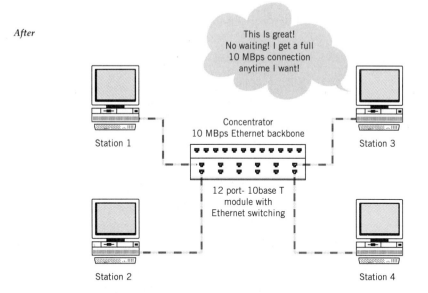

Figure 5-21 Switching HUBs.

1. Expandability
2. Supported network architectures
3. Supported media types
4. Extended communications capabilities
   a. terminal support
   b. internetworking options
   c. wide area networking options

Characteristic/Feature	Options/Implications
Expandability	*Options:* ports, LANs, slots Remember, most standalone hubs are not expandable, although they may be cascaded. Concentrators may vary in their overall expandability (number of open slots), or in their ability to add additional ports. Several concentrators allow only one LAN backbone module. Have you anticipated growth in 2- and 5-year horizons?
Network Architecture	*Options:* Ethernet, Token Ring, Arcnet, FDDI, Appletalk Some concentrators allow only one type of LAN module with ethernet being the most widely supported type of LAN module. Before purchasing a concentrator, make sure all of the necessary LAN types are supported.
Media	*Options:* Unshielded twisted pair, shielded twisted pair, thin coax, thick coax, fiber. Remember that each of these different media will connect to the hub with a different type of interface. Make sure that the port modules offer the correct interfaces for attachement of your media—also, remember that a NIC (network interface card) is on the other end of the attached media. Is this concentrator/hub compatible with your network adapter cards?
Extended Communications Macintosh support	Can an Apple Macintosh be linked to the hub?
Terminal support	Are modules available that support direct connection of "dumb" asynchronous terminals? What is the interface? (i.e., DB-25, RJ-45)
Internetworking	*Options:* Internetworking to: Ethernet, Token Ring, Arcnet, FDDI, Appletalk. As demonstrated in the next chapter, internetworking solutions are unique, dependent on the two LANs to be connected. In other words, unless a concentrator offers a module that specifically internetworks Ethernet module traffic to a token ring LAN, this communication cannot take place within the concentrator.
Wide Area Networking	*Options:* Interfaces to different carrier services—DDS, DS-0, T-1, X.25, frame relay, SMDS, ATM. We will learn how to determine effectively wide area networking requirements in Chapter 7. Once you know your wide area networking requirements, you must assure that your concentrator can seamlessly interface to those required wide area networking services.

Management	*Options:* Different standards for hub management exist. We will explore these in detail in the next chapter. For now, the possible options include: SNMP, CMIP, CMOT
	Options: What level of management is offered?
	  1. Can individual ports be managed?
	  2. Is monitoring software included?
	  3. Can wide area as well as local area link performance be analyzed/monitored through the concentrator?
	  4. What level of security in general or regarding management functions specifically is offered?
	  5. Can ports be remotely enabled/disabled?
	  6. Can the hub/concentrator be controlled from any attached workstation? Via modem?
	  7. Can management/monitoring functions be included through a graphical user interface?
	  8. How are alarm thresholds set?
	  9. How are faults managed?
	  10. Can port access be limited by day and/or time?
	  11. What operating systems can the management software run on? DOS, OS/2, Windows, UNIX, APPLE?
	  12. Can a map of the network be displayed?

Reliability	*Options:*
	  1. Is integrated UPS included?
	  2. Are there multiple, redundant power supplies?
	  3. Can individual modules be swapped out "hot," without powering down the entire hub?

Figure 5-22 Wiring center technology analysis table.

5. Hub/concentrator management capabilities

6. Reliability features

As new technical features are introduced, add them to Figure 5-22, being sure to consider the implications or benefits of such technical advances.

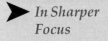

In Sharper Focus

FUTURE TRENDS IN WIRING CENTERS

Beyond the trends cited in the earlier section on LAN Superboxes, what can be expected in the evolution of hubs and concentrators?

ATM   The full implications of widespread ATM implementation is hard to imagine. Although ATM will be studied in greater depth shortly, a key characteristic of the transmission method is its transparency to transmission source. In other words, ATM just switches and transmits digital data *very* quickly (1.5Mbps to 2 or 3 Gbps) regardless of whether the source of that digital "data" was voice, video, or conventional data. ATM can be implemented within the LAN superbox for multimedia or full-motion video transmission while simultaneously transmitting voice and data. These same services may someday be available from carriers should the wide area network architecture get upgraded to ATM capability.

MAUs Become CAUs   In the Token Ring arena, single purpose, single media, inflexible MAUs (multistation access units) are becoming multipurpose, multimedia, flexible **CAU**s (controlled access units). A CAU is really just a modular, more flexible, more sophisticated MAU. For example, a CAU manufactured by either IBM or third-party vendors may include a CAU management module as well as an assortment of modules offering access to the token ring network over various types of media such as shielded and unshielded twisted pair, coax, and fiber.

These port expansion or station modules are known as either **LAMs** (lobe attachment modules) or **LACs** (lobe attachment concentrators). CAUs can offer fault recovery features and network management from remote terminals. Besides providing the Token Ring backbone for the ports on the LAMs, the CAU can also provide composite output for connection to other CAUs for inter-CAU communications via bridges or routers.

Hub Becomes a Server   Continuing with the "one stop shopping" notion that produced the LAN superbox, some vendors have chosen to put a CPU and a RAM memory into a hub/concentrator module. That's right, the hub is now also the CPU.

Specific applications written for this hub-based CPU might include NLMs (netware loadable modules) for Novell Netware to perform such network related functions as modem pooling or sharing. Remember the importance of market demand on technology success as reviewed in Chapter 1. If the data comm consumer is uncomfortable with the notion of loading system or networking software into their hub, the technology will not succeed, regardless of its scientific or networking merit.

Server Becomes a Hub   If a hub can take on the role of a server, why can't a server take on the role of a hub? In fact, recent updates to Netware allow hubs to be directly attached to the Netware server in a similar manner to network interface cards. 3Com Corporation, a major manufacturer of Ethernet adapter cards, offers the Etherlink TP (twisted pair) HubAdapter, a 12-port managed hub tied to a 16-bit bus master network adapter.

The HubAdapter (what a great example of modularity of design) is expandable to 48 ports, can be used with any Netware 3.11 or higher server or DOS-based PC, and comes with drivers for Netware 2.X, 3.X and LAN Manager. The HubAdapter can also accommodate numerous types of media besides twisted pair, such as thin and thick coax as well as fiber optic cable.

Other important software compatibility considerations are support of Novell's hub management interface **(HMI),** which defines the hub management extensions to Novell's ODI (open data-link interface) network adapter drivers, and HUB-CON, Novell's hub management utility.

Media Choices

Media characteristics, media interfaces or connectors, and the electrical specifications for transmission of data over any particular media, are defined in the physical layer or layer 1 of the OSI 7-Layer model. Figure 5-23 displays the important characteristics of most popular types of media.

Besides examining the comparative characteristics of various media options, the following will also be explored:

1. Which terminators, connectors, and interfaces are associated with which type of media?
2. Which type of media is associated with different network architectures?

Five Phone-Related Media   The distinctions between five closely related media choices will offer an excellent opportunity to explore the impediments and remedies to clear error-free data transmission. These five closely related media choices are:

1. Four-wire phone wire
2. Flat gray modular wire
3. Voice-grade unshielded twisted pair
4. Data-grade unshielded twisted pair
5. Shielded twisted pair

Not Twisted Pair   The type of phone wire installed in most homes consists of a tan plastic jacket containing four untwisted wires: green, red, yellow, and black and is also known as *four-conductor station wire.* This type of wire is not suitable for data transmission and is *not* the unshielded twisted pair (UTP) so often referred to.

Another popular type of phone wiring is referred to as *flat gray modular* wiring, also known as gray satin or silver satin. Inside this flat gray jacket are either four, six, or eight wires, which get crimped into either RJ-11 (four or six wire) or RJ-45 plugs (eight wire) using a specialized crimping tool. Now that divestiture has allowed homeowners to own and maintain their own premises' phone wiring as well as phones; crimp tools, RJ-11 plugs, and flat gray modular wire are attainable at nearly any hardware or department store.

Flat gray modular wire is not the same as twisted pair and is only suitable for carrying data over short distances. For instance, this type of cable is often used between a PC or workstation and a nearby RJ-11 jack for access to premises wiring systems or LAN backbones. Modular adapters with RJ-11 input jacks mounted

Architectures

Media Type	Also Called	Bandwidth	Distance Limits	Connectors	Comments/Applications	Token Ring	Ethernet	Arcnet	FDDI	CDDI	Price ($)
4-wire phone station wire	Quad RYO-B	3kbps	200 feet	RJ-11 jacks	4 insulated wired—red, green, yellow, black. Home phone wiring. Voice applications						0.09/foot
Flat gray modular	Flat satin, telephone cable, silver satin	14.4 kbps	10–20 feet	RJ-11 or RJ-45 plugs	Comes with 4, 6, 8 conductors. Used for short data cables using modular (mod-tap) adapters						0.09–.18/foot
Unshielded twisted pair, voice grade	UTP	14.4 kbps	100 feet	RJ-45	Twists prevent interference, increase bandwidth. Voice grade usually not suitable for data						0.10/foot
Unshielded twisted pair, data grade	UTP	16 mbps	100 feet	RJ-45 or IBM data connectors	Higher bandwidth than voice-grade UTP	■	■	■		■	0.12/foot
Shielded twisted pair	STP	16 mbps	100 feet	RJ-45 or IBM data connectors	Shielding reduces interference but complicates installation	■	■	■		■	0.42/foot
Coax—thick	Frozen yellow garden hose	10 mbps	500 feet	AUI (attachment unit interface)	Original Ethernet cabling		■				1.10/foot
Coax—thin	RG-58, thinnet, cheapernet	10 mbps	200 feet	BNC connector	Looks like cable TV cable. Easier to work with than thick coax		■				0.32/foot
Coax—thin	RG-62	2.5 mbps	200 feet	BNC or IBM data connector	Similar to RG-58 (thinnet) but different electrical characteristics make these cables NOT interchangeable	■		■			0.32/foot
Fiber-optic cable	Fiber Glass	several gbps	several kilometers	SI or SMA 905 or SMA 906	Difficult to install but technology is improving. High bandwidth, long distance, virtually error free, high security	■	■		■		1.00/foot

Figure 5-23 Media technology analysis grid.

within RS-232 hoods are available to quickly construct data cables of various pin-out configurations without having to crimp RS-232 pins on individual conductors.

Twisted Pair   Twisted pair wiring consists of one or more pairs of insulated copper wire twisted at varying lengths, from two to 12 twists per foot, to reduce interference both between pairs and from outside sources such as electric motors and fluorescent lights. Interference can cause data errors and necessitate retransmission. These individually twisted pairs are then grouped together and covered with a plastic or vinyl covering or jacket. No additional shielding (explained shortly) is added before the pairs are wrapped in the plastic covering. Thus, the completed product is known as *unshielded twisted pair* or UTP. Two, three, four, and 25 pairs of twisted copper wire are the most common numbers of pairs combined to form the unshielded twisted-pair cables.

All UTP is not created equal. One of the common appeals of UTP is that it is often already installed in modern buildings for the purpose of carrying voice conversations through the voice PBX. Most often, when the twisted-pair wiring for the voice PBX was installed, extra pairs were wired to each office location. Some people then jump to the conclusion that they don't need to invest in any new wiring to carry data transmission throughout their buildings, they'll just use the existing extra pairs of unshielded twisted-pair wiring.

The problem lies in the fact that there are five distinct varieties or grades of UTP. Two of the most common are **voice-grade** (also known as level 3 UTP) and **data-grade** (also known as level 4 UTP). Although voice-grade need only carry voice conversations with reasonable clarity, data-grade cable must meet certain predefined electrical characteristics that assure transmission quality and speed. Most 100Mbps high speed LAN standards specify UTP level 5.

Before assuming that the UTP in a building is adequate for data transmission, have its transmission characteristics tested, and assure that these characteristics meet listed data-grade UTP specifications.

STP—Shielded Twisted Pair   These data transmission characteristics, and therefore the data transmission speed, can be improved by adding **shielding** both around each individual pair as well as around the entire group of twisted pairs. This shielding may be a metallic foil or copper braid. The function of the shield is rather simple. It "shields" the individual twisted pairs as well as the entire cable from either EMI (electromagnetic interference) or RFI (radio frequency interference). Installation of shielded twisted pair can be tricky.

Remember that the shielding is metal and is therefore a conductor. Often, the shielding is terminated in a drain wire which must be properly grounded.

The bottom line is that improperly installed shielded twisted-pair wiring, or **STP,** can actually increase rather than decrease interference and data transmission problems. Given these installation difficulties, why would anyone bother with STP? The answer is speed. Transmission speeds of 100Mbps are possible using shielded twisted-pair wiring. However, recent specifications for the **CDDI** (copper distributed data interface) network architecture outline 100 Mbps performance over *data-grade* unshielded twisted pair.

Three Varieties of Coaxial Cable   Coaxial cable, more commonly known as coax or cable TV cable, has specialized insulators and shielding separating two conductors, allowing reliable, high-speed data transmission over relatively long distances. Figure 5-24 illustrates a cross-section of a typical coaxial cable. Coax

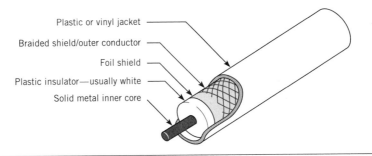

Plastic or vinyl jacket

Braided shield/outer conductor

Foil shield

Plastic insulator—usually white

Solid metal inner core

Figure 5-24 Coax cable: cross-section.

comes in various thicknesses and is used both in Ethernet as well as ARCNET network architectures. In some cases, these network architecture specifications include required characteristics of the (physical layer) coaxial cable over which the (data-link layer) MAC-layer protocol is transmitted.

For instance, Ethernet 10Base2 specifies a coaxial cable commonly known as Thinnet with an industry specification of RG-58, while ARCNET uses a very similar looking, but not interchangeable cable with an industry specification of RG-62. These facts, along with many other performance-related characteristics of various media choices are displayed in the media technology analysis grid (Figure 5-23).

Ethernet 10Base5 specifies coaxial cable called Thick Coax, or more affectionately known as "frozen yellow garden hose," giving a hint as to how easy this media is to work with.

Fiber—The Light of the Future   Coax was at one time the medium of choice for reliable, high-speed data transmission. But times and technology change, and people now often turn to fiber-optic cable when seeking reliable, high-bandwidth media for data transmission. Price is still a factor, however, as one can see from Figure 5-23, fiber-optic cable is still the most expensive medium option available. This expensive medium delivers high bandwidth in the range of several Gigabytes (billions of characters) per second over distances of several kilometers.

Debate in the professional press rages as to the proper application of fiber-optic cable and how much fiber is enough. For instance, should fiber be used only for inter- and intra-building backbones or should fiber be extended to every desktop?

Fiber-optic cable is also one of the most secure of all media as it is relatively untappable, transmitting only pulses of light, unlike all of the aforementioned media, which transmit varying levels of electrical pulses. The presence of a pulse of light is a logical 1 while the absence of a pulse of light is a logical 0. And because fiber optic is really a thin fiber of glass rather than copper, this medium is immune to electromagnetic interference contributing to its high bandwidth and data transmission capabilities. Another important thing to remember is that it is, in fact, glass and requires careful handling. Fiber-optic cable made of plastic is under development, but does not deliver nearly the speed and bandwidth of the glass fiber cable.

Fiber-optic cable comes in a number of varieties. Figure 5-25 illustrates a cross-section of a fiber-optic cable.

Light Transmission Modes   Once a pulse of light enters the core of the fiber-optic cable, it will behave differently depending on the physical characteristics of the core and cladding of the fiber-optic cable.

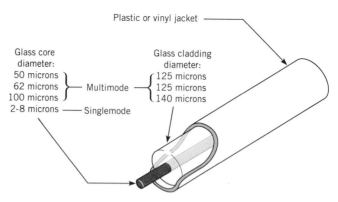

Note: A micron is a millionth of a meter

Figure 5-25 Fiber-optic cable: cross-section.

In a **multimode** or **multimode step index** fiber-optic cable, the rays of light will bounce off the cladding at different angles and continue down the core, while others will be absorbed in the cladding. These multiple rays at varying angles cause distortion and limit the overall transmission capabilities of the fiber. This type of fiber-optic cable is capable of high bandwidth (200 Mbps) transmission, but usually over distances of less than 1 kilometer.

By gradually decreasing a characteristic of the core known as the refractive index from the center to the outer edge, reflected rays are focused along the core more efficiently yielding higher bandwidth (3 GBps) over several kilometers. This type of fiber-optic cable is known as **multimode graded index fiber.**

The third type of fiber-optic cable seeks to focus the rays of light even further, so that only a single wavelength can pass through at a time, in a fiber type known as **single mode.** Without numerous reflections of rays at multiple angles, distortion is eliminated and bandwidth is maximized. Single mode is the most expensive fiber-optic cable, but can be used over the longest distances.

Core Thickness   The thickness of fiber-optic cable's core and cladding is measured in microns (millionths of a meter). The three major core thicknesses are 50, 62, and 100 microns, with their associated claddings being 125, 125, and 140 microns respectively. The increasing core thicknesses generally allow transmission over longer distances at a greater expense, however.

Light-Source Wavelength   The wavelength of the light that is pulsed onto the fiber-optic cable is measured in nanometers (nm), with the optimal light transmitting wavelengths coming in three distinct windows of 820 nm, 1310 nm, and 1500 nm. 820nm and 1310nm are most often used for local and campus-wide networking such as FDDI, while 1310nm and 1500nm are used by carriers to deliver high-bandwidth, fiber-based service over long distances. The higher frequency light emitting sources carry a higher price tag.

One trend seems certain, fiber-optic cable and its associated components continue to drop in price. Combined with a growing demand for increased bandwidth, these trends seem to predict increased deployment of fiber-optic cable in the foreseeable future.

Three Varieties of Wireless Transmission

The final media option to be examined is wireless transmission (which is really the absence of any media) for local area networks. In future chapters, various other wireless technologies for internetworking or wide area networking solutions will be covered.

There are currently three popular wireless transmission technologies in the local area network technology area. They are:

1. Microwave transmission
2. Spread spectrum transmission
3. Infrared transmission

The truth is, these are all just radio transmissions at varying frequencies. These frequencies, along with other comparative technical information are listed in Figure 5-26.

Wireless LAN Applications   Although **wireless LANs** may have been initially marketed as a means of replacing wirebound LANs, that marketing strategy has not been reflected in their applied uses to date. First of all, rather than buying several wireless adapters and setting up an entirely wireless LAN, many users are linking two wire-based LANs via a wireless connection. This application is illustrated in Figure 5-27.

Obviously, fewer wireless adapters get sold this way, which doesn't make the wireless adapter manufacturers very happy. Connecting two LANs in this fashion is really the domain of internetworking, which will be studied further in Chapter 6.

Another application of wireless LANs optimizes the ease of access of the wireless technology. Portable or notebook PCs equipped with their own wireless LAN adapters can create an instant LAN connection merely by getting "within range" of a server based wireless LAN adapter or wireless hub. In this way, a student or employee can sit down anywhere and log into a LAN as long as he/she is within range of the wireless hub and has the proper wireless adapter installed in their portable PC.

Meeting rooms could be equipped with wireless hubs to allow spontaneous workgroups to log into network resources without running cables all over the meeting room. Similarly, by quickly installing wireless hubs and portable PCs with wireless adapters, temporary expansion needs or emergency/disaster recovery situations can be handled quickly and with relative ease. No re-running of wires, or finding the proper cross-connects in the wiring closet.

Finally, wireless LAN technology allows entire LANs to be pre-configured at a central site and shipped "ready to run" to remote sites. The non-technical users at the remote site literally just have to plug the power cords into the electrical outlets and they have an instant LAN. For companies with a great number of remote sites and limited technical staff, such a technology is ideal. No pre-installation site visits are necessary. Also avoided are costs and supervision of building wiring jobs and troubleshooting building wiring problems during and after installation.

Wireless LANs are a relatively new technological phenomena. Although they have been called a technology looking for a market or, perhaps more aptly, a solution looking for a problem, they do offer significant flexibility and spontaneity not possible with traditional wire-bound LANs.

Product Name/ Manufacturer	Supported Network Architecture				Wireless Transmission Technology	Data Throughput	Set-up Restrictions	Network Management	Maximum Distance
	Ethernet	Token Ring	Appletalk	Arcnet					
Altair/Motorola	■				Microwave @18–19 gHz	3.3 mbps	Will not penetrate concrete or steel	Supports SNMP	130 feet
Freeport/ Windata	■				Spread spectrum 902–928 mHz	5.7 mbps			260 feet
InfraLAN/ BICC Communications		■			Infrared 870 nm	4 mbps	Optical transmitters and receivers must be aligned along an unobstructed path		80 feet
Photolink/ Photonics Corporation			■		Reflected infrared 870 nm.	230 kbps	Does not require line-of-sight set up		70 feet
Vistapoint/ Motorola	■						Building to building transmission		500 feet
Easyspan/ Armatek	■	■		■	TDMA microwave 902–928 mHz	2–3 mbps			1 mile
WaveLAN NCR Corporation	■				Spread spectrum 902–928 mHz	2 mbps	Can penetrate concrete but not steel walls		800 feet

Figure 5-26 Wireless LANs technology analysis grid.

What the Manufacturers Pictured   *"Wireless LANs replace wire-bound LANs"*

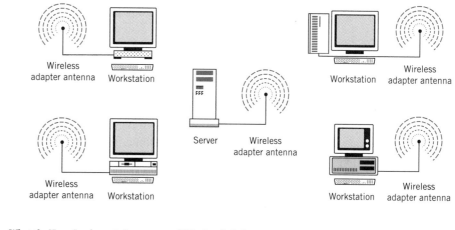

What the Users Implemented   *"Wireless links between LANs"*

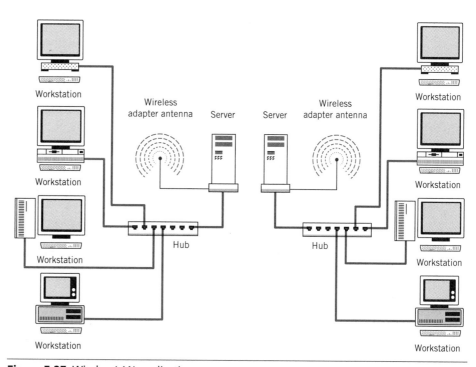

Figure 5-27 Wireless LAN applications.

Wiring System Choices

Faced with the prospect of wiring, or rewiring, an entire building rather than an office, one may wonder where on earth to start. Luckily, several well-structured "building **wiring systems**" have been developed over the past few years. Although these building wiring systems may favor one type of computer or network over another, in general, they are designed to carry voice and data effectively regardless of equipment manufacturer.

Most building wiring systems include **wiring closets** or **satellite equipment**

rooms where office connections are concentrated and cross-connected. These systems most often also include some type of higher capacity transmission medium such as a backbone network between these wiring closets and/or between floors. This system offers a structured, well-documented, and manageable wiring plan rather than a "rat's nest" or "wire jungle."

IBM Wiring System   The IBM wiring system starts by specifying physical and electrical characteristics of the various types of cabling to be used in the IBM wiring system. It goes on to identify all wiring components necessary to transmit data or voice from a user's work area to computers or voice PBXs, including everything from wiring closet equipment to wall plates. Originally designed to provide a network backbone for token ring networks, the IBM wiring system has evolved into a comprehensive building wiring system for the transportation of numerous types of data as well as voice transmission.

DEConnect   Not to be outdone, DEC (Digital Equipment Corporation) announced its building wiring system, DEConnect, at roughly the same time IBM announced its building wiring system. In a similar fashion, DEConnect details and specifies every piece of equipment and type of cable required to transmit data and voice throughout a building in an organized, well-managed, and traceable format.

AT&T Systimax PDS   AT&T Systimax Premises Distribution System (PDS) takes a very organized approach to building wiring by logically dividing the system into three functional subsystems, each with their own specifications:

> Administrative subsystem
> Horizontal subsystem
> Work location subsystem

AT&T uses unshielded twisted pair in combination with fiber optic cabling to provide proper bandwidth requirements at various points in the premises distribution system. A key advantage to this system is that it is not biased toward one type of computer implementation or another. It is designed to carry voice and data as effectively as possible, regardless of equipment manufacturer. Again, all components of each of the three subsystems are specified, assuring interoperability and compatibility.

Standards for Premises Wiring   A standard known as **EIA/TIA 568** (Electronics Industries Association/Telecommunications Industries Association) could have a significant impact on the premises wiring market. For the first time, a *nonproprietary standard* can be adhered to by multiple vendors of various sizes. This is in stark contrast to the prestandard situation in which the market was characterized by competition among just those few companies large enough to set their own proprietary standards through the introduction of their own comprehensive premises wiring systems.

Besides opening up the market to increased competition, the EIA/TIA 568 standard defines key attributes and specifications that are common to most premises wiring systems. For instance, the standard defines the *topology* of compliant premises wiring to be a star physical topology centered in a wiring closet where internetworking devices such as routers and hubs might be housed. *Maximum cable lengths* from both the wiring closet to the jack nearest an end-user's workstation, as well as from that jack to that workstation, are defined as well. To complete the wiring architecture, the *types of cables and associated connectors* to be used to connect workstations to wiring closets are also specified. Finally, *performance specifications* for the particular types of cable and connectors used in any premises wiring architecture are detailed in the EIA/TIA 568 standard.

Independent laboratories will be enabled to certify EIA/TIA 568 compliance, thus assuring end-users installing premises wiring systems. EIA/TIA 568 will no doubt evolve as end-user's premises wiring needs change and the cable and connector technology changes to meet those needs. The importance of this standard lies in its pioneering quality in standardizing an important area of data communications previously dominated by single-vendor, proprietary premises wiring systems solutions.

CHAPTER SUMMARY

Having completed the analysis of the business, application, data, and network layers of the top-down model in Chapter 4, the analysis of the technology layer was undertaken in Chapter 5. There are many different technology choices to be made in completing a physical network design, complicated by the fact that a given choice in one technology decision may influence or limit future choices. For instance, the choice of a particular network architecture, Ethernet for example, can limit choices concerning network adapter cards, media, and wiring centers.

Network architectures such as Ethernet, Token Ring, and FDDI are products of their constituent access methodologies, logical topologies, and physical topologies. Each of the previously mentioned network architectures have both positive and negative attributes and no one network architecture is correct for all networking situations. Network adapter cards are the technological interface between the PC and the network. Specially programmed chips on the adapter card build frames of information to be loaded onto the network media according to a particular format. This format varies according to whether the network adapter card is interfacing to an Ethernet, Token Ring, FDDI, or some other network.

Network operating systems such as NetWare, Vines, and LAN Manager interface to the network adapter cards through specially written software known

as APIs. Best known among these networking APIs is NetBIOS. Network operating systems can vary according to the number of different operating systems such as UNIX, DOS, Windows, and VMS, with which their client and server software can interoperate. Network operating systems can also vary according to the network architectures such as Ethernet, Token Ring, and FDDI, over which they are able to operate.

Most network architectures are capable of running over a variety of media such as unshielded twisted pair, shielded twisted pair, coaxial cable of different types, and fiber optic cable. Wireless local area networks are also available, and are an appropriate choice in some situations. Regardless of the type of media chosen, LAN segments are often concentrated into some type of wiring center known alternatively as hubs, MAUs, concentrators, or switching hubs, depending on the configuration and capabilities of the particular device.

In order to make good choices when it comes to technology, it is essential to concentrate on delivered functionality of devices rather than on descriptive titles or manufacturers' labels. Only by concentrating on device functionality can one be assured that the solutions offered by the physical design of the technology layer will meet or exceed the requirements of the business layer. This assurance is the central premise of the top-down model.

KEY TERMS

access methodologies	baseband transmission	CDDI	data-grade UTP
access rights table	broadcast	communications servers	dedicated servers
active MAU	bus	concentrators	dense switching hubs
API	bus mastering DMA	CSMA/CD	DMA
Appletalk	bus topology	DAS	DMI
ATM	CAUs	data transfer	DOS

drivers	logical topology	physical topology	SNMP
EIA/TIA 568	MAC sublayer	preemptive multitasking	spread spectrum
EISA	MAUs	printer servers	transmission
EMI	MCA	programmed I/O	star topology
Ethernet	microwave transmission	protocol conversion	STP
external adapters	motherboard	protocol stacks	switching hubs
FDDI	multimode graded index	queues	symmetrical
file audit database	multimode step index	redirector	multiprocessing
file servers	multiprotocol computers	repeaters	task switching
HMI	multitasking	RFI	10baseT
hubs	multitasking threads	ring topology	Token Passing
IEEE 802.3	NDIS	SAS	Token Ring
IEEE 802.5	NETBIOS	satellite equipment room	TSR
infrared transmission	network architecture	scalability	UNIX
ISA	network ready servers	sequential	UTP
LAC	NIC	shared memory	voice-grade UTP
LAM	ODI	shielding	wireless LANs
LLC	OS/2	single mode	wiring closets
Localtalk	PCMCIA	SMB	wiring systems

REVIEW QUESTIONS

1. Distinguish between the major types of wiring centers in terms of the following criteria:

   Price range
   Network architectures supported
   Expandability
   Reliability
   Media choices
   Extended communications
   Management and monitoring capabilities

2. What are the three major wireless LAN transmission technologies?

3. Give an example of each major type of wireless LAN. Distinguish between these examples as to:

   Network architectures supported
   Data throughput
   Set-up or transmission restrictions
   Maximum distance

4. What effect does the twisting have in twisted pair?

5. What effect does the shielding have in shielded twisted pair?

6. Why is unshielded twisted pair often favored over the shielded variety?

7. What is a switching hub and how does it improve on network architecture bandwidth limitations?

8. What are the likely future trends of LAN-based wiring centers?

9. Distinguish between the four major types of network adapter to system memory data transfer techniques. Be sure to include the following criteria:

   Effect on system CPU and memory
   Overall efficiency and speed
   Effect on adapter card CPU and memory

10. Roughly how many times more expensive is a Token Ring card than an Ethernet card? an FDDI card than a Token Ring card?

11. How does adhering to the top-down model assure that technology layer choices will meet business layer needs?

12. What are the major categories of LAN technology and what are some of the key interdependencies between them?

13. What are the major differences between peer-to-peer and client-to-server architectures?

14. What is the limitation of DOS concerning acting as both a client and server simultaneously?

15. What is the difference between multitasking, multiprocessing, and multithreaded?

16. What is the difference between task-switching and multitasking?

17. What are the advantages and disadvantages of a dedicated server?

18. What are the three most common types of servers?

19. What is the advantage of installing a dedicated printer server?

20. What functions might a file server fulfill in addition to just managing requests for files from users?

21. How does one know when it's the right time to install a dedicated printer server?

22. What is a network-ready server and what is its cost or business advantage?

23. What is the relationship between network operating systems and operating systems?

24. Which operating systems do popular network operating systems such as Netware, Vines, and LAN Manager run over?

25. Is the operating system necessarily accessible beneath the network operating system? Why or why not?
26. What are some of the key analysis questions regarding choosing an operating system? Explain the implications of each cited question.
27. Why are expanded and extended memory for DOS important to network operating systems?
28. What factors have contributed significantly to the increased capabilities of DOS-based LANs?
29. Explain the functionality of the DOS redirector. What role does it play on the network?
30. Does the redirector converse with any network operating system? Why or why not?
31. What are the positive attributes of OS/2?
32. What are the negative attributes of OS/2?
33. What are the key positive attributes of UNIX?
34. What are the key negative attributes of UNIX?
35. What are the implications of the statement "All UNIX is not created equal"?
36. Why is scalability such an important issue in today's rightsizing frenzy?
37. What is a protocol stack?
38. How can one PC contain multiple protocol stacks?
39. What is an API and what important role does it play?
40. What is NETBIOS and what role does it play?
41. How does a standardized API, such as NETBIOS, make applications program development easier?
42. Explain the interaction between NETBIOS, the redirector, and the server message block server.
43. What are some APIs other than NETBIOS?
44. What is important to remember about network adapter card drivers?
45. What exactly does a network adapter card driver do?
46. What are NDIS and ODI and why are they important?
47. What is an access methodology?
48. What are the differences in performance at low and high traffic levels for CSMA/CD and token passing?
49. Explain why collisions are a nonissue with token passing access methodology.
50. What is the MAC sublayer?
51. What is a MAC-layer protocol?
52. What is a logical topology?
53. What is the difference between a sequential and a broadcast logical topology?
54. What is the difference between a logical and a physical topology?
55. What is the current most popular physical topology and why?
56. Classically, which physical topologies were Ethernet and Token Ring associated with?
57. What were the weaknesses of each of these classic physical topology/network architecture combinations?
58. What are the weak points of a star topology?
59. How have hub and concentrator vendors sought to overcome these weaknesses?
60. What is a MAU?
61. What is the difference between an active MAU and a passive MAU?
62. What is the difference between Appletalk and Localtalk?
63. What is the major shortcoming of Localtalk?
64. How is this shortcoming corrected?
65. What is 10BaseT?
66. What are the IEEE 802 standards?
67. What is baseband transmission?
68. Why is 10BaseT so popular?
69. What are the major positive attributes of FDDI?
70. What are the major negative attributes of FDDI?
71. What is the access methodology, logical topology, and physical topology of FDDI?
72. What is CDDI?
73. What are the positive and negative attributes of CDDI?
74. Is all UTP the same? If not, why not and why is this fact important?
75. What are some of the key differences in characteristics and performance of network adapter cards?
76. What is PCMCIA and why is it important?
77. What are some of the key criteria when performing technology analysis on wiring centers of various types?
78. What is the difference between a MAU and a CAU?
79. Distinguish between the following in terms of physical characteristics and application:

    Four-wire phone wire (RYGB)
    Flat gray satin
    UTP-VG
    UTP-DG
    STP
80. What is the significance of EIA/TIA 568?

ACTIVITIES

1. FDDI consists of two counter-rotating rings. The counter-rotating directions of the primary and secondary rings have to do with insuring reliability in the event of a primary ring failure. Investigate and report on how FDDI responds to a primary ring failure and how counter-rotation of the two rings contributes to this response.
2. Compare the cost and functionality of alternative Ethernet adapters for a notebook or laptop computer. Investigate both external adapters that attach to

the laptop's parallel port as well as PCMCIA adapters. Prepare a graph plotting maximum transmission speed versus cost.

3. Investigate wireless Ethernet adapters that use spread spectrum, microwave, and infrared transmission technology. Prepare a graph plotting maximum transmission speed, maximum transmission distance, and cost per user. Also include these same pieces of information for a "wired" 10BaseT Ethernet workstation.

4. Both Arcnet and Token Ring use a token passing access methodology. However, the actual methodologies are actually quite different. Investigate and report on how the two token passing methodologies differ.

5. Many new high-speed local area networking standards have been recently developed or are in the development stage. Investigate and report on such standards as Fast Ethernet, 100BaseVG, 100VG-AnyLAN, Fibre Channel, Isochronous Ethernet, and other standards you may encounter.

6. Investigate and report on the significant features introduced in DOS Version 6.0. How many of these features were previously available as third-party utilities?

7. Collect articles from trade publications about the current versions of various client operating systems such as DOS, WindowsNT, UNIX, and OS/2. Prepare a scrapbook or bulletin board. Plot the number of articles appearing about each operating system. Which one or two operating systems do you think will dominate the client operating system market?

8. One of the concerns with wireless transmission is security. Investigate how various wireless LANs prevent unauthorized access of data.

9. Arrange for LAN managers familiar with NetWare, Vines, LAN Manager, and WindowsNT to provide guest lectures to your class. What are the strengths and weaknesses of each network operating system?

10. Collect pieces of as many of the media types listed in Figure 5-23 as possible. Prepare a display including sources of the media, current costs, applications, etc.

Featured References

Adapter Cards

Derfler, Frank. "Ethernet Adapters: Fast and Efficient," *PC Magazine*, vol. 12, no. 3 (February 9, 1993), p. 191.

Tolly, Kevin. "Token Ring Adapters Evaluated for the Enterprise", *Data Communications*, vol. 22, no. 3 (February 1993), p.73.

Derfler, Frank and David Greenfield. "Token Ring Adapters for the PC," *PC Magazine*, vol. 11, no. 17 (October 13, 1992), p. 333.

Apple

Sidhu, Andrews, and Oppenheimer. *Inside Appletalk*, 2nd ed. (Addison Wesley, 1990).

Day, Michael. "Apple's UNIX: A Solid Technical Marvel," *LAN Times*, vol. 8, no. 7 (April 1, 1991), p.73.

Germann, Christopher. "System 7: Look Under the Hood", *LAN Times*, vol. 9, no. 13 (July 20, 1992), p. 43.

Case Studies

Maloy, A. Cory. "Wordperfect Publishing Team Clears Networking Hurdles," *LAN Times*, vol. 9. no. 3 (February 24, 1992), p. 23.

Hubs/Concentrators/MAUs/Wiring Centers

Tolly, Kevin. "Evaluating Port Switching Hubs," *Data Communications*, vol. 22, no. 9 (June 1993), p. 52.

Bowden, Eric, and Eric Harper. "Product Comparison: Intelligent Network Hubs," *LAN Times*, vol. 9, no. 16 (August 24, 1992), p. 59.

Greenfield, David. "Empire Builders: 6 Enterprise Hubs," *PC Magazine*, vol. 11, no. 19 (November 10, 1992), p. 291.

Rigney, Steve. "Wiring Hubs: The Low Cost Alternative," *PC Magazine*, vol. 11, no. 19 (November 10, 1992), p. 335.

Barrett, Ed. "The Critical Steps to Hub Selection," *LAN Technology*, vol. 8, no. 11 (October 15, 1992), p. 39.

McHale, John. "The Hub of the Future," *LAN Technology*, vol. 8, no. 11 (October 15, 1992), p. 23.

McCusker, Tom. "Here's an Ethernet That's Always a 10" (switching hubs), *Datamation*, vol. 38, no. 20 (October 1, 1992), p. 73.

Salamone, Salvatore. "Buyers Guide: The Hubbub about Hubs," *Network World*, vol. 9, no. 22 (June 1, 1992), p. 47.

Network Architectures

Sunshine, Carl (ed.). *Computer Network Architectures and Protocols*, 2nd ed. (Plenum Press, 1989).

Tanenbaum, Andrew. *Computer Networks*, 2nd ed. (Prentice-Hall, 1988).

Ethernet

Metcalf, Robert, and D. R. Boggs. "Ethernet: Distributed Packet Switching for Local Computer Networks," *Communications of the ACM*, vol. 19, no. 7 (July 1976).

Kine, Bill. "Understanding the Requirements of 10Base-T," *LAN Times*, vol. 9, no. 8 (May 11, 1992), p. 27.

Token Ring

Greenfield, David. "Token Ring Closes in on Ethernet," *Data Communications*, vol. 21 no. 2 (January 21 1992), p. 47.

Jander, Mary. "Token Ring Strategy: Exceed IBM's

Specs," *Data Communications*, vol. 21, no. 8 (May 21, 1992), p. 49.

Strole, N.C. "The IBM Token Ring Network—A Functional Overview," *IEEE Network*, vol. 1, no. 1 (January 1987).

FDDI/CDDI

Ross, F.E. "FDDI—A Tutorial," *IEEE Communications*, vol. 24, no. 5 (May 1986).

Jain, Raj. "FDDI: Current Issues and Future Plans," *IEEE Communications*, vol. 31, no. 9 (September 1993), p. 98.

Hurwicz, Mike. "LAN Buyers Guide: FDDI," *Network World*, vol. 9, no. 50 (December 14, 1992), p. 49.

Network Operating Systems/APIs

Brandel, William. "Banyan Beats Novell to the Punch ," *LAN Times*, vol. 9, no. 15 (August 10, 1992), p. 1.

Alumbaugh, Wendell. "The Netbios Programming Interface for UNIX," *LAN Times*, vol. 8, no. 11 (June 3, 1991), p. 45.

Operating Systems

Day, Michael. "UNIX, DOS, OS/2, Which One for You?" *LAN Times*, vol. 8, no. 19 (October 7, 1991), p. 144.

Livingston, Dennis. "UNIX Emerges as Unexpected Network Treasure," *Network World*, vol. 9, no. 30 (July 27, 1992), p. 33.

Premises Wiring

Saunders, Stephen. "Premises Wiring Gets the Standard Treatment," *Data Communications*, vol. 21, no. 18 (November 1992), p. 105.

Servers/Bus

Derfler, Frank. "Network Printing: Sharing the Wealth," *PC Magazine*, vol. 12, no. 2 (January 26, 1993), p. 249.

Layland, Robin. "The Superbox: A Cure for This Old LAN," *Data Communications*, vol. 21, no. 12 (September 1992), p. 103.

Lapinig, Arnie. "Special Report: LAN Print Servers," *LAN Times*, vol. 8, no. 4 (February 18, 1991), p. 48.

Derfler, Frank. "486/33 File Servers," *PC Magazine*, vol. 11, no. 5 (March 17, 1992), p. 187.

Chang, Arthur and James Wall. "Making Important Bus Architecture Decisions," *LAN Times*, vol. 8, no. 13 (July 8, 1991), p. 33.

Wireless LANs

Berline, Gary, and Ed Perratore. "Portable, Affordable, Secure: Wireless LANs," *PC Magazine*, vol. 11, no. 3 (February 12, 1992), p. 291.

Gilbert, Barry. "To Cable or Not? Wireless LANs Enter the Marketplace," *LAN Times*, vol. 9, no. 5 (March 23, 1992), p. 37.

Saunders, Stephen. "Wireless LANs: Closer to Cutting the Cord," *Data Communications*, vol. 22, no. 5 (March 21, 1993), p. 59.

Mathias, Craig. "Wireless LANs: The Next Wave," *Data Communications*, vol. 21, no. 5 (March 21, 1992), p. 83.

C A S E   S T U D Y

WordPerfect Publishing Team Clears Networking Hurdles

Many publishers now believe the Macintosh computer can lower publishing costs through electronic pagination, a process which eliminates the high cost of stripping, color separation, paste-up, camera work, and imaging.

The Macintosh has proved its superiority to other computer systems in the publishing field, mostly because it lets users write, create graphics, and design publications quickly and easily. But LocalTalk, the Mac's built-in networking scheme, is a long way from giving publishers the network efficiency they need to deal with the large graphics files desktop publishing requires. Networks bog down, and the printers don't have the resolution or the speed necessary to handle the load.

One company, however, WordPerfect Publishing Corp., in Orem, Utah (sister company to WordPerfect Corp.), has worked out most of the networking hurdles it faced during its switch to electronic pagination of *WordPerfect The Magazine* and its 2 other publications, *WordPerfect for Windows Magazine* and *The Journal for Air Medical Transport*.

The high-gloss, 4-color *WordPerfect The Magazine* has 250,000 subscribers and has produced its second completely paginated issue using Quark-XPress. The project owes its success to the work of Mike Whitehead, senior technical designer, and his 5- person design team. Whitehead created a simple, workable network that solved the team's most difficult problem: outputting many full-color, fully separated, fully paginated pages to negative film from the desktop.

Whitehead said he doesn't want to waste valuable design time constantly fighting the network. Instead, he wants his network to work completely in the background. "If I can get the network to just work, it becomes one less problem to have to worry about," he said. "Hey, that makes me happy."

The company's full-color photos and drawings, scanned on Agfa's ACS100 color scanner, can be 10- to 20MB in size and sometimes bigger. The January 1992 cover alone took up 75MB. Such large files are extremely difficult, if not impossible, to work with on a LocalTalk network, and can even slow down an active Ethernet network.

There were 4 basic problems Whitehead faced when working with such large files: they bogged down the network transmission speed; they slowed down the Mac operations; they slowed down output processing and imaging time; and they required large amounts of memory.

To speed up the network, Whitehead first upgraded the Macintoshes from LocalTalk to Ethernet. By installing Dayna Communications' DaynaPORT E/II-T 10Base-T Ethernet boards in the Macintoshes, Whitehead was able to use the twisted-pair phone wiring he already had in place and benefit from Ethernet's high bandwidth.

The team connected the Macs using the phone wiring already in the walls to a SynOptics LattisNet Model 2800 12-port hub in the phone closet. Then the hub was connected to a fiber-optic backbone in order to access a file server in another building, Whitehead said.

Next, Whitehead and his team had to solve 2 problems associated with the LocalTalk laser printers and imagesetters. They had to find a way to attach the devices to the Ethernet network, and find ways to speed up the printer processing and imaging time.

Whitehead had 4 LocalTalk printers he needed to attach to the network: an Apple LaserWriter II, an Okidata 840 laser printer, a Tektronic Phaser III color printer, and an Agfa Proset 9400 imagesetter with a 9000 PS RIP. To attach the printers to the network, Whitehead purchased 3 EtherPrint-T connectors from Dayna. EtherPrint is an EtherTalk-to-LocalTalk protocol converter that enabled Whitehead to make a direct connection to the Ethernet network from the LocalTalk printers. EtherPrint proved to be an inexpensive, but effective, alternative for connecting the printers to the network.

"We were using a $2,000 Fast-Path 4 to convert our printers to Ethernet," Whitehead said. "That's expensive and complex to set up. The EtherPrint was simply plug-and-play and a fourth of the cost."

To connect the Apple Laser-Writer II to the network, Whitehead upgraded the motherboard to a LaserWriter IIg with built-in Ethernet, giving him direct Ethernet connectivity and PostScript Level II.

To free up the workstations faster from printing, Whitehead set up a print queue on the server. He also set up one Macintosh to be a "print slave" used only for printing. This enabled him to print jobs to the queue from the slave while having no wait time on his design terminals.

Whitehead then needed to find a faster way to output his pages. The printers currently on line were used for proofing the job as the magazine was designed. The Agfa Proset 9400 imagesetter, though considered a reliable "workhorse-of-a-backup," was not fast enough, nor did it provide the registration for the quality of work needed and expected. The imaging time of the 9400 was slow and subsequently affected the entire system. In addition, it could not process the next page or separation while it imaged the page preceding it. It was used only as a backup and

for outputting on positive paper rather than negative film.

To solve this problem, Whitehead turned again to Agfa. He purchased an Agfa Proset 9800 imagesetter with Agfa's new Star Plus SX RIP. The SX has 32MB of RAM and a 650MB hard disk to go along with its MIPS R-3000 RISC processor and a MIPS R-3010 coprocessor. It utilizes Adobe's Emerald technology and Agfa's Balanced Screening technology for high-resolution capabilities. It has AppleTalk, Ethernet, Centronics, and RS232-C/422-C serial input interfaces.

Under the new system, each document is queued to the server. From the server, the print job goes to the hard disk on the SX RIP via fiber-optic cable. With the document completely copied to the RIP, the network is freed, causing less network congestion and slowdown. The RIP then processes the document and begins imaging it on the 9800. While one page is imaging, the next is being processed.

The 32MB cache on the RIP lets the imager work constantly with no waiting. "I've had up to 50 jobs queued up," Whitehead said. "I just let it run itself."

Whitehead said the 75MB January front cover took only 15 minutes to output all 4 separations. Another project, a 22-page product directory, contained 300 full-color photos. The entire project was 900MB in size and was printed all at once. Imaging at 2,400 dots per inch (dpi) and 150 lines per inch (lpi), the job took 82 feet of film and 8 hours to output. That's only 1.6 minutes per photo—creating all 4 separations.

"Doing it [the product directory] ourselves in-house saved us about $20,000 just in separation costs," Whitehead said. "It took us about 2 days to scan all of the photos and about one day to lay out the directory, then 8 hours to output. It was a simple layout, but if we would have sent the job out-of-house to get separated, the separations would have taken a week or longer to complete, and would have to go back if there were any corrections to be made."

Whitehead plans to upgrade the Agfa Proset 9800 to a SelectSet 7000, which will give even faster imaging times and the ability to impose many pages on the film.

The next challenge facing WordPerfect Publishing was data volume control. Whitehead estimates that each issue took about 1.2- to 1.8GB of storage space. The network's NetWare 3.11 server has one 3GB hard drive with a second 3GB mirroring hard drive. Each of the network's 6 Macintosh workstations have 412MB of hard disk space using NuPort Card drives, and 32MB of RAM. Each issue is archived on 5GB DG90M tapes with MicroNet tape backup.

The Macintosh Quadra 900 graphics terminal has two 412MB arrayed hard drives and 128MB of RAM. Connected to the Quadra by SCSI interface is an Agfa ACS100 32-bit color scanner, which allows full-color images to be scanned at up to 3200dpi.

"We plan to add another 64MB RAM card to increase our usable RAM to 192MB," said Gary Whitehead, a design assistant. "Having all this RAM allows me to scan and manipulate the color photos in RAM instead of having to access the hard disk. The 2 arrayed hard disks are fast, but working in RAM is a lot faster. [Adobe] PhotoShop has a feature that lets me work in RAM."

Whitehead has designed a network that isn't a technology break-

through, but one that is virtually trouble free and saves money. According to Whitehead, he has spent about $250,000 on the system. However, by paginating, the bottom line is a cost savings of $15,000 to $20,000 per issue over conventional methods. In a year's time, Whitehead estimates the savings will more than pay for the cost of the system.

He also has "jumped feet first" into an efficient networking solution. Finally, he has worked closely with vendors, both to do beta testing and to stay abreast of the latest software and hardware.

"We're always upgrading and changing to make the system better," he said.

Source: "WordPerfect Publishing Team Clears Networking Hurdles," *LAN Times,* vol. 9, no. 3 (February 24, 1992), p. 23. Reprinted with permission of McGraw-Hill, *LAN Times.*

Business Case Study Questions

Activities

1. Prepare a top-down model for this business case by gleaning all pertinent facts from the case and placing them in their proper layer within the top-down model.
2. Specific financial information related to the payback period on technology investment is given in this case. Compute the payback period based on the information and plot this information on a graph.

Business

1. What specific operational problems prompted the investigation for a networking solution?
2. Find a quote that typifies the business perspective of the role played by the network in this case.
3. Exactly what business activities were being accomplished in this case?
4. What opportunities for increases in productivity had been identified?

Application

1. What were the major applications that users executed in this case?
2. What problems, if any, were they having with these applications?
3. On what platform or workstation were these applications being executed?
4. What were some of the printer related problems with these user applications?

Data

1. How large might the typical files in this case be?
2. What are the geographic issues related to data distribution in this case?
3. How can the data be archived effectively?

Network

1. How many different network architectures are involved in this case? What are they?
2. Were upgrades conducted? If so, how?
3. What was the network operating system(s) in this case?
4. What were the functional requirements of the networking layer in this case?

Technology

1. What role did the hub play in this case?
2. Were any protocol converters required in this case? Explain.
3. What equipment other than "typical" servers, printers, and workstations was also attached to the network? How was this equipment used?
4. Did the installed technology deliver on the outlined business requirements? Defend your answer.
5. Were multiple types of media used? How and where were each used?

CHAPTER · 6

Connecting LANs: Internetworking

Concepts Reinforced

Top-Down Model
Local Area Network Logical Design
Local Area Network Physical Design

Extended Communications
OS I 7-Layer Model

Concepts Introduced

LAN Dial-in/Dial-out Access
Micro–Mainframe Connectivity
LAN-to-LAN Connectivity
TCP/IP and the Internet Suite of
    Protocols
Role of the OS I 7-Layer Model
    in Internetworking

SNA and APPN
DECnet
UNIX/LAN Integration
Macintosh Integration
Internetworking Design

OBJECTIVES

After mastering the material in this chapter, you should:

1. Understand the rationale, methodology, technology, and business analysis for standalone PCs accessing a LAN remotely for either use of LAN services or LAN management purposes.

2. Understand the rationale, methodology, technology, and business analysis for standalone PCs accessing a mainframe remotely.

3. Understand the rationale, methodology, technology, and business analysis for connecting two or more local area networks.

4. Understand the additional consequences, advantages, and limitations involved when connecting LANS of differing topologies, network operating systems, media, or protocols.

5. Understand how micro–mainframe PC connectivity solutions may vary in different technological environments such as Apple Macintosh, Digital's DECnet, and IBM's SNA.

6. Understand the major characteristics of IBM SNA and the direction of the architecture in terms of its integration with the local area networking environment.

7. Understand the current state of internetworking technology as well as future trends in internetworking and the forces affecting those trends.

8. Understand the importance of the OSI 7-layer reference model to effective internetworking analysis and design.

☐ INTRODUCTION

Having fully analyzed the logical and physical design of local area networks as well as the necessary technology to implement these networks, the many possibilities for transmission of data *into* and *out of* a local area network will now be explored. This area of networking is commonly known as **internetworking**.

Several times in the study of local area network design the topic of internetworking was mentioned. For instance, a key differentiating criterion among network operating systems is the sophistication of their extended communications, or internetworking, capabilities. Second, as the features of intelligent hubs were investigated, it was revealed that modular or integral internetworking devices such as bridges and routers are often built into these "superhubs."

In this chapter, the various categories of internetworking will be first established and then investigated. The following five major categories of internetworking have been identified and will each be addressed in a separate section of the chapter:

1. Dialing into and out of a LAN
2. LAN-to-LAN connections
3. Micro-to-mainframe/minicomputer connectivity
4. Integration with UNIX workstations
5. Integration with Macintosh workstations

Subsequently, for each category of internetworking identified above, the following will be analyzed:

a. The business motivation for internetworking
b. The internetworking design methodology
c. The logical internetworking solution
d. The currently available internetworking technology to be employed in the implementation of this logical internetworking solution

In order to better understand the internetworking category commonly known as micro-to-mainframe connectivity, the IBM mainframe environment and its **SNA** (systems network architecture) network will be investigated in respect to how PCs and LANs can be integrated into this mainframe environment.

Likewise, **DECNET** and the **DNA** (digital network architecture) network architecture will be explored before investigating the integration of PCs and LANs into this popular Ethernet-based networking architecture.

The integration of Macintosh computers into various LANs as well as connectivity to the SNA and DECNET environments will also be examined.

Although every possible internetworking opportunity that may ever be encountered cannot be examined, an internetworking design methodology will be stressed which should continue to serve the reader well as internetworking needs and technology continue to evolve.

As internetworking design solutions and technology are explored in this chapter, the need to integrate these designs with wide area networking services and technology will often be encountered. Although mentioned briefly in this chapter, the majority of the study of Wide Area Networking Analysis and Design will be reserved for Chapters 7 and 8.

It is the author's opinion that no area of data communications is more challenging or full of opportunity than internetworking. In order to take advantage of this opportunity, one must be equipped with both a structured approach to internetworking problem solving as well as a knowledge of currently available internetworking technology. This chapter seeks to offer both of these requirements for success.

☐ INTERNETWORKING CATEGORY 1: DIALING INTO AND OUT OF THE LAN

As information has come to be seen as a corporate asset to be leveraged to competitive advantage, the delivery of that information to users working at remote locations has become a key internetworking challenge.

Business Uses of Remote Computing

The business motivation for remote access to local LAN resources falls into about three general categories. The first category of remote LAN access is often referred to as **telecommuting**, or more simply, working from home with all the information resources of the office LAN at one's fingertips.

A variation of telecommuting, **mobile computing**, addresses the need for field representatives to be able to access corporate information resources in order to offer superior customer service while working "on the road." These field reps may or may not have a corporate office PC into which to dial.

The third major use of remote computing is for *technical support* organizations that must be able to dial-in to client systems with the ability to appear as a local workstation, or take control of those workstations, in order to diagnose and correct problems remotely.

LAN Dial-in/Dial-out Design Methodology

There are basically only four steps to designing a dial-in/dial-out capability for a local LAN:

1. Needs analysis
2. Physical topology choice
3. Logical topology choice
4. Current technology review and implementation

Each of these four steps will be briefly introduced below. A more detailed explanation of the implications and interactions of these choices in various dial-in/dial-out implementation scenarios will round out the remainder of this section of the chapter.

Needs Analysis: What Do We Want to Do Once We're Connected?

The information sharing needs of remote users can be summarized as follows:

1. Exchange E-mail
2. Upload and download files
3. Run interactive application programs remotely
4. Utilize LAN attached resources

The purpose in examining information sharing needs in this manner is to validate the need for the remote PC user to establish a connection to the local LAN that offers *all* of the capabilities of locally attached PCs.

In other words, if the ability to upload and download files is the extent of the remote PC user's information sharing needs, then *file transfer software*, as reviewed in Chapter 4, will suffice at a very reasonable cost.

Likewise, if E-mail exchange is the total information sharing requirement, then *E-mail gateway software* (explained in a later chapter) loaded on the LAN will meet that requirement.

However, in order to run LAN-based interactive application programs or utilize LAN-attached resources—such as high-speed printers, CD-ROMs, mainframe connections, or FAX servers—a full-powered remote connection to the local LAN must be established. From the remote user's standpoint, this connection must offer *transparency*. In other words, the remote PC should behave as if it was connected locally to the LAN. From the LAN's perspective, the remote user's PC should *virtually* behave as if it was locally attached.

In order to provide this transparent, virtual connection, the following is required:

1. Decide how to physically connect the remote PC to the LAN.
2. Decide how the connected remote PC is to interact with the LAN.
3. Combine elements of hardware and software technology in order to implement the connection.

Physical Topology

Access Points: Where does a Remote User Gain LAN Access? As Figure 6-1 illustrates, there are three basic ways in which a remote PC user can gain access to the local LAN resources:

1. Serial port of a LAN-attached PC
2. Communications server
3. LAN modem

It is important to understand that the actual implementation of each of these LAN access arrangements may require additional hardware and/or software. They may also be limited in their ability to utilize all LAN attached resources, or to dial *out* of the LAN through the same access point. These alternative implementations will be explored in detail shortly.

Logical Topology

Remote Operation Mode: Where Does the Processing Occur? A second variable of remote connectivity to LANs that will be investigated further is that of the operation mode chosen by the remote PC. In other words, once the remote PC is attached to the local LAN through one of the aforementioned access points, how does the remote PC *interact* with the local LAN? This operation mode choice is independent of the LAN access point chosen as outlined above. The two major remote PC operation mode possibilities are:

1. Remote client operation mode
2. Modem remote control operation mode

Figure 6-2 outlines some of the details, features, and requirements of these two remote PC modes of operation. Each of these operations modes is not necessarily possible in each of the access point arrangements and may require additional hardware or software.

Technology

Current Technology Review and Implementation The hardware and software technology involved with remote PC access to LANs can be summarized as follows:

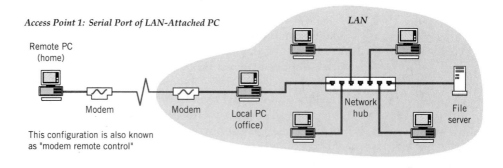

Access Point 1: Serial Port of LAN-Attached PC

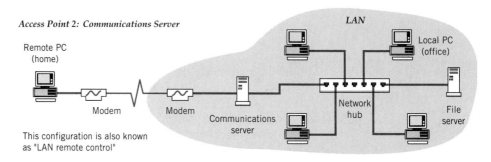

Access Point 2: Communications Server

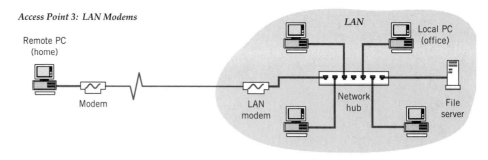

Access Point 3: LAN Modems

Figure 6-1 Remote LAN connectivity: Three primary access points.

Hardware	Software
Modems	Remote control software
Communications servers	Comm server software
LAN modems	Redirector software
Redirector hardware	

How these hardware and software elements are combined to form networking solutions which meet identified remote PC user's information sharing needs will be the topic of the next several sections of this chapter.

☐ ACCESS POINT 1: REMOTE PC TO LOCAL LAN-ATTACHED PC

Diagram 1 in Figure 6-1 portrays a remote PC attached to a local LAN-attached PC via modems over a dial-up line. Modems and their comparative features and operational characteristics have already been reviewed thoroughly in Chapter 3.

Characteristic	Remote Client Operation Mode	Modem Remote Control Operation Mode
Is redirector hardware and / or software required?	Yes	No
Where do the applications actually execute?	On the remote PC	On the local LAN-attached PC or communications server
What is the nature of the data traffic over the dial-up line?	All interaction between the LAN server and remote PC travels over the dial-up link	Only keystrokes from the remote PC keyboard and output for the remote PC monitor travel over the dial-up link
Network interface:	Actually using the remote PC's serial port and modem as a substitute NIC. This option provides a very low speed interface	Uses installed NIC on local LAN attached PC or communication server to interface to the LAN at a very high speed
Relative performance	Slower than modem remote control operation mode with substantially more traffic, depending whether application programs are stored remotely or on the LAN	Faster than remote client mode; generates substantially less traffic
Also called:	Remote LAN node LAN remote control	

Figure 6-2 Remote LAN connectivity: remote PC operations mode.

Therefore, the only new element to this implementation is the **remote control software**.

This software, specially designed to allow remote PCs to "take-over" control of local PCs, should not be confused with the asynchronous communications software reviewed in Chapter 3. Remote control software allows the keyboard of the remote PC to control the actions of the local PC with screen output being reflected on the remote PC's screen.

Remote Control Software

Modem operation, file transfer, scripting languages, and terminal emulation are the primary features of asynchronous communications software. Taking over remote control of the local PC is generally available only via remote control software. The terms remote and local are often replaced by *guest* (remote) and *host* (local), when referring to remote control software.

Operating remote control software requires installation of software programs on both the guest and host PCs. Remote control software does not interoperate. The same brand of remote control software must be installed on both guest and host PCs. Be sure that both pieces (guest and host) are included in the software package price. Remote control software must have modem operation, file transfer, scripting language, and terminal emulation capabilities similar to those of asynchronous communications software. However, in addition, remote control software should possess features to address the following situations unique to its role:

1. Avoid lockups of host PCs.
2. Allow the guest PC to disable the keyboard and monitor of the host PC.
3. Additional security precautions to prevent unauthorized access.
4. Virus detection software.

Additionally, Windows-based applications pose a substantial challenge for remote control software. The busy screens of this graphical user interface can really bog down, even with V.32 or V.32bis modems. Some remote control software vendors have implemented proprietary Windows screen transfer utilities, which allow Windows-based applications to run on the guest PC as if they were sitting in front of the host PC, while others do not support Windows applications remotely at all.

Figure 6-3 summarizes the important features of remote control software as well as their potential implications. Among the most popular remote control software packages are:

Software	Vendor
CO/Session	Triton Technologies
PCAnywhere	Symantec/Peter Norton
Close Up	Norton/Lambert
Carbon Copy for Windows	Microcom

Prices range from $129 to $295, with most in the $195-to-$199 category.

Utilizing LAN-Attached Resources

In order for the guest (remote) PC to utilize LAN resources such as a file server, database server, or printer, that PC must log on to the network. How this connection is physically made is illustrated in Figure 6-4.

As can be seen in Figure 6-4, first the guest PC gains remote control of the host

Characteristic/Feature	Options/Implications
Memory requirements	Remember: This software must be installed on both the guest (remote) as well as the host (local) PCs. Can the software be loaded into expanded memory?
Modem support and file transfer support terminal emulation	These issues were covered in Chapter 3, discussion of communications software (see Figures 3-13 and 3-14).
Host reboot on remote hangup	In this way, you can get a fresh start from the remote PC if the local/host PC should hang.
Log-off after inactivity timeout; remote log-in restrictions	These can be real money-savers if the call is a long-distance one.
Scripting languages	See implications in Chapter 3
Host keyboard disabling and monitor blanking from guest PC	If I am working from home and logged into my office PC, I want to prevent: a. Anyone seeing what programs I am running via my office PC monitor (monitor blanking) b. Anyone from hitting a key on my office PC keyboard and interrupting program execution (keyboard locking).
Security	Similar to communications software criteria in Chapter 3. Look for callback capabilities, user IDs and passwords, access restriction by drive, directory or file, user notification of remote access attempts, call logging, and data encryption.
Windows support	How are Windows applications supported? Are full bit-mapped screens transmitted, or only the changes? Proprietary coded transmissions?
Printer support	Can I print on printers attached to the host (office/local) PC? Can I print on networked printers?
Network operating systems supported	It is really the transport protocol of the network operating system we are worried about: IPX—Netware; also NETBIOS—LAN Manager, IP, NETBEUI, AppleTalk.
LAN versions available	A special version of the software may be required to install it on a communications server/access server instead of a LAN attached PC

Figure 6-3 Remote control software.

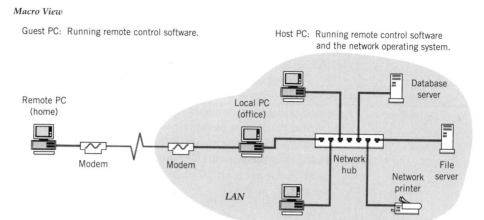

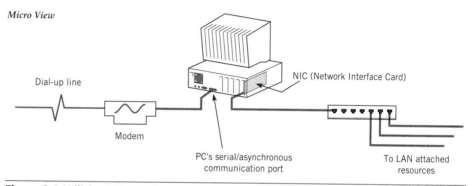

Figure 6-4 Utilizing LAN-attached resources.

PC by using the remote control software installed on each PC. Transmission between the guest and host PCs is via modems and a dial-up line with entry into the host PC through its serial port.

In order to access the network resources, the guest PC transparently logs into the network through the host PC. Communication between the host PC and network is via the network interface card installed in the host PC and connected to the network hub. After successfully logging into the network, the guest PC really employs the host PC as both a processor and as a sort of bridge. The host PC runs the application program as well as receiving data from the guest through its serial port, passing it along the bus to the network adapter card and out onto the network media to the network hub and beyond.

The data communications network illustrated in Figure 6-4 is sometimes called **modem remote control,** because the remote control software is loaded onto a single LAN-attached PC and accessed via a single modem attached to that PC. This set-up might represent a person communicating between their PC at home and their PC at their office. Figure 6-1, diagram 1, is an example of modem remote control.

☐ ACCESS POINT 2: COMMUNICATIONS SERVERS

But what if this businessperson does not have a dedicated PC at the corporate office, but still needs access to the corporate network and its attached resources? In a setup known as **LAN remote control,** or **remote client operation mode,** remote users attach to a dedicated shared PC, known as an **access server** or **communications server,** through one or more modems. In this case, the remote control software is loaded on the LAN-attached access server for all to share, rather than on the LAN-attached personal PC workstation as in the previous example.

The remote control software loaded onto the communications server is not the same as the remote control software loaded onto a remote PC as in the previous example. Communications servers' remote control software has the ability to handle multiple users, and in some cases, multiple protocols. Because of this, it is considerably more expensive than the single PC variety. Prices for this **remote LAN node** setup range from $795 for 2 users to $6850 for 16 users. Examples are Remote LAN Node from Digital Communications Associates and Close Up/LAN from Norton/Lambert.

Figure 6-1, diagram 2, is an example of LAN remote control. In fact, Figure 6-1, diagram 2, actually depicts two different possible remote LAN connections. Most communications servers answer the modem, validate the user ID and password, and log the remote user onto the *network.* Some communications servers go beyond this to allow a remote user to access and remotely control a *particular networked workstation.* This scenario offers the same access capabilities as if the networked workstation had its own modem and software, (as in Figure 6-1, diagram 1), but also offers the centralized management, security, and possible financial gain of a communications server.

☐ ACCESS POINT 3: LAN MODEM OR DIAL-IN SERVER

Another alternative is to install a specialized device known as a **LAN modem,** also known as a **dial-in server,** to offer shared remote access to LAN resources. LAN modems come with all necessary software preinstalled and, therefore, do not require additional remote control software. LAN modems are often limited to a single network architecture such as Ethernet or Token Ring, and/or to a single network operating system protocol such as IP, IPX (Netware), NetBIOS, NetBEUI, or AppleTalk.

Examples of LAN modem of dial-in servers include:

LAN Modem	Manufacturer	Protocols
Gatorlink	Cayman	Appletalk
LANRover/E	Shiva	Ethernet, Netware, Appletalk
NetBlazer	Telebit	IP

A LAN modem installation is illustrated in Figure 6-1, diagram 3. LAN modem comparative features are reviewed in Figure 6-10.

Communications Servers: Centralized Access, Processing and Control

As is often the case in the wonderful but confusing world of data communications, **communications servers** are also known by many other names. In some cases these names may imply, but don't guarantee, variations in configuration, operation, or application. Among these varied labels for the communications server are:

Access servers
Telecommuting servers
Network resource servers
Modem servers (usually dial-out)
Asynchronous communications servers

Communications Server's Role in the LAN

What is the role of the communications server in a LAN?

What is the cost justification for acquiring a communications server at a cost of between $12,000 and $21,000?

These are a few of the questions to be answered before exploring currently available technology and server configuration.

A communications server offers both management advantages as well as financial payback when large numbers of users wish to gain remote access to/from a LAN. Figure 6-5 illustrates two scenarios: one with a communications server installed, and one without. Cost categories are identified. Because of variances in modem features/prices and dial-up line charges, these costs could be filled in with realistic figures for a particular business situation.

Besides the cost savings of a reduced number of modems, phone lines, and software licenses, perhaps more important are the gains in control over the remote access to the LAN and its attached resources. By monitoring the use of the phone lines connected to the communications server, it is easier to determine exactly how many phone lines are required to service those users requiring remote LAN access.

16-User LAN without a Communications Server

Management

Users are free to use whichever remote control software they wish

No central control over network access and security

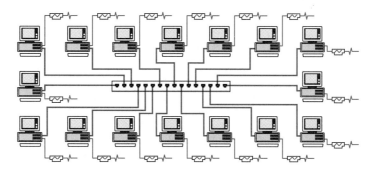

Costs

16 remote control software licenses

32 modems (one at each end of every line)

16 business lines which will incur:
    1. installation
    2. monthly flat charges
    3. long-distance charges

16-User LAN with a Communications Server

The big decision is how many modems/phone lines will be required to service 16 users–in other words, how many *simultaneous* data transmissions are likely to occur?

Management

Remote control software choice controlled by LAN administrator

All remote access traffic is subject to security and monitoring by LAN administrator

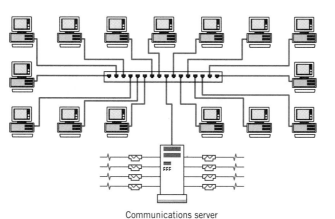

Communications server

Costs

1 remote control software network license

16 modems (one at each end of every line leaving the communications server)

8 business lines which will incur:
    1. installation
    2. monthly flat charges
    3. long-distance charges

Figure 6-5 Why bother with a communications server?

Multiple remote users can dial into a communications server simultaneously. Exactly how many users can gain simultaneous access will vary with the sophistication and cost of the communications server. Most communications servers service at least four simultaneous users. Recalling the remote PC-to-LAN-attached PC connection, the communications server must supply two key components:

1. CPU for processing requested applications
2. Access to the network and shared network resources

An I-P-O (input-processing-output) diagram for a communications server is illustrated in Figure 6-6.

Communications Server Configurations   As can be seen in Figure 6-6, the key hardware components of the communications server are:

Serial ports
CPU(s)
Network interface card(s)

The relative number of each of these three components included in a particular communications server is a key differentiating factor in communications server architectures or configurations.

Figure 6-7 summarizes the most popular communications server configurations.

As can be seen in Figure 6-7, the major categorization has to do with the number of system CPUs in the communications server. These major categories are known as *multitasking* (single CPU) and *multiprocessing* (multiple CPUs). A variation on the simple multitasking configuration is the addition of a **multiport serial board** with on-board CPU to handle the data I/O (Input/Output) to and from the serial ports, allowing the system CPU to concentrate on processing applications.

Whereas Figure 6-7 outlined the comparative features of the various communications server configurations, Figure 6-8 attempts to illustrate graphically how these configurations might be physically implemented.

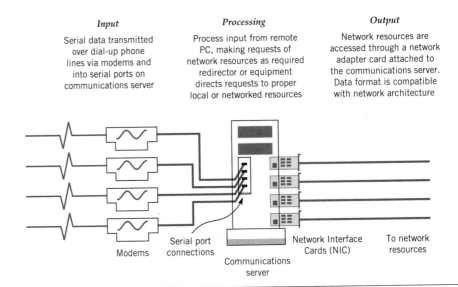

Input

Serial data transmitted over dial-up phone lines via modems and into serial ports on communications server

Processing

Process input from remote PC, making requests of network resources as required redirector or equipment directs requests to proper local or networked resources

Output

Network resources are accessed through a network adapter card attached to the communications server. Data format is compatible with network architecture

Modems   Serial port connections   Communications server   Network Interface Cards (NIC)   To network resources

Figure 6-6 I-P-O diagram for a communications server.

Configuration Name	Number of Relative Serial Ports	Number of Relative CPUs	Number of Relative NICs	Advantages/Disadvantages/Comments
Multitasking (also called Shared CPU)	Many	1	1	Requires 386 or 486 CPU. Advantage: lower cost. Disadvantage: two potential bottlenecks with 4 or more users—1. Single CPU trying to control multiple serial ports with high-speed modems; 2. Multiple processing—intensive application sessions will bog down the CPU. Not all application programs execute predictably in multitasking environment. Runs host portion of remote control software
Router-based Configuration (also called Multiple CPUs, Standard Bus)	Many	Many *one-to-one ratio*	1	Special software required (included) to mediate between the multiple CPUs for access to the single network interface card. Multiple CPUs improve processing performance. Single LAN adapter card must be shared. Each CPU runs host portion of remote control software
Independent Processor Configuration (also called Multiple CPUs, Custom Bus)	Many	Many *one-to-one ratio*	Many	Dedicated network adapter card for each CPU assures clear sailing to network resources. No special software necessary to share NIC. Each CPU runs the host portion of the remote control software
Multiport Serial Boards (also called asynchronous Redirectors)	Many	1	1	Example: Digiboard for Novell accesses server and Novell Asynchronous Communications Server software. Major difference with "plain" multitasking configuration: dedicated CPU on-board the multiport serial board handles all I/O to/from the serial ports and relieves the system CPU of this responsibility

Figure 6-7 Communication server considerations.

Communications Servers Comparative Features

In order to choose a communications server effectively, one must look beyond the previously mentioned configurations and architectures to the operational features of the communications server.

Compatibility with Network Operating System   Perhaps the most important operational feature to be scrutinized is the compatibility of the communications server with the installed network operating system. Don't assume the two will be compatible. Nearly all communications servers are compatible with Netware, but be aware of compatibility in respect to the particular versions of Netware installed. Fewer communications servers are compatible with NetBIOS networks such as LAN Manager and Lantastic.

NOS Access Server Software: Guaranteed Compatibility   One way to assure compatibility between the network operating system and the remote con-

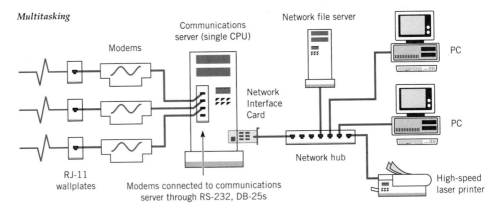

Multitasking

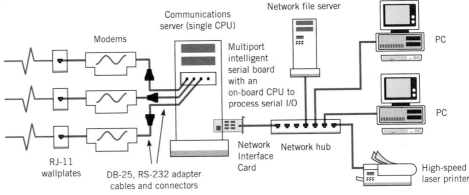

Multitasking with Multiport Intelligent Serial Board

Figure 6-8 Communications server architectures. (Figure 6-8 continues on next page)

trol software that runs on the communications server is to purchase that communications server hardware and/or remote control software from the network operating system manufacturer. For instance, Novell distributes Netware Access Server: a four-port communications server card and remote control software. Other multiport serial boards such as those manufactured by Digiboard can be substituted for the Novell card. Likewise, LAN Manager distributes remote access software which allows remote users to log into a LAN Manager network.

Management and Error Handling Capabilities   Once the compatibility issues are settled, it is desirable for the communications server to run reliably. Management features such as fault location and isolation, usage statistics gathering, and user ID and privilege management are key to smooth operations. Likewise, error or exception handling capabilities such as automatic rebooting of CPUs on hang-up, and prevention of access to that rebooting CPU via busy signal generation, are important.

The ability of certain communications servers to notify managers of problems or suspicious activities is a welcome added feature. These features along with several others are summarized in Figure 6-9.

Multiprocessing with Independent Processors

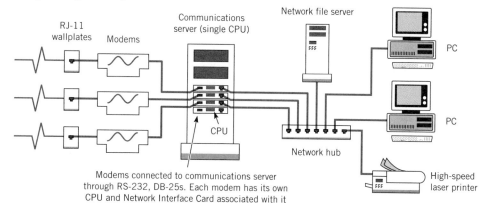

Modems connected to communications server
through RS-232, DB-25s. Each modem has its own
CPU and Network Interface Card associated with it

Multiprocessing, Router Based

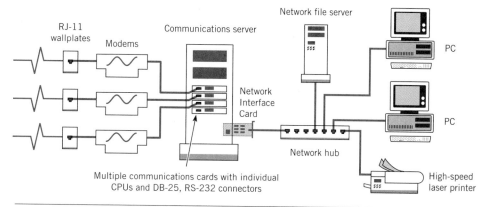

Multiple communications cards with individual
CPUs and DB-25, RS-232 connectors

(Figure 6-8 continued from previous page)

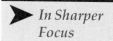

DIALING OUT FROM THE LAN

Some communications servers also manage dialing out from the LAN and sharing a pool of modems among the numerous LAN workstations. Communications servers dedicated to this dial-out task are known as **modem servers.**

Dialing out from a LAN can be more complicated than dialing into one. As can be seen in Figure 6-8, the modems are attached to the communications servers, not to the networked workstations. Most asynchronous communications software (reviewed in Chapter 3) expects a modem to be installed internally or attached directly to the serial port of the PC on which the software is installed.

Since this is not the case with a networked PC, the communications with the modem must be *redirected*. Rather than talking to the modem via the local *serial port*, the data transmission must be redirected out the local **network interface card** through the network media to the communications server and subsequently out to a modem attached to the communications server.

This *redirector* for dialing out from LANs may be either hardware or software based. Several of the communications packages reviewed in articles cited in Chapter 3 support network use. Be sure to inquire specifically whether they sup-

Features/Characteristics	Options/Implications
Capacity	How many in-coming phone lines can the communication server process simultaneously? Is this number expandable?
Management/error prevention	Location and isolation of problems? Detect and notify manager of locked CPUs? Usage statistics collected? Automatically reboot CPUs on hang-up? Prevent access to CPUs while rebooting? Can multiple CPUs be controlled/managed from a single point? Can a busy signal be generated while the CPU is rebooting?
Security	Are there user IDs with privilege restrictions? Are passwords available? Is a dial-back capacity available?
Other	Can Macintoshes and dumb (ASCII) terminals log in? Are there redundant power supplies? Are cards "hot-swappable"? Does this communications server require installation of Novell BRGEN (bridging software) in order to operate? Which network operating systems are supported?
Advanced functions	Can the communications server also manage dialing-out from the LAN (function as a modem server)? Can the communications server perform advanced internetworking tasks (i.e., bridge, router, protocol converter . . .)?

Figure 6-9 Comparative communications server features.

port networked *dial-out* use before purchase. Procomm Plus Network and Crosstalk MK.4 are two such programs.

Advanced Communications Server Capabilities

Data communications users often demand an "all-in-one" solution. Therefore, data communications manufacturers implement Goldman's modularity of design scheme and package several devices into a communications server. For instance, some communications servers can also include internetworking devices such as bridges, routers, or gateways. Wide area links to x.25 packet switching networks and T-1 (1.544 Mbps) high-speed digital transmission circuits are also possible. These wide area networking topics will be discussed in Chapters 7 and 8.

LAN Modems: No PC Required

A fairly new approach to remote LAN connectivity is illustrated in Figure 6-1, diagram 3, the *LAN modem*. A LAN modem, also occasionally known as a dial-up server, could be thought of as a modem with a network adapter card or alternatively as a standalone communications server. Included security and management software is installed on the LAN modem. Two examples of LAN modems are LANMODEM from Microtest and Shiva Corporation's NetModem/E. The features of these two LAN modems are compared in Figure 6-10.

As can be seen from the chart, LAN modems can offer a great deal of sophistication for about one-tenth the price of a communications server. The key difference is that some LAN modems are *shared single-user devices,* while other more expensive models can handle multiple simultaneous users. They are an ideal data communications solution for those situations in which many networked users need infrequent or occasional dial-in or dial-out access. LAN modems often work with

Features	LANmodem	Netmodem/E
Manufacturer	Microtest	Shiva
List price	Ethernet—$1995 Token Ring—$2595	Ethernet—$1699
Network architectures	Ethernet ArcNet Token Ring—4 mbps Token Ring—16 mbps	Ethernet only
Network operating systems	Netware	Netware Appletalk
Remote client operating systems	DOS	DOS Windows Macintosh
Dial-out?	Yes	Yes
Act as a router?	Yes	Yes
Serial port for connection of second modem?	Yes	No
Interfaces	Ethernet: thick coax thin coax 10BaseT Token Ring: type 1 STP Arcnet: RG62 coax	Ethernet: thick coax thin coax 10BaseT
Modem standards	v.32 bis with v.42 bis data compression	v.32 bis with v.42 bis data compression

Other features to consider:

Callback capability
Utilization statistics, call records kept
Are special modems required at the remote PC?
Is more than one simultaneous connection possible?
Have proprietary data transfer techniques to speed transmission of Netware facilities been installed?
Can all Netware security information be automatically loaded into the LAN modem?
What must the networked PCs install for the communication software to dial out?
Are dial-out redirectors supported?

Figure 6-10 LAN modems comparative features.

only a particular network operating system. For example, the two LAN modems compared in Figure 6-10 work *only* with Netware LANs. The routing capability of the LAN modem to transparently connect two Netware LANs will be discussed in more detail in the next section of this chapter. ◀

☐ INTERNETWORKING CATEGORY 2: LAN-TO-LAN CONNECTIONS

Now that dialing into and out of a LAN by a single workstation has been explored, LAN-to-LAN connectivity will be investigated. The key to LAN-to-LAN connectivity is that to the end-user sitting at a LAN-attached workstation, that connectivity should be completely *transparent*.

In other words, an end-user should not need to know the physical location of a database server or disk drive that they need access. All the user needs to know is a node name or drive indicator letter (A:, C:, H:, etc.), and the fact that when these node name or drive letters are entered, data is properly accessed from wherever it may be physically located. That physical location may be across the room or across the country.

As information has become increasingly recognized as a corporate asset to be leveraged to competitive advantage, the delivery of that information in the right form, to the right person, at the right place and time has become the goal of information systems and the role of internetworking.

Mergers, acquisitions, and enterprise partnerships have accelerated the need to share information seamlessly across *geographic* or *physical* LAN boundaries. Intelligent *inter-LAN* devices perform the task of keeping track of what network attached resources are located where, and how to get a packet of data from one LAN to another.

This task is further complicated by the fact that LANS can differ in any of the following categories:

Network architecture
Media
Network operating system
Operating system

This collection of differences is defined by rules or **protocols.** When LANs that need to share information operate according to different protocols, an inter-LAN device with **protocol conversion** capabilities must be employed. In cases such as this, the inter-LAN device transmits data across *logical,* as opposed to physical or geographic, boundaries.

Among the inter-LAN devices to be explored in this section are:

Repeaters
Bridges
Routers
Brouters
Gateways

Once again, although the capabilities of these devices will be distinguished from a technical stand-point, there is no guarantee that manufacturers will follow this differentiation. Don't purchase inter-LAN devices according to what they are called—purchase them according to what they do. Functional analysis of data communications devices is the best way to assure that purchased inter-LAN devices will meet LAN-to-LAN connectivity needs.

The OSI Model and Internetworking Devices

The OSI model was first introduced in Chapter 1 as a common framework or reference model within which protocols and networking systems could be developed with some assurance of interoperability. In this chapter, the OSI model provides a most effective framework in which to distinguish between the operational characteristics of the previously mentioned internetworking devices. Figure 6-11 depicts the relationship between each type of internetworking device and its related OSI layer. Each device, as well as the related OSI model layer, will be explained in detail.

Repeaters: Layer 1—The Physical Layer

Remember that all data traffic on a LAN is in a digital format of discrete voltages of discrete duration traveling over one type of *physical* media or another. Given this, a **repeater**'s job is fairly simple to understand:

1. To *repeat* the digital signal by regenerating, retiming, and amplifying the incoming signal.

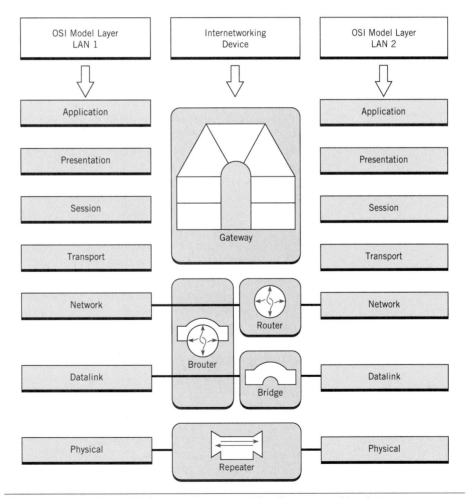

Figure 6-11 The relationship between the OSI model and internetworking devices.

2. To *pass all* signals between all attached segments.
3. To *not* read destination addresses of data packets.
4. To allow for the connection of *different types of media*.
5. To *extend* overall LAN distance effectively by *repeating* signals between LAN segments.

A repeater is a nondiscriminatory internetworking device. It does not discriminate between data packets. Every signal that comes into one side of a repeater gets regenerated and sent out the other side. Repeaters are available for both Ethernet and Token Ring network architectures for a wide variety of media types. A repeater is a *physical layer device* concerned with physical layer signalling protocols relating to signal voltage levels and timing. The primary reasons for employing a repeater are to:

1. Increase the overall length of the network media by repeating signals across multiple LAN segments. In a Token Ring LAN, several MAUs can be linked together by repeaters in order to increase the size of the LAN.
2. Isolate key network resources onto different LAN segments.

Figure 6-12 represents a simple illustration of repeater installation and functionality.

Bridges: Layer 2—The Data Link Layer

Functionality   When users on one LAN need occasional access to data or resources from another LAN, an internetworking device which is more sophisticated and discriminating than a repeater is required. From a comparative outlook on the functionality of **bridges** versus repeaters, one could say that bridges are more discriminating.

Rather than merely transferring *all data* between LANs or LAN segments like a repeater, a bridge reads the **destination address** of each data frame on a LAN, decides whether the destination is local or remote (on the other side of the bridge), and only allows those data frames with nonlocal destination addresses to cross the bridge to the remote LAN.

How does the bridge know whether a destination is local or not? Data-link protocols such as Ethernet contain **source addresses** as well as the destination addresses, mentioned in the previous paragraph, within the predefined Ethernet Frame layout. A bridge also checks the source address of each frame it receives and adds that source address to a table of **known local nodes**. After each destination address is read, it is compared with the contents of the known local nodes table in order to determine whether the frame should be allowed to cross the bridge or not (whether the destination is local or not). Bridges are sometimes known as **"forward-if-not-local"** devices.

This reading, processing, and discriminating indicates a higher level of sophistication of the bridge, afforded by installed software, and also implies a higher price tag than repeaters. (repeaters: $1000 and up; bridges: $4000 and up).

Categorization   Bridges come in many varieties. Physically, bridges may be cards that can be plugged into an expansion slot of a PC, or they may be standalone devices. In terms of bridge capabilities and performance, in order to decide which variety of bridge is correct for a given situation, it is easiest to employ the I-P-O or input-processing-output model.

Although it is known that the bridge will do the internetwork processing between two LANs, the exact nature of that processing, as well as the bridge's input and output interfaces, will be determined by the characteristics of the two

Installation — Ethernet Fiber-Optic Multiport Repeater

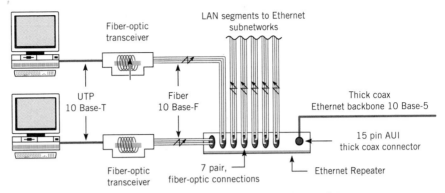

Repeaters can support multiple media types

Functionality

Installation — Token Ring

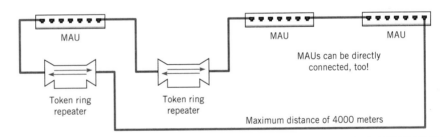

Figure 6-12 Repeater installation and functionality.

LANs that the bridge is internetworking. Figure 6-13 outlines the LAN attributes that should be considered when determining required bridge characteristics.

In determining the attributes of the input and output bridge, one must consider the following issues.

MAC Sublayer Protocol: Types of Bridges

1. Transparent bridges
2. Translating bridges
3. Encapsulating bridges
4. Source routing bridges

First and foremost, are the two LANs to be bridged Ethernet or Token Ring? You may have heard that bridges only connect LANs of similar MAC sublayer protocols (Ethernet to Ethernet or Token Ring to Token Ring). Bridges that connect

MAC Sublayer protocol	Ethernet to Ethernet	Token Ring to Token Ring			Ethernet to Token Ring	
Speed of LANs	10 Mbps to 10 Mbps	4 Mbps to 4 Mbps	16 Mbps to 16 Mbps	4 Mbps to 16 Mbps	10 Mbps to 4 Mbps	10 Mbps to 16 Mbps
Proximity of LANs	Local				Remote	
Wide Area Bandwidth requirements			T1	DS-0 64K	DDS leased-line 19.2K,56K	X.25 packet network
Media	Thin coax, thick coax, UTP, STP, fiber					

Figure 6-13 Bridge categorization: What are we bridging?

Bridge Type	LAN Segments Linked
Transparent	Ethernet to Ethernet Nonsource routing Token Ring to nonsource routing Token Ring
Translating	Ethernet to Token Ring and vice-versa
Encapsulating	Ethernet to FDDI and vice-versa
Source Routing	Source routing Token Ring to source routing Token Ring
Source Routing Transparent	Source routing Token Ring to Ethernet and vice-versa
Adaptive Source Routing Transparent	Ethernet to Ethernet Source routing Token Ring to source routing Token Ring Source routing Token Ring to Ethernet and vice-versa

Figure 6-14 Bridges link LAN segments.

LANs of similar data link formats are known as **transparent bridges.** The truth is that a special type of bridge, which includes a **format converter,** can bridge Ethernet and Token Ring. These special bridges may also be called *multiprotocol bridges* or **translating bridges.**

A third type of bridge, somewhat like a translating bridge, is used to bridge Ethernet and FDDI networks. Unlike the translating bridge, which must actually manipulate the data link layer message before repackaging it, the **encapsulating bridge** merely takes the entire Ethernet data link layer message and stuffs it in an "envelope" (data frame), which conforms to the FDDI data link layer protocol.

Source routing bridges are specifically designed for connecting Token Ring LANs. Bridges that can support links between source routing Token Ring LANs and nonsource routing LANs, such as Ethernet, are known as **source routing transparent bridges**. Finally, bridges that can link transparent bridged Ethernet LAN segments to each other, source routing token ring LAN segments to each other, or any combination of the two, are known as **adaptive source routing transparent bridges.** Figure 6-14 outlines these various bridge possibilities.

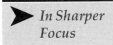
In Sharper Focus

SOURCE ROUTING

Source routing bridges are not considered routers because the capture of the routing information which delineates the chosen path to the destination address is done by the source device, usually a LAN-attached PC, and not by the bridge. The PC sends out a special **explorer packet,** which determines one or multiple paths to the intended destination of its data message. After storing this path in memory for possible future use, the PC sends the data message along with the path instructions to the local bridge which forwards the data message according to the received path instructions.

Data messages arrive at a source routing bridge with a detailed map of how they plan to reach their destination. As will be seen in the next section, when data messages arrive at a router, they ask the router for suggested directions to their intended destination address.

One very important limitation of source routing bridges as applied to large internetworks is known as the **seven-hop limit.** Because of the limited space in the **RIF** (router information field) of the explorer packet, only seven hop locations can be included in the path to any remote destination. As a result, routers with larger routing table capacity are often employed for these larger internetworks.

◄

Speed of LANs Ethernet is a 10Mbps LAN, while Token Ring comes in two varieties, 4Mbps and 16Mbps. The speeds of the input and output LANs must be known in order to determine what speed conversion, if any, must be performed by the bridge.

Local or Remote Having determined the MAC-layer protocol and speed of the LANs, their geographic proximity to one another must be taken into consideration. If the two LANs are not in close enough proximity to link via traditional LAN media such as UTP, coax, or fiber, the bridge must be equipped with an interface appropriate for linking wide area carrier services.

Wide Area Service and Media For example, **local bridges** have output connections for UTP (RJ-45), coax (BNC or AUI), or fiber (ST or SMA), while **remote bridges** usually have a DB-25 for connection to a CSU/DSU which interface to the high-speed data circuit (T-1: 1.544Mbps, DS-0:64Kbps, DDS: 56Kbps). Perhaps more importantly, *two remote bridges* are required to internetwork remote LANs, while only one bridge is required to internetwork local LANs. Figure 6-15 illustrates the differences in installation between local and remote bridges.

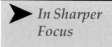
In Sharper Focus

DATA STORMS

When installing multiple bridges in a complex internetworking arrangement, a looping topology could be accidentally introduced into the internetwork architecture. These loops can be added inadvertently by end-users who install their own modems as well. In Figure 6-15, the thin Ethernet LAN segment is connected to the 10BaseT Ethernet hub via a local bridge. Unbeknownst to the network manager, two end users install a dial-up modem link creating a loop between the two LAN segments. What can result is known as a **data storm** in which data packets can circulate endlessly between LAN segments degrading overall LAN performance.

In order to prevent this, an algorithm known as the **spanning tree algorithm (IEEE 802.1)** can sense multiple paths and disable one. In addition, should the primary path between two LANs become disabled, the spanning tree algorithm can reenable the previously disabled redundant link, thereby preserving the inter-LAN link. This algorithm is built into the bridge software and is a feature worth looking for.

◄

Bridge Performance Bridge performance is generally measured by two criteria:

1. *Filtering rate:* Measured in packets/second or frames/second. When a bridge reads the destination address on an Ethernet frame or Token Ring packet and decides whether or not that packet should be allowed access to the internetwork through the bridge, that process is known as **filtering.** Filtering rates for bridges range from 7000 to 60,000 frames per second.

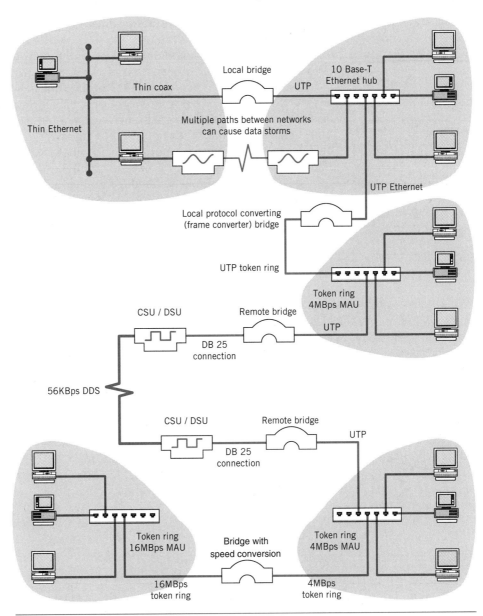

Figure 6-15 Local and remote bridge installation.

2. *Forwarding rate:* Also measured in packets/second or frames/second. Having decided whether or not to grant a packet access to the internetwork in the filtering process, the bridge now must perform a separate operation of **forwarding** the packet onto the internetwork media, whether local or remote. Forwarding rates range from as little as 700 packets per second for some remote bridges to as much as 30,000 packets per second for RISC-based high-speed local bridges.

Bridges, Protocols, and the OSI Model Bridges read the destination addresses within data frames of a predefined structure or protocol. In other words, Ethernet and Token Ring network architectures define a bit-by-bit protocol for formation of data frames. The bridge can rely on this protocol and therefore knows just where to look within the Ethernet data frames to find the bits which represent the destination addresses.

In terms of the OSI model, Ethernet and Token Ring are considered MAC (media access control) sublayer protocols. Remember that the MAC sublayer is one of two sublayers of OSI model layer 2—the data link layer. The other data link sublayer is known as the logical link control sublayer. Because the protocols that a bridge reads and processes are located on the MAC sublayer, bridges are sometimes referred to as MAC-layer bridges. Remember, in this case, MAC stands for media access control and has nothing to do with Macintosh computers. Figure 6-16 illustrates an Ethernet frame format and highlights the fields read by a bridge.

As Figure 6-16 indicates, embedded within the data field of the Ethernet frame are all of the higher OSI layer protocols. These higher layer protocols can vary independently of the data link layer Ethernet protocol. In other words, the *data link* layer protocols such as Ethernet and Token Ring are *network architectures,* whereas the *network layer* protocols could be from any one of a number of different *network operating systems*. Bridges only pay attention to network architecture (MAC sublayer) protocols or formats. They completely ignore upper level protocols. Figure 6-17 illustrates this important distinction.

Most network operating systems actually consist of stacks of protocols. In some cases, this *protocol stack* may consist of a separate protocol for each of layers 3–7. Each protocol of a network operating system performs a different networking-

Preamble Address	Destination Address	Source Address	Type	Data	32 bit CRC
64 bits	6 bytes	6 bytes	2 bytes	46 to 1500 bytes	4 bytes

Area Read by Bridge

Preamble	Used for timing and synchronization.
Destination Address	If the destination address is not local, the bridge will forward the data frame across the internetwork link.
Source Address	Used by the bridge to build its "known local nodes" table, which is used to determine whether or not individual data frames should be allowed across the bridge.
Type	The type field identifies which network layer protocol is contained in the data field. This information is particularly important to routers that process network layer protocols.
Data	This contains all embedded data packets from higher level protocol layers.
CRC	Cyclic Redundancy Check (also known as a frame check sequence). Used primarily for error detection.

Figure 6-16 Ethernet frame format.

related function corresponding to the generalized functional definition for the corresponding layer of the OSI model.

As an example, in Figure 6-17, the network layer protocol for TCP/IP networking operating system for UNIX is known as **IP**, an acronym for *internet protocol*. On the other hand, the network layer protocol of Novell Netware is known as **IPX**, which stands for *internet packet exchange*. Each of these protocols work equally well over Ethernet, a data link protocol. Frankly, Ethernet couldn't care less which network layer protocol is embedded in the data field of its data-link layer frame.

The Network Layer

Either of these two network layer protocols, IP or IPX, perform the basic functional definition of layer 3, the network layer of the OSI model. The responsibility of the network layer is to establish, maintain, and terminate the link between two points (nodes, stations) on a network. These source and destination addresses may be on the same LAN or they may be located on networks across the world from each other.

Routers: The Network Layer Processors

The delivery of data packets to destination addresses across multiple LANs and perhaps over wide area network links, is the responsibility of a class of internetworking devices known as **routers.**

Functionality   Although they both examine and forward data packets, routers and bridges differ significantly in two key functional areas.

First, although a bridge reads the destination address of every data packet on the LAN to which it is attached, a router only examines those data packets specifically addressed to it.

Secondly, rather than just merely allowing the data packet access to the internetwork in a manner similar to a bridge, a router is both more cautious as well as more helpful. Before indiscriminately forwarding a data packet, a router first confirms the existence of the destination address as well as the latest information on available network "paths" to reach that destination.

Next, based on the latest traffic conditions, the router chooses the best path for the data packet to reach its destination and sends the data packet on its way. The word "best" is a relative term, controlled by a number of different parameters to be examined shortly.

The router itself is a destination address, available to receive, examine, and forward data packets from anywhere on any network to which it is either directly or indirectly internetworked.

How do data packets arrive at a router? The destination address on an Ethernet or Token Ring packet must be the address of the router which will handle further internetwork forwarding. Thus, a router is *addressed* in the data-link layer destination address field. The router then discards this MAC sublayer "envelope," which contained its address, and proceeds to read the contents of the data field of the Ethernet or Token Ring frame.

Just as in the case of the data-link layer protocols, network layer protocols dictate a bit-by-bit data frame structure which the router understands. What looked like just "data" and was ignored by the data link layer internetworking device, the bridge, is "unwrapped" by the router and examined thoroughly in order to determine further processing. Figure 6-18 illustrates how network layer protocols are embedded within a data-link layer protocol "envelope."

Internetworking Device	OSI Model Layer	OSI Model Sublayer	Network Component	Examples	OSI Layer Function
Gateway	Application (layer 7)		The rest of the Network Operating System	TCP/IP or Internet Suite of Protocols	
Gateway	Presentation (layer 6)				
Gateway	Session (layer 5)				
Gateway	Transport (layer 4)				
Router	Network (layer 3)		Network Operating System, Network Layer Protocol	Internet Protocol (IP) / Internet Packet Exchange (IPX)	Establishes, maintains, and terminates connections between computers across a network. Destination address processing and routing take place here.
Bridge	Data Link (layer 2)	Logical Link Control / Media Access Control	Network Architecture	Ethernet IEEE 802.3 / Token Ring IEEE 802.5	Assures reliability of the physical link by providing error detection and control, so that the network layer can assume error-free transmission.
Repeater	Physical (layer 1)				

Figure 6-17 Data link versus network layer protocol.

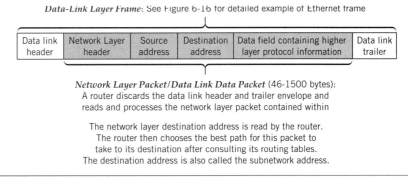

Figure 6-18 Network layer protocol in a data-link envelope.

After reading the network layer destination address and the protocol of the network layer data, the router consults its **routing tables** in order to determine the best path on which to forward this data packet. Having found the best path, the router has the ability to repackage the data packet as required for the delivery route (best path) it has chosen.

As an example, if a packet-switched data network (X.25) was chosen as the wide area link for delivery, then the local router would **encapsulate** the data packet in an X.25 compliant envelope. On the other hand, if the best path was over a local Ethernet connection, the local router would put the data packet back into a fresh Ethernet envelope and send it on its way. This is not unlike the generally followed mailing rules such as addressing envelopes in compliance with Postal Service regulations.

Unlike the bridge, which merely allows access to the internetwork (forward-if-not-local logic), the router specifically addresses the data packet to a distant router. However, before a router actually releases a data packet onto the internetwork, it confirms the existence of the destination address to which this data packet is bound. Only once the router is satisfied with both the viability of the destination address as well as with the quality of the intended path, will it release the carefully packaged data packet. This meticulous processing activity on the part of the router is known as **forward-if-proven-remote** logic.

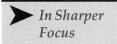

In Sharper Focus

DETERMINATION OF THE BEST PATH

The best path can take into account variables such as:

1. Number of intermediate hops; that is, how many other routers will the packet have to be processed by before it reaches its final destination? Every router takes time to process the data packet. Therefore, the fewer routers, the faster the overall delivery.
2. The speed or condition of the communications circuits. Routers can dynamically maintain their routing tables keeping up-to-the-minute information on network traffic conditions.
3. The protocol of the network operating system; for instance, remembering that multiple protocols can be "sealed" within Ethernet "envelopes." We may ask the router to open the Ethernet envelopes and forward all Netware (IPX) traffic to one network and all TCP/IP (IP) or Appletalk (AFP) to another. In some cases, a certain protocol may require "priority" handling.

Routers are made to read specific network layer protocols in order to maximize filtering and forwarding rates. If a router only has to route one type of network protocol, then it knows exactly where to look for destination addresses every time and can process packets much faster. However, realizing that different network layer protocols will have different packet structures with the destination addresses of various lengths and positions, some more sophisticated routers known as **multiprotocol routers** have the capability to interpret, process, and forward data packets of multiple protocols.

In the case of an Ethernet data link frame, the multiprotocol router knows which network layer protocol is contained within from the TYPE field in the Ethernet frame. (See Figure 6-16.)

Some common network layer protocols and their associated network operating systems or upper layer protocols are listed below:

Network Layer Protocol	Network Operating System or Protocol Stack Name
IPX	Netware
IP	TCP/IP
VIP	Vines
AFP	Appletalk
XNS	3Com
OSI	Open Systems

Other protocols which are actually data-link control protocols processed by some routers:

LAT	Digital DecNet
SNA/SDLC	IBM SNA
Netbios	DOS-Based LANs

Advanced Functionality Has Its Price

All of this processing obviously takes the router, and especially multiprotocol routers, a fair amount of time. In general, bridges, while less sophisticated, perform at two or three times the rate (measured in packets per second) of routers. As a general rule, not surprisingly, routers cost two to three times the price of bridges. Understand, however, that nearly any level of required performance can be delivered for a price. For instance, Wellfleet manufactures routers with forwarding rates of 480,000 pps.

Processing is only one of the performance issues related to routers. As has been mentioned, routers use constantly updated tables to keep up-to-the-minute information as to the best path available to reach other routers. This current information is obtained by transmitting and processing **discovery packets** or **request packets,** which help determine the best route to any distant router.

The best route information may include number of "hops" as well as time between hops, which would take into account the bandwidth of the connecting circuits. This building and maintaining of the routing information tables not only means more processing for the routers, but more traffic for the network as well.

Routing Protocols

Routers manufactured by different vendors need a way to talk to each other in order to exchange the previously mentioned discovery information concerning current network conditions. Every protocol stack mentioned above which has a need to have data processed by routers, contains an associated **routing protocol** as part of its protocol stack. Figure 6-19 lists common routing protocols and their associated protocol suites.

RIP, *routing information protocol,* at one time the most popular router protocol standard, is largely being replaced by **OSPF**, *open shortest path first.* OSPF offers several advantages over RIP including its handling of larger internetworks as well as a smaller impact on network traffic for routing table updates.

A major distinction between routing protocols has to do with the method or algorithm by which routing information is gathered by the router. For instance, RIP uses a **distance vector** algorithm, which only measures the number of hops to a distant router, to a maximum of 16, while the OSPF protocol uses a more comprehensive **link state** algorithm, which can decide between multiple paths to a given router based on variables other than number of hops, such as delay, capacity, throughput, and reliability of the circuits connecting the routers. Perhaps more importantly, OSPF uses much less bandwidth in its efforts to keep routing tables up to date.

Point-to-point protocol (**PPP**) provides a fully defined standard for routing serial data over wide area network links. PPP is associated with the internet suite of protocols (TCP/IP) and replaces the **SLIP** *(serial line internet protocol).* The significance of this protocol lies in the independence and transparency it offers in three key areas:

1. Type of wide area link
2. Type of network architecture
3. Type of network-layer protocol

To elaborate, PPP will allow the accomplishment of the most common internetworking requirements, namely:

1. Exchange electronic mail
2. Access and/or transfer remote files
3. Access remote networked resources such as printers
4. Log-in and execute applications programs on remote computers

Most significantly, PPP will allow the accomplishment of the previously mentioned activities in any combination of the following possibilities:

1. Type of wide area link: dial-up lines or leased lines up to T/1 (1.544Mbps) or T/3 (approx. 45Mbps) capacity

Routing Protocol Acronym	Routing Protocol Name	Associated Protocol Suite(s)
RIP	Routing Information Protocol	XNS, IPX(Netware), TCP/IP
OSPF	Open Shortest Path First	TCP/IP
IS-IS	Intermediate System to Intermediate System	DECNET, OSI
RTMP	Routing Table Maintenance Protocol	AppleTalk
PPP	Point-to-Point Protocol	New Internet standard supported by most router and network operating system vendors
RTP	Router Table Protocol	VINES

Figure 6-19 Routing protocols and their associated protocol suites.

2. Type of network architecture: Ethernet, Token Ring, Arcnet, Localtalk, or FDDI
3. Type of network layer protocol: IP, IPX, AppleTalk, OSI

What PPP really offers is multivendor support for the interoperability of bridges, routers, and hosts over serial links. More importantly, PPP offers support for *simultaneous transmission of multiple protocols* across the same network link. This is especially important to multiprotocol routers that are internetworking network segments of various network architectures and network layer protocols.

The PPP protocol is implemented on internetworking devices such as bridges and routers. Decisions as to whether to include this protocol in a particular bridge or router is at the discretion of the internetworking device manufacturer. PPP implementations can vary slightly between vendors, and may or may not be interoperable. A PPP vendor consortium has been formed to work out interoperability problems.

Router Configuration

Like bridges, routers generally take one of three physical forms:

1. PC card for installation in PC expansion bus
2. Standalone variety, self-contained
3. Modularized for installation in a slotted chassis

What would a network with installed routers look like? Routers may be installed to link LAN segments either locally or remotely. Figure 6-20 illustrates both a local and a remote router configuration.

☐ INTERNETWORKING CATEGORY 3: MICRO-TO-MAINFRAME/MINICOMPUTER CONNECTIVITY

In the list of protocols that could be processed by multiprotocol routers, there were a few entries that didn't look like they belonged in the PC arena: namely, SNA and DECnet. **SNA** (systems network architecture) is IBM's proprietary networking architecture while **DECnet** is Digital Equipment Corporation's networking architecture. Each is the dominant networking architecture in the mainframe and minicomputer environments, respectively. In this section, what is involved in *internetworking* to these two enormously popular networking architectures will be explored. Before discussing the implications of internetworking to these environments, a bit more of each of the networking architectures themselves must be understood.

In this section of Chapter 6, the role of **gateways** in connecting different types of networks will also be discussed. Recent advances in **multiprotocol software** and internetworking devices known as **SDLC converters,** which offer interesting alternatives to mainframe internetworking solutions will also be explored.

Micro-Mainframe versus Peer-to-Peer Internetworking

Strictly speaking, micro-mainframe connectivity and internetworking are two different concepts. In *micro-mainframe connectivity*, the micro (standalone or LAN-attached PC) pretends to be or "emulates" a mainframe terminal such as an **IBM 3270** attached and logged into the mainframe. Although file transfer utilities may allow more capability than mere remote log-in, this is not the peer-to-peer networking implied by the term internetworking.

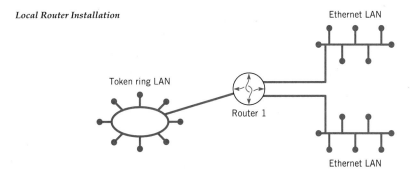

Local Router Installation

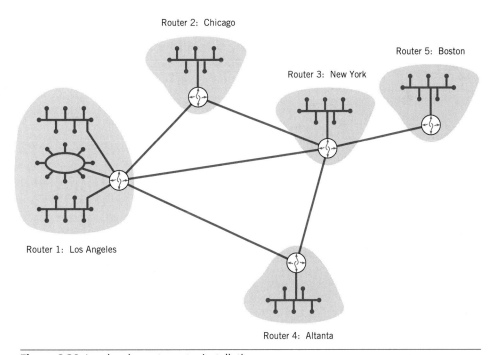

Remote Router Installation

Figure 6-20 Local and remote router installations.

With full *peer-to-peer internetworking*, the PC can exchange data with any mainframe or any other PC on a host-to-host level rather than acting like a "dumb" terminal as in the case of micro-mainframe connectivity.

Although these two mainframe connectivity alternatives have their differences, they still have much in common. The truth is that most "IBM Shops" have a mixture of 3270 terminal connections, mainframes, and LANs which must communicate with each other on a number of different levels.

Hierarchical Networks and Peer-to-Peer Networks

A **hierarchical** network structure such as the "classic" SNA centers around the mainframe. If two devices other than the mainframe on an SNA network wanted to communicate, they would have to establish, maintain, and terminate that communication through the mainframe. This model is in direct contrast to a **peer-to-peer** network structure, typical of most LANs, in which any device may communicate directly with any other LAN-attached device.

Classic SNA Architecture

Figure 6-21 illustrates a simple SNA architecture and introduces some key SNA network elements with which to become familiar.

Two devices in a classic SNA environment as illustrated in Figure 6-21 are:

1. **Front-end processor** (FEP)—**(IBM 3745)**   A front-end processor is a computer that offloads the communications processing from the mainframe, allowing the mainframe to be dedicated to processing activities. A high-speed data channel connects the FEP to the mainframe locally, although FEPs can be deployed remotely as well. The FEP, also known as a communications controller, can have devices such as terminals or printers connected directly to it, or these end-user devices may be concentrated by another device known as a cluster controller.
2. **Cluster controller—(IBM 3174, 3274)**   A cluster controller is a device that allows connection of both 3270 terminals as well as LANs with possible wide area links to packet switched networks (X.25) or high-speed leased lines. A cluster controller concentrates the transmissions of its numerous input devices and directs this concentrated data stream to the FEP either locally or remotely.

The hierarchical nature can be seen in Figure 6-21 as data received from the lowly terminals is concentrated by multiple cluster controllers for a front-end processor which further manages the data for the almighty mainframe. As additional processors and minicomputers such as an IBM AS/400 are added, the hierarchical nature of classic SNA can be seen even more clearly.

The network illustrated in Figure 6-21 will be modified one step at a time until

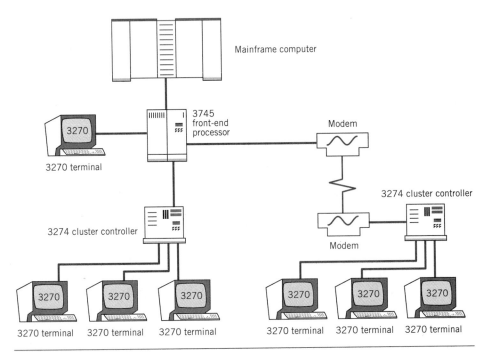

Figure 6-21 The classic SNA architecture.

the goal of an architecture which seamlessly transports SNA as well as LAN traffic is reached.

PCs as 3270 Terminals

The first step of PC or LAN integration with classic SNA is allowing a *standalone* PC to emulate a 3270 terminal and conduct a communication session with the mainframe. In order to accomplish this, *protocol conversion* must take place to allow the PC to appear to be a 3270 terminal in the eyes of the mainframe.

A *3270 protocol conversion card* is inserted into an open expansion slot of a PC. Additional protocol conversion software, which may or may not be included with the protocol conversion card, must be loaded onto the PC in order to make the PC keyboard behave like a 3270 terminal keyboard (keyboard remapping). The media interface on the card is usually RG-62 thin coax for local connection to cluster controllers. Synchronous modems could also be employed for remote connection. Figure 6-22 illustrates possible configurations for stand-alone PC-**3270 terminal emulation.**

LAN-Attached PCs as 3270 Terminals

The next scenario to be dealt with is how to deliver mainframe connectivity to LAN-attached PCs. One way would be to mimic the method for attaching standalone PCs; that is, for *every* LAN-attached PC, buy and install the *3270 protocol conversion hardware and software*. Whereas most of these LAN-attached PCs only need mainframe connectivity on an occasional basis, this would not be a very cost-effective solution. Not only would this be wasteful in terms of the number of PC boards purchased, but also in the number of cluster controller ports monopolized but under-utilized.

Instead, it would be wiser to take advantage of the shared resource capabilities

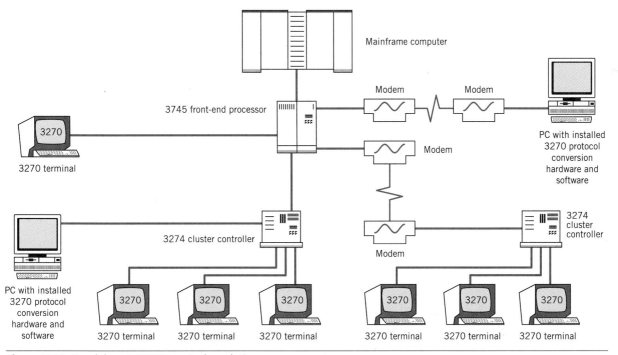

Figure 6-22 Standalone PC 3270 terminal emulation.

of the LAN to share a protocol conversion attachment to the mainframe. Such a LAN-based, shared protocol converted access to a mainframe is known as a **gateway**. Figure 6-23 illustrates both a LAN-based local as well as remote gateway.

As can be seen in Figure 6-23, a gateway configuration can allow multiple simultaneous 3270 mainframe sessions to be accomplished via a single gateway PC and a single port on the cluster controller. A remote PC-based LAN gateway needs

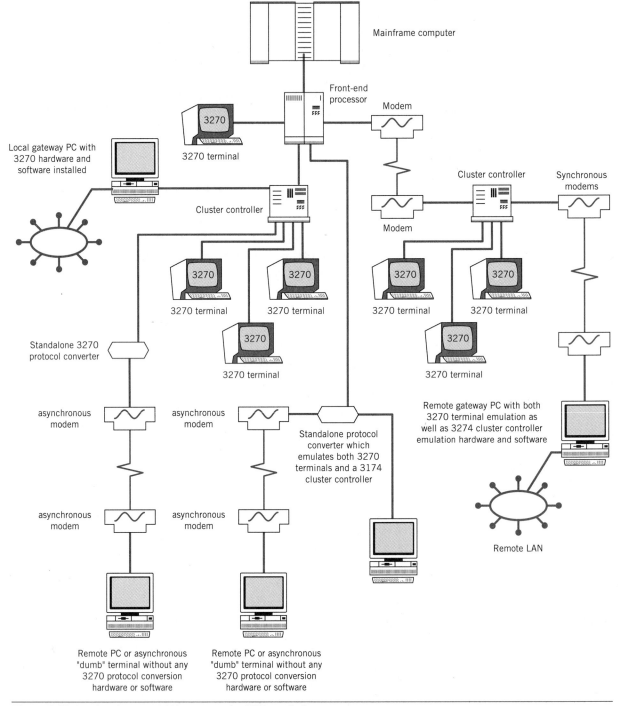

Figure 6-23 Local and remote LAN gateways for 3270 emulation.

additional hardware and software in order to emulate not only the 3270 terminal but also the 3274 cluster controller. Such Remote 3274 cluster controller boards and software are as readily available as 3270 terminal emulation hardware and software.

As a slight variant on the PC-based emulation hardware and software previously mentioned, *standalone protocol conversion devices* for both 3270 terminal as well as 3274 cluster controller emulation are available. Each of these possibilities is also illustrated in Figure 6-23.

Coax, Coax Everywhere: Coax Muxes and Baluns

3270 terminals and PC-based terminal emulation cards are normally connected to cluster controllers via RG-62 thin coax. With hundreds of terminals attached to the typical mainframe, this can constitute a tremendous amount of coax and a significant burden both in terms of cost as well as the sheer bulk of that much coax.

Predictably, two different classes of devices have evolved to cope with the situation. **Coax muxes** take the numerous coax inputs from a group (2,4,8,16) of 3270 terminals and concentrate their traffic onto a single output interface. Depending on the particular coax mux installed, that concentrated output channel may use coax, fiber, or UTP (unshielded twisted pair). Depending on the capability of the cluster controller, a matching coax multiplexor may or may not be necessary to "de-multiplex" the concentrated signal at the cluster controller end of the circuit. Figure 6-24 illustrates possible implementations of coax muxes.

Baluns are much less expensive devices that perform no multiplexing but convert media interfaces at each 3270 terminal from coax to unshielded twisted pair. By sending all 3270 traffic over UTP in this manner, the 3270 media can be incorporated with the rest of the UTP building wiring for voice and data. UTP is also five to 10 times cheaper than coax. RJ-45s, the UTP connector, are far easier and quicker to fasten than the BNC connectors required for coax termination. Figure 6-24 illustrates possible implementation of baluns.

Peer-to-Peer Internetworks Meet Hierarchical SNA

In order to understand how SNA corporate wide area networks and LAN-based internetworks can somehow cooperate to share network links and thereby reduce costs, a closer look at the overall SNA architecture in general, and the SDLC protocol in particular, must first be taken.

The SNA Architecture

Figure 6-25 illustrates a 7-layer model of the SNA (systems network architecture) hierarchy. Like the OSI model, the SNA model starts with media issues in layer 1—the Physical Control Layer—and ends up at layer 7—the Transaction Services Layer, which interfaces to the end-user. The layers in between, however, do not match up perfectly with the corresponding numbered layer in the OSI model, although general functionality at each layer is similar.

"Similar general functionality" will not suffice when it comes to internetworking. As a result, options will be seen for merging SNA (SDLC) and LAN-based data transmissions on a single internetwork involving various methods to overcome the discrepancies between the two architectures.

The SDLC Protocol

Figure 6-26 illustrates the structure of the **SDLC** (synchronous data link control) protocol. Although the protocol structure itself does not look all that unusual, the fact that the information block of the SLDC frame does not contain anything equiv-

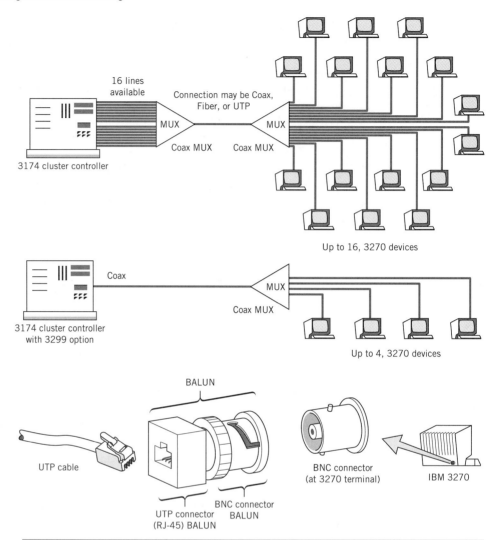

Figure 6-24 Coax multiplexors and baluns.

alent to the OSI network layer addressing information for use by routers makes SDLC a **nonroutable protocol.** SDLC is nonroutable because there is simply no network layer address information available for the routers to process. This shortcoming can be overcome in a number of different ways, as will soon be seen. However, it is important to understand that this nonroutability is one of the key challenges facing SNA-LAN integration.

SDLC's Nonroutability Yields Multiple Networks

Given that SDLC cannot be routed, network managers had no choice but to implement multiple networks between corporate enterprises. One network would carry SDLC traffic between remote cluster controllers and FEPs to local cluster controllers, FEPs and mainframes; while a second network would support remote bridged/routed LANs linking with local LANs between the same corporate locations. If only there was a way to somehow get the SDLC and the LAN traffic to share a network link. Figure 6-27 illustrates this multiple network scenario.

Layer Number	Sublayer Number	Layer/Sublayer Name	Function
7		Transaction Services	Provide network management services. Control document exchange and distributed database access.
6		Presentation Services	Formats data, data compression, and data transformation.
5		Data Flow Control	Synchronous exchange of data supports communications session for end-user applications, assures reliability of session.
4		Transmission Control	Matches the data exchange rate, establishes, maintains, and terminates sessions. Guarantees reliable delivery of data between end points. Error control, flow control.
3		Path Control	Overall layer: Creates the link between two end-points for the transmission control protocols to manage. Divided into 3 sublayers.
	3	Virtual Route Control	Create virtual route (virtual circuit), manage end-to-end flow control.
	2	Explicit Route Control	Determines actually end-to-end route for link between end nodes via intermediate nodes.
	1	Transmission Group Control	If multiple possible physical paths exist between the end-points, this protocol manages to use these multiple lines to assure reliability and load balancing.
2		Data Link Control	Establishes, maintains, and terminates data transmission between two *adjacent* nodes. Protocol is SDLC.
1		Physical Control	Provides physical connections specifications from nodes to shared media.

Figure 6-25 The SNA model.

Overcoming Incompatibilities

In order to understand what might be done, the incompatibilities between SNA and Token Ring LANs must first be delineated. The first characteristic of SNA that can cause trouble on a LAN is the great amount of *acknowledgment and polling traffic* between SNA processors and SNA end-user devices. This constant chatter could quickly monopolize the better part of the LAN bandwidth.

The second SNA characteristic that can cause problems when run over a shared LAN backbone is that SNA has *timing limitations* for transmission durations between SNA hosts and end-user devices. Thus on wide area, internetworked LANs over shared network media, SNA sessions can "time-out," effectively terminating the session.

Another traffic contributor comes from the LAN side of the house. Token Ring LANs use an internetworking device known as a *source routing bridge*. A routing bridge may sound incongruous but the key is to note that it is the *source* (PC) that

Flag	Address	Control	Information	Frame Check Sequence	Flag
1 byte	1 byte	1 byte		2 bytes	1 byte

The information segment does not contain embedded addresses for interpretation by routers according to higher level (OSI-Network layer) protocols. Contrast this with Figure 6-18.

Figure 6-26 SDLC protocol: an SDLC frame.

routes, or defines the internetwork path, and passes this route along to the *bridge.* Hence, the name *source* routing bridge. In order to define these internetworking paths, source PCs send out numerous **exploratory packets** as a means of gaining a sense of the best route from source to destination. All of these discovery packets mean only one thing—significantly more network traffic.

Given the aforementioned obstacles, it is clear that there are three major challenges to allowing SNA and LAN traffic to share an internetwork backbone.

Three SNA/LAN Integration Challenges

1. Reduce unnecessary traffic.
2. Find some way to prioritize SNA traffic to avoid time-outs.

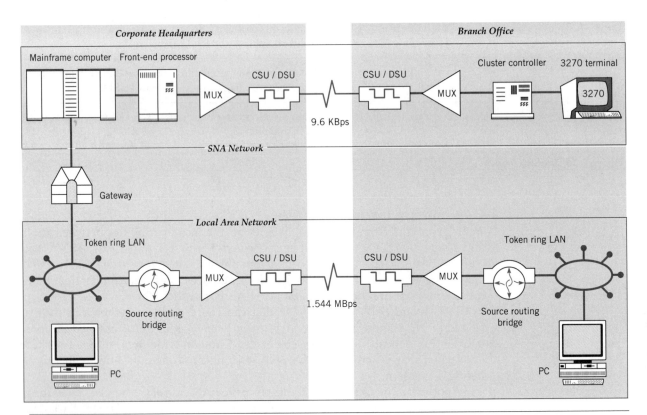

Figure 6-27 SNA/LAN incompatibilities yield multiple networks.

3. Find a way to allow internetwork protocols to transport, or route, SDLC frames.

Currently, there are at least four hardware/software solutions to integrating SDLC traffic with Token Ring traffic over a LAN internetwork. Figs. 6-28 to 6-31 illustrate these four different internetwork topologies.

Four Possible SNA/LAN Integration Solutions

The first method (Figure 6-28) is the least expensive and, predictably, also the least effective in terms of meeting the three SNA/LAN integration challenges. A Token Ring network adapter is attached to an available cluster controller port, and attached to a Token Ring network. The SNA traffic is transported using the standard source route bridging (SRB) to its destination.

However, that is only one of the three challenges to be met. The failure to deal with unnecessary traffic and prioritization of SNA traffic make this a less than ideal solution. Notice, however, the significant potential reduction to hardware and networking costs by this simple approach.

The second method is known alternatively as **encapsulation, passthrough,** or **tunneling.** Simply stated, each SDLC frame is "stuffed" into an IP "envelope" for transport across the network and processing by routers supporting **TCP/IP** internetworking protocol. This IP passthrough methodology for SDLC transport is a common feature or option on internetworking routers. Figure 6-29 illustrates a passthrough architecture. Upon close examination of Figure 6-29, it may become obvious that, in fact, there is no SNA/LAN integration. What the SNA and LAN traffic share is the T-1 wide area network between routers. The SNA traffic never

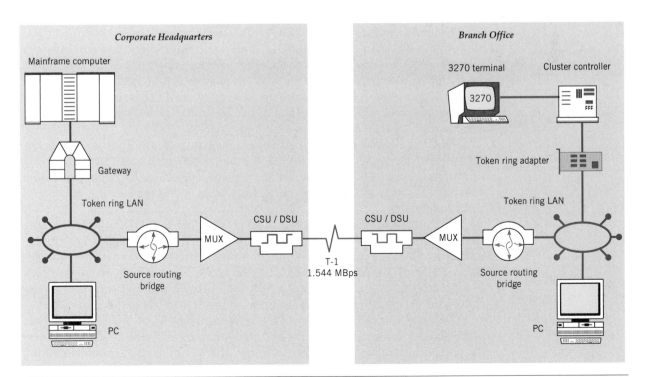

Figure 6-28 SNA/LAN traffic integration (solution 1: token ring adapter for cluster controller).

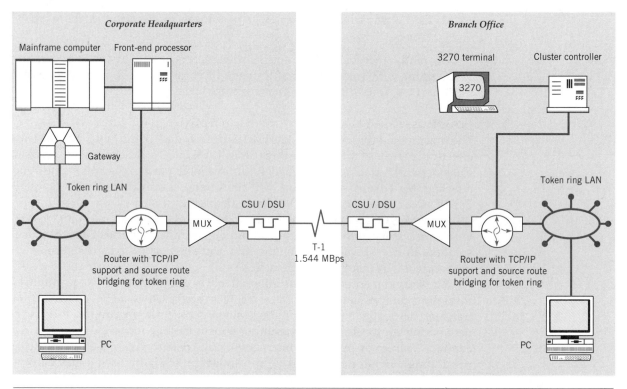

Figure 6-29 SNA/LAN traffic integration (solution 2: TCP/IP encapsulation, also known as tunneling, passthrough).

travels over shared LAN media. Cost savings includes eliminating one wide area link and two routers.

The third possible solution to SNA/LAN traffic integration is known as *SDLC conversion* and is characterized by SDLC frames actually being converted to Token Ring frames by a specialized internetworking device known as a SDLC Converter. The SDLC converter may be a standalone device or may be integrated into a bridge/router. As can be seen in Figure 6-30, in the SDLC conversion configuration, the cluster controller is attached to the Token Ring LAN via a standalone or integrated SDLC converter.

SDLC frames are converted to Token Ring frames, transported across the Token Ring internetwork, and routed to a gateway which transforms the token ring frames back into SDLC frames and forwards them to the mainframe. Also notice the absence of the FEP from the illustration, a potential savings of several thousand dollars.

The fourth and final currently available solution is a class of internetworking devices known as **protocol independent routers,** not to be confused with multi-protocol routers. A protocol independent router does no conversion, nor encapsulation. Rather, it simply adds a MAC (media access control) layer address to each frame received, whether that frame is SDLC or Token Ring. This protocol independent router architecture is also known as a *universal router architecture.*

The key to this solution, however, is how these new MAC layer addresses are processed. A protocol independent address processor reads the newly added destination addresses, not the addresses imbedded within the SDLC or Token Ring frames, and routes them to their destination according to information contained in its own address directory.

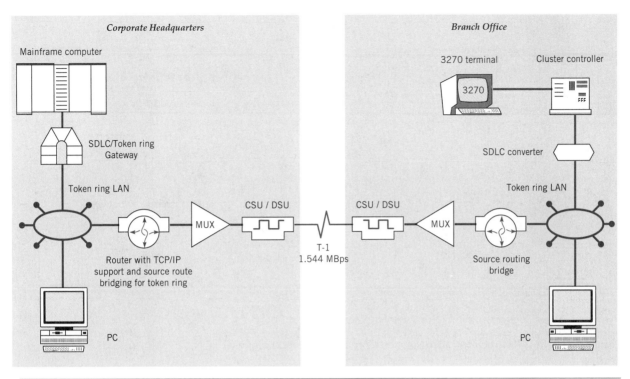

Figure 6-30 SNA/LAN traffic integration (solution 3: SDLC conversion).

Two internetworking devices were eliminated from the SDLC conversion configuration (Figure 6-30) by the protocol independent routing solution in Figure 6-31. At the branch office node, the SDLC converter is no longer needed because no SDLC conversion takes place with protocol independent routing. Because the SDLC is never converted to Token Ring frames, there is no need to convert it back to SDLC at the corporate headquarters node, thus eliminating the need for a gateway.

Meeting the SNA/LAN Integration Challenge

All of the previously mentioned SNA/LAN integration solutions are relatively new and there is no clear dominant technology among them. Figure 6-32 summarizes how each of the solutions met (or didn't meet) the previously listed SNA/LAN integration challenges. Under the "reduce unnecessary traffic" challenge are a few new terms which deserve explanation.

Poll spoofing is the ability of an internetworking device, such as an SDLC converter or router, to respond directly to the FEP's constant polling messages to the remote cluster controller. By answering these status check messages locally, the inquiry and its answer never enter the wide area link portion of the internetwork. **Proxy polling,** on the other hand, emulates the FEP's polling messages on the remote side of the network, thereby assuring the remote cluster controller that it is still in touch with an FEP.

Broadcast filtering addresses a bad habit of the LAN side of SNA/LAN integration. In Token Ring source route bridging, individual PCs send out multiple broadcast packets or **exploratory packets**, causing potential congestion on the internetwork links. Instead of allowing these packets onto the internetwork,

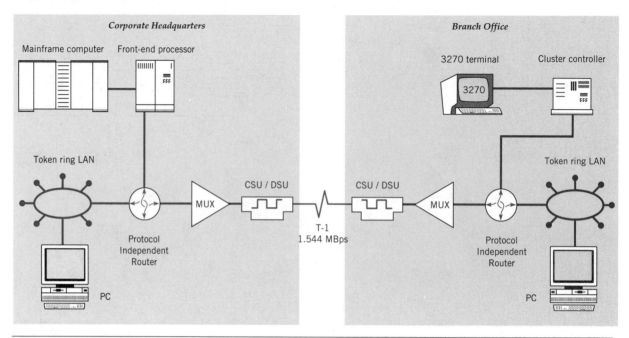

Figure 6-31 SNA/LAN traffic integration (solution 4: protocol independent routers).

	Challenges		
Solution	**Reduce Unnecessary Traffic**	**Prioritize SNA Traffic**	**Allow Internetwork Routing of SDLC Frames**
1. Token ring adapter for cluster controller			SNA traffic is formatted into Token Ring frames. Routed over internetwork using source routing protocol.
2. TCP/IP encapsulation	Broadcast Packet Filtering; Poll Spoofing/Proxy Polling	SDLC traffic assigned higher priority.	SDLC frames encapsulated in TCP/IP frames and routed.
3. SDLC conversion	Broadcast Packet Filtering; Poll Spoofing/Proxy Polling	SDLC traffic assigned higher priority.	SNA traffic is formatted into Token Ring frames. Routed over internetwork using source routing protocol.
4. Protocol independent routing	Broadcast Packet Filtering; Poll Spoofing/Proxy Polling	Traffic can be prioritized based on destination and varying priority levels switch to faster links to avoid SNA session loss.	SDLC (SNA) packets and NETBIOS (Token Ring) packets are *both* given additional Mac-layer addressing, which is processed by compatible address processor.

Figure 6-32 Measuring up SNA/LAN integration solutions.

routers can *filter* these broadcast packets out of the traffic, read the destination address to which the PC is seeking a route, and supply the PC directly with that information after consulting its own routing tables.

APPN: IBM's Alternative to LAN-Based SNA/LAN Integration

APPN (advanced peer-to-peer network) is IBM's answer to multiprotocol networking on a peer-to-peer basis rather than SNA's hierarchical approach. Simply put, attached computers, whether PCs, AS/400s, or mainframes, are welcome to talk directly with each other without having the communications session established, maintained, and terminated by the almighty mainframe.

APPN consists of three basic components:

End nodes are end-user processing nodes, either clients or servers without any information on the overall network, available internetwork links or routing tables.

Network nodes are processing nodes with routing capabilities. They have the ability to locate network resources, maintain tables of information regarding internetwork links, and establish a session between the requesting end-node and the internetwork service requested.

Central directory servers save time as well as network traffic for the network nodes. Instead of each network node on an internetwork doing their own information gathering and internetwork exploration and inquiry, they can simply consult the central directory server.

If the functionality of the three components just described sounds a lot like what was just reviewed in the SNA/LAN integration solutions, that should come as no surprise. IBM is not proposing any radical new methodologies. Rather, they are offering an IBM-backed migration from the hierarchical SNA network to a more effective peer-to-peer environment.

APPN and The New SNA

More significant than IBM's APPN announcement is the blueprint of **"The New SNA"** open architecture. It would seem that IBM has realized that customers want the ability to integrate multivendor, multiplatform, multiprotocol information systems and do not want to be locked into one vendor's proprietary network architecture.

The New SNA architecture is illustrated in Figure 6-33. Although many of the protocols listed will be covered in future chapters on wide area and enterprise networking, the protocols on the *multiprotocol transport networking layer* should be somewhat familiar. A significant event on this layer is that SNA/APPN is just one of several transport protocols supported in the new SNA.

The **common transport semantics** layer offers independence between the applications and the transport protocols, which deliver those applications across the internetwork.

One thing to bear in mind: This is only a *blueprint*. When the bricks and mortar to support this proposed architecture start to appear, then The New SNA may warrant closer attention.

Beyond SNA– Token Ring Integration: Crossing Company Boundaries

Unlike IBM's SNA which is evolving toward a peer-to-peer network architecture, *Digital Equipment Corporation's DECNET* is, and has always been, a peer-to-peer

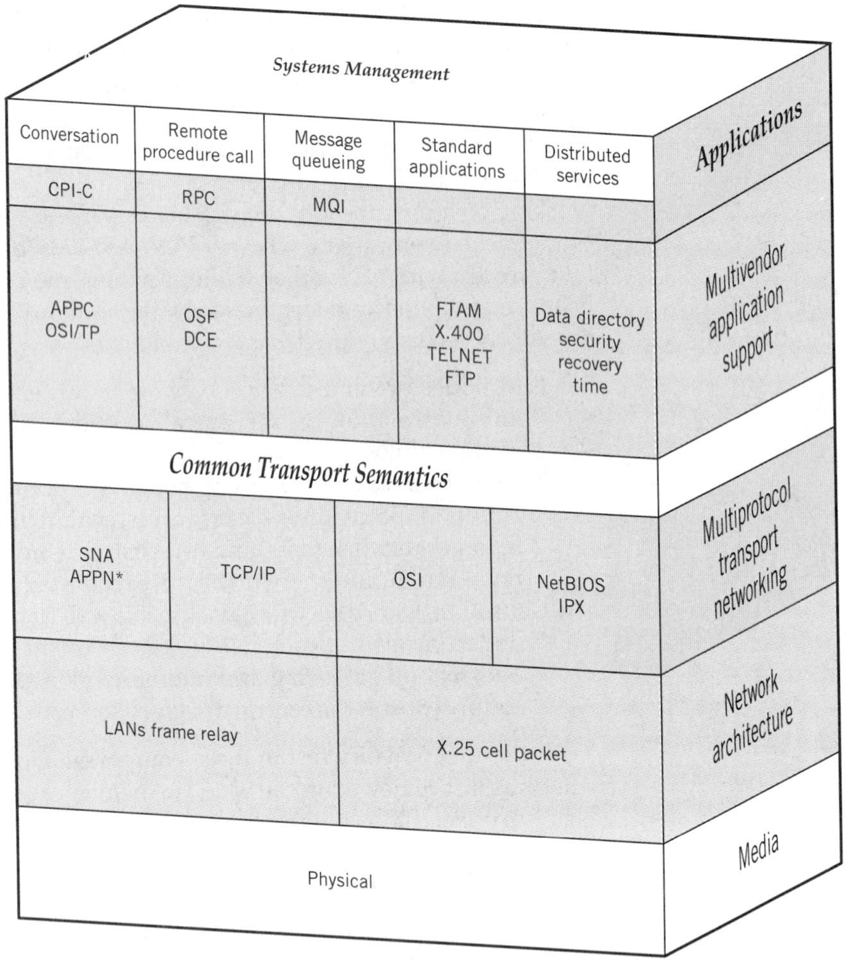

Systems Management					Applications
Conversation	Remote procedure call	Message queueing	Standard applications	Distributed services	
CPI-C	RPC	MQI			
APPC OSI/TP	OSF DCE		FTAM X.400 TELNET FTP	Data directory security recovery time	Multivendor application support
Common Transport Semantics					
SNA APPN*	TCP/IP	OSI		NetBIOS IPX	Multiprotocol transport networking
LANs frame relay			X.25 cell packet		Network architecture
Physical					Media

Figure 6-33 The new SNA.

network. Based on an Ethernet network architecture, and a proprietary network operating system known as DECnet, this networking architecture has become increasingly open to connectivity with not only other DEC computers, workstations, LANs, and terminals of different varieties, but also with UNIX machines, Token Ring LANs, third-party bridges/routers, Macintoshes, and the SNA environment as well.

Digital's network operating system for PC-based LANs is called **Pathworks** and is a licensed version of Microsoft's LAN Manager. Among its unique features is the ability to use DEC's VAX minicomputers as LAN Manager servers. Gateways are available to SNA, UNIX, and X.25 packet-switched environments.

Asynchronous terminals are connected to a DECnet architecture via **terminal servers** which offer the terminals full access to shared network resources. It is important to note, however, that LAN-attached terminals use a transport layer protocol (layer 4) known as **LAT** (local area transport) while using an Ethernet frame as a data link layer (layer 2) protocol. There is no network layer (layer 3) protocol or addressing for a router to work with. As a result, LAT traffic must be bridged. DEC offers several combination bridge/multiprotocol routers as internetworking devices. Figure 6-34 illustrates some of the connectivity options possible with a Ethernet-based DECnet architecture.

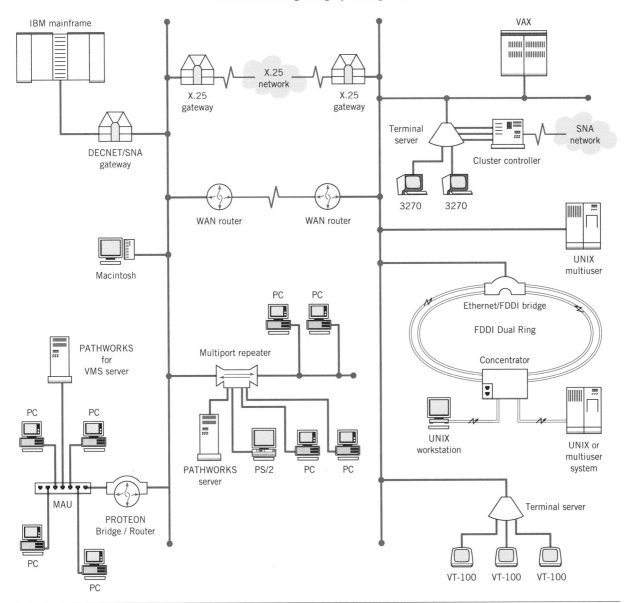

Figure 6-34 DECnet connectivity crosses company boundaries.

☐ INTERNETWORKING CATEGORY 4: INTEGRATION OF LANS AND THE UNIX ENVIRONMENT

One key feature of the DECnet internetworking architecture illustrated in Figure 6-34 is interoperability with UNIX-based machines. DEC happens to offer their own flavor of UNIX known as *Ultrix*. As the need to internetwork has grown, so has the need for PCs to be able to use **TCP/IP** (transport control protocol/internet protocol), the de facto standard for open systems internetworking.

TCP/IP and the Internet Suite of Protocols

TCP/IP is actually an acronym for Transmission Control Protocol/Internet Protocol, two protocols which are part of the **internet suite of protocols**, also known as the **TCP/IP protocol suite.** These protocols are part of a layered architecture much like the 7-layer OSI model. However, in this case, the full functionality of internet communications is divided into four layers rather than seven. Figure 6-35 compares the 4-layer internet suite of protocols model with the OSI 7-layer model.

Business Motivation for UNIX/LAN Integration

Before exploring TCP/IP and the rest of the internet suite of protocols in detail, the business motivation, uses, and applications of UNIX/LAN integration will first be examined.

Several factors have actually combined to form an opportunity for the emergence of UNIX from its traditional stronghold in the engineering and academic domain.

First, the increased global and domestic competition in the face of a downturned economy have forced businesses from all industries to seek ways to significantly reduce costs. It is no secret that the information systems departments of large corporations are a very visible consumer of corporate financial resources.

At the same time as the pressure to reduce MIS (management information systems) costs was increasing, the cost of computing power was decreasing with the introduction of high-powered microprocessors such as the Intel 386, 486, and Pentium chips. Although DOS, or perhaps OS/2, is immediately assumed to be the only possibility for microcomputer operating systems, the fact of the matter is that UNIX offers some distinct advantages over DOS. As was described in the discussion of operating systems, UNIX is inherently a *multitasking,* and therefore *multiuser* operating system.

UNIX is also a *multiplatform,* open systems operating system capable of running on computers of various sizes manufactured by various vendors. This openness and flexibility was also intriguing to the cost-conscious IS executives. A phenomenon known as **downsizing** or **rightsizing** has bloomed as a result of the demand to cut

Layer	OSI	INTERNET	Data Format	Protocols
7	Application	Application	Messages or Streams	TELNET FTP TFTP SMTP SNMP CMOT MIB
6	Presentation			
5	Session			
4	Transport	Transport or Host–Host	Transport Protocol Packets	TCP UDP
3	Network	Internet	IP Datagrams	IP
2	Data Link	Network Access	Frames	
1	Physical			

Figure 6-35 Internet suite of protocols versus OSI 7-layer model.

costs and the power of microcomputers and UNIX. Downsizing, rightsizing, and the client–server architecture will be discussed in greater detail in Chapter 9.

UNIX and *scalable computer architectures* such as those offered by the AT&T/NCR line of computers offer varying degrees of processing power up to the equivalent of today's most powerful mainframe, all based on a single architecture, the Intel X86 chip, and a single operating system, UNIX. There is virtually no possibility of outgrowing either hardware capability or software compatibility. This powerful attribute is known as **scalability.**

Basically, what this all boils down to is that UNIX workstations offer powerful computing at a reasonable cost. They make excellent LAN servers of various types requiring high amounts of processing power such as: file servers, database servers, and E-mail servers. These UNIX servers must then be able to communicate with their LAN-based DOS clients. Furthermore, UNIX workstations used for engineering purposes may need to share project information with computerized marketing or accounting departments via a LAN in order to facilitate effective project management.

This kind of UNIX/LAN integration is sometimes referred to as *cross-platform workgroup* computing. TCP/IP and the rest of the protocols listed in Figure 6-35, which comprise the internet suite of protocols, are the vehicles by which UNIX servers and non-UNIX clients are able to communicate and interoperate.

Typical Uses of LAN Access to UNIX Servers

Before examining the individual protocols of the TCP/IP family, the typical uses of UNIX servers by non-UNIX clients as well as the implications of those uses on the set of protocols that must arbitrate the communication of data between these two different environments must be considered. It should be pointed out that UNIX/LAN integration implies UNIX workstations possessing the ability to access LAN servers as well.

The uses of UNIX servers by non-UNIX clients are very similar to the initial needs of LAN users as established in Chapter 4; namely, *file access* and remote login. As previously mentioned, due to their superior processing power, UNIX workstations make excellent LAN servers. The Computer Technology Department at Purdue University has several UNIX servers running AT&T/NCR StarGroup (LAN Manager) Network Operating Systems and serving numerous DOS-based clients running Windows. In this capacity, the servers provide file access to application files as well as shared database files. Thanks to TCP/IP, users can also log into any accessible UNIX server, appear to be a UNIX terminal, and run native UNIX applications on that UNIX Server.

Protocol Requirements for UNIX/LAN Integration

Given the previously mentioned two primary uses of UNIX/LAN integration:

1. UNIX workstations accessing LAN servers
2. DOS/Windows clients accessing UNIX servers

What might be the requirements of the protocols that will be employed to establish, maintain, and terminate communications sessions between UNIX and LAN environments?

File Management System Compatibility

First of all, in order to provide compatibility of file access across these different platforms, the internetwork protocol must be able to communicate with the different file management systems on the UNIX and LAN platforms. Depending on the LAN operating system, DOS may be used as the file management system or it may be a modified or proprietary file management system embedded in the network operating system itself.

What file management system arbitrates between the two platforms? TCP/IP is actually a combination of transport and network layer protocols, not file management utilities. The FTP (file transfer protocol) included in the TCP/IP protocol stack is a limited function protocol, unable to mount UNIX disks and make them appear local on DOS clients. The most popular and powerful file management system associated with TCP/IP and UNIX is known as **NFS**. NFS stands for *network file system*, was originally developed by Sun Microsystems, and is now included in many TCP/IP for PCs software packages. NFS is also available as an NLM (netware loadable module) known as Novell Netware Network File System, which is designed to let UNIX systems access Netware File Servers via NFS.

Terminal Emulation

Secondly, in order to support remote log-in of LAN-based PC workstations to UNIX servers and vice-versa, those workstations must appear to be "native" or "normal" workstations to the server. In other words, if a LAN-based workstation is to log successfully into a UNIX server it must appear to be or *emulate* a UNIX workstation. Likewise, if a UNIX workstation is to log into a LAN, then it must emulate a LAN-based PC.

Transport and Network Layer Protocols

Finally, the transport and network layer software, OSI model layers 4 and 3 respectively, on the UNIX machine must be able to communicate with, or translate the transport and network layer software of the LAN's network operating system. After all, it is at the network (layer 3) and transport (layer 4) layers of the OSI model where the internetworking between UNIX-based systems and LAN-based PCs is actually taking place. Figure 6-36 lists some of the more popular network operating systems and their transport and network layer protocols.

UNIX/LAN Integration Implementation Alternatives

Now that it has been concluded *why* to integrate UNIX and LANs as well as what applications could be accomplished and what obstacles must be overcome or compatibility issues addressed, the alternative ways of *how* this integration can be accomplished can now be studied.

UNIX Versions of Network Operating Systems   First of all, as illustrated in Chapter 5, Figures 5-5 to 5-7, most popular LAN operating systems are available in versions that run directly over UNIX. This set-up allows UNIX workstations to access UNIX servers and receive LAN type services such as those offered by Netware, Vines, or LAN Manager.

UNIXWARE, the product of a joint-venture between Novell and Univel Corporation, integrates Netware with UNIX as well as TCP/IP with SPX/IPX. This implementation of Netware allows clients based on DOS, Macintosh, OS/2, or Windows as well as UNIX, to all access the UNIXWARE server transparently and simultaneously. The transparency of the client portion of UNIXWARE should not be taken lightly.

The importance of this feature is that users at a Macintosh client continue working in their familiar Macintosh environment even though they are accessing files off a UNIX server running a special version of Novell Netware known as UNIXWARE.

This *client transparency* is seen as an important step in the development and deployment of multivendor, multiplatform, distributed computing client–server information systems. UNIXWARE is totally scalable, meaning it can run on any UNIX-based computer, whether a desktop workstation, or a mainframe equivalent enterprise server.

Multiple Protocol Stacks A second method of providing UNIX/LAN integration is to provide a means to translate between the TCP/IP protocol and the LAN network and transport layer protocols *within* each LAN-based or client PC. In other words, two protocol stacks exist in each PC, one TCP/IP and one unique to the installed network operating system such as SPX/IPX for Novell Netware. This approach of loading multiple protocol stacks in a single client PC is known as **multiprotocol software**.

However, merely having multiple protocol stacks is not enough. Somehow, the PC must sense which protocol stack should be used at any point in time and somehow have the ability to switch back and forth between the various networking protocols as appropriate. Two multiprotocol device driver standards, **NDIS** (network driver interface specification) and **ODI** (open data-link interface) are the keys to a PC's ability to manipulate multiple protocol stacks. Another popular multiprotocol device driver written for DOS-based PCs is known as **PDS**, or packet driver specification.

The importance of these device driver standards is their ability to arbitrate between multiple protocol stacks, or allow multiple protocol stacks to run simultaneously for a single network adapter card. After installing a device driver that can support multiple protocols, a software package to supply these multiple protocols must be purchased and installed.

Multiple protocol stacks is the best solution when frequent access between PCs and UNIX servers is required. Recalling the LAN Manager installation in the Department of Computer Technology at Purdue, in order to allow our DOS-based clients to communicate with our UNIX servers, we have purchased and installed Wollongong Pathway Access TCP/IP, which operates with the NDIS multiprotocol device driver specification.

With the installation of StarGroup LAN Manager Version 2.1, the third-party TCP/IP protocol stack was no longer necessary as NFS TCP/IP was included with the new version of the network operating system. Fully-integrated multiple protocol stacks remove the possibility of incompatibilities with third-party software.

Network Operating System	Transport Protocol
UNIX	TCP/IP or UDP
LAN Manager	NETBEUI
Netware	SPX/IPX
DECNET	LAT
VINES	VIPC/VIP (Vines Interprocess Communication Protocol/ Vines Internet Protocol)
DOS-based LANs	NETBIOS
APPLETALK	ATP (APPLETALK Transaction Protocol)

Figure 6-36 Network Operating Systems Transport Protocols.

TCP/IP Gateway A third solution to the UNIX/LAN integration issue, best suited to occasional access between DOS-based clients and UNIX servers, is to install the multiprotocol software on the server only, thus creating a TCP/IP **gateway.**

As an example, Novell offers an NLM (netware loadable module) known as Netware NFS, which allows UNIX systems to access Netware file servers transparently. Figure 5-5 illustrated a Netware NFS installation. The gateway is accessible to both LAN-based PCs as well as UNIX servers. Protocol translation takes place in the gateway. In most cases, the gateway software is installed on a workstation capable of supporting multiple simultaneous sessions so that more than one user can access the gateway simultaneously.

It should be restated that a gateway is the best solution for *occasional* needs for UNIX/LAN integration. Frequent use of such protocol translation should be reserved for client-installed multiprotocol software. Figure 6-37 summarizes the alternative methods for implementing UNIX/LAN integration as well as the applications and implications of each alternative method.

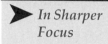 *In Sharper Focus*

IMPORTANT FEATURES AND OPTIONS FOR MULTIPROTOCOL SOFTWARE

Figure 6-38 summarizes some of the available features and options available on various vendor's offerings of multiprotocol (also known as TCP/IP for DOS, or UNIX services for DOS) software.

Which Protocols Need Supporting?

It should be pointed out that the most important criterion in selecting multiprotocol software is that it supports the required protocols. In other words, if a multiprotocol software that supports DECnet as well as IPX (Netware) and TCP/IP (UNIX)

Method	Requirements/Applications/LAN Integration
Install and run UNIX version of LAN network operating system	How many different client platforms are supported? DOS, OS/2, MAC, Windows, UNIX? Can the network be run on any version of UNIX? On any vendor's UNIX platform of any size? Was the network operating system adapted or completely rewritten for UNIX and/or UNIXWARE? Is UNIX accessible beneath the network operating system?
Client-based multi-protocol software	Must have network adapter card drivers such as NDIS, ODI, or PDS that can support multiple protocols Must purchase multiprotocol software Multiprotocol device drivers allow you to load and swap multiple protocols on a single network adapter. (See Figure 6-38 for important features and options of multiprotocol software)
Server-based multi-protocol gateway software	For occasional use only Gateway software usually available as option from network operating system vendors (example: Netware for NFS, NLM) Should be installed on PC that allows multiple, simultaneous sessions in order to support multiple occasional users accessing the gateway

Figure 6-37 Alternative methods of accomplishing UNIX/LAN integration.

Feature	Options/Implications
Protocols supported	Be sure the protocols of your client and servers are supported by the multiprotocol software. Popular protocols: TCP/IP, IPX, NFS, NETBIOS, NETBEUI Others: DECNET, X.25, OSI, XNS, UDP, RARP
Operating systems supporting	Will this software run on your client and server operating system? Options: DOS, OS/2, Windows, Macintosh, UNIX
Multiprotocol device drivers	Options: NDIS—Microsoft ODI—Novell (Note: Many multiprotocol software packages support both)
Operational features	*Ease of use/transparency:* Remote disks appear local. DOS commands can access UNIX drives. *File transfer:* NFS ⎫ FTP ⎬ Possible file transfer TFTP ⎭ protocols Can file transfer be done from server to client? *E-Mail:* SMTP protocol Build SMTP commands from E-mail entry? *Printer support:* Can LAN-based clients print to printers attached to UNIX servers? *Terminal emulation:* VT-100 (DEC) ⎫ VT-220 (DEC) ⎬ Options IBM 3270 ⎭ *Remote execution commands:* Allow commands entered in DOS to execute on UNIX server without using native UNIX commands via TELNET connection and terminal emulation? Support for multiple sessions?

Figure 6-38 Important features and options for multi-protocol software.

is required, choices are far more limited than if multiprotocol software which supported IPX(Netware) and TCP/IP are required. Don't ever assume that multiprotocol software supports a certain protocol.

What Is the Client Operating Environment?

An equally important question is: What is the operating system of the client workstation on which the multiprotocol software will be loaded?

It could be DOS, Windows, OS/2, or Macintosh. A multiprotocol software package must be found which is certified to run over the client PCs operating system.

Compatible Device Drivers and Network Adapters

In order to run multiprotocol software, a device driver that can either swap the multiple protocol stacks and/or allow them to run simultaneously, must also be installed on the client PC. NDIS and ODI are the two primary multiprotocol adapter drivers. Multiprotocol software should support either or both of these drivers.

Ease of Use/Transparency

Perhaps the most important operational feature of those listed in Figure 6-38 is their ease of use/transparency. Some multiprotocol software make the fact that a DOS client is linked to a UNIX server completely transparent to the DOS user. The user is able to address remote files physically located on disk drives attached to UNIX servers as if they were mounted locally by typing in DOS commands, not UNIX commands. Simply put, from a user's perspective, a transparent multiprotocol software package will keep DOS looking like DOS.

Cross-Platform E-Mail Support

Another occasion for ease of use comparison is the functionality afforded by the E-mail support portion of multiprotocol software. Most multiprotocol software packages support the **SMTP** (simple mail transfer protocol) protocol for UNIX-based E-mail servers. However, some packages expect the user to interface with SMTP via UNIX or UNIX-like E-mail systems, while others allow the user to interact with DOS or Windows-based E-mail programs transparently to the underlying SMTP protocol. The multiprotocol software handles the translation tasks of converting the user's DOS/Windows E-mail input into SMTP-based output.

Terminal Emulation

A final transparency issue involves terminal emulation and the ability to type in DOS commands on the local DOS client and have those commands translated into UNIX commands on the remote UNIX server. These remote commands and utilities preclude the need to log into the UNIX server via a TELNET session and terminal emulation to type in native UNIX commands.

A complete summary of the aforementioned considerations as well as operational features of multiprotocol software is included in Figure 6-38.

☐ INTERNETWORKING CATEGORY 5: MACINTOSH INTEGRATION

Rationale—Business Uses

The rationale for integrating Apple's Macintosh PCs with PC-based LANs, SNA, DECnet, or the UNIX environment is no different than that which has been articulated for other integration initiatives. In many cases, users have installed Macintoshes within a given department in a company, very often an editorial or publishing related department owing to the MAC's strength in desktop publishing. The Macintoshes very often are already networked to each other (81 percent, according to a recent survey).

The need for Mac-extended communications arises when information must somehow be shared with non-MAC systems and networks. The specific information sharing needs of the MAC environment are not unlike other networking environments previously analyzed:

File sharing
Printer sharing
File transfer
E-mail

Compatibility Issues to be Overcome

If the business uses or motivation for MAC-extended connectivity are so like that which has already been seen, what is the nature of the connectivity problem or opportunity? In other words, what protocol stack incompatibilities must be overcome in order to integrate Macintoshes with PCs, PC-based LANs of various network operating systems, the SNA environment, and the DECnet environment?

MAC versus DOS Data Formatting   The first incompatibility to be overcome is the difference in *data formatting* and *storage*. Macintoshes format data disks in one format while MS-DOS formats data disks in a different format. Even if both systems use the same media, 3.5 inch diskettes for instance, the disks are still unreadable in anything but their "native" computer. Several technology-based solutions to this compatibility hurdle have been developed and will be explored shortly.

Extending the notion of data incompatibilities, the *application software* and the *data files* which that software produces are not compatible or readable by anything but their "native" computer. Data translation software as well as other technological solutions have been introduced to meet this internetworking challenge as well.

The Spectrum of MAC Interoperability Opportunities

Now that the obstacles to MAC integration have been outlined, the solutions will be proposed. There are many opportunities of varying degrees of complexity and sophistication for internetworking with Macintoshes. A summary outlining the opportunities and possible solutions or options is featured in Figure 6-39.

Interoperability Category	Options/Features
Non-LAN connectivity	Printer sharing devices File sharing devices File transfer software LAN modems Communications software Data transmission software
Network architectures	LocalTalk Ethernet Token Ring FDDI
Peer-to-Peer networks	TOPS by Sitka
Internetworking	PC LANs/Macs SNA/Mac DECNET/Mac UNIX/Mac Network Management Ethernet/LocalTalk hubs AppleTalk routers Gateways
Macintosh integration with full-featured network operating systems	Netware for Macintosh VINES option for Macintosh LAN Manager services for Macintosh

Figure 6-39 The spectrum of Macintosh interoperability opportunities.

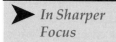

NON-LAN CONNECTIVITY

Printer-sharing devices: Most manufacturers of printer-sharing devices support Macintosh computers, but don't assume anything. At least some of the switches manufactured by leading printer-sharing device vendors, such as Fifth Generation Systems, Inc. (The Logical Connection), Buffalo Products, Inc. (Buffalo SL-512), and Digital Products, Inc. (Print Director Series) support Macintosh computers transparently.

File-sharing software and/or hardware: File sharing implies wanting to be able to run application programs written for one computer platform (DOS) on a different computer platform (Mac), or in some other way directly reading files not originally formatted for the "reading" PC. Dayna, a leader in Apple internetworking, offers DOS-mounter software, which allows Macintoshes to mount and use DOS-formatted diskettes in a Macintosh diskdrive. Hardware solutions include adding a DOS co-processor to a Mac along with the associated software to run DOS applications on the Mac. Conversely, MatchMaker from MicroSolutions and several other products/vendors offer a hardware and software combination which allows Macintosh diskettes to be read on a MS-DOS PC.

File translation software: The biggest problem with sharing files between Macs and DOS machines is that the data files written by application programs on the respective computers are unreadable to each other. Specific translations must take place between data files written by a particular application program on a Mac before a DOS-based application (in some cases the same program) can read and process the Mac's data file and vice-versa. As a result, the translation package with the most translations is often the best package. MacLink Plus/PC by DataViz is frequently mentioned in software reviews as the best Mac translation software with over 400 translation routines for not only Mac, but DOS, Windows, and UNIX data formats as well.

Applications programs which have implementations for both DOS and Mac platforms preclude the need for third-party translation packages through the use of built-in import/export utilities included in their software packages. Examples include Lotus 1-2-3 and Microsoft Excel spreadsheets and Microsoft Word and Wordperfect word processors.

File transfer software: Most Macintosh file translation software packages also handle the file transfer chores. MacLink Plus/PC, previously mentioned, handles the transfer as well as the translation tasks. Macintosh and PC computers are linked via serial or null modem cables. It should be noted that Macintosh serial ports are not the familiar DB-9 or DB-25 of the PC community. The serial port on a Macintosh is what is known as an 8-pin mini DIN plug, which looks very similar to the plug on most PC keyboard cables. Specially made 8-pin mini-DIN to DB-25 serial cables are available and often included in Mac file transfer packages.

Communications software/hardware: Many communications packages support file transfer via a number of different protocols in addition to offering remote log-in capabilities to Macs from PCs and vice versa. Among the packages that support remote communications with Macs are Microphone II by Software Ventures and White Knight Telecommunications Software from Freesoft.

LAN-attached modems such as the Shiva Net Modem/E mentioned earlier in this chapter may also allow access both to-and-from Macs. Remember that the NetModem/E attaches only to Netware or Appletalk-based networks running over Ethernet or Apple's Ethertalk network architectures. It also supports DOS, Macintosh, and Windows remote users, provided they have installed Shiva's end-user communications software or an equivalent. Also remember that the

NetModem/E can be configured to support *either* Appletalk *or* Netware, but not both at the same time.

In case some of these non-LAN connectivity MAC integration implementations were difficult to picture, Figure 6-40 illustrates many of the possibilities. ◀

Network Architecture

To obtain physical connectivity between Macs and PCs in a more sophisticated and faster manner than the serial cable connection used for file transfer software, network adapter cards and shared network media must be employed. Macintosh's native network architecture is known as **Localtalk** and suffers from two shortcomings. A speed of 230.6 Kbps is the first problem, while the second major problem with LocalTalk is that the connectors used to attach the media to the interface are miniature DIN plugs similar to PC keyboard connectors.

These connectors are very prone to coming loose and bringing down the network in the process. As a result, several alternatives have emerged to correct both the speed and connector issue.

First, as to the matter of the connectors: Farallon markets an entire line of adapters, connectors, media, and software for Localtalk under the brand name of *PhoneNet*. The phone net connectors are either RJ-11 or RJ-45 plugs, not at all prone to coming loose accidentally.

File Sharing Hardware/Software

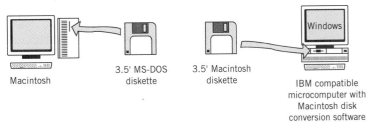

LAN Modems with Macintoshes

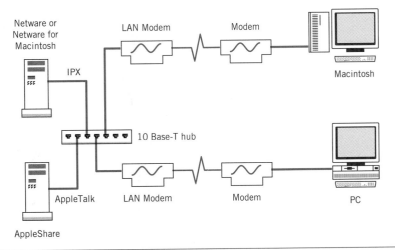

Figure 6-40 Macintosh integration: non-LAN connectivity.

Secondly, thanks in no small part to the Appletalk suite of protocols compliance with the OSI 7-Layer Model, **AppleTalk** can run quite successfully over numerous network architectures infinitely faster than Localtalk.

The most popular alternative network architecture for AppleTalk is Ethernet. As a matter of fact, Ethernet is expected to be the network architecture of choice, even over Mac's own (and free) Localtalk, by 1996. (See Figure 6-41)

Token Ring will probably always have some following especially where Macintosh and IBM integration activities are in a largely IBM environment. FDDI and its 100Mbps desktop speed is a possibility for Macs as FDDI adapter cards and the FDDITalk data link protocols are delivered. CDDI cards are likely to follow. The FDDI cards will support **A/UX**, Apple's version of UNIX for the Mac, as well as Appleshare network operating system.

Peer-to-Peer or Low-End Networks

Remembering the overall goal of linking Macintoshes and PCs for sharing information, the next logical step after non-LAN connectivity would be the equivalent of DOS-based LANs in the Mac world. However, low-cost LANS that interconnect only MACs are not sufficient. Macintosh integration has not really been accomplished unless they can be inexpensively integrated with PCs on a peer-to-peer LAN.

Added functionality offered by these low-cost LANs includes:

1. Ease of integration of PCs and Macs for file transfer and printer sharing.
2. E-mail capability between Macs and PCs.

Figure 6-42 summarizes the features of three popular peer-to-peer LANS for Macs and PCs. TOPS is a multiplatform network operating system that works by installing its own redirector software. The Sitka TOPS redirector not only redirects requests for remote data to the remote server via local network adapters, but also arbitrates or translates between file management systems on the clients and servers whether Macs or PCs.

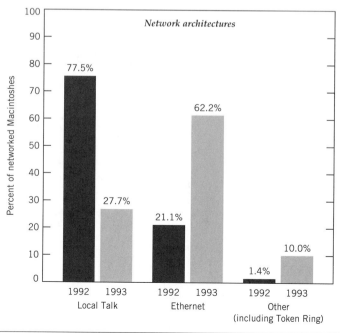

Figure 6-41 AppleTalk network architectures of choice.

Network or Systems Product Name	Vendor Name	PC	Macintosh	Additional Platforms
MacTOPS	Sitka	Network interface card (LocalTalk) and software required	Built-in Macintosh LocalTalk, additional software added. Includes MacLink Plus file transfer and translation software	Will also run over Ethernet or Token Ring. Software also available for SUN (UNIX)
PhoneNetTalk	Farallon Computing	LocalTalk interface card and software required	Built-in Macintosh LocalTalk	Will also run over Ethernet or Token Ring
DaySTAR Digital	LT 200 Connection	Requires hub in addition to LocalTalk interface cards	Built-in Macintosh LocalTalk	

Figure 6-42 Macintosh/PC peer-to-peer networks.

The Appletalk Suite of Protocols and the OSI Model

This redirector software sits at the OSI session (layer 5) and presentation (layer 6) layers. The OSI model and its relation to the Macintosh suite of protocols are central to the ability of products like TOPS to be able to run with AppleTalk over multiple network architectures such as Ethernet and Token Ring as well as Localtalk. Figure 6-43 illustrates the AppleTalk suite of protocols in comparison to the OSI 7-layer model. Notice the one-to-one correspondence of AppleTalk layers and OSI layers. Remembering the transparency of layers in the initial OSI design, it should come as no surprise that AppleTalk runs over numerous types of media (physical layer) as well as over numerous network architectures (data-link layer).

Gateways Offer Occasional Mac/PC LAN Connectivity

A gateway converts between the different protocol stacks of two different networks allowing each to share in the use of the other's network resources transparently. Often the gateway is a PC with adapter cards of each supported network architecture and each network operating system installed. For instance, an AppleTalk-to-LAN Manager Gateway would probably have both a Localtalk as well as an Ethernet adapter card installed.

A gateway allows multiple simultaneous sessions (limit varies) between users and resources connected to networks on either side of the gateway. In deciding what processing the gateway must perform it must first be decided which network operating systems and architectures it must be able to translate or provide a gateway to. A simple I-P-O (input-processing-output) diagram as shown in Figure 6-44 illustrates some of the possibilities.

Once it has been decided what types of networks will be situated on either side of the gateway, a gateway must be found which services these required protocols. For instance:

Avatar has a MacMainframe series of gateways which support connectivity between either standalone or networked Macs and SNA/SDLC hosts via 3270 terminal emulation.

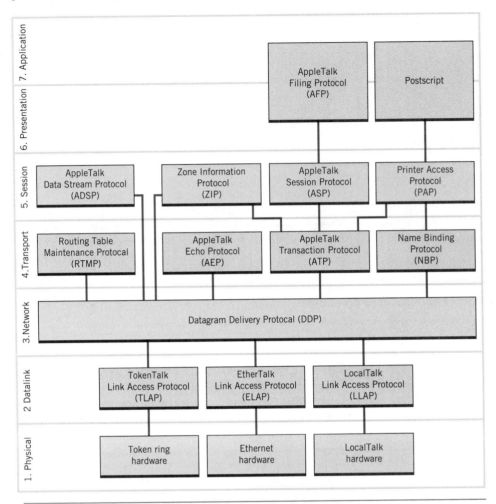

Figure 6-43 AppleTalk suite of protocols versus the OSI model.

Andrew Corporation offers the NetAxess Gateway for connectivity between AppleTalk networks running over Localtalk, Ethernet, or Token Ring to IBM's System 36, 38 or AS/400 mid-range computers.

Routers Support AppleTalk Protocols

Once AppleTalk is onto an Ethernet network it can get routed like any other Ethernet protocol (IP,IPX, etc) by any routers that support AppleTalk protocols. The important distinction to take note of between a router and a gateway, as the terms are used here, is as follows:

Any router which supports the AppleTalk protocol can make decisions as to the best way to send that packet of data across the internetwork or around the world based on two key criteria:

1. The current state of the alternative paths to reach the packet's final destination address.
2. The "flavor" of the Ethernet frame, in this case AppleTalk.

In other words, a router has the ability to recognize that the upper-level protocols embedded in an Ethernet frame are AppleTalk, and make routing decisions

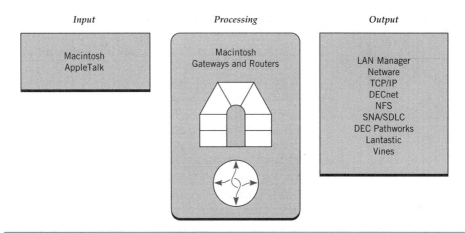

Figure 6-44 Macintosh gateways: "What do we need to connect to?" (Input-Processing-Output).

based upon that fact. However, it is a gateway which *translates* one protocol into another, allowing an AppleTalk client to talk transparently to a SNA or DECnet host.

Unfortunately, the terms gateway and router are often used interchangeably.

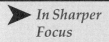

▶ *In Sharper Focus*

10BASET HUBS SUPPORT APPLETALK OVER LOCALTALK AND ETHERNET

Another Ethernet device that now supports AppleTalk running over either Localtalk or Ethernet is the Ethernet 10BaseT Hub for the Mac, manufactured by both AppleTalk vendors such as Dayna, Farallon, and Macnet, as well as traditional Ethernet hub vendors such as David Systems, Cabletron, and Synoptics.

The hubs offer Mac users UTP wiring and SNMP management capabilities in addition to the 10Mbps speed. The SNMP management can be run on Macs, allowing these hub-based networks to be all Mac for the Mac purists in the crowd. Conversely, these hubs can instantly solve PC/Mac integration issues by simply installing 10BaseT adapter cards into each of the PCs and plugging them into the hub along with the Mac Localtalk and Ethernet connections.

Because these latest hubs can handle *both* Localtalk (230.6Kbps) as well as 10BaseT Ethernet (10Mbps) Macintosh users are allowed to upgrade to Ethernet network adapter cards as the needs and financial means materialize.

The Final Frontier of Mac Integration—Full-Featured LANs

As can be seen in Figure 6-39, the final stage of the spectrum of Mac interoperability opportunities is the total integration of Mac support into a full-featured network operating system such as Netware, Vines, or LAN Manager. As a matter of fact, each of these network operating systems features either a special version or option for the Macs as follows:

Network Operating System	Macintosh Version/Option
Novell Netware	Netware for Macintosh
Banyan Vines	Vines Option for Macintosh
Microsoft LAN Manager	LAN Manager Services for Macintosh

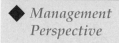

In a nutshell, what these high priced ($1000 to $2000 per server) options offer is
transparency. Users on Macintoshes transparently use networked resources such
as LAN-based file servers and printers.

Another business motivation for investing in one of these full-featured NOS
Mac options has to do with the current level of investment in a given network operating system. If a business had a large established network running Microsoft LAN
Manager and needed to integrate Macs, then there is little doubt that LAN Manager services for Macintosh would be worth looking into.

If, however, a company was about to install its first network for a grand total of
six PCs and four Macs, then most likely one of the Mac/PC peer-to-peer networks
such as TOPS would be worth looking into. ◆

SERVER-BASED OPTIONS

Most full-featured network operating systems require different sets of software to
be loaded on the server(s) and clients. The client piece is usually smaller, but no less
significant. A key differentiating point with these Mac options for full-featured
LANs is that no client software needs to be added to the Macs. Instead, the existing
client software, which is included as part of the Mac operating system and known
as *Appleshare Workstation,* serves as the client software and familiar-user interface
for the Mac user.

The fact that all three of these full-featured Mac options—LAN Manager, Vines,
and Netware—all offer completely transparent use of network resources to Mac
users by allowing them to remain in their familiar Appleshare Workstation environment, from the users perspective at least, there truly is no difference between the
three Mac integration options. Thus, the decision really comes down to network
installation and management issues—or, perhaps more accurately, which full-featured NOS (LAN Manager, Vines Netware) a business currently has installed.

Client-Based Options

An interesting twist on the "no-client software installation necessary" characteristic of these three NOSs is offered by the Apple networking company Dayna with
their NetMounter software. Rather than installing the software on a server, this
software installs on individual clients and allows Macintosh users access to files on
Netware servers without the need (and expense) of loading Netware for
Macintosh on the server.

The NetMounter software is accessed transparently through the Apple's icon
system and displays all available Netware servers. After proper user ID log-in and
security checks, any file on the Netware server may be accessed by the Mac client.
Obviously a detailed cost/benefit analysis with particular attention paid to numbers of Mac users requiring access to Netware servers should be conducted before
a decision is made regarding the server or client based alternative. ◀

☐ INTERNETWORKING IN PERSPECTIVE

At this point in the chapter, many different internetworking opportunities have
been introduced. As each new area has been explored, the *logical internetworking
design* and decision-making issues, such as business motivation and compatibility

challenges, have been separated from the more *physically-oriented internetworking design* issues, such as currently available technology. Wide area networking aspects of internetworking have been purposely left for Chapter 7.

Enough technical information in each aspect of internetworking could not possibly have been supplied in order to qualify one as an expert in these areas. Indeed, numerous books have been written on each of the topics which were covered here by a few pages. Instead, the logical and problem-solving aspects of internetworking have been concentrated upon.

Internetworking Design

In order to reinforce the methodology employed throughout this chapter, a general internetworking design strategy will be outlined which should serve well as new and unexplored internetworking challenges materialize in the future.

Start at the Top: Business Motivation

Any internetworking design should only be undertaken because of a clearly stated and hopefully measurable business opportunity or goal. Otherwise, nothing will have been done other than throwing expensive technology at an unclearly defined target. Remember that, in today's business climate, the delivery of the right information to the right decision makers at the right place and time can constitute a significant competitive advantage.

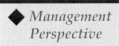
Management Perspective

This is where the demand for internetworking solutions should start:

1. What key decision maker is lacking timely information and where is that decision maker located in relation to the required information?
2. What competitive advantage would the delivery of that information afford that decision maker?
3. Is the business opportunity or competitive advantage delivered by the internetworking solution measurable in terms of market share, sales dollars, expense reduction, and bottom-line impact?
4. How do the strategic business projections of one, two, and five years from now affect the need for distributed information?

The Application and Data Layers: Deliver Business Interoperability Requirements

The business layer should offer the internetworking designer a sense of what *business solutions* are being sought. End-users do not talk in terms of routers or interoperability, nor should they be expected to. Armed with an understanding of *what* needs to be accomplished from a business perspective, the internetwork designer must go about deciding *how* these business solutions could be reached from an end-user perspective.

In other words, how do the end-users picture themselves accessing the "right" information that will lead to business solutions? Are they sitting at their Macintoshes? At home or in the office? What does the "right" information look like on the user's screen?

The effort at this level is to define the level of interoperability sought by the decision maker as well as the applications necessary to deliver that required level of interoperability. Levels of interoperability can be defined in a roughly parallel manner with the OSI 7-layer model.

For example, does the user merely need dial-in access from home or on the road to the corporate LAN (layers 1–3)? Or does the user require seamless integration between his/her Macintosh and the corporate Netware servers as well as access to the IBM mainframe (layers 1–7)?

For the purposes of this internetworking design summary, the key *data layer* concerns are:

1. Where is the location of the data required to produce the "right" information?
2. How does the data source location relate physically to the "right" information destination location?
3. In what format (database) is the required data?
4. How much data must be transported over what distances at what speed in order to ensure delivery of the "right" information at the "right" time.

The Network Layer: Protocol Mix and Match

Now that it is clearer *what* business goal to accomplish, *how* the users wish to accomplish this business goal, and *where* the data to deliver the "right" information is located, the next job is to examine these locations to be internetworked more carefully in order to produce an internetworking *"to do"* list.

The technique is relatively simple but not necessarily easy. Using the OSI 7-layer model, a 7-layer protocol stack map is made for each node that is likely to be a candidate for internetworking. One of the key outcomes of this phase is the identification of those elements of a node's protocol stack, or of the overall internetworking plan, which are *unknowns*.

In internetwork design, unlike the popular expression, it is often the things that you don't know that will hurt you.

Once protocol stack maps have been completed for all known nodes, protocol comparison between those nodes that must communicate is undertaken. Protocol discrepancies on a layer-by-layer basis are identified, and protocol conversion possibilities are proposed.

The outcome of this phase is a *logical* network design outlining *what* needs to be accomplished along internetwork links. Capacity issues and wide area networking issues will be discussed in later chapters. This logical network design is independent of the currently available technology which will be employed to *physically* implement the internetwork structure.

The Technology Layer: Delivering the Business Solution

If the network layer produces the logical network design which describes *what* internetworking tasks must be accomplished, then the technology layer analysis determines *how* the required internetwork functionality will be delivered. Discussions in this chapter have introduced a number of different categories of internetworking technology including communications servers, LAN modems, bridges, routers, gateways, repeaters, and converters, to name but a few. In most cases, these internetworking devices have been examined from a functional standpoint, concentrating on what types of internetworking solutions were delivered by a given classification of devices.

Once a logical internetworking design has been determined, one faces the rather tedious chore of matching *internetworking opportunities* (the logical design) to *internetworking solutions* (the technology or physical design). One internetwork

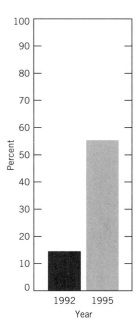

Figure 6-45 Internetworking demand: Percent of Fortune 1000 companies with LAN-based corporate networks. (*Source:* Forrester Research)

link at a time, one must review the required functionality of the logical design versus the delivered functionality of the vast array of internetworking devices.

Remember, there is always more than one way to internetwork devices. The "right" way is the way that works best for a given organization, both from a financial as well as functional standpoint. This entire internetworking design process must be conducted without losing sight of the real justification for deploying internetworking technology: The business advantage gained by supplying the right decision maker with the right information at the right place and time.

The Future of Internetworking

It is hard to overstate the opportunities for internetworking analysis, design, and implementation in the future. If the driving forces which support expanding opportunities in this area were to be reexamined, one would be certain that demand for internetworking has yet to reach its full potential.

Beyond the previously mentioned recognition of information as both a corporate asset as well as a tool to be leveraged to competitive advantage, the forms and delivery modes of that information are changing in ways to support expansion of internetworking opportunities as well.

The graph represented in Figure 6-45 represents growth in just one area of internetworking: Corporate InterNetworks Based on LAN Architectures. There are many other potential opportunities for increased internetworking activities.

For example, multimedia and desktop videoconferencing are two emerging technologies whose impact on day-to-day business are yet to be realized. Imaging activities supporting workgroup productivity and document routing and tracking applications will increase internetwork traffic as well as internetwork design sophistication requirements significantly. The increased integration of voice traffic with data traffic will lead to singular integrated desktop communications requirements for the home and office. The challenges of internetworking with the "mobile worker" of the future will open new internetworking opportunities as well. Internetworking trends will be examined further in the context of overall trends in the field of data communications in Chapter 13, "Where Do We Go From Here? Trends to Watch."

CHAPTER SUMMARY

The overall topic of internetworking was divided into five major areas of study, including:

> Dialing into and out of LANs
> LAN-to-LAN Connection
> Integration with the minicomputer and mainframe environment
> Integration with the UNIX environment
> Integration with the Macintosh environment

While studying the options for dialing into and out of LANs, the capabilities and limitations of remote control software, as well as the role of communications and remote access LAN servers and LAN modems in fulfilling remote communications needs for network-based workstations, were explored.

The study of LAN-to-LAN connection introduced a multitude of internetworking devices, including repeaters, bridges, routers, and gateways. The importance of the OSI model in the analysis, design, and implementation of LAN-to-LAN connectivity was heavily stressed.

In order to understand the implications of integrating LANs with an SNA mainframe environment, it was first necessary to learn a bit more about SNA and its protocols. Integration levels from simple terminal emulation to integrated LAN/SNA traffic on shared backbones were studied. LAN integration with IBM's SNA environment was contrasted with the methodology as well as technology involved with integrating LANs with Digital Equipment Corporation's DECnet environment.

LAN integration with the UNIX environment began with a study of TCP/IP and the internet suite of protocols. TCP/IP for DOS-based machines was explored as a method enabling connection between LANs and UNIX-based servers and workstations. The many issues surrounding installation and use of multiprotocol software were outlined and explained.

Macintosh integration with LANs was approached by delineating varying levels of integration from simple file transfer or dial-in, to full and transparent integration with full-featured LAN network operating systems such as Netware, Vines, and LAN Manager.

Finally, many of the design methods introduced throughout the chapter were summarized and enhanced as the chapter closed with a look at the future opportunities in the field of internetworking.

KEY TERMS

access server	filtering	multiprotocol software	RIF
adaptive source routing transparent bridge	forward-if-not-local	NDIS	RIP
Appletalk	forward-if-proven-remote	network interface card	routers
APPN	forwarding	network node	routing protocols
A/UX	front end processor	NFS	routing table
balun	gateway	nonroutable protocols	scalability
broadcast filtering	hierarchical	ODI	SDLC
central directory server	IBM 3174, 3274	OSPF	SDLC converter
cluster controller	IBM 3270	passthrough	7-hop limit
coax mux	IBM 3745	Pathworks	SLIP
Common transport semantics	Internet suite of protocols	PDS	SMTP
communications server	internetworking	peer-to-peer	SNA
data storm	IP	poll spoofing	source address
DECnet	IPX	PPP	source routing bridge
destination address	known local nodes	protocol	source routing
dial-in server	LAN modem	protocol conversion	transparent bridge
discovery packets	LAT	Protocol Independent Routers	Spanning tree algorithm
distance vector	link state	proxy polling	TCP/IP
DNA	Localtalk	remote bridge	telecommuting
downsizing	local bridge	remote client operation mode	terminal server
encapsulate	mobile computing	remote control software	The New SNA
encapsulating bridge	modem remote control operation mode	remote LAN node	3270 emulation
end node	modem server	repeater	transparency
explorer packet	multiport serial board	rightsizing	transparent bridge
	multiprotocol routers		tunneling

REVIEW QUESTIONS

1. Describe typical business needs that might lead to an implementation of dial-in/dial-out capabilities to a LAN.
2. What are the advantages and disadvantages of installing a communications server or access server on a LAN?
3. Describe how a remote user can gain access to a particular LAN-attached workstation rather than just to a LAN server.
4. Draw a model of the OSI 7-layer model matching internetworking devices of various types to their corresponding OSI layer.
5. Differentiate between the different types of bridges in terms of functionality and the types of LANs they connect.
6. Differentiate between bridges (local and remote), routers, and multiprotocol routers in terms of proper internetworking application as well as implementation.
7. Explain the potential impact on internetwork traffic and performance of the RIP, OSPF, and PPP router protocols.
8. Explain the difference in terms of internetwork impact, potential financial savings, and performance, of the following SNA/LAN integration alternatives: token ring adapters for cluster controllers, TCP/IP passthrough, SDLC conversion, and protocol independent routing.
9. Explain the key aspects of multiprotocol software, including any compatibility issues with device drivers or network adapter cards.
10. Explain why many Macintoshes are now networked via Ethernet in terms of protocols, impact of the OSI model, relative performance of alternatives, and enabling technology.
11. What are the key differences, advantages, and disadvantages of multiprotocol routing versus protocol independent routing?
12. What are the five major categories of internetworking?
13. What are the four major information sharing needs of remote computing users?
14. What are the three major access points for remote users to gain access to a LAN?
15. What is the difference between a LAN modem and a dial-in server?
16. What are the key differences and similarities between the two logical topologies or operation modes of remote computing?
17. Outline the similarities and differences between communications software and remote control software.
18. What are the key differences in terms of capabilities and cost/benefit between client-based remote control software and server-based remote control software?
19. What are some of the key features that remote control software should possess which are unique to the remote computing environment?
20. What is required in terms of hardware and software for a remote PC to utilize LAN-attached resources?
21. What are the advantages and disadvantages of installing a communications server?
22. Compare the technological differences, functional capabilities, and relative cost/benefit of the four major communication server architectures.
23. Why can dialing out of a LAN be more complicated than dialing in?
24. What is required of communications software in order to function correctly on a LAN?
25. What is protocol conversion and how does it relate to the OSI model?
26. Why is a repeater known as a physical layer device?
27. What advantage does a repeater offer to Ethernet or Token Ring networks?
28. Describe the logic employed by a bridge.
29. How does a bridge know whether or not a given destination address is local?
30. Draw an I-P-O model for a translating bridge. Describe the processing step fully.
31. What is the cause and effect of the 7-hop limit of source routing bridges?
32. What impact do source routing bridges have on network traffic levels?
33. What are the key physical configuration differences between remote and local bridges?
34. How does the spanning tree algorithm prevent and utilize redundant links?
35. What is the difference between filtering rate and forwarding rate?
36. Would a bridge or router be more likely to have a higher filtering rate? Defend your answer.
37. A bridge works at which sublayer of the OSI model?
38. Explain how higher level protocols can be embedded in an Ethernet frame in terms of processing performed by bridges and routers.
39. What are the differences and similarities between IP and IPX?
40. Explain how routers maintain and use routing tables.
41. How does a router's forwarding logic differ from a bridge's forwarding logic?
42. What are the implications in terms of physical design and cost/benefit of the differences cited in the previous question?
43. What is meant by the term "best path" and how does a router determine such a thing?

44. What is the source of any negative impact that routers may have on networks?
45. What are the two major categories of best-path algorithms?
46. What are some of the significant advantages of the PPP protocol?
47. How does a gateway differ from a router?
48. Why is a classic SNA network known as hierarchical?
49. What are the roles of the front-end processor and cluster controller in a classic SNA environment?
50. What is required for a PC to converse with an IBM mainframe?
51. What is required for a LAN-attached PC to act as a gateway to an IBM mainframe?
52. How can a coax mux be cost-justified?
53. What is meant by the term "nonroutable"?
54. How can a nonroutable protocol be transferred effectively between networks?
55. Explain the three challenges to SNA/LAN traffic integration.
56. Compare the four alternatives for SNA/LAN integration presented in terms of functionality, protocols employed, and cost/benefit.
57. At which OSI model layer does a protocol independent router work? Explain your answer fully.
58. What is the difference between proxy polling and poll spoofing?
59. What impact do proxy polling and poll spoofing have on network traffic?
60. What is the relationship between APPN and SNA?
61. What is meant by The New SNA?
62. What are the key characteristics of a DECnet network?
63. What are some of the reasons why UNIX/LAN integration is of such interest?
64. What are some of the key applications and obstacles of UNIX/LAN integration?
65. What is the advantage of operating a PC with multiple protocol stacks?
66. What are the hardware and software requirements of running a PC with multiple protocol stacks?
67. What is a proper business application of a TCP/IP gateway?
68. What are some of the key analysis questions and their implications on the choice of multiprotocol software?
69. What are the key technical challenges to Macintosh/LAN integration?
70. What is the advantage of the AppleTalk's suite of protocols complementary structure to the OSI model?
71. What is the key advantage from the Mac user's perspective of Mac integration with a full-featured LAN?
72. How can the OSI, I-P-O, H-S-M, and top-down models be used in internetworking analysis and design? Explain the role and advantages of each model individually.

ACTIVITIES

1. Gather product literature on the category of internetworking devices known as LAN Modems. Prepare a chart or bulletin board highlighting distinguishing characteristics such as network architectures and network operating systems supported, number of simultaneous users, cost, interfaces, etc.
2. Design an alternative to the LAN modem. Include all required software and hardware components. Price out these components in order to support comparative cost analysis versus the LAN modem.
3. Go to the computer section of a local bookstore. Count the number of books and periodicals available for each of the different categories of internetworking as listed in this chapter. Display your results in graphic form.
4. Research articles that describe both the pros and cons of TCP/IP as a suite of internetworking protocols. Prepare an objective report on TCP/IP and alternative internetworking protocols.
5. Read *The Cuckoo's Egg* by Cliff Stoll; then share your feelings about it with your professor and classmates.
6. Find an opportunity requiring internetworking design. Use the methodology described in the final section of this chapter. Don't be intimidated. The objective is to organize known facts within a framework in order to provide structure for questions and further investigation. View the assignment as practice in asking questions rather than a forced march to find answers.
7. Inquire at your campus computer center about the possibility of acquiring a computer account with access to the Internet. Send me some E-mail and let me know what you think of the book. (Profanity is not allowed on the Internet.) My E-mail address is GOLDMAN@VM.CC.PURDUE.EDU
8. Internetworking devices such as bridges and routers can be very confusing. Gather product literature on a variety of bridges and routers. Read this literature carefully and prepare a comparative functionality chart detailing the operational differences, as well as price differences, between these broad categories of internetworking devices.

Featured References

Bridges

Bradner, Scott. "Ethernet Bridges & Routers: Faster than Fast Enough," *Data Communications*, vol. 21, no. 3 (February 1992), p. 58.

St. Clair, Melanie. "Broadening the Scope of Bridges," *LAN Times*, vol. 9, no. 6 (April 6, 1992), p. 49.

Tolly, Kevin. "Local Token Ring Bridges: Speed and Simplicity Make Shopping a Snap," *Data Communications*, vol. 21, no. 11 (August 1992), p. 94.

Feldman, Robert. "Classic Bridges Can't Cope With Internetworking Maze," *LAN Times*, vol. 10, no. 11 (June 14, 1993), p. 1.

Case Studies

Molloy, Maureen. "Bank Buys into Cisco Plan for Handling SNA Traffic," *Network World*, vol. 9, no. 45 (November 9, 1992), p.1.

Wright, David. "Agency Takes 'Collapsed' Approach and Saves Time," *LAN Times*, vol. 9, no. 17 (September 14, 1992), p. 51.

Hume, Barbara. "Out with the Iron: LANs Take Control at U-Haul," *LAN Times*, vol. 9, no. 20 (October 26, 1992), p. 48.

Feldman, Robert. "Coldwell Banker Upgrades LAN-WAN Links," *LAN Times*, vol. 9, no. 13 (July 20, 1992), p. 41.

Hume, Barbara. "pcAnywhere Links Dean Witter Offices," *LAN Times*, vol. 9, no. 9 (May 25, 1992), p. 37.

Walker, Robyn. "Roadway Works to Reduce MIS Costs at Remote Sites," *LAN Times*, vol. 9, no. 2 (February 10, 1992), p. 47.

Didio, Laura. "Green Spring Ends the Paper Chase," *LAN Times*, vol. 10, no. 10 (May 24, 1993), p. 59.

Gateways

Brandel, William. "Banyan Announces VINES Enhancements" (VINES/SNA Gateway), *LAN Times*, vol. 9, no. 8 (May 11, 1992), p. 14.

Tolly, Kevin. "Mac to SNA Gateways:Picking Apple–IBM Products," *Data Communications*, vol. 21, no. 2 (January 21, 1992), p. 12.

Hubs

Tolly, Kevin. "Grading Smart Hubs for Corporate Networking," *Data Communications*, vol. 21, no. 17 (November 21, 1992), p. 56.

Greenfield, David. "Switching Hubs Give Ethernet New Life," *Data Communications*, vol. 21, no. 3 (February 1992), p. 41.

Internetwork Design

Lippis, Nick. "The Internetwork Decade," *Data Communications*, vol. 20, no. 14 (October 1991).

Barrett, Ed. "The Critical Steps to Hub Selection, *LAN Technology*, vol. 8, no. 11 (October 15, 1992), p. 39.

Derfler, Frank, and Steve Rigney. "From LAN to WAN: Bringing Your Networks Together, *PC Magazine*, vol. 10, no. 15 (September 10, 1991), p. 106.

Tomlinson, Gary. "Redefining Interoperability in the 90's," *LAN Times*, vol. 8, no. 15 (August 19, 1991), p. 50.

Internetwork Architectures

Biery, Roger. "Collapsed Backbones: Next Step in Premises Networks," *LAN Times*, vol. 9, no. 17 (September 14, 1992), p. 47.

Digital Equipment Corporation, *DECnet Digital Network Architecture (Phase IV)*, Order no. AA-149A-TC, 1982.

LAN Modems

Johnson, Johna. "Putting Remote Sites on the LAN," *Data Communications*, vol. 21, no. 6 (April 1992), p. 47.

Johnson, Johna. "LAN Modems: The Missing Link for Remote Connectivity," *Data Communications*, vol. 22, no. 4 (March 1993), p. 101.

White, Roger, and Dave Doering. "The Netmodem/E: Shiva's Next Generation of Modem," *LAN Times*, vol.9, no. 8 (May 11, 1992), p. 84.

Williams, Dennis. "A Plug-n-Play Solution to Modem Sharing," *LAN Times*, vol. 9, no. 15 (August 10, 1992), p. 63.

Bachus, Kevin, and Elizabeth Longsworth. "Road Nodes," *Corporate Computing*, vol. 2, no. 3 (March 1993), p. 55.

Macintosh

Carrell, Jeffrey, and David Greenfield. "Across the Great Divide: PC-to-Mac Connections," *PC Magazine*, vol. 11, no. 9 (May 12, 1992), p. 173.

Derfler, Frank. "MAC/Lantastic Connectivity," *PC Magazine*, vol. 11, no. 14 (August 1992), p. 551.

Didio, Laura. "GatorStar GX Marries Router and Repeater in a Single Box" (MAC/Ethernet Connectivity), *LAN Times*, vol. 9, no. 1 (January 20, 1992), p.18.

Bowden, Eric. "Dayna Gives Macs Direct Access to Netware Servers," *LAN Times*, vol. 9, no. 5 (March 23, 1992), p. 1.

Wylie, Margie. "Mac Networks to Snub Localtalk for E-Net," *Network World*, vol. 9, no. 30 (July 27, 1992), p. 13.

Molloy, Maureen. "User Resolves Appletalk Routing Woes," *Network World*, vol. 9, no. 28 (July 13, 1992), p. 1.

Carr, Jim. "The Mac Moves to Ethernet," *Data Communications*, vol. 21, no. 14 (October 1992), p. 115..

Maloy, A. Cory. "DOS and Macintosh Overcome Barriers," *LAN Times*, vol. 9, no. 6 (April 6, 1992), p. 31.

Salamone, Salvatore. "Merging the Macintosh into Enterprise Nets," *Data Communications*, vol. 21, no. 18, p. 49.

Multiprotocol Software

Lam, S. S. (ed.). *Tutorial: Principles of Communication and Networking Protocols* (IEEE Computer Society Press), 1984.

Kine, Bill. "Options for Supporting Multiple Protocols," *LAN Times*. vol. 8, no. 24 (January 6, 1992), p.50.

Hancock, Bill. "Multiprotocol Networking: Advantage DEC," *Data Communications*, vol. 21, no. 4 (March 1992), p. 91.

Salamone, Sylvester. "Multiprotocol Software Moves up the Stack," *Data Communications*, vol. 21, no. 11 (August 1992), p. 121.

Jander, Mary. "Netware Gets Some Mainframe Aid," *Data Communications*, vol. 21, no. 2 (January 21, 1992), p. 74.

Mohen, Joe. "OSI Interoperability: Separating Fact from Fiction," *Data Communications*, vol. 21, no. 2 (January 21, 1992), p. 41.

Bowden, Eric. "Netware Connectivity Adds Red to LAN Manager Palette," *LAN Times*, vol. 9, no. 6 (April 6, 1992), p. 68.

Remote Access Software

Ellison, Carol. "Productivity from Afar: Modem Remote Control Software," *PC Magazine*, vol. 11, no. 4 (February 25, 1992), p. 189.

Bowden, Eric. "LAN Manager Remote Access Manages Communication," *LAN Times*, vol. 9, no. 6 (April 6, 1992), p. 69.

Duncan, Thom. "RLN: The Office Away from Home," *LAN Times*, vol. 9, no. 7 (April 20, 1992), p. 1.

Bachus, Kevin, and Elizabeth Longsworth. "Road Nodes," *Corporate Computing*, vol. 2, no. 3 (March 1993), p. 55.

Repeaters

McCullough, Thomas. "Don't Forget Repeaters for Connectivity," *LAN Times*, vol. 9, no. 11 (June 22, 1992), p. 31.

Routers

Feldman, Robert. "Can PC-based Routing Replace Standalone Boxes?," *LAN Times*, vol. 10, no. 11 (June 14, 1993), p. 110.

Williams, Dennis, and Blaine Homer. "Routers: LAN 'Shakers and Movers'," *LAN Times*, vol. 9, no. 20 (October 26, 1992), p. 69.

Koss, Gregory. "Combining SNA, LAN Data over One WAN Connection," *LAN Times*, vol. 8, no. 24 (January 6, 1992), p. 33.

Molloy, Maureen. "Packet Forwarding Not the Only Measure of Routers," *LAN Times*, vol. 9, no. 27 (July 6, 1992), p.1.

Layland, Robin. "IBM's Multiprotocol Router: Worth the Wait," *Data Communications*, vol. 21, no. 4 (March 1992), p. 69 .

Bradner, Scott, and David Greenfield. "Routers: Building the Highway," *PC Magazine*, vol. 12, no. 6 (March 30, 1993), p. 221.

Hindin, Eric. "Mutiprotocol Routers:Small Is Getting Big," *Data Communications*, vol. 21, no. 8 (May 21, 1992), p.79.

Tolly, Kevin, and Eric Hindin. "Can Routers Be Trusted with Critical Data?," *Data Communications*, vol. 22, no. 7 (May 1993), p. 58.

Router Protocols

Molloy, Maureen. "OSPF: Addressing RIP's Shortcomings," *Network World*, vol. 9, no. 28 (July 13, 1992), p. 13.

Moy, John. "OSPF Meets Growing Demands on TCP/IP," *LAN Times*, vol. 9, no. 7 (April 20, 1992), p. 35.

Brown, Bob. "Vendors Unite to Back PPP Router to Router Protocol," *Network World*, vol. 9, no. 27 (July 6, 1992), p. 29.

Gotelli, Debra, and Greg Linn. "A Point-by-Point Investigation of PPP," *LAN Times*, vol. 9, no. 21 (November 9, 1992), p. 35.

Salamone, Salvatore. "OSPF Routing: Better, but Not Good Enough," *Data Communications*, vol. 21, no. 14 (October 1992), p. 53.

Gotelli, Debra, and Greg Linn. "Point-to-Point Protocol," *Netware Connection*, (Nov./Dec. 1992), p. 26.

Servers—Communication

Bowden, Eric. "LAN Times Looks at Comm Servers," *LAN Times*, vol. 8, no. 24 (January 6, 1992), p. 61.

Derfler, Frank, and Susan Thomas. "Asynchronous Communications Servers: Dialing in at Large," *PC Magazine*, vol. 11, no. 18 (October 27, 1992), p. 169.

SNA and APPN

Martin, James. *SNA: IBM's Networking Solution* (Prentice Hall, 1987).

IBM Corporation. *Systems Network Architecture Concepts and Product* (IBM, 1986).

IBM Corporation. *Systems Network Architecture Technical Overview* (IBM, 1986).

Fernandez, Joseph, and Kathryn Winkler. "Using SMI to Model SNA Networks," *IEEE Communications*, vol. 31, no. 5 (May 1993), p. 60.

Salamone, Salvatore. "Playing 'Beat the Clock' with SNA," *Data Communications*, vol. 21, no. 16 (November 1992), p. 57.

Kapoor, Atul. *SNA: Architecture, Protocols, and Implementation* (New York: McGraw-Hill, 1992).

Tolly, Kevin. "The Long Goodbye: FEPs and Internetworks," *Data Communications*, vol. 21, no. 10 (July 1992), p. 43.

Tolly, Kevin. "Testing the New SNA," *Data Communications*, vol. 21, no. 8 (May 21 1992), p. 58.

Tolly, Kevin. "SDLC Conversion: We Have a Winner," *Data Communications*, vol. 21, no. 10 (July 1992), p. 87.

Tolly, Kevin. "Diagnosing SNA Gateways," *Data Communications*, vol. 21, no. 5 (March 21 1992), p. 59.

Bowman, Michael. "Rationally Migrating SNA to Multiprotocol Intenetworks," *LAN Times,* vol. 9, no. 2 (February 10, 1992), p. 63.

Keough, Lee. "APPN: IBM's Bid for Multiprotocol Nets," *Data Communications,* vol. 21, no. 7 (May 1992), p. 55.

Hindin, Eric. "Channel Extenders Get a Critical Boost," *Data Communications,* vol. 21, no. 1 (January 1992), p. 71.

Lippis, Nick. "APPN for 3270 Traffic? Better Think Twice," *Data Communications,* vol. 21, no. 7 (May 1992), p. 27.

Kerr, Susan. "How IBM Is Rebuilding SNA," *Datamation,* vol. 38, no. 20 (October 1, 1992), p. 28.

Connor, Deni. "Who Will Support APPN?," *Datamation,* vol. 38, no. 20 (October 1, 1992), p. 46.

Tolly, Kevin, et al. "Checking out Channel Attached Gateways," *Data Communications,* vol. 22, no. 8 (May 21, 1993), p. 75.

UNIX/PC Integration—TCP/IP

Rose, Marshall. *The Simple Book: An Introduction to Management of TCP/IP-based Internets* (Prentice Hall, 1991).

Comer, Douglas. *Internetworking with TCP/IP: Principles, Protocols, and Architecture, second edition* (Prentice Hall, 1991).

Derfler, Frank. "TCP/IP Packages for Netware 3.11," *PC Magazine,* vol. 11, no. 13 (July 1992), p. 415.

Dostert, Michele. "Integrating PC LANs with UNIX Systems," *LAN Times,* vol. 9, no. 9 (May 25, 1992), p. 23.

Dostert, Michele. "PC-to-TCP/IP Products Flood the Networking Marketplace," *LAN Times,* vol. 9, no. 10 (June 8, 1992), p. 22.

Snell, Ned. "Why TCP/IP Still Has the Edge," *Datamation,* vol. 38, no. 20 (October 1, 1992), p.38.

CASE STUDY

Mail Access Made Easy Via Chameleon TCP/IP Package

Global communications takes on new meaning when communicating with coworkers means exchanging E-mail and sharing files with individuals scattered across the world.

For software developers and managers at Siemens Nixdorf Information Systems Inc.'s Santa Clara, Calif.-based Research and Development Division, exchanging mail and transferring files over the corporate Unix mail network is the primary means of communicating with their colleagues at the U.S. company's Burlington, Mass., headquarters and with Siemens Nixdorf Information Systems' 51,000 employees worldwide.

For users of the Santa Clara facility's Unix-based machines, sending and receiving mail to and from the corporate Unix mail system was simple. Initiating the Unix remote login command allowed

them to access the U.S. division's Unix mail-distribution server in Boston via the corporation's WAN. But for the lab's PC-based workgroup, gaining access was a slow and frustrating process until it found Chameleon, a Windows-based TCP/IP communications package developed by NetManage Inc. of Cupertino, Calif.

"Here in Santa Clara, we have two worlds: a Unix world, which is a TCP/IP Ethernet with Unix PCs and servers, and a PC world—which consists of Siemens 386 and 286 machines, a Novell file and database server, a fax server, and an optical disk server running on a Novell NetWare LAN," said Dr. Olaf Kaestner, director of Technology & Special Projects at Siemens Nixdorf. "Linking the two worlds is a filtering bridge."

Access to the outside world—the Siemens Nixdorf corporate net-

work and the TCP/IP internet—is through the TCP/IP LAN, which is linked to the company's Boston office via a Cisco router and a dedicated 56Kbps telephone line. A satellite link ties the Boston Unix mail-distribution server to a similar mail server at the Siemens Nixdorf corporate headquarters in Paderborn, Germany.

To utilize Siemens Nixdorf's corporate mail network and to gain access to the Internet, Kaestner and the other PC users at the Santa Clara center needed to send and receive mail and transfer files to and from their local Unix mail server, a Nixdorf Targon/35, residing on the TCP/IP network.

When the Santa Clara office first opened, the group's 286 and 386 machines were directly tied to the host by RS-232 lines. Before a PC user could send a file to or retrieve a file from the Unix server, software installed on the host needed to communicate with the terminal emulation program resident on the PC.

"Not only was the program slow and character-oriented, but it also forced us to be tied to the specific machine that the program supported," said Kaestner. "For us, it was very important to have a more open system since we needed to have software that would be supported worldwide."

Today Chameleon, a comprehensive applications package for Windows 3.X TCP/IP communications, allows users to exchange mail messages and files to and from the Unix mail server via the Novell and TCP/IP networks.

The package's NetMail facility enables users to create and send mail messages to the server from within Windows, using dialog boxes and point-and-click buttons. Incoming messages, which are forwarded from the Targon/35 to the mailbox on the user's personal computer, can be saved, edited, or forwarded to any other PC user on the network. Chameleon also enables PCs on the Novell network to transfer files to and from the server using the File Transfer Protocol command.

When Kaestner began his evaluation of TCP/IP communica-tions programs, his intent was to make a purchase decision based on what he calls user feeling—"Is this a product I want to work with?"—rather than on a technical analysis of the protocols. "I was much more interested in how the product worked within my environment, rather than analyzing how its protocols were implemented," Kaest-ner said.

To be successful in his Windows environment, the program had to be Windows 3.1-based, run Novell IPX protocols and TCP/IP protocols in parallel, and support domain name service—the Internet directory service.

"We looked at several DOS packages, but our work environment here is more graphics-oriented," he said. "Our goal was to be able to send files locally to the Novell file server and to communicate with the Unix server within Windows, without having to switch from IPX to TCP/IP. Since many of us are on several standards committees, we also wanted a program that allowed us to route messages to Internet subscribers."

Chameleon not only met these requirements, but it was also able to do so without exacting a stiff price in memory. Because Chameleon implements the TCP/IP stack as a Windows dynamic link library (DLL) and not a TSR pro-gram, the application requires only 6.1KB of the PC's lower 640KB memory.

"There are many things, such as the network shell, that must be loaded in to memory," said Kaestner. "Although the introduc-tion of DOS 5.0 eased things a bit by providing access to upper memory blocks, it is only a partial solution. The Chameleon Windows TCP/IP communications applications pro-gram frees us the PC's base mem-ory for programs that cannot be loaded elsewhere."

Today the package is running on 11 of the facility's 12 Windows 3.1 PCs, allowing them to exchange E-mail and files with employees in the East Coast research and devel-opment lab, as well communicate with Siemens Nixdorf employees worldwide.

"Chameleon allows those of us on the PC LAN to communicate with anyone on the corporate Unix network," Kaestner added. "We now can receive a file transfer from a Siemens Nixdorf engineer in Germany or send mail to a project manager in Singapore as easily as we exchange E-mail messages among ourselves."

Source: Angie Mongillo, "Mail Access Made Easy via Chameleon TCP/IP Package," *LAN Times,* vol.9, no. 17 (September 14, 1992), p. 77. Reprinted with permission of McGraw-Hill, *LAN Times.*

Business Case Study Questions

Activities

1. Prepare a top-down model for this case by extracting pertinent facts from the case and placing them in their respective layers within the top-down model.

Business

1. What was the business motivation for this internet-working design effort?
2. What business problem was adversely affecting productivity?

Applications

1. List all applications performed by users as well as the nature of the workstation platform on which these applications were performed.
2. How was transparency from underlying networking protocols achieved for users?
3. Were clear evaluation criteria or success measure-ments established prior to the evaluation of technol-ogy? If so, what were they?

Network

1. What were the exact multiprotocol requirements of this network? Draw protocol stacks to illustrate which protocols were required on which workstation platforms.
2. Are there unknown protocol issues? If so, what are they?

Technology

1. List all hardware and software technology employed before and after the internetwork design.

Seamless Communications Over a Diverse Network

As the case study's network diagram is examined, note each LAN segment and the internetworking devices that connect those LAN segments.

To Do:

For each internetworking device employed:
1. Explain why a given internetworking device was employed in a particular location joining any two LAN segments.
2. If the choice cannot be explained, identify questions which, when answered, would provide the necessary information to understand the internetworking design decisions that led to the diagrammed internetwork implementation.

C A S E   S T U D Y

Coldwell Banker Upgrades LAN-WAN Links

Since its formation after the 1906 San Francisco earthquake, Coldwell Banker, the third-ranking residential real estate franchise in the United States, has built a solid foundation. During 1991 Coldwell listed more than 437,000 residential properties and transacted more than $44.5 billion in home sales.

In the past, communicating information to more than 1900 real estate offices with nearly 40,000 sales associates was a formidable task for the real estate giant. Particularly daunting was the task of economically integrating remote sales offices into the information flow of the company's central-site, IBM Token-Ring LAN located in Mission Viejo, Calif. More often than not, Coldwell Banker reverted to "sneaker net" and courier service.

To further complicate the task, as a member of the Sears Financial Network, Coldwell also had to report the same information, after it had been analyzed by Coldwell Banker headquarters staff, to the corporation's IBM mainframe in Dallas.

For a real estate company, information exchange is crucial. Yet, even though Coldwell's brokerage offices already had DOS-based, IBM PS/2 computers, personnel used to manually fill out forms that would then be sent to a metropolitan or regional office where data would in turn be keyed into a 3270 host data entry terminal. The large metropolitan and regional offices used leased lines to communicate with the Texas-based mainframe. Delays were inherent due to courier and keyboarding time; mistakes were introduced during keying; and the leased lines and mainframe processing were expensive.

Jason Shane, director of distributed services for Coldwell Banker, and his staff started an exhaustive, two-year search for a wide-area communication system that would tie together all the isolated LANs and other computing resources, be economically viable, and provide an automatic and streamlined system that could be easily used by a multitude of non-technical personnel. They finally settled on XcelleNet Inc.'s Remote-Ware Communications Management System, a set of software tools, providing manageable connections on low-cost telecommunications across both WANs and LANs.

"This may seem obvious, but there are two ways to increase profitability: generate more revenue and decrease overhead costs," said Shane. "Although I can't directly affect a specific sale, I can provide our agents the automation to do a more effective job, and then we can drive down the costs of communications. It is difficult for me to compare our new dial-up network with our previous mainframe data entry methods with its limited communications options. Our new system has opened a door that wasn't available previously because all the options were literally multimillion-dollar choices."

Remote PCs to a Central LAN

"Our initial plan was to provide remote communications to our 500 company-owned brokerage offices with subsequent roll-out to our 1,400 franchised locations," explained Shane. "Dedicated leased lines, which can be economical if you are moving large amounts of data on a continuing basis, just didn't make sense for our remote offices because—although we were transferring mission-critical information such as number, value, and expiration of real estate listings—that data exchange needed to occur only intermittently."

In 1990 Shane began installing RemoteWare to send and receive information over standard dial-up telephone lines. In this case, Coldwell Banker uses industry-standard 9600bps V.32bis dial-up modems. This combination of RemoteWare and dial-up connections for a "network on demand" is a critical element in helping the firm keep costs in line.

The software at the 500 brokerage offices automatically calls the central site each week. The central-site server consists of an IBM PS/2 running OS/2 with 16 communications ports. Two additional servers are dedicated for communications with Coldwell's franchised locations and its Relocation Services division. All three central-site servers are connected to the Mission Viejo IBM Token Ring, which also supports about 250 PCs for corporate personnel. The final link is a 3174 Token-Ring gateway to the IBM mainframes in Dallas.

When he began providing electronic communications to the 1900 remote offices, Shane had three primary reasons, in addition to cost savings, for moving to the RemoteWare dial-up system. First, with predominantly non-technical staff members at the remotely-located sites, an automatic, one-

step communication process was a necessity. "We've made communications transparent to our users," said Shane. "They simply fill out an online form and press a single key to automatically transmit the information to Mission Viejo. But, in addition to our initial 500 corporate-owned installations, we have to provide the 1400 independent franchises a simple communications method that they can make ready use of."

Second, with so many remote locations, Coldwell Banker needed a network that was easy to support from the central site. "We've transferred the setup and day-to-day support of the Remote-Ware system from the information systems staff to our customer service representatives. With very basic training, they are able to add remote nodes, reconfigure telephone numbers, and deploy new definition files. Occasionally they can't complete some of the very technical tasks, and we supply backup support. By using the customer support staff that already has daily contact with our remote offices, we are able to support and maintain a large network that wouldn't have been possible with our limited technical staff."

Coldwell Banker has also found the system to be highly reliable—with automatic error recovery that restarts at the specific packet where the communication was interrupted—even for longer sessions. "Several large offices are transferring nearly 20 megabytes every night in less than two hours," said Shane. "Because of the data compression algorithms in RemoteWare, we are getting an actual data rate of nearly 25Kbps, which is almost double the rated capacity of the 14.4Kbps modems used at these large offices."

"This solution has been so successful that new projects continue to come in at an increasing rate

from divisions such as the brokerage finance group. This group wants to electronically communicate its budget spreadsheets across the country, have the remote sites enter data, and then send them back to Mission Viejo for consolidation," continued Shane. "It's a relief to know that we have a one-button solution that's easy to use and won't be a nightmare for us to support," he said.

Third, with so many independent locations, Coldwell Banker needed a system that could flexibly support a variety of computing resources including DOS, Windows, OS/2, Macintosh, Unix, and others. "Even if an office has a minicomputer, if they can hang a PC from the LAN, we can still give them cost-effective central-site connectivity. We had to have the most versatile connections for the diverse environments of our franchised offices."

Advanced Applications

Coldwell Banker is beginning to look at the RemoteWare system for a variety of new advanced applications. For example, a new project being considered by the company is the further automation of relocation services, especially for Fortune 500 companies that are clients of Coldwell Banker Relocation Services Inc. In order to achieve instant access to information such as current expenses or whether a transferee's house has been sold, the human resources departments of these companies expect to communicate electronically with the real estate companies handling their employees' relocations. If that information were resident only on the Sears Financial Network mainframe and Systems Network Architecture (SNA) network, some clients who are not SNA-based could encounter cumbersome and difficult procedures to access such data.

"We are now in the position to easily make our relocation clients nodes on our RemoteWare network, regardless of their computing resources," said Shane. "At virtually no incremental cost to us, we can provide them one-button access to their data. This will provide a marketing advantage to Coldwell Banker as we are able to provide value-added services that will allow our clients to continuously track and manage their relocation expenses."

Several layers of security ensure that clients cannot access one another's information. For example, with the RemoteWare software at both Coldwell Banker's central site and on the client's PCs,

a "hand-shake" comparison of registration numbers and encoded passwords makes access to anyone's information except a client's own, impossible.

Shane also considers the RemoteWare network a "retaining tool" for both independent franchises and agents. "This isn't just a one-way road of information into the corporation," said Shane. "Simply put, we've built a data freeway to our field offices and personnel. Everything we do is designed to keep the agents away from administrative overhead and give them access to data that will help them sell."

Also, his staff is planning how to integrate the laptop computers

of 50 Coldwell Banker consultants who travel around the country to work with local offices. And, by having the remote offices, which are the revenue-generating entities, call in rather than having the central site placing calls this particular cost of doing business is distributed among profit centers, rather than shouldered solely as a corporate expense.

"Whatever we put out to the field offices, our first consideration is the communications themselves, and secondly how we can support the process," said Shane. "We're convinced we have the most accurate, efficient, and low-cost system available, and it is a strategic element of our ability to compete."

Source: "Coldwell-Banker Interconnects 1900 Offices," *LAN Times,* vol. 9 no. 13 (July 20, 1992), p. 41. Reprinted with permission of McGraw-Hill, *LAN Times.*

Business Case Study Questions

Multiple Platforms

Three distinct platforms are involved in this case study even though there are nearly 2000 actual nodes or locations involved.

1. Identify the three computing platforms involved in this case study.
2. Using the model of your choice (OSI, I-P-O, H-S-M, or top-down), prepare a profile of each of the three major platforms identified in question 1. Include all known technology including hardware or software. Highlight any key unknown items on any of the three platforms.
3. Prepare an I-P-O model for the 3174 Gateway shown in the network diagram. Be sure to include all known information regarding protocols and technology on either side of the gateway as well as processing performed by the gateway whether known or inferred.
4. Trace the information flow before and after network implementation from a remote office, through Coldwell Banker's central office to Sears headquarters. Be especially careful to note network and transport layer protocols.

Project Management

Managing large network analysis and design projects will be studied in depth in Chapter 12, "The Network Development Life Cycle." Nonetheless, many of the

tools of network analysis and design have already been introduced. Using what you aleady know regarding the models (OSI, I-P-O, H-S-M, or top-down) of network analysis and design, as well as a large dose of common sense and basic organization and communications techniques, answer the following questions:

1. Sears has sold Coldwell Banker as part of its restructuring. You have been given the assignment to develop transparent connectivity from Coldwell-Banker's remote and central offices to the new corporate headquarters. Develop a detailed plan outlining the step-by-step approach to your network analysis.
   a. Where will you start?
   b. What questions must be asked?
   c. What models will you employ, and how, in order to structure the analysis?
   d. What might be included in the network analysis and design in order to maximize network flexibility in the event that Coldwell Banker is resold?
   e. At what point will you begin examining technology options or inviting vendor demonstrations and sales calls?
2. Coldwell Banker wishes to extend the network of its Relocation Services Division to several hundred of its largest clients who are running a wide variety of LAN-based, minicomputer and mainframe systems. You are project manager for this wonderful opportu-

nity, which will offer a distinct competitive advantage to Coldwell Banker. This is a very important project and highly visible to senior management. Prepare a detailed overall project plan.

a. Where will you start?
b. What questions must be asked?

c. What models will you employ, and how, in order to structure the analysis?
d. How must the network be designed in order to avoid redesigning customized network applications for every new client?

CHAPTER ▪ 7

Basic Principles of Wide Area Networking

Concepts Reinforced

Top-Down Model
OSI 7-Layer Model
Multiprotocol Routing

Concepts Introduced

Basic WAN Principles
Switching Architectures
Transmission Architectures
Multiplexing
Packetization

X.25 Packet-Switched Networks
Frame Relay
Cell Relay
ATM

OBJECTIVES

After mastering the material in this chapter you should:

1. Understand the concept of multiplexing in general as well as several multiplexing techniques and related technology and applications in particular.

2. Understand the relationship between business motivation, available technology, and carrier services in creating wide area networking solutions.

3. Understand the advantages, limitations, and technology of current and forthcoming packet-switching networks.

4. Understand the importance of standards as applied to wide area networking.

5. Understand the interrelationships and dependencies between the components of any wide area network architecture.

6. Understand the impact of the evolution in switching methodologies as it applies specifically to frame relay and cell relay.

☐ INTRODUCTION

The study of internetworking in Chapter 6 provided a convenient bridge (no pun intended) to the study of wide area networking in Chapters 7 and 8. Network managers linking LANs and data traffic of various sources and types are often faced with the challenge of transmitting that data over large geographic distances.

The analysis, design, implementation, and management of wide area networks require both knowledge and skills unique to this area of study.

One of the most significant differences between wide area networks and the local area networks that have been studied previously, is the dependency, in most cases, on third-party carriers to provide wide area transmission services. The ability to understand the transmission and switching architecture that underlies and enables the wide area transmission services offered by these carriers is of critical importance to successful wide area network managers.

In order to understand wide area switching and transmission architectures, one must first understand some basic principles of wide area networking such as multiplexing, packet switching, and circuit switching, as well as the current and emerging technology associated with these WAN principles.

In-depth analysis of the emerging wide area network architectures being deployed by both familiar phone companies as well as new competitors will be conducted. As this analysis unfolds, particular attention will be paid to both current and projected levels of deployment of new switching and transmission architectures in an effort to project the impact of technology deployment on the availability of wide area network services. An attempt to differentiate between somewhat confusing terms and concepts will also be made. These topics will be covered in this chapter.

Emerging Wide Area Network Services and Technology will be studied in Chapter 8. Having gained a better understanding of the evolution of wide area network *architectures* in this chapter, most currently available and proposed wide area network *services* will be analyzed from a business application as well as financial perspective in Chapter 8. Once again, attention will be paid to current as well as proposed deployment levels of wide area network services.

Once a thorough understanding of both the current as well as the emerging wide area network architecture and services has been gained, the focus will turn toward the top of the top-down model to consider the *Business Uses of Wide Area Network Services* in the second major section of Chapter 8. Particular interest will be paid to the business impact of the use of WAN services such as EDI (electronic data interchange) and electronic mail.

Having gained a significant level of understanding in local area networks (Chapters 4 and 5), Internetworking (Chapter 6), and Wide Area Networking (Chapters 7 and 8), this knowledge and its associated technology will be tied together in the exploration of enterprise-wide networking opportunities in Chapter 9, "Enterprise Networking and Client/Server Architectures."

☐ BASIC PRINCIPLES OF WIDE AREA NETWORKING

WAN Technical Principles Are Motivated by Business Principles

In order to understand the basic *technical* principles of wide area networking, one must really start by looking at the basic *business* principles of wide area networking. In wide area networking as in most areas of business, the desire to maximize the impact of any investment in technology is a central focus.

Figure 7-1 illustrates the underlying business motivation of wide area networking principles. Given five information systems of some type (LANs, computers, terminals to mainframes) which need to be linked over long distances, there are basically two choices of physical configurations. A dedicated wide area link can be provided for each system-to-system connection (Figure 7-1*a*) or, somehow, both the principles and technology necessary to share a single wide area link among all five system-to-system connections can be found (Figure 7-1*b*).

The basic principles and technology involved in establishing, maintaining, and terminating multiple wide area system-to-system connections over a single wide area link constitute the topics covered in the remainder of this chapter.

A. Dedicated Multiple Wide Area System to System Connections

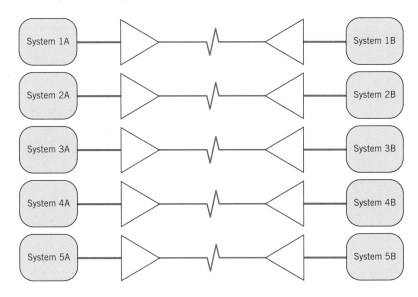

B. Single Wide Area Link Shared to Provide Multiple System to System Connections

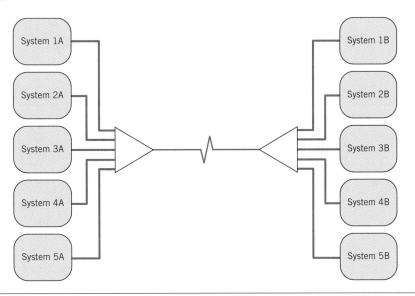

Figure 7-1 WAN technical principles are motivated by business principles.

Packetizing and Multiplexing

The two most basic principles involved in sharing a single data link among multiple sessions, as illustrated in Figure 7-1*b*, are *packetizing* and *multiplexing*.

Packetizing is the segmenting of data transmissions between devices into structured blocks or packets of data which contain enough "overhead" or management information in addition to the transmitted data itself, to assure delivery of the packet of data to its intended destination.

Multiplexing then takes this packet of data and sends it over a shared wide area connection along with other packetized data from other sources. At the far end of the single wide area network link, this stream of multiple source, multiplexed data packets are de-multiplexed and sent to their respective destination addresses. There are several different multiplexing techniques available and each has its respective applications and associated technology.

Both packetizing and multiplexing will be further explored shortly. Each of these terms is used in a general sense at this point in order to introduce the basics of wide area transmission principles. In addition, the "shared wide area connection" mentioned in the multiplexing explanation can take a number of different forms.

The two broadest categories of wide area connections are *packet-switched networks* and *circuit-switched networks*. Each of these will be explored in depth later in the chapter. A long-distance parcel shipping analogy, illustrated in Figure 7-2, may help clarify the concepts of packetizing and multiplexing.

A Parcel Shipping Analogy

As can be seen in Figure 7-2, multiple packages of several presents each are transported over a long distance via a single transport mechanism and subsequently delivered to their individual destinations. The equivalent wide area data transmission events are listed along the top of Figure 7-2, illustrating several packets of data from multiple sources being transmitted over a single, shared wide area communications link, and subsequently de-multiplexed and delivered to their individual destination addresses. As the specific parts of this wide area data transmission are examined in more detail, this parcel shipping analogy will be recalled for further analysis.

Generalized Packetizing

As stated previously, at this point a **packet** is being described as a group of data bits organized in a predetermined, structured manner, to which overhead or management information is added in order to assure error-free transmission of the actual data to its intended destination. These generalized packets are sometimes known as frames, cells, blocks, data units, or several other names. The differences between these various "packet-like" data organization structures as well as the various transmission methodologies and protocols which have been designed to transport these structured data packets will be differentiated.

The "predetermined, structured" nature of a packet should not be overlooked. Recall that all of the raw data, as well as any address information or error control information, are nothing more than bits of data, 1's and 0's, which will be processed by some type of programmed, computerized communications device. This programmed data communications device must be able to depend on exactly where certain pieces of key information, such as destination address and error check numbers, are located within a packet containing both raw data as well as overhead information.

By knowing exactly which bits within a packet represent a destination address and which bits represent data to be forwarded, the data communications device can process incoming data packets more quickly and efficiently. As different protocols for different types of packetized data are examined, the individual packet structures or layouts will be used as a point of differentiation.

A parcel shipping analogy also illustrates the need for "pre-determined, structured" packets. When shipping a parcel with nearly any parcel shipping company, one must fill out one of their standardized "structured" shipping forms, putting all data in the properly marked spaces. By doing so, the wide area transport mechanism, the parcel shipping company, can process packages more quickly and effi-

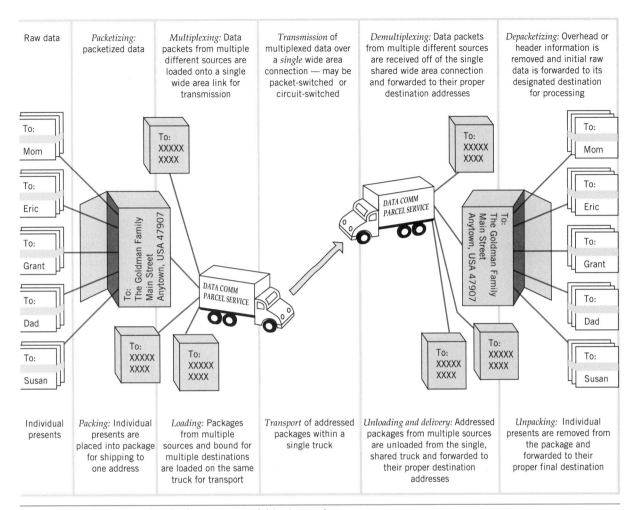

Raw data

Packetizing: packetized data

Multiplexing: Data packets from multiple different sources are loaded onto a single wide area link for transmission

Transmission of multiplexed data over a *single* wide area connection — may be packet-switched or circuit-switched

Demultiplexing: Data packets from multiple different sources are received off of the single shared wide area connection and forwarded to their proper destination addresses

Depacketizing: Overhead or header information is removed and initial raw data is forwarded to its designated destination for processing

To: Mom
To: Eric
To: Grant
To: Dad
To: Susan

To: The Goldman Family Main Street Anytown, USA 47907

DATA COMM PARCEL SERVICE

To: XXXXX XXXX

Individual presents

Packing: Individual presents are placed into package for shipping to one address

Loading: Packages from multiple sources and bound for multiple destinations are loaded on the same truck for transport

Transport of addressed packages within a single truck

Unloading and delivery: Addressed packages from multiple sources are unloaded from the single, shared truck and forwarded to their proper destination addresses

Unpacking: Individual presents are removed from the package and forwarded to their proper final destination

Figure 7-2 Packetizing and multiplexing: A parcel shipping analogy.

ciently by reading only one type of form and knowing where specific data is located on that form.

Regulations pertaining to maximum and minimum package size, as well as packaging techniques, also serve to allow the parcel shipping company to perform more efficiently. As will be seen, maximum and minimum packet lengths in wide area data transmission are important to overall transmission efficiency as well. Figure 7-3 summarizes some of the possible areas of standardization for generalized packets.

The term "generalized packets" implies that the diagram in Figure 7-3 does not necessarily represent any particular actual protocol, but rather a list of possible pieces of useful information that may be included in actual packet protocols or structures. Remember that the purpose of any packet protocol definition is to enable the data communications devices which must process these data packets to do so as efficiently and quickly as possible.

As particular packet, frame, and cell structures are defined throughout the chapter, elements of those data structures will be selected from among those listed in Figure 7-3, explaining both the rationale for the inclusion of these bits of data as

Starting Flag	Source Address	Destination Address	Type	Length	Control	Data	Error Control	Closing Flag

Data field length may be fixed or variable

Overall packet length may be fixed or variable

Flags (starting and ending):	Unique sequence of bits to signal beginning and ends of packets.
Addresses:	
Source Address:	On which node (system) did this data originate?
Destination Address (ultimate):	What is the *final* destination of this data?
Destination Address (next stop):	What is the address of the next data communications device that must process this data packet on its journey to its ultimate destination?
Error Checking Code:	Also known as frame check sequence, cyclic redundancy check.
Type:	May indicate higher level protocols embedded within the data as in an Ethernet frame.
Length:	Used to indicate the total length of the overall packet, or the length of the data portion.
C ontrol:	May be used to set up, monitor, and control the connection over which the data is transmitted.
Data:	Length may be fixed or variable; dependent on protocol may contain embedded upper layer protocols (TCP/IP embedded in an Ethernet frame).

Figure 7-3 Possible areas of standardization for generalized packets (not necessarily representative of an actual protocol).

well as the methodology by which the associated data communications device will process these structured bits of data. As a matter of fact, some specific examples of packet or frame definitions have already been seen. In Chapter 6, both an Ethernet frame structure (Figure 6-16) and an SNA SDLC frame structure (Figure 6-26) were examined.

Having introduced the overall structure of a wide area data communications transmission session as well as the relationship between the constituent parts of that transmission process, each of the constituent parts of this wide area transmission can now be examined in more detail. A thorough examination of multiplexing will start the process, followed by an elaboration on packetizing, also known as **packet assembly/disassembly.** In each case, both the process as well as the associated technology which performs the featured process will be examined.

Multiplexing in Detail

Recall that multiplexing is simply transmitting two or more signals over a single channel. It will be seen that different types of multiplexing can vary in a fairly limited number of ways. For example:

1. *How* is the actual multiplexing performed? How are the second and higher input signals loaded onto and taken off of the single output channel?
2. *How many input devices* or incoming signals, in terms of either number of devices or aggregate bandwidth, can be multiplexed?
3. *How large a composite output* channel can be handled by the multiplexing technique and/or technology?
4. *What type of source* information can be multiplexed? Data only? Voice? Fax? Video?

As each type of multiplexing and its associated technology is explored, keep in mind the preceding four major points of comparison.

Basic Multiplexing Techniques   To answer question 1 above, two basic techniques are employed in multiplexing:

>   Frequency division multiplexing (FDM)
>   Time division multiplexing (TDM)

A variation of TDM known as **statistical time division multiplexing (STDM)** is also commonly employed.

Frequency Division Multiplexing   In frequency division multiplexing (FDM), multiple input signals are modulated to different frequencies within the available output bandwidth of a single composite circuit, often a 3000 Hz dial-up line, and subsequently demodulated back into individual signals on the output end of the composite circuit. Sufficient space in between these separate frequency channels is reserved in **guardbands** in order to prevent interference or **crosstalk** between the two or more input signals sharing the single circuit. Figure 7-4 illustrates a simple FDM configuration.

The communications device that employs frequency division multiplexing is known as a *frequency division multiplexer* or FDM. At one time, FDMs were employed to transmit data from multiple low-speed (less than 1200 bps) terminals over dial-up or leased lines. As the speed of frequency division multiplexed terminals increases, the guardband width between channels in the shared composite circuit must increase also. As terminal speeds and demand for more bandwidth per terminal have risen, frequency division multiplexing is no longer the most practical multiplexing method employed.

Data Over Voice is FDM   Although FDM is seldom if ever still used to multiplex data from multiple terminals, it is still employed in devices known as **data over voice units** or **DOV** units. DOV units are most often used where data transmission is desired in a location currently wired for phones but which cannot be easily or affordably rewired for data.

In these cases, both the data and the voice transmission are *simultaneously* transmitted over the existing phone wiring. In addition, the data and voice transmissions are independent of one another. A person can be talking to someone else across the country while being on-line with a data transmission to the local computing center.

It is important to point out that DOV units cannot be used over the PSTN (public switched telephone network). In other words, they must be used in environments served by a local PBX (private branch exchange). College campuses are probably the most popular environment for DOV unit usage. At Purdue University, students rent DOV units from the Computing Center to allow the exist-

Overall Configuration

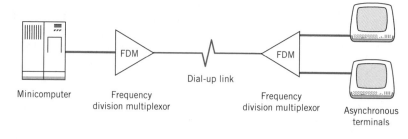

Minicomputer   Frequency
                 division multiplexor

Dial-up link

                 Frequency
                 division multiplexor   Asynchronous
                                          terminals

Inside the Dial-up link

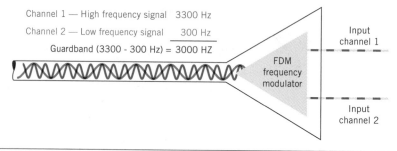

Channel 1 — High frequency signal   3300 Hz
Channel 2 — Low frequency signal   300 Hz
Guardband (3300 - 300 Hz) = 3000 HZ

FDM
frequency
modulator

Input
channel 1

Input
channel 2

Figure 7-4 Frequency division multiplexing.

ing phone wiring in their dorm rooms to function simultaneously as both a data and a voice transmission circuit. Figure 7-5 illustrates a typical DOV unit installation. DOV units will be discussed in more detail in Chapter 10, "Voice Transmission and Data/Voice Integration."

Time Division Multiplexing   In FDM, the total bandwidth of the composite channel is divided into multiple subchannels by frequency. With FDM, from a connected terminal's point of view, a *portion* of the total *bandwidth* is available *100 percent* of the time, yielding the appearance of a dedicated circuit. As a result, the *tim-*

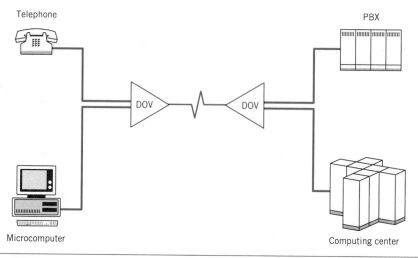

Telephone

PBX

DOV

DOV

Microcomputer

Computing center

Figure 7-5 Data over voice (DOV) unit installation.

ing of signals between a connected terminal or device and the centralized processor is not effected.

In **time division multiplexing (TDM),** just the opposite is true. With TDM, from a connected terminal's point of view, *100 percent* of the *bandwidth* is available for a *portion* of the time.

The portion of time available to each connected input device is *constant* and controlled by the time division multiplexer. A key point to understand about time slots in a TDM environment is that a fixed portion of time, measured in milliseconds, is reserved for each attached input device *whether the device is active or not.* As a result, efficiency is sacrificed for the sake of simplicity.

There are times in a TDM environment, when a terminal with nothing to say is given its full time allotment, while other busy terminals are waiting to transmit. A TDM is really a fairly simple device employing many familiar elements such as buffer memory and flow control. A TDM can affect the timing of signals between a connected terminal and its associated remote processor in a predictable way, thanks to the nondiscriminating nature of the TDM. Figure 7-6 illustrates simple time division multiplexing.

As can be seen in Figure 7-6, each input channel has a fixed amount of *buffer memory* into which it can load data. *Flow control,* either *XON/XOFF* or *CTS/RTS,* tells the terminal to stop transmitting to the buffer memory when the buffer memory fills. A central clock or timing device in the TDM gives each input device its allotted time to empty its buffer into an area of the TDM where the combined data from all the polled input devices is conglomerated into a single message frame for transmission over the composite circuit. This process of checking each connected terminal in order to see if any data is ready to be sent is known as **polling.**

If a terminal is inactive and has nothing in its input buffer to contribute to the consolidated message frame, that input terminal's allotted space in the *composite message frame* is filled with blanks. The insertion of blanks, or null characters, into composite message links is the basis of TDMs' inefficient use of the shared composite circuit connecting the two TDMs.

Although the data from the various input terminals is combined into a single message frame, each individual terminal's data is still identifiable by its position within that composite message frame. This fact is important, because once the com-

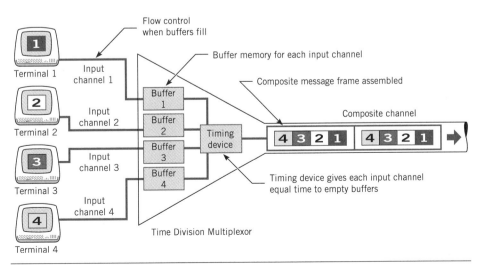

Figure 7-6 Time division multiplexing.

posite message frame has finished its journey down the transmission link, it must be resegmented back into the individual terminal's original data format.

Bit-Interleaving versus Byte or Character Interleaving   The polled input data from the various input terminals is combined into a composite message block in one of two ways:

> **Bit-interleaving**
> **Byte-interleaving** (also known as *character-interleaving)*

Figure 7-7 illustrates the two interleaving techniques for the Figure 7-6 example of four input devices.

Byte-interleaving requires more buffer memory than bit-interleaving in order to assemble the larger composite message frames. Remember that when these composite message frames are received at the destination TDM, they must be broken apart, with an individual terminal's data reassembled from the pieces transported in numerous composite message frames.

Most TDMs on the market today are byte- (character-) interleaved if they work with asynchronous modems, and bit-interleaved if they work with synchronous modems. The inefficiency of the TDM time allocation methodology hampers multiplexing more than two devices in most cases. Some TDMs seek to overcome the strict, and sometimes wasteful, time allocation scheme by allowing the TDM to be programmed. In these cases, the TDMs may handle up to four input devices, with the programming allowing the channels to be assigned fixed percentages of the total time allotment in multiples of 25 percent. For example:

> 1 device could get 100 percent allocations
> 2 devices could get 50 percent each or 75 percent/25 percent
> 3 devices could get 50 percent for one and 25 percent each for the other two
> 4 devices could get 25 percent each

TDMs today transmit over composite links of 9600bps to 38.4Kbps.

As will be seen in the next section, many more than four input devices can be multiplexed onto composite lines of 9600bps to 38.4Kbps. That increased capacity, however, comes as a result of more sophisticated, and expensive, multiplexing techniques.

Statistical Time Division Multiplexing   Statistical time division multiplexing (STDM) seeks to offer more efficient use of the composite bandwidth by employing increased monitoring and manipulation of input devices to accomplish two major goals:

> **1.** Eliminate "idle time" allocations to inactive terminals.
> **2.** Eliminate padded blanks or null characters in the composite message blocks.

In a *stat mux*, time is allotted to input devices dynamically. As terminals become more active, they get more time to send data directly to the stat mux. As terminals become less active or inactive, the stat mux polls them for input less frequently. This dynamic time slot allocation takes both processing power and additional memory. *Statistics* are kept regarding terminal activity over time and hence the name: statistical time division multiplexers. Specially programmed microprocessors and additional buffer memory are key upgrades to STDMs and contribute to their increased costs over the simpler TDMs.

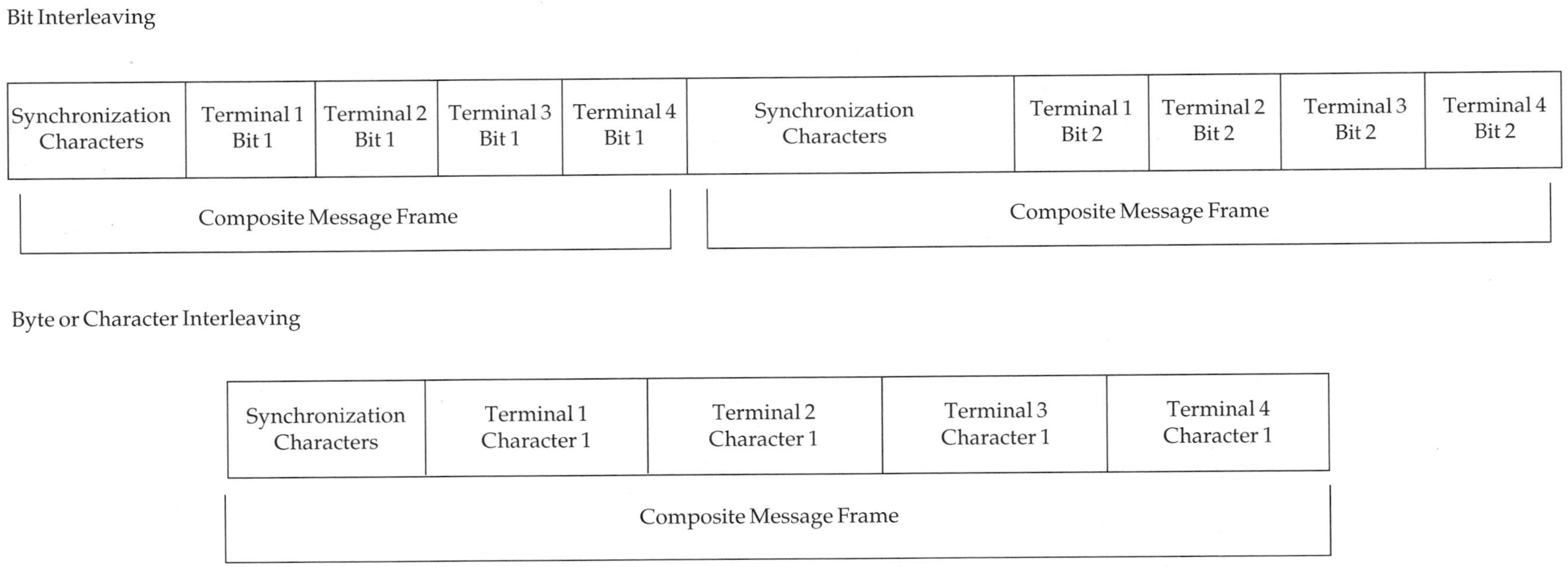

Bit Interleaving

Synchronization Characters	Terminal 1 Bit 1	Terminal 2 Bit 1	Terminal 3 Bit 1	Terminal 4 Bit 1	Synchronization Characters	Terminal 1 Bit 2	Terminal 2 Bit 2	Terminal 3 Bit 2	Terminal 4 Bit 2

Composite Message Frame

Composite Message Frame

Byte or Character Interleaving

Synchronization Characters	Terminal 1 Character 1	Terminal 2 Character 1	Terminal 3 Character 1	Terminal 4 Character 1

Composite Message Frame

Figure 7-7 Bit interleaving versus byte interleaving.

313

Two important points about stat muxes:

1. The time allocation protocols and composite message frame building protocols are proprietary and vary from one manufacturer to the next. As a result, *multiplexers from different manufacturers are not interoperable.*
2. The dynamic allocation of time afforded to individual terminals or devices by the STDM can interfere with any timing that might have been previously set up between the remote device and the central processor. This is particularly important in manufacturing or process control operations.

STDM's Improve Efficient Use of Composite Link   To increase the efficiency of the composite link, padded blanks and null characters are not inserted into message frames for inactive terminals. Remember the purpose of the blanks: to occupy the space in the composite message frame assigned to that particular device. In an STDM, rather than assign space to input devices in the composite message frame by position regardless of activity, the STDM adds control information to each terminal's data within the composite message frame, which indicates the source terminal and how many bytes of data came from that terminal. Figure 7-8 illustrates composite message block construction in STDMs.

STDM Cost/Benefit Analysis   From a business standpoint, what does a cost/benefit analysis of an STDM reveal? The STDM's increased costs are due to increased buffer memory, more sophisticated programming, and an integral microprocessor. On the benefits side of the equation, STDMs produce increased efficiency in time-slot allocation and composite bandwidth usage. Some STDMs also include proprietary data compression techniques as well. These increased efficiencies in STDMs seem to produce "something for nothing."

For example, it is not unheard of for STDMs to *seemingly* transmit data at four or even eight times the speed of the composite link. For instance, I have installed 16-port STDMs with four printers running at 2400bps and 12 async terminals running at 4800bps for an apparent bandwidth requirement of 67.2Kbps (2400x4 plus 4800 x 12). The fact of the matter is, these 16 devices ran just fine over a 9600bps leased line!

This apparent discrepancy is largely due to the "statistical" nature of data

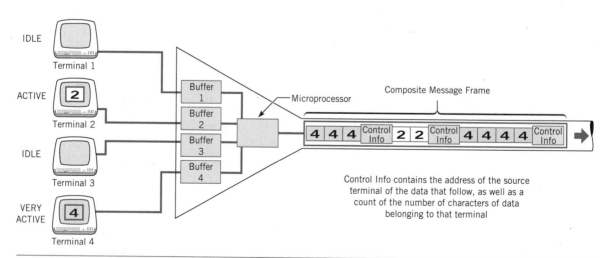

Figure 7-8 STDMs make efficient use of composite bandwidth.

transmission from terminals, which demonstrates the likelihood that only a relatively small percentage of terminals will be transmitting data at any split second in time. It is the STDM's sophisticated dynamic time-slot allocation capabilities that take advantage of this relatively large "idle time." Figure 7-9 illustrates the STDM's apparent ability to offer something for nothing.

Specialized Multiplexers Specialized multiplexers that build on the sophistication of the STDM, as well as offering increased capacity and/or flexibility in input devices or increased output bandwidth capacity will be studied either later in this chapter or in subsequent chapters. Among these specialized muxes are so-called *"fast-packet muxes"* that can multiplex not only data, but also voice, and fax transmissions. Fast-packet muxes, as well as the high-capacity *T-1 muxes* will be examined in Chapter 10, "Voice Transmission and Data/Voice Integration." In Chapter 11, "Networking Aspects of Videoconferencing, Imaging, and Multimedia," the *inverse mux*, sometimes called the backwards mux or the mux "stood on its head," will be examined.

Switching: Getting Voice or Data from Here to There

The examination of multiplexing and packetizing has illustrated two general concepts aimed at getting multiple messages from multiple sources *onto a transmission medium*. In order to further the understanding of wide area networking principles, the next logical step is to manipulate or *switch the transmission medium* in such a way to assure delivery of the data message to its proper destination.

Switching of some type or another is necessary because the alternative is unthinkable. To explain: Without some type of switching mechanism or architec-

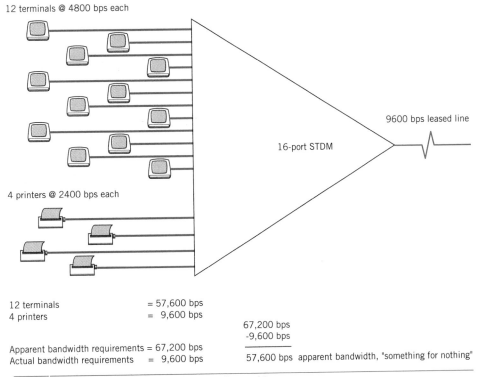

12 terminals	= 57,600 bps
4 printers	= 9,600 bps

67,200 bps
-9,600 bps
—————
57,600 bps apparent bandwidth, "something for nothing"

Apparent bandwidth requirements	= 67,200 bps
Actual bandwidth requirements	= 9,600 bps

Figure 7-9 STDMs seem to offer something for nothing.

ture, every possible source of data in the world would have to be *directly* connected to every possible destination of data in the world, a very unlikely prospect.

Switching allows temporary connections to be established, maintained, and terminated between message sources and message destinations, sometimes called *sinks* in data communications. In the case of the voice-based phone network with which most people are familiar, a call is routed through a Central Office piece of equipment known as a *switch*, which creates a temporary circuit between the source phone and the phone of the party to whom one wishes to talk. This connection or *circuit* only lasts for the duration of the call.

Circuit-Switching versus Packet Switching

Circuit Switching   **Circuit switching** is one of two primary switching techniques used to deliver messages from here to there. In a circuit-switched network, a switched dedicated circuit is created to connect the two or more parties, eliminating the need for source and destination address information such as that provided by the packetizing techniques explored earlier.

The "switched dedicated circuit" established on circuit switched networks makes it appear to the circuit user as if a wire has been run directly between the phones of the calling parties. The physical resources required to create this temporary connection are dedicated to that particular circuit for the duration of the connection. If system usage should increase to the point where insufficient resources are available to create additional connections, users will not get a dial tone. Circuit switching will be explored further in Chapter 10, "Voice Transmission and Data/Voice Integration."

Packet Switching   The other primary switching technique used to deliver messages from here to there is known as **packet switching.** Packet switching differs from circuit switching in several key areas. First, packets travel one at a time from the message source through a **packet switched network (PSN),** otherwise known as a **public data network (PDN),** to the message destination. A packet switched network is represented in network diagrams by a symbol resembling a cloud. Figure 7-10 illustrates such a symbol as well as the difference between circuit switching and packet switching.

The cloud is an appropriate symbol for a packet-switched network because all that is known is that the packet of data goes in one side of the PDN and comes out the other. The physical path that any packet takes may be different than other packets, and in any case, is unknown to the end users. What is beneath the cloud in a packet switched network is a large number of **packet switches,** which pass packets among themselves as the packets are routed from source to destination. Figure 7-10 illustrates such a packet-switched network.

Remember that packets are specially structured groups of data that include control and address information in addition to the data itself. These packets must be assembled (control and address information added to data) somewhere before entry into the packet-switched network, and must be subsequently disassembled before delivery of the data to the message destination. This packet assembly and disassembly is done by a device known as a **PAD** or **packet assembler/disassembler.** PADs can be standalone devices or can be integrated into specially-built modems or multiplexers.

These PADs may be located at an end-user location, or may be located at the entry point to the packet-switched data network. Figure 7-10 illustrates the latter scenario in which the end users employ regular modems to dial-up the value-added network (VAN) or on-line information service which provides the PADs to

Circuit Switching

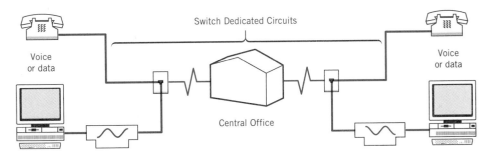

All data or voice travel from source to destination over the *same* physical path.

Packet Switching

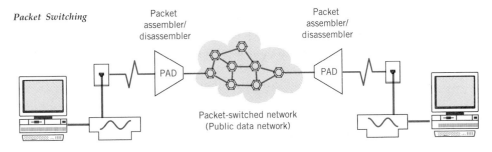

Data enter the packet-switched network one packet at a time;
Packets may take *different* physical paths within packet-switched networks.

Figure 7-10 Circuit switching vs. packet switching.

properly assemble the packets prior to transmission over the packet-switched network. This set-up is often more convenient for end-users as they can still employ their modem for other dial-up applications as well.

Packet-Switched Networks The packet switches illustrated inside the PDN cloud in Figure 7-10 are generically known as **DSE**s, data switching exchanges, or **PSE**s, packet switching exchanges. DSE is the packet switching equivalent of the DCE and DTE categorization, which were first encountered in the study of modems and dial-up transmission. These networks are also alternatively known as PSNs, packet-switched networks, or PDNs, public data networks.

Another way in which packet switching differs from circuit switching is that as demand for transmission of data increases on a packet-switched network, additional users are *not* denied access to the packet-switched network. Overall performance of the network may suffer errors and retransmission may occur, or packets of data may be lost, but all users experience the same degradation of service. This is because, in the case of a packet-switched network, data travels through the network one packet at a time, travelling over *any* available path within the network rather than waiting for a switched dedicated path as in the case of the circuit-switched network.

In order for *any* packet switch to process *any* packet of data bound for *anywhere,* it is essential that packet address information be included on each packet. Each packet switch then reads and processes each packet by making routing and forwarding decisions based upon the packet's destination address and current network conditions. The full destination address uniquely identifying the ultimate destination of each packet is known as the **global address.**

Because an overall data message is broken up into numerous pieces by the packet assembler, these message pieces may actually arrive out of order at the message destination due to the speed and condition of the alternate paths within the packet-switched network over which these message pieces (packets) traveled. The data message must be pieced back together in proper order by the destination PAD before final transmission to the destination address. These self-sufficient packets containing full source and destination address information plus a message segment are known as **datagrams.** Figure 7-11 illustrates this packet-switched network phenomenon.

Connection-Oriented versus Connectionless Packet-Switched Networks

The switching methodology described in the previous paragraph in which each datagram is handled and routed to its ultimate destination on an individual basis resulting in the possibility of packets traveling over a variety of physical paths on the way to their destination is known as a **connectionless** packet network. It is called connectionless because packets do not follow one another, in order, down an actual or virtual circuit or connection.

There are no error-detection or flow-control techniques applied by a datagram-based or connectionless packet-switched network. Such a network would depend on end-user devices (PCs, modems, comm software) to provide adequate error and flow control. Because datagrams are sent along multiple paths to the destination address, there is no guarantee of their safe arrival. This lack of inherent error-detection or flow-control abilities is the basis for connectionless packet networks also being known as **unreliable** packet networks.

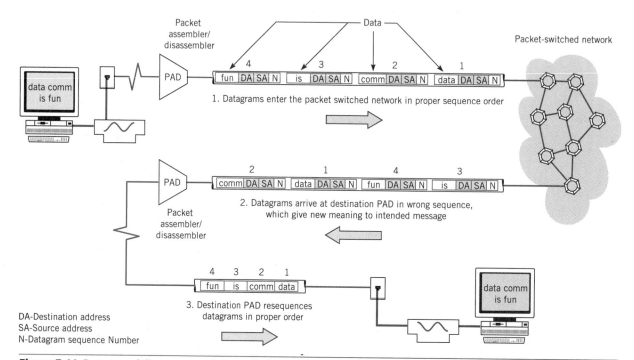

DA-Destination address
SA-Source address
N-Datagram sequence Number

Figure 7-11 Datagram delivery on a packet switched network (a connectionless network).

In contrast to the connectionless packet networks, **connection-oriented** or **reliable** packet networks establish **virtual circuits** enabling message packets to follow one another, in sequence, down the same connection or physical circuit. This connection from source to destination is set up by special packets known as **call set-up packets.** These call set-up packets are not unlike the explorer packets encountered in the study of internetwork bridging and routing.

Once the call set-up packets have determined the best path to the destination and established the virtual circuit, the message-bearing packets follow one another in sequence along the virtual circuit from source to destination.

Unlike a connectionless service, a connection-oriented service, because of the establishment of the virtual circuit, can offer check-sum error detection with ACK/NAK retransmission control and flow control. These services can be offered by the packet network itself rather than depending on the end-user devices.

Because connection-oriented packets all follow the same path, or **logical channel,** from source to destination, they do not require the full global addressing on each packet as in the case of the connectionless datagram networks. Instead, connection-oriented network packets have an abbreviated *logical channel number,* or *LCN* included with each packet. The details which relate the LCN to a physical circuit consisting of an actual series of specific packet switches within the packet switched network are stored in a **virtual circuit table.**

Switched Virtual Circuits and Permanent Virtual Circuits

Connection-oriented packet switching networks actually define two types of virtual circuits: **switched virtual circuits (SVC)** and **permanent virtual circuits (PVC).** The *switched* virtual circuit connection is terminated when the complete message has been sent and a special *clear request packet* causes all switched virtual circuit tables related to this connection to be erased. The virtual circuit table of the *permanent* virtual circuit is not erased, making the PVC the equivalent of a "virtual" circuit-switched leased line.

Overhead in Connection-Oriented Networks

While the use of LCNs as opposed to full global addressing reduces overhead in connection-oriented packet networks, the following elements add to that overhead:

1. Connection set-up
2. Network-based, point-to-point error detection and flow control

Figure 7-12 contrasts the overhead of connectionless versus connection-oriented packet-switched networks as well as several other key criteria.

The truth is that unless a company plans to set up its own packet-switched network, decisions regarding the relative merits of connectionless versus connection-oriented packet-switched networks will not have to be considered. It is more likely that a company will access a major commercial packet-switched network such as Compuserve, Tymnet, Prodigy, or Internet. In that case, what goes on "inside the cloud" is invisible to the users of that packet-switched network. In such a case, an end-user's only concern is how to **interface** to "the cloud".

☐ X.25 DEFINES STANDARD INTERFACE TO PACKET-SWITCHED NETWORKS

X.25 is an international CCITT standard which defines the interface between terminal equipment (DTE) and any packet-switched network (the Cloud). It is important to note that X.25 does *not* define standards for what goes on *inside* the cloud.

	Overhead	Greatest Strength	Call Set-up	Addressing	Also Known As...	Virtual Circuit	Error Correction	Flow Control
Connectionless	Less	Ability to dynamically reroute data	None	Global	Datagram unreliable	None	Left to end-user devices	Left to end-user devices
Connection-oriented	More	Reliability	Yes	Local logical channel number	Reliable Virtual circuit	Created for each call, virtual circuit table established	By virtual circuit	By virtual circuit

Figure 7-12 Connectionless versus connection-oriented packet-switched networks.

One of the most common misconceptions is that the X.25 standard defines the specifications for a packet switching network. On the contrary, X.25 only assures that an end-user can depend on how to get information into and out of the packet-switched network.

X.25 is a three-layer protocol stack corresponding to the first three layers of the OSI model. The total effect of the three layer X.25 protocol stack is to produce packets in a standard format acceptable by any public packet-switched network. X.25 offers network transparency to the upper layers of the OSI protocol stack.

X.25 requires data to be properly packetized by the time it reaches "the cloud." Terminals and computers that do not possess the X.25 protocol stack internally to produce properly formatted packets employ a PAD (packet assembler/disassembler) to packetize their output data into X.25 format for entry into the cloud. Figure 7-13 illustrates the relationship of the X.25 protocol stack to the OSI model as well as a representation of the X.25 standards scope of influence.

Inside the X.25 Protocol Stack

The X.25 standard consists of a three-layer protocol that assures transparent network access to OSI layers 4-7. In other words, applications running on one computer that wish to talk to another computer do not need to be concerned with anything having to do with the packet-switched network connecting the two computers. In this way, the X.25 compliant packet-switched network is nothing more than a transparent delivery service between computers.

The physical layer (layer 1) protocol of the X.25 standard is RS-232, which we were first introduced to in Chapter 2. The data-link layer (layer 2) protocol is known as **HDLC** or high-level data link control. HDLC is very similar to IBM's SDLC in structure. Functionally, HDLC accomplishes the same things as any other data-link layer protocol, such as Ethernet or Token Ring:

1. Organizes data into structured frames that may contain more than one packet.
2. Assures reliable delivery of data via error checking.
3. Provides *point-to-point* data delivery between adjacent nodes.

Figure 7-14 illustrates an HDLC frame. In the case of HDLC and X.25, error checking is achieved via a 16-bit *frame check sequence,* while the *control field* transports important management information, such as frame sequence numbers and requests for retransmission. Newer implementations of X.25 use **LAP-B,** or link access procedure-balanced, a subset and functional equivalent of the full HDLC frame, as a data-link layer protocol.

The network layer (layer 3) X.25 protocol is known as **PLP** or *packet layer protocol.* Remembering that the job of any OSI layer 3, network layer protocol is the establishment, maintenance and termination of *end-to-end* connections, PLP's main job is to establish, maintain, and terminate virtual circuits within a connection-oriented packet switched network.

Important Standards Related to X.25

Listed below are important standards related to X.25 and a brief explanation of their importance:

> **X.121**—global addressing scheme: As packet switching networks have become global in nature, a global addressing scheme was necessary to allow transparent global access to these networks. X.121 defines zone codes, country codes, and PSN codes within countries. This four-digit global addressing

Protocol Stack

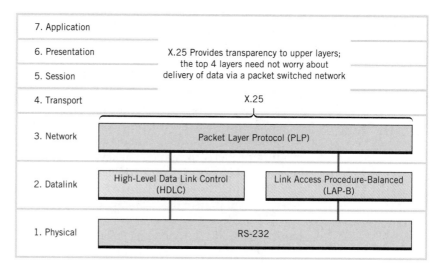

7. Application	
6. Presentation	X.25 Provides transparency to upper layers;
5. Session	the top 4 layers need not worry about delivery of data via a packet switched network
4. Transport	X.25
3. Network	Packet Layer Protocol (PLP)
2. Datalink	High-Level Data Link Control (HDLC) / Link Access Procedure-Balanced (LAP-B)
1. Physical	RS-232

X.25 Implementation

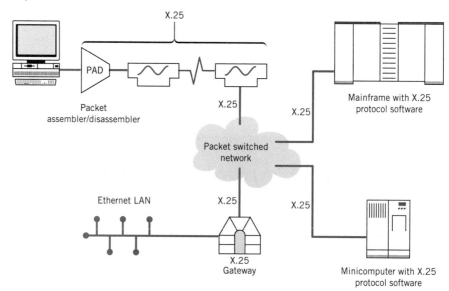

Figure 7-13 X.25 packet switching interface standard.

Flag	Address field	Control field	Information field	Frame check sequence	Flag
8 bits	8 bits	8 bits	Variable	16 bits	8 bits

Figure 7-14 X.25 Datalink layer protocol: HDLC.

prefix is followed by up to 10 digits to uniquely identify the destination address node.

X.28 and X.32—Dial-up Access Directly into PADs X.28 (asynchronous) and X.32 (synchronous) define standards that allow users to dial-up a PAD and subsequently place a call over the packet-switched network.

X.75—Internetworking packet switched networks: X.25 defined the interface from the end-user device into the packet-switched network cloud. But what if the ultimate destination node is attached to a different cloud? A standard was required to define a standardized interface between different packet-switched networks. X.75 is that standard and has been referred to as the packet-switched network "gateway" protocol.

A Business Perspective on Circuit-Switching versus Packet Switching

If the top-down model is applied to an analysis of possible switching methodologies, **circuit switching** and **packet switching** can be properly placed on either the network or technology layers. In either case, in order to make the proper switching methodology decision, the top-down model layer directly above the network layer, namely, the *data* layer must be thoroughly examined.

The key data-layer question becomes:

What is the nature of the data to be transmitted and which switching methodology best supports those data characteristics?

The first data-related criterion to examine is the *data source.*

What is the nature of the application program (application layer) which will produce this data?
Is it a transaction-oriented program or more of a batch-update or file-oriented program?

A transaction-oriented program, producing what is sometimes called *interactive data,* is characterized by **bursty data** followed by variable length pauses due to users reading screen prompts or pauses between transactions. This *bursty transaction-oriented traffic,* best categorized by banking transactions at an AnyTime Money machine, must be delivered as *quickly* and *reliably* as the network can possibly perform. In addition to *data burstiness, time pressures,* and *reliability constraints,* are other important data characteristics which will assist in switching methodology decision making.

Applications programs more oriented to large file transfers or batch updates have different data characteristics than transaction-oriented programs. Overnight updates from regional offices to corporate headquarters or from local stores to regional offices are typical examples. Rather than being bursty, the data in these types of applications is usually large and flowing steadily. These transfers are important, but not often urgent. If file transfers fail, error detection and correction protocols such as those examined in the study of communications software can retransmit bad data or even restart file transfers at the point of failure.

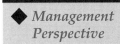
Management Perspective

From a business perspective, the two switching techniques vary as well. While both circuit-switched and packet-switched services usually charge a flat monthly fee for access, the basis for *usage charges* differs. In general, circuit switched connections are billed according to *time connected* to the circuit. Packet-switched networks usually charge according to *packet transfer volume.*

To analyze further, if a company gets charged for connection time to the circuit-switched service whether they use it or not, they had better be sure that while they are connected, their data is steady and taking full advantage of available bandwidth.

One other switching difference is worth noting before some conclusions are drawn. In terms of the need to deliver bursty, transaction-oriented data quickly and reliably, *call set-up time* can be critical. With circuit-switched applications, a dial-tone must be waited for, the number must be dialed and switched through the network. With connection-oriented packet-switched networks, call set-up packets must explore the network and build virtual circuit tables before the first bit of data is transferred. Datagrams don't require call set-up, but offer no guarantee of safe delivery.

So which switching method is best for which type of data? Although business application of wide area networking will be explored further in Chapter 8, and in the case studies, Figure 7-15 summarizes key data characteristics in relation to major switching methodologies.

WIDE AREA NETWORK SWITCHING AND TRANSMISSION ARCHITECTURES

In order to better understand all of the current and emerging wide area networking technologies and services, a simple model defining the major segments and inter-relationships of an overall wide area network architecture are included in Figure 7-16.

Major Components of a Wide Area Network Architecture

As can be seen in Figure 7-16, User Demands are the driving force behind the current and emerging wide area Network Services offered to business and residential customers. Companies offering these services are in business to generate profits by

	Circuit Switched Preferred	Packet Switched Preferred
Data Characteristic	**Characteristic Value**	
Application source	Overnight batch jobs File transfers	Transaction oriented Interactive data
Data flow	Large and steady	Large and bursty
Delivery pressure	No great hurry	Seconds count
Reliability	Communication software for error detection	Error detection and flow control built into network itself
Business Characteristic	**Characteristic Value**	
Usage charge basis	Per TIME connected	Per PACKET transferred

Figure 7-15 Data and business characteristics verus switching methods.

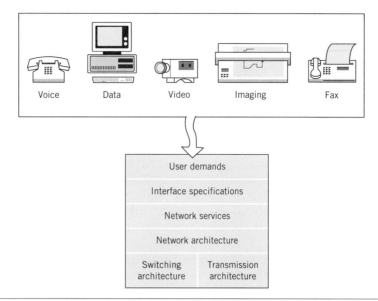

Figure 7-16 Major components of a wide area network architecture.

implementing the underlying architectures that will enable them to offer the wide area networking services which users are demanding at the lowest possible cost.

It has been mentioned, as early as Chapter 1, that users are demanding simple, transparent access to variable amounts of bandwidth as required. In addition, this wide area network access must offer support for transmission of data, video, imaging, and fax as well as voice. One of the primary driving forces of increased capacity and sophistication for wide area network services is *LAN interconnection.*

Recall in the study of internetworking devices in Chapter 6, that inter-LAN routers are now being manufactured with integrated wide area network interfaces in order to offer transparent inter-LAN connectivity for widely dispersed LANS. Inter-LAN traffic requires not only high bandwidth, but also highly reliable data delivery as well. Wide-area routers will be studied in more detail later in this chapter.

In order for users to take advantage of network services, standardized **interface specifications** must be developed to ensure interoperability among different manufacturer's end-user equipment. As an example, the X.25 interface specification ensures that users can purchase packet assembler/disassemblers from any manufacturer, and be able to interface successfully to a packet switched network service.

Furthermore, these network services cannot be offered unless the underlying infrastructure of the carriers and companies wishing to offer these services is technically capable of doing so. The combination of sophisticated switches and transmission facilities that comprise this infrastructure is known as the network architecture.

Switching and Transmission Capabilities Determine Services

Companies offering wide area network services, whether familiar phone companies or not, have two major architectures or sets of technology to integrate into a cohesive network architecture in their attempt to offer wide area network services at an affordable price. This relationship between switching architectures, transmission architectures, network architectures, network services and interface specifications can be seen in Figure 7-16.

Switching architectures, or methods, such as circuit switching or packet switching, assure the proper routing of information (data, voice, video, etc.) from the data's source to its destination. **Transmission architectures,** or methods, are the circuits or data highways over which the information is actually delivered.

To return to the parcel shipping analogy, *switching* is the activity that takes place inside depots and warehouses, while *transmission* takes place in the trucks on the highways and in the planes in the air. By adjusting depot organization, human-power, floorspace, or equipment, a parcel shipping company can adjust its switching capacity or sophistication. By utilizing varying numbers of planes or trucks, or changing truck or plane routes, the same parcel shipping company can adjust its transmission capacity or sophistication.

In the case of wide area or packet-switched networks, the copper, fiber, microwave, and satellite links and the protocols which control access to and monitoring of these circuits constitute the *transmission architecture* of wide area networks.

The central office switches and packet switches which build connections from source to destination utilizing these transmission circuits constitute the *switching architecture* of the wide area or packet-switched network.

The importance of the relationship between the two architectures is well illustrated by the parcel shipping company analogy as well. If the parcel shipping company increases switching capacity and sophistication by building several new depots, but does not upgrade its transmission capacity by increasing numbers of trucks and planes, the result will be less than optimal. Similarly, providers of wide area network services are in the process of upgrading *both* their switching and transmission facilities in order to be able to meet future user demands for sophisticated and reasonably-priced wide area network services.

Switching Architectures: Current and Emerging

Two of the major current switching technologies, namely circuit-switched and packet-switched, have already been explored. For LAN interconnection, neither switching architecture is ideal.

Circuit-switched options include dial-up lines or leased lines. Dial-up speeds can be up to 14.4Kbps with a V.32bis modem. V.42bis data compression may increase this throughput to something less than 57.6Kbps (14.4Kbps x 4:1 compression max.) Even 57.6Kbps falls far short of offering transparency to typical LAN speeds, Token Ring at 4Mbps or 16Mbps and Ethernet at 10Mbps. Most inter-LAN connections will not tolerate the call set-up time associated with dial-up access, nor the possibility of dial-tone denial in the case of network resource shortage.

Leased-line circuits are not an ideal inter-LAN connection either. Inter-LAN traffic tends to be bursty, with large amounts of inter-LAN data being transmitted for short bursts of time followed by random amounts of little or no traffic. Leased lines need to be configured to handle the maximum data bandwidth needs of the bursts, leaving excess capacity sitting idle for long periods of time. Leased lines are billed at a flat rate based largely on distance covered by the circuit and overall bandwidth of the circuit. As a result, users employing leased lines for inter-LAN connection will pay a great deal for unused or under-used leased line capacity.

Current *packet switching* technologies based on the X.25 protocol stack can satisfy both the guaranteed availability and charge-per-packet requirements of inter-LAN connection. However, the maximum bandwidth that most X.25-based packet networks can deliver is 64Kbps, still far short of inter-LAN transparency. Given that it seems as if some type of packet switching will be the answer to the inter-LAN connectivity challenge, two new packet-switching technologies are emerging and being tested by wide area network services providers. Figure 7-17 illustrates the relationship between the various "new" and "old" switching methodologies.

From the preceding paragraph, it can be concluded that packet switching might be the ideal inter-LAN switching methodology if it were only faster. As can be seen from Figure 7-17, two new **fast packet switching** methodologies have emerged for inter-LAN connection consideration.

Fast Packet Switching: Frame Relay and Cell Relay

X.25's Hop-by-Hop Error Checking   In order to understand how these new packet services can be made faster, the source of the overhead or "slowness" of the existing X.25 packet switching networks must first be examined. Recall from the previous discussion of connection-oriented packet switched networks, that error-checking and retransmission requests were done on a point-to-point basis, between adjacent packet switches. This *point-to-point oriented error checking* is sometimes also called *hop-by-hop error checking*.

At the time X.25 was first introduced about 20 or so years ago, the long-distance circuits connecting the X.25 packet switches were not nearly as error free as they are today. Transmission errors are measured by **bit error rate (BER).** As a result, in order to guarantee end-to-end error-free delivery, it was necessary to check for errors and request retransmissions on a point-to-point or hop-by-hop basis at every X.25 packet switch in the network. Although necessary, this constant error checking and correction added significant overhead, and therefore delay, to the X.25 packet transmission process.

Frame Relay   Today's long-distance digital transmission systems are largely fiber based and far less error prone than those of 20 years ago. As a result, new packet switching methodologies, such as **frame relay,** were introduced which sought to take advantage of the decreased bit error rate on today's transmission systems. The basic design philosophy is simple:

> Given the quality of the transmission system, stop all point-to-point error correction and flow control within the network itself and let the end-nodes worry about it!

The end nodes, such as PCs, servers, mainframes, etc., would use higher level (layers 4–7) protocols to perform their own error checking. In the case of a PC, this would likely be a sliding window file transfer protocol such as those we studied in Chapter 3. This philosophy works fine as long as the basic assumption, the low bit error rate of today's transmission system, holds true. If not, then retransmissions are *end-to-end,* spanning the entire network, rather than point-to-point between adjacent packet switches.

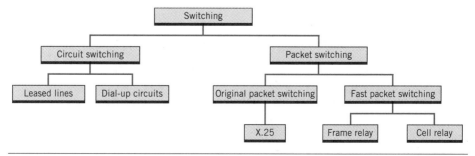

Figure 7-17 Switching methodology evolution.

Error Detection and Correction with Frame Relay It is important to distinguish between **error detection** and **error correction.** Both frame relay and X.25 perform point-to-point error detection by comparing generated **CRCs** (cyclic redundancy checks) with transmitted CRCs, also known as **FCSs** (frame check sequences). The difference and resultant processing time savings for frame relay occurs in the action taken upon the detection of an error.

An X.25 switch will always send either a positive ACK or negative NAK acknowledgement upon the receipt of each packet and will not forward additional packets until it receives an ACK or NAK. If a NAK is received, the packet received in error will be retransmitted. Packets are stored in X.25 switches in case a NAK is received, necessitating retransmission. This is why X.25 packet switching is sometimes called a **store-and-forward** switching methodology.

On the other hand, if a frame relay switch detects an error when it compares the computed versus transmitted FCSs, *the bad frame is simply discarded.* The correction and request for retransmission of bad frames is left to the end node devices; PCs, modems, computers and their error correction protocols. Technically speaking, in frame relay, there is *point-to-point error detection, but only end-to-end error correction.*

As can be seen in Figure 7-18, the technology configuration for the X.25 packet-switched network and the frame relay network are amazingly similar. In the case of the frame relay network, the access device is known as a **FRAD** or *FAD* (frame relay or frame assembler/disassembler) rather than a PAD, while the switching device is known as a **frame relay switch,** rather than a packet or X.25 switch. FRADs are also known as *frame relay access devices.* FRADs and frame relay switches are available in numerous configurations and integrated with numerous other internetworking devices such as bridges, routers, multiplexers, and concentrators.

In terms of the OSI model, the difference between X.25 packet switching and frame relay is simple. Frame relay is a two-layer protocol stack (physical and data link) while X.25 is a three-layer protocol stack (physical, data-link, and network). There is no network layer processing in frame relay, accounting for the decreased processing time and increased throughput rate.

Frame Relay Flow Control Although end node devices such as PCs and modems can handle the error detection and correction duties shed by the frame relay network with relative ease, *flow control* is another matter. End nodes can only manage flow control between themselves and whatever frame relay network access device they are linked to. There is no way for end nodes to either monitor or manage flow control within the frame relay network itself. Some frame relay

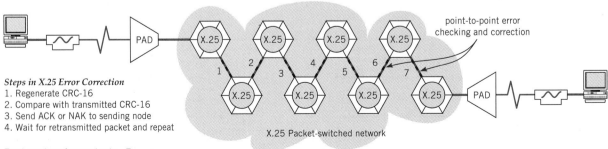

Steps in X.25 Error Correction
1. Regenerate CRC-16
2. Compare with transmitted CRC-16
3. Send ACK or NAK to sending node
4. Wait for retransmitted packet and repeat

Total number of error checks: 7

Figure 7-18a Point-to-point vs. end-to-end error control (X.25 packet swtiched network).

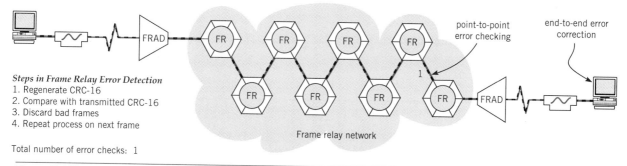

Steps in Frame Relay Error Detection
1. Regenerate CRC-16
2. Compare with transmitted CRC-16
3. Discard bad frames
4. Repeat process on next frame

Total number of error checks: 1

Figure 7-18*b* Point-to-point vs. end-to-end error control (frame relay network).

switch vendors have implemented their own flow control methodologies, which is sufficient only if that vendor's switches are being used.

Referring to the frame relay frame structure diagram in Figure 7-19, there are three bits in the frame definition known as **BECN, FECN,** and **DE**, which stand for *backward explicit congestion notification,* forward explicit congestion notification, and *discard eligibility.* These bits are the elements of a scheme to allow frame relay devices to adjust flow control dynamically. Some frame relay devices even have the ability to read or write to these fields.

The only problem is, no one has decided what action should be taken by a given device in the event that any of these bits indicate a flow control problem. Unless you are responsible for setting up your own frame relay network, you might not think much of this problem. On the other hand, it represents the need to have a healthy dose of cynicism when shopping for data communications devices, even when those devices "support all applicable standards."

Frame Relay Frame Definition   In a similar manner to X.25 packet formation, frame relay frames are formatted within the FRAD, or in computers or PCs that have frame relay protocol software loaded to build frame relay frames directly. The **frames** that a frame relay network forwards are *variable* in length with the maximum frame transporting nearly 8000 characters at once. Combining these potentially large, variable length frames with the low overhead and faster processing of the frame relay switching delivers a key characteristic of the frame relay network: *High throughput with low delay.*

Figure 7-19 illustrates the frame definition for frame relay networks. This frame definition is said to be a subset of the LAP-D protocol. **LAP-D** stands for *link access protocol-D channel,* where the D channel refers to the 16Kbps data channel in BRI (basic rate interface) ISDN (integrated services digital network). The relationship between ISDN and frame relay will be explored further in Chapter 8.

Implications of Variable Length Frames   The variable length frames illustrated in Figure 7-19, can be a shortcoming, however. Because there is no guarantee as to the length of a frame, there can be no guarantee as to how quickly a given frame can be forwarded through the network and delivered to its destination. In the case of data, this lack of guaranteed timed delivery or maximum delay is of little consequence.

However, in the case of more *time sensitive information,* such as voice or video, it can be a real issue. Voice and video can be digitized as will be seen in later chapters. This digitized voice or video can be packetized or put into frames like any other

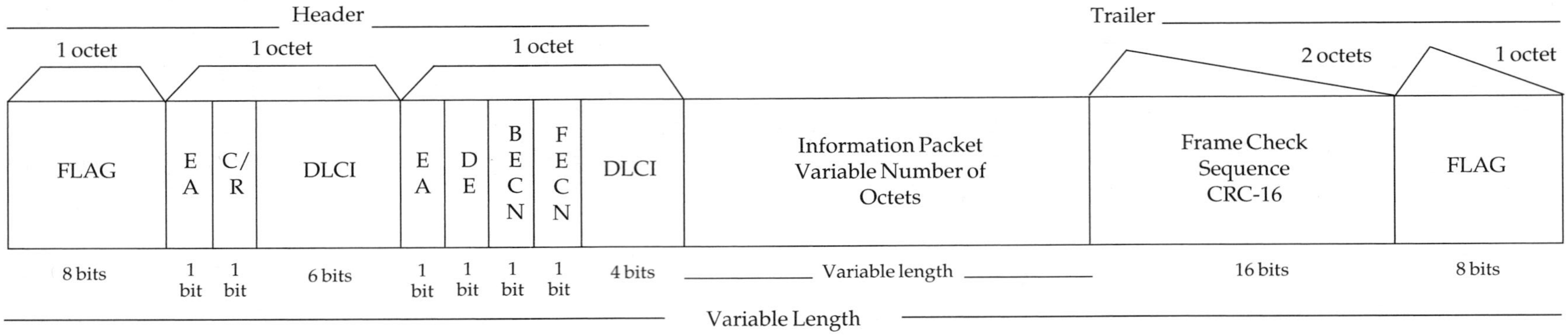

	Header							Trailer	
1 octet	1 octet		1 octet					2 octets	1 octet
FLAG	EA	C/R	DLCI	EA	DE	BECN	FECN	DLCI	Information Packet Variable Number of Octets	Frame Check Sequence CRC-16	FLAG
8 bits	1 bit	1 bit	6 bits	1 bit	1 bit	1 bit	1 bit	4 bits	Variable length	16 bits	8 bits

Variable Length

FLAG   indicates beginning of frame
EA   extended address
C/R   command or response
DLCI   data-link connection identifier (address)
EA   extended address
DE   discard eligibility
BECN   backward explicit congestion notification
FECN   forward explicit congestion notification
DLCI   data-link connection identifier (address)
INFORMATION   minimum number of octets—enough to make total frame at least 7 octets long. Maximum number of octets is 8000
FCS   frame check sequence for error detection—also called cyclic redundancy check
FLAG   indicates end of frame

Figure 7-19 Frame relay structure: subset of LAP-D—Link Access Protocol, D channel.

data. The problem arises when framed voice and video do not arrive in a predictable timed fashion for conversion back to understandable voice and video.

As a result, frame relay is often described as a *data only* service. That's not exactly true. Options do exist to transport digitized, compressed voice transmissions via a frame relay network.

Frame Relay Switching Architecture Advantages

Frame relay networks currently employ **PVCs** (permanent virtual circuits) to forward frames from source to destination through the frame relay cloud. **SVC** (switched virtual circuit) standards have been defined but not implemented. Remembering that an SVC is like a dial-up call, in order to transport data over an SVC-based frame relay network, a LAN NOS such as Netware has to communicate call set-up protocol information to the frame relay network before sending a data request or transaction update to a remote server.

Frame relay transmission rates are as high as 1.544 Mbps. Remembering that multiple PVCs can exist within the frame relay network cloud, another key advantage of frame relay over circuit-switched options such as leased lines is the ability to have multiple PVCs supported from only one access line. From a cost justification standpoint, this allows a frame relay user to replace multiple leased-line connections with a single access line to a frame relay network. Remember also that frame relay network charges are based on usage, whereas circuit-switched leased lines charges are based on flat monthly fees whether they are used or not. Figure 7-20 illustrates the concept of multiple PVCs per single access line.

A secondary, but no less important characteristic offered by the many transmission options available with the mesh network of the frame relay cloud is the ability to allocate bandwidth dynamically. In other words, up to the transmission limit of the access line and the circuits between the frame relay switches (usually 1.544M), the frame relay network will handle bursts of data by simply assembling and forwarding more frames per second onto the frame relay network, over multiple PVCs if required.

Frame Relay and Bursty Inter-LAN Traffic

This ability to handle bursty traffic is especially appealing for LAN interconnection. Inter-LAN communication tends to be bursty with intermittent requests for data and file transfers. Remembering that this inter-LAN communication should be as transparent as possible, frame relay's ability to handle bursty traffic by dynamic bandwidth allocation is especially appealing. In the case of frame relay network access for LAN interconnection, the internetwork bridge or router is often integrated with a frame relay assembler/disassembler or frame relay protocol software.

A word of caution, however. Bursty traffic is difficult to define. How large a burst, in terms of maximum bandwidth demand, and of what duration, is the frame relay network expected to be able to handle?

An attempt has been made to structure *burstiness* with the two terms. **CIR** or *committed information rate* refers to the minimum bandwidth guaranteed to users for "normal" transmission, while **CBS** or *committed burst size* defines the extent to which a user can exceed their CIR over a period of time. If a user exceeds their CBS, the frame relay network reserves the right to discard frames in order to deliver guaranteed CIRs to other users.

Other Frame Relay Positives and Negatives

Another frame relay feature that is appealing for LAN interconnection is that frame relay merely encapsulates

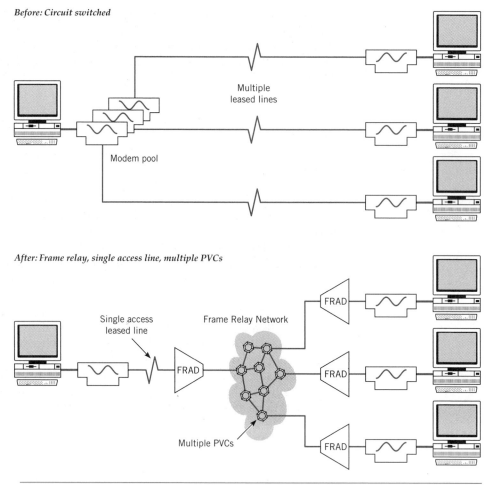

Figure 7-20 Multiple PVCs (Permanent Virtual Circuits) per access line.

user data into frames and forwards it to the destination. Frame relay is merely a delivery service. It does not process user data and is therefore *protocol independent* or *protocol transparent*. It can forward SNA/SDLC traffic just as easily as it can forward TCP/IP or Novell IPX traffic.

An issue hindering the widespread global use of frame relay is the need for better coordination among the different frame relay network vendors in order to offer transparent access between them in a manner similar to the standard interfaces developed by phone companies for voice traffic. A conceptual standard known as **NNI** or *network-to-network interface* would be the functional equivalent of the X.75 internetwork standard for X.25 packet switched networks.

Conclusion: What Is Frame Relay?   Figure 7-16 listed the components of a wide area network architecture which interact to hopefully meet user demands for WAN services. Where does frame relay fit in such an architecture?

The unfortunate truth is that it could fit in several places. First and foremost, frame relay is an *interface specification*. The LAP-D data link layer protocol defines a frame structure which contains destination address, error checking, control information, and user data all in a single protocol layer frame. It is this interface specification which allows faster processing to take place within the frame relay network.

Secondly, frame relay is also a *network service,* offered by several regional and long-distance phone companies primarily for the purpose of LAN interconnection. Frame relay's ability to dynamically allocate bandwidth over a single access line to the frame relay network make it particularly well-suited for the bursty nature of inter-LAN traffic. Private frame relay networks can be established as well.

Finally, frame relay can also be considered a *switching architecture.* What goes on inside the frame relay network cloud really remains transparent to end-users, as long as the interface specification causes frame relay frames to enter the cloud and frame relay frames to exit the cloud. However, there are *true frame relay switches* designed specifically to forward frame relay frames at an optimal rate. A mesh network comprised of these "native" frame relay switches can legitimately be considered a switching architecture.

Cell Relay: A Switching Alternative to Frame Relay

As seen in Figure 7-17, **cell relay** is another "fast-packet" switching methodology and a key part of future network architectures. The key physical difference between cell relay, sometimes known as a *"switching fabric,"* and frame relay is that, unlike the variable length frames, all cells are of a *fixed length,* 53 octets long. (An octet is 8 bits.) Forty-eight of the octets are reserved for user data or information from higher layer protocols, plus a five octet header.

Constant Cell Length Yields Performance Results   Because of the constant-sized cells, cell relay switches can perform much faster by being able to depend upon constant cell length, since more instructions for processing can be included in firmware and hardware. The constant-sized cells also lead to a predictable and dependable processing rate and forwarding or delivery rate. The lack of a predictable maximum delivery delay was a key weakness in frame relay.

This *predictable delivery time* of each and every cell makes cell relay a better choice for transmission of voice or video applications as well as data. Cell relay *switching* can provide switching capability on a similar scale to the highest capacity transmission alternatives, such as T-3s (45Mbps) and fiber optic transmission circuits with capacity of up to 2.4 gigabytes per second.

Cell Relay Standards   Cell relay is unique in that most of its standards were developed prior to the deployment of cell relay technology. Some important standards-related issues remain. The excitement surrounding cell relay centers around its ability to carry voice, video, data, image or fax transparently. It can even carry more than one of these media or information types simultaneously.

The key standard developed for the cell relay switching methodology is known as **ATM** (asynchronous transfer mode). ATM is presently defined by two different cell formats. One is called the **UNI** (user-network interface) and carries information between the user and the ATM network. The second cell standard is known as **NNI** (network-network interface) and carries information between ATM switches. Figure 7-21 illustrates the structure of these two ATM cells.

In Sharper Focus

ATM CELL STRUCTURES

To clarify a few of the field definitions of the ATM cell structures:

> *GFC: generic flow control*—Multiple devices of various types (voice, video, data) can gain access to an ATM network through a single access circuit. These different devices may require different flow control signalling.

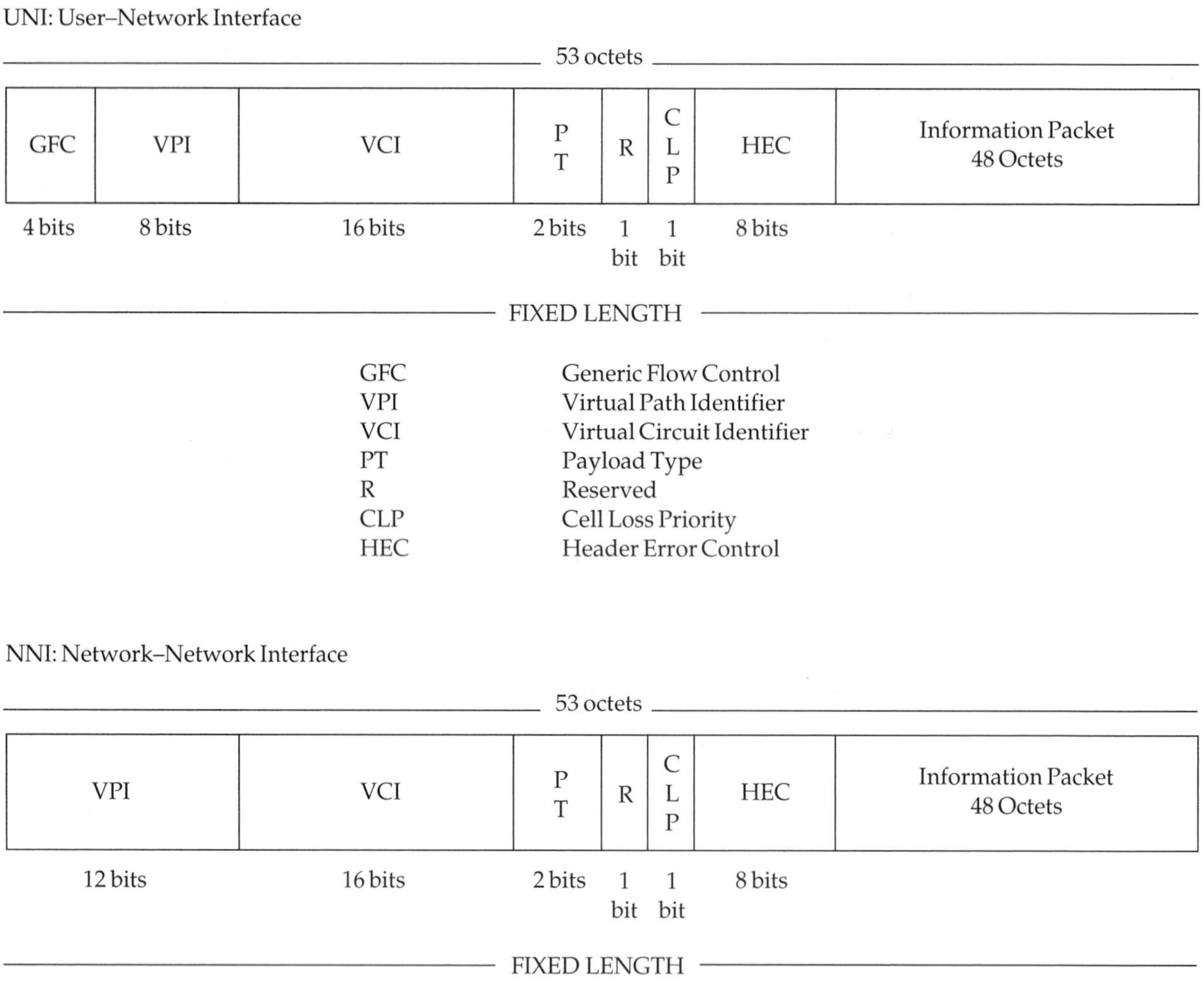

UNI: User–Network Interface

53 octets							
GFC	VPI	VCI	P T	R	C L P	HEC	Information Packet 48 Octets
4 bits	8 bits	16 bits	2 bits	1 bit	1 bit	8 bits	

FIXED LENGTH

GFC	Generic Flow Control
VPI	Virtual Path Identifier
VCI	Virtual Circuit Identifier
PT	Payload Type
R	Reserved
CLP	Cell Loss Priority
HEC	Header Error Control

NNI: Network–Network Interface

53 octets						
VPI	VCI	P T	R	C L P	HEC	Information Packet 48 Octets
12 bits	16 bits	2 bits	1 bit	1 bit	8 bits	

FIXED LENGTH

Figure 7-21 ATM cell structures.

VPI: virtual path identifier—The virtual path identifier uniquely identifies the connection between two end-nodes and is equivalent to the virtual circuits of X.25 networks. A VPI consists of several VCIs. (see below)

VCI: virtual channel identifier—Because ATM can carry multiple types of information (voice, video, data), several channels of information could be traveling along the same end-to-end connection simultaneously. The VCI uniquely identifies a particular channel of information within the virtual path.

PT: payload type—Indicates whether a cell contains user information or network control information.

CLP: cell loss priority—If an ATM transmission exceeds its allotted bandwidth, including concessions for burstiness, a cell can be marked by the ATM network in a process known as policing. If congestion occurs on the network, these marked cells are the first to be discarded.

HEC: header error control—Assures that header information contains no errors. The biggest concern is that the VPI and VCI are correct. Can you imagine the possibilities if video or voice transmissions were sent to the wrong network end-node?

ATM Implementation

An implementation of an ATM-based network consists of ATM access devices as well as a "cloud" of ATM switches. The ATM access devices take user information in the form of variable length data frames from a LAN or workstation, digitized voice from a PBX, or digitized video from a video codec and format all of these various types of information into fixed-length ATM cells. The local ATM switch routes information to other locally-connected ATM devices as well as to the wide area ATM network.

ATM-LAN hubs are an exciting prospect that extend the basic design of the Ethernet switch explored in Chapter 5. Rather than share media with other workstations as in the case of Ethernet and Token Ring, every workstation connected to the ATM-LAN hub has the potential of gigabytes of bandwidth available at all times.

In a sense, the general makeup of the ATM network is not unlike the X.25 or frame relay networks. Access devices assure that data is properly formatted before entering "the cloud" where the data is forwarded by switches specially designed to handle that particular type of properly formatted data. However, the functionality that an ATM network can offer far exceeds that of either the X.25 or frame relay networks. Figure 7-22 illustrates a possible implementation of an ATM Network.

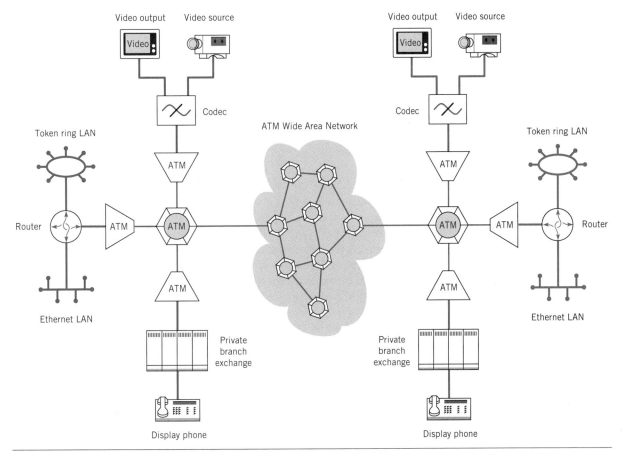

Figure 7-22 ATM network implementation.

Added Functionality Offered by ATM

ATM offers all of the advantages of frame relay such as dynamic bandwidth allocation and fast forwarding rates. It also offers significant additional functionality directly attributable to the fixed length cells of the ATM standard.

As has been previously stated, the fixed cell length and **low latency,** or minimum delay, allow voice and video transmissions to be forwarded over the ATM switching fabric. More importantly, these voice and video transmissions can be taking place simultaneously with data transmissions.

The second major unique feature of ATM is its scalability. Thusfar, only the use of ATM as the switching methodology within an "ATM cloud" wide area network has been mentioned. As will seen in Chapter 8, ATM can also be the underlying switching fabric for *metropolitan* area network services such as SMDS (switched multimegabit data service). Finally, ATM *local* area network switches are offering 100Mbps bandwidth to attached workstations. Unlike FDDI, in which the 100Mbps must be shared among all workstations, with the ATM-LAN switch, each workstation gets a full 100Mbps of bandwidth. Although the technology is very young and standards are still being developed, there exists the possibility that ATM may prove to be the homogeneous switching fabric that will deliver voice, video, and data traffic whether the destination is across the room or across the globe.

When this "deliver anything" switching methodology (cell relay) is combined with fiber optic transmission methodologies such as SONET (Synchronous Optical Network), the network architecture of the future, capable of delivering transparent universal information services becomes a reality.

Conclusion: Where Does ATM Fit in the Larger Scheme?

Figure 7-23 illustrates ATM's place within the hierarchical model of today's emerging networking environment.

ATM, asynchronous transfer mode, is a standard for cell relay switching. Another cell relay switching methodology standard, IEEE 802.6, otherwise known as distributed queue dual bus will be studied in Chapter 8. Although not identical, these two cell relay standards are compatible. As can be seen in Figure 7-23, DQDB-based services such as SMDS can run over ATM with the use of an SMDS interface.

Unlike frame relay, cell relay is *not* a network service. As a matter of fact, as can be seen in Figure 7-23, frame relay is one of the network services available over an ATM cell relay switching fabric. This is not as strange as it may seem. Remember that frame relay is an *interface specification*. Once those frames are built according to specification, they can be quickly delivered over the ATM mesh network just as quickly and easily as any other data, voice, or video.

The potential scalability of ATM should also be evident from Figure 7-23. Although the interoperability between many of these products and platforms is yet to be tested, from an architectural standpoint, ATM certainly seems to be an all-encompassing switching fabric. The final test of any network architecture will be the level of inherent flexibility required to respond to changing user demands. The transparency as to both source (data, voice, video, image, fax) and protocol (SNA/SDLC, IP, IPX, etc.) that ATM offers certainly bodes well for its flexibility. As to its ability to deliver, on a large scale, network services that meet user demands, only time will tell.

Networking hierarchy level

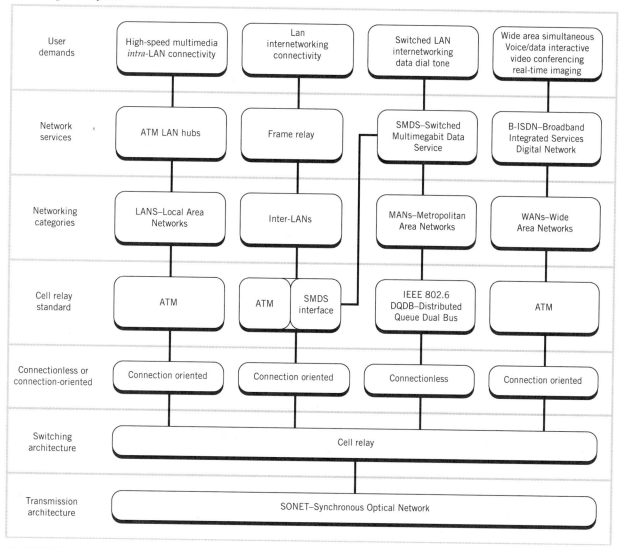

Figure 7-23 ATM: The switching fabric for tomorrow's network?

CHAPTER SUMMARY

Having studied local area networks (LANs) in Chapters 4 and 5 and the methods for connecting LANs, or internetworking in Chapter 6, the overall networking view was extended by examining the concepts, architectures, and basic principles of wide area networks (WANs) in Chapter 7.

Key concepts such as multiplexing, packetizing, and switching were first explained as a basis for building the underlying architectures of wide area networking. Switching and transmission were introduced as the two key components of any wide area network.

The mechanics of packet switching in general and X.25 packet switched networks in particular were studied in detail. Frame relay was introduced as a variation of the basic X.25 packet-switched network with diminished point-to-point flow control and error correction overhead.

Cell relay and ATM were discussed as the possible underlying switching fabrics that will support many of the emerging network services of the future.

KEY TERMS

ATM	DE	logical channel	store-and-forward
BECN	DSE	low latency	switched virtual circuit
Bit Error Rate (BER)	error correction	multiplexing	(SVC)
bit-interleaving	error detection	NNI	switching architectures
bursty data	fast packet switching	packet	TDM
byte-interleaving	FCS	Packet Assembler/	time division multiplexing
call setup packets	FDM	Disassembler (PAD)	transmission architectures
CBS	FECN	packetizing	UNI
Cell relay	FRAD	packet switch	unreliable
CIR	frame	packet-switching	virtual circuit table
circuit switching	frame relay	Packet Switched Network	X.25
clear request packet	frame relay switch	(PSN)	X.28
connectionless	frequency division	permanent virtual circuit	X.32
connection-oriented	multiplexing	(PVC)	X.75
CRC	global address	polling	X.121
crosstalk	guardbands	Public Data Network	
datagram	HDLC	(PDN)	
Data Over Voice units	interface	reliable	
(DOV)	interface specification	statistical time division	
Data Switching Exchange	LAP-B	multiplexing	
(DSE)	LAP-D	STDM	

REVIEW QUESTIONS

1. Differentiate between the following multiplexing techniques in terms of mechanics, technology, and application:
   a. Frequency-division multiplexing
   b. Time-division multiplexing
   c. Statistical time-division multiplexing
2. What is fast-packet multiplexing and how does it differ from STDM?
3. Are multiplexers from different manufacturers interoperable? If not, why not? What limitations in network design or operation would a lack of interoperability cause?
4. What is the difference between an X.25 packet-switched network and a frame-relay network?
5. What are frame relay's underlying assumptions regarding transmission media and services?
6. Frame relay is an interface specification, a network service, and a switching architecture. Explain both the implication as well as the independence of each of the aforementioned designations.
7. What types of information are included in packets other than the actual data message itself?
8. Differentiate between FDM, TDM, and STDM in relation to each one's effect on timing signals between the end-user device and the central processor.
9. What is a common application of FDM technology?
10. What is the current geographic limitation associated with DOV units?
11. How is it possible with a DOV unit that the voice

and data don't necessarily have to share the same destination?
12. What are the key shortcomings of TDM and how does STDM seek to overcome these weaknesses?
13. What additional technology and expense is required to support the advanced functionality of an STDM?
14. What is polling and what does it have to do with multiplexer efficiency?
15. What is the difference between bit-interleaving and byte-interleaving?
16. Which transmission methodology is most likely to employ bit- or byte-interleaving?
17. Why is it sometimes said that STDMs appear to offer something for nothing?
18. What is the difference between switching and transmission and how do the two architectures compliment each other?
19. What is circuit-switching?
20. What is packet-switching?
21. What are the key differences between circuit switching and packet switching from an end-user's perspective?
22. What is the difference between a packet assembler/disassembler and a packet switch?
23. How might X.25 packets be assembled other than by a stand-alone X.25 PAD?
24. Why is a packet-switched network represented by a cloud?

25. What are the positive and negative aspects of a datagram packet delivery service?
26. What is the difference between connectionless and connection-oriented packet services in terms of overhead, transmission paths, and reliability.
27. What do connection-oriented services use instead of global addressing?
28. What overhead is involved with the establishment and maintenance of logical channel numbers?
29. What benefits are realized from the use of logical channel numbers?
30. What are the differences between SVCs and PVCs in terms of establishment, maintenance, and termination?
31. Which part of the packet-switched network does X.25 actually define?
32. What are the other important standards related to X.25 and what area of the packet-switched network do each of them define?
33. What is HDLC and what does it accomplish?
34. What is PLP and what does it accomplish?
35. What is the packet-switched network gateway protocol and why is it so named?
36. What is meant by the term "bursty data" and what unique transmission challenges does it pose?
37. What is a typical source of bursty data?
38. Name the seven major components of a wide area network environment or architecture and the significance of each.
39. Give examples of typical switching and transmission architectures in today's network architecture.

40. What are the advantages and disadvantages of hop-by-hop error checking?
41. How are transmission errors measured?
42. Why is an X.25 packet-switched network known as a store-and-forward messaging system?
43. How does frame relay handle error detection and error correction?
44. How does frame relay currently handle flow control?
45. How might frame relay handle flow control in the future?
46. What are the significant features of the frame definition for frame relay?
47. Why is frame relay sometimes referred to as a data-only service?
48. Why is dynamic allocation of bandwidth an important feature of frame relay?
49. How are carriers which offer frame relay services attempting to deal with the burstiness of data?
50. Why are both circuit-switched and "typical" packet-switched networks unsuitable for bursty data?
51. What are the primary differences between cell relay and frame relay?
52. What is the relationship between cell relay and ATM?
53. What do the functional characteristics of cell relay offer in terms of the types of data that can be transported effectively?
54. What is low latency and what effect does it have on data transmission requirements?

ACTIVITIES

1. Gather articles on ATM from trade journals. Create a bulletin board or prepare a research topic summarizing the current issues on ATM, focusing particularly on obstacles to widespread deployment, such as the pace of the standards development process.
2. Contact the ATM forum and request literature concerning current standards development issues.
3. Investigate the cost and installation specifics of using an X.25 packet-switched network such as Compuserve. What is the controlling factor when considering maximum transmission speed in such an arrangement?
4. Choose two cities within your local LATA. Contact your local carrier for a quote on the cost for a leased line between those two cities. Compare pricing for both analog and digital lines at a variety of speeds. Are switched digital services available? What are the installation or nonrecurring costs?

5. Now choose another city just outside your local LATA. Contact multiple long-distance carriers for quotes similar to that in the previous question. How do the quotes from the various carriers compare? How do the long-distance carrier quotes compare with the local carrier quotes? What was the impact of leaving your LATA for the additional city? Graph your results.
6. Investigate the availability of frame relay data services in your area. How are such services tariffed? How are committed information rates (CIR) negotiated? What happens if you exceed your CIR? How does this CIR compare with available transmission capacity via X.25 packet-switched networks? Graph your results.
7. Investigate the expense of a frame relay interface for a router. How does its cost compare with other WAN interfaces for routers such as CSU/DSU?

Featured References

ATM

Zegura, Ellen. "Architectures for ATM Switching Systems," *IEEE Communications,* vol. 31, no. 2 (February 1993), p. 28.

Pattavina, Achille. "Nonblocking Architectures for ATM Switching," *IEEE Communications,* vol. 31, no. 2 (February 1993), p. 38.

Jajszcyk, Andrezej, and H. T. Mouftah. "Photonic Fast Packet Switching," *IEEE Communications,* vol. 31, no. 2 (February 1993), p. 58.

Farkouh, Stephen. "Managing ATM-Based Broadband Networks," *IEEE Communications,* vol. 31, no. 5 (May 1993), p. 82.

MacAskill, Skip. "ATM Emerging as LAN Hub Alternative," *Network World,* vol. 9, no. 29 (July 20, 1992), p. 21.

MacAskill, Skip. "ATM Threatens to Usurp FDDI as Backbone Choice," *Network World,* vol. 9, no. 29 (July 13, 1992), p. 1.

Klessig, Bob, and George Prodan. "FDDI and ATM: No Sibling Rivalry," *LAN Times,* vol. 9, no. 21 (November 9, 1992), p. 35.

Johnson, Johna. "Putting ATM on the Premises," *Data Communications,* vol. 21, no. 10 (July 1992), p. 51.

Johnson, Johna. "ATM: A Dream Come True?" *Data Communications,* vol. 21, no. 5 (March 21 1992), p. 53.

Lippis, Nick. "A First Look at ATM Means Second Thoughts about FDDI," *Data Communications,* vol. 21, no. 9 (June 1992), p. 39.

Broadband Switches

Johnson, Johna. "A Low Cost Switch with SONET in Its Future," *Data Communications,* vol. 21, no. 5 (March 21, 1992), p. 49.

Case Studies

Eckerson, Wayne. "J. P. Morgan Takes Simpler Approach to E-Mail Unity," *Network World,* vol. 9, no. 51 (December 21, 1992), p. 1.

Bancroft, Bruce. "Cancer Institute Builds Enterprise Network," *LAN Times,* vol. 9, no. 1 (January 20, 1992), p. 21.

Duncanson, Jay. "Standing the Multiplexer on Its Head," *LAN Times,* vol. 9, no. 17 (September 14, 1992), p. 47.

Maxwell, Kimberly. "Agency Bridges E-Mail Gap Between Netware and UNIX," *LAN Times,* vol. 9, no. 21 (November 9, 1992), p. 40.

Walker, Robyn. "Jet Propulsion Labs Investigates ISDN," *LAN Times,* vol. 9, no. 1 (January 20, 1992), p. 29.

Eckerson, Wayne. "Federal Express Uses EDI to Streamline Its Billing," *Network World,* vol. 9, no. 21 (May 25, 1992), p. 29.

Brown, Bob. "A&P Setting up VSAT Net to Register Service Gains," *Network World,* vol. 9, no. 26 (June 29, 1992), p. 17.

Case Studies—International

Bancroft, Bruce. "TackBoard Supplies Commodities News," *LAN Times,* vol. 9, no. 1 (January 20, 1992), p. 37.

Heywood, Peter. "Ford Puts ISDN in the Driver's Seat," *Data Communications,* vol. 21, no. 11 (August 1992), p. 91.

Cell Relay

McQuillan, John. "Cell Relay Switching," *Data Communications,* vol. 20, no. 11 (September 1991, p. 58.

Schultz, Beth, and Chris Roeckl. "Trio Targets Packet, Cell Interoperability," *Communications Week,* no. 427 (November 2, 1992), p. 1.

Digital Leased Line

Briere, Daniel. "Buyer's Guide: Digital Private Line Services," *Network World,* vol. 9, no. 24 (June 15, 1992), p. 47.

Wallace, Bob. "AT&T Adds Array of High-Speed Net Links (fractional T-3)," *Network World,* vol. 9, no. 48 (November 30, 1992), p. 1.

Frame Relay

Muller, Nathan, and Robert Davidson. *The Guide to Frame Relay* (New York: Telecom Library, 1991).

Johnson, Johna. "Frame Relay Products: Sorting out the 'Simple' Technology," *Data Communications,* vol. 21, no. 7 (May 1992), p. 69.

Heywood, Peter. "Global Public Frame Relay: Risky Business," *Data Communications,* vol. 21, no. 18 (November 1992), p. 85.

Duffy, Jim. "Frame Relay Technologies Unveils New Access Switch," *Network World,* vol. 9, no. 27 (July 6, 1992), p. 9.

Flanagan, William. *Frames, Packets and Cells in Broadband Networking* (New York: Telecom Library, 1991).

Lippis, Nick. "Frame Relay Takes a Multiprotocol Tack," *Data Communications,* vol. 21, no. 11 (August 1992), p.27.

Strizich, Martha. "FastComm Access Device Will Get Frame-Relay Networks Talking", *Communications Week,* no. 428 (November 9, 1992), p. 36.

Feldman, Robert. "Frame Relay Rollout Picks up Speed," *LAN Times,* vol. 9, no. 22 (November 23, 1992), p. 1.

Brown, Bob, and Bob Wallace. "Users, Carriers Engage in Frame Relay SVC Tug-of-War," *Network World,* vol. 9, no. 50 (December 14, 1992), p. 1.

Briere, Daniel, and Christopher Finn. "Frame Relay Selection Is No Picnic," *Network World,* vol. 10, no. 5 (February 1, 1993), p. 45.

HSSI—High Speed Serial Interface

Schultz, Beth. "Adaptive to Add HSSI Bandwidth Management Feature to SONET Switch," *Communications Week*, no. 428 (November 9, 1992), p. 13.

Hindin, Eric. "HSSI Sizzles," *Data Communications*, vol. 20, no. 15 (November 1991), p. 49.

Internet

Homer, Blaine. "Beat the Competition by Accessing Info on Internet," *LAN Times*, vol. 9, no. 15 (August 10, 1992), p. 55.

International WANs

Heywood, Peter. "A Fast Start Means a Big Lead in Global LAN Interconnect," *Data Communications*, vol. 20, no. 17 (December 1991), p. 114.

Dern, Daniel. "Linking LANs Internationally with TCP/IP Based Internet," *LAN Times*, vol. 8, no. 18 (September 16, 1991), p. 45.

Packet Switches and PSDNs

Bransky, Jonathan, and Dean Wolf. "Buyers Guide:X.25 Switches—Vendors Aim to Transform X.25 Switches," *Network World*, vol. 9, no. 29 (July 20, 1992), p. 46.

Schlar, Sherman. *Inside X.25: A Manager's Guide*, (New York: McGraw-Hill, 1990).

Derfler, Frank, and Kimberly Maxwell. "Reliable Relays," *PC Magazine*, vol. 10, no. 15 (September 10, 1991), p. 377.

SONET

Davidson, Robert, and Nathan Muller. *The Guide to SONET*, (New York: Telecom Library, 1991).

Gareiss, Robin. "SONET Vendors Grapple with Net Management," *Communications Week*, no. 385 (January 13, 1992), p. 18.

Sweeny, Terry. "SONET Support Key to Emerging Digital Cross-Connects," *Communications Week*, no. 427 (November 2, 1992), p. 32.

Messmer, Ellen. "Ameritech Unit, MCI Use SONET to Maximize Nets," *Network World*, vol. 9, no. 47 (November 23, 1992), p. 25.

Switched Services

Glossbrenner, Kenneth. "Availability and Reliability of Switched Services," *IEEE Communications*, vol. 31, no. 6 (June 1993), p. 28.

Fagerstom, Richard, and John Healy. "The Reliability of LEC Telephone Networks," *IEEE Communications*, vol. 31, no. 6 (June 1993), p. 44.

Wallace, Bob. "User Says Switched 384 Service Exceeds Expectations," *Network World*, vol. 9, no. 3 (January 20, 1992), p. 4.

Wallace, Bob. "AT&T Simunet Line Lets the 5ESS Support Switched T-1," *Network World*, vol. 9, no. 30 (July 27, 1992), p. 21.

VSATs—Very Small Aperture Terminals

Johnson, Johna. "Users Rate VSAT Networks," *Data Communications*, vol. 21, no. 4 (March 1992), p. 85.

WAN Protocol Analyzers

Jander, Mary. "WAN Protocol Analyzers," *Data Communications*, vol. 21, no. 6 (April 1992), p. 65.

WAN Routers

Jander, Mary. "Frame Relay Switch, Router to Wed," *Data Communications*, vol. 21, no. 7 (May 1992), p. 121.

Feldman, Robert. "Novell Sharpens Wide-Area Focus," *LAN Times*, vol. 9, no. 15 (August 10, 1992), p. 1.

Cooney, Michael. "IBM Details Role of Its 3172 Controller," *Network World*, vol. 9, no. 30 (July 27, 1992), p. 11.

Johnson, Johna. "A WAN Service Interface That Gets Around," *Data Communications*, vol. 21, no. 3 (February 1992), p. 112.

C A S E   S T U D Y

Bank Goes Global with Frame Relay

Banco de Brasil, the largest bank in Brazil, plans to funnel voice traffic over a global frame relay network as part of its strategy for cutting network costs.

The bank is installing the frame relay network and expects to reduce its monthly telecommunications expenses, which are total more than $1 million, by 30%. Voice traffic will share the same access and backbone circuits with facsimile and data.

Sending voice over frame relay networks has not met with widespread adoption for fear of transmission delay, jitter and discarded packets due to congestion. But Banco de Brasil's network may convince the naysayers that there is no need to worry, said Tom Spadafora, vice president of marketing for Advanced Compression Technologies, Inc. (ACT), the bank's frame relay equipment provider.

ACT's access muxes and backbone switches will link 32 sites in 26 countries over leased 56K and 64K bit/sec lines. In a few cases, dial-up lines will link remote sites with a small amount of backbone-bound traffic to hub sites, Spadafora said.

ACT's ACTnet MS-1000 frame relay switch will be installed in five hub sites to form the backbone. The sites—Brasilia; Buenos Aires, Argentina; London, New York, and Tokyo—will be interconnect-ed in a near-mesh topology over 64K bit/sec circuits. Tokyo will be connected only to New York, but all other backbone sites will be connected to at least two other locations for redundancy.

The MS-1000 switches will be able to dynamically reconfigure the network to route around failed backbone circuits, Spadafora said. The switch can detect when a physical port or a permanent virtual circuit is down, and route to another available trunk.

Branch office sites will be equipped with ACT's ACTnet SDM-FP frame relay access muxes. The multiplexer will take in voice, fax, local-area network and terminal data traffic, wrap it into variable-length frames and send it to the backbone over 56K bit/sec access lines in the U.S. and 64K bit/sec lines overseas.

Currently, the bank uses public-switched services for voice and fax, and a few leased lines for data transmission, an ACT spokeswoman said. The private frame relay network will generate savings by allocating bandwidth on a single trunk to voice, data and fax.

For voice transmission, ACT has tuned its equipment to address the delay, jitter and congestion concerns. The SDM-FP muxes will first digitize and compress voiced signals before mapping them into variable-length frames. To ensure minimal transmission delay, ACT developed a so-called "fair share" algorithm that assigns a high priority to voice traffic, medium priority to fax and low priority for data.

The fair share algorithm also eliminates packetization of silent pauses in voice, which increases bandwidth efficiency, ACT said.

In addition, the algorithm includes Digital Speech Interpolation, which allocates high-priority bandwidth to fax and data when speech is not detected.

The SDM-FP limits voice frames to 83 bytes, which further minimizes delay and jitter because the small frames are easier to buffer.

To handle congestion, ACT developed a "predictive" congestion management algorithm that enables the endpoint SDM-FP muxes to sense a congestion situation.

When buffer queues start to fill up, the SDM-FP sends a frame to the transmitting node telling it to lower its transmission rates.

Banco de Brasil is now funneling voice over frame relay between the Brasilia and New York hubs, and up to the New York switch from SDM-FPs in Chicago, Los Angeles, Miami, San Francisco, and Washington. This marks the completion of the first phase of the bank's network project.

The other hub sites are expected to come on-line by the end of this year.

Business Case Study Questions

Activities

1. Construct a top-down model by placing the pertinent facts from the case in their respective layers within the top-down model. Use the following layer-by-layer questions as a guide.

Business

1. The implementation of the frame relay network was part of what overall corporate strategy?
2. What is the expected expense reduction from the frame relay network?
3. Estimate the capital investment and nonrecurring expenses involved in establishing the frame relay network. Prepare a graph showing the estimated payback period based on anticipated expense reduction.

Data

1. What is the extent of the geographic distribution of the network nodes?
2. Which sites will be hub sites and how will all of the various sites be interconnected?
3. Draw a network diagram showing hub sites, known end-nodes, muxes, and access switches as well as interconnecting circuits.
4. How are data, fax, and voice actually put onto the frame relay network?

Network

1. What characteristic of frame relay networks causes it to be a bad choice for voice transmission?
2. Why is the Bank of Brazil not concerned about this traditional weakness of frame relay?
3. What is a mesh network? What does it look like and what is the purpose of such a network topology?
4. What types of disaster recovery mechanisms, if any, were built into the design?
5. How does the proposed network differ from the current configuration?

Technology

1. What is the difference in terms of functionality between an access mux and a backbone switch?
2. How does the proposed technology overcome frame-relay's traditional inability to handle voice traffic?

Analysis

1. What are some of the questions that occur to you regarding the case?
2. Based on what you have read, do you think that the network design, as described in the business case, will meet the business layer requirements of the Bank of Brazil? Why or why not?

CHAPTER · 8

Emerging Wide Area Networking Services and Technology

Concepts Reinforced

Top-Down Model	Switching Architectures
OSI 7-Layer Model	Transmission Architectures
Multiprotocol Routing	ATM
Network Architectures	Frame Relay

Concepts Introduced

SMDS	Transmission Services
ISDN	SONET
B-ISDN	E-Mail Interoperability
MANs	Electronic Data Interchange
DQDB	Value-Added Networks
Signalling System 7	

OBJECTIVES

After mastering the material in this chapter you should:

1. Understand the advantages, disadvantages, limitations, and proper application of wide area network services such as SMDS, ISDN, and B-ISDN.

2. Understand the requirements for offering emerging network services in terms of switching and transmission architectures.

3. Understand the challenges and possible solutions to E-mail and EDI integration and interoperability opportunities.

4. Understand the importance of standards in the successful implementation of emerging network services.

5. Understand the technology, advantages, disadvantages, limitations, and application of SONET as a transmission architecture.

6. Understand the advantages, disadvantages, limitations, and applications of various possible MAN architectures.

7. Understand the role of Signalling System 7 (SS7) in providing the Software Defined Network (SDN) and Intelligent Network (IN) features of the future.

INTRODUCTION

The basic principles of wide area networking, including an understanding of switching and transmission architectures, were introduced in Chapter 7. The wide area network services that can be offered via that network architecture will now be covered in Chapter 8. Some of these WAN services include SMDS, ISDN, and B-ISDN.

Different possible implementations of metropolitan area networks, or MANs, will be explored with an applications-oriented perspective. The importance of SONET as a transmission architecture of the future will be examined as well.

From a business applications standpoint, the challenge of E-mail integration will be investigated. EDI, or electronic data interchange, will be explored in respect to the technology as well as cost/benefit. Finally, the features and services offered by value-added networks (VANs) will be compared.

☐ DATA DIAL-TONE: SMDS—SWITCHED MULTIMEGABIT DATA SERVICE

By referring back to Figure 7-23 and "reading the SMDS stack," **SMDS,** *switched multimegabit data service,* can be defined as a connectionless network service delivering switched LAN internetworking and data dial tone in a metropolitan area network deployment while adhering to the IEEE 802.6 and DQDB protocols by delivering fixed length cells of data to their destinations via a SONET transmission system.

In the following analysis of SMDS, each layer of the SMDS stack in Figure 7-23 will be examined, followed by a discussion of current deployment levels of SMDS and possible business outlooks for the service.

First and foremost, SMDS is a *network service.* The standards for SMDS were developed by **Bellcore,** the research and development arm of the regional Bell operating companies. The service standards were designed with full implementation and smooth internetworking between carriers in mind from the start.

Rather than just defining the technical aspects—and worrying about the management, billing and troubleshooting aspects later—SMDS was developed from its inception to be fully standardized and defined before the first SMDS product was built or SMDS service offered.

The business and management side of telecommunications services is often referred to as **OAM&P,** or *operation, administration, maintenance, and provisioning.* OAM&P systems are also known as operational support systems or OSSs. OAM&P systems allow telephone companies to utilize new technology effectively in the deployment of new telecommunications services. As more advanced and customer responsive services such as the *advanced intelligent network* are installed, more advanced and sophisticated OAM&P systems will be required to support these flexible, customer-defined services.

It could be said that, in the case of SMDS, the OAM&P as well as the underlying architecture were fully developed prior to deployment. Security and privacy issues were of particular concern as SMDS utilized a shared-media architecture. Although shared-media *local* area networks have been explored earlier, as in the case of Ethernet and Token Ring, the shared media implemented in a *metropolitan* area network has the potential of carrying data of competing corporations over a single network.

What Is a MAN? Metropolitan Area Networks

A *metropolitan area network* **(MAN)** provides network services, such as SMDS, to users within a "metropolitan" area of usually less than 50 kilometers. Most often, the services offered over these MANs are utilized for inter-LAN connectivity, allowing companies with multiple locations within a metropolitan area to share data quickly, easily, and cost-effectively among their various offices.

The LAN-interconnection offered by MAN services such as SMDS must possess characteristics such as reliability, security, and transparency. How each of these criteria are met in MAN implementations will be explored shortly. Although MANs can technically carry voice and video as well as data, these multimedia implementations are more complicated. The architecture and standards underlying the MAN will be investigated in order to explain why data-only MAN services are currently the most common. Finally, the current level of field trials and deployment of SMDS will be summarized.

Metropolitan Area Network and SMDS Are Not Synonymous

One of the first things to understand about SMDS is that it is just one service that can be offered in a metropolitan area network environment. It is currently the most popular one in the United States, but other MAN implementations and services do exist. Figure 8-1 outlines some of the currently implemented MAN services and a small amount of information about each.

As can be seen from Figure 8-1, a variety of underlying architectures contribute to a variety of service levels. The two most common *architectures* employed for MAN services are **FDDI** (fiber distributed data interface) and **DQDB** (distributed queue dual bus). Metropolitan Fiber Systems, Inc. offers the Metrofiber Multimegabit Data Service (MMDS) over its existing fiber network in certain metropolitan areas. Fiber is run directly to users homes or businesses. Connections are circuit-switched, supporting 100 Mbps LAN interconnection data traffic.

FDDI offers 100Mbps shared media connections for data-only LAN interconnection. FDDI consists of a dual-ring counter-rotating data architecture and was studied in Chapter 5. In the metropolitan area network domain, FDDI is most often used by a single corporate or academic institution to establish "campus-wide" LAN interconnection. FDDI is not the choice of the phone companies entering the MAN arena.

Distributed Queue Dual Bus: IEEE 802.6

The architecture of choice for the phone companies' MAN efforts is DQDB/IEEE 802.6. The **IEEE 802.6** designation signifies that this MAC (media access control) sublayer protocol is a member of the same family of IEEE media access protocols as Ethernet and Token Ring. Although the "DB" in DQDB stands for **dual bus,** in fact, this MAN architecture is most often deployed in a **dual ring** physical topology. How the dual ring implementation of the dual bus architecture contributes to greater MAN reliability will be explored shortly.

The DQDB protocol, as specified in the IEEE 802.6 standard, seeks to exhibit

MAN services	Switched multimegabit data service (SMDS)	Fiber distributed data interface (FDDI)	Deutsche Bundepost Telecom (DBP Telecom)	Metrofiber multimegabit data service (MMDS)
Current speed	44.736 MBps (T-3)	100 MBps	2.048 MBps (E-1)	100 MBps
Currently Transporting	Data only	Data only	Data, voice, and video	Data only
Underlying Architecture	DQDB	FDDI	DQDB	Fiber backbone
Architecture type	Switched access	Shared media	Switched access	Circuit switched

Figure 8-1 MANs and MAN services.

the best characteristics of both Ethernet and Token Ring when it comes to access methodologies. Recall that at low traffic levels, Ethernet's CSMA/CD access methodology works very well, getting packets quickly onto the shared media without collisions, timeouts, and retransmissions. On the other hand, Token Ring, with its explicit required permission of token possession before accessing the shared media, worked best at high traffic levels.

DQDB strives for an access methodology that will get messages onto the bus quickly with a minimum of overhead at low traffic levels and efficiently without collisions at high traffic levels. Stated simply, DQDB accomplishes this access methodology goal by "calling ahead for reservations" and keeping track of how many reservations have already been called in. Although somewhat difficult to explain, the access methodology is really quite simple. Although explanations of DQDB often make analogies to bus stops and chair lifts, this explanation will be phrased in terms of dual buses instead. Study Figure 8-2 as the explanation of the DQDB/IEEE 802.6 access methodology is begun.

DQDB Access Methodology Basic Components   Before explaining the functionality of the DQDB access methodology, the components that contribute to that functionality must first be identified. DQDB is comprised of *two buses*, each carrying traffic (*data* and *reservations*) in one direction only. *Access units* are able to read from and write to both of these buses. Upon careful examination of the access arrows between a bus and an access unit, it will be seen that each access unit reads from each bus *before* it writes to that bus. This is how the access unit knows that a "slot" on a bus is empty or unreserved.

The slots on a bus in DQDB are actually preallocated *53-octet cells*, just waiting for preformatted data packets of 53 octets to jump on the bus and fill them up. The empty cells are put onto each bus by the two **head of bus** access units. Each head of bus access unit formats cells for only one of the two buses. The two head of bus units are synchronized so that cells are generated on each bus in a simultaneous manner. It will be seen shortly how DQDB's ability to let any access unit be a head of bus access unit adds significantly to the reliability of the network architecture.

The Role of Counters in DQDB   In this simplified diagram, each access unit also has two *counters*. In order to understand the role of these counters, two terms dealing with relative position on the bus must first be defined: *downstream* and

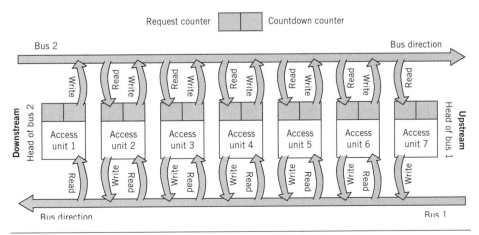

Figure 8-2 Distributed queue dual-bus access methodology: basic components.

upstream. Quite simply, in Figure 8-2, access units 2 and 3 are downstream from access unit 4 and access unit 5 is upstream from access units 2, 3, and 4. One of the counters is known as the **request counter** and keeps track of how many downstream access units have already made reservations on future empty cells (slots on the bus). The second counter is known as the **countdown counter** and holds the number of queued reservations that were in the request counter when a user attached to that particular access unit and made a reservation for an empty cell. In other words, how many users were already in line for empty cells when this access unit's user showed up, or how many reservations had already been called in ahead?

As mentioned in the previous paragraph, Figure 8-2 is a simplified diagram of a DQDB access methodology especially in the area of counters. In this example, counters will make reservations for cells in one direction only. The real DQDB access units have counters for both bus directions and for three different traffic priorities. Data traffic and reservations normally flow on both buses.

DQDB Functionality at Low and High Traffic Levels   Now that the components of the DQDB access methodology are understood, its functionality under two circumstances will be investigated: low traffic levels in which Ethernet's CSMA/CD performed well, and high traffic levels in which Token Ring's token passing access methodology performed admirably.

Low Traffic Functionality   Figure 8-3 illustrates the DQDB access methodology at low traffic levels. In this scenario, a user attached to access unit 5 wishes to send a message to access unit 3, a downstream station. This task is accomplished quickly and easily. Access unit 5 buffers the 53-octet data message from the user while it does three things:

1. It reads the cell immediately in front of it on bus 1, the downstream bus, to determine if it's empty. Given that this is a low traffic example, we assume it is indeed empty.
2. Given that an empty cell is available in the "loading area," access unit 5 next checks the request counter to see how many, if any, downstream access units already had reservations in for the next empty cell.

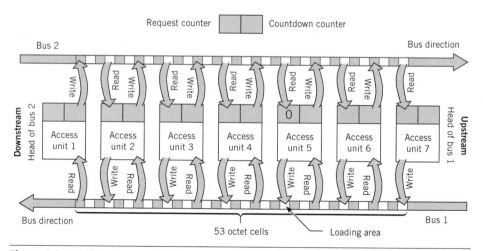

Figure 8-3 Distributed queue dual-bus access methodology: low-traffic access.

3. Again, given that this is a low traffic condition, the request counter is read as zero, and access unit 5 immediately loads its 53-octet data message into the empty 53-octet cell.

Result: Immediate access to a shared media in a low traffic situation—the best characteristic of Ethernet CSMA/CD.

High Traffic Functionality Figures 8-4 and 8-5 illustrate the effectiveness of the DQDB access methodology in high traffic situations. Once again, a user attached to access unit 5 wishes to send a message to access unit 3. Access 5 reads the cell in the loading area on bus 1, the downstream bus, and once again it is empty. However, this time when access unit 5 checks its request counter, it sees that two downstream units have already made reservations for the next empty cell. (See Figure 8-4.)

Step 2: Seeing that two downstream stations have priority on the next two empty cells, access unit 5 moves the "2" from the request counter into the countdown counter and resets the request counter to 0. (See Figure 8-5.)

Because an empty cell was not immediately available, access unit 5 puts a request (makes a reservation) on the *upstream* bus, bus 2, for a reservation on the next available empty cell not previously reserved. Access units 6 and 7 respond by increasing their "downstream request counter" by one.

Access unit 5 continues to read each passing cell. Some may be occupied given that this is a high traffic situation. The first empty cell that access unit 5 encounters, it knows belongs to a downstream access unit. It lets the empty cell pass and decrements its countdown counter by one. When the next empty cell passes, it decrements its countdown counter to zero, which means that the next empty cell which is encountered is *guaranteed* to belong to access unit 5 because it waited its turn (waited until the countdown counter went to zero) and notified other access units of its reservation for an empty cell (set reservation flag on upstream bus).

As can be seen, even under heavy traffic conditions, access to the media is arbitrated and orderly by reservations for empty cells waiting for their turn in a queue. As a matter of fact this type of access to DQDB is known as **queue arbitrated access.** The wait for an empty cell, even under heavy traffic conditions, would only be a matter of milliseconds or perhaps even microseconds.

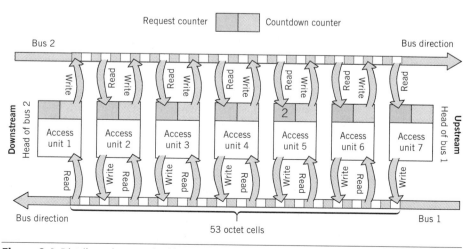

Figure 8-4 Distributed queue dual-bus access methodology: high traffic access—step 1.

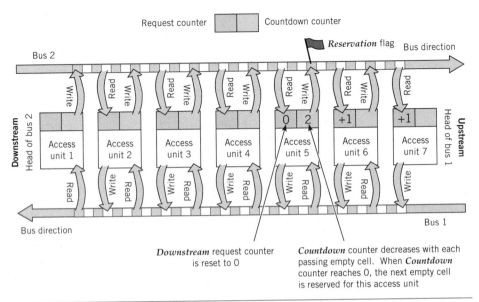

Figure 8-5 Distributed queue dual-bus access methodology: high traffic access—step 2.

Effects of Variable Traffic Conditions

As traffic conditions vary, the wait for an empty cell varies. For most data traffic, this variable waiting period is no problem. However, for some types of timing-sensitive traffic, such as digitized voice or video, this variable waiting period can be a major problem. Voice may become unintelligible and video transmissions may freeze without reliable timed transmission.

DQDB/IEEE 802.6 have a way to cater to the timing sensitive traffic by *prereserving* or *prearbitrating* empty cells on a timed basis (every 125 microseconds). In this way, the voice or video traffic has a guaranteed prereserved cell on a timed basis. This timed, continual, guaranteed arrival of an empty cell by **prearbitrated access** becomes a type of timing device in itself, which can provide synchronization for the timing sensitive traffic. Traffic that derives its timing from the signal (arrival of empty cells) itself is known as **isochronous** traffic. Isochronous traffic as well as voice and video transmission will be studied in later chapters.

FDDI-II

FDDI is an alternative for private networks of a metropolitan area network scale, most often used in college or corporate campus environments. FDDI and its twisted-pair relative CDDI, are *data only* services. A standard under development known as **FDDI-II** seeks to add the capability of isochronous circuit-switched traffic such as voice to the original FDDI standard. In order to accomplish this, FDDI-II is incompatible with current FDDI standards and equipment. Given this incompatibility, it becomes debatable why the new standard should be called FDDI-II.

DQDB Reliability

Reliability was mentioned earlier as a key operational characteristic of metropolitan area networks. DQDB/IEEE 802.6 has a unique way of assuring continued reliable service in the event of a cable break or failure. Figure 8-6 illustrates the physical topology of DQDB before and after a cable break. Notice how that even though the break causes the *dual rings* to become *dual buses,* the overall topology remains

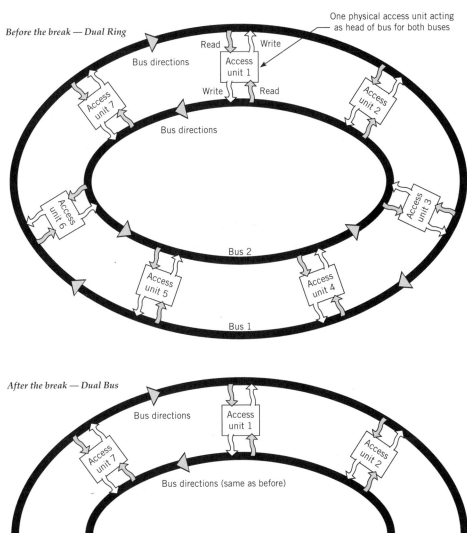

Figure 8-6 Cable break causes head of bus shift.

operational by having the ability to enable any access unit to act as a head of bus access in charge of generating cells.

This logic seems to make perfect sense: if the access unit closest to the cable break can no longer receive cells, just make it the new head of bus access unit and let it be in charge of generating new cells.

SMDS Interfaces User Data with the MAN

DQDB/IEEE 802.6 defines the underlying network architecture of a metropolitan area network. These MANs are established by phone companies or alternative communications vendors such as Metropolitan Fiber Services (MFS). End users do not generally set up and maintain metropolitan area networks. In fact the actual metropolitan area network architecture is completely transparent to the end user, one of the key MAN operational criteria which was established earlier. From a physical perspective, the dual fiber optic buses of DQDB/IEEE 802.6 may not even be employed but instead replaced by a hardware device known as an SMDS switch, which supports the MAC sublayer protocols of DQDB/IEEE 802.6.

End users purchase MAN services which interface between the user's data, usually LAN traffic, and the transparent MAN architecture via a high speed (1.544 or 44.736 Mbps) access line from phone companies or alternative carriers. Eventually, as **SONET** (synchronous optical network) is deployed, SMDS will run at SONET rates of 155Mbps. SMDS, switched multimegabit data service, is the most common MAN service currently available in the United States.

SMDS is a switched, connectionless datagram service wherein no time or overhead is spent for call set-up, virtual circuit table creation, call termination, etc. In that sense, it has many of the advantages of X.25 datagram packet-switching networks. For instance, the potential savings over circuit-switched alternatives in the reduced number or required circuits can be significant.

Rather than having to connect all sights to each other with multiple leased point-to-point lines, SMDS requires one leased, point-to-point access line, usually a 1.544 Mbps T-1, from each sight into the "SMDS cloud" where datagrams, in this case 53-octet cells, are delivered quickly and securely. SMDS users reach other SMDS users via special SMDS phone numbers. Remember this is *switched* multimegabit data service. Figure 8-7 illustrates a possible SMDS MAN configuration.

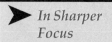
In Sharper Focus

HIGHLIGHTS OF SMDS ARCHITECTURE AND STANDARDS

Interface Specifications

Figure 8-7 highlights several important aspects of SMDS. First, as was stated earlier, SMDS was highly standardized and well-defined prior to its first field trial. As can be seen in Figure 8-7, specific *interface specifications* have been defined for:

> User data to SMDS data: *SIP*—SMDS interface protocol
> User equipment to SMDS network: *SNI*—subscriber network interface
> Among SMDS switches within the same MAN: *ISSI*—inter-switching system interface
> Between SMDS service on different MANs: *ICI*—inter-carrier interface

Security

Second, *security* is a vital concern in SMDS. SMDS access devices, which interface the SMDS network with the user's access line, read the address of all incoming and

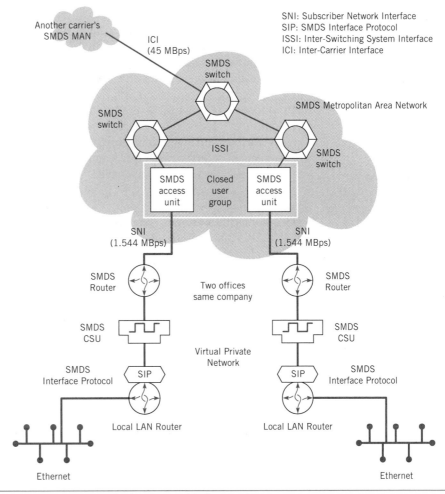

Figure 8-7 SMDS—Switched multimegabit data service.

outgoing cells. Only cells with authorization to send to a particular destination are forwarded to that destination. Users are allowed to adjust their group tables to specify which local users are allowed access to the MAN and from which remote MAN users' data will be accepted.

These *closed user groups* constitute what is known as a **virtual private network,** which seeks to replace the user maintained circuit-switched point-to-point network connecting all user sights. Both of these concepts are illustrated on Figure 8-7.

In conclusion, as SMDS services are deployed over additional MANs, inter-MAN links will turn MAN services into WAN services. With the forethought that Bellcore put into interface specifications concerning MAN-to-MAN connectivity, this MAN-to-WAN migration should become a reality. In fact, a long-haul SMDS transport trial connecting a long-distance carrier with two different regional carriers was completed in October 1992. For SMDS to succeed, users cannot be limited as to what areas of the region or country they may transport their inter-LAN traffic.

☐ ISDN: INTEGRATED SERVICES DIGITAL NETWORK

ISDN is somewhat of a phenomenon in the telecommunications industry. Opinions on it range from consideration of it as a revolutionary breakthrough to an absolute conviction that it won't ever materialize. ISDN has brought more humor to telecommunications than nearly any other topic with the various interpretations of the ISDN acronym such as: *It Still Does Nothing* or *I Still Don't Need it.*

In this section, what ISDN is and what it isn't will be investigated. Its underlying architecture as well as its current and potential services will be studied. Current deployment levels and future possibilities will also be explored. The technical aspects of interfacing to ISDN in comparison to other existing or imminent alternative telecommunications services will also be analyzed.

What Is ISDN?

ISDN is sometimes known as **narrowband ISDN** as opposed to *broadband ISDN* or **B-ISDN**. B-ISDN operates at 155Mbps, or about 10 times narrowband ISDN, and will be explored in the next section of this chapter. ISDN is *switched* digital network service offering both voice and nonvoice connectivity to other ISDN end users. Voice, video, and data are all transportable over a single ISDN connection. Depending on bandwidth requirements, voice, video, and data may even be transported simultaneously over a single network connection. Figure 8-8 illustrates a high-level view of possible ISDN use.

Two Service Levels: BRI and PRI

Narrowband ISDN, which will be referred to as simply ISDN from now on, is deliverable in two different service levels or interfaces. *Basic rate interface,* or **BRI,** is also referred to as **2B+D.** This 2B+D label refers to the channel configuration of the BRI service in which 2 *Bearer* channels (64Kbps ea) and one *Data* channel (16Kbps) are combined into a 144Kbps interface. The *bearer channels* are intended to "bear" or carry services such as voice, video, or data transport, while the *data channel* is

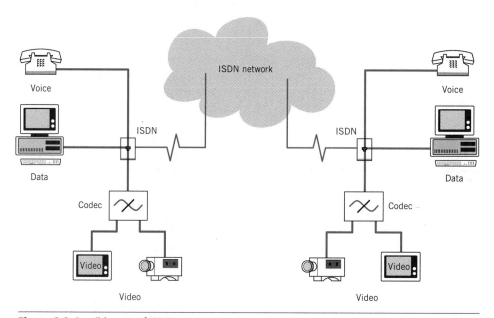

Figure 8-8 Possible uses of ISDN.

intended for network management data for call set-up and teardown, calling number identification and other ISDN specific network signals.

The use of this side D channel for carrying signal data is known as **out of band signalling** and is one of the key features of ISDN. The "out of band" refers to the fact that the signal control information does not have to be intermingled with the user data, thereby maximizing the available bandwidth for user data. Prior to ISDN, control information was passed over the network within the user channels in a technique known as *in-band signalling.* This is why many so-called ISDN services, such as **automatic number identification,** can be offered without ISDN.

A second ISDN service level known as **PRI,** or *primary rate interface,* also known as **23B+D** is comprised of 23 64Kbps bearer channels and one 64Kbps data channel for a combined bandwidth of 1.536Mbps. With a small amount of additional overhead, PRI maps nicely onto the 1.544Mbps **T-1** circuit. In Europe, ISDN is offered in a *30B+D* configuration yielding 1.984Mbps. Additional overhead in this case maps nicely to the **E-1** (European digital signal level 1) of 2.048 Mbps. Figure 8-9 summarizes much of the narrowband ISDN architectural information.

Services	Video freeze-frame Voice Data	LAN Interconnect Full motion video Voice Data
Transport category	BRI (Basic Rate Interface)	PRI (Primary Rate Interface)
Transport capacity	2 B + D 2 × 64Kbps 128Kbps + 16Kbps 16Kbps 144Kbps	23 B + D (23 × 64k) B channels + 64k D channels 1.536Mbps
Transport architecture	2-wire Dial-up	T-1
Inter-switch protocol and switching architecture	Signalling System 7 (SS7)	

Figure 8-9 Narrowband ISDN.

ISDN Uses and Services

ISDN can be used for anything that a point-to-point leased digital line of equivalent bandwidth can be used for. This was supposed to be one of ISDN's major selling points: An all-digital *circuit-switched* network that could deliver leased-line transmission quality and bandwidth with usage-based rates. In other words, whereas leased lines are billed on a flat monthly fee regardless of utilization, with ISDN, one pays only for the time the switched circuit is operational.

One of the early problems with ISDN, however, is that the ISDN rates in many cases, do not represent a savings as opposed to a leased-line alternative. What a marvelous top-down model example of perceived *business* layer effects dooming a *technology* layer carrier service.

Dial-up voice calls, data transfer, and videoconferencing over the two 64Kbps of the 2B+D BRI channels are all possible. The 23+D PRI interface yielding a 1.54Mps transmission rate may also be suitable for LAN interconnection, although a quick comparison shows that this inter-LAN rate is significantly below most LAN transmission rates. This disparity in transmission rates can produce a bottleneck for live interactive inter-LAN communication. On the other hand, this rate may be very suitable for nightly backup or batch-oriented file transfer between remote LAN servers.

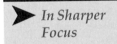

In Sharper Focus

ISDN VOICE-RELATED SERVICES

In addition to the aforementioned generalized uses, several voice-related services are available through ISDN. As previously mentioned, these services are currently offered in many cases over non-ISDN phone networks. Sometimes generalized as "Smartphone" services, among the specific possible offerings are:

Caller ID: Identifies the phone number of the incoming call before the call is answered. Requires a display unit to display the phone number. In an ISDN implementation, this incoming phone number is transmitted over the D channel. Phone companies can then leverage additional services through the use of this number. For instance, certain incoming numbers can be blocked or forwarded, or alternatively, only certain numbers can be allowed to ring through.

Call forwarding, call hold, and *automatic callback* are but a few of the other services possible with ISDN.

Frame Relay Is an ISDN Service

As confusing as it may sound, frame relay is in fact an ISDN service. Its formal ISDN name is frame relaying bearer service, with "bearer service" just meaning that it runs over one (or both) of the 64K B channels. This is the exact same frame relay service studied earlier, seeking to improve performance in comparison to X.25 packet-switched networks by foregoing the point-to-point acknowledgment, error correction, and retransmission in light of higher quality, low error-rate digital circuitry.

Recall that frame relay is a connection-oriented fast packet-switched service. Calls must be set up prior to frame relay sessions and torn down following frame relay sessions. ISDN is a circuit-switched network offering a fast, dependable service for call set up and termination for frame relay via ISDN's D channel. In other words, ISDN is acting as a *transport mechanism* to deliver a frame relay service.

Alternatively, it could be said that frame relay is a packet-switched service running over a circuit-switched network.

Once ISDN has transported the frame relay frames into the ISDN network, the actual frame relay switching can only be done by switches understanding the frame relay protocol. This may be accomplished in at least three different ways:

1. The ISDN switches may also be frame relay "literate" and process the frames directly.
2. A frame relay switch may be present within the ISDN network, in which case the ISDN switch passes the frames to the frame relay switch for further processing.
3. The ISDN switch may pass the frames outside of the ISDN network to a frame relay network for further processing.

The advantage to vendors of ISDN services for offering frame relay as a data transfer service should be clear. The more options that ISDN can offer over its single access line, the more likely users are to avail themselves of this service.

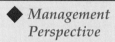

Management Perspective

ISDN Network Service Availability

The first and foremost requirement for ISDN connection is that the ISDN service is provided by one's local telecommunications vendor. This is by no means a given. The most commonly expressed opinion as to ISDN's lack of acceptance has been its sporadic deployment by local phone companies leading to "ISDN Islands of Isolation." In other words, it may be great to have local ISDN service, but if it isn't possible to communicate with the remote sights that a company needs via the ISDN service, of what use is it?

The only sure way to determine if ISDN service is available locally is to call one's local phone company. Figure 8-10 summarizes data concerning ISDN deployment by the RBOCs.

ISDN Incompatibilities

The "islands of ISDN isolation" were largely due to incompatibilities in individual ISDN implementations. The heart of an ISDN network is the ISDN switch. Two competing ISDN switches, AT&T 5ESS Switch and Northern Telecom's DMS100 switch had slightly different interface specifications with *customer premises equipment* (**CPE**). Customer premises equipment which supported the AT&T specification would not operate on Northern Telecom switches and vice-versa.

This brings up another key reason for less than spectacular adoption of ISDN: existing phone equipment and modems do not work on ISDN. Significantly more expensive ISDN-ready phones (digital as opposed to analog) must be purchased to carry voice traffic over ISDN. Alternatively, so-called **terminal adapters** can make existing phone equipment ISDN-ready.

SS7 Provides Intelligent Network Interoperability

In order to offer transparent, long-distance ISDN service, a standard or protocol was required by which ISDN switches could exchange management and control information. Incompatible switches or implementations led to situations where services available in one ISDN network were not available in others, leading to a further lack of long-distance transparency and interoperability. A standard known

Local availability of ISDN depends on C.O. capability

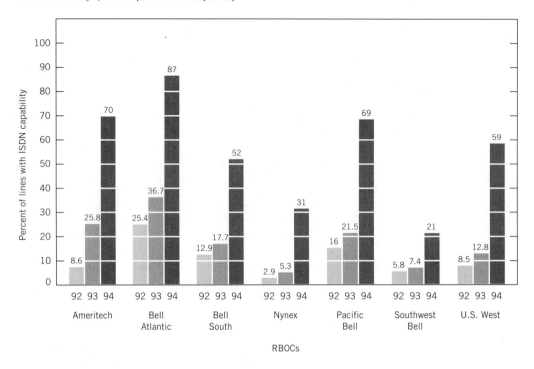

Long-distance ISDN depends on inter-C.O. Signalling System 7 (SS7)

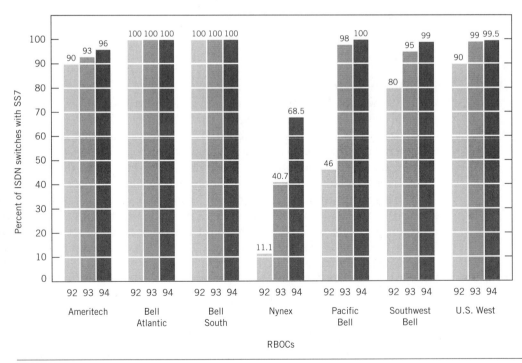

Figure 8-10 ISDN deployment by RBOC.

as **signalling system seven** or **SS7** defines specifications for the out of band signalling by which ISDN switches exchange information.

In fact, it is SS7 which captures all of the caller ID and other call control information. ISDN merely delivers the control information and network intelligence generated and transported by SS7.

Transcontinental ISDN Project 1992

If the "islands of incompatibility" stigma was ever to be lifted, a coordinated effort, international in scope, would have to be launched. Such an effort was produced by the Corporation for Open Systems International and the North American ISDN Users Forum in an effort entitled Transcontinental ISDN Project 1992, and nicknamed **TRIP '92.** The objectives of this event were two-fold:

1. Define necessary specifications to eliminate incompatibilities between ISDN networks.
2. Establish a multivendor national ISDN network as a demonstration of ISDN's viability.

The interoperability specification developed is known as **NISDN-1** (National ISDN-1). It defines a national standard for ISDN switches as well as interswitch communication.

A trans-continental videoconference over an ISDN network was established for the event. However, perhaps indicative of ISDN's troubled past, there were technical difficulties with the network and portions of the audio were garbled.

ISDN to X.25 Interfaces

Another problem plaguing significant deployment of ISDN is the number of network users currently attached to X.25 packet-switched networks. No one is going to switch to ISDN if it means they either can no longer communicate with remote X.25 network sights, or must maintain two separate network links, one to ISDN and the other to the X.25 network.

An interconnect specification known as **LPN-ISDN** (local packet network-integrated services digital network) has been developed and demonstrated at TRIP '92. This interconnect will allow ISDN network-attached users to transparently access X.25 networks over a single ISDN network access line.

Getting Data onto ISDN

In order to get data onto the ISDN network, the equivalent of an ISDN modem known as an *ISDN terminal adapter* must be employed. These ISDN terminal adapters are available both as PC cards for installation into a PC's expansion bus, as well as in standalone units. ISDN terminal adapters very often have a jack for a phone to be attached as well. By attaching a "regular" phone through the terminal adapter it becomes an "ISDN" phone.

Standalone single PC terminal adapters are available for $1300 to $1400. Although this may seem more expensive than an average modem, remember that transmission speeds of up to 64Kbps are possible over ISDN. If both B channels and the D channel can be combined by the terminal adapter, then the full 144Kbps is available. Figure 8-11 illustrates a single PC and phone hooked to an ISDN network via a terminal adapter.

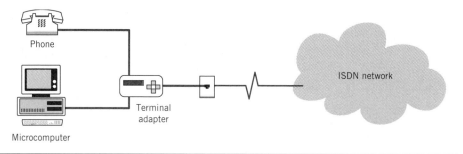

Figure 8-11 PC and phone access to ISDN.

ISDN/LAN Interconnection

In order to connect an entire LAN to the ISDN network there are basically three options:

1. ISDN/LAN gateway
2. ISDN/LAN bridge/router
3. ISDN/LAN server

The **ISDN gateway** is most often a LAN-attached PC with both a NIC card and an ISDN interface card installed. Some type of bridging or routing software may be required in order for the network operating system's redirector to know which frames should be forwarded over the ISDN link. Figure 8-12 illustrates ISDN/LAN gateway configuration.

The **ISDN/LAN bridge or router** is a dedicated standalone device that takes LAN frames as input, processes them into ISDN compliant packets, and outputs them to an ISDN interface. This is a good example of the I-P-O Model of data com-

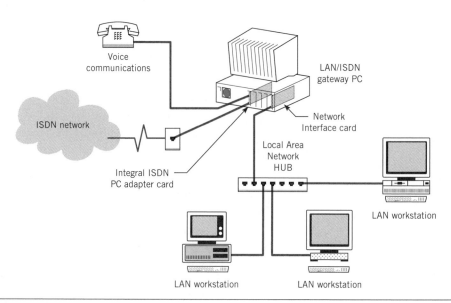

Figure 8-12 ISDN/LAN PC gateway.

munications device analysis that has been employed throughout the text. Without even knowing that such a device existed, a network analyst would be able to articulate its functional requirements and interfaces.

As a matter of fact, such a device does exist. The **ISDN to MAC sublayer (IMAC) Bridge** from Digiboard interfaces between Ethernet networks and ISDN networks. The IMAC works like any other bridge with an added feature for ISDN. It examines the destination address on every Ethernet frame and if the destination is not local, the IMAC dials the proper remote ISDN node and forwards the ISDN packets out over the ISDN link. Multiple IMACs can be linked to a single LAN for additional internetwork transmission capacity to the ISDN network. Figure 8-13 illustrates an ISDN/LAN bridge installation.

By installing multiple ISDN PC adapter cards in the expansion slots of a LAN server, an ISDN/LAN server can be created in order to offer multiple simultaneous connections to the ISDN network. As a matter of fact, remembering that a BRI ISDN link offers two 64K B channels, each ISDN adapter card can actually create, and support two simultaneous calls to the two different remote nodes via the ISDN network.

This ability to create *multiple simultaneous connections per single access line* is a key attribute of ISDN. Given this ability, it should follow that an **ISDN server** with four ISDN PC adapter cards can support eight simultaneous sessions to the ISDN network. Figure 8-14 illustrates an ISDN/LAN server installation.

Operational Features of ISDN PC Adapters

Important operational features of ISDN PC adapters are summarized in Figure 8-15. Some of the features listed relate to the ISDN PC adapter card's use of a PC as an ISDN/LAN bridge. In those cases, the desired operational feature, such as explorer packet filtering, is no different than what would be desirable in any bridge.

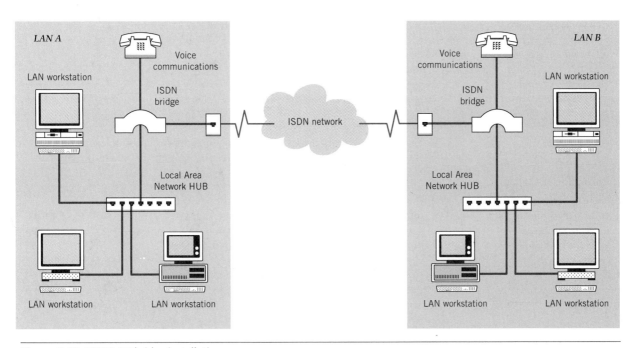

Figure 8-13 ISDN/LAN bridge installation.

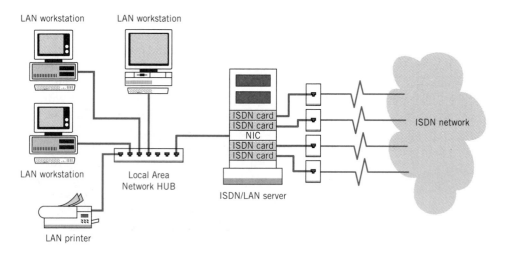

Figure 8-14 ISDN/LAN server installation.

Feature	Options/Implications
Multiple calls per access line	A standard feature of ISDN. Not necessarily supported on all cards
Use of D channel for automatic call set-up and termination	ISDN expects out of band signalling. Some PC adapter cards require manual call set-up and termination
Filtering of explorer or broad-cast packets	Standard bridge/router feature not necessarily included on PC card to be used as ISDN gateway. Can save money on usage based billing
Multiprotocol support	A standard router feature, but is this PC/ISDN adapter compatible with your network operating system?
Auto reestablishment of failed calls	Especially helpful during late-night unattended server to server backup sessions
SNMP support	Like any internetwork device, performance and alarm conditions must be monitored. Can this card or ISDN device output management information in standardized SNMP format?
Synchronization of multiple calls to the same location	Can separate ISDN calls to the same location be synchronized to produce higher aggregate bandwidth?
Data compression	Are V.42bis data compression standards supported?
PRI support	Is this card/device also operational or upgradable to 23B+D PRI interface?
Multivendor support	Recalling our earlier discussion of incompatibility across different vendors' ISDN switches, which vendors' equipment will this operate with?

Figure 8-15 ISDN PC adapter card features and options.

Multirate ISDN: Bandwidth on Demand?

Before moving on to broadband ISDN and its multimegabit bandwidth capacity, it might be worthwhile to take a look at a relatively new and unknown type of ISDN known as **multirate ISDN.** Initially proposed as a service and proprietary specification by U.S. Sprint, multirate ISDN is undergoing standardization by both Bellcore and the CCITT.

With multirate ISDN and a T-1 (1.544Mbps) access line, users may dial up as many 64K increments of bandwidth as required up to the 1.544 access line limit. The interesting thing is that this is all accomplished via one phone call over one D-channel rather than one call for each incremental 64K of bandwidth.

Alternatively, "bandwidth on demand" can be provided through the use of a device known as an *inverse multiplexer*, which will be studied further in Chapter 11 on videoconferencing. Using the inverse mux, users place individual calls for each incremental 64K of bandwidth and multiplex the individual 64K channels into a single composite channel of the desired bandwidth, usually 128K or 384K for the purposes of videoconferencing.

Remember, multirate ISDN is a *dial-up*, usage-based billing, circuit-switched service. Incremental 64K channels are also available on a *leased* point-to-point basis through a service known as **fractional T-1,** which we will review shortly.

A LOOK AT TRANSMISSION SERVICES

Because the power and appeal of B-ISDN is so closely linked to SONET, its underlying *transmission architecture,* various transmissions alternatives, standards, and concepts will be examined before studying B-ISDN.

Figure 8-16 illustrates the various categories and offerings of transmission services.

Circuit-Switched Transmission Services

Circuit-switched transmission services imply that circuits are set up, utilized, and torn down or disassembled for each requested connection. Long-distance circuit-switched connections may travel through multiple COs (central offices) or POPs (point of presence). The facilities that support and comprise the circuit-switched connection are dedicated to that connection for its entire duration. It is possible, although in most circumstances unlikely, for the phone companies to have insufficient resources to handle requested circuit-switched services. Such a situation would manifest itself as a lack of dial-tone.

The circuit-switched network was originally designed to be an efficient way to handle voice communication. A manually operated switchboard in which the call-

Circuit Switched	Leased/Private Lines	Packet Switched
POTS—plain old telephone service	Analog Leased (3002 circuit)	X.25
Switched 56K	DDS—Digital 1200bps - 56K	Frame Relay
Switched 64K	DS-0 64K	SMDS
Switched 384K	Fractional T-1 (FT-1)	B-ISDN
Switched T-1	T-1	
ISDN—BRI	T-2	
ISDN—PRI	T-3	
ISDN—multirate	SONET	

Figure 8-16 Transmission services.

ing (source) party was "patched through" to the called (destination) party is a primitive form of circuit switching. In some ways, very little has changed except the speed and the capacity of the devices doing the "patching through."

Circuit-switched connections are most often billed based on duration of the connection and end-to-end distance of the connection. Therefore, the most cost-effective uses of circuit-switched connections are those applications that can use as close as possible to 100 percent of the available bandwidth for the duration of the connection. One way to achieve this efficiency is to use the circuit-switched connection to carry data or information from multiple sources simultaneously by either multiplexing or combining data and voice channels as in the case of ISDN.

All of the circuit-switched transmission services listed in Figure 8-16 have been reviewed previously with the exception of the switched T-1. Before reviewing the digital transmission standards of which T-1 is a part, it should be pointed out that not all services listed are universally available on either a local or long-distance basis. For example, switched 56K may only be available to NYNEX customers for intra-LATA traffic while switched 384K may only be available to AT&T customers for inter-LATA traffic.

Digital Transmission Standards

In order to establish and manage long-distance telecommunications links effectively between multiple vendors, standards were required to outline both the size and organization of high-capacity digital communications links between carriers.

The organization portion of the task involved dividing the high-capacity (1.544Mbps) transmission lines into several separate identifiable transmission channels. The technique involved is known as *framing* and is an adaptation of the *TDM* (time division multiplexing) techniques explored in Chapter 7.

In a technique known as **periodic framing** or **synchronous TDM,** every 193rd bit transmitted represents a marker indicating the end of one frame and the beginning of another. Each frame is then divided into *24 channels of 8 bits* each. The mathematics behind the 24 channels of 8 bits each and the 1.544Mbps overall transmission capacity has to do with the bandwidth required to transmit toll-quality digitized voice. Each of the 24 channels is able to carry a single digitized voice transmission.

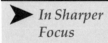 *In Sharper Focus*

FRAMING MULTIPLE CHANNELS PER T-1

Remembering that voice conversation is a naturally occurring analog signal, in order to have the digitized voice sound reasonable, the analog voice signal must be sampled, or have a digital value assigned to analog frequency at a given moment in time, at a sampling rate of 8000 times per second. The resultant mathematics follows:

> 24 channels × 8 bits/channel = 192 bits
> Plus one framing bit for every 24 channels = 193 bits/frame
> Multiplied by 8000 samples or completed frames/sec for toll-quality digitized voice:
> 193 bits/frame × 8000 frames/sec = 1,544,000 bits/sec. or 1.544Mbps = the capacity of a T-1.

Framing will be explored further in Chapter 10, "Voice Transmission and Data/Voice Integration." Figure 8-17 illustrates the concepts of TDM and multiple voice channels.

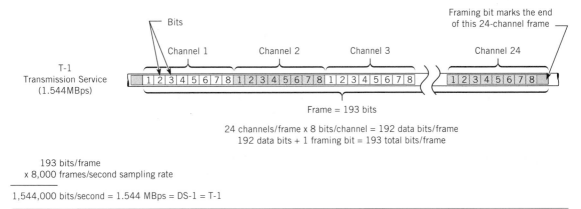

24 channels/frame x 8 bits/channel = 192 data bits/frame
192 data bits + 1 framing bit = 193 total bits/frame

193 bits/frame
x 8,000 frames/second sampling rate

1,544,000 bits/second = 1.544 MBps = DS-1 = T-1

Figure 8-17 TDM yields multiple channels per frame.

Digital Service Hierarchy

The 1.544Mps standard is part of a hierarchy of standards known as the **digital service hierarchy** or **DS** standards. These standards are independent of the transmission services that may deliver the required bandwidth of one of the standards. For instance, technically speaking DS-1 is not the same as T-1, but the two terms are very often used interchangeably. To be exact, a T-1 transmission service delivers DS-1 equivalent bandwidth. Figure 8-18 summarizes the digital service hierarchy for North America as well as the CCITT standards for international digital service. Although numerous transmission service designators may be listed, T-1 and T-3 are by far the most common service levels delivered.

Digital Service Level	Number of Voice Channels	Transmission Rate	Corresponding Transmission Service
DS-0	1	64 Kbps	DS-0 or switched 64K
DS-1	24	1.544 Mbps	T-1 or switched T-1
DS-1C	48	3.152 Mbps	T-1C
DS-2	96	6.312 Mbps	T-2
DS-3	672	44.736 Mbps	T-3
DS-4	4032	274.176 Mbps	T-4

Figure 8-18a Digital service (DS) hierarchy.

Digital Service Level	Number of Voice Channels	Transmission Rate	Corresponding Transmission Service
1	30	2.048 Mbps	E-1
2	120	8.448 Mbps	E-2
3	480	34.368 Mbps	E-3
4	1920	139.264 Mbps	E-4
5	7680	565.148 Mbps	E-5

Figure 8-18b CCITT digital hierarchy.

Leased/Private Lines

Use of leased or private lines, also known as dedicated lines, differs from circuit-switched line usage in several ways:

With leased lines there is no dial tone. The circuit is always open and available. The end-user is billed for the circuit, 24 hours a day, 7 days a week. With leased lines, it is even more imperative than with circuit-switched lines to assure sufficient data traffic to utilize as close to 100 percent capacity as possible 100 percent of the time in order to assure cost-justification of circuit costs.

◆ *Management Perspective*

Before the advent of high-speed packet services, and high-speed modems that work over dial-up (circuit-switched) lines, leased lines were the only available means of high-speed data transfer over a wide area network. Network managers did their best to get the most out of these relatively expensive leased lines through the use of STDMs, explained earlier in Chapter 7.

Leased lines do not get set up in a matter of seconds in a manner such as circuit switched lines. In most cases, a 4 to 6 week lead time is required for the installation of a leased line. Leased lines are constructed to circumvent central office switch facilities so as not to monopolize limited circuit-switching capacity.

In some cases the multiple 64K channels within a T-1 transport circuit can be manipulated or utilized on an individual basis. A service which offers such capability is known as **fractional T-1** or *FT-1*. The fact of the matter is that the full T-1 must be physically delivered to the customer premises, but only a given number of 64K channels within the T-1 are enabled. Fractional T-1 is really just a creative marketing practice on the part of the carriers as a means of increasing sales of digital transmission services.

◆

The only leased-line service listed on Figure 8-16 which has not already been discussed is SONET or Synchronous Optical Network. SONET is the transmission architecture underlying B-ISDN, the only packet-switched service not previously explained.

SONET: Synchronous Optical Network

SONET is an optical transmission service delivering multiple channels of data from various sources thanks to periodic framing or TDM much like the T-1 transmission service just reviewed.

The differences between T-1 and SONET transmission services lie chiefly in the higher transmission capacity of SONET due to its fiber optic media and the slightly different framing techniques used to channelize this higher transmission capacity.

Just as the digital service hierarchy defined levels of service for traditional digital service, optical transmission has a hierarchy of service levels as well. Rather than being designated as DS levels, optical transmission is categorized by *OC* or **optical carrier levels.**

Because SONET will eventually carry voice, video, and image as well as data, the basic unit of measure is referred to as an **octet** or 8 bits rather than a byte of 8 bits. Byte is usually reserved for referring to data only and is often synonymous with a character.

SONET Framing   In many ways, SONET framing is the same as T-1 framing. The basic purpose of each is to establish markers with which to identify individual chan-

OC-Level	Transmission Rate
OC-1	51.84 Mbps
OC-3	155.52 Mbps
OC-9	466.56 Mbps
OC-12	622.08 Mbps
OC-18	933.12 Mbps
OC-24	1.244 Gbps
OC-36	1.866 Gbps
OC-48	2.488 Gbps

Figure 8-19 SONET's OC (Optical Carrier) standards.

nels. Because of the higher bandwidth of SONET (51.84 vs. 1.544Mbps) and potential for sophisticated mixed-media services, more overhead is reserved surrounding each frame than the single bit reserved every 193rd character in a T-1 frame.

Rather than fitting 24 channels per frame delineated by a single framing bit, a single SONET frame or "row" is delineated by 3 octets of overhead for control information followed by 87 octets of "payload." Nine of these 90 octet rows are grouped together to form a SONET **superframe.** The 87 octets of payload per row in each of the time rows or the superframe is known as the **synchronous payload envelope** or *SPE.* The electrical equivalent of the OC-1, the optical SONET superframe standard is known as the STS-1, or synchronous transport signal.

Figure 8-19 defines the OC or optical carrier standards of SONET while Figure 8-20 defines SONET frame structure.

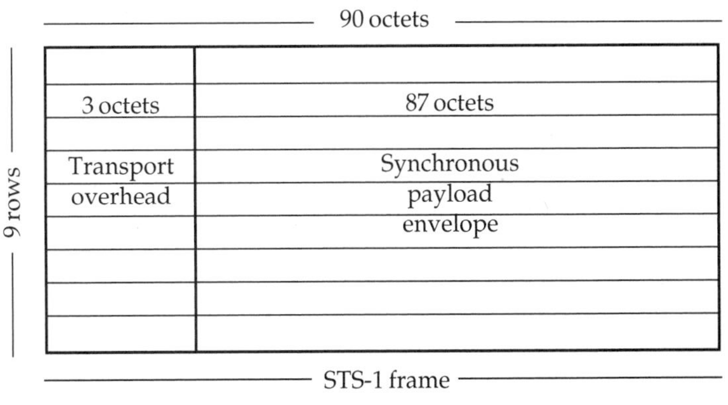

90 octets/row $\times$ 8 bits/octet = 720 bits/row

720 bits/row $\times$ 9 rows/frame = 6480 bits/frame

6480 bits/frame $\times$ 8,000 frames/second (sampling rate) = 51,840,000 bits/second

Transfer Rate of 51.84 Mbits/second

Figure 8-20 SONET framing: OC-1 = STS-1 = 51.84 Mbps.

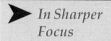

VIRTUAL TRIBUTARIES IN SONET

Unlike the T-1 frame with its 24 predefined 8-bit channels, SONET is flexible in its definition of the use of its payload area. It can map DS-0 (64Kbps) channels into the payload area just as easily as it can map an entire T-1 (1.544Mbps). These flexibly defined channels within the payload area are known as **virtual tributaries** or *VTs*.

For instance, a T-1 would be mapped into a virtual tributary standard known as VT-1.5, with a bandwidth of 1.728Mbps, the difference between that figure and the 1.544Mbps T-1 being accounted for by the additional SONET overhead.

The virtual tributaries of SONET are equivalent to circuit-switched transmission services. In addition to the 3 octets per row of transport overhead in OC-1 there is also a variable amount of path overhead embedded within the SPE to keep track of which virtual tributaries start where within the SPE payload boxcar. This path overhead brings the total overhead to about 4 percent before any additional overhead embedded within the SPE payload boxcar is considered.

Management Perspective

Conclusion: So What Is SONET?

SONET is a service independent *transport* function that can carry the services of the future such as B-ISDN, FDDI, or HDTV (high-definition television), as easily as it can carry the circuit-switched traffic of today, such as DS-1 and DS-3. It has extensive performance monitoring and fault location capabilities. For instance, if SONET senses a transmission problem, it can switch traffic to an alternate path in as little as 50 msec. (1000ths of a sec.). Based on the OC hierarchy of standard optical interfaces, it has the potential to deliver multigigabyte bandwidth transmission capabilities to end-users.

SONET + ATM = B-ISDN

SONET is the optical **transmission** interface and mechanism that will deliver broadband ISDN services. ATM is the *switching* architecture which will assure that video, voice, data, and image packets delivered by B-ISDN services are delivered to the proper destination. Together, ATM and SONET form the underlying network architecture of the B-ISDN of the future. ATM provides the cell relay switching fabric providing **bandwidth on demand** for bursty data from any source (voice, video, etc.), while SONET's synchronous payload envelope provides empty boxcars for ATM's cargo.

Much of the excitement concerning B-ISDN is due to its ability to support existing services (T-1, T-3), emerging services (SMDS, frame relay), as well as future services (HDTV, medical imaging) and services as yet undiscovered. B-ISDN should be the service that finally delivers true bandwidth on demand in an uncomplicated, transparent, and hopefully affordable manner.

B-ISDN Services

Broadband ISDN services fall into two general categories: interactive and broadcast. Interactive services might include such things as meeting room videoconferencing, desktop videoconferencing, multimedia computing, LAN interconnection, medical imaging distribution and consulting, MAN interconnection, video window shopping (interactive home shopping network) and videophone. Broadcast or distributed services might include high-definition TV, pay-per-view events, or on-line news services.

Bandwidth on demand services for data access or transfer will include SMDS, switched T-1, switched T-3 and permanent virtual circuit T-1 and T-3.

Putting It All Together

Simply stated, SONET possesses the flexibility to carry multiple types of data cargo (voice, video, etc.) simultaneously while ATM has the ability to switch multiple types of data simultaneously. The fact that the complementary nature of the two architectures produce a network service known as B-ISDN should come as no surprise. Figure 8-21 illustrates the coming evolution of transmission and switching architectures and the relationship of the two.

Figure 8-22 takes the general categories of user demands first outlined in Figure 7-16 and fills in the blanks with the wide area network architecture of the future.

☐ BUSINESS USES OF WIDE AREA NETWORK SERVICES

Among the important business uses of wide area networks mentioned previously were: voice traffic, interactive transaction processing, LAN interconnection, and video conferencing. Perhaps the most popular use of wide area network services not previously mentioned is **electronic mail,** more commonly known as **E-Mail.** In fact, E-mail is very often the first LAN-based application that end-users learn and

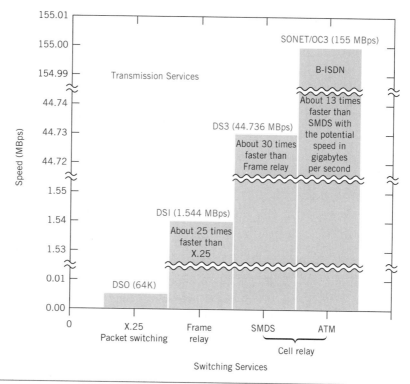

Figure 8-21 Wide area network services: Switching services versus transmission services.

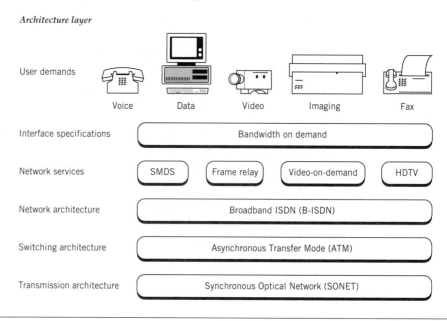

Figure 8-22 Wide area network architecture of the future.

use. When used correctly, E-mail can have a definite positive impact on the overall productivity and effectiveness of a business.

Very often, different LANs installed different E-mail systems. Sharing E-mail across the internetwork or wide area network became an issue not only of connectivity (OSI layers 1–3), but translation or interoperability as well (OSI layers 4–7). In this section, wide area E-mail networks will be explored from a number of perspectives:

1. What is the overall architecture of a wide area E-mail network?
2. What are the cross-platform integration issues associated with wide area E-mail networks?
3. What are the possible solutions to these integration opportunities from both a technology as well as a standards standpoint?
4. How do any of the above issues relate to EDI (electronic data interchange) or the client/server architecture?

Overall Wide Area Network E-Mail Architecture

E-mail can run as an application program on computers of any size. For example, Quick Mail may run over Appletalk, CC:Mail may run over a Netware LAN, All-in-One may be running on DECnet and PROFS (professional office system) may be running on an IBM mainframe. The problem arises when any of the users on any of these E-mail platforms wish to send E-mail to each other. The E-mail systems are simply not compatible.

Following is a sampling, but by no means an exhaustive list, of mail systems or protocols and their native platforms:

Platform	Mail System/Protocol
LANs (Apple and PC)	Quick Mail
	cc: Mail
	Microsoft Mail
	DaVinci Mail

DEC Minicomputers
(DECnet)
UNIX Workstations

PCs and MACs
IBM Minis and Mainframes

All-in-One
SMTP (Simple Mail Transfer Protocol)
UUCP (Unix-to-Unix Communication Protocol
POP (Post Office Protocol)
PROFS (Professional Office System)

OSI Model Uncovers E-Mail Incompatibilities

In order to diagnose E-mail incompatibilities, the OSI model is employed, filling in what is known about each E-mail implementation. This is the same procedure employed in Chapter 6 to analyze and design internetwork links. In some cases, additional research within a particular OSI layer such as the application layer (layer 7), which holds the E-mail applications, will be required in order to uncover all existing incompatibilities. Figure 8-23 illustrates an initial attempt at employing the OSI model for incompatibility identification.

The solutions to the kinds of incompatibilities identified through the use of the OSI model in Figure 8-23 were covered in depth in Chapter 6. Through a combination of software and hardware technology such as protocol conversion, bridges, routers, gateways and encapsulation, almost any of the OSI related incompatibilities can be overcome.

Wide Area E-Mail Integration Challenges

The remaining problem then, is the incompatibilities between the various E-mail packages themselves. In order to find solutions to these incompatibilities, they must first be categorized and better understood. Figure 8-24 outlines these wide area E-mail integration challenges.

Figure 8-24 can be looked on as the equivalent of the OSI model for E-mail systems. Incompatibilities on each layer must be resolved in order for transparent E-mail system interoperability to be achieved. There are four general approaches to resolving wide area E-mail incompatibilities.

		Platforms			
		Macintosh	PC LAN	Minicomputer	Mainframe
	Application	QuickMail	CC:Mail	All-In-1	PROFS
	Presentation				
	Session				
OSI Layer	Transport		SPX	LAT	
	Network	AppleTalk	IPX		
	Data-Link	IEEE 802.3 CSMA/CD LocalTalk or Ethernet	IEEE 802.5 Token Passing	IEEE 802.3 CSMA/CD	SDLC
	Physical	Twisted pair	Twisted pair	Twisted pair	Coax

Figure 8-23 OSI model uncovers wide area E-Mail incompatibilities.

Challenge	Explanation/Implication
Network architecture and network operating system	OSI model analysis reveals what layers of the OSI model possess incompatibilities. Multiprotocol routers, gateways, and protocol conversion solve most of these problems. (See Chapter 6.)
Message addressing	Formats for user addresses vary widely among different E-mail systems. How will these addresses be translated across E-mail platforms?
Directory-related issues	E-mail directories, like phone directories, keep current user address information. How will these directories be shared, remain synchronized across multiple E-mail platforms?
System features (the bells and whistles)	How will special system features such as ability to append multiple document types as attachments or request a return receipt or delivery confirmation be supported across multiple E-mail platforms if not all E-mail systems offer such features?
System management and administration	As numbers of E-mail users grow, there arises a need for sophisticated management and administrative features. In a multiplatform environment, which E-mail system is in charge?

Figure 8-24 Wide area E-mail integration challenges.

E-Mail Single Solution Gateways

The first approach is known as an E-mail gateway, or more accurately as a *single solution gateway*. These gateways are known as "single solution" because they perform complete translation or protocol conversion through all 7 layers of the OSI model as well as meeting all of the E-Mail integration challenges between two, and only two, distinct E-mail systems. If a company needs to only translate between two different E-mail systems, such a solution may be ideal. However, if translation between multiple E-mail platforms is desired, then a more sophisticated solution is required.

E-Mail Universal Backbones

The second approach to E-mail interoperability starts with the notion that rather than "hard-wiring" two E-mail systems together, let's find a neutral, third-party device or protocol to which all E-mail systems can speak, a sort of "universal" E-mail language or standard. This E-mail translation architecture is known as a *mail backbone* or *shared LAN backbone*.

However, the shared media backbone only provides physical connectivity. The "universal" mail protocol is still needed.

In addition to the neutral third-party protocol, each E-mail system on the mail backbone must have a gateway to the **universal protocol backbone.** The gateways in this case are primarily software translation programs that interpret syntax and commands between the mail systems and the universal mail protocol. Several such protocols have been proposed and deployed with varying degrees of success. Three have their roots in a particular vendor's architecture while a fourth is a product of a more neutral industry-wide consortium.

From IBM's SNA world comes the SNA distribution service or SNADS, while DEC has produced MAILBUS. Varying numbers of third-party e-mail systems vendors support each of these two "universal" mail protocols or backbones. MHS, or message handling service, is Novell's Netware LAN-based universal mail protocol. Perhaps the word universal is misleading in MHS's case as it only runs over Netware. A fourth universal mail protocol proposed by the CCITT is known as **X.400.**

A problem with all of these universal protocols is that in order to be universal, they must be concerned with the support of only those features that all attached E-mail systems are likely to possess. As a result, the universal backbone becomes a "least common denominator" among competing E-mail systems, thereby negating many of the most powerful features of any particular E-mail system.

X.400   X.400 has been designed as an international standard to allow international users to exchange E-mail. Recalling the 5 E-mail integration challenges, X.400 is most concerned with *message addressing,* and the ability of mail systems to interpret each other's users'mail addresses easily. Two recent versions of X.400 are known as *X.400 1984* and *X.400 1988.* The 1988 version of X.400 added several key features that allowed it to become the universal mail protocol of choice for most **EDI** (electronic data interchange) transmissions.

Among these enhancements were security related issues that could authenticate both the source and contents of an EDI delivery as well as provide proof of delivery to the sending party. Another X.400 1988 upgrade allowed documents with both text and graphics to be transmitted between X.400 compliant systems. EDI refers to the electronic exchange of business documents such as purchase orders, shipping papers, invoices, and payments. The business impact of EDI and the value-added networks which often deliver EDI will be studied later on in this chapter.

> ▶ *In Sharper Focus*

A CLOSER LOOK AT X.400

Remember that any E-mail system that wishes to use the X.400 mail backbone as its universal mail protocol must possess a gateway to that protocol. The phrase often seen depicting the support of such gateways is *X.400 compliant.* However, even X.400 is open to interpretation and, as a result, X.400 compliant E-mail systems may not necessarily be interoperable.

X.400 is defined by an architecture employing three layers or logical function blocks. The three areas of specialization within X.400 are:

Message User Agent: Interfaces between the user's E-mail or message-enabled application program and the X.400 backbone.
Message Router: Locates the address of the destination E-mail system and user and supplies the corresponding path information.
Message Transfer Agent: Forwards the message in proper format to the proper destination application or end-user.

Figure 8-25 illustrates the single solution gateway and shared mail backbone approach to overcoming E-mail integration problems.

E-Mail Messaging APIs   As can be seen in Figure 8-25, each separate E-mail system, otherwise known as a *messaging application,* must be able to communicate with the universal mail protocol backbone. An *API,* application program interface, is required to complete this communication. Several **messaging APIs** have been proposed by various member groups, although no standard has been adopted.

Solution 1 — Single Solution Gateway

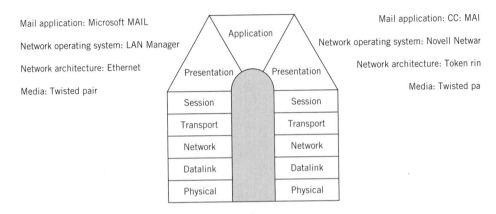

Mail application: Microsoft MAIL

Network operating system: LAN Manager

Network architecture: Ethernet

Media: Twisted pair

Mail application: CC: MAI

Network operating system: Novell Netwar

Network architecture: Token rin

Media: Twisted pa

Solution 2 — Shared Mail Backbone

Mail systems with proprietary gateways to universal backbone protocol

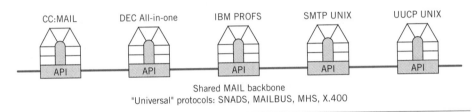

Shared MAIL backbone
"Universal" protocols: SNADS, MAILBUS, MHS, X.400

Figure 8-25 Overcoming E-mail integration challenges: Single solution gateway and shared mail backbone.

Stated in terms of the X.400 components identified above, no interface has been defined between the user application and the X.400 message user agent.

These interfaces to X.400 are crucial for transparency and ease of operation. X.400's addressing scheme can be cumbersome and overwhelming with up to 14 attributes assigned to each X.400 address. Applications developers offer easy-to-use front-ends, which build X.400 compliant command strings transparently to the user through the use of messaging APIs.

A messaging API is not to be confused with a universal mail protocol. X.400 is a universal mail protocol. In order for a messaging application or E-mail to communicate with the X.400 backbone, it must send a message through a messaging API which both it and the universal mail protocol understand. Listed below are five popular messaging APIs and their respective industry supporters. Significant standards development activity in this area is likely to take place in the near future.

Messaging API	Sponsors
MAPI—Messaging Application Programming Interface	Microsoft, Banyan, DEC, HP, Compuserve, Soft-Switch
VIM—Vendor Independent Messaging	Apple, Lotus, Borland, Novell
OCE—Open Collaborative Environment	Apple
SMF—Netware Standard Message Format API	Novell
CMC—Common Mail Calls	XAPIA (X.400 API Assoc.)

X.500 X.500 is the directory-related counterpart of X.400. Whereas X.400 provides the ability to transfer mail between any X.400 compliant proprietary E-mail system, X.500 provides the ability to integrate the directories of the various proprietary E-mail systems. In other words, X.500 can give the full address and other related information about any E-mail end-user attached to an X.500 compliant directory, while X.400 will allow the delivery of E-mail to that person through the X.400 compliant E-mail system. X.500 can link public directory services with private corporate directory services. X.500 can be thought of as the world's ultimate phone book.

▶ *In Sharper Focus*

X.500 ARCHITECTURE

Like X.400, X.500 is defined as an architecture or a pair of logical function blocks. In the case of X.500, the two logical function blocks are as follows:

DSA (directory service agent): Accesses and maintains a database of names and attributes of addressable end-users on various E-mail systems. Among the attributes that can be stored for each address are names, digitized photographs, and routing information.

DUA (directory user agent): Requests address information services from the directory services agent on behalf of end-user applications or E-mail systems.

E-Mail Messaging Servers

A third possible solution to overcome the E-mail integration challenges is to improve on the "least common denominator" nature of the universal mail backbone approach. By adding intelligence to the backbone in the form of a mail server that will keep track of the advanced features available on all attached E-mail systems, the **messaging server** can deliver the *maximum* functionality possible between any two attached E-mail systems.

Such centralized mail transfer intelligence also has the ability to overcome another key integration challenge, namely **directory reconciliation.** Directory and configuration information is stored and maintained in a database on the messaging server. By having all messages travel through this one server, all addresses and routing tables can be kept up to date.

Figure 8-26 illustrates both the configuration of such an E-mail system integration solution as well as an I-P-O diagram for the messaging server. Remembering the principle of modularity of design, it should be possible to see that a messaging server is the equivalent of an "E-mail system-aware" router.

To repeat somewhat, by having all messages travel through this one server, a marvelous single point of failure has been created.

An example of such a server would be the Netware global messaging server, which is actually implemented as an NLM (Netware loadable module) on Netware 3.11 servers. This messaging server supports *MHS* (message handling service), the LAN market leader for "universal" mail backbone protocols. Another more "open" example is the Retix OpenServer 400 which supports at least a dozen different PC-based E-mail systems and provides access to IBM, Digital, X.400, Compuserve, and MCIMail E-mail networks. Open Server 400, like MHS, is a software package which gets loaded onto the server of your choice. Retix is the leading vendor of X.400 software.

Solution 3 — Messaging Server

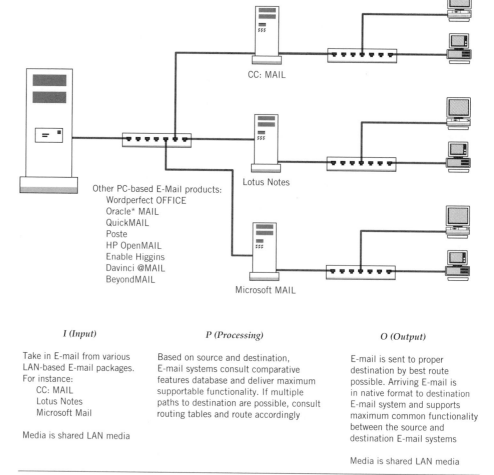

I (Input)	P (Processing)	O (Output)
Take in E-mail from various LAN-based E-mail packages. For instance: CC: MAIL Lotus Notes Microsoft Mail	Based on source and destination, E-mail systems consult comparative features database and deliver maximum supportable functionality. If multiple paths to destination are possible, consult routing tables and route accordingly	E-mail is sent to proper destination by best route possible. Arriving E-mail is in native format to destination E-mail system and supports maximum common functionality between the source and destination E-mail systems
Media is shared LAN media		Media is shared LAN media

Figure 8-26 Overcoming E-mail integration challenges: Messaging server.

E-Mail Backbone Switches

A fourth possible solution is to combine the backbone and server into a single device while adding multiple connections for redundancy in a device known as an **E-mail backbone switch.** These E-mail backbone switches, otherwise known as *global messaging backbone switches,* provide directory services, mail switching, and delivery for otherwise incompatible E-mail systems. This functionality represents a great deal of processing for each E-mail message. In order to deliver that processing power, these switches are based on powerful multiprocessor computers, often RISC-based UNIX machines operating at speeds of up to 117MIPS (millions of instructions per second). An added feature of some messaging backbone switches is their ability to convert Fax to E-mail and vice-versa.

A company by the name of Soft-Switch dominates this market. Figure 8-27 illustrates both the configuration of such an E-mail system integration solution as well as an I-P-O diagram for the E-mail backbone switch. Remembering the principle of modularity of design, it should be possible to see that an E-mail backbone switch is the equivalent of an "E-mail system-aware" Ethernet switch or data PBX.

Solution 4 — E-mail Backbone Switch

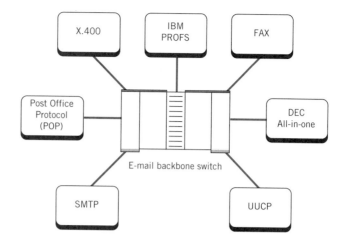

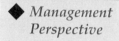

I (Input)	P (Processing)	O (Output)
Input is various E-mail protocols. Input over high speed lines possibly destined for any other E-mail protocol connection supported by this switch	A switch-based rather than LAN-based solution	Delivery to proper destination in proper E-mail format with maximum common functionality between source and destination E-mail systems
Collapsed backbone switch, no shared LAN media	Process each received E-mail message quickly. Convert E-mail protocols as necessary. Maximize functionality. Complete circuit (switch) to destination node and deliver converted E-mail message. Convert E-mail to FAX and vice versa	Collapsed backbone switch, no shared LAN media

Figure 8-27 Overcoming E-mail integration challenges: E-mail backbone switch.

◆ *Management Perspective*

Important Attributes of E-Mail Interoperability Products

Whether investigating the purchase of an E-mail gateway, server, or backbone switch, there are certain important characteristics to consider in making the decision. These attributes are outside of the more "typical" performance and financial criteria, such as messages processed per second or cost per user.

Figure 8-28 summarizes important E-mail interoperability products features and their implications.

◆

E-Mail Goes Client-Server

Traditionally, a single E-mail package provided a total E-mail solution. In other words, the single E-mail package provided both the user interface (the client side) as well as the E-mail transfer agents or messaging software (the server side). In much the same way as the database world has now separated into product specialization, whereby database engines or back-ends on the server side are developed and marketed separately from the query tools and fourth generation development environments on the client side, the E-mail system environment is evolving into a similar product specialization.

Part of the motivation for this separate development is a category of end-user software known as **mail-enabled applications.** Instead of having to go to a dedi-

Feature	Options/Implications
Standards Compliance	Which revision of X.400 and X.500 does the product support? Does it support 100% of that revision's features?
Directory synchronization	How does this E-mail device keep its directory synchronized with other E-mail devices? Two popular methods are master/slave directory propogation in which all changes are stored in a single master directory and downloaded, or peer-to-peer directory propogation in which directories update one another on an equal basis. Is the directory synchronization automatic or must it be manually attended?
Address translation	Does this E-mail device translate E-mail addresses to X.400 or another proprietary format? Must an additional gateway/translation product be purchased to perform such a task?
Security	Is the ability to encrypt E-mail included? Is digital signature authentication supported in order to verify the validity of the source and contents of the message? Are passwords required for wide area E-mail access?
Performance features	How many and what type of attachments can be appended to an E-mail message? Can the system support delivery confirmation requests and nondelivery notification? Can connection (E-mail sending) scripts be customized, saved, and revised? Can the E-mail device be administered remotely?
Performance monitoring/statistics	What type of statistics are kept for performance monitoring or accounting/charge-back purposes? **Management Statistics** Number of messages sent out Number of messages received Gateway/server shutdowns/performance problems Time/day/source/destination address of each E-mail sent/received

Figure 8-28 E-mail interoperability products important features: E-mail servers, gateways, backbone switches.

cated E-mail program to send mail, users are able to do so from their word processing, spreadsheet, or productivity software programs. These mail-enabled programs form the group of client-side or E-mail front-end programs. The key attributes of such programs are transparency and ease of use. Examples include BeyondMail, and @Mail which work from within Lotus 1-2-3 and Symphony.

On the back-end or E-mail engine side, key characteristics are more performance related. Efficient message transfer accompanied by thorough management and administrative services characterize this class of software. Novell MHS (message handling service) is a LAN-based example of such an E-mail back-end. As E-mail users continue to migrate to a LAN-based environment, the client–server E-mail architecture should continue to grow in popularity.

The two independent component pieces, client and server, of the E-mail system will communicate over the previously mentioned universal mail backbone via gateways and messaging APIs. X.400 could be the universal mail protocol of this client–server backbone if standards-making bodies can increase its functionality thereby shaking its image as a "least common denominator functionality" E-mail standard. Figure 8-29 illustrates an E-mail client–server architecture, while the graph in Figure 8-30 illustrates the supporting trend toward LAN-based E-mail users.

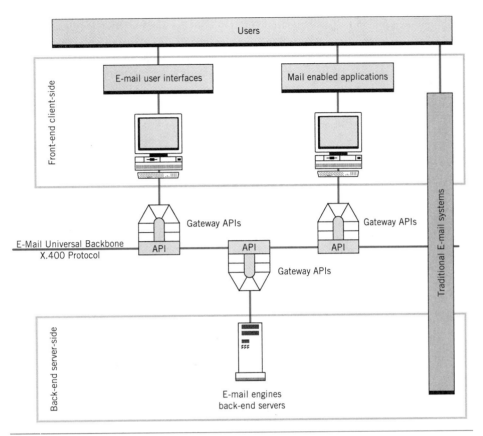

Figure 8-29 Client–server based E-mail systems.

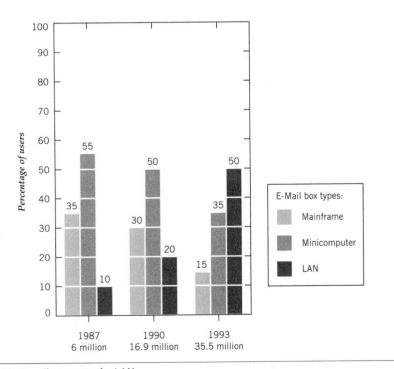

Figure 8-30 E-mail moves to the LAN.

EDI—Electronic Data Interchange

First mentioned in Chapter 1 as an excellent example of how networking technology can solve business problems, **EDI** (electronic data interchange) involves the transfer of business documents by electronic rather than traditional means. EDI is sometimes considered a subset of **IES** (inter-enterprise systems), which incorporate E-mail, fax, electronic funds transfer, and other multimedia transfers among trading partners.

EDI can be looked upon as an application layer overlaying the E-mail architecture just described, or alternatively as one of the "mail-enabled" applications previously described. EDI transfer is often offered as a service by companies known as **VAN**s (value-added networks). By utilizing a VAN, companies can avoid the expense of establishing and maintaining their own EDI networks and support organizations.

EDI is the "nervous system" or supporting architecture of many of today's latest business productivity trends. **JIT** (just-in-time) ordering and inventory control is one technique for reducing costs by only ordering, and paying for, those items that will be either used in manufacturing or reshipped in a relatively short period of time.

In other words, materials are ordered so that they arrive "just in time" to be included in a manufacturing process or reshipped. In any case, a successful JIT implementation depends heavily on a successful EDI implementation to transfer business correspondence such as purchase orders, shipping papers, invoices, and payments in a "just-in-time" manner.

The top-down model of such an implementation is illustrated in Figure 8-31.

EDI can make business more equitable as well as more profitable. For example, the Department of Defense has implemented an EDI system through which vendors can access RFQs (requests for quotes) for items of less than $25,000. This enables equal access for all vendors through EDI to the bidding process, correcting former practices of less-open bidding processes.

Business	Reduce expenses in order to become more profitable. Reduce inventory on-hand in order to reduce expenses.
Application	Implement a "just-in-time" inventory system in cooperation with enterprise trading partners, vendors and suppliers, and customers.
Data	Decide on which business documents will be transmitted electronically via EDI. Decide where enterprise partners are located geographically.
Network	Implement an EDI network for electronic delivery of business documents among enterprise partners.
Technology	EDI standards Security/encryption standards EFT (electronic funds transfer) standards Use of VANs (value added network) vs. establishment of its own EDI network.

Figure 8-31 Top-down model: EDI supports JIT.

EDI Standards

EDI standards had to be able to conform to the unique information requirements of different industries if they were to be widely supported and successful. For instance, paint manufacturers or auto parts dealers need to transmit different information from food processors or apparel manufacturers. Some industry specific groups established their own EDI standards. In most cases, *EDI standards* are now rolled under the category heading of **ANSI X.12.**

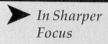
In Sharper Focus

EDI STANDARDS DEVELOPMENT

Within X.12, industry specific data requirements can be accommodated. **Transaction sets** refer to the various types of business documents that trading partners may need to exchange. The next step in the standards making process is much like a database definition process. First, the elements, or fields, which comprise a transaction set or business document are established. Next, just as in database definition, the format or characteristics of each of these fields is determined. For instance:

> How many characters?
> Is it an alphabetic or numeric field?
> Is it a date field? If so, what is the date format?
> Are there restrictions as to valid answers on any fields?
> If so, what are the range or validity checks for each field?
> What is the purpose of each field?
> Is the field required or optional?

EDI standards such as X.12 can be looked upon as neutral or universal data definitions between proprietary business application systems much as X.400 was conceived as a universal E-mail standard to support communication between proprietary E-mail systems.

EDI Translation and Transmission

Once the data from the proprietary business application, perhaps an order-entry system, has been translated into the "neutral" X.12 format, it is then transmitted to the proper destination's business trading partner. *Translation* and *transmission* are the two basic processes of EDI. These processes are often offered as a service by specialized EDI VANs (value-added networks). Figure 8-32 summarizes the relationship of the various components of EDI.

Some Potential Pitfalls of EDI

EDI presents a unique set of business problems. Given electronic transmission's occasional glitches and susceptibility to unauthorized access, there is the potential with EDI for documents to be delivered which have been miscommunicated or tampered with. To deal with these situations as well as other contingencies inherent to EDI, companies that do business via EDI often sign trading partner agreements which very carefully outline definitions, liabilities, and responsibilities for these EDI-related contingencies. **EFT** (electronic funds transfer) also requires very clearly defined trading partner agreements. EDI can reduce costs and increase productivity. However, it can also introduce new risks for fraud and financial miscalculation that must be addressed and controlled.

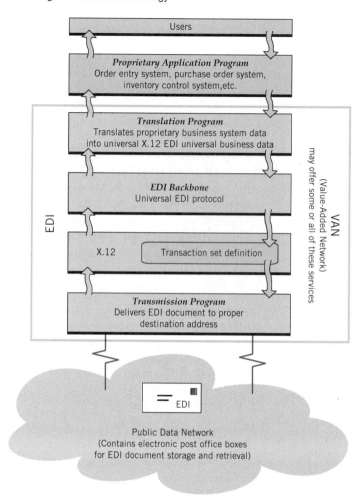

Figure 8-32 EDI components and architecture.

VANs—Value Added Networks Save Time and Effort: For a Price

Value-added networks, otherwise known as PDNs (public data networks), offer everything from simple X.25 packet-switched transmission of data to complete turnkey EDI solutions. In many cases, the EDI services are established in a manner comparable to Post Office boxes inside a Post Office.

For a fee, the VAN will rent an electronic P.O. Box on their network. They will also supply the order entry program, or any other required transaction generating program to allow trading partners to enter standard format transactions into this electronic mailbox. Automated communications scripts to empty the P.O. Box and transfer all contents to a company's local computer for further processing can also be supplied.

Remembering that frame relay can be thought of as a second generation of X.25, it should come as no surprise that many VANs are offering frame relay as well as X.25 service. This higher bandwidth transmission will no doubt be required as multimedia EDI, combined data and image, becomes the norm. Figure 8-33 summarizes a representative sample of VANs and their services.

Network Name	Company	Services/Comments
InfoLAN	Infonet—Brussels Services Belgium Corporation	Global LAN interconnect services up to 2.048 Mbps. Router-based rather than X.25 network which is better for LAN interconnect. X.25 network service is also available
AccuNET	AT&T	Offers AccuNET X.25 packet service internationally. Also offers: high-speed (up to T-1) circuit-switched services—AccuNET switched digital service. Information Access Service Interspan Frame Relay Service AT&T EDI Service
BT Tymnet	British Telecomm	Currently offers X.25/frame relay with plans to migrate to B-ISDN ATM—over 4500 nodes worldwide
Sprintnet	U.S. Sprint	Offers X.25/frame relay/multirate ISDN. Absorbed former TeleNET network. Asynchronous services also available
Wilpak	Wiltel	Frame relay service for LAN interconnection.
Compuserve	Compuserve, Inc.	Primarily an information services network. Does provide X.25 packet switching network. Plans to build public frame relay service
Datapac	Telecomm Canada	Provides X.25 services—global connectivity from Canada—asynchronous services also available
IBM Information Network	IBM	Full-service international PDN operating LAN interconnection as well as information services
Marknet	General Electric	Global X.25 transmission services

Figure 8-33 VANs (PDNs) and their services.

VAN Access and Pricing

If a company is located outside large metropolitan areas, network analysts will need to be especially careful when inquiring about charges for the use of value-added networks. A review of the process involved in interfacing to a VAN will reveal the potential for high costs.

A person or business accesses the VAN through some type of *access line*. Depending on the bandwidth requirements of the services purchased, that access line can be anything from a dial-up line to a T-1. Someone is going to have to pay for that access line to the VAN, most likely the company wishing to subscribe to the VAN's services.

The next important question is: What distance must this access line travel? Remember that circuit-switched or leased lines are most often priced according to distance. Most VANs have access points or POPs (points of presence) in nearly all metropolitan areas. If it is a local call from a place of business to the VAN access point, then the *access charges* may be quite reasonable.

If a POP or access point is not nearby, a company will probably have to pay for data to be transmitted to the VAN's POP. The charge incurred by this hauling of one's data to the VAN's POP is sometimes known as a **backhauling charge.** Depending on the bandwidth requirements and distance, this can be a significant charge.

The aforementioned charges are only access charges. Any usage of the VAN's services has still not been charged for. Usage charge criteria vary widely and should be investigated thoroughly. However, generally speaking, usage charges consist of both a flat monthly rate plus an additional rate based on actual usage. The actual usage is often based on a unit of measure known as a **kilopacket,** meaning 1,000 packets. Total monthly charges can be calculated as:

Access and Backhauling Charges + Flat Monthly VAN Fees + Incremental Usage-Based Monthly VAN Fees = Total Monthly Bill

Shop carefully. Hopefully a given geographic area is served by more than one VAN. Competition can do wonders for the reasonability of telecommunications rates.

CHAPTER SUMMARY

Metropolitan area network architectures such as DQDB and services such as SMDS were introduced as viable alternatives for transparent LAN interconnection. The implementation issues for such networks including underlying switching and transmission architectures prompted the introduction of ATM (asynchronous transfer mode) and SONET (synchronous optical network).

Wide area digital services such as ISDN and B-ISDN (broadband ISDN) were explored as to underlying architecture and offered functionality, as well as current and short-term deployment levels.

Finally, business uses of wide area networks such E-mail and EDI were explored from both technology-oriented as well as potential business impact perspectives.

KEY TERMS

ANSI X.12
automatic number
　identification
backhauling charge
bandwidth on demand
Bellcore
B-ISDN
BRI
countdown counter
CPE
digital service hierarchy
directory reconciliation
DQDB
dual bus
dual ring
E-1
EDI
EFT
electronic mail

E-mail backbone switch
E-mail gateway
FDDI
FDDI-II
fractional T-1
head of bus
IEEE 802.6
IES
ISDN
ISDN gateway
ISDN/LAN bridge/router
ISDN server
ISDN to MAC sublayer
　bridge
isochronous
JIT
kilopacket
LPN-ISDN
mail-enabled software

MAN
messaging API
messaging server
multirate ISDN
narrowband ISDN
NISDN-1
NREN
OAM&P
octet
optical carrier levels
out of band signalling
periodic framing
PRI
queue arbitrated access
request counter
signalling system 7
SMDS
SONET

SS7
superframe
synchronous payload
　envelope
synchronous TDM
T-1
terminal adapters
transaction set
TRIP '92
2B+D
23B+D
universal protocol
　backbone
VANs
virtual private networks
virtual tributaries
X.400
X.500

REVIEW QUESTIONS

1. What are the major differences between SMDS and frame relay in terms of standards development, industry backing, and deployment levels?
2. What are the differences between SMDS and frame relay in terms of business uses, technical limitations, and future outlooks?
3. What are the differences between ISDN and B-ISDN?
4. How does ISDN fit among other WAN service alternatives in terms of offered functionality versus implementation costs?
5. What is the relationship between frame relay and ISDN?
6. Explain how frame relay can be an interface specification, network service, and switching architecture.
7. What have been the traditional stumbling blocks to wide-spread ISDN deployment and what progress has been made in overcoming each of these stumbling blocks?
8. What is SONET and how does it fit into the vision of tomorrow's network?
9. What is ATM and how does it fit into the vision of tomorrow's network?
10. What are some of the stumbling blocks to implementation of an EDI network among trading partners?
11. What are the potential benefits to trading partners from the implementation of an EDI network?
12. What is the relationship of SS7 to ISDN?
13. What are possible future deployment possibilities for SS7?
14. Evaluate narrowband ISDN as a LAN interconnection service.
15. What effect does the burstiness of LAN data have on WAN service selection?
16. What is OAM&P and what role does it play in a WAN service?
17. Do the terms MAN and SMDS mean basically the same thing? Explain.
18. What are the major differences between the two primary MAN architectures?
19. What are the key characteristics of DQDB/IEEE 802.6 that contribute to its reliability?
20. How does DQDB try to offer the best characteristics of both Ethernet and Token Ring?
21. Explain the role of the request counter and countdown counter in DQDB.
22. What is queue arbitrated access?
23. Why is DQDB with queue arbitrated access considered a data only service?
24. What types of traffic would prefer prearbitrated access and why?
25. How does FDDI-II differ from FDDI?

26. What is a head of bus shift and how does it contribute to DQDB reliability?
27. What is the relationship between DQDB and SMDS?
28. Can SMDS only be offered over DQDB? Explain.
29. Given that SMDS is a switched service, how are connections between source and destination actually made?
30. Why are closed user groups or virtual private networks important to SMDS?
31. What are the advantages of out-of-band signalling as opposed to in-band signalling?
32. How can "ISDN-like" services such as caller ID be offered without ISDN?
33. What are some of the issues surrounding ISDN CPE?
34. What is the difference between a T-1 and an E-1?
35. What do the terms 2B+D and 23B+D stand for?
36. What are some of the business layer issues surrounding ISDN?
37. Explain how a frame relay service could be offered to subscribers without the use of frame relay switches.
38. What is the significance of NISDN-1?
39. How can users effectively migrate from X.25 networks to ISDN networks?
40. Describe the three major ways in which LANs can interface to an ISDN network.
41. What is multirate ISDN and what are its applications and significance?
42. What is the purpose of periodic framing on a T-1?
43. What is the difference between a DS-1 and a T-1?
44. What is fractional T-1 and what is the business motivation behind such a service?
45. How does an octet differ from a byte?
46. What is the purpose of the synchronous payload envelope?
47. Can SONET transmit isochronous traffic? Why or why not?
48. What are the roles of virtual tributaries within SONET?
49. What are SONET's current and potential transmission capabilities?
50. What are some of the services that may be available over B-ISDN?
51. What are some of the key E-mail interoperability challenges?
52. How can the OSI model be used to organize an approach to E-mail incompatibilities?
53. Describe the four major approaches to solving E-mail incompatibilities.
54. What are the important standards regarding E-mail interoperability?
55. What is the role of a messaging API?

56. What is directory reconciliation and why is it important?
57. Why is X.400 considered a least common denominator standard?
58. Which E-mail interoperability solution offers a greatest common factors approach? How?

59. How is a client–server deployment of an E-mail system different from a typical E-mail program?
60. How does X.12 cater to the different data requirements of different industries?

ACTIVITIES

1. Consult trade journals and gather articles about deployment of MANs. Construct a chart or bulletin board that contrasts the various underlying network architectures, protocols, and services offered by these implementations. What do each of the MANs offer, if anything, as far as interconnection to WAN services or seamless integration with other MAN services?
2. Contact several VANs (value added networks) or third-party EDI providers. Survey the range of services offered and compare pricing. Are industry specific forms and/or standards supported? How much programming and set-up is provided by the service agency?
3. Review product specifications and/or contact vendors of corporate E-mail systems to establish the level

of support of X.400 and X.500 protocols by these E-mail systems.
4. Contact your local phone carrier. Is ISDN available in your local calling area? What are the nonrecurring and monthly charges for such a service? What special equipment is required? What is the cost of such equipment and must it be purchased from the carrier? Are both PRI as well as BRI service available? What are the differences in cost? What intelligent services are available via ISDN?
5. Contact your long-distance carrier. Determine the availability of long-distance ISDN in your local calling area. Is this ISDN service interoperable with other long-distance carriers' ISDN services?

Featured References

ATM

Neighbors, Ken. "Driving ATM to the Edge," *Telephone Engineer & Management*, vol. 97, no. 16 (August 1993), p. 48.

MacAskill, Skip. "ATM Emerging as LAN Hub Alternative," *Network World*, vol. 9, no. 29 (July 20, 1992), p. 21.

Rebman, Kevin. "ATM—A Wolf in Sheep's Clothing?" *LAN Times*, vol. 9, no. 20 (October 26, 1992), p. 43.

MacAskill, Skip. "ATM Threatens to Usurp FDDI as Backbone Choice ," *Network World*, vol. 9, no. 29 (July 13, 1992), p. 1.

Klessig, Bob, and George Prodan. "FDDI and ATM: No Sibling Rivalry," *LAN Times*, vol. 9, no. 21 (November 9, 1992), p. 35.

Johnson, Johna. "Putting ATM on the Premises," *Data Communications*, vol. 21, no. 10 (July 1992), p. 51.

Johnson, Johna. "ATM: A Dream Come True?" *Data Communications*, vol. 21, no. 5 (March 21, 1992), p. 53.

Lippis, Nick. "A First Look at ATM Means Second Thoughts about FDDI," *Data Communications*, vol. 21, no. 9 (June 1992), p. 39.

Broadband Switches

Johnson, Johna. "A Low Cost Switch with SONET in Its Future," *Data Communications*, vol. 21, no. 5 (March 21, 1992), p. 49.

Case Studies

Eckerson, Wayne. "J.P. Morgan Takes Simpler Approach to E-Mail Unity," *Network World*, vol. 9, no. 51 (December 21, 1992), p. 1.

Bancroft, Bruce. "Cancer Institute Builds Enterprise Network," *LAN Times*, vol. 9, no. 1 (January 20, 1992), p. 21.

Duncanson, Jay. "Standing the Multiplexer on Its Head," *LAN Times*, vol. 9, no. 17 (September 14, 1992), p. 47.

Maxwell, Kimberly. "Agency Bridges E-Mail Gap between Netware and UNIX," *LAN Times*, vol. 9, no. 21 (November 9, 1992), p. 40.

Walker, Robyn. "Jet Propulsion Labs Investigates ISDN," *LAN Times*, vol. 9, no. 1 (January 20, 1992), p. 29.

Eckerson, Wayne. "Federal Express Uses EDI to Streamline Its Billing," *Network World*, vol. 9, no. 21 (May 25, 1992), p. 29.

Brown, Bob. "A&P Setting up VSAT Net to Register Service Gains," *Network World*, vol. 9, no. 26 (June 29, 1992), p. 17.

Case Studies—International

Bancroft, Bruce. "TackBoard Supplies Commodities News," *LAN Times*, vol. 9, no. 1 (January 20, 1992), p. 37.

Heywood, Peter. "Ford Puts ISDN in the Driver's Seat," *Data Communications*, vol. 21, no. 11 (August 1992), p. 91.

Cell Relay

McQuillan, John. "Cell Relay Switching," *Data Communications*, vol. 20, no. 11 (September 1991), p. 58.

Schultz, Beth, and Chris Roeckl. "Trio Targets Packet, Cell Interoperability," *Communications Week*, no. 427 (November 2, 1992), p. 1.

Digital Leased Line

Briere, Daniel. "Buyer's Guide: Digital Private Line Services," *Network World*, vol. 9, no. 24 (June 15, 1992), p. 47.

Wallace, Bob. "AT&T Adds Array of High-Speed Net Links (fractional T-3)," *Network World*, vol. 9, no. 48 (November 30, 1992), p. 1.

Electronic Data Interchange—EDI

Cummings, Joanne. "Cost Savings Not a Factor for Firms Moving to EDI," *Network World*, vol. 10, no. 5 (February 1, 1993), p. 37.

Messmer, Ellen. "EDI Suppliers to Test Fed Purchasing Net," *Network World*, vol. 9, no. 25 (June 22, 1992), p.43.

Bolles, Gary. "Gearing up for EDI: A Primer on Electronic Data Interchange," *Network Computing*, vol. 2, no. 9 (September 1991), p. 88.

Messmer, Ellen. "ABA Offers Model Plan for Electronic Payment Partners," *Network World*, vol. 9, no. 27 (July 6, 1992), p.1.

Eckerson, Wayne. "Federal Express Uses EDI to Streamline Its Billing," *Network World*, vol. 9, no. 21 (May 25, 1992), p. 29.

Messmer, Ellen. "New NIST Digital Signature Encryption to Bow," *Network World*, vol. 9, no. 27 (July 6, 1992), p. 2.

Scott, Karyl. "EDI and X.400 Electronic Mail Come Together," *Data Communications*, vol. 20, no. 6 (May 1991), p. 72.

Cummings, Joanne. "EDI Proponents Sign up AT&T for Demo," *Network World*, vol. 9, no. 32 (August 10, 1992), p. 27.

ISDN and B-ISDN

Verbiest, Willem. "FITL and B-ISDN: A Marriage with a Future," *IEEE Communication*, vol. 31, no. 6 (June 1993), p. 60.

Sutherland, Scott, and John Burgin. "B-ISDN Internetworking," *IEEE Communications*, vol. 31, no. 8 (August 1993), p. 60.

Martz, Ellen. "ISDN Deployment Moves Slowly but Surely," *Telephone Engineer & Management*, vol. 97, no. 16 (August 1993), p. 36.

Duc, N. Q. "ISDN Protocol Architecture," *IEEE Communications*, vol. 23, no. 3 (March 1985).

Korostoff, Kathryn. "ISDN Applications Are Kicking in with Users," *Communications Week*, no. 459 (June 21, 1993), p. 49.

Korostoff, Kathryn. "PRI: The Other Kind of ISDN Service," *Communications Week*, no. 459 (June 21, 1993), p. 50.

Briere, Daniel, and Mark Langner. "Users Wonder if ISDN Can Endure," *Network World*, vol. 9, no. 51 (December 21, 1992), p. 29.

Stallings, William. *ISDN and Broadband ISDN*, 2nd ed. (New York: Macmillan, 1992).

Morris, Larry. "Integrated Services Digital Network Defined," *LAN Times*, vol. 9, no. 1 (January 20, 1992), p. 29.

Johnson, Johna. "ISDN Goes Nationwide, but Will Users Want It?" *Data Communications*, vol. 20, no. 18 (November 1992), p. 93.

Derfler, Frank. "Digiboard's IMAC: An Inexpensive ISDN Bridge to Distant LANs," *PC Magazine*, vol. 11, no. 12 (June 30, 1992), p. 56.

Sweeny, Terry. "NYNEX Trial to Tie Frame-Relay & ISDN," *Communications Week*, no. 428 (November 9, 1992), p. 39.

Kirvan, Paul. "ISDN CPE: Ready and Willing," *Telephony*, vol. 223, no. 15 (October 12, 1992), p. 26.

Stokesberry, Dan. "ISDN in North America," *IEEE Communications*, vol. 31, no. 5 (May 1993), p. 88.

Guenther, Wolfgang. "Object Oriented Design of ISDN Call Processing Software," *IEEE Communications*, vol. 31, no. 4 (April 1993), p. 40.

International WANs

Heywood, Peter. "A Fast Start Means a Big Lead in Global LAN Interconnect," *Data Communications*, vol. 20, no. 17 (December 1991), p. 114.

Dern, Daniel. "Linking LANs Internationally with TCP/IP Based Internet," *LAN Times*, vol. 8, no. 18 (September 16, 1991, p. 45.

Mail Switches and Gateways/ BBS Software

Jander, Mary. "An E-Mail Switch That Delivers Anywhere," *Data Communications*, vol. 21, no. 9 (June 1992), p. 115.

Strom, David. "How to Make E-Mail Gateways Work," *Network Computing*, vol. 3, no. 1 (January 1992), p. 83.

Denny, Bob. "E-Mail: Now Come the API Wars," *LAN Times*, vol. 9, no. 22 (November 23, 1992), p.60.

Messmer, Ellen. "Friendly Gopher Reduces Complexity of Messaging," *Network World*, vol. 9, no. 48 (November 30, 1992), p. 1.

Duffy, Jim. "DEC Set for Unveiling of E-Mail Tools," *Network World*, vol. 9, no. 23 (June 8, 1992), p. 1.

Brown, Bob. "Microsoft Seeks to End Mail API War," *Network World*, vol. 9, no. 25 (June 22, 1992), p. 1.

Salamone, Salvatore. "Delivering E-Mail for the Enterprise," *Data Communications*, vol. 21, no. 18 (December 1992), p. 49.

Ayre, Rick, et al. "E-Mail Systems: Can They Keep Their Customers Satisfied?" *PC Magazine*, vol. 11, no. 18 (October 27, 1992), p. 261.

Managed Data Network Services

Roussel, Anne-Marie. "MDNS: In-House Management of Outsourced Networks," *Data Communications*, vol. 21, no. 10 (July 1992), p. 78.

Manfield, David. "Congestion Control in SS7 Signalling Networks," *IEEE Communications*, vol. 31, no. 6 (June 1993), p. 50.

Metropolitan Area Networks—MANs

Gasparro, Daniel. "Waiting for SMDS? Here's a New MAN," *Data Communications*, vol. 21, no. 9 (June 1992), p. 29.

Heywood, Peter. "MANs Make Their Mark in Germany," *Data Communications*, vol. 21, no. 7 (May 1992), p. 63.

Johnson, Johna. "MFS Makes a MAN out of FDDI," *Data Communications*, vol. 20, no. 14 (October 1991), p. 57.

Multiplexers—Inverse

Duncanson, Jay. "Standing the Multiplexer on Its Head," *LAN Times*, vol. 9, no. 17 (September 14, 1992), p. 47.

Johnson, Johna. "Curbing the Cost of LAN Interconnect," *Data Communications*, vol. 21, no. 18 (December 1992), p. 37.

Multiplexers—T1

Johnson, Johna. "Users Rate T1 Multiplexers," *Data Communications*, vol. 21, no. 10 (July 1992), p. 107.

Multirate ISDN—Bandwidth on Demand

Gareiss, Robin. "Sprint Plans Own Multirate ISDN," *Communications Week*, no. 385 (January 13, 1992), p. 1.

Packet Switches and PSDNs

Bransky, Jonathan, and Dean Wolf. "Buyers Guide: X.25 Switches—Vendors Aim to Transform X.25 Switches," *Network World*, vol. 9, no. 29 (July 20, 1992), p. 46.

Schlar, Sherman. *Inside X.25: A Manager's Guide* (New York: McGraw-Hill, 1990).

Derfler, Frank, and Kimberly Maxwell. "Reliable Relays," *PC Magazine*, vol. 10, no. 15 (September 10, 1991), p. 377.

SMDS—Switched Multimegabit Data Service

Wallace, Bob. "User Trial Called Major Step in Evolution of SMDS," *Network World*, vol. 9, no. 36 (September 7, 1992), p. 1.

Johnson, Johna. "SMDS: Out of the Lab and Onto the Network," *Data Communications*, vol. 21, no. 14 (October 1992), p. 71.

Killette, Kathleen. "US West to Start Data Trial," *Communications Week*, no. 385 (January 13, 1992), p. 18.

Sweeny, Terry. "Long Haul SMDS Trial Makes a Point about Options," *Communications Week*, no. 428 (November 9, 1992), p. 40.

Wallace, Bob. "Bell Atlantic Leads the Way; First to File Tariff for SMDS," *Network World*, vol. 9, no. 29 (July 20, 1992), p. 4.

Johnson, Johna. "Long-Distance SMDS Goes on-Line," *Data Communications*, vol. 21, no. 17 (November 23, 1992), p. 37.

SONET

Ching, Yau-Chau. "SONET Implementation," *IEEE Communications*, vol. 31, no. 9 (September 1993), p. 34.

Klein, Michael. "Network Synchronization—A Challenge for SDH/SONET?," *IEEE Communications*, vol. 31, no. 9 (September 1993), p. 42.

Allmis, Susanna. "Implementing a Flexible Synchronous Network," *IEEE Communications*, vol. 31, no. 9 (September 1993), p. 52.

Wu, Tsong-Ho. "Cost-Effective Network Evolution," *IEEE Communications*, vol. 31, no. 9 (September 1993), p. 64.

Henderson, Scott, and Randy Jones. "Synchronizing SONET," *Telephony*, vol. 225, no. 13 (September 27, 1993), p. 26.

Davidson, Robert, and Nathan Muller. *The Guide to SONET* (Telecom Library, 1991).

Gareiss, Robin. "SONET Vendors Grapple with Net Management," *Communications Week*, no. 385 (January 13, 1992), p. 18.

Sweeny, Terry. "SONET Support Key to Emerging Digital Cross-Connects," *Communications Week*, no. 427 (November 2, 1992), p. 32.

Messmer, Ellen. "Ameritech Unit, MCI Use SONET to Maximize Nets," *Network World*, vol. 9, no. 47 (November 23, 1992), p. 25.

Switched Digital Services

Wallace, Bob. "User Says Switched 384 Service Exceeds Expectations," *Network World*, vol. 9, no. 3 (January 20, 1992), p. 4.

Wallace, Bob. "AT&T Simunet Line Lets the 5ESS Support Switched T-1," *Network World*, vol. 9, no. 30 (July 27, 1992), p. 21.

WAN Protocol Analyzers

Jander, Mary. "WAN Protocol Analyzers," *Data Communications*. vol. 21, no. 6 (April 1992), p. 65.

WAN Routers

Jander, Mary. "Frame Relay Switch, Router to Wed," *Data Communications*, vol. 21, no. 7 (May 1992), p. 121.

Feldman, Robert. "Novell Sharpens Wide-Area Focus," *LAN Times*, vol. 9, no. 15 (August 10, 1992), p. 1.

Cooney, Michael. "IBM Details Role of Its 3172 Controller," *Network World*, vol. 9, no. 30 (July 27, 1992), p. 11.

Johnson, Johna. "A WAN Service Interface That Gets Around," *Data Communications*, vol. 21, no. 3 (February 1992), p. 112.

WAN Services

Weismann, David. "Interoperable Wireless Data," *IEEE Communications*, vol. 31, no. 2 (February 1993), p. 68.

Ramaswami, Rajiv. "Multiwavelength Lightwave Networks for Computer Communications," *IEEE Communications*, vol. 31, no. 2 (February 1993), p. 78.

Sivey, Russell. "Planning Services for the Intelligent

Network," *Telephone Engineer & Management*, vol. 97, no. 16 (August, 1993), p. 40.

Finnie, Graham. "OA&M Out from the Back Room," *Communications Week International*, no. 098 (February 1, 1993), p. 14.

Molloy, Maureen. "Dial-up Links Finding New Role in Internets," *Network World*, vol. 9, no. 27 (July 6, 1992), p. 19.

Johnson, Johna. "Rebuilding the World's Public Networks," *Data Communications*, vol. 21, no. 18 (December 1992), p. 60.

Derfler, Frank. "Making the WAN Connection: Linking LANs," *PC Magazine*, vol. 12, no. 5 (March 16, 1993), p. 183.

X.400/X.500

Saunders, Stephen, and Peter Heywood. "X.400's Last Window of Opportunity," *Data Communications*, vol. 21, no. 8 (May 21, 1992), p. 73.

Heywood, Peter. "X.500: A Directory with No Unlisted Numbers?" *Data Communications*, vol. 21, no. 10 (July 1992), p. 63.

Salamone, Salvatore. "Messaging Backbones: Making Sure the Mail (and More) Gets Through," *Data Communications*, vol. 22, no. 8 (May 21, 1993), p. 54.

CASE STUDY

Jet Propulsion Labs Investigates ISDN

The futuristic world of spacecraft development has set the stage for an innovative project at Jet Propulsion Labs (JPL) to research and analyze the future of advanced communications.

Initially, the study was aimed at investigating ISDN.

"We are in a constant state of change due to the nature of our business," said Jim Jacobson, ISDN project manager at JPL, in Pasadena, Calif. "Every time a new project comes into vogue, it requires that we move that complete project into the area that can best serve them.

"Every employee move or new hire requires that we address both voice and data due to the nature of our business. The ability to do both simultaneously, address voice and data, was very appealing to us."

According to Jacobson, initial studies indicated that a considerable cost savings could be accrued using ISDN. Before looking at ISDN, JPL was providing its network users with telephone instruments, called electronic business

sets, and access to the institutional LAN (ILAN) either by modem or by a network interface unit at 9600 baud.

"If you take the equipment purchase price, installation or relocation costs, and the yearly operation costs for those [phones and modems] and you compare them against the same costs for basic rate ISDN, it comes out to a 20 to 40 percent savings over the way we were currently doing business," Jacobson said.

These initial findings convinced JPL to implement a testbed scenario of ISDN to see if it would satisfy the center's other computing requirements.

"This [ISDN] turned out to be the only emerging technology that might satisfy our requirements," Jacobson said.

In the Lab

Jet Propulsion Labs is NASA's lead center in unmanned space exploration. The lab has built and flown many of the unmanned spacecraft that have been sent to the moon,

Mars, and Venus. According to Jacobson, its most notable projects have been the Viking program, which landed a craft on Mars and took soil samples, and the Voyager project, which made a "grand tour" of the planets in our solar system.

The network that helps make this all possible is comprised of more than 12,000 computers, including micros, minis, and mainframes, all networked together using broadband and fiber backbone topologies. The network serves literally hundreds of scientific and engineering and office automation local area networks, according to Jacobson.

From the voice telecommunications side of the house, JPL has 13,500 voice lines served by a Northern Telecom DMS100 supermode switch that is dedicated to the lab. The service is provided by Pacific Bell.

The main lab is set in a campus environment of hundreds of buildings, but the network also serves a number of off-campus facilities. All off-campus facilities are within a 10-mile radius of the main campus, including the processing center that houses the host computer systems. JPL is an operating division of the California Institute of Technology.

ISDN Trials

According to Jacobson, most of the ISDN trials to this point had been focused on voice communications. For data transmissions, it had primarily been used as a modem replacement technology.

"We decided to look at the data side of the house in all facets of the way we were doing business," Jacobson said. "We wanted to use it [the technology] for LAN-to-LAN interconnects, remote access to LANs, and replacement of dedicated 56 kilobit lengths.

"And we also wanted to look at it in our IBM SNA environment, our Sun TCP/IP environment, and, obviously, as a device called a PCTA (PC terminal adapter) in our local area networking environment. We have done all of that."

According to Jacobson, JPL uses "all the operating systems"—DOS, Macintosh, and Unix, plus all those for host computers, including those made by IBM, Unisys, Cray, and Digital. JPL's office automation network runs NetWare 386 and is actually made up of about 70 such Novell networks. The lab also has approximately an equal number of MS-Net networks.

The ILAN is divided into 4 separate channels based upon the protocols they carry. One channel is for the DEC protocol, another is for TCP/IP, a third for lowspeed asynchronous (19.2Kbps) communications, and a fourth carries a mix, including IPX, AppleTalk, and XNS.

Findings from the trial were mixed. "Basically, we found out that 64 kilobit [ISDN] appeared to be a suitable adjunct to our existing infrastructure," Jacobson said. "We found that it satisfied certain niche

requirements better than any other technology."

The lab's basic requirement was the ability to get high-speed communication to its remote locations, and ISDN met that need, Jacobson said. But when the lab considered institutional support of the technology, some concerns were raised.

"These concerns are not unique to JPL: they were unique to the ISDN industry prior to the announcement of ISDN I," he said.

These concerns included limited vendors, which generally means higher prices; no guarantee of vendor interoperability; and no end-to-end knowledge continuity.

"Which basically meant to put up a new configuration would require as many as 5 or 6 people on the phone at one time because no one person understood the entire end-to-end configuration," Jacobson said.

ISDN and NASA

Jacobson said the lab did an initial analysis of these institutional support questions, which led it to the next problem: Where did basic-rate ISDN fit into the NASA picture?

The solution to this problem meant that JPL might finally be a part of the NASA family, which Jacobson characterized as being a group of "islands," unable to connect to other centers.

"The phone infrastructure could not handle ISDN from Pasadena to Washington, D.C.," said Jacobson. "We took off here."

What the investigators discovered was that, through the turn of the century, NASA was going to be acquiring and archiving more than 4,200TB of data annually, he said. That information would consist of primary data acquired from a spacecraft, a space probe, or satellite; it would then be archived at one of NASA's archive centers.

"So we used a peak busy minute formula to roughly determine what size of network would be required to handle that type of volume," Jacobson said, "and it basically pointed to about a 300Mbps network."

The investigators then looked at what the lab might be doing during that same timeframe.

"During the 1995–1996 timeframe, NASA's accumulation of data begins to shoot almost straight up from the turn of the century from the previous gigibit [of information], all the way through terabits," Jacobson said. "That is going to be the result of what may turn out to be NASA's most important mission ever—and that is a mission to the planet Earth."

That mission will entail putting a number of Earth observation satellites in orbit to observe environmental changes and effects on Earth.

"That increase is also very important data," Jacobson said. "It may be the data that will help save the planet."

The researchers found that the lab, starting from a bandwidth of 20Mbps, would need to implement fiber (FDDI) at 100Mbps by 1992–93, and high-performance parallel interface (HPPI) at 800Mbps by 1994–95. From these findings, the lab would like to be part of a national research and education network.

The investigators felt that the other NASA centers would have similar needs.

"The final, most important question in that same timeframe was, 'Where was the public service sector going?'" Jacobson said.

The lab found that public service, starting with basic rate ISDN, would move to primary-rate ISDN, then to SMDS (switch multimegabit data service) at 44.7Mbps, and finally onto broadband ISDN (BISDN) and SONET at 2.5Gbps.

"So now we're faced with a whole different scenario," Jacobson said. "It appeared that the fiber networks that we were putting up within JPL were rigid in nature—that is to say, they were inflexible—they did not have the same characteristics of a switched environment.

"It appeared that it would be a long way off when we would be able to reach the 2.5 gigibits that the public service would be offering in the 1995–96 timeframe."

So a few more factors went into the lab's decision-making process, and the lab finally decided to create an environment suitable to implement all advanced communications technologies. The result: JPL's Advanced Communications Laboratories.

Three Functions

According to Jacobson, the ACL consists of 3 unique laboratories. The configuration analysis lab investigates and evaluates customer premise equipment (CPE) configurations.

"We wanted to use the lab to verify end-user configurations prior to installation," Jacobson said. "Wring it out in the lab first. This proved to be the single most valuable characteristic [of the lab]."

The second function of the lab is to serve as a prototype laboratory. This lab serves 2 purposes: to cultivate a vendor/user/service-provider relationship and to provide end-to-end verification in an operational environment.

The third function is to serve as a demonstration lab. "We decided in our demonstration lab to differentiate for potential users the 'dream from reality' by demonstrating contemporary configurations based on commercially available CPE and applications," Jacobson said.

Evolution

Plans call for the lab to share the information it gathers with NASA,

Jacobson said. A paper Jacobson wrote on the project, entitled "Navigating JPL's Bandwidth Requirements through the '90s," won the 1991 Call for Innovation from Network World magazine.

The lab, which was Jacobson's brainchild, has come some distance from there.

"As a result of this [the lab], we got a growing list of CPE vendors for the configuration analysis lab, and we've initiated a memorandum or understanding between JPL and Pac Bell to allow JPL to be a trial site for these technologies," he said.

The lab is currently involved in a frame relay trial with Pacific Bell. The lab has also received a request from the City of Los Angeles to monitor the modeling of the ISDN technology in the IBM SNA environment. There has also been some discussion that the lab might acquire a prototype asynchronous transfer mode (ATM) switch for analysis, which would provide the broadband ISDN capabilities the lab will eventually require, Jacobson said.

"It appears that we've provided a forum for all advanced communications implementers," Jacobson said. "It appears that it will allow JPL to acquire expert knowledge on these technologies possibly years before commercial availability."

The lab will also permit JPL to apply the correct technology to any given JPL or NASA bandwidth requirement and provide a migration path for JPL's increasing bandwidth requirements.

"So you begin to see that we started out with ISDN and we're still doing a lot with ISDN," Jacobson said. "But it's [ISDN] the most rudimentary of some advanced technologies in the public service arena, and we have to look at all of them. That's what comes out loud and clear."

Currently, JPL has implemented 120 ISDN lines. It has also procured another 100 lines from Pacific Bell and will be implementing those over the next 2 years. "We're not pushing ISDN as fast as we could because of the pending infrastructure issues that need to be addressed," Jacobson said.

Essentially, ISDN is just a piece in a much bigger high-speed connectivity puzzle, according to Jacobson.

"What we ran across was that people are riding different technology horses," he said. "In reality, you've got to look at the much bigger picture.

"Each technology satisfies a number of requirements better than the other technologies, but they all really have to fit together. Even broadband ISDN isn't the end-all technology."

Jacobson has spent the past year on the ISDN project and found that there's still much more to learn.

"Implementing this new technology requires that we look at our current infrastructure and see what it takes to bring our infrastructure up to speed," Jacobson said. "That's a whole other area we have to look at—how much it's going to cost us."

The goal, he said, is to achieve complete compatibility by the year 2000. This goal should also be shared by other computer users, he said. As networks incorporate such technologies as ISDN, SMDS, and frame relay, every business is going to have to do an infrastructure upgrade, Jacobson contends. He said that the lab hopes to carry out this mission in an open lab environment.

Jacobson also hopes to open the doors to the lab and its knowledge base to academia.

"What we have here is a real-world operation dealing with real-world issues, and we're attempting to bring in advancing or state-of-the-art technology," Jacobson said. "It's a piece of the puzzle that students have not been able to put their hands on—the real-world slant. And that's what we're hoping to provide them."

For example, Jacobson said that the City of Los Angeles mentioned that it may take 3 to 5 years before a graduate with a master's degree in communications is productive in a working environment.

JPL has also become involved in the North American ISDN Users Forum and is chairing the transcontinental ISDN project for this year called TRIP '92. The project is a national and international exposition of users, demonstrating ISDN capability in open-house fashion, said Jacobson.

A simple search into the realm of ISDN has spawned an entire career for Jacobson, who has become somewhat of an expert in the area. He has been making on average about one speaking engagement per month to computer organizations on the subject.

Even though his initial search unlocked numerous paths and goals in the area of advanced communications, Jacobson did make an important discovery about the impetus of the entire adventure—ISDN.

Emphasis on Telecommuting

Jacobson said he sees primary-rate ISDN's best fit being in the area of telecommuting. In the future, Jacobson sees telecommuting becoming mandatory in major metropolitan areas throughout the United States. Jacobson jokingly refers to telecommuting as an Intelligent Solution to Driving Needlessly (ISDN).

"Here's another angle that the [public service] industry hasn't picked up on," Jacobson said. "There's something looming that may act as a tremendous driver for this entire industry, and that is the environmental issues."

According to Jacobson, the public service sector has not been promoting telecommuting, or the

environmental factors in its ISDN rollouts—factors that he contends are going to drive ISDN.

"It's an issue that the industry needs to start looking at," Jacobson said. "They only have to look in their own areas to realize the need for telecommuting and that it is an eventuality, so the quicker they provide the infrastructure for telecommuting, the quicker they can satisfy the demand."

Jacobson said his enthusiasm for telecommuting is not influenced by a particularly strong environmental viewpoint. "I was just trying to get more bandwidth," he quipped. "But I do realize that those who are [environmentalists] and those who need to make these changes to fix this dilemma are going to have to use this technology. This technology really is timely."

Jacobson expects his involvement with ISDN is far from over. "My whole attitude about this [ISDN] is that this is 'to be continued.' I've got a feeling that we've just scraped the surface."

Source: Robyn Walker, "Jet Propulsion Labs Investigates ISDN," *LAN Times,* vol. 9, no. 1 (January 20, 1992), p. 29. Reprinted with permission of McGraw-Hill, *LAN Times.*

Business Case Study Questions

Activities

1. Prepare a top-down model of this case by extracting pertinent facts and placing them in the proper layer within the top-down model. Use the questions below as guidelines.
2. After having completed the top-down model, summarize the results of the pilot study including, but not limited to, on-going concerns, projected architecture timetables, and additional needs identified.

Business

1. What were the business issues or needs which prompted the pilot study?
2. What were the results of the preliminary cost–benefit analysis?
3. How did the Jet Propulsion Lab's relationship with NASA affect the pilot study?

Application

1. What were some of the ways in which the pilot study sought to employ ISDN beyond simple modem replacement?

Data

1. What range of data volume was JPL to be acquiring and archiving each year?

Network

1. What operating systems, network operating systems, and network transport protocols were in need of support by the new network?
2. In terms of capacity, how many computers, voice lines, buildings, etc., needed to be supported by the new network?
3. What effect did concerns over availability of wide area ISDN from carriers have on the overall study?

4. What was the purpose of the advanced communications lab?

Technology

1. List as many aspects of the physical implementation of the existing network as possible. Pay particular attention to currently supported transport protocols.

Further Analysis

1. How many of the concerns identified above would be addressed if the NISDN-1 standards are widely adhered to?

2. Do you feel that the Jet Propulsion Labs took a top-down approach to this study? Defend your answer.

3. How did NASA see ISDN fitting into its long-range WAN plans, if at all?

4. What do you believe was the overall outcome of the pilot study?

CHAPTER · 9

Enterprise Networking and Client/Server Architectures

Concepts Reinforced

Top-Down Model	Internetworking
OSI 7-Layer Model	Wide Area Networking
Cost/Benefit Analysis	Multiprotocol Software
Local Area Networking	Importance of Standards

Concepts Introduced

Corporate Downsizing	Distributed Databases
Information Systems Downsizing	Front-End Tools
Applications Rightsizing	SQL
Client/Server Architectures	Middleware
Distributed Computing	Enterprise Network Management
Object-Oriented Programming	Open Systems Architectures

OBJECTIVES

After mastering the material in this chapter you should:

1. Understand the business forces motivating the emphasis on information systems downsizing and application rightsizing.

2. Understand the relationship between client–server architectures and the implementation of distributed computing, application rightsizing, database distribution, and enterprise networking.

3. Understand the major hardware and software components of a client–server architecture and the role that middleware plays in integrating these components to form a working architecture.

4. Understand the additional difficulties and decision making as well as the currently available solutions involved in implementing client–server architectures involving multiple vendor's systems.

5. Understand the role of open systems in client–server implementation and the approach that major computer vendors have taken toward open systems client–server architectures.

6. Understand the current state of the actual implementation of client–server architectures in industry, the problem areas or limiting factors affecting these implementations, and the outlook for resolution of these limiting factors.

7. Understand the unique problems encountered in the management of multivendor, multiplatform client–server architectures and the current state of available distributed enterprise network management systems.

INTRODUCTION

In this chapter the knowledge of local area networks, internetworking, and wide area networks gained thus far will be integrated in an attempt to demonstrate how networking technology truly is the foundation of today's "rightsized" information systems. Using the top-down model as a frame of reference, the chapter will start with a brief overview of the business forces currently influencing information systems engineering.

Current information systems trends that have emerged in response to these business forces, such as application rightsizing, distributed computing, database distribution, client/server architectures, and enterprise networks, will be introduced and related to the top-down model as well as to each other. Once the overall architecture of tomorrow's enterprise network-based information system is understood, the issues involved in implementing such an architecture will be more specifically discussed.

The role of standards, either de facto or actual, in such an "open system" architecture, as well as the existence or absence of any required standards, will be discussed. Major implications exist in the implementation of such systems in the areas of people and systems management. The human and administrative aspects of the enterprise networking and application rightsizing phenomena will be thoroughly explored as well.

Finally, currently available software and hardware technology which exists to implement an enterprise network-based information system will be analyzed. Deficiencies, if any, in the current enabling technology will be identified as the integration of LAN, internetwork, and WAN technologies builds a foundation for distributed information systems. Having identified any potential technological or administrative pitfalls affecting the smooth establishment and operation of such distributed information systems architectures, the chapter will close with an examination of possible future trends in the areas of enterprise networking, applications rightsizing, and client/server architectures.

THE BUSINESS OF DOWNSIZING

As companies have sought a competitive advantage in the downturned economy of the early 1990s, information has been increasingly recognized as a corporate asset to be leveraged for that sought-after competitive advantage. More precisely, the timely delivery of the right corporate information, in the right format, to the right decision-maker at the right place and time can be the differentiating factor between success and failure in today's business world. It is important to add one additional criterion to the previous sentence: That information must also be delivered at the right *price.*

As profits have dwindled and pressures to decrease expenses have mounted, the cost of maintaining corporate information systems have come under increased scrutiny. The mainframe computer and its associated hierarchical network and maintenance/development budget have been singled out, perhaps unfairly, as the biggest consumer of information systems departments' budgets. As will soon be seen, mainframe computers still have their rightful place in some corporate information systems environments.

Corporate downsizing, not to be confused with **information systems downsizing,** has involved elimination of positions within a corporation through attrition, early retirement, closed operations, or forced lay-offs. The duties of the eliminated positions are either assumed by remaining employees or deemed "dispens-able" and not assumed by anyone.

In many cases, it is the information systems of these "downsized" corporations that must pick up the slack and deliver better information more efficiently to the remaining employees. "Accomplishing more with less" is one of the aims of the properly "rightsized" application.

☐ ELEMENTS OF DISTRIBUTED INFORMATION SYSTEMS ARCHITECTURE

It is important to understand that "information systems downsizing" and **"application rightsizing"** are not merely about saving money. As will be seen, a combination of events, including the introduction of reasonably-priced, powerful personal workstations, and the emergence of UNIX as an acceptable operating system in the business world, have combined with the demands of today's business climate to produce an entirely new **distributed architecture** for information systems processing and delivery. As cited case studies will illustrate, these distributed or rightsized information systems not only save money, but also deliver better information more flexibly, as well as enable quicker business level responses to competitive situations.

This distributed information systems architecture consists of the three main elements of any information system, namely,

>Processing
>Data
>Networks

The distributed nature of these three basic elements have been described in the following terms:

>Distributed processing or distributed computing
>Database distribution
>Distributed networks or enterprise networks

The combination of these three distributed architecture elements are often referred to collectively as a **client–server architecture.** Figure 9-1 summarizes the relationship between many of the key concepts of this chapter as they relate to the familiar top-down model. The exploration of each of the elements contained in Figure 9-1 will constitute the majority of the material presented in the chapter.

A Physical Outlook on Client–Server Architectures

Figure 9-1 presents a diagram of the *functional* relationships between the elements of distributed information systems. In order to understand the full impact of client–server architectures, it is necessary to comprehend the *physical* relationship or generic implementation configuration of the elements of a typical client–server architecture as well.

To expand on the list of main elements of any information system noted in Figure 9-1, the following key components can be added:

>Presentation of data to user
>Formatting of data for presentation to user
>Application program request for data
>Data retrieval
>Data storage

Business	Increased competition on a global scale Corporate downsizing Information systems downsizing Business process redesign/reengineering		
Application	Application rightsizing Distributed computing Distributed applications	Middleware	Client–server Architecture
Data	Distributed databases		
Network	Enterprise networks Distributed network management		
Technology	Software: UNIX as operating system of choice Hardware: Powerful, reasonably priced multitasking CPUs		

Figure 9-1 The top-down model and key components of distributed information systems.

Transport of data requests
Transport of actual data

Client–Server versus Mainframe-Terminal Architectures

To understand the significant differences between a client–server architecture and a more traditional mainframe-terminal architecture, where each of the elements listed above is accomplished must be located. Figure 9-2 illustrates the differences in location of these key information systems elements between client–server and mainframe-based architectures.

The client–server illustration in Figure 9-2 is somewhat of an oversimplification of client–server architectures. First, *multiple servers* are commonplace in such an architecture. Secondly, servers are very likely to be distributed geographically with some servers being located remotely and linked to geographically dispersed clients via wide area network routers, sometimes referred to as **enterprise routers.**

Several key facts should be evident in Figure 9-2. First, in the client–server architecture, the processing necessary to produce application program requests for data may take place on either the client workstation or the shared system server. This characteristic of client–server architecture is known as **distributed processing.**

Secondly, data may be stored and/or retrieved on either the client workstation or the shared system server in a process generally referred to as *database distribution* or **distributed databases.**

Finally, the network of the client–server architecture must have sufficient sophistication to transport those data requests to the remote server as necessary, while allowing data requests to be fulfilled locally to remain on the client workstation for processing. The **enterprise network** handles the transportation of data requests and actual data for the client–server architecture with the help of a specialized category of interface software known as **middleware.**

In contrast, as can be seen in Figure 9-2, the mainframe-terminal environment requires *all processing* of any type to be performed on the mainframe with terminals acting only as "dumb" input/output devices. In order to enhance processing

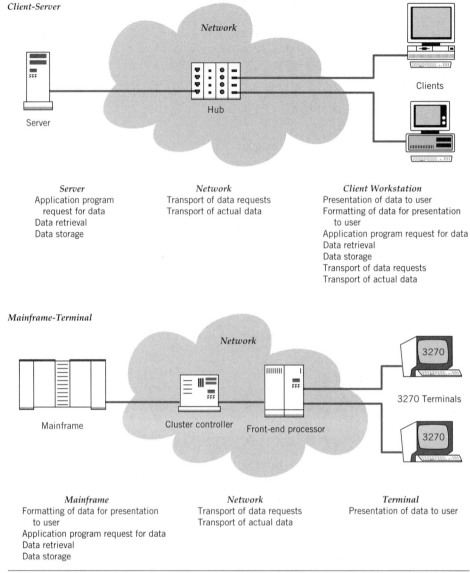

Client-Server

Server	*Network*	*Client Workstation*
Application program request for data	Transport of data requests	Presentation of data to user
Data retrieval	Transport of actual data	Formatting of data for presentation to user
Data storage		Application program request for data
		Data retrieval
		Data storage
		Transport of data requests
		Transport of actual data

Mainframe-Terminal

Mainframe	*Network*	*Terminal*
Formatting of data for presentation to user	Transport of data requests	Presentation of data to user
Application program request for data	Transport of actual data	
Data retrieval		
Data storage		

Figure 9-2 Client–server versus mainframe-terminal architectures.

power in a mainframe-terminal environment, one's only choice is to increase the power of the mainframe.

On the other hand, in the distributed processing environment of the client–server architecture, one can increase the overall processing power of the architecture at a far lower cost by increasing the power of the PC-based client workstations.

Obviously, this is only taking into account the hardware side of the equation. In order to take advantage of the power of distributed processing, specially-written software able to divide processing and database tasks across multiple processors located in both clients and servers, must be either written or purchased.

Enterprise Network Delivers Client–Server Independence

Each of the key client–server topics just mentioned will be explored in detail later in this chapter. Figure 9-3 illustrates a physical stack relationship between the elements of a client–server architecture. The key point of Figure 9-3 is the *total independence of client and server*. Ideally, any client workstation running any network operating system, operating system, and other software components, will be able to communicate *transparently* with any server running any database system, network operating system, operating system combination.

As can be seen from Figure 9-3, if this ideal scenario is to ever become a commonplace reality, it will be largely due to the sophistication of the enterprise network and the rather loosely-defined category of software known as middleware, which serves as an interface between clients, servers, and the enterprise network. The importance of the independence of clients and servers will be expanded upon as the chapter progresses.

This diagram will be expanded and elaborated on throughout the remainder of the chapter.

Why Rightsize? Some Success Stories

The distributed nature of the application, processing, and data distribution for client–server architectures, as well as the independence of clients and servers, as illustrated in previous figures, are at the heart of many of the advantages and benefits of such an information system architecture.

Although sometimes overshadowed by the more concrete benefits such as per-

Major Element	Sub-Element	Examples	Also Known as
Client	Graphical User Interface Development tools	Windows Object-Vision Visual Basic Powerbuilder	Front-End
	End-user tools Groupware Data inquiry tools	Excel Lotus Notes Q&E Forest & Trees	
	Network Operating Systems Operating Systems	see Chapter 5	
Middleware	RPC—Remote Procedure Calls Command Translation	To be explained further	
Enterprise Network	Transparent Transport Facilities	Combined elements of LAN, Internetworking, and WAN technologies (Chapters 5, 6, 7)	
Middleware	RPC—Remote Procedure Calls Command Translation	To be explained further	
Server	Distributed Database	ORACLE SQL RDBMS	Back-End
	Network Operating Systems	see Chapter 5	
	Operating Systems		

Figure 9-3 The physical relationship of client–server elements.

formance improvements or budget decreases, the flexibility of design afforded by the distributed nature of the client–server architecture holds the key to the most significant benefits of this new computing paradigm.

Distributed architectures and application rightsizing are far more subjective than most topics studied thus far. Topics such as these do not lend themselves well to objective performance measurement in units such as bits per second. In light of this, implementation and performance issues from actual case studies will be used to maintain the "real world" orientation of the text. Accordingly, this chapter also includes a significantly greater number of case studies in the featured references section than most other chapters.

The primary focus in this chapter will be on the skills involved in planning, implementing, and maintaining the enterprise network that must support these distributed information systems. However, in order to fully understand enterprise networks, it is necessary to first understand the distributed information systems architectures which they are supporting.

Before introducing specific elements of the distributed information system as outlined in Figure 9-1, a brief examination of a few case studies may shed some light on some of the reasons why companies undertake rightsizing projects. All instances cited below have been gathered from case studies listed in the featured references section of this chapter.

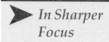

In Sharper Focus

CLIENT–SERVER SUCCESS STORIES

Motorola's Computer Group has shifted in-house written applications based on an IBM mainframe to primarily packaged software running on distributed UNIX processors. In the process they have reduced their budget by 40 percent and shortened application development cycles. These systems are also valued for their flexibility and their ability to adapt to changes in the business environment.

Flexibility and the ability to initiate new business ventures are two of the key outcomes sought by Kash n'Karry's 112-store grocery business' investment in a new object-oriented, distributed computing environment. These goals are not without their inherent cost however. The new distributed information systems initiative will require a 12 percent increase on an annual information systems budget of $6 million. The relationship between object-oriented programming and distributed computing will be investigated later in this chapter.

Reader's Digest is optimizing mainframe use while distributing information over a global LAN internetwork, and is reducing its number of data centers from 17 to three, a reduction of 82 percent in the process. Improved information accessibility will be a key outcome of the project, as authorized users will be able to access subscriber information on any mainframe, rather than just on the mainframe to which they are locally connected.

Financial Guaranty Insurance Company has reduced its system budget by 80 percent and reduced its programming staff by 71 percent as a result of its downsizing initiative from a mainframe to a client–server architecture employing 200 Intel 386-based clients and 4 Intel 486-based servers.

Finally, and perhaps most significantly, better, faster information from the City of San Antonio's Emergency Dispatch System has saved lives. Using 386-based clients and multiprocessor 486-based servers, dispatchers can get ambulances faster to where they are needed due to the increased speed and flexibility of the system.

Benefit	Examples/Explanation
Reduced costs in comparison to mainframe-based information systems	Budget reductions of 40–80% are possible, along with the possibility of significant staff reductions
Flexibility	Cited as a benefit in nearly every case study. Information is more accessible and display formats more flexible thanks to client–server architecture
Support/respond to business environment changes	Beyond flexibility. Demonstrates potential for proactive use of information systems in business. Significantly reduced time to develop new applications is a contributing factor
Improved information accessibility.	Information stored on distributed LANs is more easily accessible to a wider user group than information stored on a mainframe–based hierarchical network
Faster information	Distributed processing allows combined power of client PC and server PC to increase processing speed by as much as a factor of 10 over the mainframe based solutions
Better information	The "right" information. Produced as a result of a combination of faster processing, more flexible formatting, and improved access to a wider array of information
Open architecture	The typical PC-based client–server architecture offers unlimited potential for multi-vendor solutions to information systems opportunities. Mainframe-based, single vendor information systems lock out the competition and, in many cases, innovative solutions
Empowered users	Perhaps most significantly, users will play a larger role in information systems design and development as client-based, easy-to-use systems development tools are employed in the client–server architecture

Figure 9-4 Benefits of distributed information systems.

Figure 9-4 summarizes the significant benefits of successful distributed information system implementation.

The Negative Side of Rightsizing: Wrongsizing?

Just as there are often many sides to every story, there are drawbacks and potential pitfalls to information systems rightsizing efforts. Some of these negatives are unique to client–server or rightsizing efforts, while others are true for any shift in information systems design or architecture.

Since cost savings is often the key positive attribute of rightsizing, it seems only fitting that a closer examination of rightsizing efforts sometimes reveals that this cost savings is often minimized when **transition costs** are taken into account. If the new "rightsized" system is to replace an existing system, then both systems must be maintained and supported for some period of time. In addition, the cost of writing new software or converting old software should be taken into account, as should the cost for development of new user or management software "tools."

Several case studies cite the *lack of existing management tools for the distributed computing architecture* as a serious impediment to client–server deployment. Such tools must automatically and transparently cater to system backup, disaster recovery, and security issues such as user log-in and user access management over the entire distributed computing network. In short, users expect all of the functionality of the sophisticated operating systems of standalone mainframes on the distributed platform of the client–server architecture.

Because of the increased sophistication and processing power available to the end-user at the client workstation, increased end-user training is a reality and an additional cost that must be considered by client–server architecture implementation teams. It should follow that these same more powerful end-user workstations require increased on-going technical support as well.

As can be seen from a thorough review of the case studies, there can be many negative aspects or potential pitfalls to the shift from traditional information systems architectures to client–server architectures. Figure 9-5 summarizes the results of a survey of 750 large companies to the primary benefits and shortcomings of client–server implementations.

The People Architecture of Client–Server

The distribution of processing power, coupled with the distribution of corporate data and the distribution of application development via a client–server architecture can raise fundamental issues regarding the "ownership" of and responsibility for different aspects of these distributed systems. For instance, are local department personnel responsible for the maintenance, backup, and disaster recovery of local servers, or do these functions remain in the domain of the centralized MIS

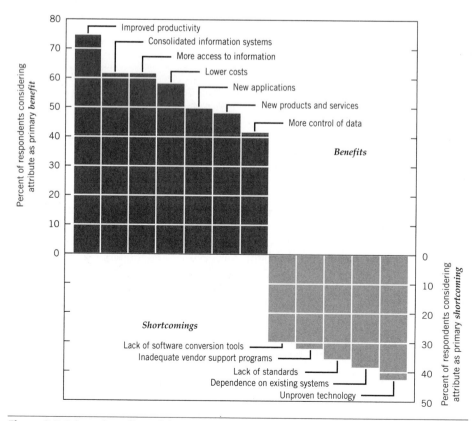

Figure 9-5 Primary benefits and shortcomings of client–server implementations.

department? Which organization is responsible for which aspects of the enterprise network?

All of these people-related issues form the basis of a **people architecture** which is a reflection or a result of a related **system architecture.** This relationship between systems architectures and the organization of people to support these systems architectures is nothing new and is not unique to the age of applications rightsizing or client–server architectures.

Major Paradigms of the Information Age

These unique combinations of systems architectures and people architectures are often referred to as *paradigms* of information systems. There have been at least two or three major paradigms in information systems prior to the introduction of the client–server model. Depending on which information systems philosopher is consulted, any or all of these may be seen as major paradigms of the Information Age:

1. The Age of the Mainframe
2. The Introduction of the Minicomputer
3. The Introduction of the Personal Computer
4. The Dawn of the Client–Server Architecture and Applications Rightsizing

The period of time when information systems professionals are madly scrambling to gain competitive advantage for their companies by implementing the "new" paradigm is known as a **paradigm shift.** A paradigm shift is not merely the introduction of new technology. It is much more than that. A paradigm shift occurs when the fundamental underlying processes and environment change to such an extent that *significant changes in behavior are required.* In short, a completely new way of doing things results from a completely new way of looking at the world of information systems.

The key point of a paradigm shift is to realize that in addition to major technological or systems architecture shifts, there are also correspondingly large shifts in people architectures. Thus, it should not be surprising that the dawn of the client–server age is uncovering a great many people-related issues as the centralized MIS departments of the "old" paradigm are faced with the reality of the distributed systems of the "new paradigm." Much of the debate in today's evolving people architecture centers around which functions of an MIS department should be distributed, to match the systems architecture, and which must remain centralized.

There are no easy answers to these questions. The people architecture of the client-server age is still evolving. Figure 9-6 summarizes some of the people architecture features and issues of the client–server or applications rightsizing paradigm.

After reviewing Figure 9-6, it should be obvious that the people architecture changes resulting from the client–server/applications rightsizing paradigm shift are potentially at least as dramatic as the changes in systems architecture. These people architecture changes will cause anxiety as people worry about changing job descriptions and long-term security. A predictable reaction on the part of many will be to resist the change aggressively. Coping with negativism and overall effective management of the people side of the client–server architecture will be addressed more fully later in the chapter.

The Importance of People Issues to Data Communications Professionals

Why is the people architecture of a particular paradigm important to data communications professionals? Hopefully, the answer to that question is fairly obvious by now. If, as data communications professionals, we are expected to build the net-

Feature/Characteristic	Issues/Explanation
The Dawn of the Empowered User	Powerful, easy-use, front-end client-based tools will empower end-users to meet many more of their own information needs, thanks to access to distributed data via the client–server architecture and enterprise networks
Cross-functional, User Department-Based Application Development	No longer totally centralized, application development will be distributed to end-user departments. Empowered users of the departments, rather than MIS staff, may be project leaders
MIS Personnel in Consultative Roles	No longer the sole "owners" of all corporate data and applications development expertise, MIS personnel will work in a more distributed, consultative, or "loaned" basis for individual end-user department projects for extended periods of time
Changing Role for Centralized MIS Department	A smaller, centralized MIS department must still be responsible for certain "global" concerns such as: Centralized, coordinated user support Centralized, coordinated user training Maintenance of the enterprise network Quality assurance in the areas of database design, applications development, and departmental networking projects Data administration standards development and enforcement by defining standard, global data definitions for globally used data elements Standards testing—test new technology for adherance to corporate standards before allowing global deployment

Figure 9-6 People architecture issues of the client–server and applications rightsizing paradigm.

works that will smoothly and transparently transport all required data and information to the distributed members of this people architecture, then we had better have a thorough understanding of how these people are likely to be distributed. In addition, we will also need to know which users are using which distributed processing and distributed database "tools," as this will have a direct bearing on the distributed network requirements for each of these distributed users.

☐ DISTRIBUTED COMPUTING: CLIENTS AND SERVERS SHARE PROCESSING LOAD

The first component of the client–server architecture, as illustrated in Figure 9-1, to be explored will be **distributed processing,** also known as **distributed computing.** Simply stated, distributed processing is nothing more than dividing an application program into two or more pieces, and subsequently distributing and processing those **distributed applications** on two or more computers, either clients or servers. The division of application programs for optimal use by a client–server environment can be a major undertaking. As the chapter progresses, many complexities of distributed processing will be introduced.

The client portion of the program is often called the **front-end,** and is primarily used to:

Provide a user interface.
Format requests for data or processing from the server.
Format data received from the server for output to the user.

The server portion of the program is often called the **back-end** or **engine** and is primarily used to retrieve and store data as requested, perform computation and application processing, and provide necessary security and management functions. Simply stated, the back-end does all processing except the interface and formatting-related tasks performed by the front-end. Relatively speaking, this back-end distributed application represents the majority of the total required processing, leading to the term "processing engine." Figure 9-7 summarizes some of the key characteristics of front-end and back-end distributed applications.

Key Attributes of Distributed Computing: Transparency, Scalability

Two of the most important attributes of distributed processing are *transparency* and *scalability*. The extent to which each of these attributes is true can vary from one distributed processing installation to another.

Transparency refers to the ability of distributed processing systems to combine clients and servers of different operating systems, network operating systems, and protocols into a cohesive system processing distributed applications without regard to the aforementioned differences. Complete transparency is still a largely unrealized goal of distributed processing. As will be seen when specific distributed processing solutions are explored, limited transparency among a finite number or vendors' equipment, operating systems, and network operating systems is currently possible.

This transparency is achieved via a category of software known as **middle-**

Characteristic	Front-End	Back-End
Also called . . .	Client-Portion	Engine
Runs on . . .	Client workstation	Servers
Primary functions	User inteface Format requests for data or processing from server Format data received from server	Store and retrieve data Perform computation and application processing Provide security and management functions
Runs . . .	. . . as needed or as activated by user	. . . constantly.
Services . . .	. . . individual user at single client workstation	. . . multiple users sending requests for processing/data from multiple client workstations
Examples	E-Mail Systems	
	Receive, read, send personal E-mail messages as desired	Provide on-going E-mail delivery service for all attached clients
	Database Systems	
	Format requests for data from data server	Services data requests from multiple clients

Figure 9-7 Distributed processing: Front-end vs. back-end distributed applications.

ware. Middleware resides in the middle of the distributed processing system, serving as a transparent insulator surrounding the enterprise network over which the client–server communication actually travels. Middleware will be explored in detail later in the chapter.

Scalability refers to the ability of distributed processing systems to add clients without degrading the overall performance of the system. This is possible due to the fact that as each client is added, the incremental processing power of that client's CPU is added to the overall processing power of the entire distributed processing system.

This distributed processing attribute of scalability should be contrasted with the effect on the mainframe-terminal architecture of the addition of incremental terminals to the mainframe. Because all processing power is concentrated in the mainframe, overall system performance is degraded for each terminal added. When overall system performance is seriously degraded, the customary solution to increase overall processing power is to buy a bigger mainframe. Obviously, the cost of a bigger mainframe is significantly more than the cost of client workstations.

This is not to say that mainframes don't have their rightful place in a distributed computing environment. The changing role of the mainframe will be explored in the next section on database distribution. It is also worth repeating that the scalability of a distributed processing system is only significant if application programs can be split, or distributed, between clients and servers. As will be seen, this is by no means a trivial task. With this distributed application hurdle overcome, massive amounts of processing power and storage capability can be merged via the enterprise backbone to effectively form one massively powerful and flexible computer. Figure 9-8 illustrates transparency and scalability, the key attributes of distributed processing systems.

Distributed Processing: Basic Communications

A closer look at how distributed processing is actually accomplished will reveal a process simple in design, yet often complicated in implementation. Figure 9-9 illustrates the elements of and process of a client–server communication session.

Figure 9-9 is purposefully depicted without specific technology identified in any hardware or software category. The purpose of the diagram is to show what general elements are involved in client-server communication, and how that communication is accomplished.

As can be seen in Figure 9-9, a piece of the distributed application is processed on both the client (front-end) and server (back-end). The overall communication process starts when the client-portion of the distributed application needs a service which the server portion of the distributed application can provide. The particular nature of this service will vary depending on the distributed application. It may be a request for a database lookup, a request to forward some E-mail, or a request to process a particular routine or subroutine. The nature of the particular request is not important at this point.

What is important is how that request for service is constructed and relayed to the servicing distributed application. As can be seen in Figure 9-9, the client portion of the distributed application issues a specially formatted packet of data known as a **RPC** (remote procedure call), which contains, among other things, the destination server address and the requested service. This remote procedure call passes through an **API** (application program interface) which reformats the remote procedure call as appropriate for the network operating systems of the

Transparency: Clients and servers cooperatively share processing load *without regard for operating system or protocol differences*

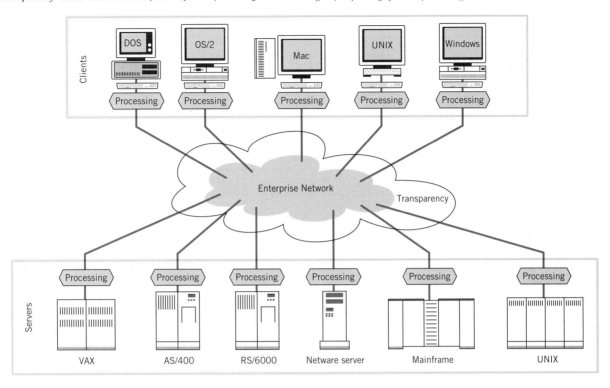

Scalability: Additional clients are added to system with little or no effect on processing load due to *incremental processing power added by each client*

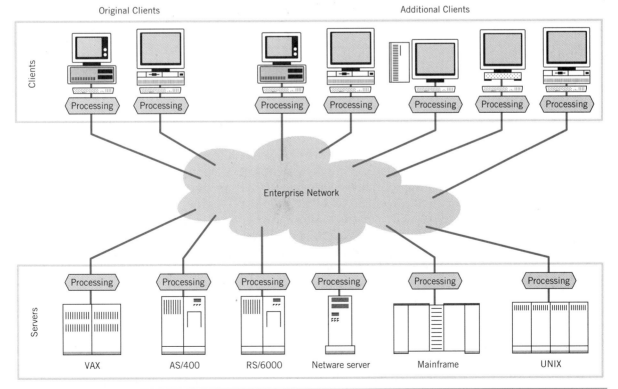

Figure 9-8 Key attributes of distributed processing.

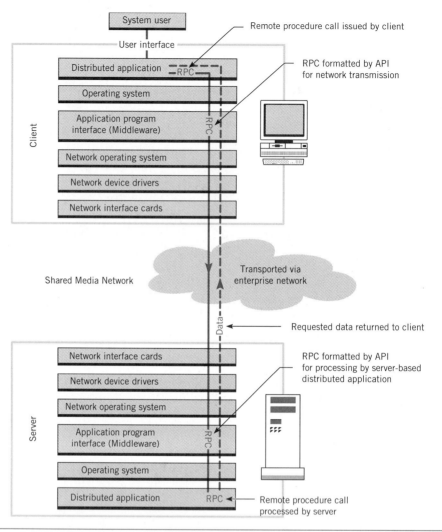

Figure 9-9 Distributed processing basics: client/server communications.

client and destination server. RPCs and APIs constitute the heart of middleware and will be examined in a dedicated section later in the chapter.

The appropriately-formatted RPC is then transported over the enterprise network to the intended back-end processing engine. The RPC is reformatted by the API present in the server into a form that can be understood and processed by the network operating system, operating system, and distributed application of the server. Processed results or requested data is returned to the client workstation's distributed application via a similar process in which actual network communication and other protocols are satisfied via the API portion of the transparency-producing middleware.

Communication between distributed applications can be from server to server as well as from client to server. Examples include complex database inquiries involving distributed databases physically located on multiple servers, or E-mail delivery which involves transfer of E-mail across several E-mail servers in order to reach the final user destination address. **Server-to-server communication** is most often transparent to the client workstation requesting the initial service which triggered the server-to-server communication. Figure 9-10 illustrates server-to-server communication among distributed applications, again, in a nontechnology-specific manner.

As can be seen in Figure 9-10, the initial remote procedure call (RPC) is generated by a client, and directed to server 1. After analyzing the original RPC, server 1 realizes that required data or processing must be supplied by server 2, and issues a new RPC accordingly. Having processed the RPC and supplied the requested data or services, server 2 transmits that data back to server 1. Combining this data received from server 2 with any locally processed data, server 1 forwards the results of the original RPC to the client workstation.

Client-Based Tools for Distributed Application Development

Although an entire book could be written on the currently available as well as future tools for the development of distributed applications, the focus will be kept on basic distributed processing functionality in the context of its integration with database distribution, enterprise networks, and the middleware that ties it all

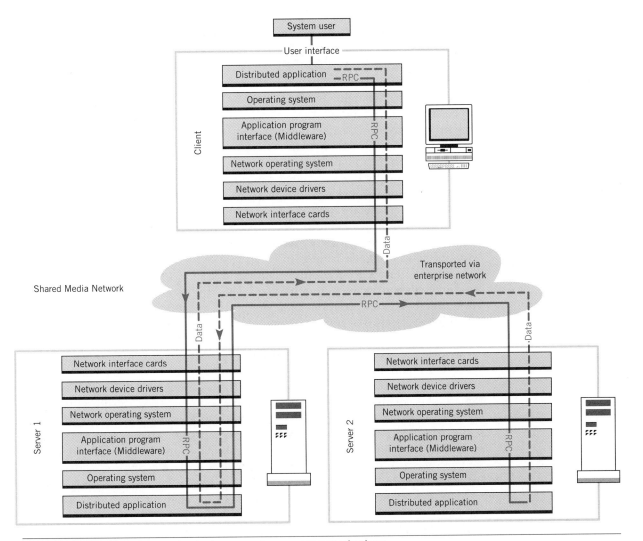

Figure 9-10 Distributed processing basics: server-to-server communications.

together. As a result, only an awareness of a wide range of client-based tools for distributed applications development and implementation which fall into the following broad categories will be offered:

Category	Example
4th Generation Languages	Visual Basic
Object-Oriented Programming	Objectvision
	Powerbuilder
Groupware	Lotus Notes
Multiple Platform Client–Server	
Software Development System	NCR Cooperation
	Uniface Open 4GL

The assumption as the chapter continues is that one or a combination of these tools have been used to develop a distributed application. The more detailed studies will include that distributed application's interaction with distributed databases, the enterprise network, and the role of middleware in enabling those interactions.

☐ DATABASE DISTRIBUTION: THE SUBSTANCE OF DISTRIBUTED PROCESSING

Referring back to Figure 9-1 in which the top-down model was used as an overall architecture for organizing the key concepts of distributed information systems, it can be seen that distributed processing on the applications layer depends on distributed databases on the data layer. If specially designed distributed applications are split to run as separate client (front-end) and server (back-end) portions, then it stands to reason that database management systems (DBMS) somehow have to be specially adapted for the distributed environment as well.

In a distributed environment, data must be able to be stored in multiple physical locations, on different types of server computers in a manner which is transparent to the end-user. These multiple database servers must be able to communicate with each other, even if they are not running the same database management system. Specially designed front-end, client-based, tools perform distributed database inquiry, report generation, and application development. **Distributed database management systems** and their associated front-end tools serve as additional variables, together with application programs, operating systems, and network operating systems, that must interoperate transparently over the enterprise network.

In order to achieve end-user transparency with such an enormous number of possible combinations of DBMS, NOS, OS, and application programs, the role of *standards* for interprocess communications is absolutely critical. Due to the evolutionary state of distributed processing and client–server architecture, it should come as no surprise that applicable standards are evolving as well. Figure 9-11 summarizes the relationship between the various aspects of database distribution, each of which will be covered in detail. Additional components such as operating system, network operating system, API, network device drivers, and network interface cards are assumed but not listed for clarity's sake.

Figure 9-11 illustrates the overall process for client workstations accessing data located on distributed database servers via the use of front-end tools. The generic illustration makes no assumptions as to specific examples of front-end tools or database management systems. Because a single front-end tool may need to access several different database management systems running on different

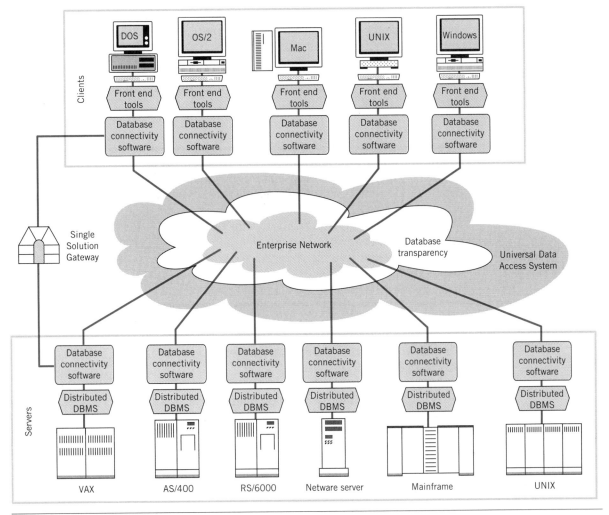

Figure 9-11 Key components of database distribution.

server types, a "database distribution-specific" middleware layer consisting of data connectivity software and a more general universal data access system have been included. As the chapter progresses, specific examples of currently available products and standards will be examined in each of the following categories:

Distributed database management systems
Front-end tools
Data connectivity software
Universal data access systems

To reiterate, the object of this review is not to present an exhaustive presentation of database concepts or distributed database technology. Rather, it is to gain sufficient insight into distributed database management systems in order to enable effective analysis and design of the enterprise networks on which these data management systems depend.

Distributed Database Management Systems: Database Engines

Simply stated, in order to qualify as a true *distributed* database management system, the product in question must offer *data transparency* to the end-user. Although specific required characteristics will be explored shortly, generally speaking, a true distributed database management system should allow a user to access data without regard for:

Front-end tool or distributed application
Type of server computer (Intel-based, minicomputer, mainframe, etc.)
Physical location of the server
Physical details and protocols of the network path to the server

◆ *Management Perspective*

In addition to data transparency, the *distribution-related characteristics* largely center around the distributed database management system's ability to divide and distribute portions of databases in a flexible manner while maintaining all of the security, integrity, and control functionality of a single site database management system. This last point, the ability to effectively *manage* distributed databases is perhaps the single most important issue in the implementation of distributed database management systems. As will be seen, financial considerations of single-site versus distributed database management systems play a large role in final purchase decisions as well.

◆

Key Characteristics of Distributed Database Management Systems

Characteristics of distributed databases and their influence on networking considerations were first introduced in Chapter 4, local area networks (LANs) and LAN lookalikes.

The transparency of distributed database management systems mentioned above depends on that DBMS's ability to easily interoperate with a variety of operating systems, network operating systems, as well as other DBMS.

Operating System Compatibility

The *multiplatform* aspect of a DBMS refers to its ability to run on a variety of different server computers from the microcomputer, minicomputer, and mainframe classes. *Operating system compatibility* is the key issue when it comes to multiplatform operation. Listed below are the most popular operating systems in each of the three main categories of server computers.

Operating Systems

Microcomputer: DOS, OS/2, UNIX, Mac, Windows, Windows NT
Minicomputer: DEC VAX/VMS, DEC Ultrix, IBM AS/400 OS/400, IBM AIX, UNIX
Mainframe: IBM MVS, IBM VM

Start a DBMS search by considering only those systems with proven compatibility with the operating systems of choice. Do not depend on promises of the future delivery of enhanced software releases.

Transport Protocol Compatibility

The second compatibility issue has to do with the network operating system. More specifically, the *transport layer protocols* which will carry database requests and transactions across the enterprise network, must be compatible with the DBMS issuing those requests and transactions. Transport layer protocols were covered extensively in Chapters 5 and 6. The following is a listing of some of the transport-layer protocols with which a DBMS may need to be compatible and their associated networking environment.

Possible Transport Protocols

TCP/IP	Internet/UNIX
IPX/SPX	Novell Netware
SNA	IBM
ATP	Appletalk
DECnet	DEC
Netbios	DOS-Based LANs
VIPC	Vines
NetBEUI	LAN Manager

Database-to-Database Interoperability

The third compatibility issue concerns *database-to-database interoperability*. In cases where microcomputer-based servers must interact with minicomputer or mainframe-based servers, the microcomputer-based DBMS must be able to interoperate with the native database implementation on the minicomputer or mainframe. Just how this interoperability is accomplished can vary and will be explored in more depth in the database connectivity section of this chapter.

Two of the most popular minicomputer and mainframe-based database management systems are listed below. The two DBMS listed are distributed by the computer manufacturers themselves. Many additional third-party DBMS are installed on both the minicomputer and mainframe platforms. The real issue here is that if interaction is required between a microcomputer-based DBMS and a minicomputer or mainframe-based DBMS, make sure that the microcomputer-based DBMS has a proven methodology for providing such interoperability.

Minicomputer and Mainframe DBMS

Minicomputer: DEC Rdb
Mainframe: IBM DB2

Database Distribution Issues

The key distribution-related characteristics generally fall into two major categories:

Optimization of resources
Assurance of data integrity

Distributed Query Optimization When a database inquiry involving data which is physically located at multiple widely-distributed servers is generated, the impact on the overall resources of the distributed information system can vary significantly depending on exactly how that query is processed. Most distributed DBMS have some method for **distributed query optimization** which takes into account the three major elements of any distributed database inquiry:

Processing
Data
Network

These optimization routines determine the best method to retrieve the data, the best location at which to process that data, and the best network links over which to transport that data in order to maximize the effective use of the processing, database, and networking system resources. Exactly how the optimization is achieved may vary from one DBMS to another. Be sure that the distributed query optimization routine meets today's needs while offering the flexibility to continue to meet the future's distributed database query needs.

Distributed Database Integrity Issues In order to keep track of which data is stored on which distributed server, **global dictionaries** and **directories** must be maintained. How these global directories are updated and kept "in sync" with each other is a very important DBMS characteristic. Be especially aware of the network traffic generated in order to keep the global directories synchronized and up to date.

Many database integrity issues such as locking granularity and transaction rollback were addressed in Chapter 4. One integrity issue of particular importance to distributed DBMS is the transaction-related integrity process known as **two-phase commit.** When multiple distributed databases which are physically located on widely dispersed servers must all be updated as part of a transaction update, two-phase commit basically assures that either *all* required databases will be updated or *none* of the required databases will be updated. What happens to the "failed" two-phase commit transactions can vary from one DBMS to another and should be looked at very carefully.

If one server on a multiserver network goes down, or if the network link to a particular server goes down, no transactions will be posted during that time with a two-phase commit transaction process in place. This may not be acceptable in every business situation. Some businesses may prefer for the transaction to continue posting to those distributed servers that can be reached successfully. The posting of transactions to multiple databases that are connected via local or wide-area networks is an area of analysis requiring in-depth study before any distributed DBMS purchase decisions are reached. It is also an area of DBMS development which continues to evolve.

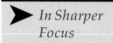 *In Sharper Focus*

DISTRIBUTED DATABASES TRIGGERS AND STORED PROCEDURES

When data located in multiple databases is related in some way that must be maintained as transactions are posted to any of the databases involved, the *integrity* of the data must be checked in some way. In this case, integrity refers to an assurance that the relationship between the data in multiple databases has been maintained. There are basically two ways in which integrity among distributed databases can be assured.

Triggers can be built into the application program that causes the transaction to be posted in the first place. The trigger creates an "integrity-assurance subroutine" to run that checks all the necessary distributed database fields involved and verifies that their current contents are correct based on the latest transaction.

Rather than have the transaction posting application program trigger the integrity check, the database definition itself can be written in such a way that if any particular field in the distributed database is updated, then the DBMS initiates a **stored procedure** or *declarative structure,* which performs all necessary integrity checking on the distributed databases involved. **Dependency tables** can be included in a database definition to indicate which fields depend on which other fields for database integrity assurance.

Front-End Tools Transform Distributed Data into Useful Information

Front-end tools and user programming environments were first introduced in Chapter 4. Although many client-based front-end tools exist for interaction with particular DBMSs, two approaches to front-end tools that take a much more open approach to front-end distributed DBMS interoperability will now be explored.

DDE Add-On Utilities

DDE (dynamic data exchange) utilities, also known as relay-point applications, provide a transparent interface between Windows applications and database servers. As an example, Microsoft Excel, a Windows-based front-end spreadsheet program, can query a variety of different database servers thanks to the transport services of a DDE utility by Pioneer known as Q+E. DDE is actually a protocol for the transfer of data between Windows-based applications.

The transport provided by these DDE utilities is the delivery of **SQL** (structured query language) statements, first introduced in Chapter 4, from the Windows application to the database server via the enterprise network. The delivery over the network is assured by encapsulating that SQL statement in the proper network transport protocol envelope. As discussed earlier, depending on the network operating system in question, that transport envelope may be TCP/IP, IPX/SPX, etc. Figure 9-12 illustrates the mechanics of such a Windows application-to-database server inquiry.

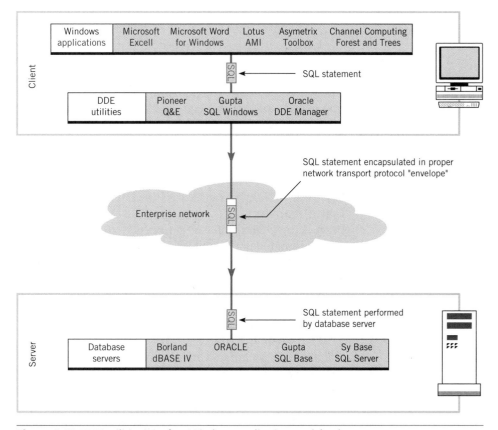

Figure 9-12 DDE utilities interface Windows applications and database servers.

This database server access from the Windows application is transparent to the user. For instance, from within Excel, a user can execute Q+E, choose which database is to be accessed, and build complex database queries within the point-and-click Windows environment. Meanwhile, Q+E is building the SQL (structured query language) statement without any need for the user to have any knowledge of proper SQL syntax. Upon execution, the SQL statement is transferred to the proper database server via the enterprise network.

The SQL statement is processed on the back-end database engine and only those records meeting the criteria specified in the SQL statement are returned to the client via the enterprise network. These records can then be received into the Excel spreadsheet for further analysis or manipulation. This entire process can be automated for nightly or weekly transfer and analysis of sales figures, inventory usage, etc.

▶ *In Sharper Focus*

EMERGING WINDOWS CONNECTIVITY STANDARDS: ODBC AND WOSA

Highlighting the evolution of client–server architectures and the connectivity schemes contained therein, DDE utilities may be deemed obsolete by a new interface, or API, added directly to Windows itself known as **ODBC** (open database connectivity). Microsoft, Oracle, and Sybase have jointly developed the ODBC driver to allow Windows applications to interact directly with database servers. Just as a network device driver prepares output for transport through the network interface card to the shared network media, the ODBC database driver formats Windows application output to be transported across the enterprise network for processing by database servers.

ODBC is the database-specific portion of a more encompassing Windows interoperability standard known as **WOSA** (windows open systems architecture). WOSA includes other APIs to allow Windows-based clients transparent access to distributed E-mail systems and other enterprise-network-based connectivity options. The primary objective of WOSA is to allow Windows-based clients to be used as transparent front-ends to any number of different back-end server platforms.

Front-End Tools for MultiPlatform Client–Server Applications Development

Besides the DDE utilities mentioned in the previous section, more sophisticated application development tools are required to enable users to develop their own customized client–server applications. Application development tools are available for most database servers, provided by either the database server vendor or by third parties. However, more significant are those front-end application development tools with the sophistication to develop applications for *multiple* database server environments.

One such multiple-platform application development tool is known as Uniface 4GL by Uniface Corporation. One of the unique features of Uniface 4GL is the wide choice of platforms supported by applications developed using Uniface 4GL. In addition to numerous operating systems, network operating systems, and database engines supported, through a feature known as the **universal presentation interface** (UPI), applications can be developed for numerous graphical user interfaces (GUI) other than the popular Windows GUI.

The UPI actually resides on each client on which Uniface-developed applications are deployed, offering full support of native GUI features, while running multiplatform database applications transparently to the user. For the application programmer, the UPI allows freedom from concern over the particular GUI of the client workstations on which the application will eventually be deployed. Figure 9-13 illustrates how Uniface's UPI allows application programmers to focus on applications development from the GUI, down.

Distributed Database Connectivity via SQL

SQL (structured query language) has been mentioned several times before as a structured language used to access data from relational databases. One problem with SQL, however, has to do with *extensions,* which were first mentioned as a standards-related issue in Chapter 1. SQL, as originally defined, offered options for vendor extensions to the basic language functionality. As a result, different vendor's versions of SQL cannot interoperate easily, if at all.

In an effort to rectify this situation, the *SQL Access Group* was formed. A consortium of database management users and vendors, the SQL Access Group has issued specifications to overcome the problems caused by vendor-specific SQL implementations. When evaluating products for SQL compatibility levels, be sure to look for *SQL Access Group Phase Level* compatibility.

Two of the recent proposed specifications from the SQL Access Group are

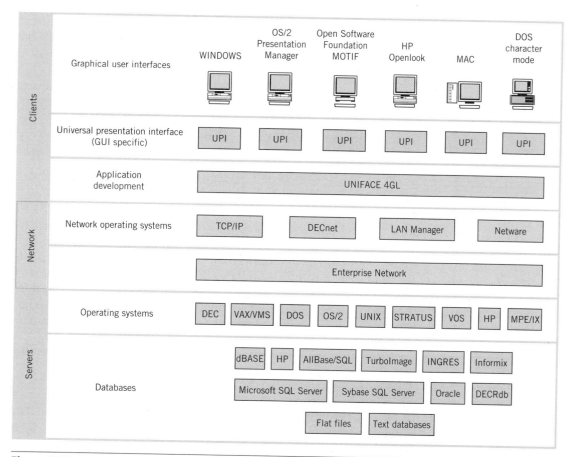

Figure 9-13 A multiple-platform, multiple GUI applications development platform: UNIFACE 4GL.

known as Phase II and Phase III. Phase II proposed the establishment of a **CLI** (call level interface), which would control the syntax of the SQL statements issued from a SQL-compliant client or server as an alternative to the vendor-specific, imbedded SQL APIs which have caused all of the incompatibility headaches. Microsoft Windows ODBC, Open Database Connectivity, includes the SQL Access Group's CLI specification. Phase II also specified support for TCP/IP as an internetwork transport protocol for SQL statements.

Phase III specifications include standardized procedures for stored procedures and two-phase commits, two distributed DBMS characteristics reviewed earlier in the distributed DBMS section. When and if all SQL distributed databases products are SQL Access Group Phase Level compliant, then any compliant client should be able to work with any compliant server in a truly *database-transparent* manner.

Lack of SQL Standardization Provides Market Opportunity

The lack of SQL standardization created by the numerous vendor-specific versions of the database access language, provided a market opportunity for a sort of *SQL middleware* which could translate transparently between the many versions of SQL implemented on different platforms and databases.

A product known as **EDA/SQL** (enterprise data access/SQL) from Information Builders Inc., has taken advantage of that market opportunity. Calling itself a universal data access system, EDA/SQL acts as a middleware layer, trapping SQL requests from clients and reformatting them as necessary before transporting them to the appropriate server.

Portions of the specially written software are deployed on clients, in order to interface to PC-based products such as Lotus 1-2-3. Server portions of the software are also available for IBM mainframes, DEC and HP minicomputers, UNIX processors such as IBM RS/6000, Sun, Pyramid, DEC, NCR, and Data General; and IBM OS/2 Lan Server and Novell Netware Servers. SQL data access to over 50 databases deployed on the previously mentioned servers is supported. EDA/SQL routing software, which runs on the mainframe, mini, and UNIX servers listed; is able to transport EDA/SQL queries to their appropriate servers on widely distributed database management systems.

◆ *Management Perspective*

A comprehensive transparent SQL middleware layer such as EDA/SQL is represented by the "universal data access system layer" in Figure 9-11. EDA/SQL represents a single vendor solution to the SQL incompatibility problem. However, any single vendor solution can be a problem in itself. Single vendor solutions are generally proprietary solutions, lacking in support of open systems standards and unable to guarantee wide-ranging interoperability. Be sure to carefully weigh the pros and cons of proprietary solutions such as EDA/SQL versus the standards-based solutions as proposed by the SQL Access Group before making any purchase decisions. ◆

Simpler Solutions for Simpler SQL Connectivity

If SQL connectivity needs do not entail several different distributed database management systems running on several different server platforms, then a simpler **SQL gateway** will probably meet SQL transport needs more easily and affordably. A gateway, as its name implies, is a single solution device linking a particular database/server combination with a different database/server combination while performing the necessary SQL syntax translation between the two. Such gateways are widely available, most often from one or both of the database vendors in question. Micro Decisionware is also a major database gateway vendor.

Software that goes beyond insuring merely SQL interoperability by providing transparent client–server links among various operating systems, network operating systems, and user interfaces fall more into the category of middleware, which will be studied shortly. Uniface 4GL is more than just middleware as it also offers a full-powered application development environment as well. Two other products that offer database transparency and then some, Oracle SQL*Net and Oracle Glue, will be analyzed further in the middleware section of this chapter.

THE ROLE OF ENTERPRISE NETWORKS: DELIVERING DISTRIBUTED PROCESSING AND DATABASES

The enterprise network is the transportation system of the client–server architecture. Together with middleware, it is responsible for the transparent cooperation of distributed processors and databases. In an analogy to a powerful standalone mainframe computer, the enterprise network would be analogous to that computer's system bus, linking the processing power of the CPU with the stored data to be processed.

The role of the enterprise network is to deliver the integration and interoperability enabled by the client–server architecture. Further, the enterprise network often also incorporates host-terminal traffic, voice traffic, and videoconferencing traffic in an integrated and well-managed fashion.

What Is an Enterprise Network?

What exactly does an enterprise network look like? That depends on what the business enterprise looks like. If the business enterprise is comprised of regional branches or subsidiaries widely dispersed geographically, then the enterprise network will obviously contain wide-area network links. From a physical standpoint, the enterprise network is most often the combination of network devices and connections of the following categories:

> Local area network (LAN)
> LAN-to-LAN or Inter-LAN
> Wide Area Network (WAN)

> Plus:

> Associated network management hardware and software capable of effectively supporting corporate requirements for distributed information systems.

From this description, it can be seen that there is not a great deal of new technology or concepts involved with enterprise networking, but rather a synthesis of many of the areas of data communications and networking which have been studied to this point.

Basic Concepts of Enterprise Networks

Enterprise networks are most often described in terms of *architecture* and *backbones*. Although the terms are often used arbitrarily or interchangeably, the two terms will be differentiated with the help of the OSI model. Figure 9-14 illustrates the relationship of *enterprise network architectures* and *enterprise network backbones*.

OSI Model Layer	Enterprise Network Element	Options
Application		Centralized Hierarchical Distributed Peer-to-peer Hybrid
Presentation	Architecture	
Session		
Transport		
Network		
Data Link	Backbone	Distributed Collapsed Hybrid
Physical		

Figure 9-14 Enterprise network architectures and backbones.

Architectures

Enterprise Network architectures are most often described as *centralized* or *distributed*.

Centralized   **Centralized architectures,** also known as hierarchical architectures, are similar to the classic IBM SNA architecture in which all use of the network was controlled by a single computer. It is important to differentiate between computer usage for simple processing or network control. A centralized or hierarchical network may include several computers or processors. However, only *one* of those processors is loaded with the appropriate software to negotiate all possible network connections between all attached devices. Figure 9-15 illustrates a centralized or hierarchical network architecture.

Distributed   **Distributed architectures,** also known as peer-to-peer architectures, equip *all* networked processors with the necessary software required to set up network connections to any other network attached device. In other words, every device is network-capable and network-aware. DECnet, DEC's Ethernet network operating system, is an example of a distributed network architecture. Figure 9-16 illustrates a distributed or peer-to-peer network architecture.

Hybrid   Each of the previous examples are single vendor networks. The multivendor, multiprotocol, open systems more common to the client–server architectures do not lend themselves as easily to categorization as either a centralized or distributed network architecture. Depending on the particular combination of clients, servers, operating systems, network operating systems, databases, and E-mail systems, some combination of centralized and distributed network architecture elements may be combined in order to deliver required functionality and interoperability to the end-users. Such a network is known as a **hybrid network architecture.** Figure 9-17 illustrates a hybrid network architecture. Note the distributed and centralized elements within the hybrid architecture.

These network architecture categories are really for descriptive or discussion purposes only. One does not start an enterprise network design by deciding which network architecture to employ. On the contrary, the network architecture is the

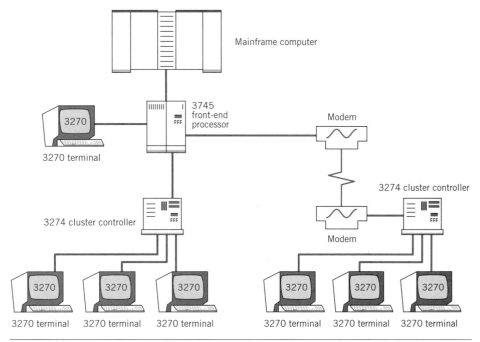

Figure 9-15 Centralized or hierarchical enterprise network architecture.

end-product rather than the starting point of enterprise network design. As stated in the previous paragraph, functionality and interoperability as required by end-users are the driving forces behind enterprise network design. Delivering the right information, in the right format, to the right decision-maker, at the right time and place, for the right price, remains the goal of any enterprise network. How the top-down model once again plays a major role in helping to structure this enterprise network design process will be reiterated shortly.

Backbones

While architectures are concerned with the installation and distribution of networking and connectivity *software* and its associated functionality, backbones are more concerned with networking and connectivity *hardware* and its associated functionality. Enterprise network backbones are normally categorized as either *distributed* or *collapsed*. As with enterprise network architectures, a combination of the two concepts yields a *hybrid* enterprise network backbone.

All backbones, whether distributed or collapsed have certain things in common. For instance, a true enterprise network backbone should provide most if not all of the following capabilities:

Carry different types of traffic (voice, video, LAN data, host/terminal data, fax)
Carry multiple data protocols (SNA/SDLC, TCP/IP, IPX)
Provide intra-LAN connections
Provide inter-LAN connections
Provide WAN connections
Operate reliably and securely
Support multiple media type connections

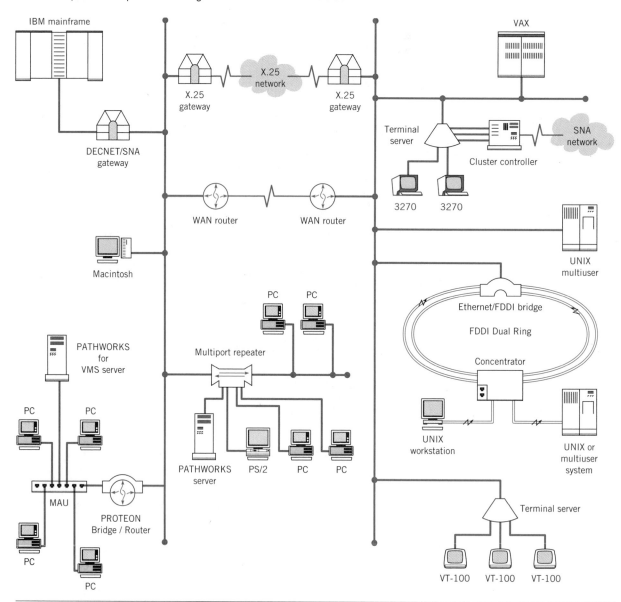

Figure 9-16 Distributed or peer-to-peer enterprise network architecture.

Operate at speeds sufficient to support business operations effectively, ideally at speeds that allow the backbone to achieve transparent operation

Distributed   Traditionally, enterprise network backbones have been of the distributed variety. An Ethernet backbone running between the floors of a building with each individual floor's LAN segment attached to it via repeaters or bridges is a good example of a distributed backbone. Figure 9-18 illustrates such a distributed backbone.

Collapsed   A recent enterprise networking phenomenon, known as the **collapsed backbone,** has come about through the development of internetworking

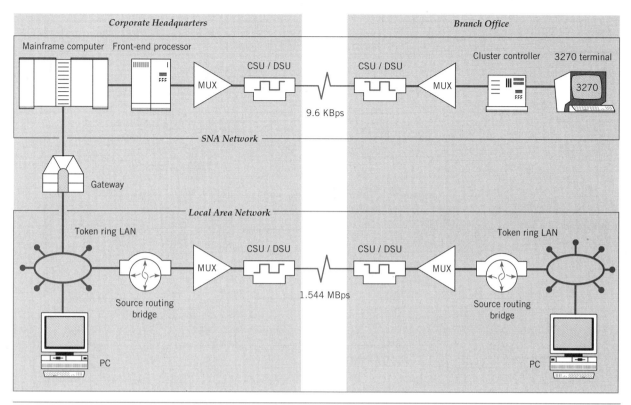

Figure 9-17 Hybrid enterprise network architecture.

devices such as hubs and routers. The backbone portion of the device is referred to as "collapsed" because the entire building backbone, which once spanned several floors, has now been "collapsed" onto the backplane of a specially-designed, high-powered internetworking device. These collapsed enterprise network devices are often called LAN superhubs and were first introduced in Chapter 5. Figure 9-19 highlights both the collapsed backbone of such a device as well as an implementation scenario to be contrasted with the distributed network backbone pictured in Figure 9-18.

◆ *Management Perspective*

The collapsed backbones within these superhubs transport internetwork traffic at speeds according to MAC layer protocols. In other words, Ethernet is transmitted at 10Mbps, Token Ring at 4 or 16Mbps, and FDDI at 100 Mbps. In order to prevent bottlenecks over this collapsed backbone, the backbone itself has much higher transmission capacities, in the range of 320 Mbps to 1Gbps. This total actual backbone bandwidth is important when evaluating the potential performance of collapsed backbone devices.

The overall hub backplane actually consists of multiple physical channels for each protocol's backbone. Furthermore, actual collapsed backbone and hub backplane design often varies by vendor and is proprietary. Although the design can have a great effect on performance, the best assurance of appropriate purchase choice is an in-house trial, with a company's own unique mix of network traffic.

◆

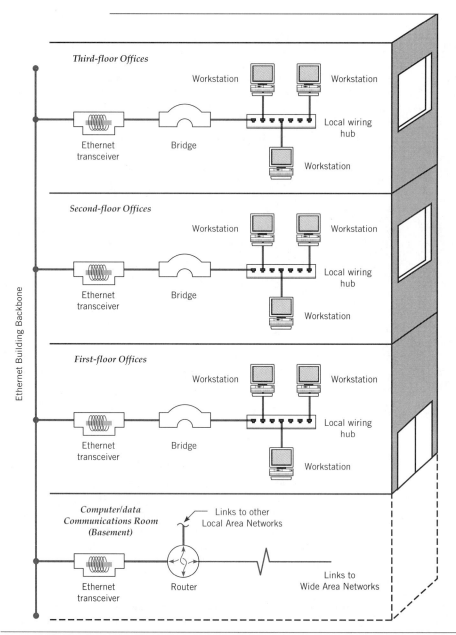

Figure 9-18 Distributed backbone.

▶ *In Sharper*
   Focus

ADVANTAGE OF COLLAPSED BACKBONES IN SUPERHUBS

It should be obvious from Figure 9-19 that all network and internetwork processing is completed by various modules within the superhub via the collapsed backbone. In other words, *all* network traffic travels through the hub. The advantage of this is that it presents a wonderful opportunity for intelligent network monitoring and management. Less sophisticated network management techniques such as looking at the LEDs on any superhub for alarm conditions are also possible. With all bridges in a single location there is no need for a network technician to run to the third floor to see what the lights on the bridge are doing.

"Collapsed" onto a Hub Backplane

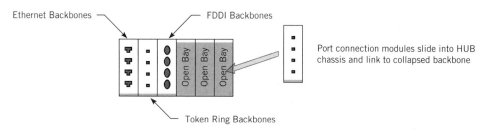

Ethernet Backbones

FDDI Backbones

Port connection modules slide into HUB chassis and link to collapsed backbone

Token Ring Backbones

Implementation

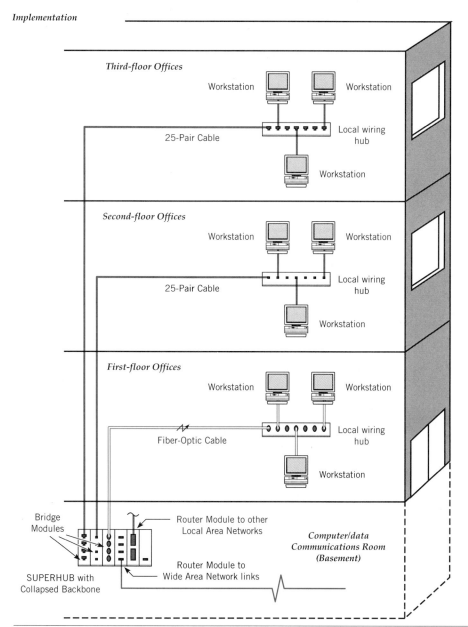

Figure 9-19 Collapsed backbone.

What better spot to monitor and manage data than where one is guaranteed that all data must travel? As a result, sophisticated enterprise network management modules are also available to be slid into empty slots of the superhub chassis.

Another advantage of the modular approach taken by many superhub vendors is that as new, improved networking technology is introduced, that technology can be distributed to the entire enterprise network by simply sliding a new module into the superhub.

One such new technology is ATM (asynchronous transfer mode), which was discussed in detail in Chapter 8. As bandwidth demands increase, switched rather than shared media backbones will become the enterprise network backbones of the future. The Ethernet switch discussed in Chapter 6 is an example of a current implementation of a switched LAN backbone. ATM with its enormous potential bandwidth and ability to carry voice and video as well as data, looks as if it may be the enterprise network backbone of the future.

The Disadvantage of Collapsed Backbones in Superhubs

The fact that all traffic flows through the collapsed backbone is a double-edged sword. As may have been guessed, the superhub also represents a marvelous *single point of failure*. To overcome this, vendors of collapsed backbone superhubs have built in several reliability features. Besides the multiple backbones for redundancy mentioned previously, other superhub reliability features might include multiple redundant power supplies, built-in uninterruptable power sources, and "hot-swappable" cards that allow one bad module to be swapped out without shutting down the entire superhub.

◄

Structured Enterprise Network Design

Although many of the overall aspects of network design will be covered in Chapter 12, "The Network Development Life Cycle," it is important to introduce at this point a few structured techniques for organizing enterprise network requirements. As was first seen in Figure 9-14, any enterprise network can be easily related to the OSI 7-layer reference model.

In order to begin to document networking requirements for an enterprise network, one must first have a node-by-node protocol stack analysis for each and every node to be connected to the enterprise network.

However, when it comes to client–server architectures, the truly unique aspect of enterprise networks, the OSI model does not structure all required information about each client or server in an easy to use format.

The Client Server Top-Down Model for Enterprise Network Analysis and Design

An enhancement of the top-down model becomes an easy-to-use yet well structured tool for the documentation of client–server architecture requirements. Like the OSI model, the client–server top-down model can help uncover unknown connectivity problems or highlight areas requiring further investigation. Figure 9-20 illustrates the client–server top-down model for enterprise network analysis and design.

Figure 9-20 should be looked upon as a starting point or framework for the structured documentation of client–server architecture requirements. As can be seen, once overall business issues and justification have been addressed, subsequent layers are subdivided into those issues surrounding:

Business	What business activity will this client/server link be engaged in? Optional: What is the financial justification or priority of this business activity? How important is this client–server link? Can the costs of this link be justified?			
Application	**Client**	**Middleware**	**Server**	**Management**
	Client tools? E-mail processing requirements?	E-mail gateways?	Distributed processing server? E-mail server?	How will this particular client/server interaction be monitored/ managed?
Data	Database front-end?	Database connectivity software? SQL? EDA/SQL? SQL*NET?	Database server/ engine?	How will this particular client/server interaction be monitored/ managed?
Network	Client network operating system?	APIs? Named pipes? NETBIOS? Transport protocol? TCP/IP? IPX/SPX?	Server network operating system?	How will this particular client/server interaction be monitored managed?
Technology	Client operating system? Media?	Compatibility problems? Gateway solutions? Media interface converters?	Server operating system Media?	How will this particular client/server interaction be monitored/ managed?

Figure 9-20 Client/server top-down model for enterprise network analysis and design.

> Client
> Middleware
> Server
> Management of the client–server interaction

One such model would be completed for each potential client–server link on an enterprise network. As an example: if a network had Windows, MAC, and UNIX clients and UNIX, Netware, and VAX servers, and all three client types were going to need to interact with all three servers in some manner, then a total of nine such models would be completed (3 clients × 3 servers = 9 client–server links). The exact nature of each of the client–server interactions would be detailed on individual models. Thus if the UNIX client needed file transfer, E-mail, and database access to the netware server, but only E-mail access to the VAX, that could be clearly documented on the respective models.

When filling out such models, don't feel as if all the answers must be known or that all blocks must be filled in. A blank block only represents a data communications solution yet to be found. The management aspects of the *entire* client–server architecture, not just the enterprise network, will be explored in the next section. At that time, the top-down model may be further modified in order to more accu-

Business	**Management**		
	Who will be responsible for the management of the various elements of the client–server architecture? Does a distributed information system suggest a distributed management structure or is this a job for a centralized MIS department?		

Application	Management		
	Client	Middleware	Server
	Client tools E-Mail	E-Mail. Gateways	Distributed processing server E-Mail server

Data	Management		
	Client	Middleware	Server
	Database front-end	Database connectivity software	Database server

Network	Management		
	Client	Middleware	Server
	Network operating system Multiprotocol software	APIs	File server Communications server

Technology	Management		
	Client	Middleware	Server
	Client operating system Media	Gateways Media interface converter	Server operating system

Processing Elements

	Management		
	LAN	Inter-LAN	WAN
	Hubs	Repeaters Routers Bridges Gateways	WAN routers PADS/packet Switches FRADS/frame relay Switches ISDN terminal Adapters MUXES/modems

Networking Elements

Figure 9-21 Manageable elements in a client–server architecture.

rately reflect the management requirements and solutions of the client–server architecture.

The use of such structured requirements models or frameworks will be incorporated into the discussion of the process of client–server architecture analysis and design later in this chapter.

☐ MANAGEMENT OF THE CLIENT–SERVER ARCHITECTURE

Client–Server Components to be Managed

In order to understand the complexity of a *comprehensive* management system for a client–server architecture, one only needs to examine the vast array of components within that architecture that can potentially require management. Figure 9-21 takes the client–server adaptation of the top-down model and lists a representative sample of manageable elements. Although many of these elements first appeared in Figure 9-20, several networking devices and links have been added to the technology layer.

Most, if not all, of the client–server architecture elements listed in Figure 9-21 are available with some sort of management system or software. The problem is that there is little if any similarity or consistency in management system design among various vendors, even for elements of similar function. In addition, the multiple layers of management evident in Figure 9-21 present a management system integration problem of major proportion.

Users do not want "piecemeal" system management caused by the distributed nature of their information systems. They do not wish separate management consoles or systems for database systems, operating systems, network operating systems, and networking hardware. Furthermore, since the client–server architecture can feature multiple client and server operating systems and network operating systems, it can be seen how one could potentially need an entire room just for systems consoles for the management of the various client and server possibilities.

The solution to the management system integration problem comes down to a few key questions surrounding *standards:*

Can management system standards be developed that lend themselves especially well to distributed information systems?

More importantly, can and will these standards be adhered to by the manufacturers of the various elements of the client–server architecture as listed in Figure 9-21?

In the remainder of this section on the management of client–server architectures, the extent to which existing and emerging management standards define an integrated management structure for client–server management will be examined. Recent attempts to deliver *integrated* client–server management tools as well as current implementations of various vendor's enterprise network management systems will also be investigated.

Integrated Client–Server Management

It is important to distinguish between **integrated client–server management** and **enterprise network management.** Further summarizing the elements of Figure 9-21, integrated client–server management systems can be defined as being able to manage the following major components:

Distributed processing system
Database distribution system
Enterprise network

Although there are many multivendor enterprise network management systems, most so-called integrated client–server management systems are still in the "vaporware" stage. Note that enterprise network management is only one component of the overall integrated client–server management.

In order to parallel the distributed nature of the processing, database, and network as listed above, it should stand to reason that the management of these distributed systems should be distributed as well. Distributed management systems must manage a wide variety of networking and processing devices manufactured by numerous manufacturers. Standards for the gathering, structuring, and reporting of this distributed management data are essential to the success of any distributed information system.

The Role of Standards in Client–Server Management: Management Architecture Basics

In order to understand the standards that govern the management of enterprise networks and other elements of the client–server architecture, one must first understand the environment in which these standards must operate. There are really only three basic pieces to the enterprise network management puzzle.

Agents are software programs that run on networking devices such as servers, bridges, and routers to monitor and report the status of those devices.

Agents from the numerous individual networking devices forward this network management information to **managers** which compile and report network operation statistics to the end user, most often in some type of graphical format. Managers are really management application programs running on a management server.

The network management information gathered must be stored in some type of database with an index and standardized field definitions so that network management workstations can easily access this data. A **MIB** (management information base) as these databases are known, can differ in the fields defined for different vendor's networking devices. These fields within the MIBs are known as **objects.** One fairly standard MIB is known as the **RMON MIB,** which stands for remote network monitoring MIB. Figure 9-22 illustrates the relationship between agents, managers, and MIBs.

Standards for Agents, Managers, and MIBs

Although the entities of managers, agents, and MIBs may be named differently in different network management systems, the basic functions of these entities and the relationship between them are fairly universal. What can differ from one network management system to another are the protocols or standards that govern the structure and transmission of the network management information shared by the managers and agents.

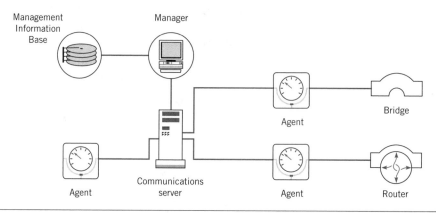

Figure 9-22 Agents, managers, and MIBs.

Several multiprotocol, multivendor network management systems exist. Among the most popular of these multivendor network management platforms, sometimes known as distributed management systems, are:

Network Management System	Vendor
Netview	IBM
DECmcc	DEC
Openview	HP
Sunnet Manager	Sun
Netware Management System	Novell

These various network management platforms differ in a relatively small number of ways:

Client (network management workstation) operating system and GUI supported (Windows, OS/2, Motif)

Server operating system supported (OS/2, VMS, UNIX)

Type(s) of databases supported for storage of network management information (proprietary, SQL compliant, Btrieve)

Management information and transport protocols

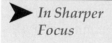
In Sharper Focus

STANDARDS FOR MANAGEMENT INFORMATION TRANSPORT PROTOCOLS

The most important way in which distributed management systems may differ is in the management information structure and transport protocols supported. Figure 9-23 summarizes information regarding the primary standards for distributed network management protocols.

As the various acronyms in Figure 9-23 are examined, some patterns should be obvious. There are basically two camps in the nonproprietary network management protocol world:

CMIP and its variations: **CMOT** and **CMOL**

SNMP and its recent update: **SNMP2,** also known as **SMP.**

This polarization of network management protocols corresponds to the long-standing philosophical arguments between the supporters of the overall protocol stacks associated with network management protocols, namely:

Protocol Acronym	Protocol Name	Transport Protocol (runs over)
SNMP	Simple Network Management Protocol	TCP/IP
CMIP	Common Management Information Protocol	OSI
CMOT	CMIP Over TCP/IP	TCP/IP
CMOL	CMIP Over LLC (Logical Link Control) (IEEE 802.2)	LLC (Part of Data Link Layer of most LANs)
SNMP2	SNMP2 is also called SMP: Simple Management Protocol	TCP/IP IPX OSI AppleTalk

Figure 9-23 Distributed network management protocols.

OSI, or open systems interconnect protocol stack
TCP/IP, also known as the internet suite of protocols

Since this book is about *applied* data communications, those network management protocols most often applied will be stressed, thus avoiding the philosophical arguments between the two camps. SNMP is deployed over ten times as often as CMIP. This is due largely to the popularity of the transport protocol that delivers SNMP data, namely TCP/IP.

SNMP and SNMP2

SNMP (simple network management protocol) is nothing more than a standard that defines the formatting of packets containing network management information. These SNMP packets are then transported over TCP/IP networks through the use of a connectionless datagram service known as UDP (user datagram protocol), part of the TCP/IP stack. It may be recalled from Chapter 7 that the most efficient way to send numerous, short messages quickly over a network is connectionless datagrams.

All of these network management datagrams constantly being transmitted between managers and numerous agents over enterprise networks can lead to a significant amount of network traffic. It should follow that as the size of the network increases, the number of networked devices increases, the number of network device agents increases, and the number of network management information datagrams increases, thus leading to an escalating network traffic problem.

SNMP2 Solves SNMP's Problems and Shortcomings

The need to reduce network traffic caused by the SNMP protocol, as well as deal with several other shortcomings, led to a proposal for a new version of SNMP known as SNMP2, or SMP (simple management protocol).

SNMP2's major objectives, which will be explained individually, can be summarized as follows:

Reduce network traffic
Segment large networks
Support multiple transport protocols
Increase security
Allow multiple agents per device

Reduce Network Traffic: Through a new SNMP2 procedure known as **bulk retrieval mechanism,** managers can retrieve several pieces of network information at a time from a given agent. This precludes the need for a constant request and reply mechanism for each and every piece of network management information desired. Agents have also been given increased intelligence that enables them to send error or exception conditions to managers when requests for information cannot be met. With SNMP, agents simply sent empty datagrams back to managers when requests could not be fulfilled. The receipt of the empty packet merely caused the manager to repeat the request for information, thus increasing network traffic.

Segment Large Networks: SMNP2 allows the establishment of multiple manager entities within a single network. Therefore, large networks that were managed by a single manager under SNMP, can now be managed by multiple managers in a hierarchical arrangement in SNMP2. Overall network traffic is reduced as network management information is confined to the management domains of the individual network segment managers. Information is only passed from the segment managers to the centralized network management system via manager-to-manager communication upon request of the central manager or if certain predefined error conditions occur on a subnet. Figure 9-24 illustrates the impact of SNMP2 manager-to-manager communications.

Support Multiple Transport Protocols: SNMP was initially part of the internet suite of protocols and therefore was only deployed on those networks equipped with the TCP/IP protocols. Those networks that did not possess "native" TCP/IP could employ multiprotocol software as explored in Chapter 6. SNMP2 precludes

Before: Manager-to-Agent Communications

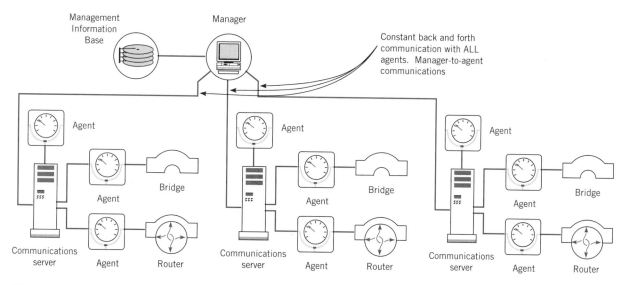

After: Manager-to-Manager Communications

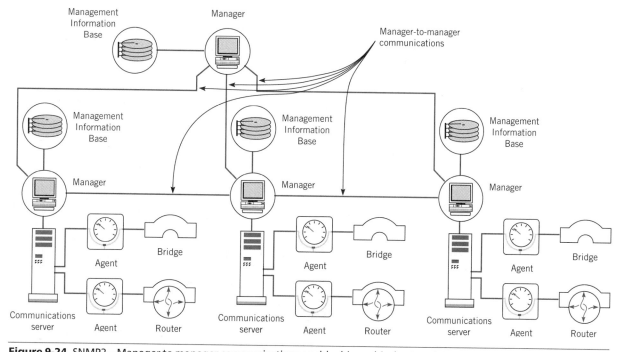

Figure 9-24 SNMP2—Manager to manager communications enables hierarchical network management.

the need for this extra software on Appletalk, Novell Netware, and OSI networks by now working transparently with Appletalk, IPX, and OSI transport protocols.

Increased Security: Increased security in SNMP2 allows not just monitoring and management of remote network devices, but actual *remote configuration* as well. Furthermore, SNMP2 or a variation of SNMP known as **secure SNMP,** will allow users to access carriers' network management information and incorporate it into the wide area component of an enterprise network management system. This ability to actually access data from within the carrier's central office has powerful implications for users and enables many advanced user services such as SDN (software defined network), which will be explored in the next chapter. SDN is just one of several services that will take advantage of increased transparency for users into carriers' central offices in an overall trend known as "The Intelligent Network."

Multiple Agents/Device Holds Promise for Client–Server Management

Perhaps the most significant SNMP2 development in terms of implication for distributed client–server management is the ability to deploy *multiple agents per device.* As a practical example, on a distributed server, one agent can monitor the processing activity, a second agent can monitor the database activity, and a third can monitor the networking activity, with each reporting back to their own manager!

In this way, rather than having merely distributed enterprise *network* management, the entire *distributed information system* can be managed, with each major element of the client–server architecture managed by its own management infrastructure.

Referring back to Figure 9-21, which represents a logical model of each element of the client–server architecture managed by its own management infrastructure, it can be seen that SNMP2 may be the enabling standard which will turn this logical model into a physical reality.

SNMP and SNMP2: NonProprietary Protocols

Because SNMP and SNMP2 are nonproprietary protocols, independent software and hardware developers can create products that incorporate SNMP agents and/or managers. One such product which deserves mention is LANlord by Microcom, the company responsible for the MNP classes of modem communication protocols.

LANlord extends SNMP management protocol beyond the typical networking devices such as servers, bridges, and routers, all the way to end-user workstations. Using its own MIB definition with over 200 defined objects, LANlord is able to monitor and control the software and hardware for up to 500 PCs running on a Novell network.

APIs available for LANlord allow other programs to react to the conditions which LANlord reports via SNMP. The possibilities for applications are limited only by the imagination.

The 500-device limit, the limitation to Netware, or this particular product are not really what's important here. What's important to grasp is the potential power of standards such as SNMP and SNMP2 when put to creative use. If client–server architectures are to ever become the standard information-systems architecture, or paradigm, then comprehensive, integrated, distributed management systems are a prerequisite. Nonproprietary distributed management information standards such as SNMP and SNMP2 are the fuel which will power the drive to these powerful management systems of the future.

☐ MIDDLEWARE: HOLDING TOGETHER THE CLIENT–SERVER ARCHITECTURE

Now that the respective roles of distributed applications, distributed data, and the enterprise network are understood, it is time to investigate how distributed information systems can be developed to interconnect the myriad combinations of client and server platforms.

Applications, whether the client or server portion, will only run on a given platform if all of the protocols in the 7-layer OSI reference model protocol stack for that particular node are compatible with each other. Recalling discussions from earlier in the text, upper-level protocols are encapsulated within lower-layer protocols. As each successive upper layer is "removed" from its lower layer "envelope," the current layer's protocol contents within that envelope must be capable of being processed properly in order to assure continued communication up and down the protocol stack.

One way in which assurance that a given application will run on a given client or server platform can be gained, is for the programming team to write not only the application layer software but also the *communications software* necessary for this application to interface properly to the enterprise network. This process is very tedious and must be rewritten for each different combination of client and server platforms.

If a company decides to bring in a new server or client platform, all applications programs would have to be rewritten since the communications software was imbedded within the applications software. It is not difficult to see the impracticality of this method of distributed application development.

What could improve this situation would be a transparency layer similar to the data transparency layer pictured in Figure 9-11, which would provide transparency between the *distributed application layer* and the *enterprise network layer* in the client–server architecture. This transparency providing layer has been termed **middleware.** The need for such a layer of transparency was first introduced in Figure 9-8. The relative position of middleware within the client–server architecture is illustrated in Figure 9-25.

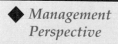

Middleware Functionality

From a functional standpoint, middleware allows distributed applications to communicate across the enterprise network transparently to the particular hardware platform, operating system, or networking protocols installed on a particular client or server. In doing so, middleware assures interoperability of distributed applications regardless of the configuration of the underlying enterprise network backbone.

From a business perspective, middleware allows applications programmers to program distributed applications without having to also program the highly technical underlying network communications software as well.

♦

Middleware and the OSI Model

The transparency offered by middleware to distributed applications can be delineated in terms of the OSI model. This transparency has to span the OSI layers and their associated implementation issues as illustrated in Figure 9-26.

Middleware Establishes Multiple Sessions Realizing that a single client or server may be running multiple applications (multitasking) or that a single appli-

Architectural

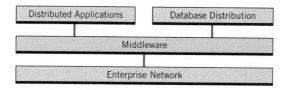

Functional

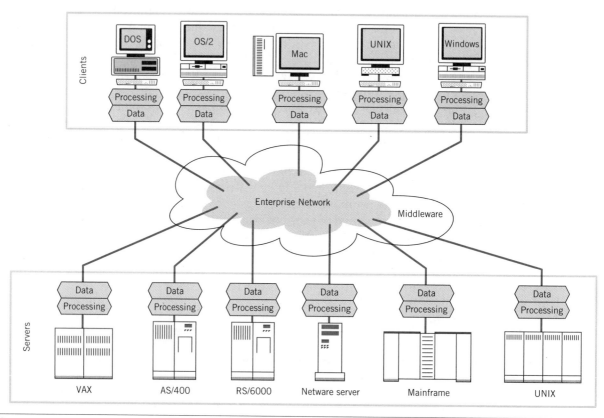

Figure 9-25 Middleware's role in the client–server architecture.

cation may have a need to communicate to more than one other program simultaneously (multithreading), how does middleware address this issue in terms of the OSI model? The answer is *by establishing multiple sessions.*

Individual sessions, which are called **TCP sockets** in the TCP/IP world, are established for each required communication between distributed processes. These communications between processes can take many different forms but are often referred to generically as **inter-process communications** or **IPC**s. Figure 9-27 illustrates the establishment of multiple sessions in relation to the OSI model.

To summarize, in terms of the OSI model, middleware offers transparency between distributed applications (layer 7) and the enterprise network (layers 1–4). In addition, middleware can establish multiple sessions (layer 5) in order to support multiple interprocess communications (IPCs) for each distributed application (layer 7).

No.	OSI Layer	Implementation Issue	Example(s)
		Middleware—Delivered Transparency	
4	Transport	Network transport protocols	TCP/IP, IPX
3	Network	Network Operating Systems	Netware, DECnet
2	Data-Link	Network Architecture	Ethernet, Token Ring
1	Physical	Media	UTP, Coax, Fiber

Figure 9-26 Middleware and the OSI model: Transparency delivered.

Delivering Network Transparency

Before fully understanding the functionality of middleware, one must first understand how distributed applications communicate with each other without the benefit of middleware. As has been previously stated, *network protocol dependent* communications programming has to be added to the applications programming.

A fitting analogy might be that if in order to place a long-distance call, each user would have to first delineate which central office switches and which interswitch protocols should be employed to establish the connection before beginning a conversation. In this case, the phone switch software that reads the source and

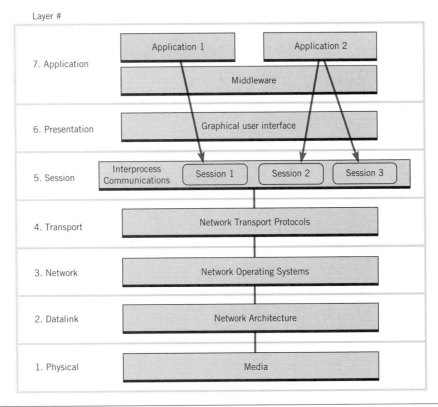

Figure 9-27 Middleware and the OSI model: Multiple sessions established.

destination phone numbers and establishes the circuit-switched connection, *transparently to the user*, is fulfilling the role of middleware.

Network Transport Protocols APIs

To return to the client–server architecture, each network transport protocol offers an API (application program interface) to which commands can be passed from application programs. The syntax of this command includes sufficient information to indicate the location of and path to the destination server, establish a session to the destination server, and authorize the requesting application's authority to access that destination server.

As stated previously, the real drawback is that each of the network transport protocol APIs follows a different syntax, obligating application programmers to customize application programs dependent on client and server technology deployment at any point in time. Figure 9-28 illustrates network transport APIs and their relationship to API-specific application programs.

Some of these network transport protocol APIs are quite complicated, employing over 30 different commands, or verbs, as well as several possible error conditions for each and every verb.

Middleware Replaces Network Specific APIs

In comparison, most middleware employs less than ten verbs, with some products featuring less than five. This full-functionality without over-complication is compounded by the fact that these same few middleware verbs are used *regardless of the network protocol API or server platform*. The real demand for middleware stems from the impracticality of developing and supporting several unique versions of every distributed application, dependent on client, network, and server combinations.

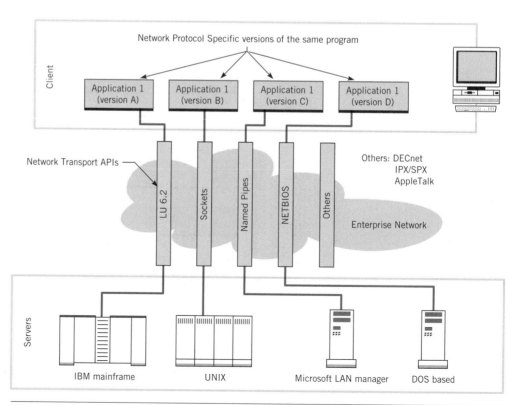

Figure 9-28 Network transport APIs require unique programming.

As a matter of fact, it is probably safe to say that were it not for middleware, the widespread deployment of client–server architectures would be called into serious question. Middleware delivers network transparency by offering a single set of commands which, in turn, interface to the various network protocol APIs previously mentioned, and write the network protocol specific commands on behalf of the end-user.

Middleware itself is really a "super-API" which interfaces to the network-specific APIs. By delivering network transparency to distributed applications, middleware is able to eliminate the need for and expense of development of network-specific distributed applications. Client and server portions of distributed applications can be developed independently. In fact, client-based applications can be developed without regard for the server which will interact with this client.

Figure 9-29 illustrates how middleware interacts with a variety of network protocol APIs to yield network transparency for distributed applications.

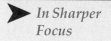

In Sharper Focus

MIDDLEWARE DELIVERS A VARIETY OF INTERPROCESS COMMUNICATIONS NEEDS

Middleware is actually a fairly general category of software. The general category of middleware can be broken down into several subcategories based upon the nature of the interprocess communication enabled by the middleware. Four major subcategories of middleware can be identified in this manner. Most middleware products deliver only one of these subcategories of functionality, although a few deliver multiple functional subcategories. The subcategories of middleware are illustrated in Figure 9-30 and summarized below.

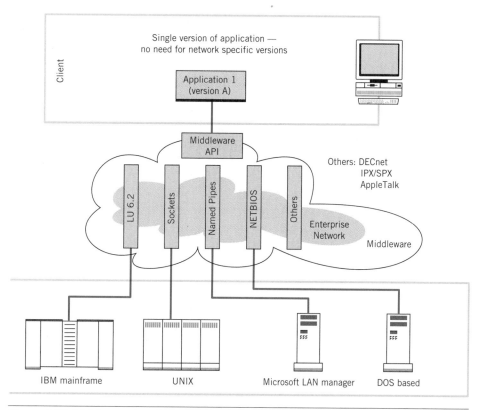

Figure 9-29 Middleware interfaces with Network Transport Protocol APIs.

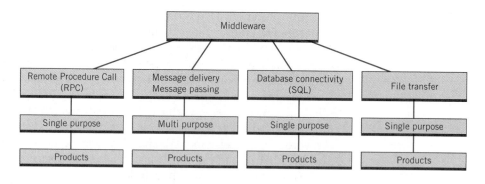

Most Middleware products fulfill only one functionality category

Figure 9-30 Major subcategories of middleware.

RPC: Remote Procedure Call

RPC (remote procedure call) middleware works in a manner similar to a locally run application program which activates, or calls, a subroutine stored outside of the application program itself, but usually in a subroutine library on the same computer. The major difference with the remote procedure call is that the call for the execution of a subroutine is made to a remote procedure located on a distributed processor via the enterprise network. Where that particular server is located and how the remote procedure call will get transported are the concerns of the RPC middleware rather than the applications programmer.

RPCs are like local subroutines in at least one other characteristic as well. When an application program branches to a subroutine, whether a local or a remote procedure, that application program waits for the local or remote procedure to complete execution and return either data or some type of status message before continuing with its own program execution. This style of interprocess communication can be categorized as **send-and-wait.**

The RPC middleware actually consists of the application development tools necessary to build separate client and server-based distributed applications with imbedded remote procedure calls. **Stubs** are specially coded lines of the applications program added by the RPC tool to allow the client and server portions of distributed application to interface to the network transport protocol API as illustrated in Figure 9-29.

SQL: Structured Query Language for Database Interaction

SQL, mentioned earlier in the Database Distribution portion of this chapter, is roughly the equivalent of a more specialized version of RPC. Rather than just initiate a remote application or procedure, SQL initiates *database* interaction with remote database servers and returns database server responses to the inquiring client. This style of interprocess communication can still be characterized as *send-and-wait.* SQL connectivity products, or SQL middleware, is often supplied by the vendors of the databases themselves.

For instance, Oracle's SQL*Net allows clients on virtually any platform to access databases on nearly any server, via any network protocol. In some cases, SQL middleware goes beyond database inquiry transparency over the enterprise network. Oracle also markets a product known as PL(procedural language)/SQL. Stored procedures associated with particular database fields can be written in this language. When a field with a stored procedure is accessed or updated, that stored procedure is executed.

None of this may sound out of the ordinary until it is considered that the stored procedure can access remote servers transparently as well. Thus, a local client could transparently update the database on a remote server which would, in turn, cause a stored procedure to update other databases on other remote servers, all completely transparent to the original end-user.

File Transfer

Not all distributed information systems require on-line, realtime, up-to-the-minute, record-by-record updates of data. Many systems only require daily or nightly transfer or backup of updated files from one platform to another. These platforms may be from various manufacturers, running various operating systems, and be connected to enterprise networks employing a variety of network transport protocols.

File transfer middleware seeks to ease the burden of initiating and managing file transfers in a multiplatform environment. The word multiplatform is key here. As was seen earlier in the text, there are a large assortment of excellent file transfer packages for the PC and LAN world. Most minicomputer and mainframe operating systems come with their own file transfer utilities. The problem arises when one breaks out of the boundaries of the local platform into the multiplatform file transfer arena.

File transfer middleware offers APIs, just like the previous two types of middleware examined, so that multiplatform file transfer functionality can be built into distributed applications without regard to the underlying network complexities. File transfer middleware offers many of the same features mentioned in our reviews of PC-based file transfer and communications packages. Timed batch jobs, multiple simultaneous transfers, format conversion, and error detection/correction are but a few of the features to be found in file transfer middleware.

Message Delivery: More than Just APIs

Message delivery, also known as message passing, message queueing, and distributed messaging, differs significantly from the previously mentioned middleware subcategories in its ability to establish various types of interprocess communications modes other than the send-and-wait mode of the previously mentioned middleware APIs.

For instance, distributed applications programs can communicate indirectly with the help of message queues, which are roughly equivalent to post offices. In this scenario, a distributed application generates a message for another distributed application, forwards it to the message queue, and resumes its own processing activity. This type of interprocess dialogue is known as *asynchronous*, not to be confused with asynchronous transmission.

Another interprocess dialogue type supported by message delivery middleware is broadcast (or multicast) dialogues. A broadcast sends messages to all clients and/or servers on an enterprise network, whereas multicast sends to a selected group.

Message delivery middleware is flexible as to the content of interprocess communication messages as well. For instance, message handling middleware can deliver RPC or SQL as its message. Security checking, encryption, data compression, and error recovery can all be supported features of message delivery middleware. Message handling middleware often has the network savvy to navigate the enterprise network intelligently by responding to changing network conditions.

Possible Future Directions for Middleware

Where might middleware be going in the future? Before answering that question, it is prudent to ask another: What user demands or trends are most influential on middleware's future? If the answers to this question were limited to just two, they would be:

Transparency
Ease of use

These two driving forces are really related as one could argue that with increased transparency comes increased ease of use.

Increased transparency for the middleware of the future implies that users need not worry that their particular combination of hardware, operating system, networking operating system, and internetworking transport protocols are supported by any particular middleware product.

Self-configuring or *network aware* middleware is easy to install and configures itself to provide the required enterprise network transparency regardless of the client and server protocol stacks attached to the network. It also doesn't matter whether the enterprise network spans LAN, inter-LAN, or WAN connections, the middleware would self-configure and manage accordingly.

Distributed network management was mentioned previously in the chapter as a key challenge to widespread deployment of the client–server architecture. New standards for interoperability and *intermanageability* may be required. It will be an extended version middleware that will finally deliver intermanageability for distributed information systems. Emerging standards for intermanageability such as **DME** (distributed management environment), developed by the Open Software Foundation (OSF) will be discussed in the next section of this chapter.

Middleware as a separately purchased software product may actually disappear in the name of ease of use. Network transparency can easily be interpreted as the responsibility of the network operating system. Thus, the day could come when every client and server included all necessary, self-configuring middleware, in the installed network operating system.

Finally, for both transparency and ease of use, electronic mail, so-called mail-enabled applications, and middleware produced interprocess communication should all operate within a single, easily manageable architecture. Single function middleware will probably merge its best features into a multipurpose middleware such as message delivery middleware. Currently, E-mail has its own standards, such as X.400 and X.500, many of which are vague and/or extended beyond standardization as we discovered in Chapters 7 and 8. Middleware operates with few standards at the present time, adhering primarily to de facto standards in supporting certain network operating systems or internetwork transport protocols.

◀

◆ *Management
Perspective*

Without a doubt, middleware is the enabling technology of the client–server paradigm. As middleware goes, so goes client–server. The size of the task is enormous. The possible combinations of devices and associated protocols attached to the enterprise network for which middleware is responsible for supplying transparency is staggering. The opportunity to develop the "glue" of client–server is both challenging and exciting. This opportunity belongs to those individuals who understand the proper application of data communications and networking technology to distributed information systems. Only people well-versed in the use of the top-down model and OSI model as analysis tools are qualified to meet such a challenge. People like you.

◄

☐ STANDARDS AND THE CLIENT–SERVER ARCHITECTURE

Standards for client–server architectures, distributed computing, and open systems have been under various stages of development from three major sources:

> Major computer vendors
> Official standards organizations
> "Unofficial" user/vendor consortia

After a brief introduction of the major players in each of these categories, a more detailed discussion of the various comparative architectures will follow.

Digital Equipment Corporation (DEC) and IBM have both defined so-called open architectures in order to support multivendor computing. DEC's architecture is known as **NAS** (network application support), while IBM's open architecture is known as **SAA** (systems application architecture). It is somehow ironic to reconcile that these two companies each have their own *proprietary open* system architecture.

◆ *Management Perspective*

As an end-user, one must be cautious when analyzing a computer vendor's architecture. An architecture is nothing more than a verbalization of a vision. It does not necessarily imply the deliverability of products to implement that architecture nor even a promise to develop such products. Proposed delivery dates should not be taken as firm commitments on which end-users can base their own implementation plans.

◄

In IBM's case, the **new SNA** as reviewed in Chapter 6, seems to be currently getting more attention than SAA. In either case, product delivery is the only real measure of commitment to a software architecture, open or otherwise.

As far as the definition of open systems architectures by an officially recognized standards-making organization, the ISO (International Standards Organization) has been slowly developing standards for various aspects of distributed computing for layers 3 and above in its famous OSI 7-layer model. Internetworking standards such as router-to-router protocols have also been produced by the ISO.

Finally, a consortium of UNIX vendors and users known as the Open Software Foundation, Inc., have taken it upon themselves to produce their own wide ranging specifications for distributed computing known as **DCE** (distributed computing environment). As will be seen, this nonproprietary, unofficial approach to standards generation has produced standards and gained voluntary compliance for those standards in relatively short amounts of time. Contrast this approach with the "standards generation lag time" associated with official standards-making organizations mentioned in Chapter 1.

ISO Produces OSI Model, Protocols

Throughout the text, the OSI reference model has been constantly mentioned and utilized. Its value as a basic analysis tool for network analysis and design has been thoroughly demonstrated. Not mentioned to this point is the fact that the ISO has also been developing their own set of protocols to fit within the various layers of their famous model. Alas, these protocols have not nearly gained the fame of the model in which they sit.

The relatively slow development of OSI standards, protocols, and protocol-compliant products have forced users to search for other *nonproprietary* or open standards. The internet suite of protocols, better known as TCP/IP, was the logical choice. Originally seen as a temporary fill-in for the developing OSI protocols, TCP/IP and its associated protocols have gained wide acceptance and continue to evolve and gain in sophistication. Supporters of OSI and TCP/IP have argued for years over the relative merits of each other's protocol stacks.

Confrontation has yielded to cooperation in more recent years as the two protocol stacks have begun to interoperate. For instance, OSI's management protocol, CMIP, now runs over TCP/IP in an adaptation known as CMIP over TCP/IP or CMOT. Multiprotocol routers are now able to route both OSI and TCP/IP protocols, allowing the two protocol stacks to coexist on the enterprise network. Just as TCP/IP can be added to netware-based LANs with the use of multiprotocol software, OSI and TCP/IP can exist on the same workstation or server with the same "dual-stack" approach.

Some of the OSI protocols or standards previously mentioned include:

X.400 and X.500 E-mail standards
CMIP network management protocol
IS-to-IS router-to-router protocol

Other OSI protocols will be included in a summary analysis of open systems standards later in this section.

One of the major driving forces behind OSI and OSI-compliance is the U.S. Government. Through its **GOSIP** (government OSI profile) procurement directives, the NIST (National Institute of Standards and Technology) insures that so-called OSI products have actually passed OSI compliance testing. The NIST compiles the *GOSIP Register* to keep track of which vendor's products are fully OSI-compliant.

OSF: Nonproprietary, Consortium-Based Standards

The Open Software Foundation, Inc, or **OSF,** headquartered in Cambridge, Massachusetts, set out to develop a comprehensive set of standards for distributed computing in a UNIX environment in an effort to increase the use of UNIX platforms in a commercial setting. The result of their efforts has moved beyond the UNIX environment to include a multivendor, multiplatform approach to distributed computing.

Known as DCE (distributed computing environment), this architecture is supported by major computer vendors such as IBM and DEC as well as networking companies such as Novell and Banyan. DCE seeks to define a comprehensive distributed computing environment to preclude the need to add third-party, nonstandard products in order to deliver required functionality or performance. DCE defines the following major components:

Interprocess communications with RPC
Distributed file system
Security system
Distributed directory

What was missing from DCE was a direction or set of standards on how to manage effectively the distributed computing environment created with DCE. As a result DME (distributed management environment) was created to define standards for the management of the full client–server architecture based on DCE. As pointed out in the discussion of middleware, there is much more to manage in a client–server architecture than just the enterprise network. DME defines standards for the management of:

> Enterprise network including internetworking devices
> Servers
> Operating systems
> Distributed applications
> Distributed databases

In many ways the comprehensive DME set of standards seeks to offer information systems *management personnel* the same thing that the client–server architecture seeks to offer information systems *end-users:* The right information (management information) to the right decision-maker (systems and network managers) at the right place and time (wherever they need it, whenever they need it). Figure 9-31 illustrates the relationship of the distributed management environment to the client–server architecture.

One of the unique aspects of DME is that it will be implemented as *object-oriented* software. Objects which contain information about network resources will be paired with methods, which are routines, or small programs, for managing those network resources. Global objects which describe an entire class of networking devices as well as local objects which describe a particular network attached device will both be defined.

An **object server,** much like a database server, will maintain the objects and methods as well as answer requests for their services. Those requests for services will come from a **MRB** (management request broker), which will receive those service requests from management application programs via a DME-supplied API. **ORB**s (object request brokers) are sometimes considered another category of middleware,

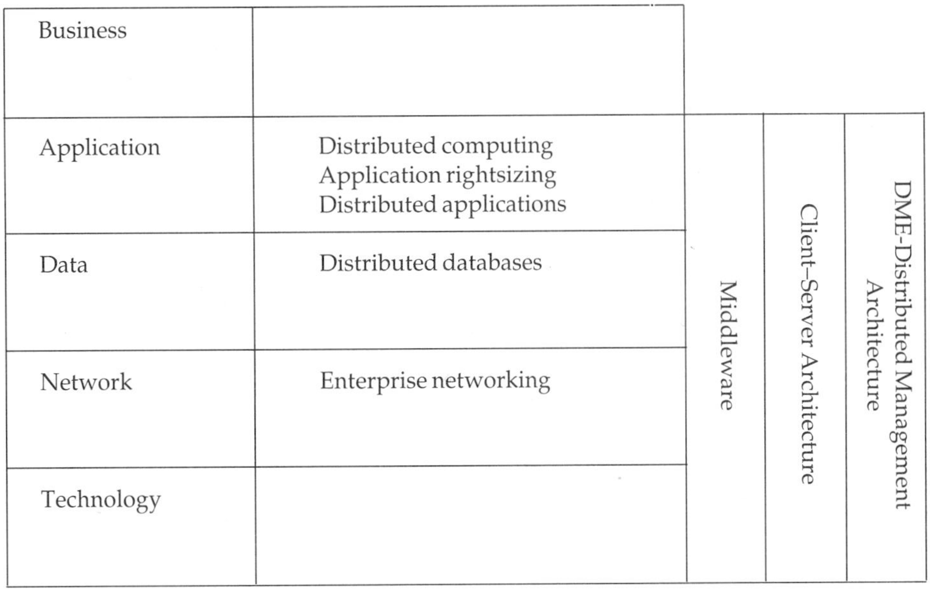

Business		Middleware	Client–Server Architecture	DME-Distributed Management Architecture
Application	Distributed computing Application rightsizing Distributed applications			
Data	Distributed databases			
Network	Enterprise networking			
Technology				

Figure 9-31 Distributed management environment (DME) manages client–server architecture.

similar to the database request category. Figure 9-32 illustrates the logical relationship of the various elements of the OSF's distributed management environment.

SAA and NAS: Proprietary, Open Standards

SAA, IBM's systems application architecture, and NAS, DEC's network application support, both attempt to outline their respective company's vision for multivendor, multiplatform, distributed computing. As stated previously, each should be judged both on products delivered as well as support for nonproprietary open systems architectures such as those proposed by OSI and OSF.

As seen in Chapter 6 on internetworking, DEC has been supporting multivendor networks with its DECnet architecture for many years. On the other hand, IBM's first challenge with SAA was to first get its own many incompatible operating system platforms to communicate and coexist before it could incorporate multivendor platforms into the SAA architecture.

An Open-Systems Architecture Analysis Methodology

Rather than compare the two proprietary open architectures on a feature-by-feature basis, a more functional approach to the analysis of **open systems architectures** will be taken. The first step in such an analysis is to identify functional categories within a distributed computing environment that might benefit from standardization. Next, any current nonproprietary, open standards for that func-

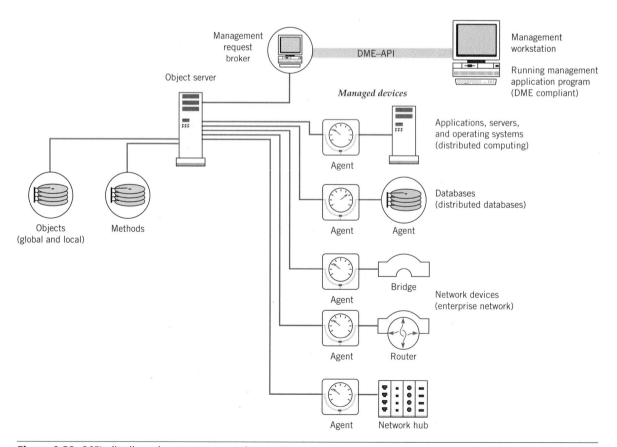

Figure 9-32 OSF's distributed management environment.

tional category will be listed. This open systems architecture analysis grid can then be employed to evaluate any so-called open systems architecture.

In addition, as new open standards or functional categories are created, they can be added to the analysis grid. Figure 9-33 identifies the functional categories and current open standards for open system architectures.

Functional Category	Open Standards	Compliance of Evaluated Architecture
Support of Open Standards Organizations and Future Standards	Organizations: ISO–International Standards Organization OSF—Open Software Foundation	
E-Mail	X.400 X.500 SMTP	
File Transfer and Management Systems	OSI FTAM (File Transfer, Access, Management) FTP TFTP NFS	
Network Management	SNMP CMIP CMOT CMOL	
Internetworking Transport	TCP/IP UDP OSI Transport Class 4	
User Interface	TELNET Virtual Terminal Protocol (OSI)	
Distributed Database Connectivity	SQL	
Router-to-Router Protocols	RIP OSPF PPP ES-IS (OSI model) IS-IS (OSI model)	
Comprehensive Distributed Computing	DCE (OSF) RPC Security Directory File system	
Comprehensive Distributed Management	DME (OSF) API Object server Management request broker	

Figure 9-33 Open systems architecture analysis grid.

CHAPTER SUMMARY

A business-oriented top-down analysis of a client–server architecture finds that flexibility of design and the ability to respond quickly to changing business conditions, rather than drastically reduced information systems budgets, are the key benefits of implementing such an information systems architecture.

A client–server architecture is actually comprised of three subsystems (distributed processing, distributed databases, and enterprise networks) as well as the middleware that ties these three sub-systems together. Variables on each client and server include: operating system, network operating system, and database management system, to name a few. Since differing combinations are nearly infinite, standards-based middleware is required in order to prevent programmers from having to rewrite application software for every possible client/server combination.

The role of the enterprise network is central to the successful implementation of client/server information systems. Enterprise networks must be designed and implemented in such a way as to offer transparency to the end-user from any of the underlying networking protocols required to deliver messages from client workstations to server processors or database engines.

Client/server information systems will only be widely deployed in the future if management systems can be developed that can effectively manage widely distributed client/server information systems effectively. Although multi-vendor, multiprotocol enterprise network management systems are available, distributed management environments that also incorporate the management of processing and database activities are still largely in the developmental stages.

KEY TERMS

agent
API
application rightsizing
back-end
bulk retrieval mechanism
centralized architecture
CLI
client–server architectures
CMIP
CMOL
CMOT
collapsed backbone
corporate downsizing
DCE
DDE
dependency tables
distributed applications
distributed architectures
distributed backbone
distributed computing
distributed databases
distributed database
   management system

distributed processing
distributed query
   optimization
DME
EDA/SQL
engine
enterprise network
enterprise network
   management
enterprise routers
front-end
global dictionaries
GOSIP
hybrid network
   architecture
information systems
   downsizing
integrated client–server
   management
interprocess
   communications
IPC

management request
   broker
manager
message delivery
methods
MIB
middleware
MRB
NAS
new SNA
object server
objects
ODBC
open systems architecture
ORB
OSF
paradigm shift
people architecture
RMON MIB
RPC
SAA
scalability

secure SNMP
send-and-wait
server-to-server
   communications
SMP
SNMP
SNMP2
SQL
SQL gateway
stored procedures
stubs
system architecture
sockets
transparency
transition costs
triggers
two-phase commit
universal presentation
   interface
WOSA

REVIEW QUESTIONS

1. What are the major business forces motivating the interest in client–server architectures?
2. What is application rightsizing and what are its key enabling technologies and benefits?
3. Define each of the following in terms of their contribution to a client–server architecture:
   Distributed computing
   Distributed applications
   Front-end
   Engine
   Database distribution
   Enterprise network
4. If middleware did not exist, how would applications programmers have to adjust?
5. What are the key differences between RPCs and message handling APIs?
6. What people architecture changes or issues are likely to accompany wide-scale deployment of client–server architectures?
7. What is SQL and what role does it play in database distribution?
8. What is the difference between an enterprise network backbone and an enterprise network architecture?
9. What are the differences, advantages, and disadvantages of distributed backbones versus collapsed backbones?
10. What are some of the issues that make management of distributed information systems more difficult than centralized information systems?
11. What are the key differences between SNMP and SNMP2 and what implication do these differences have for comprehensive client–server architecture management?
12. What is IPC and how is it enabled?
13. What do LU 6.2, sockets, and named pipes have in common? How do they differ?
14. What are the four major types of middleware? Compare and contrast them in terms of functionality and flexibility.
15. What is the OSF and how does it differ from other open systems standards making organizations?
16. What are DCE and DME and why are they significant to client–server architectures?
17. What is the function of the object server in the DME environment?
18. What approach would you take in evaluating a "proprietary" open systems architecture such as SAA or NAS?
19. What is the difference as well as the relationship between corporate downsizing and information systems downsizing?
20. Explain the contribution of each of the major components of a client–server architecture.
21. What are some of the key differences between a client to server and a mainframe to terminal architecture?
22. What is the role of middleware in relation to the enterprise network and distributed applications?
23. Explain how the concept of total independence of client and server is a key benefit of the client–server architecture.
24. How is the flexibility of design offered by client–server architectures considered a business-layer benefit?
25. What are some of the key potential negatives of the rightsizing phenomenon?
26. How does the top-down model relate to application rightsizing efforts?
27. What is a paradigm and how does one know when a paradigm shift has occurred?
28. What is the relationship between systems architectures and people architectures?
29. What is the major system architecture of today and how does the current people architecture correspond?
30. Why are people architectures and people issues important to network analysts in charge of application rightsizing projects?
31. What are the respective roles of the front-end and back-end in distributed processing?
32. Why are transparency and scalability considered the two key attributes of distributed computing?
33. Explain the basic communications required between front and back ends in order to accomplish distributed computing.
34. What is the relationship between RPCs and APIs in delivering distributed computing?
35. Why are server-to-server communications also considered a major part of distributed computing?
36. Why is a section on distributed database management systems included in a data communications text?
37. What are some of the compatibility issues surrounding database distribution?
38. How are database requests between different databases accomplished?
39. Explain both the importance and accomplishment of distributed query optimization.
40. What are some of the pros and cons of two-phase commit as a database integrity function?
41. What do triggers and stored procedures have in common? How are they different?
42. How does DDE deliver database transparency to Windows applications?

43. What important standards issues regarding SQL should be kept in mind when purchasing a database system?
44. What is an enterprise network?
44. What is the difference between a network architecture and a network backbone?
45. What are the different possible network architecture categories?
46. What are the advantages and disadvantages of collapsed network backbones?
47. How does the client–server top-down model for enterprise network analysis and design assist in client–server architecture design?
48. What is the difference between integrated client–server management and enterprise network management?
49. What is the relationship of agents, managers, and MIBs in distributed management systems?
50. What are some of the key challenges to integrated client–server management?
51. What are some of the most promising technologies or standards for integrated client–server management?
52. How did two different sets of "open" distributed management protocols get developed?
53. What is the significance of SNMP2 to integrated client–server management?
54. How can ever increasing amounts of network management traffic be avoided as networks continue to grow?
55. What are the major subcategories of middleware?
56. What is the relationship between RPC and message passing middleware?
57. What is meant by asynchronous message passing?
58. Why is RPC considered a send-and-wait inter-process communication?
59. What are some possible future developments of middleware?
60. What developments in related technologies could eliminate the need for middleware?
61. What is the significance of DCE and DME and how are they related?

ACTIVITIES

1. Contact the Open Software Foundation (11 Cambridge Center, Cambridge, MA 02142) regarding the current status of DCE and DME environments. Ask for any free white papers which they may offer.
2. Survey current trade journals and prepare a report or bulletin board indicating industry's support of DCE and DME environments for open systems. From an industry perspective, what are the pros and cons of DCE and DME?
3. Prepare a technology survey for department, company, or campus-wide computing resources. This is not a top-down network analysis and design. We are not planning a new network. It is a simple survey to determine the variety of client and server platforms in a given network. For every computer (client or server) encountered, record the following:
   1. Make and model of hardware
   2. CPU architecture (Intel, RISC, etc.)
   3. Operating system
   4. Network operating system
   5. Network architecture (Ethernet, Token Ring, etc.)
   6. Network transport protocols supported
   7. Installed databases
   8. Major applications
4. After completing the survey, compile information by categories in order to determine how many different operating systems, networking operating systems, etc., must be integrated.
5. Review trade journals or product literature to determine possible products and technology that might be able to link these various platforms. Pay particular attention to a group of software products known as middleware.
6. Prepare a cost–benefit analysis for the purchase of any middleware products identified in previous steps of the study. List any intangible benefits as well.
7. Gather product literature and cost information on client–server databases such as Oracle or Sybase. Do these databases support transparent data distribution? Is integrated database middleware available for these products?

Featured References

Business Related Issues

Eckerson, Wayne. "Mgmt. Concerns Slow Distributed Systems," *Network World,* vol. 9, no. 29 (July 20, 1992), p. 25.

Brown, Bob. "Client/Server Move May Alter Industry," *Network World,* vol. 9, no. 29 (July 20, 1992), p. 31.

Rymer, John. "Users Could Benefit from Downsizing's Hidden Costs," *Network World,* vol. 9, no. 29 (July 20, 1992), p. 43.

Eckerson, Wayne. "Hidden Costs May Come with Downsizing Savings," *Network World,* vol. 9, no. 26 (June 29, 1992), p. 41.

Conliffe, Alison. "Jan Scites: Facing the Future Headfirst" (Business Process Re-Design), *Network World*, vol. 10, no. 1 (January 4, 1993), p. 31

Case Studies

Microsoft Corporation. *Microsoft–Texas Instruments Case Study* (1992).

Martin, Mary. "Reaping the Rewards," *Network World*, vol. 9, no. 46 (November 16, 1992), p. 63.

Duffy, Jim. "Reader's Digest Plots Global Net, Data Center Merger," *Network World*, vol. 9, no. 23 (June 8, 1992), p. 17.

Eckerson, Wayne. "Intrepid User Braves Risks of Distributed Object World," *Network World*, vol. 9, no. 23 (June 8, 1992), p. 1.

Cooper, Geoff. "Exabyte on Cutting Edge of Client/Server Technology," *LAN Times*, vol. 9, no. 6 (April 6, 1992), p. 29.

Tolly, Kevin. "A Methodology to Our Madness," *Data Communications*, vol. 21, no. 9 (June 1992), p. 47.

Eckerson, Wayne. "User Downsizes in an Off-the-Shelf Way," *Network World*, vol. 9, no. 28 (July 13, 1992), p. 19.

Warren, Sheila. "Firm Improves Management of Internals," *LAN Times*, vol. 9, no. 7 (April 20, 1992), p. 36.

Walker, Robyn. "Roadway Works to Reduce MIS Costs at Remote Sites," *LAN Times*, vol. 9, no. 2 (February 10, 1992), p.47.

LaPlante, Alice. "K-Mart's Client/Server Special," *DBMS*, vol. 5, no. 13 (December 1992), p. 56.

Chowning, David. "MDBS Speeds Fermi Accelerator Lab," *DBMS*, vol. 5, no. 13 (December 1992), p. 58.

Schnapp, Marc. "Dunkin's Downsizing: A Piece of Cake," *DBMS*, vol. 5, no. 13 (December 1992), p. 59.

Frank, Maurice. "Developer Follows CA's Downsizing Path," *DBMS*, vol. 5, no. 13 (December 1992), p. 60.

Moazami, Mohsen. "Acius Races on Cross-Country Network," *DBMS*, vol. 5, no. 13 (December 1992), p. 61.

Darling, Charles. "From CICS to InterBase," *DBMS*, vol. 5, no. 13 (December 1992), p. 63.

Brownstein, Mark. "Client/Server Saves Lives in San Antonio," *DBMS*, vol. 5, no. 13 (December 1992), p. 64.

Darling, Charles. "With Oracle and Novell, Talk Is Cheaper," *DBMS*, vol. 5, no. 13 (December 1992), p. 65.

Longsworth, Elizabeth, and John Montgomery. "Network Puzzle," *Corporate Computing*, vol. 2, no. 1 (January 1993), p. 98.

Client/Server

Ewald, Alan, and Mark Roy. "The Evolution of the Client/Server Revolution," *Network World*, vol. 9, no. 46 (November 16, 1992), p.75.

Keough, Lee. "APPN: IBM's Bid for Multiprotocol Nets," *Data Communications*, vol. 21, no. 7 (May 1992), p. 55.

Brown, Bob. "Client/Server Move May Alter Industry," *Network World*, vol. 9, no. 29 (July 20, 1992), p. 31.

Milliken, Michael. "A Client–Server Success Story," *Data Communications*, vol. 21, no. 10 (July 1992), p. 39.

Milliken, Michael. "DEC and Microsoft: The New Client–Server Power Pair," *Data Communications*, vol. 21, no. 9 (June 1992), p. 43.

Eckerson, Wayne. "User Wrestles with Client/Server Mgmt.," *Network World*, vol. 9, no. 32 (August 10, 1992), p. 19.

Brandel, William. "Digital Is Sticking Close to Microsoft with its LAN Strategy," *LAN Times*, vol. 9, no. 9 (May 25, 1992), p. 14.

Cooney, Michael. "IBM Targets Host in Client/Server Push," *Network World*, vol. 9, no. 25 (June 22, 1992), p. 1.

Distributed Computing

Linnell, Dennis. "Windows NT: Can Microsoft Make the Jump from the Desktop to Distributed Computing?," *Data Communications*, vol. 22, no. 6 (April 1993), p. 68.

Ezzell, Ben. "Windows NT: The Power Under the Hood," *PC Magazine*, vol. 12, no. 11 (June 15, 1993), p. 173.

Derfler, Frank, and Steve Rigney. "Windows for Workgroups," *PC Magazine*, vol. 11, no. 21 (December 8, 1992), p. 255.

Rymer, John. "Distributed Computing Meets Object-Oriented Technology," *Network World*, vol. 10, no. 9 (March 1, 1993), p. 28.

Hindin, Eric. "Distributed Applications: Unix and Beyond," *Data Communications*, vol. 21, no. 3 (February 1992), p. 44.

O'Brien, Timothy. "HP Exec Details Role of Object Technology," *Network World*, vol. 9, no. 51 (December 21, 1992), p. 17.

Milliken, Michael. "Why Smart Users Are Taking Notes," *Data Communications*, vol. 21, no. 8 (May 21, 1992), p. 33.

Carr, Jim. "Novell Upgrades Netware for the Enterprise," *Data Communications*, vol. 21, no. 9 (June 1992), p. 63.

Eckerson, Wayne. "Firm to Offer Utility to Tie Object-Oriented Applications," *Network World*, vol. 9, no. 50 (December 14, 1992), p. 4.

Ferris, David. "A Look at Mail-Enabled Applications," *Network World*, vol. 9, no. 50 (December 14, 1992), p. 41.

O'Brien, Timothy. "Development System Supports Many GUIs," *Network World*, vol. 9, no. 27 (July 6, 1992), p. 25.

Ferris, David. "Windows NT Promises to Ease Net Integration," *Network World*, vol. 9, no. 26 (June 29, 1992), p. 41.

Rymer, John. "Needed: A Comprehensive Approach to Development," *Network World*, vol. 9, no. 3 (January 27, 1992), p. 37.

Salamone, Salvatore. "An Easier Way to Build Distributed Applications," *Data Communications*, vol. 21, no. 11 (August 1992), p. 131.

Distributed Databases

The, Lee. "A Client/Server 4GL With Mix and Match GUIs," *Datamation*, vol. 38, no. 20 (October 1, 1992), p. 49.

Brandel, William. "Oracle 7 Lets Applications Query, Access Data on a Variety of Servers," *LAN Times*, vol. 9, no. 13 (July 20, 1992), p. 59.

Nitzsche, Kyle. "Guide to Strategic Purchase Decisions: Distributed DBMS," *Network World*, vol. 9, no. 48 (November 30, 1992), p. 43.

Eckerson, Wayne. "Info Builders Expands Data Access Horizons," *Network World*, vol. 9, no. 49 (December 7, 1992), p. 1.

Eckerson, Wayne. "Cincom Eyes New 2-Phase Commit Plan," *Network World*, vol. 9, no. 50 (December 14, 1992), p. 1.

O'Brien, Timothy. "SQL Access Group Rolls out Phase II Technical Specs," *Network World*, vol. 9, no. 23 (June 8, 1992), p. 15.

Dostert, Michelle. "Sybase Intros SQL Server for Netware," *LAN Times*, vol. 9, no. 9 (May 25, 1992), p. 1.

Gillooly, Caryn. "DAL Server Connects MACs to IBM RS/6000 Databases," *Network World*, vol. 9, no. 27 (July 6, 1992), p. 6.

O'Brien, Timothy. "Microsoft, Apple to Forge Common Database Access," *Network World*, vol. 9, no. 29 (July 20, 1992), p. 2.

Morris, Larry. "Front Ends Support Netware SQL 3.0," *LAN Times*, vol. 9, no. 5 (March 23, 1992), p. 25.

O'Brien, Timothy. "Windows Opens Wider to New Data Sources," *Network World*, vol. 9, no. 26 (June 29, 1992), p. 1.

Anderson, Ron. "SQL Databases: High-Powered, High-Priced," *PC Magazine*, vol. 11, no. 15 (September 15, 1992), p. 369.

Eckerson, Wayne. "IBI's EDA/SQL Software Leads the Data Access Pack," *Network World*, vol. 10, no. 1 (January 4, 1993), p. 25.

Distributed Multivendor/Multiplatform Management

Jander, Mary, and Johna Johnson. "Managing High Speed WANs: Just Wait," *Data Communications*, vol. 22, no. 7 (May 1993), p. 83.

Waldbusser, Steve. "SNMP Management Goes Down to the Wire," *Data Communications*, vol. 21, no. 7 (May 1992), p. 111.

Jander, Mary. "Beyond RMON: Making Sense of Remote Data," *Data Communications*, vol. 21, no. 9 (June 1992), p. 51.

Jander, Mary. "MIB Tools: Coping with the Not-So-Simple Side of SNMP," *Data Communications*, vol. 21, no. 3 (February 1992), p. 79.

Molloy, Maureen. "On the Winding Road to SNMP Version 2," *Network World*, vol. 10, no. 1 (January 4, 1993), p. 17.

Heywood, Peter. "Bringing SNMP to End-Node Management," *Data Communications*, vol. 21, no. 10 (July 1992), p. 47.

Herman, James. "Distributed Network Management," *Data Communications*, vol. 21, no. 9 (June 1992), p. 74.

Jander, Mary. "SNMP 2: Coming Soon to a Network Near You," *Data Communications*, vol. 21, no. 18 (November 1992), p. 66.

Duffy, Jim. "DEC, Systems Center to Deliver Management Link," *Network World*, vol. 9, no. 25 (June 22, 1992), p. 1.

Eckerson, Wayne. "New Software Targets Client/Server Mgmt.," *Network World*, vol. 9, no. 27 (July 6, 1992), p. 1.

Jander, Mary. "IBM Gets Serious about SNMP," *Data Communications*, vol. 21, no. 4 (March 1992), p. 47.

Enterprise Networks

Longsworth, Elizabeth, and John Montgomery. "Network Puzzle," *Corporate Computing*, vol. 2, no. 1 (January 1993), p. 98.

Zeile, Mike. "Expanding the Enterprise by Collapsing the Backbone," *Data Communications*, vol. 21, no. 17 (November 21, 1992), p. 71.

Hindin, Eric. "Netware Gears up for the Enterprise," *Data Communications*, vol. 21, no. 13 (September 21, 1992), p. 50.

O'Brien, Timothy. "Object Orientation to Push Networking to Next Zenith," *Network World*, vol. 9, no. 30 (July 27, 1992), p. 1.

Cooney, Michael. "APPC/MVS Fighting for Industry Respect," *Network World*, vol. 9, no. 27 (July 6, 1992), p. 9.

Cooney, Michael. "Companies Report Success with APPC Implementation," *Network World*, vol. 9, no. 51 (December 21, 1992), p. 5.

E-Mail

Salamone, Salvatore. "Delivering E-Mail for the Enterprise," *Data Communications*, vol. 21, no. 18 (December 1992), p. 49.

Middleware

Eckerson, Wayne. "Middleware Offers Server Link Options," *Network World*, vol. 9, no. 48 (November 30, 1992), p. 4.

Eckerson, Wayne. "Smack Dab in the Middle," *Network World*, vol. 10, no. 25 (June 21, 1993), p. 43.

O'Brien, Timothy. "Replication, Naming Added to NetWeave," *Network World*, vol. 9, no. 50 (December 14, 1992), p. 35.

Dostert, Michelle. "Netwise Intros Multiprotocol RPC Development Tool," *LAN Times*, vol. 9, no. 8 (May 11, 1992), p. 10.

King, Steven. "Middleware!" *Data Communications*, vol. 21, no. 4 (March 1992), p. 58.

King, Steven. "Message Delivery APIs: The Message Is the Medium," *Data Communications*, vol. 21, no. 6 (April 1992), p. 85.

Milliken, Michael. "An Object-Oriented Middleware Strategy That Works," *Data Communications*, vol. 21, no. 6 (April 1992), p. 35.

Milliken, Michael. "RPCs vs. Message-Based: The Great Nondebate," *Data Communications*, vol. 21, no. 3 (February 1992), p. 37.

DeBoever, Larry, and Max Dolgicer. "Middleware's Next Step: Enterprise Wide Applications," *Data Communications*, vol. 21, no. 12 (September 1992), p. 157.

DeBoever, Larry, and Max Dolgicer. "Middleware: IBM's View," *Data Communications*, vol. 21, no. 17 (November 21, 1992), p. 31.

Conniff, Michael. "Middleware: Networking's Postal Service," *Network World*, vol. 9, no. 36 (September 7, 1992), p. 59.

Eckerson, Wayne. "Wanted: Middleware Mgmt. Capabilities," *Network World*, vol. 10, no. 9 (March 1, 1993), p. 19.

Multiprotocol Software

Layland, Robin. "Assessing IBM's Blueprint for Multiprotocol Nets," *Data Communications*, vol. 21, no. 12 (September 1992), p. 139.

Kine, Bill. "Options for Supporting Multiple Protocols," *LAN Times*, vol. 8, no. 24 (January 6, 1992), p. 50.

Hancock, Bill. "Multiprotocol Networking: Advantage DEC," *Data Communications*, vol. 21, no. 4 (March 1992), p. 91.

Salamone, Sylvester. "Multiprotocol Software Moves up the Stack," *Data Communications*, vol. 21, no. 11 (August 1992), p. 121.

Jander, Mary. "Netware Gets Some Mainframe Aid," *Data Communications*, vol. 21, no. 2 (January 21, 1992), p. 74.

Mohen, Joe. "OSI Interoperability: Separating Fact from Fiction," *Data Communications*, vol. 21, no. 2 (January 21, 1992), p. 41.

Bowden, Eric. "Netware Connectivity Adds Red to LAN Manager Palette," *LAN Times*, vol. 9, no. 6 (April 6, 1992), p. 68.

Rightsizing

VanName, Mark, and Bill Catchings. "The Road to Rightsizing," *PC Week*, (March 8, 1993), p. 84.

Standards

Messmer, Ellen. "NIST Explains GOSIP Procurement Rules," *Network World*, vol. 9, no. 50 (December 14, 1992), p. 9.

Messmer, Ellen. "X/Open Draws up 1993 Interoperability Road Map," *Network World*, vol. 9, no. 50 (December 14, 1992), p. 39.

DeBoever, Larry, and Max Dolgicer. "Microsoft Moves Beyond the Desktop," (WOSA), *Data Communications*, vol. 21, no. 18 (December 1992), p. 31.

Mohen, Joe. "OSI Interoperability: Separating Fact from Fiction," *Data Communications*, vol. 21, no. 2 (January 21, 1992), p. 41.

Messmer, Ellen. "Feds Issue Buyers' Guide for OSI Mgmt.," *Network World*, vol. 9, no. 30 (July 27, 1992), p. 1.

Jander, Mary. "Can CMOL Challenge SNMP?" *Data Communications*, vol. 21, no. 8 (May 21, 1992), p. 53.

Eckerson, Wayne, and Ellen Messmer. "Is OSI Dead?" *Network World*, vol. 9, no. 24 (June 15, 1992), p. 1.

C A S E   S T U D Y

User Down sizes in an Off-the-Shelf Way

TEMPE, Ariz.—Last year, Motorola, Inc.'s Computer Group (MCG), based here, embarked on a two-year migration from IBM mainframes running applications developed in-house to distributed Unix processors using primarily packaged applications.

While the project will not be completed until the first quarter of 1993, MCG is already reaping considerable benefits. The group has been able to cut its information systems (IS) budget by 40%, while shortening applications development cycles, sometimes from months to minutes.

"To meet Motorola's overall quality and cycle-time reduction goals, we needed to make a paradigm shift in our approach to systems development," said Paul Watz, director of information technology at MCG, located here. "We need systems that are flexible and can adapt to rapid changes in our business environment."

MCG is one of three groups within Motorola's General Systems Sector that is downsizing from IBM hosts to Unix processors. The other groups are the Cellular Subscriber Group, which makes cellular phones, and the Cellular Infrastructure Group, which makes cellular switches. Together, the three groups have cut more than $40 million from the sector's annual IS budget, according to William Connor, director of information technology for the General Systems Sector.

For Motorola, the key to gaining systems flexibility in a distributed environment is to rely as much as possible on packaged software.

"We have made a commitment to avoid purchasing or developing proprietary software because our business moves too fast to justify the investment in time or money," Connor said.

Packaged software relieves the in-house development staff from having to upgrade applications to support each new release of an operating system or a new hardware platform. It also makes it easier to standardize a single set of applications for accounting, inventory and other general operating functions that can be used across departments, reducing costs significantly.

But MCG has had to weigh the cost savings that come from standardizing software packages throughout the group against the individual needs of each division in the group.

"We try to balance our business and systems requirements with what's available. But there are times when it isn't appropriate to change the business to fit the software," Watz said.

In order to customize packaged software to meet end users' needs, MCG established a set of criteria for evaluating off-the-shelf software.

To start, the software had to be written in a pure fourth-generation language and had to come with computer-aided software engineering tools so MCG could maintain and modify the applications as needed, Watz said.

MCG also decided the software should support triggers, which are pieces of code that can be added to software programs without fundamentally altering the core application. Triggers allow users to modify software without having to assume responsibility for

supporting the entire application. Users have to support only the trigger code, while the vendor maintains the rest.

Finally, the software had to run on either Oracle Corp. or Informix Software, Inc. relational databases, and the vendor had to have a worldwide network of value-added resellers that can support the software in place.

MCG chose software from FourGen, Inc., a small developer in Redmond, Wash., to provide shipping, inventory, purchasing and order-entry applications running on Informix relational databases and a suite of financial applications from Oracle that run on Oracle's Oracle Server relational database.

According to Watz, FourGen's software is designed so customers can modify the applications without changing the source code. This allows MCG to tailor FourGen applications to different business environments without losing the benefits of off-the-shelf software.

MCG developed a close partnership with FourGen so that many of Motorola's requirements get written into new releases of FourGen applications or development tools.

FourGen's software as well as the relational databases from Informix and Oracle run on Motorola's own Delta Series Unix processors running AT&T Unix Version 5.3. MCG will soon upgrade to Version 5.4, Watz said.

Currently, MCG has 25 Unix servers supporting about 1,000 X terminals on an Ethernet linked to a campus fiber backbone running Transmission Control Protocol/ Internet Protocol. Another 10 Unix servers and 250 X terminals are located in a Dallas office, which is linked to Tempe via Motorola's corporate peer-to-peer network.

MCG has more than 100 other sites around the world—mainly sales offices—that will be linked into the client/server network via dial-up lines or dedicated links, depending on traffic volumes.

Watz said that in addition to carefully choosing software, downsizing users also need to establish procedures and safeguards for protecting distributed data.

"Our production Unix systems need to be managed in a secure, controlled environment with proper procedures for data backup, storage, security and recovery, just as in the IBM mainframe environment," Watz said. "We can't afford a free-lance distribution of data."

MCG runs a dozen or more Unix servers in a single area so they can be more easily managed and controlled by trained systems administrators.

MCG is also developing a number of tools and operating procedures that will help it better manage a distributed Unix processing environment. These include automated backup and restoral programs that can work across a network and directory services that automate the task of establishing and changing user accounts on multiple servers, said Ken Ridgely, a network and systems manager at MCG.

Source: Wayne Eckerson, "User Downsizes in an Off-the Shelf Way," *Network World,* vol. 9, no. 28 (July 13, 1992), p. 19. Copyright July 1992 by Network World, Inc., Framingham, MA 01701. Reprinted from *Network World.*

Business Case Study Questions

Activities

1. Prepare a top-down model for this case by identifying pertinent facts from within the business case and placing these facts in their respective layers within the top-down model framework. Use the layer-by-layer analysis questions as a guide.

Business

1. Why was this downsizing effort undertaken?
2. What were the strategic directions articulated by the parent company that affected this effort?

Applications

1. What stated characteristics must applications possess in order to qualify for consideration in this downsizing effort?
2. How was the purchase of off-the-shelf software justified from a business perspective?
3. What were the evaluation criteria established for evaluating application software?

Data

1. What were the client–server databases over which the application software must run?

Network

1. What network architectures were used in the case?
2. What were the wide area networking requirements?
3. What were the unique management issues involved in managing a distributed network?

Technology

1. What were the processors, operating systems, network operating systems and numbers of users at all involved sights?
2. Investigate some of the other business cases listed in this chapter's reference section. Categorize them into one of the four downsizing categories mentioned below. If any cases don't seem to fit one of these four categories, debate whether additional categories should be established.

Downsizing Categories

1. Simple change of platform
2. Change of application development environment
3. Business process or systems re-engineering
4. Purchase off-the-shelf distributed applications

CHAPTER 10

Voice Communications and Voice/Data Integration

Concepts Reinforced

Top-Down Model
OSI 7-Layer Model
Cost–Benefit Analysis
Wide Area Networking

Importance of Standards
ISDN
SS7

Concepts Introduced

Voice Digitization
Voice Compression
Voice/Data Integration
PBX Architectures
PCS—Personal Communication
    Systems
Network Bypass

Network Services
Cellular, VSAT, and Microwaves
    Technologies
Computer Integrated Telephony
Software Defined Networks
Advanced Intelligent Networks

OBJECTIVES

After mastering the material in this chapter you should:

1. Understand the underlying technical concepts for voice transmission, voice digitization, voice compression and data/voice integration.

2. Understand currently available voice-related technology including PBXs, voice digitizers, and voice/data multiplexers.

3. Understand the different network transport methodologies available including copper-based, fiber-based, VSAT, cellular, microwave, PCS, and others.

4. Understand the advantages, limitations, and proper business utilization of the network services offered by the carriers for voice or voice/data transmission.

5. Understand the advantages, methodology, and limitations of user-created private or bypass networks including, but not limited to, microwave and VSAT.

6. Understand how available technology and business demand will combine to foster network services of the future such as Software Defined Networks and Advanced Intelligent Networks.

INTRODUCTION

After having had an introduction to wide area networks and services in Chapters 7 and 8, the wide area networking implications and requirements of voice communication and data/voice integration will now be further explored.

Once voice related concepts such as voice digitization and voice compression are understood, the next area of study will be the key voice management technology component known as the PBX (private branch exchange). After a review of the functionality provided by the PBX and its alternatives such as Centrex, the voice that is transmitted out onto the wide area network will be followed.

Network alternatives of ownership (public or private), as well as transmission methodology will be explored in detail. New and emerging network infrastructures such as VSAT, cellular, wireless, and PCS (personal communications systems) will be examined from both a voice transmission as well as a data/voice integration perspective.

As network infrastructures change, so can the services offered for transport over those networks. Although new and emerging data services were explored in Chapter 8, additional voice and data/voice services will be explored here in Chapter 10.

Voice communications technology and the application of that technology for meeting business objectives will be better understood as topics such as computer integrated telephony are explored.

In summary, by further explaining voice communications and data/voice integration, this chapter will add to your existing knowledge of wide area networks, as well as the services enabled by those networks and the technology which interfaces to them.

☐ VOICE TRANSMISSION BASIC CONCEPTS

Now that we have covered analog transmission, modulation techniques, and digital transmission in previous chapters, a few voice-specific topics will be elaborated upon to begin the study of voice transmission and data/voice integration.

As previously studied, a voice conversation consists of sound waves of varying frequency and amplitude and represented as a continuously varying analog waveform. The POTS (plain old telephone service) network employed analog transmission methodologies to transmit the voice signals from source to destination.

Getting Voice Onto and Off of the Network

But how does this analog waveform get from a person's mouth, the human transmitter, onto the analog network and subsequently into the ear, the human receiver, of the person called? Figure 10-1 illustrates the mechanics of a typical phone handset, which consists of both transmitter and receiver components.

The telephone handset, consisting of both a transmitter and receiver is really a fairly simple device that works largely based on the properties of electromagnetism. The *transmitter,* or mouthpiece contains a movable diaphragm which is sensitive to changes in voice frequency and amplitude. The diaphragm is made of carbon granules which have the ability to conduct electricity. As the human voice spoken into the transmitter varies, the amount of carbon granules striking the electrical contacts in the mouthpiece varies, sending a varying analog, electrical signal out onto the voice network.

This constantly varying electrical analog wave is transmitted over the voice network to the phone of the receiving person. The *receiver* or earpiece portion of the handset basically works in the opposite fashion of the mouthpiece. The varying electrical waves produced by the transmitter are received at the receiver by an electromagnet. Varying levels of electricity produce varying levels of magnetism

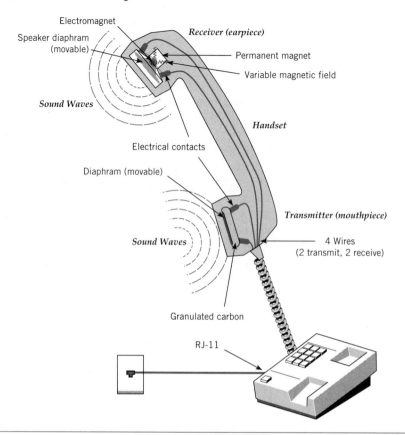

Figure 10-1 Getting voice on and off the voice network.

which cause the movable diaphragm to move in direct proportion with the magnetic variance. The moving diaphragm produces varying sound waves corresponding to the sound waves which were input at the transmitter. The electromagnetically reproduced sound resembles the actual sound waves input at the transmitter closely enough to allow for voice recognition by the receiving party.

Signalling the Central Office: Dialing

As discussed in previous chapters, the switch at the central office routes calls from source to destination via circuit switching. Requested destinations for phone calls are indicated to the central office switch by dialing a series of numbers. These numbers tell the switch whether the call to this destination will be local, intra-LATA (local access transport area), or inter-LATA and subsequently, which circuits must be accessed and combined to complete the call as requested.

The dialed numbers can be generated in two ways. Older-style rotary phones, like the one which was taken apart in order to draw Figure 10-1, have a round dial which causes a certain number of pulses of electricity to be generated depending on the number dialed. Dialing "1" produces one electrical pulse, dialing "2" produces two electrical pulses, and so on. Many of today's phones no longer have rotary dials.

Instead, today's phones contain 12 buttons that correspond to the 10 numbers on the rotary dial plus two other characters, the star (*) and the pound (#). A switch is often included which can be set to **pulse** in order to emulate the dialing process of the older style of phone. This may be necessary in areas where central office switches have not been upgraded to understand **tone,** more commonly known as touch-tone dialing.

Touch-tone dialing is technically known as **DTMF,** or (dual-tone multi-frequency), because the tone associated with each number dialed is really a combination of two tones selected from a matrix of multiple possible frequencies. Figure 10-2 illustrates the numbers and symbols found on a typical telephone touch panel and their associated dual-tone frequencies.

The tones generated by DTMF phones are used for much more than merely dialing. As will be seen later in the chapter, these same tones can be used to enable specialized services from PBXs, carriers, banks, information services, and retail establishments.

Voice Digitization

Although the *local loop* between the local CO and a residence or place of business may be an analog circuit, it is highly unlikely that the continuously varying analog signal representing a person's voice will stay in analog form all the way to the destination location's phone receiver. Rather, it is very likely that high-capacity digital circuits will be employed to transport that call, especially between COs or carriers.

Converting analog voice signals for transmission over digital circuits is the exact opposite of the situation faced in earlier chapters when digital data had to be converted into analog form for transmission over the voice network. The fact that carriers may be converting a voice conversation to digital format and reconverting it back to analog form before it reaches its destination is completely transparent to phone network users.

The basic technique for **voice digitization** is relatively simple. The constantly varying analog voice conversation must be *sampled* frequently enough so that when the digitized version of the voice is converted back to an analog signal, the resultant conversation resembles the voice of the call initiator. Most voice digitization techniques employ a sampling rate of 8000 samples per second.

Digital Signals Represent Analog Waves   Recalling that a digital signal is just a discrete electrical voltage, there are only a limited number of ways in which the electrical pulses can be varied to represent varying characteristics of an analog voice signal.

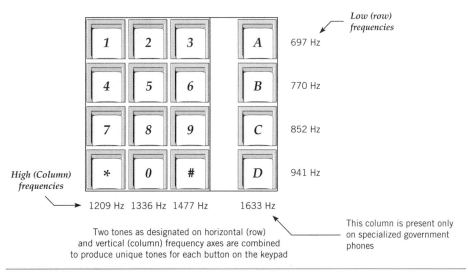

Figure 10-2 Tone dialing with DTMF.

PAM (pulse amplitude modulation) varies the amplitude or voltage of the electrical pulses in relation to the varying characteristics of the voice signal. PAM was the voice digitization technique used in some earlier PBXs.

PDM (pulse duration modulation), otherwise known as **PWM** (pulse width modulation), varies the duration of each electrical pulse in relation to the variances in the analog signal.

PPM (pulse position modulation) varies the duration between pulses in relation to variances in the analog signal. By varying the spaces in between the discrete electrical pulses on the digital circuit, PPM focuses on the relative position of the pulses to one another as a means of representing the continuously varying analog signal. Figure 10-3 illustrates these three voice digitization techniques.

PAM: Pulse Amplitude Modulation

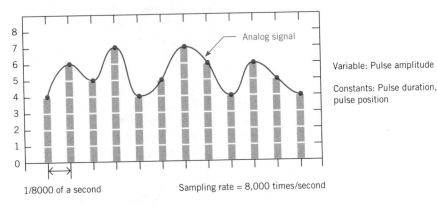

PDM: Pulse Duration Modulation

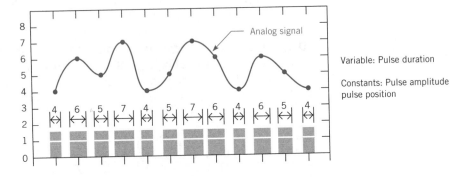

PPM: Pulse Position Modulation

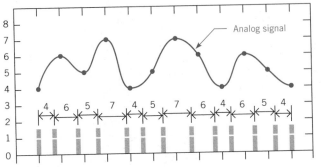

Figure 10-3 Voice digitization: PAM, PDM, PPM.

PCM   Although any of these methods can be used for voice digitization, the most common voice digitization technique in use today is known as pulse code modulation or **PCM**. A variation of this digitization technique known as **ADPCM** (adaptive differential pulse code modulation) is also very popular employing roughly half the bandwidth for each digitized conversation as compared to PCM. Figure 10-4 illustrates the basics of PCM.

> ➤ *In Sharper Focus*

VOICE DIGITIZATION BANDWIDTH REQUIREMENTS

As can be seen from Figure 10-4, eight bits or one byte are required in order to transmit the sampled amplitude of an analog signal. Some simple mathematics will reveal the bandwidth required to transmit digitized voice using PCM. This computed required bandwidth will, by no coincidence, correspond exactly to a very common digital circuit bandwidth.

Recalling that 8000 samples per second are required to assure quality transmission of digitized voice and that each sample requires eight bits to represent that sampled bandwidth in binary (1's and 0's) notation, the following equation reveals that 64,000 bits per second is the required bandwidth for transmission of digitized voice via PCM. A DS-0 circuit is exactly 64K. Twenty-four DS-0's are combined to form a T-1, yielding the fact that a T-1 can carry 24 simultaneous digitized voice conversations.

$$8000 \ \frac{\text{samples}}{\text{second}} \times 8 \ \frac{\text{bits}}{\text{sample}} = 64,000 \ \frac{\text{bits}}{\text{second}}$$

$$64,000 \ \frac{\text{bits}}{\text{second}} = 64 \ \text{Kbps} = \text{DS-0 Circuit}$$

$$(24 \times \text{DS-0} \ (64\text{K each})) + 1 \ \text{8-bit framing character} = \text{T-1} = 1.544 \ \text{Mbps}$$

ADPCM   ADPCM (adaptive differential pulse code modulation) takes a slightly different approach to coding sampled amplitudes in order to use transmission bandwidth more efficiently. By transmitting only the approximate *difference* in amplitude of consecutive amplitude samples, rather than the absolute amplitude, only 32Kbps of bandwidth is required for each conversation digitized via ADPCM, thereby allowing 48 simultaneous digitized voice conversations per T-1.

Voice Compression

ADPCM is also known as a **voice compression** technique because of its ability to transmit 24 digitized voice conversations in half of the bandwidth required by PCM. Other more advanced techniques employ specially programmed microprocessors known as **DSPs** (digital signal processors), which take the digitized PCM code and further manipulate and compress it. In doing so, DSPs are able to transmit and reconstruct digitized voice conversations in as little as 4800 bps per conversation, an increase in transmission efficiency of more than 13 times over PCM!

Numerous voice compression technological approaches exist. Voice compression can be performed by stand-alone units or by integral modules within multiplexers. The particular method by which the voice is compressed may be according to an open standard or by a proprietary methodology. Each voice compression

Analog Signal to be Digitized:

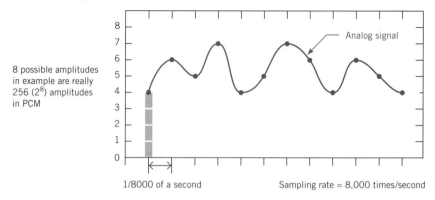

8 possible amplitudes in example are really 256 (2^8) amplitudes in PCM

1/8000 of a second

Sampling rate = 8,000 times/second

Step 1: Sample Amplitude of Analog Signal

Amplitude in example at sample position 1 (the gray shaded box) is 4

Step 2: Represent Measured Amplitude in Binary Notation

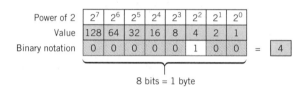

Step 3: Transmit Coded Digital Pulses Representing Measured Amplitude

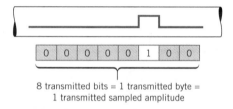

Figure 10-4 Voice digitization: Pulse Code Modulation (PCM).

technique seeks to reduce the amount of transmitted voice information in one way or another.

Some voice compression techniques attempt to synthesize the human voice, other techniques attempt to predict the actual voice transmission patterns, while still others attempt to transmit only changes in voice patterns. Loading information from multiple conversations is done primarily by two familiar techniques. One is simple time division multiplexing; the other involves packetization of voice packets prior to transmission.

Regardless of the voice compression technique or circuit-loading technique employed, one thing is certain: The quality of compressed voice transmissions does not match the quality of an analog voice transmission over an analog dial-up line or a full 64K of digital line. The transmission quality degradation will vary from one instance to another. However, only the end-users of the compressed voice system can determine whether the reduced voice quality is worth the bandwidth and related cost savings.

Coder/Decoder   A device known as a coder/decoder, or **CODEC,** is the technology employed to sample analog transmissions and transform them into a series of binary digits. In addition, many codecs also multiplex several digitized voice conversations onto a single channel and are an integral part of T-1 multiplexers. As will be seen in the chapter on videoconferencing, CODECs are also employed to digitize video for transmission over high bandwidth digital circuits. In some sense, a CODEC can be considered the opposite of a modem. CODECs are also employed in PBXs, as will be seen in the next section of this chapter.

☐ PBX BASIC CONCEPTS

In order to provide flexible voice communications capability among people within a business organization as well as with the outside world, a switching device known as a **PBX** (private branch exchange) is often employed. Sales of PBXs in the United States represent approximately a $1.5 billion annual market. The I-P-O model of PBX functionality illustrated in Figure 10-5 delineates the major functional requirements of a PBX.

The switching of calls within a PBX is really just circuit-switching as described in earlier chapters. To elaborate, a PBX is really just a privately-owned, smaller version of the switch in central offices which can control circuit switching for the general public. Depending on the requested destination, switched circuits are established, maintained, and terminated on a per call basis by a portion of the PBX known as the **switching matrix.**

Basic PBX Architecture

Beyond the switching capabilities of a PBX, programmable features offer advanced functionality to users. These features and the overall performance of the PBX are controlled by software programs that reside in and are executed on specialized computers within the PBX in an area sometimes referred to as the **PBX CPU, stored program control** or **common control area.**

Physically, most PBXs resemble the high-powered internetworking concentrators described in previous chapters. Starting with an open chassis or cabinet with power supply and backbone or backplane, modules or cards are added to increase PBX capacity for either user extensions or connections to the outside network. Additional cabinets can often be cascaded to offer PBX expandability.

Phone lines to users' offices for phone connection are terminated in the PBX in slide-in modules or cards known as *line cards, port cards,* or **station cards.** In order to increase capacity of connections to the outside network, cards known as **trunk cards** are added to the PBX. Some trunk cards are specialized to a particular type of network line, T-1 or DDS lines, for instance. Some PBXs allow any chassis slot to be used for any type of card or module, while other PbXs specify certain slots for line cards and others for trunk cards. Figure 10-6 illustrates the physical attributes of a representative PBX.

I (Input)	P (Processing)	O (Output)
End-users access PBX capabilities and network connections through their phones.	Provide necessary switching to allow connection between PBX users or to outside network connections. Provide additional capabilities to track PBX usage and offer advanced functions such as conference calling, call forwarding, least cost routing, automatic call distribution, automated attendant, etc.	Private or public network connections.

Figure 10-5 I-P-O model of PBX functionality.

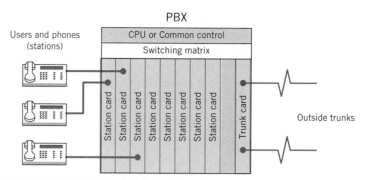

Figure 10-6 Physical attributes of a PBX.

PBX Installation

In an actual PBX installation, station lines would probably not terminate directly into station cards in the PBX as shown in Figure 10-6, but rather would be "punched-down" on a Telco punch-down block, or 66M block, which would be located in a secure telecommunications closet. A single 25-pair Telco cable would carry multiple station lines to a given station card with far less clutter than individual connections for each station. Outside lines from the telephone network would also, in all likelihood, be punched down before being attached to PBX trunk cards.

PBXs installed in geographically separate locations can be tied together to form one virtual PBX with the use of a special type of outside line known as a **tie line.** This setup is especially useful to companies with a main office and several branch offices within a metropolitan area. Conference calls across multiple PBXs can be accomplished transparently with the use of these tie lines.

A tie line allows a user on a remote PBX to access extensions or services of a main PBX as if they were locally attached to that main PBX. Rather than dialing a full phone number at the remote PBX to reach the main PBX, a single digit or button can be pushed. Tie lines do not have outside network dial tones. They are quite similar to the voice equivalent of a point-to-point data line. Figure 10-7 illustrates a standard PBX installation with remote PBX attached via tie lines.

Digital PBXs Offer Additional Benefits

Most modern PBXs are known as digital PBXs due to their digitizing of analog voice signals prior to switching and transmission. The digitization is usually done by a CODEC using PCM as described earlier in this chapter. The CODECS are located either in the phones or in the PBX. The fact that many PBXs are digital in nature with specially-designed digitizing phones is important in that "regular" phones purchased at a local department store will not work on a digital PBX. The digital PBX phones are many times more expensive than the readily available analog models.

A digital PBX does not necessarily imply connection to digital outside network trunks such as T-1s. The digitization is primarily for improved internal operation of the PBX. Specifically, digitization offers the following benefits to PBX operations:

1. Digitization of voice allows the same switching and transmission equipment to handle voice, fax, and data. This eliminates the need for special analog switching equipment and reduces the overall cost of the PBX.
2. Since all voice, fax, and data is in digital format, the various types of information can be multiplexed or interleaved over the same transmission cir-

cuits eliminating the need for redundant circuits and further reducing transmission costs. The benefits of this data/voice integration will be further explored later in this chapter.

3. Over long distances, digital information, whether voice, data, or fax, tends to be more error free than analog transmissions. As stated in previous chapters, this is largely due to the fact that digital signals are merely regenerated, while analog signals along with inherent background noise and interference are simply amplified.

PBX FEATURES AND SERVICES

PBX features and services tend to fall into three broad categories:

Features and services that provide users with flexible usage of PBX resources.
Features and services that provide for data/voice integration.
Features and services that control and monitor the use of those PBX resources.

Although providing data/voice integration can be considered a type of flexible PBX resource usage, the increased emphasis on this category of features warrants a separate listing.

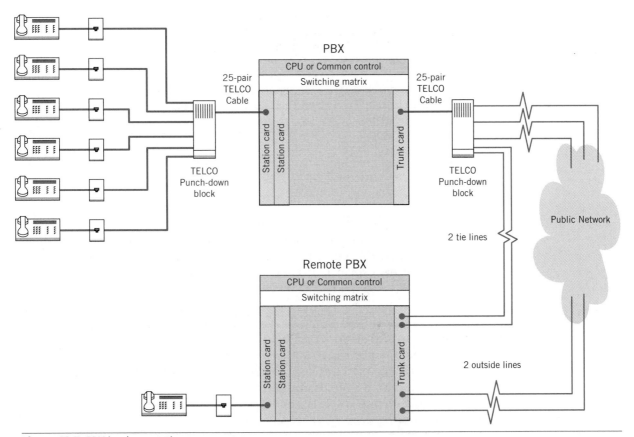

Figure 10-7 PBX implementation.

Feature/Service	Description
Least Cost Routing (LCR)	Using routing and pricing information supplied by the user, the PBX chooses the most economical path for any given call. This feature was more important when WATS (wide area telecommunications service) lines were more prevalent. These days, thanks to competition and discount programs among long-distance carriers, PBXs can access any outgoing trunk rather than trying to get certain calls onto certain trunks
Automatic Call Distribution (ACD)	Incoming calls are routed directly to certain extensions without going through a central switchboard. Calls can be routed according to the incoming trunk or phone number. Often used in customer service organizations in which calls may be distributed to the first free agent
Call Pickup	Allows a user to pickup or answer another user's phone without the need to actually forward calls
Paging	Ability to use paging speakers in a building. May be limited to specific areas
Direct Inward Dialing (DID)	Allows calls to bypass the central switchboard and go directly to a user's phone
Hunting	Hunt groups are established to allow incoming calls to get through on alternate trunks when a primary trunk is busy. For example, most businesses publish only one phone number. If that trunk is busy, the PBX hunts for an open incoming trunk in a manner unknown to the customer
Prioritization	Individual extensions can be given priority access to certain trunks or groups of trunks. In most cases, PBXs are not equipped with equal numbers of user extensions and outgoing trunks. If certain users *must* have access to outside lines, prioritization features are important
Night Mode	Many companies close their switchboards at night but still have employees working who must be able to receive and make phone calls. Programming night mode features offer this flexibility

Figure 10-8 Voice-based PBX features and services.

Voice-Based Features and Services

In the flexible-usage category, features such as conference calling, call forwarding, call transfer, speed dialing, redialing, and call hold are commonplace and should not require further explanation. Other voice-based PBX features and services that support flexible usage of PBX resources are summarized in Figure 10-8.

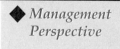 *Management Perspective*

Data/Voice Integration   Data/voice integration by PBXs is increasingly common but should not be assumed merely because a PBX is categorized as digital. Differences in data interfaces and whether or not those interfaces and associated software represent an upgrade at additional cost should be investigated thoroughly before any PBX purchase. Data and data/voice integration related features and issues are summarized in Figure 10-9.

Feature/Service	Description
ISDN support	Are ISDN interfaces and support included in PBX or available as upgrades?
T-1 support	Are T-1's supported? Are CODECS included? Are channel banks included?
Data interfaces	Are data interfaces to host computers provided on a card in the PBX chassis, or are they provided as part of the digital phone equipment? Which interface standards are supported? Are these interface standards supported by your computer equipment? Are LAN interfaces (Ethernet, Token Ring) provided on the PBX? RS-232? How many of the following are supported: fax transmission modem pooling printer sharing file sharing video conferencing

PBX-to-Host Interfaces (PHI)	PBX Vendor	PHI Name
	Northern Telecom	Meridien Link
	Northern Telecom/DEC	Computer PBX Interface (CPI)
	ROLM	CallBridge
	IBM	CallPath
	AT&T	Adjunct Switch Applications Interface (ASAI)
	Siemens	Applications Connectivity Link (ACL)
	MITEL	Host Command Interface (HCI)

Figure 10-9 Data and data/voice integration: PBX features and services.

PBX to Computer Interfaces   Access by computers to the PBX may be via ports in a card installed in the PBX chassis or through data ports included in specially configured digital phones. Remote users can then dial into the PBX and access computers attached via these data interfaces. Each PBX vendor has their own proprietary interface to computers from various manufacturers. Although some of the more popular PBX-to-host interfaces are listed in Figure 10-9, the more generic terms for these interfaces are either open application interfaces **(OAI)** or PBX–host interfaces **(PHI).** Many computer vendors have written corresponding interfaces from their computers to a particular PBX vendors PHI specification. Establishing, maintaining, and terminating switched connections between data users and host computers via a PBX according to the specifications of a PBX–host interface is only the first stage of PBX/computer integration.

Computer Integrated Telephony

Passing actual information such as incoming or outgoing phone numbers along these switched connections to or from the attached computer for subsequent processing by the computer or PBX is the next stage in PBX–host integration and is generally known as computer integrated telephony **(CIT).** Customer service and telemarketing departments are ideal applications for CIT.

For instance, in an in-bound customer service setting the PBX can pass the caller's phone number to the computer via automatic number identification **(ANI)** or calling line identification display **(CLID)** upon receipt of the call. The computer can query the computer's database for the records of the customer with that phone number and have the information displayed on the screen as the call is put through

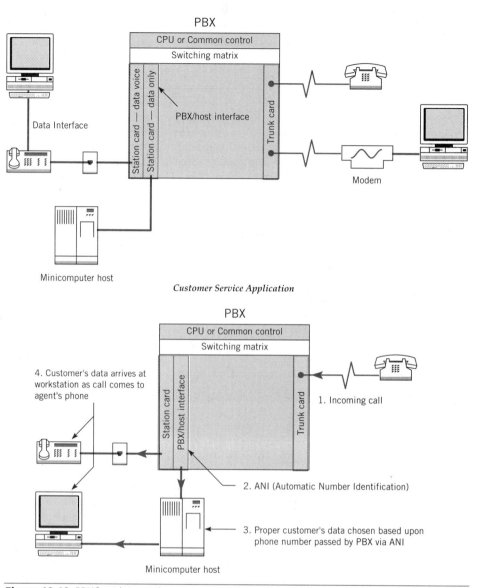

Figure 10-10 PBX/host integration.

to the agent. In an order taking setting, if the phone number dialed by the customer indicates which product or service they'll be ordering, then the PBX can pass that dialed number to the computer via the dialed number identification service **(DNIS)** standard.

In an outbound telemarketing setting, phone numbers can be fed from the computer's database to special auto-dialing equipment that interfaces to the PBX. If the call is answered, the PBX triggers the computer to display the associated data record on the data terminal of the telemarketing agent as they begin their conversation with the called party. Figure 10-10 illustrates some PBX–host integration possibilities.

Control and Monitoring Features   Control and monitoring features range from the simple, such as limiting access to outside lines from certain extensions, to the complex, such as entire standalone **call accounting systems.** Call accounting systems are often run on separate PCs which interface directly to the PBX and execute specially written software. Accounting reports or bills sorted by department or extension can be run on a scheduled basis or on demand. Exception reports can be generated to spot possible abuses for calls over a certain length or cost, or calls made to a particular area code. Incoming as well as outgoing calls can be tracked. Call accounting systems can pay for themselves in a short amount of time by spotting and curtailing abuse as well as allocating phone usage charges on a departmental basis.

The information on which such a call accounting system depends is generated by the PBX. In a process known as **SMDR** (station message detail recording), an individual detail record is generated for each call. This data record can then be transferred from the PBX to the call accounting system computer, usually from an RS-232 DB-25 port on the PBX to the serial port on the PC. Data records can be stored and summarized on the call accounting system computer dependent on available disk space. Figure 10-11 illustrates the setup of a call accounting system.

Auxiliary Voice-Related Services

Just as the previously mentioned call accounting systems are most often an add-on device for PBXs, other auxiliary systems exist to enhance PBX capability. The auxiliary nature of these systems implies that they are often not included as standard features on PBXs but may be purchased separately from either the PBX vendor or third-party manufacturers. Figure 10-12 lists and describes a few of the more popular auxiliary PBX systems.

Voice Processing

Voice processing, listed in Figure 10-12, has seen an increase in usage thanks to readily available development hardware and software for voice processing systems. Formerly only delivered as "turn-key" solutions by a limited number of vendors, voice processing cards for PCs and associated application development lan-

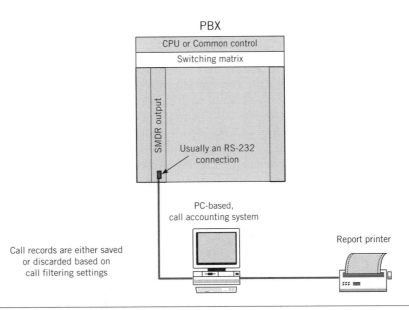

Figure 10-11 Call accounting systems integration.

Service/device	Description
Automated attendant	A recorded message system that works with touch-tone (DTMF) phones. Rather than having an operator answer all calls, the automated attendant first answers and requests callers to press the extension number they wish to reach. Those wishing to speak to the operator are transferred. Sometimes also connected to voice-mail systems.
Voice mail	Voice mail systems can vary widely in cost and sophistication. After recording an initial message for someone, voice mail systems may allow the voice mail to be handled like a written phone message. It can be forwarded, copied, have comments added to it, saved, and recalled.
Voice Response Units (VRU)	Also called interactive voice response unit. Could perhaps be more correctly called touch-tone response units. The voice part is synthesized voice which offers menu selections to be chosen via a touch-tone phone. As an example, some answering machines include VRUs which allow the owner of the answering machine to check for messages from a remote location. The VRU offers choices such as save messages, rewind the tape, record a new outgoing message, etc.
Voice processor	Performs same basic functions as voice response units but may also recognize and process applications software or menu selections based on actual voice responses, speech recognition, or touch tone.
Voice server	A LAN-based server which stores, processes, and delivers digitized voice messages. Translates digitized voice into analog form before transmission to recipients. Often used as the processing and storage component of a voice mail system.
Music/ads on hold	When customers are put on hold, music plays or, alternately, a tape recorded sales message interrupts periodically with messages such as, "Your call is important to us, please stay on the line."

Figure 10-12 Auxiliary voice-related services/devices.

guages or APIs are allowing customers to develop their own interactive voice response systems. Any organization receiving a large number of calls which must be properly routed can develop their own automated attendant system with voice processor hardware and software.

After responding with one's voice or touching the proper key on a touch-tone phone, a user of such a system might be routed to a customer service agent, access particular data records off a server, or access voice mail or fax services. An example of data access and processing through a voice response system is a banking service that allows an account holder to check current account balances or transfer funds between accounts via any touch-tone phone. Figure 10-13 illustrates the elements of a user-developed voice processing system.

PBX Trends

As PBXs become more highly integrated into information systems in applications such as computer integrated telephony, it stands to reason that PBX trends will follow some of the trends currently affecting the computer industry. Two of the most prevalent PBX trends, interoperability between PBXs of various manufacturers and integration with wireless phone systems, are testaments to the symmetry of PBX and computer development trends.

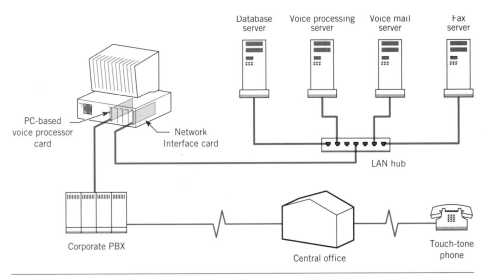

Figure 10-13 User-developed voice processing systems.

Multivendor Interoperability Standards Just as open systems has become a major emphasis in the computer industry, interoperability between PBXs from various manufacturers has been receiving increased attention. An international standard sponsored by the ISO known as **Q.Sig** seeks to allow PBXs of any manufacturers to interoperate with each other and with ISDN networks. As a matter of fact, Q.Sig is an extension of an ISDN standard known as *Q.931*, which allows PBX features to interoperate with public switched network features. This fading line of demarcation between customer equipment and the carrier's equipment is another important trend which will be explored later in this chapter when such topics as the software defined network (SDN) and the advanced intelligent network (AIN) are studied.

Q.Sig standardizes features among different PBX manufacturers and delivers those standardized features within the limitations of the feature set offered by ISDN. Among the standardized PBX features are call establishment and termination, call waiting, caller ID and caller ID blocking, as well as other ISDN supported features. In some ways, Q.Sig is analogous to the X.400 standard in the E-mail world. X.400 defines standardized features among various E-mail systems and delivers these arbitrated features via an X.400 compliant E-mail backbone.

PBX Integration with Wireless Phones It seemed inevitable that with the explosion in the use of portable wireless telephones a demand would arise for transparent integration of those wireless phones with the traditional PBX architecture. Northern Telecom, one of the world's largest and most successful PBX manufacturers, has created such a link between wireless phones and PBXs.

Their system, called the Companion, allows wireless phones to take advantage of PBX features such as call forwarding, conference calling, speed dialing, etc. In addition, a person's portable phone can be "twinned" with their office phone so that both ring when the extension is called. The portable phone becomes just another PBX extension, rather than an unintegrated remote phone, reachable only by dialing a full seven-digit number.

Standards support is important in wireless phones as in any other aspect of data communications. These PBX-integrated wireless phones support the **CT2** (cordless telephony generation 2) common air interface **(CAI)** global standard for low-power wireless transmission. Such systems are especially useful in large hospitals, hotels, convention centers, and office buildings where key support people spend a great deal of time at various locations throughout the building.

☐ VOICE NETWORK CONCEPTS

The basic architecture and operation of the PSN (public switched network) was introduced in Chapter 2 as part of the discussion of dial-up data connections. Terms such as central office (CO), local access transport area (LATA), and point of presence (POP) were introduced at that time. In this section, a more in depth look at the operation of the PSN will be taken while focusing on two areas in particular.

First, a concept or architecture known as the **network hierarchy** and its implication on call routing and delivery will be explored. Secondly, a key element in the control and management of this network hierarchy known as signalling system 7, or **SS7,** introduced in Chapter 8 as part of the study of ISDN, will also be studied.

Network Hierarchy

As can be seen in Figure 10-14, a residential or business call is first processed in the local *central office,* also known as an end office or local office. In terms of the network hierarchy, an end office is known as a **class 5 end office.** This local central office contains a switch which processes incoming calls, determines the best path to the call destination, and establishes the circuit connection.

Local calls come into the local central office via a local loop and travel to their local destination via a local loop. Calls that are not local but still within the same LATA are known as **intra-LATA** calls and are handled by a local carrier, most often an RBOC's operating company. Technically, these are long-distance calls and a local CO may not have a direct trunk to the destination CO. In this case, the call is routed through a **tandem office** which establishes the intra-LATA circuit and also handles billing procedures for the long-distance call.

Inter-LATA calls must be turned over from a local carrier to a long-distance carrier such as AT&T, MCI, or U.S. Sprint. In most cases, the particular inter-exchange carrier (IXC) employed will have been chosen by individual residential and business subscribers. The local CO still receives such inter-LATA calls from subscribers. However, rather than the local carrier routing the call to its final destination, the call is merely forwarded to the local switching office of the long-distance carrier of choice.

Such a long-distance switching office is known as a *POP* (point of presence) and also as a **class 4 toll center.** The term toll center implies that long-distance billing calculation as well as switching activities are performed at these locations. A given local CO may have trunks to more than one toll center. As will be seen, circuit redundancy offering multiple alternative paths for call routing is a central premise of the voice network hierarchy.

If the local toll center can find adequate space on a trunk headed to the destination CO, then the connection between source and destination COs is completed. If no paths to the destination are directly available to the local toll center, then the call is escalated up the network hierarchy to the next level of switching office. The overall desire is to keep the call as low on the hierarchy as possible. This provides both quicker call completion for the subscriber as well as a cost effective use of the lowest, and least expensive switching offices possible.

Higher levels on the network hierarchy imply greater switching and transmission capacity as well as greater expense. When calls cannot be completed directly, class 4 toll centers turn to **class 3 primary centers** for backup, which subsequently turn to **class 2 sectional centers,** which turn finally to **class 1 regional centers.** Not all inter-LATA or long-distance carriers have a five level network hierarchy. These categories of switching and transmission centers were originally AT&T's, but have become industry standard terminology.

Although Figure 10-14 illustrates the relationship among various levels of switching centers, Figure 10-15 more clearly illustrates why higher level offices

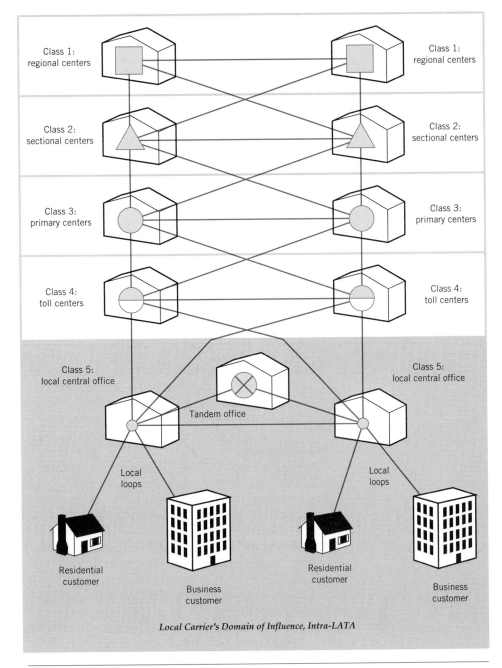

Figure 10-14 Voice network hierarchy.

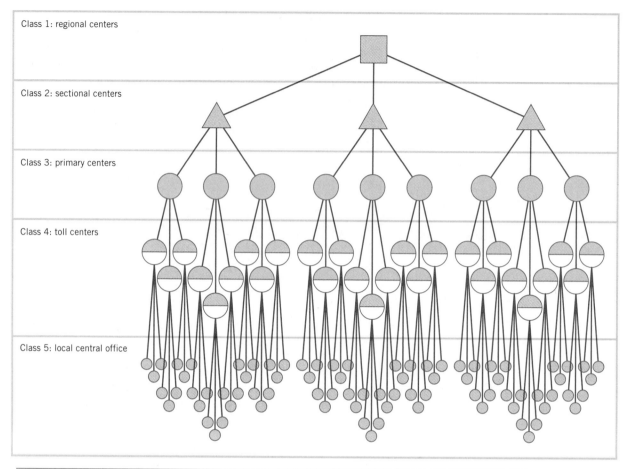

Class 1: regional centers

Class 2: sectional centers

Class 3: primary centers

Class 4: toll centers

Class 5: local central office

Figure 10-15 Voice network hierarchy: a logical pyramid.

have greater routing flexibility. As can be seen in Figure 10-15, the network hierarchy is more of a logical pyramid, with numerous toll centers serviced by a single class 3 primary center and so on. Although the numbers of centers on any given level in Figure 10-15 are for illustrative purposes only, the basic proportions may be valid. In fact, while there are over 9000 class 5 centers, there are only 12 class 1 regional centers.

As an interesting sidenote, Figure 10-14 could change in the intra-LATA or local carrier area. In some jurisdictions, intra-LATA competition has now been allowed. This implies that business and residential subscribers will not only be allowed to choose among long distance carriers, but local carriers as well.

Network Interoffice Signalling Standards

As residential and business subscribers not serviced by PBXs begin to expect PBX-like intelligent services from network offerings such as ISDN, the network itself must become more "intelligent." End-to-end signalling between carrier's switches and customer premises equipment **(CPE),** regardless of what local or long-distance carrier might be involved, is the first step toward delivering intelligent services such as **ANI** (automatic number identification).

There are two key requirements of this inter-switch signalling methodology. First, it must be standardized. Secondly, it must not travel over the same logical channel as the voice conversation itself. In other words, the signalling should travel out of the voice conversation's band or channel in a process known as **out-of-band signalling.** A more official name for out-of-band signalling is common channel interoffice signalling **(CCIS).**

Out-of-band-signalling was introduced during the discussion of the D channel's use in ISDN. Besides delivering incoming phone numbers to residential and business users, the out-of-band signalling is used to manage the network itself by handling the routing of calls and circuit establishment as well as the monitoring of circuit status and notification and rerouting in the case of alarms or circuit problems.

Signalling System 7 The worldwide, CCITT-approved standard for out-of-band signalling is known as signalling system 7 (SS7). Signalling system 7 is closely related to ISDN. As an underlying architectural component of ISDN, SS7 delivers the out-of-band signalling over ISDN's D channel, delivering both intelligent services to the end user as well as network management information to network administrators. Signalling system 7 can exist without ISDN, but transparent, inter-switch services cannot be delivered via ISDN without SS7.

But what exactly *is* signalling system 7? SS7 is nothing more than a suite of protocols, not unlike others suites of protocols examined earlier, which controls the structure and transmission of both circuit-related and noncircuit related information via out-of-band signalling between central office switches. Like most protocol suites, SS7 can be modeled in comparison to the OSI 7-layer reference model. Figure 10-16 summarizes the major characteristics of the signalling system 7 protocols and compares the SS7 protocol suite to the OSI model.

SS7 Enables AIN and SDN

Signalling system 7 and the intelligent services it enables are often described as part of an all-encompassing interface between users and the PSTN (public switched telephone network) known as **AIN** (advanced intelligent network). Among the major components of the advanced intelligent network is **SDN** (software-defined network). A software-defined network implies that the user has some control over the flexible configuration of their telecommunications service and network. By extending SS7 out-of-band signalling to the end users, voice networks can be reconfigured as business activities dictate.

The most common application to date of SDN is customer controlled 800 services for in-bound customer service or calling center applications. For instance, with AT&T's intelligent call processing **(ICP)** service, customers are able to reroute incoming 800 calls among multiple customer service centers in a matter of seconds. This rerouting is done completely transparently to the calling customer and is actually accomplished by the ICP user having direct access to AT&T's switching network via SS7 out-of-band signalling. Such a service as ICP allows multiple call centers geographically dispersed throughout the country to function as one logical call center, with the overall number of incoming calls distributed in a balanced manner across all centers.

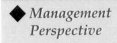

Network Architectures and Services Respond to User Demands
User-oriented network services such as AIN and SDN are being offered in response to user demands for in-house control over a key element of their business: their telecommunications systems and the links from those systems to the wide area public switched telephone network. Catalog sales organizations are literally

Protocol Name	Description/Function
Message Transfer Part (MTP)	MTP provides standards for routing of signalling messages between switches. A connectionless, datagram service
Signalling Connection Control Part (SCCP)	SCCP provides standards for routing and management of signalling messages. *Not* related to call set-up between switches. A connection-oriented service providing reliable message delivery
ISDN User Part (ISUP)	ISUP provides standards for routing and management of signalling messages as specifically required by ISDN and its services
Transaction Capabilities Application Part (TCAP)	TCAP provides standards for routing and management of noncircuit related information for transaction processing applications requiring out-of-band signalling
Operations Maintenance Application Part (O&MAP)	O&MAP provides standards for routing and management of messages related to network operations and maintenance

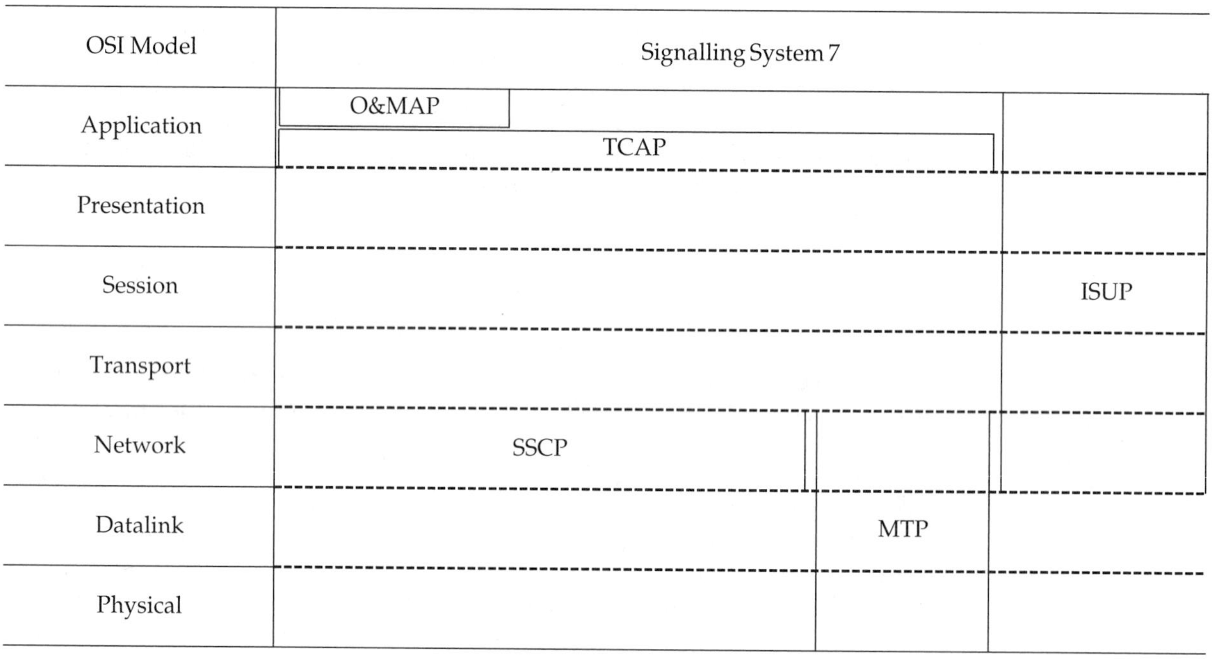

OSI Model	Signalling System 7		
Application	O&MAP / TCAP		
Presentation			
Session			ISUP
Transport			
Network	SSCP		
Datalink		MTP	
Physical			

Figure 10-16 Signalling system 7 protocols.

out of business without their phones and must have contingency plans and disaster recovery plans in place in order to deal with and hopefully avoid possible catastrophes.

Bandwidth on demand was first introduced as a driving force on the evolution of data network architectures and services in Chapter 1. At that time, bandwidth on demand was articulated as, "I want all the bandwidth I need, only when I want it, at a price I want to pay." The evolution of the voice-based network architecture and services is responding to a slight modification of this initial bandwidth on demand definition.

Emerging network architectures and services that will eventually transport voice, data, and image are responding to additional user demands for not just connectivity at *any time*, but also *anywhere*.

PCS: PERSONAL COMMUNICATIONS SERVICES

PCS (personal communications services) is a visionary concept of an evolving all-digital network architecture that could deliver a variety of telecommunications services transparently to users at any time regardless of their geographic location. PCS is not a totally new "from the bottom up" telecommunications architecture. In fact, it is the integration of a number of existing telecommunications environments. PCS seeks to combine the capabilities of the PSTN, otherwise known as the **land-line telephone network,** with the cellular network, paging network, and satellite communications network.

The need for the seamless delivery of a combination of all these is easily illustrated by the plight of today's mobile professional. A single person has a phone number for their home phone, a voice and fax number for their office, a cellular phone number for their automobile, a pager phone number for their pager, and perhaps even another phone number for their satellite service phone for use outside cellular phone areas. The premise of PCS is rather straightforward: *one person, one phone number*.

Personal Phone Numbers

This **PTN** (personal phone number) would become the user's interface to PCS and the vast array of transparently available telecommunications services. This personal phone number is a key concept to PCS. It changes the entire focus of the interface to the telecommunications environment from the current orientation of a number being associated with a particular location regardless of the individual using the facility to a number being associated with a particular individual regardless of the location of the accessed facility. Figure 10-17 illustrates the basic elements of PCS.

As Figure 10-17 is examined, it is difficult not to be struck by the similarity of the PCS architecture with earlier diagrams illustrating database, E-mail, and network connectivity. In fact, PCS serves as a type of *telecommunications middleware* transparently connecting users via their PTN (personal telephone number) API to a variety of telecommunications services.

Challenges to Widespread Deployment

Although PCS, sometimes referred to as a network of networks, may make a great deal of sense in theory, the actual implementation of a seamlessly integrated telecommunications environment faces several significant challenges.

Spectrum Wireless transmissions such as those included in the PCS vision transmit over certain frequencies as designated by domestic or international agencies responsible for spectrum allocation. It is estimated that PCS would require over 300 Mhz of spectrum allocation, not just in the United States, but worldwide in order to provide the true geographic independence of the PCS vision. Such large amounts of bandwidth are not available and would therefore have to be allocated to PCS by the displacement of current governmental or industrial users from that bandwidth.

At the World Administrative Radio Conference in 1992, sponsored by the International Telecommunications Union (ITU), a worldwide allocation of

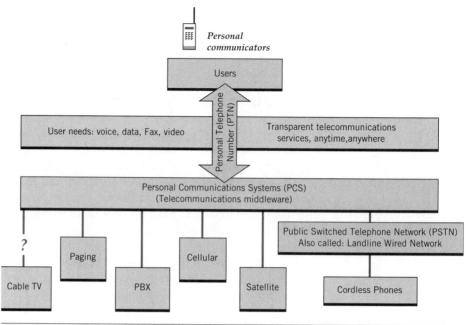

Figure 10-17 Basic elements of PCS.

240MHz of bandwidth was recommended for PCS. Compliance with the recommendation is at the discretion of individual countries. This bandwidth allocation was part of an overall effort to define PCS on a worldwide basis through a program sponsored by the **CCIR** (Consultative Committee for International Radio) known as Future Public Land Mobile Telecommunications Systems **(FPLMTS).** The relationship between CCITT, CCIR, ITU, and WARC is illustrated in Figure 10-18.

Operational Standards **Roaming** is a term derived from the cellular transmission industry which implies that as a mobile telecommunications user moves, or roams, beyond the transmission range of a particular cell, the call is handed off to a neighboring cell offering uninterrupted service transparently to the user. One of the goals of PCS is transparent worldwide roaming implying the need for not just worldwide bandwidth allocation but also worldwide standards for transmission and handing off. The CCITT is currently developing such standards known as universal personal telecommunications (UPT).

Societal and User Issues Required changes in thinking and behavior on the part of PCS users should not be overlooked. For instance, if a person can be called regardless of their location thanks to the PTN, who should pay for that call, the called party or the calling party? Caller ID services will now display the calling party's name or *personal* number rather than the number of the phone from which that person is calling. Remember, with PCS, numbers are associated with people, not with equipment and phone lines.

If the calling party is to be responsible for payment, they would probably like to know where they are calling before placing the call. However, as a potentially called party, would you want just anybody knowing your location? Your supervisor, or even vandals, could pinpoint your location without even placing a call. Advanced call screening services could allow only certain PTN's calls to be

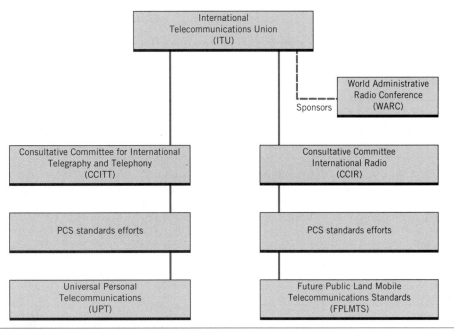

Figure 10-18 International regulatory agencies and PCS.

received on a person's personal communicator. As with any dramatically new technology, societal impact and changes will result. PCS should be no exception.

Operational, Administrative and Management Issues   More pragmatic concerns may turn out to be the most difficult to solve. For instance, how will calls be routed between cellular networks and the PSTN? How will billing be processed? Which companies will be responsible for collection of fees and how much income will each segment of the PCS architecture receive? Which company will coordinate the entire effort? How will customer problems or network problems be resolved? How can facilities changes and upgrades be coordinated in order to minimize service disruption? To summarize, it will be difficult to build an integrated, comprehensive telecommunications architecture by combining competitive network segments when each of those segments is evolving and developing according to its own strategic plan.

Who's in Charge?   The two major players in the PCS architecture have very different views of the operation of the PCS network of the future. The wire-based, PSTN industry sees themselves as the center of the PCS architecture, while the cellular industry feels that PCS is a natural extension of current cellular industry service offerings. Each industry is conducting their own field trials. Many RBOCs have their own cellular networks, which are managed by subsidiary companies, positioning the RBOCs as a logical choice for PCS field trials.

Perhaps overshadowing the RBOCs mix of cellular and landline facilities and experience is the partnership of AT&T, the largest landline network, with McCaw Cellular Communications, which controls about 20 percent of the U.S. cellular market. Plans call for the joint-venture to implement PCS field trials using individual PTNs which will be used to reach individuals regardless of their location.

Figure 10-19 summarizes some of the challenges facing PCS.

Challenge	Explanation/Implication
Spectrum Allocation	Worldwide allocation required for goal of transparent worldwide service. Little if any available bandwidth implies displacement of existing users
Operational Standards	Worldwide standards are required for issues such as service definition, numbering plan, billing, call routing, network architecture, and signalling
Societal and User Issues	Who should pay for calls? Should location be broadcast? Privacy issues? Potential misuse of PCS services?
OA&M	Operations, Administration, and Management. How will various network segments and industries transparently interoperate on a technical and business basis?
Who Is in Charge?	Which network constituency runs or coordinates PCS? What role will interexchange carriers, RBOCs, and cellular companies play?

Figure 10-19 Personal Communications Systems challenges.

Potential Benefits of PCS

Personal communicators will replace ordinary phones in the world of PCS. These devices, initially weighing between two and four pounds, will include not only a cellular phone, but also E-mail capabilities, fax capabilities, built-in modems or CSU/DSUs, and perhaps even an on-board personal organizer computer with scheduling software and electronic phone directories.

With such devices, a wide range of telecommunications related services would be available on an as-needed and where-needed basis.

Wireless Centrex   Wireless centrex would allow PCS subscribers to enjoy all the services offered by wire-based Centrex with their personal communicators. Centrex is a central office-based service offering all of the convenience and service of a PBX. Wireless Centrex would offer PCS users such functions as conference calling, call forwarding, call hold, speed dialing, call transfer, and automatic callback. Such services would offer the mobile professional all the power of a PBX-based office phone away from the office. Wireless Centrex may be especially popular in large buildings such as hospitals, hotels, and convention centers in which key personnel seldom stay at a fixed location.

Two-Way Calling   Users with personal communicators can place calls to any outgoing phone number as well as receive calls from any phone number regardless of their geographic location. The wireless or cellular portions of the PCS network would interface transparently to the PSTN for transfer of calls to and from the PSTN landline network.

Paging   Paging capabilities are integrated within the personal communicator. The personal communications services would interface to the paging company's transmission facilities and forward paging messages to the personal communicator.

Voice Mail   PCS subscribers can forward unanswered calls to their voice mailbox located in a commercial voice-mail service integrated transparently with other PCS services. This would provide for both "do-not-disturb" time as well as those times when users may not be in close proximity to their personal communicator.

Handoff and Roaming   Handoff standards between PCS networking elements will enable transparent global roaming to the PCS user. In this manner, mobile professionals will be able to conduct business on an uninterrupted basis without worry of going beyond the range of a particular transmitter or repeater.

Figure 10-20 summarizes both the networking elements of PCS as well as some of the available services.

What Will PCS Actually Look Like?

PCS has been deployed in only very limited field trials to date. One of the extensive field trials was conducted by Ameritech in 1992 and 1993. The results of that field trial may well answer what PCS might look like as deployment expands. Figure 10-21 illustrates a PSTN-based personal communications services architecture.

As can be seen in Figure 10-21, the personal communicator device can be used in both a mobile fashion as well as at the home or office. While moving, the personal communicator's signal roams and gets handed off from one PCS intelligent base station to the next. While at the home or office, the personal communicator functions like a cordless phone by communicating to the PSTN via a personal base station which is plugged into an RJ-11 jack and subsequently networked to the landline PSTN.

Wireless calls can be completed to other wireless personal communicators directly through the PCS switches or can be handed off to either wire-based PSTN services or any of the PCS services previously mentioned and illustrated in Figure 10-21. All of the handing off and network management is handled via out-of-band signalling using signalling system 7 and managed from a dedicated PCS control center.

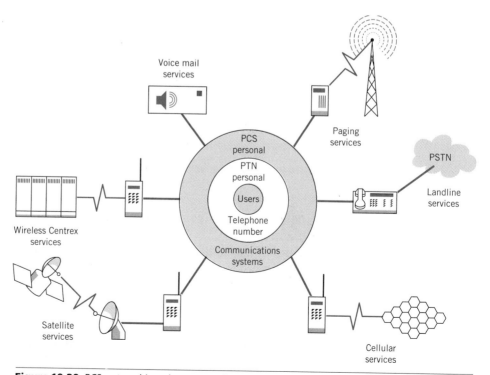

Figure 10-20 PCS networking elements and services.

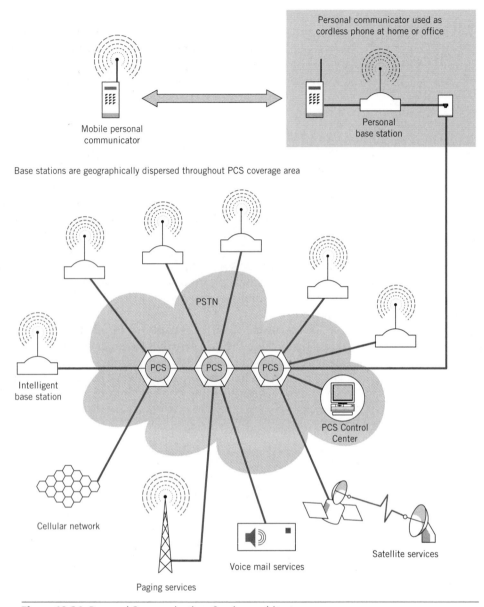

Figure10-21 Personal Communications Services architecture.

The Wireless Challenge: Maximize Calls on Minimum Bandwidth

Given the limited bandwidth allocated to PCS and the potentially large number of subscribers needed to share that limited bandwidth, a key challenge for PCS not previously mentioned is the ability to maximize the number of simultaneous conversations over a finite amount of bandwidth. Just as multiplexing was originally introduced in the study of wide area networks as a means of maximizing the use of wire-based circuits, three variations of multiplexing are being field tested as a means of maximizing the use of the allocated bandwidth of these air-based circuits.

TDMA (time division multiple access), **FDMA** (frequency division multiple access), and **CDMA** (code division multiple access) are the three methodologies currently being researched in PCS field trials. Note that the names of each of these techniques end in the words "multiple access" rather than "multiplexing." The "multiple access" refers to multiple phone conversations having access to the same bandwidth and yet not interfering with each other.

TDMA achieves more than one conversation per frequency by assigning timeslots to individual conversations. Ten timeslots per frequency often are assigned, with a given cellular device transmitting its digitized voice only during its assigned timeslot. Receiving devices must be in synch with the time slots of the sending device in order to receive the digitized voice packets and reassemble them into a natural sounding analog signal.

FDMA achieves more than one conversation per frequency by strategically deploying the various frequencies so that cells that are sufficiently geographically separated so as not to interfere with each other are allowed to use the same frequency. This technique is analogous to the FCC assigning radio stations the same frequency if the cities they service are sufficiently separated geographically.

CDMA is the newest and most advanced technique for maximizing the number of calls transmitted within a limited bandwidth by using a spread spectrum transmission technique. Rather than allocate specific frequency channels within the allocated bandwidth to specific conversations as is the case with TDMA and FDMA, CDMA transmits digitized voice packets from numerous calls at different frequencies spread all over the entire allocated bandwidth spectrum.

The "code" part of CDMA lies in the fact that in order to keep track of these various digitized voice packets from various conversations spread over the entire spectrum of allocated bandwidth, a code is appended to each packet indicating which voice conversation it belongs to. CDMA is most often used for in-building wireless PBX applications. This technique is not unlike the datagram connectionless service used by packet switched networks to send packetized data over numerous switched virtual circuits within the packet switched network. By identifying the source and sequence of each packet, the original message integrity is maintained while maximizing the overall performance of the network.

Figure 10-22 illustrates these three multiple access techniques that comprise a key area of research for PCS.

Wide Area Data Transmission on a PCS Wireless Network

Today's mobile professional not only has a need for voice transmission via cellular or satellite phone networks, but also a need to transmit data as well. Laptop, notebook, notepad, and pen-based are but a few of the categories of mobile computers which may require wireless data transmission. The ability for the mobile professional to receive and send E-mail and faxes at any time from any place is perfectly in keeping with the overall theme of PCS. Special purpose preprogrammed data collection devices such as those used by delivery personnel and parcel services may also require frequent wireless data transmission for updates to corporate headquarters.

Wireless data transmission over wide areas is still evolving. Currently, three different transmission network types offer services either nationwide or in a limited number of metropolitan areas. Those three types are basically the same as the networks carrying PCS voice transmissions: satellite, cellular, and mobile radio.

Several developmental challenges exist for improved performance of wireless PCS data transmission. First of all, current transmission rates are slow by landline

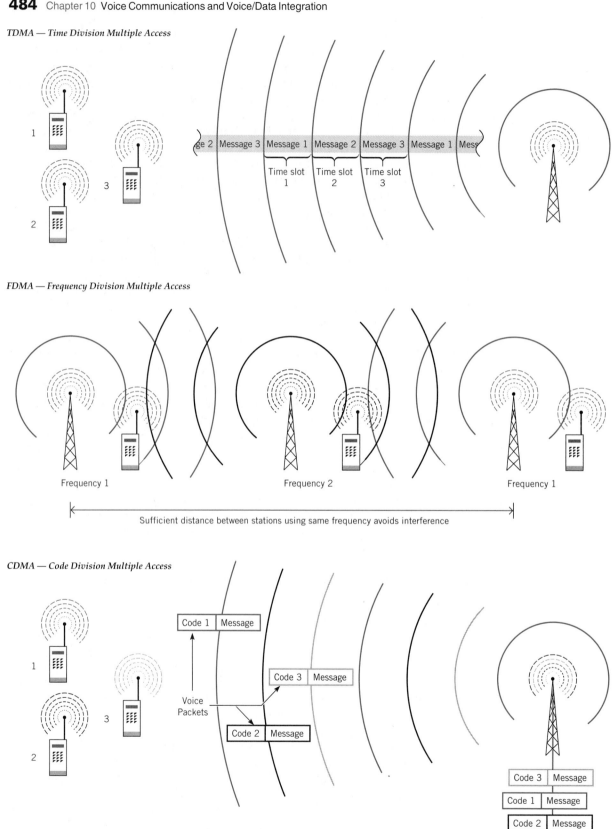

Figure 10-22 Maximizing minimum bandwidth: TDMA, FDMA, CDMA.

wire-based standards. Wireless transmission rates are in the range of 165–8000 bps. Secondly, wireless error correction and flow control methodologies are proprietary. There are no standards, and therefore, little or no interoperability among different manufacturers' equipment or different PCS data networks. Proprietary standards also imply a lack of third-party communications software to manage data transmission.

Technology development in wireless modems is still evolving. Current technology allows cellular modems to be attached between cellular phones and laptop computers. Cellular fax machines are also available. Wireless modems built into laptop computers are the new generation of PCS data transmission devices. One problem associated with cellular modems is caused by the "handoff" of cellular conversations between cells as discussed earlier. Modems and data transmission do not always tolerate the hand-off gracefully. Figure 10-23 summarizes the features and issues of PCS data transmission over wide areas.

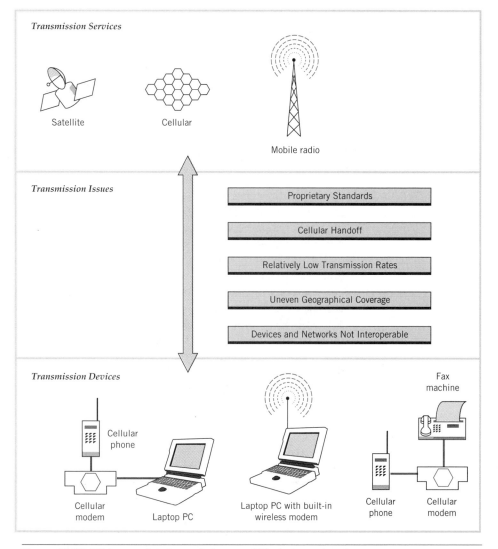

Figure 10-23 Wide area data transmission on a PCS wireless network.

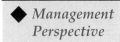

◆ *Management*
 Perspective

PCS Conclusion

PCS faces significant challenges on its way to worldwide deployment. Perhaps the most significant hurdles are the individual and, at times, conflicting business missions of the various industries that must somehow achieve a metamorphosis which will produce a comprehensive, seamless, transparent personal communications service for subscribers. Another industry with its own distinct mission and on a possible collision course with the telecommunications industry is the cable television industry. PCS spread-spectrum communicators have been successfully demonstrated on CATV networks.

Finally, future PCS deployment levels may be determined by simple market demand. There is always the possibility that a seamless, comprehensive, location independent communications system such as PCS is of more interest to the companies who stand to profit from it than to the buying public who are supposedly demanding it.

◆

☐ ### WIDE AREA NETWORK OPTIONS FOR DATA/VOICE TRANSMISSION

With all the services available for wide area data and voice transmission from carriers, third-party operators, and privately owned facilities, confusion may be guaranteed while opportunities for possible cost savings are bypassed. A further exploration of the network options for data/voice transmission should provide realistic alternatives for the majority of companies who must transmit both voice and data. The network options for data/voice transmission can really be plotted along a continuum with a completely *public* network solution at one extreme and a totally *bypassed* solution on the other. Figure 10-24 illustrates such a continuum.

A **public network** option implies that only dial-up voice and data services available on the PSTN are used by a company. With the newer usage based dial-up data services such as SMDS, frame relay, and ISDN, the public network offers more data transmission solutions than ever before. Voice transmission is via normal dial-up lines and local trunks to the local CO in a public network option for data/voice transmission.

A **private network** option implies leased lines are rented on a monthly basis by corporations for transmission of voice and/or data. A common example is leased T-1 (1.544Mbps) lines equipped with T-1 multiplexers integrating voice and data in order to optimize the use of the digital circuit. If the number of sites in an organization is relatively small, they can be fairly easily interconnected via T-1s. Private does not imply private ownership of the transmission facilities. Leased circuits of guaranteed bandwidth and quality available 24 hours a day at a flat monthly fee are the backbone of the private network. These circuits are leased from common carriers such as the RBOCs or interexchange carriers.

A *hybrid* data/voice network option includes elements of the public and private networks. A common scenario is for a company's voice traffic to be carried via the public network while data is carried over the leased lines of a private network.

A fairly new option enabled in part by the sophisticated out-of-band signalling capability of SS7 is known as *virtual private networks* or **VPN.** In such a scenario, a company maintains flexible control over its network management with the ability to adjust network capacity and obtain performance and traffic accounting reports while leaving the actual capital investment and network operations to the phone

Network Option	Public	Hybrid	Virtual Private	Private	Bypass
Examples	Carrier services—SMDS, frame relay	Combination of some public network carrier services and some leased lines	Software defined network. Centrex	Leased lines	User-owned and controlled or third party. VSAT Microwave
Characteristics	Central control. Maintained by TELCO staff. Highly redundant network	Voice is often transmitted via public network, while leased lines are used for data	Offers closed user groups on a public network. Offers control and features of private network without capital investment and operations personnel	Offers user control over guaranteed bandwidth facilities on a 24-hour-a-day basis for a fixed monetary fee	May bypass local TELCO and bring voice and data directly to POP (point of presence) of long-distance carrier

Figure 10-24 Network options for data/voice transmission.

company. Software-defined networks of various types, Centrex, and other services that offer *closed user groups* on the public network are all examples of virtual private networks.

In the case of Centrex, PBX (private branch exchange) features such as speed dialing, call forwarding, and conference calling are available even though there is no PBX physically at the customer sight. The PBX functionality is supported by central office equipment offering a *virtual* PBX to end users.

Finally, a **bypass** network represents avoidance of the public network for voice and data service. Third-party bypass companies offer alternative data and voice transmission services which in some cases merely avoid the local carrier and carry voice and data directly to the nearest long-distance carrier's POP. In the case of larger corporations that can afford the capital investment, microwave or VSAT (very small aperture terminal) satellite service is installed between corporate locations for data/voice transmission. VSAT is not the only satellite service available. Public networks, such as AT&T, sell satellite service internationally at data rates of 56K to 2.048Mbps (E-1). In some instances, depending on local regulations, voice and data may be transmitted over local cable TV facilities thus bypassing the local public network.

☐ VSAT: VERY SMALL APERTURE TERMINAL SATELLITE TRANSMISSION

Depending on the particular data application of a company, **VSAT** satellite transmission may offer a cost-effective alternative to land-based public or private network options. Careful analysis should be undertaken before going to the expense of installing VSAT satellite dishes on all corporate buildings. In particular, two classic shortcomings of VSAT transmission, which will be described in detail shortly, should be carefully investigated. These shortcomings do not necessarily eliminate VSAT transmission as a viable alternative in all cases. In some cases, VSAT technology may be able to compensate for or overcome these transmission difficulties, while in other cases, the nature of a corporation's transmission needs may be able to tolerate these transmission shortcomings.

The first of these issues is the unwavering fact that data or voice must travel a distance of over 22,000 miles from a VSAT earth station up to an orbiting satellite and another 22,000 miles down to a destination earth station. Such a trip can take as long as one second, intolerable for some data applications. The second issue which has been dealt with to varying degrees of success is the interference with satellite transmissions caused by rain (known as *rain fade*) and other inclement or severe weather.

Used correctly, VSATs can be a very effective business tool to transmit voice, data and video between multiple corporate locations. VSATs are not always used alone but may be combined with land-based leased line or dial-up data services as well. To a network manager, a VSAT link is just another circuit to be managed in combination with all other available data circuits. Multivendor network management software, discussed in previous chapters, may or may not interface to VSAT systems—a fact which should be investigated carefully.

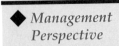 ◆ *Management Perspective*

Configuring and implementing a VSAT is a complicated and potentially very expensive undertaking. Unless a company is large enough to hire or train an in-house specialist, it is usually wise to employ a vendor who will install as well as guarantee VSAT installations.

Remembering that a VSAT is just a replacement for a land-based circuit, compatibility issues must be considered. For instance, does the VSAT support multiple transport protocols such as SNA SDLC, TCP/IP and X.25? How does the VSAT terminal interface with LANs? Does it support LAN transport protocols such as IPX/SPX?

VSAT Installation Components

The key components to any VSAT installation are the network interface unit (NIU), the local VSAT, the orbiting satellite, the remote VSAT(s), and the hub satellite station. The hub satellite station acts much like the hub in a LAN, with the ability to respond to multiple remote VSATs at higher transmission rates. These hub stations are very often installed at corporate headquarters buildings in large corporate nets. In smaller nets, hub services are often rented from a satellite service provider. The network interface unit may have interfaces to LANs, or asynchronous communications, via RS-232 or V.35 interfaces.

☐ MICROWAVE

Another bypass transmission option that has been successfully implemented for both data and voice transmission is known as microwave. **Microwave** specifically refers to the small wavelength of the high frequency (18–23GHz) bandwidth reserved for this transmission methodology. Most importantly, microwave is a line-of-sight transmission technique with ranges from five to 30 miles depending on terrain and weather conditions. Depending on transmission frequency and equipment, rain, fog, and humid air can have an adverse effect on microwave transmission.

Two factors of a practical nature that limit widespread deployment of private microwave transmission systems over long distances are availability of bandwidth and acquisition cost of land for line-of-sight towers. Frequency licensing is petitioned through the FCC following a search for available frequency. The more heavily populated and developed an area is, the less likely sufficient available microwave bandwidth will be found. The cost of installing line-of-sight towers in remote or wooded areas can be prohibitive as well. In urban areas, if frequency bandwidth can be secured, line-of-sight antennae can be installed relatively easily on the roofs of buildings.

Microwave transmission systems interface to LANs in much the same way as VSAT. Integrated into the indoor portion of the microwave is either a bridge, repeater, router, or an interface or transceiver to which the user can attach their own internetworking device. In this sense, the microwave link is just another wide area link as far as the LAN is concerned.

Channel capacity of microwave transmission systems falls roughly in the range of T-1 (1.544Mbps) to T-3 (45 Mbps). Microwave has been successfully used for LAN interconnection at 10 Mbps. A branch of the Internet in greater Boston links 100,000 users and thousands of computers of various shapes and sizes via a microwave backbone running Ethernet at 10Mbps.

☐ PUBLIC NETWORK SERVICES

Transmission services of various types offered by local and long-distance carriers have been thoroughly reviewed in previous chapters. Another group of services, sometimes referred to as value-added services, represent the carriers' attempts to add value to their own transmission services by offering additional convenience or functionality. After an analysis of the elements of influence on network services, three different network services will be examined:

> First, a well established voice transmission service in a state of significant transition: *800 service.*
>
> Second, a lesser known business-related service: *billing automation.*
>
> Finally, a carrier offered network service of possible great potential with few current offerings: information services.

Elements of Influence on a Network Service

Many interacting forces and influences determine the possibility as well as the viability and financial success of network services. Figure 10-25 summarizes these service influences.

The diagram is relatively simple. Any network service starts with a vision. If the contributing factors are positive, that vision may materialize into an actual network service. If the contributing factors are negative, the vision may never become a network service. Alternatively, despite negative contributing factors, the vision may still become a network service and face a deployment of uncertain success.

This systems diagram can be used as a diagnostic tool to examine the possible causes of failed network service offerings as well. In the case of ISDN, it could be said that with the possible exception of the regulatory component, all other potential influences have generated negative impacts on the ill-fated service at one time or another. Trials have been sporadic as the first national trial was not held until 1992. Technology played an important role as various manufacturers' ISDN equipment was incapable of interoperating. The user needs for the service have subsided in recent years as other services such as SMDS and frame relay have eclipsed much of the initial interest in ISDN. Finally, applications for ISDN have been limited due in a large part to the spotty deployment of the service.

Consider this diagram and the impact of the contributing factors as one of the most successful network services ever offered is examined: 800 service.

800 Service in Transition

Traditionally, 800 service was provided over designated trunks to a company's PBX. The trunks were used only for 800 service and the company was given an 800 number for distribution to its customers. Some carriers, such as NYNEX, recognized the advantage of offering 800 service over "normal" trunks. As a *layered service,* the 800 service could be expanded easily over existing trunks which could also be used for regular incoming and outgoing traffic.

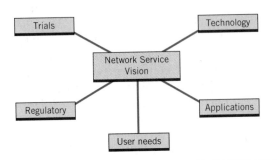

Figure 10-25 Elements of Influence on network services.

There was only one catch to this service: A user would have to change their 800 number in order to take advantage of this *valueflex 800* service. Few companies were interested in changing their 800 number, although the service was ideal for small businesses looking to break into the 800 number service.

800 Portability

800 number portability came about as a result of users' inability to change 800 carriers or services without changing their 800 numbers. Simply stated, 800 numbers were assigned in blocks to individual carriers, rather than being assigned to end-users. To be precise, the first three numbers of the 800 number (known as NNX) indicate to which carrier that particular 800 number belongs. The carriers let customers "use" one of their 800 numbers. However, if the user wanted to switch carriers, they could not take their 800 number with them.

Beyond switching carriers, users discovered the need to have multiple carriers provide 800 service for them using the same 800 number. National corporations with multiple-call service centers needed the ability to route and reroute calls as necessary over various carriers' networks.

The basic design premise of 800 portability is that a master 800 number database is set-up and accessed by all carriers via SS7 out-of-band signalling. This database contains information as to which carrier is supposed to carry how much of a particular 800 number's traffic.

User concerns have centered around a "what-if" scenario in which the central database fails. A backup database has been created to be accessed in such situations. If Figure 10-25 is referred to while analyzing 800 portability, sufficient user demand and applications should be evident. Regulatory support from the FCC has been significant. Trials are a necessity and the technology of a centralized database shared by numerous local and long-distance carriers, as well as the use of SS7 for database queries, need to be thoroughly tested.

Business Network Services: Flexible Billing Formats

For large, multilocation corporations the monthly phone bill can be literally several feet high. Processing such a stack of paper to verify billing, spot abuse, or charge-back internal departments can be both frustrating and costly. Companies that subscribe to multiple carrier services for voice and data transmission often receive separate bills for each service. In a similar fashion, multilocation companies often receive separate bills for each and every location.

In response to customers' needs for easy-to-use, consolidated billing systems, many carriers have developed **flexible billing formats** from which customers may choose. The three large long-distance companies, AT&T, MCI and Sprint have developed entire customized billing analysis applications programs to assist companies in managing their billing data effectively.

Customer needs in the billing domain are really quite straightforward. Bills must be able to be consolidated across multiple locations and multiple services. In addition, that billing data must be able to be segmented into several user-defined levels such as store, division, region, state, etc. Ad hoc report generation from the data, generation of graphics displays, or what-if analysis of data from within spreadsheet programs are also required by some corporations.

The second major category of customer needs entails the manner in which the data itself is delivered. Any of the following data delivery options may be desired by the customer and/or offered by the carrier: diskettes, magnetic tape, CD-ROM, EDI, E-mail, dial-up access with file transfer, or microfiche.

Long-distance carriers have developed sophisticated billing analysis applications programs that not only meet the requirements listed above but may also have the ability to generate bills in a selective manner in order to facilitate internal billing activity. MCI's program is known as Perspective, AT&T's is known as Detail Manager, and Sprint's is known as FONView.

The actual format of the billing data from the carrier may be important as well if the user-company plans to develop applications or use their own report generators on the data. An important category of data overlooked or missing on many bills concerns the number of and reason for uncompleted incoming calls. For sales-oriented companies that depend on customers being able to easily access available customer service reps, data concerning blocked calls can be very valuable. Customized billing arrangements are most often established through the carrier's customer service representative or account executive assigned to a particular company's account.

Information Services: Network Service of the Future?

As part of the continuing saga of deregulation, telecommunications companies were allowed to offer **value-added information services** over their own networks following a ruling in 1991. Other vendors of such services were upset by this ruling; they felt that the carriers were being given an unfair competitive advantage since they could use their own networks to transport such services.

Beyond the more familiar and well-established information services, such as Compuserve and Prodigy, carriers may also offer video-based information services. Such video-on-demand services and the network implications for supporting them will be discussed in Chapter 11. A shorter-term information service offering may more likely resemble an on-line news service. Such services can be customized for an individual's areas of interest.

Demographic data gathered by the phone company or purchased from market research organizations may be offered to companies considering opening a store or building a factory in a particular region or location. Joint ventures between the information gathering market research firms and the information distributing carriers are a strong likelihood. In any case, the telephone network of the future will carry much more than voice and will be seen as more of a source of information than an access to mere voice communications. The evolving and expanded services offered by cable television corporations could prove to be an interesting point of comparison and perhaps competition for the network carriers and their information services offerings in the coming years.

☐ WIDE AREA DATA/VOICE INTEGRATION DOES NOT IMPLY ISDN

Data/voice integration and even **data/voice/fax integration** are motivated by a strategic business decision to optimize the use of one's wide area network links. As will be seen, those wide area links can be anything from dial-up analog lines to cutting edge frame relay services. The important point to remember as the technology employed to achieve this data/voice integration is reviewed, is that none of these data/voice integration examples require ISDN. Figure 10-26 summarizes the characteristics and features of some of these non-ISDN-dependent data/voice integration technologies.

As can be seen in Figure 10-26, data/voice/fax integration technology is available for nearly any voice or data source, and capable of being interfaced to nearly

End Devices Connected	WAN Service Employed	Integration Device	Integration Elements
Voice: PBXs or channel bank *Data:* mainframe to terminal traffic or LAN traffic	Frame relay accessed via T-1	Frame relay switch	Data Voice
Voice: PBXs *Data:* mainframe to terminal traffic or LAN traffic	DDS lines to 56K or DS1 64Kbps digital leased lines	Remote bridges	Data Voice Fax
Voice: PBX *Data:* mainframe to terminal traffic	T-1, fractional T-1, DDS, or analog leased lines	Multiplexor	Data Voice Fax
Voice: single line phone *Data:* PC	Switched analog dial-up line	DOV (data over voice) unit and software	Data Voice
Voice: PBX *Data:* LAN traffic	Analog or digital leased lines to DS-0 (64Kbps)	PC expansion card	Data Voice Fax

Figure 10-26 Data/voice integration does *not* imply ISDN.

any wide area network service. As an excellent example of modularity of design, data/voice integration can be added to frame relay switches, remote bridges, statistical multiplexers, or fax boards to name but a few.

The theory or functionality behind all of these data/voice integration devices is relatively similar. Voice transmissions are digitized and compressed by various means as described earlier in this chapter. Next, the voice, data, and fax transmissions are organized in such a way as to share the access to the wide area network service. That circuit-sharing may be managed by simple TDM (time division multiplexing), or the voice, data, and fax may be packetized with additional header information being added to each packet.

Among the header information may be an indicator of the type of payload (voice, data, or fax) present within the packet. In this way, the delay-sensitive packets such as voice can be easily identified and given priority access to the wide area link in order to maximize the voice quality produced by the bandwidth-efficient data/voice integration device.

If Figure 10-25 is recalled, and the non-ISDN technology listed in Figure 10-26 is determined as meeting user needs for data/voice integration, then a large portion of the "user needs" element of influence for ISDN services disappears. Other ISDN features such as the ability to transmit caller ID, also known as automatic number identification (ANI), are offered by many carriers without the use of ISDN technology.

Finally, use of ISDN's two 64K "B" channels for videoconferencing can be achieved alternatively through the use of inverse multiplexers and dial-up 56K services, or by possible upgrades to the local loop. Both of these ISDN-alternative concepts for the delivery of videoconferencing services will be explained further in Chapter 11, "Networking Aspects of Videoconferencing, Imaging, and Multimedia."

CHAPTER SUMMARY

Basic concepts of voice transmission such as transforming the human voice into transmitted analog signals, voice digitization, and voice compression were introduced in order to complement the understanding of data transmission. The primary local area voice management device, the PBX, was reviewed as to architecture, functionality, and future design trends.

The integration of PBXs and computers to solve business problems and meet strategic business objectives through such technologies as computer integrated telephony were explored from both a technical and business viewpoint.

The structure of the voice transmission network was introduced as a hierarchical pyramid designed for both redundancy and reliability. The role of out-of-band signalling and signalling system 7 in the development and deployment of future intelligent network services was deemed essential to meeting user demands for transparent voice and data services at any time from anywhere.

PCS (personal communications services) is a concept or vision of meeting those user demands for transparent voice and data services by integrating elements of the paging, cellular phone, satellite, and landline phone networks. The realization of PCS faces many challenges from a variety of sources: technological, regulatory, and societal, to name but a few.

Choices for network usage including public, private, virtual private, as well as user-owned or bypass networks illustrated once again the need to balance business objectives and perspectives with available technical options. A network service analysis diagram was introduced to assist in the evaluation of current as well as future network service offerings.

KEY TERMS

ADPCM	CPE	out-of-band signalling	SS7
AIN	CT2	PAM	station cards
ANI	data/voice/fax	PBX	stored program control
bypass	integration	PCM	switching matrix
CAI	DNIS	PCS	tandem office
call accounting system	DSP	PDM	TDMA
CCIR	DTMF	PHI	tie line
CCIS	800 number portability	PPM	tone
CDMA	FDMA	private network	trunk cards
CIT	flexible billing format	PTN	value-added information
class 5 end office	FPLMTS	public network	services
class 4 toll center	ICP	pulse	voice compression
class 1 regional center	inter-LATA	PWM	voice digitization
class 3 primary center	intra-LATA	Q.sig	voice processing
class 2 sectional center	landline phone network	roaming	VPN
CLID	microwave	SDN	VSAT
CODEC	network hierarchy	SMDR	wireless Centrex
common control area	OAI		

REVIEW QUESTIONS

1. How do the sound waves of the human voice actually get transferred onto and off of the voice network?
2. What is DTMF and what are its potential uses beyond assisting in completing a call?
3. What are the differences between the various voice digitization techniques?
4. How does PCM differ from ADPCM in terms of bandwidth requirements?

5. How is voice compression accomplished? What technology is involved?
6. What is the business motivation for voice compression? What is the potential trade-off?
7. What are the major architectural elements of a PBX?
8. Explain how voice transmissions can be integrated with computers to produce a service known as computer integrated telephony.
9. What are some practical business applications of CIT?

10. What are some potential uses of voice processing or interactive voice response systems?
11. What is the voice network hierarchy and what are the functional implications of such a hierarchical design?
12. What is out-of-band signalling and of what importance is such a technical ability in terms of emerging network services?
13. What is PCS and what is the basic underlying paradigm shift involved from current telecommunications network services?
14. What are some of the key challenges to PCS deployment and what are some of the important benefits of such a telecommunications environment?
15. What is OA&M and what role does it play in the development and implementation of new network services?
16. What techniques are currently being tested in order to maximize the number of voice conversations in wireless or cellular networks?
17. What business decisions are involved in choosing between public, private, virtual private, or bypass network options?
18. What are some of the key limitations of VSAT and microwave transmissions for voice and data traffic?
19. What are the key elements of influence on the relative success or failure of a given network service?
20. What is 800 number portability and what are some of the obstacles to its implementation? What are the potential benefits?
21. What are some of the options for data/voice integration available without the use of ISDN network services?
22. Why might a voice conversation not be totally transmitted via analog transmission even if the source and destination loops are analog?
23. How does sampling rate in voice digitization relate to the quality of the transmitted voice signal?
24. How does ADPCM accomplish digitized voice transmission in less than 64Kbps?
25. Why is a DS-0 considered a standard circuit for the transmission of digitized voice?
26. How does PCM differ from other voice digitization methodologies such as PAM?

27. What are the benefits of PCM over other voice digitization methods?
28. What is the role of a CODEC in voice digitization?
29. What additional benefits do digital PBXs offer?
30. How can geographically dispersed PBXs be connected to form one virtual PBX?
31. What would be the advantages and disadvantages of forming such a virtual PBX?
32. What are some of the interoperability issues surrounding computer integrated telephony?
33. How can call accounting systems be cost justified?
34. What are some of the PBX characteristics required in order to support a call accounting system?
35. What are some of the issues surrounding interoperability of PBXs from various vendors?
36. What is signalling system 7 and how is it related to ISDN?
37. What is a software-defined network and what role does SS7 play in such a network?
38. What are some of the potential difficulties associated with a personal telephone number?
39. The personal communicator to be used in a PCS environment combines which current devices?
40. What is wireless Centrex and how does it relate to PCS?
41. What is the potential role of cable TV in the PCS environment?
42. What are some of the differences between cellular services and satellite services?
43. What are the international issues surrounding deployment of PCS?
44. What progress has been made to date on the international PCS issues?
45. How is CDMA like a datagram packet service?
46. What are the positive and negative attributes of a bypass network?
47. What are the advantages and disadvantages of a virtual private network?
48. What are some of the advantages and disadvantages of 800 number portability?
49. What was the motivation for the establishment of 800 number portability?
50. Analyze both ISDN and SMDS using Figure 10-25.

ACTIVITIES

1. Suppose a normal voice-grade circuit was 3000Hz. What would be the maximum sampling rate of an analog signal on such a circuit? How much bandwidth would be required to transmit a digitized conversation from such a circuit using PCM? Using ADPCM? How many such conversations could be transmitted over a T-1 using PCM? Using ADPCM?
2. Find out the nearest sales location of the following

PBX vendors: AT&T, Northern Telecom, Rolm (or other vendors of your choice). Request information about PBX functionality and pricing. Prepare presentations concerning PBX options and price ranges for small, medium, and large companies.
3. Investigate the level of support for computer integrated telephony from the major PBX vendors. Which computers are compatible with which com-

puters? Are turn-key solutions including CIT software available? What are the approximate costs of the various CIT systems? Assuming a two-year maximum payback period, how much additional revenue would the various CIT options have to generate?

4. Spread spectrum technology was first used during World War II. Investigate its military use and report on what more recent developments have allowed its use in the public domain for applications such as wireless LANs and PCS.

5. Investigate and report on the latest status of frequency allocation both domestically and internationally for PCS.

6. Investigate and report on the current status of 800 number portability. Were the users' fears of reliance on a master 800 number well-founded? How was the transition to 800 portability actually executed? From your analysis, determine who the real winners and losers were in the introduction of 800 portability.

7. Take apart a modern telephone handset and compare it to the handset illustrated in Figure 10-1. Draw a detailed diagram of your handset. Try to explain any differences between the two diagrams.

8. Investigate and report on which government agencies use the specialized keys illustrated in Figure 10-2 and for what purpose such keys are used.

9. Determine how much of the frequency spectrum is reserved for government use and which areas of bandwidth are reserved for which specific government agencies.

10. Investigate the similarities and differences between the microwaves used in a microwave oven and those used for microwave transmission. Report on the required safety precautions for working with microwave transmission. Determine which wireless LANS are actually using microwave transmission and determine whether or not such devices should be used with any special precautions.

11. Speak to the telecommuncations department of your school or business and arrange a tour of the facility's PBX. Prepare a detailed report outlining PBX functionality, installation, and architecture, as well as the PBX's ability to meet business level requirements and objectives.

12. Investigate whether WATs lines are available in your area. If not, why not? Investigate the evolution of network services offered by your local phone company. Try to map the changing network services to changes in user demands.

13. Find out if your school or business uses a call accounting system. Speak to the person in charge of the system to investigate how it is used, as well as its effectiveness at spotting and curtailing abuse of phone privileges. Report on your findings.

14. Conduct a survey on how people feel about doing business with companies which employ voice processing or automated attendant systems.

15. Contact your local phone company to investigate the nearest location of the various classes of switching centers as illustrated in Figure 10-14.

16. Investigate and report on the current status of PCS trials including key findings in the areas of services offerred and obstacles to be overcome.

17. Investigate and draw a map of the availability of cellular services in your state. Highlight those cellular services which support data transmission. Prepare a chart showing the cost of such services.

18. Investigate the issue of bypass networks. How do local phone companies feel about them? Has there been a response to bypass networks from regulatory agencies? What are leakage access charges and how are they related to bypass networks?

19. Find a local school or business that uses a VSAT network. Investigate the level of technical expertise at the local level. What is the nature of the information (voice, data) transmitted via satellite? What are the advantages and disadvantages of the network from both a business and operational perspective? Draw a diagram of the local and remote nodes of the VSAT network.

20. Investigate whether your local phone company offers Centrex or a similar service. What are the characteristics of the companies that use such a service? Draw a network diagram of a Centrex installation. What are the business and operational advantages and disadvantages of a Centrex installation?

Featured References

Case Studies

Davis, Tim. "Computer Integrated Telephony Gives UA a Competitive Edge," *LAN Times,* vol. 9, no. 21 (November 9, 1992), p. 56.

Brown, Bob. "A&P Setting up VSAT Net to Register Service Gains," *Network World,* vol. 9, no. 26 (June 29, 1992), p. 17.

Sherry, Ed. "A Law Endorsement for Cellular," *Telephone Engineering & Management,* vol. 96, no. 16 (August 15, 1992), p. 36.

Duffy, Jim. "T-1 Keeps Shaw's on Top of Grocery Game," *Network World,* vol. 9, no. 31 (August 3, 1992), p. 9.

DeVries, John. "Data/Voice Concentration Pays off for

Auto Agency," *LAN Times*, vol. 9, no. 16 (August 24, 1992), p. 37.

Data over Voice

Johnson, Johna. "Data over Voice—Without ISDN," *Data Communications*, vol. 21, no. 9 (June 1992), p. 59.

Editors of Data Communications Magazine. *Integrating Voice and Data*, (New York: McGraw-Hill, 1990).

Duffy, Jim. "Brooktrout Unveils 4-Port Voice/Facsimile/Data Card," *Network World*, vol. 9, no. 30 (July 27, 1992), p. 11.

DeVries, John. "Integrating Voice and Data on WANs," *LAN Times*, vol. 9, no. 16 (August 24, 1992), p. 37.

Mohan, Suruchi. "Voice/Data Integration Not Just for the Fortune 500," *LAN Times*, vol. 10, no. 8 (April 19, 1993), p. 1.

Intelligent Networks/Software Defined Networks

Garrahan, James. "Intelligent Network Overview," *IEEE Communications*, vol. 31, no. 3 (March 1993), p. 30.

Cancer, Emilio. "IN Rollout in Europe," *IEEE Communications*, vol. 31, no. 3 (March 1993), p. 38.

Suzuki, Shigehiko. "IN Rollout in Japan," *IEEE Communications*, vol. 31, no. 3 (March 1993), p. 48.

Russo, Peter. "IN Rollout in the United States," *IEEE Communications*, vol. 31, no. 3 (March 1993), p. 56.

Cameron, E. Jane. "A Feature–Interaction Benchmark for IN and Beyond," *IEEE Communications*, vol. 31, no. 3 (March 1993), p. 64.

Fujioka, Makoto. "Globalizing IN for the New Age," *IEEE Communications*, vol. 31, no. 4 (April 1993), p. 54.

Wallace, Bob. "AT&T Opens SS7 Net for 800 Routing," *Network World*, vol. 9, no. 49 (December 7, 1992), p. 1.

Briere, Daniel. "RBHC Puts SS7, AIN Investment to Use," *Network World*, vol. 10, no. 2 (January 11, 1993), p. 89.

Wallace, Bob. "Ireland, Finland Added to AT&T's Global SDN Roster," *Network World*, vol. 10, no. 2 (January 11, 1993), p. 89.

Wallace, Bob. "AT&T Gives Call Centers SDN Routing," *Network World*, vol. 9, no. 27 (July 6, 1992), p. 1.

International

Wallace, Bob. "European Carriers Unite in Continental Network Effort," *Network World*, vol. 9, no. 28 (July 13, 1992), p. 1.

Heywood, Peter, and Anne-Marie Roussel. "Europe's PTTs: No Heat, No Hurry," *Data Communications*, vol. 21, no. 18 (December 1992), p. 72.

Heywood, Peter. "European PBX Networks: Taking the Fortune Telling Out of the Future," *Data Communications*, vol. 21, no. 3 (February 1992), p. 70.

Heywood, Peter, and Anne-Marie Roussel. "Pacific Carriers Get a Head Start," *Data Communications*, vol. 21, no. 18 (December 1992), p. 78.

Saunders, Stephen. "U.K. Telecom: Free to Choose," *Data Communications*, vol. 21, no. 9 (June 1992), p. 86.

Roussel, Anne-Marie. "Southeast Asian Telecom: Giving Users Something to Celebrate," *Data Communications*, vol. 21, no. 7 (May 1992), p. 92.

Microwave

Theodore, David. "LAN Interconnect Takes to the Airwaves," *Data Communications*, vol. 20, no. 9 (July 1991, p. 83.

PBXs

Saunders, Stephen. "PBXs and Data: The Second Time Around," *Data Communications*, vol. 22, no. 9 (June 1993), p. 69.

Johnson, Johna. "Users Rate PBXs," *Data Communications*, vol. 21, no. 9 (June 1992), p. 93.

Wallace, Bob. "PBX Interoperability Spec Nears Int'l Standard Status," *Network World*, vol. 9, no. 51 (December 21, 1992), p. 3.

Wallace, Bob. "NTI Unveils Wireless Telephone Systems," *Network World*, vol. 9, no. 48 (November 30, 1992), p. 29.

PCS (Personal Communication Systems)

Kobb, Bennett. "Personal Communications Services," *IEEE Spectrum*, vol. 30, no. 6 (June 1993), p. 20.

Arnbak, Jens. "The European Revolution of Wireless Digital Networks," *IEEE Communications*, vol. 31, no. 9 (September 1993), p. 74.

Reed, David. "The Cost Structure of Personal Communication Services," *IEEE Communications*, vol. 31, no. 4 (April 1993), p. 102.

Hallman, Ken, and Ron Czaplewski. "Ameritech's PCS Trial: Integrating Advanced Technologies," *Telephone Engineer & Management*, vol. 96, no. 17 (September 1, 1992), p. 60.

Chao, James. "What's Next for PCS," *Telephone Engineer & Management*, vol. 96, no. 16 (August 15, 1992), p. 33.

Taff, Anita. "Ameritech Initiates Broad Testing of PCS Technology," *Network World*, vol. 9, no. 26 (June 29, 1992), p. 29.

Messmer, Ellen. "Wireless Supporters Say More PCS Spectrum Needed," *Network World*, vol. 9, no. 46 (November 16, 1992), p. 2.

Private Networks

Briere, Daniel. "Public or Private? That Is the Question," *Network World*, vol. 9, no. 29 (July 20, 1992), p. 55.

Heywood, Peter. "Europe Prepares for a VPN Service Surge," *Data Communications*, vol. 21, no. 9 (June 1992), p. 71.

Public Networks

Johnson, Johna. "Rebuilding the World's Public Networks," *Data Communications*, vol. 21, no. 18 (December 1992), p. 60.

Johnson, Johna. "U.S. Carriers: Variations on a

Rebuiding Theme," *Data Communications,* vol. 21, no. 18 (December 1992), p. 68.

Johnson, Johna. "HDSL: An Extra Boost on the Local Loop," *Data Communications,* vol. 21, no. 13 (September 21, 1992), p. 47.

Molloy, Maureen. "Dial-Up Links Finding New Role in Internets," *Network World,* vol. 9, no. 27 (July 6, 1992), p. 19.

Services

Wallace, Bob. "SW Bell Set to Move Tulsa to First Citywide Centrex," *Network World,* vol. 10, no. 3 (January 18, 1993), p. 25.

O'Brien, Bradley. "How to Plant the Right Crop of Advanced Services," *Telephone Engineer & Management,* vol. 96, no. 16 (August 15, 1992), p. 44.

Jander, Mary. "Making Voice a Choice for Data Networks," *Data Communications,* vol. 21, no. 10 (July 1992), p. 59.

Briere, Daniel, and Chris Finn. "Footing the Bill," *Network World,* vol. 9, no. 21 (May 25, 1992), p. 32.

Taff, Anita. "Users, Carriers Fret about 800 Portability," *Network World,* vol. 9, no. 31 (August 3, 1992), p. 19.

Sacerdote, George. "Where Are Those Telco Information Services?," *Data Communications,* vol. 22, no. 1 (January 1993), p. 130.

Johnson, Johna. "Users Rate Long-Distance Carriers," *Data Communications,* vol. 21, no. 11 (August 1992), p. 111.

Wallace, Bob. "MCI May Win Big after 800 Portability," *Network World,* vol. 9, no. 51 (December 21, 1992), p. 15.

Wallace, Bob. "Sprint Slips 800 Feature in Past AT&T," *Network World,* vol. 9, no. 50 (December 14, 1992), p. 1.

Wallace, Bob. "AT&T Opens SS7 Net for 800 Routing," *Network World,* vol. 9, no. 49 (December 7, 1992), p. 1.

Taff, Anita, and Bob Brown. "Nagging Questions Tarnish Allure of 800 Portability," *Network World,* vol. 9, no. 48 (November 30, 1992), p. 1.

Technology

Bennett, Ronnie. "Switching Systems in the 21st Century," *IEEE Communications,* vol. 31, no. 3 (March 1993), p. 24.

Heywood, Peter. "Mixing Voice and Data on the Backbone," *Data Communications,* vol. 22, no. 1 (January 1993), p. 116.

Johnson, Johna. "Switching Voice over Frame Relay," *Data Communications,* vol. 22, no. 1 (January 1993), p. 40.

Salamone, Salvatore. "Remote Bridge Handles Voice and Fax Calls," *Data Communications,* vol. 21, no. 10 (July 1992), p. 117.

Transmission

Bellamy, J. *Digital Telephony,* (New York: Wiley, 1982).

Berman, Michael. "Beaming It Over," *Telephone Engineering & Management,* vol. 96, no. 16 (August 15, 1992), p. 52.

VSAT

Roussel, Anne-Marie. "VSAT Service Crosses the Border," *Data Communications,* vol. 22, no. 7 (May 1993), p. 73.

Johnson, Johna. "VSAT Takes the Pain out of Picking Data Rates," *Data Communications,* vol. 22, no. 1 (January 1993), p. 42.

Cummings, Joanne. "VSATs Poised for New Internet Role," *Network World,* vol. 9, no. 37 (September 14, 1992), p. 17.

Johnson, Johna. "Users Rate VSAT Networks," *Data Communications,* vol. 21, no. 4 (March 1992), p. 85.

Wallace, Bob. "AT&T Launches New Skynet Int'l Satellite," *Network World,* vol. 9, no. 51 (December 21, 1992), p. 15.

Wireless WANs

Goldenberg, Barton, and Walter Sonnenfeldt. "The Sky's the Limit for Wireless WANs," *Data Communications,* vol. 22, no. 3 (February 1993), p. 101.

C A S E   S T U D Y

A&P Setting up VSAT Net to Register Service Gains

MONTVALE, N.J.—While large retailers were quick to adopt very small aperture terminal technology to address the networking needs of their geographically dispersed stores, supermarkets have been slow to follow suit.

However, the Great Atlantic & Pacific Tea Co, Inc. (A&P) has begun installing a VSAT net to replace its terrestrial links, a move analysts said could prompt other major players to adopt the technology. While A&P is scheduled to become the first major national chain to deploy a private satellite network, VSAT vendors report other supermarket chains are hot on A&P's heels.

Supermarkets such as A&P are looking to VSAT nets to address their growing data communications needs. Data traffic is increasing as a growing number of chains embrace new customer services, such as credit and debit cards. Supermarkets are also collecting more point-of-sale data on the merchandise they sell and need to process it faster to support electronic data interchange applications.

"Almost all the companies in the grocery industry are experimenting with credit cards," said Shelly Revin, senior vice-president of marketing and sales at Hughes Network Systems, Inc. in Germantown, Md. "This sort of application requires much faster response times than the supermarkets are used to, and VSAT networks are the platform many companies are looking at as a solution."

Credit card firms are enticing supermarkets to accept their cards by lowering the rates, said Revin, whose company recently formed

an alliance with a Florida firm that has designed a turnkey data collection system for supermarkets.

A&P, which thinks credit card rates are still too high, is rolling out support for debit cards first, said Peter Rolandelli, vice-president of information and administrative services at A&P, an $11.6 billion company. Debit cards work like checks; they let users authorize withdrawal of funds from bank accounts to pay for purchases.

A&P is looking for a more cost-effective way to handle debit card transactions than the 4.8K bit/sec dial-up terrestrial links the VSAT net will replace.

"We need to deliver good service to the customer to stay competitive, and much of that revolves around the payment area," said Rolandelli, who acknowledged that supermarkets are generally four to five years behind general retailers in supporting electronic payments." Customers increasingly are finding [debit] cards to be convenient."

A&P also plans to use the VSAT net to better monitor in-store inventory, he said.

"The amount of information supermarkets are accumulating about transactions is increasing immensely," Rolandelli said. A&P's VSAT net will deliver data to its data processing center more often than was economically feasible using pay-as-you-go dial-up lines, he said.

Updating the company's databases more frequently will speed response to customer buying patterns and help the retailer keep its shelves stocked with the most popular products.

A&P's multimillion-dollar private satellite net from Scientific-Atlanta, Inc. will feature a master hub earth station at the chain's headquarters site here. It will provide links to the company's Columbia, Md., data processing center and more than 500 stores, initially those in A&P's Super Fresh chain. Down the road, the net will serve other A&P regional chains, including Farmer Jack, Food Emporium, Kohl's and Waldbaums.

The VSAT net will support audio, data and video communications via 56K bit/sec links to and from the earth station.

In addition to credit verification, the net will support applications such as merchandise replenishment, which will be based on the collection and processing of POS information, and the Checkout Channel, a video service displaying advertisements at checkout lines.

The network hub will be installed by year end; deployment of VSATs at the 71-store Super Fresh chain based in Philadelphia has already begun, Rolandelli said. A&P officials expect to expand the VSAT net to encompass all of its 1,300 stores by the mid-1990s. Scientific-Atlanta will likely handle management of the VSAT net, Rolandelli said.

The fixed cost of the VSAT net vs. the unpredictable costs of using terrestrial nets clinched A&P's decision, Rolandelli said. "It just turned out to be a dollars and cents issue," he said, declining to provide specific savings estimates.

Philip Arst, a principal consultant with Regis McKenna, Inc., a high technology marketing consulting firm in Costa Mesa, Calif., said A&P's move to VSATs could result in other supermarkets doing the same.

"It'll depend on how A&P's sales do," Arst said. "If the company's revenue starts growing because customers are finding it more convenient to use debit cards at A&P stores, other supermarkets are certain to look at VSAT."

Source: Bob Brown, "A&P Setting up VSAT Net to Register Service Gains," *Network World,* vol. 9, no. 26 (June 29, 1992), p. 17. Copyright 1992 by Network World Inc., Framingham, MA 01701. Reprinted from *Network World.*

Business Case Study Questions

To Do

After reading the article concerning A&P's installation of a VSAT network:

1. Organize pertinent facts from the article in a top-down model.
2. Prepare two 7-layer OSI models: One for a remote VSAT site and one for the central VSAT site. Fill in all known protocols in their appropriate layers. Pay particular attention to network operating systems and network transport protocols. Note any unknown protocols. Discuss the particular implications of any unknown protocols.

Answer the Following

1. What were some of the factors that motivated A&P to investigate VSAT networks in the first place?
2. What was the nature of the network that the VSAT network replaced?
3. What was the nature of the costs (capital, expense, fixed, variable, one-time, on-going) of the terrestial network?
4. What was the nature of the costs (capital, expense, fixed, variable, one-time, on-going) of the VSAT network?
5. Propose a valid method for comparing the costs associated with the two networks.
6. Contact the long-distance carrier of your choice and price a 56K leased line from Montvale, New Jersey to Columbia, Maryland.
7. Obtain the price, including installation and usage charges, for a switched 56K circuit between the same two cities if available.

8. Contact Scientific Atlanta or the VSAT vendor of your choice to determine the initial and on-going costs for a VSAT link between Montvale, New Jersey and Columbia, Maryland.
9. Which types of companies are likely to be EDI partners of A&P?
10. What types of electronic documents are A&P and its trading partners likely to exchange?
11. What are the advantages of EDI to a business such as A&P?
12. Investigate the availability and cost of third-party EDI services.
13. How have changing consumer demands affected A&P's network planning and installation?
14. What are the network requirements of the debit card system?
15. What are the expandability issues involved with the VSAT implementation?
16. It is often said that weather can adversely affect VSAT performance. Investigate this claim with experts in the field and either support or reject the previous statement.
17. What is the maximum bandwidth and cost of that bandwidth for VSAT networks?
18. Is the VSAT network protocol transparent?
19. Does it matter which network operating systems or network transport protocols are employed at any given node?
20. What might be the implications of trying to run SNA sessions over a VSAT network?
21. How are flow control and error control handled on a VSAT network?

CHAPTER · 11

Networking Aspects of Videoconferencing, Imaging, and Multimedia

Concepts Reinforced

Top-Down Model
OSI 7-Layer Model
Cost–Benefit Analysis
Local Area Networking

Internetworking
Wide Area Networking
Importance of Standards

Concepts Introduced

Video Bandwidth Requirements
Video Digitization and Compression
Multipoint Videoconferencing
Desktop Videoconferencing
Videoconferencing Technology
Videoconferencing-Related Standards
Video Dialtone and the Local Loop

Imaging Technology
Imaging Applications
Multimedia Technology
Multimedia Applications
Impact on Local Area Networks
Impact on Public Networks

OBJECTIVES

Having mastered the material in this chapter, you should be able to:

1. Understand the underlying technical concepts for video transmission, video compression, imaging, multimedia transmission, and multipoint video-conferencing.

2. Understand current technology available to accomplish these concepts including CODECs, inverse multiplexers, multipoint control units, video bridges, videohubs, multimedia servers, and videophones.

3. Understand the advantages, availability, limitations, and compatibility of currently available videoconferencing, imaging, and multimedia technology.

4. Understand the current status of industry standards for videoconferencing, imaging, and multimedia technology.

5. Understand the availability, advantages, limitations, and proper business utilization of the network services offered by the carriers for videoconferencing, imaging, and multimedia.

6. Understand the various possible uses of videoconferencing, imaging, and multimedia technology for business applications as well as the cost–benefit analysis inherent in justifying these uses.

7. Understand the network impact of videoconferencing, imaging, and multimedia applications on LANs, inter-LANs, and WANs.

☐ INTRODUCTION

The focus of this chapter will center on the networking aspects of videoconferencing, imaging and multimedia rather than on a thorough coverage of all aspects of the aforementioned technologies. After gaining an understanding of any new technical concepts involved in these technologies, a top-down approach will be taken to further analysis of these networking requirements and implications.

An examination of the possible business impacts of these technologies on existing businesses will be followed by illustrations of possible new ventures enabled by videoconferencing, imaging, and multimedia. Implementation issues such as the following will be explored:

> Will these be services offered by phone carriers, or will carriers be barred from offering such services?
> How does the cable TV industry fit into this picture?

Currently available and possible future videoconferencing, imaging, and multimedia technology, as well as a survey of standards to which any of this technology may conform, will be explored.

Finally, and perhaps most importantly, the networking impact of these bandwidth-hungry applications will be explored. Having gained an appreciation for the general and business public's desire for transparent network services from LANs to WANs and everything in between, those changes that must occur in LAN, inter-LAN, and WAN networking technology and services in order to offer seamless desktop-to-desktop video, image, and multimedia applications will be studied.

Possible changes by carriers to the local loop in order to support such applications, as well as the impact of transmission and switching evolution to SONET and ATM, could have a great bearing on the ability to deploy these applications in any sort of universal fashion.

☐ VIDEOCONFERENCING

Basic Components

In this section on videoconferencing, the business analysis involved in the justification of a videoconferencing system as well as the required technology and network services necessary to implement such a system will be examined. First, however, basic technological concepts which underlie videoconferencing and serve as limiting factors to technical performance and cost justification must be understood. Figure 11-1 illustrates the basic components of a videoconferencing system. After gaining an understanding of the basics of videoconferencing, the study will be expanded to include enhanced features and technological advances in videoconferencing systems.

As illustrated in Figure 11-1, input devices are the microphone and camera for audio and video input, respectively. Output devices are the video monitor for the video portion of the conference and the speaker for the audio portion of the conference.

The Videoconference Processor: The CODEC

At the heart of the videoconferencing system is the video **CODEC** (COder–DECoder), not unlike the CODEC introduced in the study of voice digitization. However, a videoconferencing CODEC digitizes not only analog voice sig-

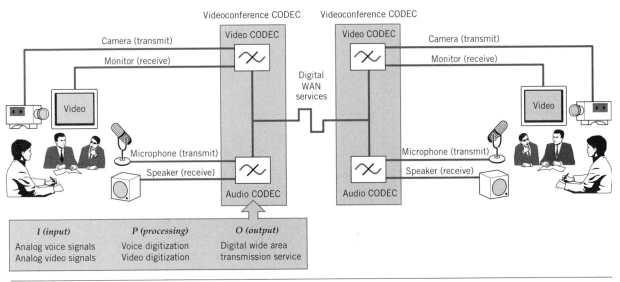

Figure 11-1 Basic components of a video conferencing system.

nals but also analog video signals. **Video digitization** is not unlike PCM (pulse code modulation) voice digitization in that a sample of a video signal is digitized into an 8-bit code.

Video Digitization

While the sampling rate of voice digitization is defined as samples per second, or baud; the sampling rate of video digitization is defined in pixels per frame. A **pixel** (PICture ELement) is a single point of video information represented by eight bits of digitized information in a video frame. **Frames** are defined in terms of the number of rows (lines) and columns of pixels per frame. The higher the number of pixels per frame, the higher resolution or picture quality of that single frame.

As a matter of fact, two pixels are required to accurately describe each point within a video frame. One pixel is coded to represent the brightness of a given point while a second pixel is required to represent the color of that same video point. Full motion video adds another variable to the equation by defining the relative quality of the full motion video in terms of *frames per second*. The higher the number of frames per second, the higher the quality of the full motion video.

Video quality can be a very subjective area of judgment. However, certain standards exist by which to measure and compare video quality. Some of these standards will be introduced as bandwidth requirements for transmission of full motion video are determined.

Computing Videoconferencing Bandwidth Requirements

Figure 11-2 illustrates a simplified calculation of bandwidth requirements for so-called "uncompressed video."

To further explain the calculations in Figure 11-2: 640 pixels per line is a common standard for video monitors while 525 lines per frame and 30 frames per second are part of the **NTSC** (National Television Standards Committee) recommendations for broadcast video. As can be seen, even without considering bandwidth requirements for the accompanying audio portion of the videoconference, bandwidth requirements already equal nearly 90 megabits per second. In terms of

Video frame resolution		640	pixels/line
	×	8	bits/pixel
	×	525	lines/frame
	=	2.688	megabits/frame
Full motion video quality	×	30	frames/second
Bandwidth required	=	80.64	megabits/second

Excluding bandwidth required for associated audio transmission.

Figure 11-2 Bandwidth requirements for uncompressed video.

WAN digital services, two T-3 circuits (approximately 45Mbps each) would be required to fill this bandwidth need. Such bandwidth is not only very costly but not necessarily available through all COs servicing all of the locations to which companies may want to conduct videoconferences.

Reducing Bandwidth Requirements

There are basically only two methods to reduce the bandwidth requirements for video transmission as calculated in Figure 11-2. One method is to reduce the transmitted coded video information by reducing the amount of video data generated in the first place. In other words, at the expense of video frame resolution and/or full motion video quality, reduce the number of pixels per line, lines per frame, and frames per second. The key decision in such a method is the limit to which any of these factors can be reduced without reducing the video quality below acceptable levels.

A second method for reducing transmitted video data is borrowed from the voice digitization world. While overall transmission of digitized voice can be reduced through such methods as ADPCM, **video compression** can reduce overall transmission of video information.

The H.261 Standard

The CCITT's **H.261** standard defines video transmission standards in terms of pixels per line and lines per frame. Such standards not only allow videoconferencing at more reasonable bandwidths, but also offer the prospect of codec interoperability among various manufacturers' videoconferencing equipment. Such interoperability is especially important if enterprise partners such as customers and suppliers are to conduct business easily via videoconferencing.

H.261 defines two different video resolution formats: **CIF** (common interface format) defines a frame at 352 pixels by 288 lines per frame, while **QCIF** (quarter CIF) defines a frame at 176 pixels by 144 lines per frame. Frame refresh rates for either format may be up to 30 frames per second.

Perhaps more important, H.261 also defines video compression algorithms which allow video transmissions between H.261 compliant CODECs at transmission rates in multiples of 64Kbps up to 2Mbps. These transmission rates are a far cry from the 45Mps and higher transmission rates required for uncompressed video. As will be seen later on when network services for videoconferencing are examined, common bandwidth requirements fall into the 128Kbps to 1.544Mbps (T-1) range.

Video Compression

Video compression seeks to minimize the amount of coded video information transmitted between remote CODECs while maximizing the picture quality produced by those CODECs. The video compression algorithms perform a balancing act between sending just enough coded video data for production of video images of acceptable quality and sending too much coded video data, thereby increasing bandwidth demand.

The major method used in reducing overall transmitted video information is to send only information relating to the parts of the present frame which have *changed* since the last frame. This **interframe coding** precludes the need to send a full frame's worth of video data 15 to 30 times per second.

Another technique, known as **motion compensation,** seeks to minimize transmission bandwidth requirements by sending information to a receiving CODEC about how to move an image which is currently known to the receiving CODEC rather than completely re-transmitting that image in motion at 30 frames per second.

Advanced Functionality: Pre- and Post-Processing

Although H.261 defines standards for video coding, compression, and transmission, many vendors have their own proprietary protocols which further decrease bandwidth usage and/or increase picture quality. Thus, although CODECs which support the H.261 standard may interoperate, improved performance may be realized through the use of the manufacturer's additional proprietary protocols. These additional techniques beyond simple video compression are known as video **pre-processing** and video **post-processing.**

In roles similar to compression and decompression, the pre-processor analyzes the video image to be transmitted and determines the most efficient way to inform the remote CODEC of changes in the most recent frame. This information is not the image itself, but information about the image and how it relates to previously transmitted frames. This information is then compressed and transmitted to the remote CODEC where it is decompressed and post-processed into the proper image. The standard versus proprietary video processing is isolated in CODECs through separation of the video compression functionality from the pre- and post-processing functionality as illustrated in Figure 11-3.

In order for two videoconferencing units to decide whether to communicate via an H.261 protocol or a proprietary protocol, a handshaking routine similar to that employed by V.32 and V.32bis modems is undertaken. Most CODECs will attempt to agree upon proprietary protocols first because of their ability, in general, to transmit higher quality images over reduced bandwidth. If mutually supported proprietary protocols cannot be found, then H.261 is employed as a lowest level of common functionality solution through the handshaking routine's fallback prioritization scheme.

Quality Audio Is Also Important

Having a clear picture of a fellow member of a videoconference is of little use if that person's voice is unintelligible. Transmitted voice quality is a key performance issue for videoconferencing systems. The analog voice signals are digitized using voice digitization techniques described in Chapter 10. Voice compression via ADPCM is quite common in videoconferencing systems.

As is the case with video, the more bandwidth available for voice transmission,

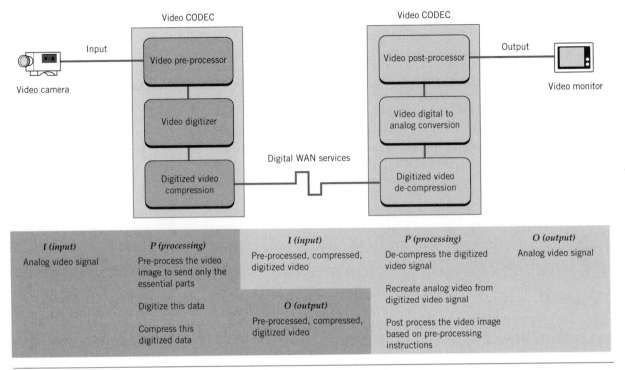

Figure 11-3 Advanced CODEC functionality.

the higher the quality of the transmitted voice. Different videoconferencing systems allocate varying amounts of bandwidth to voice. Those systems that employ a full T-1 (1.544Mbps) often allocate 64Kbps for voice while those systems that employ an ISDN BRI interface (144Kbps total) often allocate 32Kbps for voice, sufficient for ADPCM digitized voice.

A challenge to high-quality videoconference audio has to do with the varying acoustics of the rooms in which these videoconferences occur. Often, echoes are generated by audio output from speakers being picked up by remote microphones and recycled back to the echo source. **Adaptive echo cancellation,** similar to that employed by V.32 and V.32bis modems, actually subtracts transmitted audio echoes from incoming audio signals. These audio echoes are calculated based on the changing echo characteristics of the videoconferencing rooms involved.

Business Demands Dictate Additional Features

The basic purpose of a videoconference is to enable the execution of effective business meetings between widely dispersed business partners without the need for extensive travel. Ideally, the fact that these are videoconferences and not face-to-face meetings should be transparent to the participants. Anything that can be accomplished at a face-to-face meeting should be able to be accomplished at a videoconference. These additional business meeting activities and requirements are often the added features which differentiate one videoconferencing system from another.

Often at meetings, for instance, documents such as contracts or proposals are reviewed and signed. Integrated fax capabilities are one option for videoconferencing systems. Graphs or charts of one type or another are often displayed at business meetings. Again some way must be found to transmit projected graphs, charts, or even recorded video presentations as well. Most meeting rooms contain a blackboard or dry-erase white board for brainstorming, planning, or diagramming. Electronic blackboards capable of transmitting through the videoconferencing CODECs are often included in videoconferencing systems. Finally, PC-based applications such as engineering drawings, CAD/CAM output, or spreadsheets may need to be collaboratively developed. PC or LAN interfaces incorporated directly into the videoconferencing unit may offer such functionality. Videoconferencing systems with all of the previously mentioned additional capabilities are sometimes referred to as **mediaconferencing systems** or telemedia systems.

As will be seen in the section on imaging later in this chapter, medical videoconferences in which medical imaging data such as x-rays, CT-SCANS, and MRIs are transmitted in an integrated fashion, are predicted to be a significant use of videoconferencing equipment and services in the future. Ideally, these capabilities should be transparently integrated into videoconferencing systems as well.

Network Access and Network Services

Now that a better understanding of the functionality offered by a CODEC has been gained, the alternatives available for interfacing to the various digital wide area network services available for transport of digitized videoconference information can be examined. Figure 11-4 summarizes some of the CODEC's wide area network interfaces and associated services.

The interface devices listed in Figure 11-4 may be integrated within the videoconference device or may be separate standalone devices.

◆ *Management Perspective*

There are relatively few differences among all of the wide area services available for transporting videoconferences as listed in Figure 11-4. The services may be either switched or leased, otherwise known as dedicated. ISDN, if available between videoconference locations, may also be an option. All of the services are digital in nature and vary according to available bandwidth. Which service to employ will be dictated largely by the videoconferencing equipment in use. Most videoconferencing equipment can operate within a range of different bandwidths dependent on the quality desired for video and audio transmission.

A difficulty with long-distance videoconferencing which should be considered is that not all long-distance carriers offer all the services listed in Figure 11-4. Furthermore, if the local phone company is to be employed to transport videoconference traffic over the local loop to the long-distance carrier's POP, then the local phone company must also support the required digital service. Finally, even similar sounding services, such as switched 56K, from different long-distance carriers, may not interoperate.

◆

Inverse Multiplexers

The **inverse multiplexer,** sometimes known as a biplexer, has experienced a rebirth as part of the videoconferencing phenomenon. Inverse multiplexers were first used to support high-speed remote printers by combining two (or more) separate circuits into a single circuit of sufficient bandwidth to support proper operation of the remote high-speed printer. Inverse muxes function in a manner in direct contrast to "normal" muxes such as STDMs. Whereas an STDM combines several relatively low-speed local application's transmissions onto a single com-

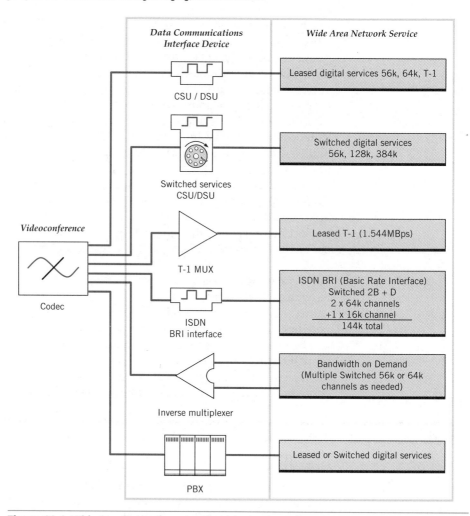

Figure 11-4 Wide Area Network services for videoconferencing.

posite high-speed network circuit, an inverse mux combines two or more network circuits to satisfy the transmission needs of a single local application such as videoconferencing.

In the videoconferencing application, inverse multiplexers can operate with either switched or leased digital services. By accumulating multiple circuits on demand, the inverse multiplexer offers the videoconference just the bandwidth it needs to maintain desired video and audio quality without requiring payment for unused or unnecessary bandwidth. For this reason, the inverse multiplexer has come to be known as a **"bandwidth-on-demand"** device. Figure 11-5 illustrates an inverse multiplexer installation.

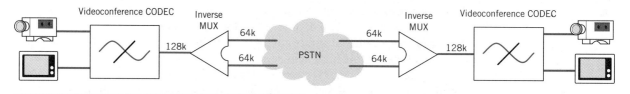

Figure 11-5 Inverse multiplexer installation.

Alternative Uses of Inverse Multiplexers

Inverse multiplexers may be standalone devices or may be integrated into other data communications devices. For instance, standard muxes which access 56K, 64K, or T-1 circuits as their composite output channel may integrate inverse multiplexers as built-in disaster recovery or backup mechanisms which would access the required amount of switched 56K services and conglomerate them into a composite channel of sufficient bandwidth to support normal operations.

Alternatively, inverse multiplexers could access varying numbers of the 24 64K channels contained within a T-1 on a switched basis. In this way, an inverse mux could access required bandwidth for videoconferences while leaving the remaining 64K channels for dedicated voice or data usage. Figure 11-6 illustrates alternative uses of inverse multiplexers.

Manufacturers of inverse multiplexers have recognized the need for guaranteed interoperability among inverse multiplexers from various manufacturers. Unlike STDMs, which used only proprietary multiplexing protocols, inverse multiplexers will conform to a standard designed by an industry forum known as **BONDING,** or Bandwidth ON Demand Interoperability Group. The standard defines how multiple 56K or 64K switched circuits are combined to deliver the desired bandwidth as well as standard disaster recovery and backup techniques.

Demand for Multipoint Conferences

Although point-to-point, or two-point, videoconferences can often be cost-justified in terms of saved travel expenses, meetings involving decision-makers from more than just two locations still involve travel on the part of some people to one of the point-to-point videoconferencing sights. The logic of traveling to a videoconferencing sight in order to save travel expenses is somewhat suspect. In response to this business demand, numerous technological alternatives for offering multipoint videoconferencing capabilities have been developed.

MCUs (multipoint control units) can be thought of as a sort of videoconferencing wide area router. Multiple CODECs from numerous videoconference network segments are attached to the MCU. With the aid of high-speed microprocessors, the MCU routes individual videoconference connections to the proper videocon-

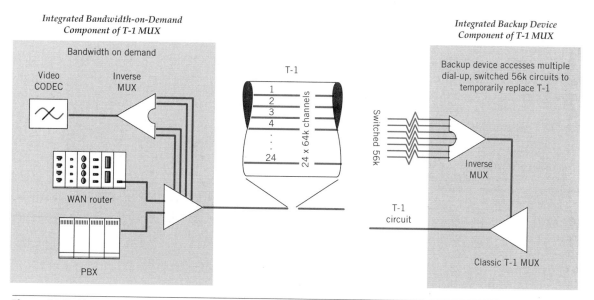

Figure 11-6 Alternate uses of inverse multiplexers.

ference location destination. In addition to allowing more than just two end-points to participate in a single videoconference, some MCUs also have the ability to support multiple multipoint videoconferences. Multipoint control units were first introduced by CODEC vendors in order to connect, or bridge, multiple CODECs to form multipoint videoconferences. The problem was that these vendor-specific MCUs would only work with CODECs of a certain manufacturer. Figure 11-7 illustrates a multipoint videoconferencing network enabled by MCUs.

Advanced Multipoint Videoconferencing

Videoconferencing will gain increased significance as an enterprise-wide management tool when enterprise partners representing multiple corporations are able to easily establish multipoint videoconferences on demand without regard for CODEC manufacturer. In order to achieve such a goal, the CCITT proposed a standard known as **H.243,** which standardized the interface between MCUs and CODECs regardless of manufacturer.

Besides varying in the number of CODECs and simultaneous videoconferences supported, MCUs can also vary in their ability to interface to a variety of wide area network services, both switched and dedicated, as well as their ability to cascade with other MCUs in a manner similar to cascadable LAN hubs. Some MCUs are integrated with inverse multiplexers for bandwidth on demand access and are known as **virtual bridges.**

As an alternative to owning and operating one's own MCUs and multipoint

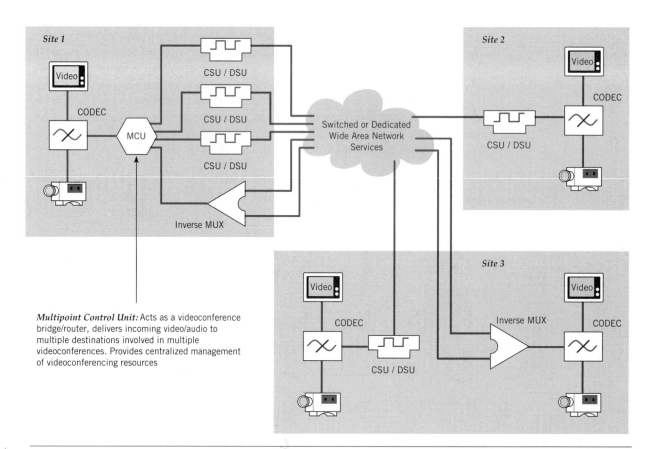

Multipoint Control Unit: Acts as a videoconference bridge/router, delivers incoming video/audio to multiple destinations involved in multiple videoconferences. Provides centralized management of videoconferencing resources

Figure 11-7 Multipoint videoconferencing.

videoconferencing network, *videoconference bridging services* are available from a number of long-distance carriers including AT&T, Sprint, and MCI. Users merely create point-to-point videoconferences to the carriers bridging equipment which can interface to a variety of manufacturer's CODECs. Videoconference transmissions are switched to the proper destination by the carriers' multipoint control units.

As an excellent example of modularity of design, a device known as a **videohub** combines the functionalities of multiple inverse multiplexers, a centralized video wiring hub, and a video switch or bridge into a single device with centralized management capabilities of multiple multipoint videoconferences. Videohubs also enable the previously mentioned carriers' videoconferencing services to interoperate as well. As a wiring hub, videohubs enable CODECs to be flexibly located throughout a facility and connected to the videohub via unshielded twisted-pair wiring which often already exists within the building for data networks. The videohub then accesses the switched or dedicated wide area network services for videoconference transmission.

Without this wiring hub functionality, CODECs and/or inverse multiplexers would need to interface directly to the wide area services, necessitating the wiring of these services into any room in which the CODEC may need to operate or a

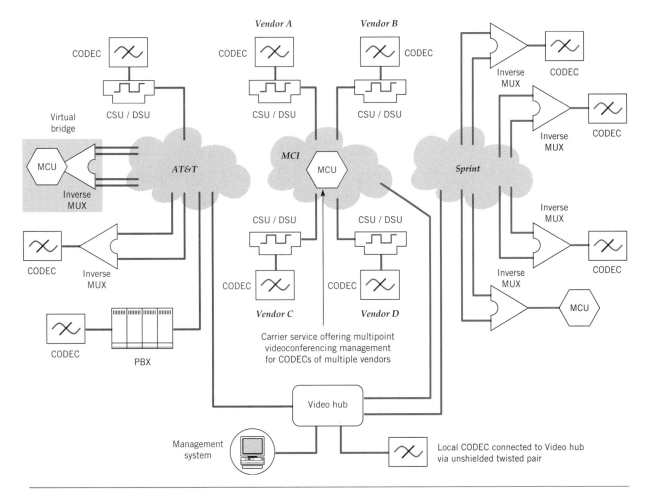

Figure 11-8 Advanced multipoint videoconferencing.

videoconference may need to be held. Videohubs might be thought of as the video-conferencing equivalent of the LAN SuperServer. Figure 11-8 illustrates some of the options for multipoint videoconferencing beyond single-manufacturer, user-controlled MCUs as illustrated in Figure 11-7.

Videoconferencing Is Not a Wide Area Only Service

Traditionally, videoconferences have been transmitted over wide area networks between specially equipped videoconferencing rooms in geographically dispersed corporate locations. As both videoconferencing and networking technology have evolved, numerous other platforms have emerged as potential purveyors of video-based business communications.

Permanently installed videoconferencing *room systems* ranging in price from $15,000 to $100,000 have been the initial platforms of videoconferencing technology. A movable version of a videoconferencing room system known as a *rollabout system* offers flexibility assuming the availability of wide area digital connections in multiple locations within a corporate building. *Standalone desktop videoconferencing* technology, such as the **videophone,** has offered face-to-face long distance meetings for a price of between $2000 and $5000 per desktop installation. Other standalone desktop videoconferencing systems consist of expansion board enhancements to existing PCs such as the Macintosh or Windows-based PCs. In between private desktop systems and large boardroom size videoconferencing systems are a category of videoconferencing systems known as *tabletop systems*, appropriate for small group videoconferences. Finally, integrated **LAN-based videoconferencing** technology is beginning to emerge as higher speed LAN standards are offering sufficient bandwidth for the simultaneous transmission of delay-sensitive video and audio. Figure 11-9 summarizes the major categories of videoconferencing platforms and their approximate price ranges.

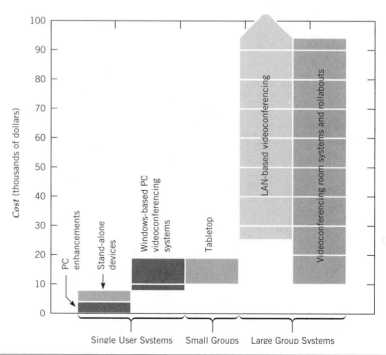

Figure 11-9 Videoconferencing platforms and price ranges.

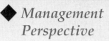

◆ *Management*
Perspective

None of the price ranges featured include additional equipment such as MCUs or videohubs required for multipoint videoconferencing. CODECs and CSU/DSUs or inverse multiplexers may or may not be included. Careful investigation should also be exercised in confirming whether room videoconferencing systems are only compatible with CODECs of a particular manufacturer.

Cost justification for videoconferencing systems is based largely on decreased travel expenses. Personal desktop videoconferencing systems have to be cost-justified on an individual basis while room videoconferencing systems can be cost-justified on overall reduced corporate travel expenses.

◆

Emerging Videoconferencing Technology

At the heart of videoconferencing's move to the desktop is the development of CODECs that are able to interface directly to Windows-based PCs and Macintoshs. Compression Labs Incorporated (CLI) developed such a CODEC and an integrated camera which is incorporated into a Macintosh and marketed under the name of Cameo Personal Video Systems. Many currently available CODECs for the desktop rely on an ISDN BRI (2B+D) interface for videoconference transmission. One of the 64K "B" channels is used for digitized voice transmission while the other "B" channel will be used for video and/or data. The 16K "D" channel will be used for call set-up and management.

Although all of this looks good on paper, the fact of the matter is that ISDN is still not very widely available and potential desktop videoconference users should investigate ISDN's availability before purchasing any equipment. Some desktop videoconference CODECs may also work over switched 56K services, however, these wide area services are by no means universally available either.

If the availability of wide area bandwidth is the limiting factor to desktop videoconferencing deployment, what videoconferencing options are available for use over the universally accessible analog switched dial-up network? The videophone, first introduced nearly 30 years ago, has been reborn as the AT&T Videophone 2500 at a price of $1500, and operates over normal analog dial-up lines. The videophone includes a 3-inch screen and a built-in camera, as well as a 19.2Kbps modem and specialized video compression/decompression chips.

These chips, which combine video and audio compression/decompression as well as modem functions, were jointly developed by AT&T and Compression Labs, Inc., manufacturer of the Cameo Personal Video System mentioned in the previous paragraph. This chip technology has been given the name **GVS** (global video standard) and is available to other manufacturers who may want to incorporate the chipset in their own videoconferencing related devices.

One possible drawback to the technology is the relatively slow frame refresh rate of only 10 frames per second as compared with the customary 30 frames per second. Perhaps more importantly, recalling that these videophones are operating over the *analog* network, they will not be able to interoperate as nodes on corporate videoconferencing networks which normally employ some type of long-distance *digital* service or another.

Local Area Networks and Videoconferencing

Video and voice, the two main components of videoconferencing, are known as delay-sensitive payloads, a fact first explored in the discussions of emerging wide area services such as SMDS, frame relay, and ATM. Local area network access methodologies are highly deterministic, allowing delays in transmission of data in the interest of maintaining overall order. Prioritization based on payload is not an inherent characteristic of Ethernet, Token Ring, or FDDI networks.

However, FDDI, with its 100Mbps bandwidth can certainly support videoconferencing applications. Several companies have demonstrated videoconferencing technology over FDDI. Perhaps a more important LAN requirement than massive amounts of bandwidth, videoconferencing traffic must be able to coexist with the equally important data traffic on local area networks. The coexistence of videoconferencing and data on local area networks can take two basic forms:

First, **LAN-enabled Videoconferencing,** allows LAN-based data and applications programs to be shared with videoconference participants connected via a wide area videoconference link.

Secondly, LAN-based videoconferencing, allows LAN-attached workstations to be full, active participants in a video conference. That video conference may be with another local LAN-attached user or may be with a remote videoconference participant via wide area links.

Standards for LAN-Based Videoconferencing

An important standard known as **IEEE 802.9,** is actually designed to define the integrated transmission of voice and data over twisted-pair local area networks. The standard defines two types of transmission channels within a LAN: one packet-based channel for the transmission of packetized data, and one circuit-based channel for simultaneous transmission of delay-sensitive voice or video.

Individual channels are 64K each, a convenient bandwidth for digitized voice. High-quality (30 frame/sec) digitized video currently requires 384Kbps, exactly six of the 64K channels. No dominant standard or technology currently exists for LAN-based videoconferencing. Other approaches include separate twisted-pair wiring and transmission methodologies for video, voice, and data to each desktop. Multimedia LANs and video servers are other possible platforms for LAN-based videoconferencing which will be explored further in this chapter.

Available Bandwidth Is the Determining Factor

Although great strides have been made in reducing the amount of videoconferencing data that must be transmitted thanks to video and voice compression as well as pre- and post-processing, the key determining factor in a videoconference system design remains bandwidth availability. Whether over a local area network or through the use of wide area network links, available bandwidth determines both the quality of the videoconference as well as the technological requirements of the attached end-devices, such as CODECs and network interfaces. Figure 11-10 contrasts current videoconference bandwidth requirements with currently available local area and wide area network services. Remember, not all listed wide area services, such as ISDN, are universally available.

◆ *Management Perspective*

Key Videoconferencing Technology Selection Criteria

As is true in any data communications opportunity, users should be especially diligent at using the top-down model when determining business objectives and requirements to be achieved by LAN-based or desktop videoconferencing. Applications to be executed at LAN-attached workstations should be clearly understood before a review of the currently available technology ever takes place.

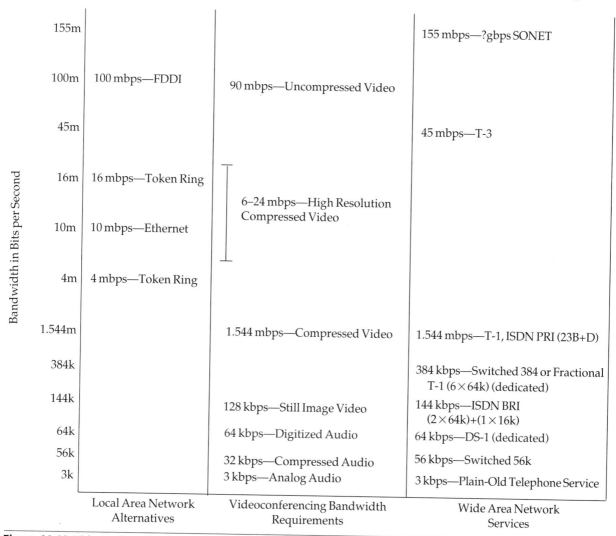

Figure 11-10 Videoconferencing bandwidth requirements versus available network bandwidth.

The level of required integration between PC-based application programs and the videoconferencing system must be determined in advance as well.

Some, but not all, videoconferencing systems are configured as complete, or turnkey, videoconferencing solutions. Included are CODECs, monitors, cameras, microphones, control units, as well as MCUs if multipoint videoconferencing is a requirement.

Figure 11-11 summarizes some of the issues to be considered in the purchase of a desktop or LAN-based videoconferencing system.

Third-Party Videoconferencing Services

Not all corporations have the need or the personnel/expertise to justify the purchase, maintenance, and operation of their own videoconferencing network. To meet this market demand, videoconferencing services have emerged which not

Characteristic	Options/Implications

Desktop components	If the desktop videoconferencing system is not delivered as a complete turnkey system, any or all of the following components may need to be added or considered:
	CODEC
	Camera—options for upgraded model allowing wide range or zoom?
	Microphones—options for lapel microphones or more than one input?
	Monitor—will the PC monitor be used? Must a special video adapter board be purchased?
	Audio/Visual Processing Card—in addition to CODEC
	Management Software—GUI based? Easy to use?
	WAN/LAN Interface—what options are available for WAN/LAN transmission services?
	  Are WAN interfaces included?
	   ISDN BRI?
	   CSU/DSU?
	   INVERSE MUX?
	  What are the bandwidth requirements?

LAN issues	How well is the videoconferencing system integrated with the PC? How well can PC software such as spreadsheets or presentation graphics be incorporated into the videoconference? Is the videoconferencing system LAN-enabled, or LAN-based?
Performance issues	Audio—What is the compression rate of the audio? How much bandwidth is required for transmission? Video—What is the *minimum* as well as the *maximum* frame refresh rate in frames/second? Full color video? Added Features—Fax capability, electronic blackboard, data exchange, graphics capabilities?
Standards compliance	Support H.261, H.243 and other videoconferencing related standards?

Figure 11-11 Videoconferencing technology characteristics.

only handle the wide area network connections or bridging requirements for multipoint videoconferences, but also install and maintain videoconferencing equipment.

Users who desire a videoconference are able to dial into the control center of the videoconference service and place an order for a videoconference through easy-to-use PC-based software programs. Videoconferences can be scheduled months in advance for regular occasions such as monthly sales meetings. Such services are sometimes known as on-demand videoconferencing.

Beyond Videoconferencing: Video Dialtone

An emerging carrier service, known as **video dialtone,** will deliver a variety of video-based services, including videoconferencing, to homes and businesses. Although largely in the test stage, video dialtone has the potential for over $120 billion dollars of annual revenue. (See Figure 11-12.) Central to the video dialtone delivery dilemma is the nature of the transmission service that can offer sufficient bandwidth to support multiple video applications to each home or business. Among the possibilities are the cable TV connection to many homes, ISDN PRI (23B+D, 1.544 Mbps), or at a later date, SONET with ATM switches.

Sometimes known as *video-on-demand,* this service can offer pay-per-view movies, information services on such topics as worldwide financial markets, or

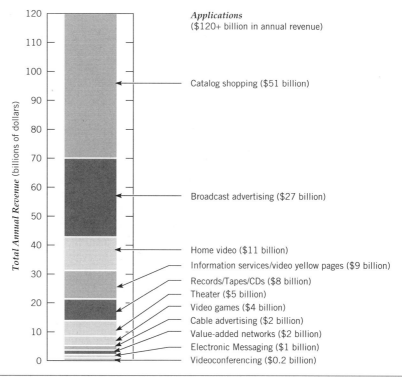

Figure 11-12 Possible video-dialtone applications.

catalog shopping. Carriers such as the RBOCs would sell transmission services, or bandwidth, to companies that wished to offer video-on-demand services to the carriers' residential and business subscribers. Carriers would also operate and maintain the network as well as handle all billing services. Such video dialtone services could prove to be in direct competition with cable TV operators currently offering similar services. Figure 11-12 illustrates just some of the possible uses of video dialtone.

Local Loop Implications of Video Dialtone

In order to determine the requirements of the local loop portion of the network that must deliver video dialtone services, one must first make some educated guesses as to the projected use of video dialtone services and their corresponding bandwidth requirements for potential residential and business subscribers.

If a home were to desire HDTV (high-definition television) at a required bandwidth of 20Mbps, four cable TV-type information services for an additional 20Mbps and two video-on-demand movies for an additional 5 Mbps, then total required bandwidth per home is in the vicinity of 45Mbps or a T-3 to every home! Recalling the "on-demand" and interactive nature of some of these video dialtone services, it is important to note that the video dialtone network must support two-way communication rather than simple one-way broadcast communication.

Even if the estimate in the previous paragraph were overly ambitious, it should still be clear that the current analog local loop technology will have to be replaced if video dialtone is to become a reality.

Some alternatives for possible upgrades to the local loop are the following:

HDSL—high bit rate digital subscriber loop: HDSL is a line encoding scheme which offers 1.544Mbps full duplex transmission over two twisted pair. The key point with HDSL that differentiates it from current T-1 technology of the same bandwidth is the fact that HDSL does not require repeaters between the CO and the customer premises, thereby reducing both cost and installation lead time.

ADSL—asymmetrical digital subscriber loop: "Asymmetrical" refers to the fact that unlike HDSL which offers 1.544Mbps in both directions, ADSL offers 1.544Mbps toward the user, but only 16Kbps from the user to the CO in order to carry information regarding control information such as requests for video dialtone services.

FITL—fiber in the loop: Fiber optic cable will be delivered "to the curb" with only the run from the pole to the subscriber's home being conventional copper. The transmission method and speed to be employed over the fiber is a separate decision with SONET and its potential 155Mbps speed being an obvious possible eventuality. Current limitations in CO switches would probably limit this local loop technology to 135Mbps in the near term. FITL is also known as fiber to the curb or FAITH (fiber almost in the home).

VHDSL—very high bit rate digital subscriber loop: VHDSL will offer full duplex transmission over two twisted pairs at a rate of between 3 and 6 Mbps.

ISDN-PRI—integrated services digital network-primary rate interface: Although the 2B+D (144Kbps) ISDN basic rate interface is out of the question, ISDN-PRI may have the potential to deliver video dialtone services with its 23B+D (1.5Mbps) capacity.

Wireless—Proposals have been prepared demonstrating the effectiveness of wireless multimedia networks in the 18GHz frequency range as local loop extensions to a copper or fiber-based distribution trunk. Motorola wireless enterprise systems is an advocate of wireless technology for the local loop.

Future Possibilities of Videoconferencing and Video Dialtone

When trying to analyze the possibilities for the future of videoconferencing and video dialtone, an equation introduced in Chapter 1 should be recalled:

Business Demand + Available Technology = Emerging Network Services

It has already been stated that reduced travel expenses form part of the cost justification of videoconferencing technology. Projections state that videoconferencing will replace 25 percent of airline business trips by the year 2010 and 33 percent of airline business trips by the year 2020.

In terms of videoconferencing and video dialtone, a few observations can be made concerning each piece of the equation. Demand for video-based services has been brought to the consumer level thereby vastly expanding potential markets beyond data communications oriented business customers. In a cyclical fashion, consumer oriented offerings and services will increase consumer demand and further expand the market. For example, the AT&T videophone which operates over analog dial up lines and video mail, the video equivalent of voice mail, are but two consumer-oriented video-related offerings.

The term video dialtone seems to be reserved for those video services that are ordered through a service offered by a traditional phone company via a special communications device attached to one's television set and transmitted over the local loop. **Interactive TV** appears to cover a wider range of implementation options most often combining cellular radio, satellite, and cable TV technologies in order to deliver on-demand video services to the customer's premises.

In terms of numbers, projected demand for videoconferencing equipment is increasing while costs and required bandwidth for videoconferencing systems are decreasing. Figure 11-13 illustrates these trends.

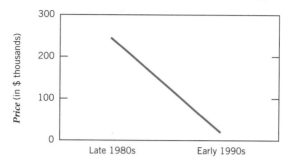

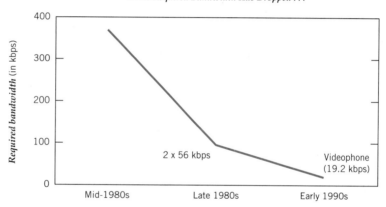

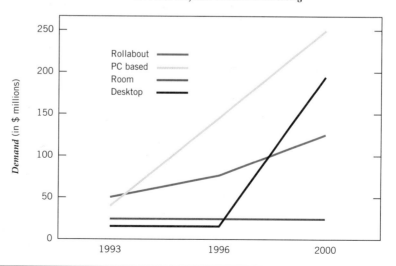

Figure 11-13 Videoconferencing trends. (*Source:* GI Consulting)

Technology has been advancing in the video networking arena but still has room to grow. Video and audio compression technology has improved remarkably as evidenced by the performance of the AT&T videophone over voice-grade dial-up lines. CODEC and high-speed modem functionality are now available on specially designed chipsets. If there were an area of technology that might have the greatest potential impact on video-network services, it would be the evolution of the local loop as previously discussed.

The RBOCs or other carriers do not have a monopoly on the delivery of video-on-demand services. Cable TV companies may offer interactive enhancements to their current broadcast-only technology or may form partnerships with carriers in order to take advantage of the current strengths of each partner. If local loops must be replaced rather than reused in order to deliver video dialtone service, then a significantly larger business and consumer demand is required in order to cost-justify such an investment.

As far as network impact on local area network platforms, videoconferencing is joined by two related demands for imaging and multimedia capabilities to be delivered to LAN-attached PCs. Both imaging and multimedia have the ability to help achieve strategic business objectives in the areas of improved productivity, improved customer service, and decreased paper shuffling.

IMAGING: PRODUCTIVITY IMPROVEMENT OR FINANCIAL BURDEN?

Imaging in its simplest implementation is merely the creation, storage, and retrieval of documents in digitized form. Documents such as contracts, invoices, bills of lading, and so on, are first scanned to produce digitized images in a similar manner to feeding a document into a fax machine. The difference in the case of imaging is that rather than being transmitted to a remote fax machine, the digitized image is stored on a local magnetic or optical disk drive for later retrieval.

In order to understand the local and wide area networking impact of imaging applications, one must really perform a top-down analysis of a particular imaging implementation beginning with the business motivation for purchasing imaging systems in the first place. In this section, such a top-down analysis of imaging's business motivations, applications availability, data requirements, network implications, and current technology alternatives will be performed. Figure 11-14 illustrates a top-down model analysis of imaging systems. Details regarding the information contained on each layer follows.

Imaging's Business Motivation

The idea of storing and retrieving images of documents rather than the documents themselves is not new. Microfilm and microfiche technology have been around for years but required specialized equipment for both image production and retrieval. The appeal of today's imaging systems lies largely in their ability to be integrated with business information systems.

What are the types of business perspectives or objectives that would motivate a company to purchase and install an imaging system at costs often estimated at over $10,000 per imaging system user? Perhaps not surprisingly, businesses heavily dependent on processing multitudes of paper forms have been the pioneers in the imaging field. Among these industries are the insurance, health-care, and shipping industries.

In these paperwork-dependent industries, efficient handling of that paper-

Business	Business Process: Business Objectives:	Business reengineering Improved customer service Increased worker productivity Increased competitive advantage Reduced paper handling	
Application	Workflow or document-flow application software Must offer both user-oriented and inter-user effective retrieval and manipulation Often custom written on a company-by-company basis at significant expense		
Data	Image compression, data distribution analysis, and dynamic image indexing help to minimize transmission requirements (see Figure 11-15 for sample calculation)		
Network	Imaging network bandwidth demand may be just a portion of the overall bandwidth demand (see Figure 11-15 for sample calculation)		
Technology	Processing Platforms	mainframe, minicomputer, LAN, client–server	
	Image Storage	proprietary image databases	image aware SQL databases
	Storage Devices	magnetic disk drives	optical juke boxes
	Network Operating Systems	image-enabled software	
	Databases Management Systems	imaging optimized or capable databases ORACLE INFORMIX	SYBASE GUPTA
	Front-end Tools	image-enabled Lotus NOTES	

Figure 11-14 Top-down analysis of imaging systems.

work translates directly into better customer service, higher employee productivity, and ultimately, competitive advantage and increased profitability. However, although an expensive imaging system may reduce paper handling, it will not improve the efficiency of a document workflow that was poorly designed in the first place. In other words, imaging systems are most effective when analyzed from a top-down approach by starting with an analysis step known as **business reengineering** rather than by jumping immediately to a technology analysis of currently available imaging systems.

Business reengineering takes a fresh, close, objective look at workflow, document flow, and process design in a business. Every aspect of every business process is subject to scrutiny and evaluation. "Because we've always done it that way" is not an acceptable justification for any current workflow or process. Only by taking a fresh look at the business processes that the imaging system will automate can one be sure that the outcome will be more than merely an automated but still inefficient system.

Specific business impacts in productivity can result from a combination of business reengineering and imaging technology. For example, it is possible for multiple geographically-dispersed workers to view a single document simultaneously with the use of an imaging system. Business reengineering may have disclosed the fact that workers who previously had to view a document one after the other were only doing so because it had been physically impossible for them to do otherwise and not because of any particular business motivation or legitimate control. The introduction of an imaging system in such a situation would have a measurable impact in terms of worker productivity.

In some cases, imaging systems may retrieve documents faster than previous paper-handling systems and may also reduce the chance of documents being misplaced or misfiled.

Application Layer: Workflow or Document-Flow Software

Once images are created and stored, they can only have real business impact if they can be retrieved and manipulated effectively. This "effectiveness" really has two dimensions. First, imaging application software must offer effective user-oriented performance by delivering functionality equivalent to or better than a paper-based system. Imaging systems activities that can be timed or compared with paper-based performance include:

1. Locating and retrieving a folder.
2. Locating and retrieving a document from within a folder.
3. Viewing multiple documents simultaneously on one's desktop.

Inter-user effectiveness is delivered by workflow or document-flow application software which is most often custom written for each industry or company implementing an imaging system. Effectiveness in this case can be measured by:

1. Length of time required to fully process a particular document.
2. Backlog of documents to be processed.
3. Level of customer complaints due to slow or ineffective processing of paperwork.

The use of such effectiveness measures should not be overlooked. Referring to the top-down model in Figure 11-14, it should be clear that business objectives will only be met if application layer processes are designed in such a way as to meet those business objectives. For instance, document-flow software should not only route a document properly from one person to another but it can also pinpoint the current status, location, progress, and expected completion date on any document as well.

If a customer calls with an inquiry regarding their paperwork, specific answers can be offered immediately. This level of service would likely represent an improvement in customer service, one of the initial business objectives for imaging systems. Without measurable, objective evaluation criteria, it will be impossible to balance the benefits to be gained from purchasing an imaging system against the costs expended to acquire that system.

The fact that workflow or document-flow application software, which forms the user interface to the imaging system, must be custom written in most cases adds significant cost to the overall imaging system implementation. As imaging platforms shift from mainframes and minicomputers to LANs and workstations, an introduction of more LAN-based, generalized, or customizable workflow automation software will likely be seen.

Data Requirements Hold the Key to Network Impact

The primary focus of this study of imaging is on the network impact, both LAN and WAN, of such systems. In order to understand networking requirements, the top-down model indicates a necessity to first understand the nature of the data requirements that imaging systems place on both local area and wide area networks.

Imaging Network Bandwidth Demand Calculation Documents are scanned or digitized into images by feeding them into a scanner. Although the exact size of this scanned image will vary from one document to another depending on the amount of typed versus blank space, the average one page scanned document occupies about 30–50K.

The next data variable to examine is the average number of pages or documents per folder. This may vary greatly by company, and should be calculated on an individual basis. For the sake of this calculation, an average of five documents per folder, yielding an average folder size of 250K (50K $\times$ 5) will be used.

Thus far, the digitized images have been only stored, but not delivered. In order to know how fast these images must be delivered, the evaluation criteria established as effectiveness measures must be recalled. If a person working with a paper-based system can open a folder on their desk and be viewing the desired document within two seconds, then the imaging system must perform at least as well. This scenario would yield a required transmission time of between 125Kbps and 250Kbps per imaging worker. Remember that these calculations are based on 50K documents and five documents per folder. Scanned photographs or gray-scale graphics can easily produce images of greater than 1MB each.

The final consideration of imaging network bandwidth calculation is how many imaging workers will be simultaneously accessing the image delivery network. Ten imaging workers simultaneously accessing documents produce an imaging network demand of 2.5Mbps, while 50 imaging workers produce an imaging network demand of 12.5Mbps.

The term "imaging network demand" was purposely used due to the fact that as imaging systems are moving away from closed mainframe and minicomputer-based systems to more open LAN-based systems, the imaging network bandwidth must be shared with the "regular" data bandwidth demands of the data processing users as well. In other words, if the imaging system is to be LAN-based, the imaging network demand can be only a small portion of the overall network bandwidth demand. Figure 11-15 summarizes the imaging network bandwidth demand calculation.

◆ *Management Perspective*

LAN and WAN Network Choices for Imaging

Having calculated an overall network bandwidth demand, one can now "shop" for those local and wide area network services capable of delivering sufficient bandwidth, with plenty of excess to spare, in order to enable imaging and data transmission. Local area networks such as 10Mbps Ethernet and 16Mbps Token Ring would seem, at first glance, to have sufficient bandwidth to support imaging services.

Do not assume this to be the case, however. If a LAN-based imaging system is being considered for purchase, insist on seeing an operational version of the system on the LAN of your choice. Alternatively, a no-obligation pilot test is another

Average size of scanned image: _____

Average number of documents per folder: × _____

Average size of folder: = _____

Maximum allowable folder delivery time: × _____

Imaging bandwidth demand per user: = _____

Number of simultaneous imaging users: × _____

Overall imaging bandwidth demand: = _____

Additional data network bandwidth demand: + _____

Total network bandwidth demand: = _____

Figure 11-15 Imaging network bandwidth demand calculation.

good way to evaluate whether or not the performance of the system meets your company's criteria for effectiveness.

Wide area network services of a reasonable cost with sufficient bandwidth to support imaging network demands effectively may be more difficult to find. Recall that a T-1 delivers 1.544 Mbps and is a leased line offering services 24 hours a day, 7 days a week. Fractional T-1 allows users to access 64K increments of the T-1 circuit, also as a dedicated leased line. Switched 56K services are available on an as-needed basis, but would probably not deliver sufficient bandwidth on a single dial-up circuit.

However, recalling videoconferencing network bandwidth solutions, an inverse multiplexer could be employed to dial-up additional switched 56K circuits as needed to provide sufficient imaging bandwidth-on-demand.

Other current or emerging wide area network services that might serve as imaging bandwidth options were explored in Chapters 8 and 10. For example:

Service	Bandwidth	Switched or Leased
ISDN-BRI	144Kbps	Switched
ISDN-PRI	1.544Mbps	Switched
Switched 384	384Kbps	Switched
Frame Relay	1.544Mbps?	Switched
SMDS	45Mbps	Switched

In any case, there is little doubt that increased implementation of imaging systems will put more pressure on carriers to offer more bandwidth-on-demand services at a reasonable price.

Data Management Techniques Apply to Images

Once digitized, an image becomes just another type of data to be stored, retrieved, and manipulated. As such, data management techniques originally developed in the database world have been applied successfully to imaging systems in order to improve the overall efficiency and performance of these systems.

Specifically, **image compression,** like data or video compression, can shrink a 1MB image down to about 25 or 30KB. This saves not only storage space but also reduces the required transmission bandwidth for networked imaging systems.

Another way to reduce the amount of imaging data that must be transported via wide area network links is achieved through *data distribution analysis.* In this technique borrowed from the field of data management and design, each image or class of images is analyzed as to the likelihood and frequency of it being retrieved in any particular corporate location. By storing the most frequently accessed images locally, the need for wide area network bandwidth is reduced. Timing of large batch image transfers between image servers can have an impact on network performance as well. If these large transfers can be done during off-hours, when the servers aren't busy processing local user requests, performance during work hours won't suffer and the image transfer will go more quickly.

Finally, **dynamic image indexing** keeps track of exactly which document images are contained in each image folder at any point in time. In many cases, just this small index of folder contents can be quickly sent to a customer service rep or imaging worker. If the inquiry only involves the verification of the existence, receipt, status or processing of a particular document, the index itself may contain sufficient information to answer such an inquiry, thereby eliminating the need for the bandwidth-intensive transfer of the image itself.

Technology: Imaging Platform Evolution

High-End   Traditionally, imaging systems have been powerful, expensive information systems that ran on mainframes and minicomputers. Although LAN-based and client/server solutions are appearing, these powerful imaging systems are still often the choice for the most demanding applications. These high-end systems come with a high-end price often starting at around $100,000. Thorough business analysis should be conducted before purchasing such a system in order justify its cost. Figure 11-16 lists the manufacturers of some of these high-end systems and the platforms on which each of these systems run.

LAN-Based   As PCs have become more powerful from both a hardware and software standpoint, increased attention has been paid to LAN-based imaging solutions due largely to their significantly lower price tag. Many LAN-based imaging systems support numerous network operating systems such as Netware, LAN Manager, Appletalk, Vines, or DEC Pathworks (LAN Manager). Client platforms include DOS, MAC, OS/2, UNIX, and Windows while server platforms include DOS, OS/2 and UNIX.

As users have demanded more open imaging systems that can be more easily integrated with their existing LANs, the database portion of the imaging system has gone through a bit of an evolution as well. Whereas image storage databases had been largely proprietary in the past, images can now be stored in numerous SQL-compliant databases such as Oracle, Informix, Gupta and Sybase to name just a few.

As a matter of fact, images can be stored in any of these databases thanks to a field type designation known as **BLOB** (binary large objects). This flexibility of SQL databases to handle "regular" data or BLOBs comes at a price in terms of performance. Specially designed proprietary imaging databases or image-supported versions of popular databases such as Oracle or Informix will outperform "regular" SQL databases supporting image management via the BLOB. Figure 11-17

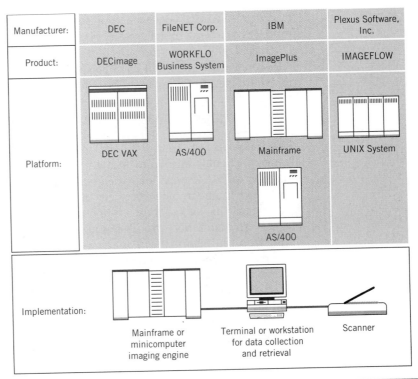

Figure 11-16 High-end imaging system platforms.

illustrates some of the major characteristics and options of LAN-based imaging systems.

Image-Enabled LANs Among the most intriguing of the LAN-based imaging solutions is a joint venture between Kodak and Novell known as **image-enabled Netware.** It is important to realize that image-enabled Netware is not an imaging system. It is a special version of Netware that allows third-party imaging application software vendors to write imaging systems which will run over Novell LANs. The "image-enabled" portion allows the application developers to interface to imaging services APIs in Novell, rather than having to write device drivers and other technical codes amounting to an imaging operating system. Simply stated, the Novell server becomes an image server as part of its role as network operating system server. Figure 11-18 illustrates a possible implementation of a third-party imaging application on image-enabled Netware.

Image-Enabled Netware Three specific image related services implemented in image-enabled Netware are:

   HCSS—High Capacity Storage Services control image access to and from the optical juke box on which the images are stored. Optical juke boxes contain several (as many as 100) optical platters which are able to store as much as 100GB of images on each platter. Imaging or document-flow applications merely issue a call to the HCSS for access to the optical juke box rather than having to write all the device drivers to access the optical juke box directly.

   DMS—Document Management Services is an object-oriented approach to document management which organizes documents into logical folders and

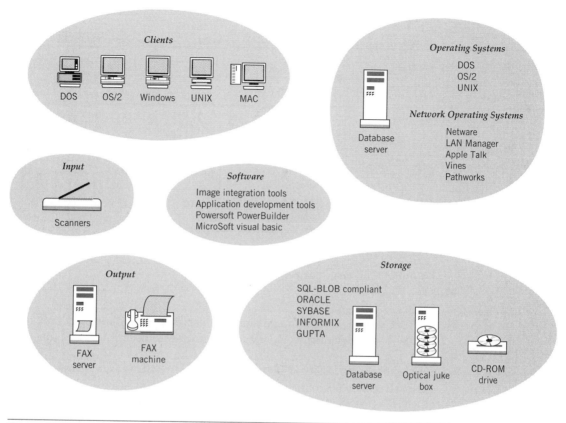

Figure 11-17 LAN-based imaging systems.

workbaskets. The icons representing these objects can then be included in document flow software as part of the graphical user interface. Logical index cards are attached to each document, folder, and workbasket in order to facilitate document retrieval, processing, and management.

IMS—Image Management Services control the access and management of the image files themselves. Image files can be stored in numerous different formats. IMS keeps track of which format each image is stored in and interprets each image appropriately according to its format before sending it to the requesting workstation. Among the possible image storage formats are the following:

> *TIFF*—Tagged Image File Format
> *PCX*—PC Graphics Format
> *JPEG*—Joint Photographic Expert Group Format

Image-Enabled Front-End Tools

Lotus Notes, often referred to as a member of a category of software known as groupware, has also entered into a partnership with Kodak in order to be able to incorporate images directly into Notes documents and applications. In addition, Notes images can be attached to other applications such as word processing, presentation graphics, spreadsheet, E-mail, or EDI as well. As Notes capabilities expand, it may offer not only the ability to scan, store, and transport images, but also offer the workflow or document management application software necessary to actually implement an imaging system effectively within a business.

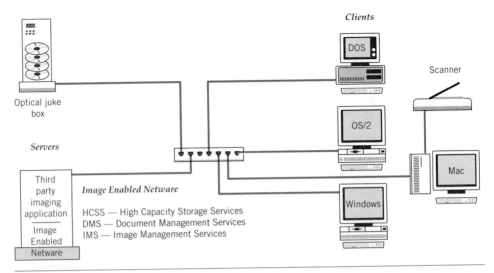

Figure 11-18 Image-enabled Netware.

Combined with image-enabled Netware, image-enabled Lotus Notes bodes well for the future of LAN-based imaging systems.

The Future: Client–Server Based Imaging Systems

Just as database management and E-mail systems have gone through a metamorphosis that took them from a LAN (server) based platform to today's distributed computing, distributed database platform, imaging systems' evolution will in all likelihood take a similar course. Given increased interest and implementation fueled by the lower cost LAN-based systems, high-powered **imaging application development front-end tools** will evolve separately from the high-performance imaging server back-end applications or **imaging engines.** Image-enabled Netware is a step towards the optimized imaging engine. Standard APIs will tie the imaging front-ends and engines together via a universal imaging backbone connectivity standard similar to SQL in the database world and X.400/500 in the E-mail world. Figure 11-19 illustrates a possible client–server imaging architecture.

Imaging can be thought of as just another type of "payload" to be transported to information workers connected via local and wide area networks. Voice and video transmission joined directly to the desktop through a single network connection are within the realm of possibility as well. *Multimedia computing* seeks to bring all of these various payload types together over a single network. Having already studied the details of the transmission of data, voice, video, and image, an attempt will be made to put it all together in terms of network implications in the next section on multimedia networking.

☐ PUTTING IT ALL TOGETHER: MULTIMEDIA NETWORKING

Multimedia computing seeks to deliver any and every known method of conveying a message or idea to the desktop. Although perhaps a bit overstated, this is not far from the truth. To the previously studied areas of videoconferencing and imaging, multimedia adds full motion video, still photographic images, animation, and the sound associated with any of these as well as "normal" data. The development, organization, delivery, and manipulation of these many information types into a

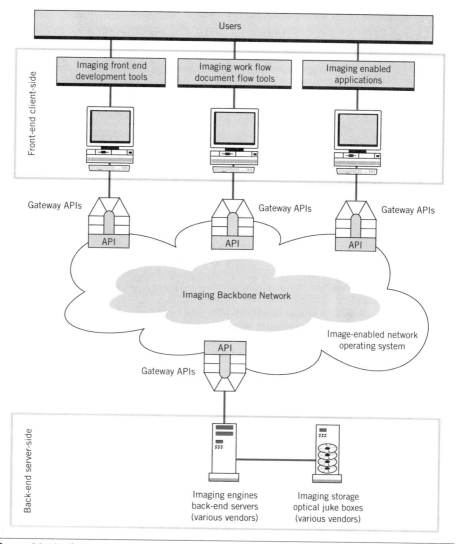

Figure 11-19 Client–server based imaging systems.

cohesive and understandable graphical user interface is the real challenge of multimedia computing.

Multimedia computing, like most data communications-based devices and/or services, is a product of at least two contributing factors as delineated in a variation of the now familiar equation:

Business(User) Demand + Available Technology = Current State of Multimedia Computing

In this section, the current business demands as well as possible future uses of networked multimedia computing will be explored. In addition, the current state of a number of different technologies affecting multimedia computing including but not limited to the following will be studied:

Multimedia applications development software
Local and wide area network implications

Computing and processing requirements

Multimedia enabled applications and network operating systems

Business Demands as a Driving Force

Without significant demand associated with proven benefits, financial or otherwise, multimedia computing will remain a topic to be read about rather than implemented. First aimed at the education and entertainment markets, multimedia computing's real impact may only be felt when coupled with the power of networking.

Transparency is a term used frequently throughout the text to connote the ability of networking or computing platforms to somehow make the user's interface to the computer less complicated or give the user one less thing to worry about. When multimedia can deliver true **user-location transparency** at a reasonable cost, then the demand side of the equation should be satisfied. User-location transparency refers to a user's ability, through networked multimedia computing, to take part in a meeting of any type, from anywhere, at any time, as effectively as if they were physically present at the meeting site. Types of meetings may range from planning sessions, to engineering sessions, to product review meetings, or marketing campaign approval meetings. Part of the transparency test is that regardless of the type of meeting, remote participants can participate as effectively as local participants.

Applications Must Meet the Business Demand

On the applications layer, user-location transparency will be enabled by a class of multimedia application software known as *distributed multimedia groupware*. Through a combination of videoconferencing, imaging, and group collaborative design utilities, as well as shared data capabilities, geographically dispersed decision makers will be able to engage in collaborative design and problem solving sessions leading to significantly reduced travel expense budgets. Although applications programs that deliver these features with complete transparency across multiple client, server, and network types may not currently exist, a few currently available applications may give a hint as to what these distributed multimedia groupware applications may offer.

IBM's P2P, Person-to-Person/2, is the closest thing to true distributed multimedia groupware, although many aspects of the application are still under development. P2P could be considered a peer-to-peer or client-based product as the P2P is loaded onto each local or remote workstation. Currently limited to five person conferences, P2P offers simultaneous videoconferencing and a **virtual meeting room.** Virtual meeting rooms include such capabilities or functions as:

A shared on-screen chalkboard on which documents can be posted.

Any conference participant may annotate or point to anywhere on the chalkboard and have those notes and points appear on all conference attendees' workstations.

Chat utilities allow conference participants to exchange text messages.

Perhaps most importantly, P2P supplies an API (applications program interface), which allows other application programs, whether new or existing, to take advantage of P2P's virtual meeting room capabilities. By simply issuing calls to the P2P API, applications can become **multimedia-enabled.** This is a similar pattern to the mail-enabled and image-enabled applications which have been created with similar APIs and studied in previous sections or chapters. Figure 11-20 illustrates a possible P2P installation.

Hardware

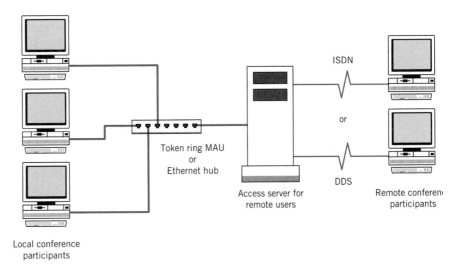

Software

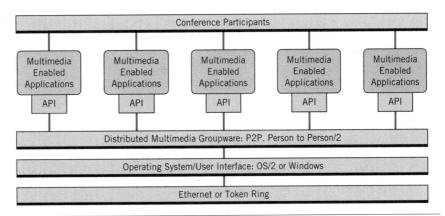

Figure 11-20 P2P and the virtual meeting room.

One existing application likely to be one of the first to become multimedia enabled via the P2P API is Lotus Notes. Notes' image-enabled capabilities were detailed in the imaging section of this chapter. Microsoft Word for the Macintosh is another example of a multimedia-enabled application.

Server-Based Multimedia Applications

Whereas P2P was really a client-based or peer-to-peer multimedia application, server-based application platforms are also emerging and generally fall into two different categories. Some multimedia servers work alongside conventional network servers transporting video via the transport protocols of a network operating system such as Novell in a software-only arrangement known as **loadable multimedia servers.** Other multimedia servers supply the entire network operating system including transport protocols as well as the server hardware and are known as **dedicated multimedia servers** or more simply **mediaservers.**

As an example of a loadable multimedia server, Fluent, Inc. markets a product known as FluentLinks, which is actually an NLM (Netware loadable module) that transforms a Netware server into a multimedia server allowing video to be played back to any Windows-based clients attached to the Netware server. This particular NLM operates only on those Netware networks running over Ethernet or FDDI. The impact of various network access methodologies on multimedia transmission will be examined shortly.

Starworks

Starlight, Inc., produces a turnkey multimedia server combining both hardware and software products. The MediaServer and Starworks operating system deliver video, audio, and data to up to 20 users simultaneously. This multimedia traffic is delivered over either 10BaseT or 10Base2(Thinnet) Ethernet LANs to Macintosh, Windows or DOS clients running the Starworks client software. End-user applications software such as spreadsheet, database, word-processing or groupware can run unmodified on the mediaserver/starworks network.

An available API to the Starworks software allows application programs to become "multimedia-enabled" simply by issuing requests for services to the Starworks software through this API. Such multimedia enabled applications are able to recall video, animation, document images or sound associated with database records, spreadsheets, or word processing documents. Figure 11-21 summarizes the hardware/software details of a mediaserver/Starworks implementation.

Two items in the Starworks protocol stack in Figure 11-21 deserve further explanation. First, rather than using a data-oriented LAN transport protocol such

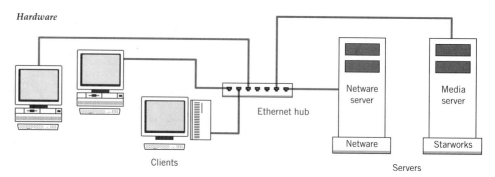

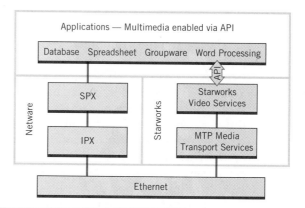

Figure 11-21 Media server/Starworks implementation.

as IP or IPX, Starworks uses its own transport protocol known as **MTP** (media transport protocol) instead. The key distinguishing characteristic of MTP is its inherent ability to handle **streaming data** such as video and audio. Streaming data is continuous in nature as opposed to packetized data, such as typical LAN traffic, which exhibits more bursty characteristics. The Starworks video services are offered to applications programs through the Starworks API for locating, enabling, and managing video and audio segments in multimedia-enabled applications.

One of the Starworks services of particular interest is known as **object management.** This service allows any multimedia source such as video, audio, data, or image to be considered as an object in order to be included in any application. Objects and object oriented programming were first discussed in terms of distributed computing in Chapter 9.

Practical applications of this multimedia application software are currently in the developmental or design stage. Multimedia mail as an extension of E-mail is an obvious possibility. Extending the current marketing technique of mailing VCR video tapes for high-priced items can lead to multimedia marketing campaigns via CD-ROMS for interactive playback on home computers.

The real limiting factor to practical multimedia applications is not the software that displays multimedia presentations, but rather the software which is employed to *produce* multimedia software presentations. This powerful yet sophisticated category of software is often referred to as **authoring software.** Although detailed descriptions and product reviews of multimedia production software are beyond the scope of this text, be aware as network managers that multimedia applications that may have a significant impact on a network must first be produced, which is a task not to be underestimated.

Client–Server-Based Multimedia Applications

Specially designed multimedia servers and operating systems such as the MediaServer/Starworks system represent one of many multimedia delivery possibilities. The client-based, peer-to-peer application described earlier known as P2P is a second alternative. Client–server-based applications are a third alternative. In typical client–server fashion, multimedia functionality is delivered to the end user's workstation via cooperative processing by software elements on both client and server processors. As has been illustrated on numerous occasions, APIs play a key role in offering transparency between client interfaces and server services. Figure 11-22 illustrates both the overall architecture as well as some of the currently available technology for creating multimedia-enabled client–server-based applications.

In comparison to client–server-based distributed database or distributed computing architectures, the distributed multimedia architecture shown in Figure 11-22 illustrates the relatively early stage of development of this architecture. Middleware-like multimedia extensions are written for particular clients and are linked to particular servers running particular network operating systems. There is no universal multimedia connectivity standard such as X.400 or SQL, and thus the enterprise network does not represent a transparent, universal delivery backbone as was the case with other client–server distributed architectures discussed earlier.

The closest thing to a universally accepted de facto standard for multimedia middleware is Microsoft's **AVI** (audio visual interleave). AVI is actually a part of the underlying structure of Microsoft's *Video for Windows*, which defines file formats for storage of video and audio payloads. Support for the AVI file definitions

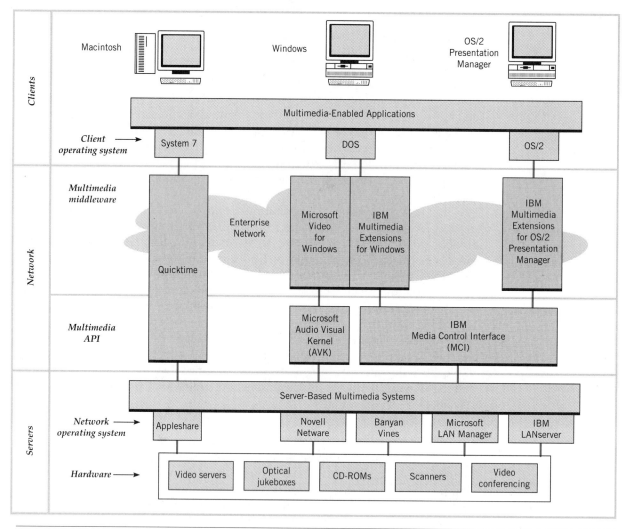

Figure 11-22 Client–server-based multimedia application architecture.

can be incorporated into multimedia middleware from other vendors, thereby assuring some measure of interoperability.

Data Layer Implications of Multimedia

Given the level of integration between "normal" applications programs and multimedia sources in the aforementioned multimedia-enabled applications, what might be the implications for storage of these multimedia archives? It is known from the study of videoconferencing and imaging that even with sophisticated compression techniques, a tremendous amount of storage is required. Two basic options exist for storage requirements of such high capacity. The first option is **optical juke boxes** containing multiple **WORM** (write once read many) platters capable of holding several gigabytes of data. Another alternative is **RAID** technology, more commonly known as redundant arrays of inexpensive disks.

In any case, once sufficient storage space has been acquired, how will video, audio, and image objects be stored, organized, indexed and retrieved? Multimedia databases must not only store the multimedia source video, audio, and image, but must also retain key information about each of the multimedia sources which is unnecessary for "normal" data. For instance, bandwidth requirements, interface requirements, circuit characteristics or LAN segment requirements for successful transmission of a given multimedia segment may be stored along with the multimedia source. In this manner, multimedia-enabled operating systems will immediately know the best way to deliver multimedia sources to requesting applications and will also know whether or not sufficient bandwidth even exists to perform such a delivery.

Network Implications of Multimedia

Although sheer bandwidth is certainly important in determining the successful transmission of multimedia applications, it is not the sole networking issue. As stated above in the discussion of transport protocols, video and audio are inherently different in nature from customary data. This difference is reflected in the access methodologies developed for local area networks. Because LAN data is bursty requiring large amounts of bandwidth for short amounts of time, access methodologies such as CSMA/CD and Token Passing were developed to bring some order to the rather unpredictable nature of this bursty LAN data.

Video and audio on the other hand are more like a continuous, steady stream of data than bursty LAN data. In order to produce smooth projection of video images on a videoconferencing unit, a *constant, guaranteed bandwidth* is the most important factor. Transmission of video or audio, unlike data, is very sensitive to even the slightest delay. This delay-sensitive video data requiring constant bandwidth is transmitted best via **isochronous transmission**, which was first introduced in Chapter 8.

In isochronous transmission, timing is kept constant by the consistently timed arrival of fixed length cells comprising the transmission signal that actually transports the time-sensitive payloads. Isochronous payloads such as voice and video may require transport protocols designed especially for the streaming characteristics of their transmission. MTP, or media transport protocol, mentioned above as part of the Starserver multimedia server is an example of such a streaming-enabled transport protocol. The differences between typical LAN data and digitized video and voice as well as the differences in available networking technology are summarized in Figure 11-23.

Shared LAN Media versus LAN Switches

Two different networking technology possibilities are illustrated in Figure 11-23. The typical shared media LAN, such as Ethernet or Token Ring, with CSMA/CD or token passing access control can only guarantee access and sufficient bandwidth when the number of simultaneous users is relatively low. On the other hand, LAN switches, such as the Ethernet switch discussed earlier in the text, offer dedicated connections of guaranteed bandwidth. 100Mbps FDDI switches are also a possibility as is the eventual introduction of an ATM switch for guaranteed bandwidth. So-called Fast Ethernet at 100 Mbps bandwidth availability may play a role in delivery of multimedia LAN services as well. LAN switches and Fast Ethernet will be discussed further in Chapter 13, "Trends to Watch: Where Do We Go from Here?"

Alternative Access Methodologies

Upon closer examination of the classic LAN scenario, a possible third technological alternative for delivery of voice and video emerges. The actual limiting factor in the use of a typical shared media LAN for video transmission is not really the media itself but rather the *access methodologies*. In other words, it is the inability of

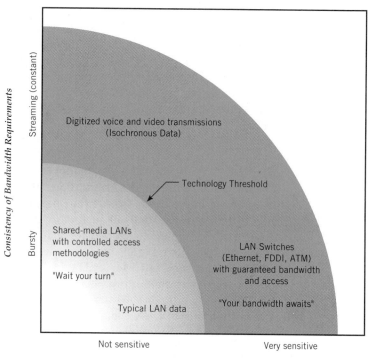

Figure 11-23 Network requirements versus available technology.

CSMA/CD and token passing to distinguish voice or video traffic from data traffic and prioritize the transmission of that voice or video accordingly which cuts to the root of the problem. It may be recalled from earlier discussions of multiplexers, that a device known as a fast packet mux can distinguish and prioritize accordingly between voice, fax, video and data.

Although ATM switches are certainly one solution to multimedia transmission, a viable alternative is a new access methodology which recognizes the unique transmission requirements of voice and video versus data and can react accordingly. **IEEE 802.9** is a new category of developing standards that seeks to deliver *both* a packet-oriented transport channel for data as well as a circuit-switched constant bandwidth channel for isochronous traffic over conventional LAN media.

Not surprisingly, proposals for these new multimedia LAN access methodologies have emerged based upon both Ethernet as well as Token Ring LANs. Figure 11-24 summarizes the comparative characteristics of these emerging multimedia LAN access methodologies.

Each of the proposed standards outlined in Figure 11-24 seeks to meet the critical low latency requirements of multimedia transmission in its own way. For instance, IsoEnet reserves a 6Mbps channel for multimedia applications and time stamps multimedia payloads to ensure timely delivery. On the other hand, multimedia-enabled Token Ring with its 32-bit adapter card, uses a packet prioritization scheme which was already part of the Token Ring standard but largely unused. Multimedia payloads are given higher priority access to Token Ring's 16Mbps bandwidth while the overall number of concurrent multimedia sessions is limited to 12 by the Network Transport/2 management software.

IEEE 802.9 Proposals		
Network Name	ISOENET (Isochronous Ethernet)	Multimedia Token-Ring
Developer(s)	National Semiconductor IBM APPLE	IBM
Network and Bandwidth	16 Mbps Ethernet	16 Mbps Token-Ring
Media	UTP	STP/UTP
Adapter Cards	Based on isochronous chip set. Single media interface	32-bit specialized adapter card
Prioritization Scheme	Video is sent in reserved 6 Mbps channel via time division multiplexing	Uses Token-Ring's built-in prioritization mechanism, sends multimedia traffic on shared media with data traffic at a higher priority
Restrictions/ Limitations	Backwardly compatible with 10BaseT, but requires new workstation adapter cards and concentrator or HUB modules	Requires client/server software called Network Transport/2 Runs only on OS/2 operating systems running LAN Server network operating system 12 multimedia sessions per LAN segment

Figure 11-24 Emerging multimedia access methodologies.

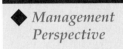

Management Perspective Although no one standard or technology appears to be the dominant choice of multimedia LAN transmission, several of the aforementioned alternatives possess the capability to deliver satisfactory multimedia service over local area networks at a reasonable cost. Wide area network transmission of multimedia services may be a bit more difficult. Referring back to Figure 11-10, it should be obvious that LAN technology is better able to transport multimedia services at a reasonable cost than current WAN alternatives. The costs of a T-3 line for multimedia transmission is extremely prohibitive in most cases.

Multimedia on the WAN

It would appear that the opportunity exists in the WAN services arena for a new series of reasonably priced, usage-based multimedia WAN transport services. WAN ATM services have been proposed as one solution although transparent, universal availability of such products may be a problem. SMDS, switched multimegabit data service, discussed earlier in the text, may also be a viable WAN transport service if the current "data only" restrictions can be overcome.

The logical alternative to increasing available WAN bandwidth for multimedia transport is to reduce the amount of bandwidth which multimedia sessions demand. The further development of sophisticated video and audio compression methodologies will play a key role in the eventual widespread use of wide area multimedia transport services. Recalling that any video or audio payload that is compressed according to a certain algorithm or formula must be decompressed by that same method, the need for standards in this area in order assure interoperability should be obvious.

Multimedia Compression

Compression/decompression can be completed most efficiently when performed by special-purpose computer chips. **DVI** (digital video interactive) is the name of a chipset from Intel which is capable of compressing and decompressing full-motion video at 30 frames per second in real-time. In plain terms, DVI is capable of compressing and decompressing video "on the fly," storing approximately 70 minutes of video on a CD-ROM.

The particular compression/decompression technique employed by the DVI chips can be programmed onto the chip, allowing for performance upgrades as more advanced compression/decompression techniques are developed. DVI chipsets also support the **AVI** (audio visual interleave) file definition for storage of audio and video payloads. By using a standard compression processing chipset such as DVI, which supports a standard file definition, such as AVI, one assures transparent interoperability with other multimedia hardware and software which either employ or support the same chipset.

Multimedia's Future

The widespread deployment of multimedia hardware and applications will, in all likelihood, be determined by the availability of multimedia applications with the following characteristics:

High-productivity
Ease of use
Reasonable price

Furthermore, these multimedia applications must be able to be employed over a wide variety of client-platforms (notebooks, laptops, notepads) and networks offering users total geographic transparency. In other words, it must not matter whether a multimedia resource is around the corner or around the world, access to that resource must be transparent from the end-user's perspective. Clearly, such a scenario offers significant opportunities for development in the areas of wide area as well as local area networking design.

Recalling the top-down model, the ultimate test for multimedia, as for any application, lies in the impact delivered to the business layer. Can multimedia provide positive cost–benefit ratios and/or increase worker productivity? The answer to that question is really the key to the future of multimedia.

CHAPTER SUMMARY

Videoconferencing, imaging, and multimedia applications must be viewed from several perspectives in order to be thoroughly understood. In this chapter these three services were studied from conceptual, technical, and financial perspectives using the top-down model as a frame of reference. Most importantly, these technologies were primarily studied with a view toward their poten-

tial impact on both local and wide area networks. The current and potential business uses of these three services were reviewed. Possible beneficial results of the deployment of such services as well as the use of an objective business analysis skill known as business reengineering were analyzed.

The applications of videoconferencing, imaging,

and multimedia services that actually deliver on stated business objectives are still in a stage which could perhaps be described as evolutionary. Solutions exist on particular platforms to accomplish specific business objectives, but flexible, multiplatform, transparent applications are in various stages of development. Some applications development tools exist to allow end-users to develop videoconferencing, imaging, and multimedia applications or to enable existing applications to interact with these advanced services.

One of the major problems of this evolutionary process is the simultaneous evolution of standards governing the interoperability of the technology which processes and delivers videoconferencing, imaging, and multimedia. These standards, or the lack thereof, were highlighted throughout the chapter.

The data formatting, storage, and transport implications of these services, as well as the impact of transmission on local area and wide area networks, was the main focus of the chapter. In order to understand potential network impact of such technologies, one must first have a thorough understanding of the technologies themselves. Current network alternatives available for the delivery of videoconferencing, imaging, and multimedia services were evaluated in terms of their ability to meet both bandwidth as well as time delay constraints of these services. Evolving network standards and technological advances that might better meet the unique network demands of video, imaging, and multimedia services in the future were analyzed as well.

Finally, given the evolutionary state of these services, some thought was given to the trends that may shape the future direction or further development of videoconferencing, imaging, and multimedia applications.

KEY TERMS

adaptive echo cancellation
ADSL
authoring software
AVI
bandwidth-on-demand
BLOB
BONDING
business reengineering
CIF
CODEC
dedicated multimedia server
DMS
DVI
dynamic image indexing
FITL
frame
GVS
H.243
H.261
HCSS
HDSL
IEEE 802.9
image compression
image-enabled Netware
imaging engines
imaging front-end tools
IMS
interactive TV
interframe coding
inverse multiplexer
isochronous transmission
LAN-based videoconferencing
LAN-enabled videoconferencing
loadable multimedia server
MCU
mediaconferencing systems
mediaserver
motion compensation
MTP
multimedia-enabled
NTSC
object management
optical juke boxes
pixel
post-processing
pre-processing
QCIF
RAID
streaming data
user-location transparency
VHDSL
video compression
video dialtone
video digitization
videohub
videophone
virtual bridge
virtual meeting room
WORM

REVIEW QUESTIONS

1. What is the trade-off in videoconferencing for increased video compression and decreased bandwidth requirements?
2. Why are inverse multiplexers such important technology?
3. What carrier services are best suited to wide area transmission of videoconferencing, imaging, and multimedia?
4. Are there wide area services that might support transport of videoconferencing, imaging, and multimedia more effectively than present offerings? If so, what are the characteristics of these wide area services?
5. What is meant by low latency?
6. How do video and voice payloads differ in their transmission requirements from "normal" LAN data?
7. What is isochronous transmission and why is it important?
8. What adjustments must be made to current LAN access methodologies in order to transport video and voice over LANs more effectively?
9. What are some of the proposals for new LAN access methodologies to transport voice, video, and data simultaneously?
10. What are the data storage and management implications for integrated videoconferencing, imaging, and multimedia services?

11. What is meant by the terms user-location transparency and virtual meeting room?

12. How do these terms relate to the overall deployment level of multimedia systems?

13. What is the difference between streaming and bursty data?

14. What impact would these characteristics have on the transport protocols employed to deliver payloads exhibiting these characteristics?

15. Which standards are most important in the area of multimedia and why?

16. How does object management and BLOBs relate to integrated videoconferencing, imaging, and multimedia?

17. In your opinion, what is the limiting factor or bottleneck in the transparent use of desktop videoconferencing, imaging, and multimedia applications among geographically dispersed end-users?

18. What are some of the potentially most significant business impacts of videoconferencing, imaging, and multimedia?

19. What are some of the potential changes which may occur in the local loop in order to support wide area access to videoconferencing, imaging, and multimedia services?

20. What are some of the future services which may be offered by carriers or other companies in the video services area?

21. How is the sampling rate of video digitization different from voice digitization?

22. How can bandwidth requirements for video transmission be calculated?

23. What challenges do the requirements for transmission of uncompressed video pose?

24. What are some of the potential solutions to the bandwidth requirements of uncompressed video?

25. What are the advantages and disadvantages of H.261 as a CODEC interoperability standard?

26. What are the similarities and differences between interframe coding and motion compensation?

27. How do pre- and post-processing further reduce videoconferencing bandwidth requirements?

28. What are the potential disadvantages of pre- and post-processing?

29. What role does adaptive echo cancellation play in videoconferencing?

30. What kinds of added features might be required in order to meet business demands in a mediaconferencing system?

31. Describe at least three cost-effective uses of inverse multiplexers. Include network diagrams.

32. What efforts toward inverse multiplexer interoperability have been achieved?

33. What additional technology is required to establish and manage multipoint conferences?

34. How can multipoint control units be cost-justified?

35. What are some alternatives to purchasing one's own multipoint control units?

36. What standardization efforts have taken place concerning multipoint control units?

37. How are MCU standardization efforts related to the growth of enterprise partnerships?

38. What are some of the positive and negative aspects of videophones?

39. What is the difference between LAN-enabled videoconferencing and LAN-based videoconferencing?

40. What is the importance of IEEE 802.9 to LAN-based videoconferencing?

41. What two industries are interested in offering video dialtone or video-on-demand services?

42. How does video-on-demand differ from interactive TV?

43. What are some possible scenarios for the evolution of the local loop to support high bandwidth requirements?

44. Which industries are most likely to benefit from imaging technology and why?

45. Why have imaging systems been traditionally deployed on mainframe and minicomputer platforms?

46. What changes have allowed imaging applications to be deployed on local area network platforms?

47. What is the importance of business process reengineering to imaging application analysis?

48. What is the relationship of workflow or document-flow software to imaging systems?

49. How can imaging network bandwidth demand be calculated?

50. What implications do such calculations have for deployment of imaging systems on LANs?

51. Which WAN services are best suited to imaging applications and why?

52. What techniques have been developed to reduce overall bandwidth demand by imaging applications?

53. How do image enabled LANs simplify the development of imaging applications?

54. Draw a diagram of how imaging applications can be deployed on image enabled LANs.

55. What is meant by the term multimedia?

56. What are some of the unique requirements demanded of multimedia transport protocols?

57. What is isochronous transmission and how does it relate to multimedia networking?

58. What are some of the data layer implications and possible solutions for multimedia networking?

59. Compare two proposed access methodologies designed for the transport of multimedia applications.

ACTIVITIES

1. Investigate and report on the efforts of Telecommunications, Inc. of Denver to upgrade its network to provide 500-channel capacity to its 10 million customers by 1996.

2. Investigate and report on the video-dialtone field trials of Bell Atlantic in New Jersey and Virginia.

3. Investigate and report on the efforts of Time-Warner, Inc. to set up a digital cable network in Orlando, Florida.

4. Contact your local phone company and determine which locally available services, if any, are suitable for videoconferencing. Determine the price for a 30-minute videoconference for the following geographic ranges: local, approximately 50 miles, approximately 250 miles, approximately 1000 miles.

5. Choose cities that are 50, 250 and 1000 miles from your present location. Determine ground and/or air travel costs to those locations. Compare these travel costs for six people in comparsion to the costs of the videoconferences determined in question 4. Is videoconferencing always cost-effective?

6. Contact the videoconferencing equipment vendor of your choice. Possibilities: PictureTel Corp., (508) 977-9500, or Compression Labs, Inc., (408) 435-3000. Request literature and price lists. Determine the capital and on-going costs involved in establishing a local and remote videoconferencing center. On-going costs include network transport services and the maintenance of the videoconference room and equipment.

7. Given the savings in the travel budget computed in question 5, at a rate of one videoconference per month, how many months will it take for the videoconferencing equipment to pay for itself based on travel expense savings?

8. Given information supplied by vendors or determined from videoconferencing buyers guides, determine the initial investment and on-going costs for an eight-point multipoint video conference. If six people from each location are involved in the video conference, determine whether a multipoint video-conference set-up has a shorter, longer, or equivalent payback period as compared to a point-to-point videoconference set-up.

9. Investigate and report on the current status of image-enabled netware. Are third-party applications currently available for this image-enabled version?

10. Investigate and report on the current status of image-enabled Lotus Notes.

11. Investigate and report on the partnership between NYNEX and Dow Jones, Inc. to deliver multimedia financial information services to brokers in New York.

12. Investigate and report on the role of the Internet standard known as MIME (multipurpose internet mail extension) in supporting multimedia transport over the Internet.

13. Distinguish between the following multimedia standards: DVI, QuickTime, Video for Windows, MPEG, JPEG, Px64

14. Investigate and report on the current status of the IEEE 802.9 standard. Has a standard been determined? Are products which support that standard currently available?

15. Investigate and report on the emerging technology known as ICR, intelligent character recognition, and its impact on the future of document imaging.

16. Research and compare the projected growth of LAN-based versus minicomputer- or mainframe-based imaging systems for the next five years.

17. Investigate and report on the category of software known as document management. Comment on this software category's relationship to imaging systems. Some document management software packages and companies:

Software	Company	Phone
SoftSolutions for Windows	SoftSolutions	(801) 226-6000
PC DOCS Open	PC DOCS Inc.	(800) 933-3627
Document Administrator	Info. Mgmt. Research	(303) 689-0022
Reference Point	Global Integrated Systems	(800) 374-6805

Featured References

Business Analysis Cases

Brandel, William. "JBS' Imaging Investment Pays Big," *LAN Times*, vol. 10, no. 12 (June 28, 1993), p. 47.

Brandel, William. "Aetna Searches for the Paperless Office," *LAN Times*, vol. 10, no. 8 (April 19, 1993), p. 43.

Morris, Larry. "UF, Varian Vacuum Take Imaging into the Mainstream," *LAN Times*, vol. 10, no. 7 (April 5, 1993), p. 59.

Cummings, Joanne. "Fiber Net Saves Video Firms Time, Money," *Network World*, vol. 9, no. 29 (July 20, 1992), p. 9.

Cummings, Joanne. "Videoconferencing Gives Recruiter Edge," *Network World*, vol. 10, no. 9 (March 1, 1993), p. 25.

Smalley, Eric. "Getting the Picture," *Network World*, vol. 9, no. 47 (November 25, 1992), p. 41.

Lazar, Jerry. "Altering Its Image," *Network World*, vol. 9, no. 47 (November 25, 1992), p. 43.

CODECs

Schwartz, Jeffrey. "Now, PC Videoconferencing," *Communications Week*, no. 385 (January 13, 1992), p. 4.

Imaging

Koleini, Pat. "Special Report: Document Imaging," *LAN Times*, vol. 10, no. 7 (April 5, 1993), p. 53.

Alsup, Mike. "Buyers Guide: LAN Imaging Systems," *Network World*, vol. 9, no. 37 (September 14, 1992), p. 41.

Reinhold, Bob, and Allen Harris. "Imaging Makes Its Mark on Nets," *Network World*, vol. 9, no. 23 (June 8, 1992), p. 43.

Brandel, William. "Lotus Tries to Bring Imaging into LAN Mainstream," *LAN Times*, vol. 9, no. 11 (June 22, 1992), p. 1.

Didio, Laura. "Kodak, Novell Plan 'Image Enabled Novell'," *LAN Times*, vol. 9, no. 11 (June 22, 1992), p. 1.

Wallace, Scott. "Image Archiving," *Corporate Computing*, vol. 1, no. 4 (October 1992), p. 75.

Mulqueen, John. "DoD Building Imaging System," *Communications Week*, no. 385 (January 13, 1992), p. 24.

Didio, Laura. "Making Document Image Processing Work on LANs," *LAN Times*, vol. 9, no. 11 (June 22, 1992), p. 41.

Bowden, Eric. "Get a Better Grip on Your Documents," *LAN Times*, vol. 10, no. 12 (June 28, 1993), p. 65.

Inverse Multiplexers

Briere, Daniel, and Christopher Finn. "Buyers Guide: Inverse Multiplexers," *Network World*, vol. 10, no. 20 (May 17, 1993), p. 41.

Johnson, Johna. "Switched or Dedicated? This Device Does Both," *Data Communications*, vol. 21, no. 4 (March 1992), p. 45.

Gold, Douglas. "Inverse Multiplexing: A Cost Effective Alternative," *LAN Times*, vol. 9, no. 7 (April 20, 1992), p. 39.

Messmer, Ellen. "Makers of Inverse Muxes Make Interoperability Push," *Network World*, vol. 9, no. 28 (July 13, 1992), p. 25.

Local Loop and Network Changes

Greenan, Jerry. "Taking HDSL to the Next Level," *Telephone Engineer & Management*, vol. 97, no. 17 (September 1, 1993), p. 33.

Johnson, Johna. "HDSL: An Extra Boost on the Local Loop," *Data Communications*, vol. 21, no. 13 (September 21, 1992), p. 47.

Wallace, Bob. "FCC Opens Spectrum for New CellularVision Offering," *Network World*, vol. 9, no. 51 (December 21, 1992), p. 15.

Karpinski, Richard. "NYNEX, Cable Company First to Test Video Dialtone Waters," *Telephony*, vol. 223, no. 15 (October 12, 1992), p. 6.

Multimedia Servers and Networks

Aoyama, Tomonori. "ATM VP-Based Broadband Networks for Multimedia Services," *IEEE Communications*, vol. 31, no. 4 (April 1993), p. 30.

Sakata, Shiro. "B-ISDN Multimedia Workstation Architecture," *IEEE Communications*, vol. 31, no. 8 (August 1993), p. 64.

Ubois, Jeff. "Preparing for the Multimedia Mix," *Network World*, vol. 10, no. 17 (April 26, 1993), p. 36.

Adam, John. "Interactive Multimedia," *IEEE Spectrum*, vol. 30, no. 3 (March 1993), p. 22.

Karpinski, Richard. "Multimedia Alliance Draws Telcos," *Telephony*, vol. 223, no. 15 (October 12, 1992), p. 12.

McQuillan, John. "Multimedia Networking: An Applications Portfolio," *Data Communications*, vol. 21, no. 12 (September 1992), p. 85.

Salamone, Salvatore. "A Special Server for Multimedia," *Data Communications*, vol. 21, no. 14 (October 1992), p. 37.

Cummings, Joanne. "NatSemi, IBM Offer Multimedia Ethernet," *Network World*, vol. 9, no. 47 (November 23, 1992), p. 1.

Salamone, Salvatore. "Hub Delivers Video over 10BaseT," *Data Communications*, vol. 22, no. 1 (January 1993), p. 78.

Hargadon, Tom. "Networked Media Sends a Message," *New Media*, vol. 2, no. 11 (November 1992), p. 27.

Salamone, Salvatore. "Sending Multimedia across the Network," *Data Communications*, vol. 22, no. 1 (January 1993), p. 75.

Salamone, Salvatore. "A Multimedia Approach to Groupware," *Data Communications,* vol. 22, no. 2 (January 21, 1993), p. 27.

Cummings, Joanne. "IBM Girds Token Ring for Multimedia Applications," *Network World,* vol. 9, no. 49 (December 7, 1992), p. 1.

Cummings, Joanne. "Phone to Become Multimedia Vehicle," *Network World,* vol. 10, no. 5 (February 1, 1993), p. 37.

Karpinski, Richard. "Multimedia Alliance Draws Telcos," *Telephony,* vol. 223, no. 15 (October 12, 1992), p. 12.

Toubagi, Fouad. "Multimedia: The Challenge Behind the Vision," *Data Communications,* vol. 22, no. 2 (January 21, 1993), p. 61.

Lippis, Nick. "Multimedia Networking: Restructuring the Enterprise for Video Traffic," *Data Communications,* vol. 22, no. 3 (February 1993), p. 60.

Murie, Michael. "Revving up Mac Network Rendering," *New Media,* vol. 2, no. 12 (December 1992), p. 49.

Technology

Johnson, Johna. "Video MCU Gets the Standard Treatment," *Data Communications,* vol. 22, no. 1 (January 1992), p. 50.

Johnson, Johna. "Mix-and-Match Videoconferencing," *Data Communications,* vol. 21, no. 11 (August 1992), p. 73.

Saunders, Stephen. "For Videophones, Light at the End of a Very Long Tunnel," *Data Communications,* vol. 20, no. 17 (December 1991), p. 116.

Videoconferencing

Johnson, Johna. "A New Look for Videoconferencing Services," *Data Communications,* vol. 22, no. 8 (May 21, 1993), p. 67.

Cummings, Joanne. "AT&T, CLI to Offer Analog Videoconferencing Chipset," *Network World.* vol. 9, no. 46 (November 16, 1992), p. 41.

Richardson, Steve. "Videoconferencing: The Bigger (and Better) Picture," *Data Communications,* vol. 21, no. 9 (June 1992), p. 103.

Guptill, Bruce, and Mark Langner. "Buyers Guide: Videoconferencing," *Network World,* vol. 9, no. 3 (January 27, 1992), p. 51.

Mangan, Tom. "Multipoint Video: The MCU in the Middle," *Data Communications,* vol. 21, no. 10 (July 1992), p. 27.

Johnson, Johna. "Videohub Cuts Costs, Opens Options," *Data Communications,* vol. 21, no. 3 (February 1992), p. 109.

Cummings, Joanne. "VTEL Joins Rush Toward Low-Cost Videoconferencing," *Network World,* vol. 10, no. 5 (February 1, 1993), p. 2.

Duffy, Jim. "Start-up Unveils Standard Videoconferencing Switch," *Network World,* vol. 9, no. 24 (June 15, 1992), p. 13.

Messmer, Ellen. "BT Offers Complete Videoconferencing," *Network World,* vol. 9, no. 27 (July 6, 1992), p. 29.

Cummings, Joanne. "Room Videoconferencing to Entice Low-End Users," *Network World,* vol. 10, no. 2 (January 11, 1993), p. 19.

Reveaux, Tony. "Videoconferencing Moves to the Desktop," *New Media,* vol. 2, no. 11 (November 1992), p. 33.

Johnson, Johna. "Mix-and-Match Videoconferencing ," *Data Communications,* vol. 21, no. 11 (August 1992), p. 73.

Video Dialtone

Karpinski, Richard. "NYNEX, Cable Company First to Test Video Dial Tone Waters," *Telephony,* vol. 223, no. 15 (October 12, 1992), p. 6.

Reed, David. "A Question of Network Evolution," *Telephone Engineer & Management,* vol. 96, no. 17 (September 1, 1992), p. 80.

Rosenthal, Steve. "Interactive TV: The Gold Rush Is on," *New Media,* vol. 2, no. 12 (December 1992), p. 27.

Rosenthal, Steve. "Interactive Network: Viewers Get Involved," *New Media,* vol. 2, no. 12 (December 1992), p. 30.

Cummings, Joanne. "Interactive TV Gains Support in Industry," *Network World,* vol. 9, no. 33 (August 17, 1993), p. 29.

Cummings, Joanne. "Phone to Become Multimedia Vehicle," *Network World,* vol. 10, no. 5 (February 1, 1993), p. 37.

CASE STUDY

Videoconferencing Gives Recruiter Edge

CLEVELAND—Videoconferencing technology is giving a recruitment firm here a competitive edge by helping the company provide its clients with a low-cost option for long-distance interviewing of job candidates.

Management Recruiters International, Inc. (MRI) is using a videoconferencing system officially unveiled by Compression Labs, Inc. (CLI) last week to conduct interviews between a client company in one of its 600 offices and a job candidate in another. For about $250 per half hour, the MRI service offers a huge cost savings for clients, who had been spending between $1,600 and $1,700 per candidate for travel, lodging and meals.

"This really gives us an edge in the recruitment field," said Stephen Fogelgren, vice president of operations at MRI. "When companies factor in the cost savings [for travel], they'll find that's more money than our total fee. None of our competitors can say that."

Videoconferencing gives employers an effective means of winnowing the field of prospective candidates, Fogelgren said.

"This won't replace the final face-to-face interview," he said. "But most firms find they need to do 10 or 12 initial interviews before they narrow down the field to the one or two people who most interest them."

The ability to see candidates and evaluate them via the videoconferencing system increases the value of the information obtained by three or four times that of telephone interviews, Fogelgren said.

"We're looking at the quality of the person's presentation," he explained. "The words we use make up less than 40% of the actual message; the rest is facial expression, eye movement, hand gestures. In an interview, you're looking for quality characteristics, like honesty and forthrightness, and you can learn a lot about those from body language."

MRI decided to make the investment in videoconferencing after evaluating systems from the top three U.S. manufacturers and several Japanese firms. In the end, it chose to base its project on CLI's new Eclipse system.

"CLI showed us what they had planned for the Eclipse, and it looked like our best option," Fogelgren said.

The Eclipse had all the features the firm needed at a very low price. "With every system, there are a series of trade-offs as to ease of use, cost and quality," Fogelgren said. "The Eclipse is one of the lowest priced systems, is very easy to use, and the quality is the same as the others we examined."

MRI uses public switched 56K bit/sec services to link its videoconferences. It has 50 units installed but plans to increase that to 250 by year end and, eventually, to all of its 600 offices.

MRI arranges more than 250,000 interviews per year, 90,000 of which involve candidate travel. "This is really going to keep costs down for everyone involved," Fogelgren said.

MRI also hopes to utilize the systems to enable small companies to perform on-campus recruiting at colleges. Since today only the largest firms can send recruiters directly to campuses, videoconferencing should help smaller firms compete for top candidates.

"Eventually, we'd like to install a videoconferencing unit in our offices near every major college campus," Fogelgren said. "That would enable the smaller firms to even the playing field and get a fair crack at the brightest candidates."

Source: Joanne Cummings, "Videoconferencing Gives Recruiter Edge," *Network World*, vol. 10, no. 9 (March 1, 1993), p. 25. Copyright 1993 by Network World Inc. Framingham, MA 01701. Reprinted from *Network World*.

Business Case Study Questions

To Do

1. After reading the article describing this business analysis case, prepare a top-down model by organizing pertinent facts into their proper layers within the top-down model.

2. Determine the potential cost savings per interview for clients who use Management Recruiters International's videoconferencing services.

3. Contact Compression Labs, Inc., (408) 435-3000, for product literature and price lists in order to determine

the acquisition costs of the Eclipse videoconferencing systems. Be sure to add the cost of CODECs if not already included.

4. At $250.00 per half-hour, how many client interviews will MRI have to book in order to cover the aquisition costs of the videoconferencing equipment? Remember: A point-to-point videoconference implies two offices have been equipped with videoconferencing equipment.

5. If an average of 20 interviews per week are booked, how long will the payback period be?

6. Assume the two MRI offices in the conference are 1000 miles apart. Contact your local or long-distance carrier to determine the costs of a switched 56K call over that distance for each half-hour interview.

7. Adding this operating expense to the acquisition costs

determined in question 3, how many half-hour interviews must be sold in order to payback the intitial investment for two locations?

8. Assuming all 600 MRI offices are equipped with videoconferencing equipment and that 90,000 out of a total of 250,000 half-hour interviews per year utilize the service, prepare a financial analysis detailing acquisition costs, transmission costs, and payback period. Assume an average videoconference distance of 1000 miles.

9. Discuss the business layer issues that make it unlikely that 100 percent of candidate interviews will be conducted by videoconferencing.

10. If you were a competitor of MRI, what might your strategic business objectives and resultant networking and technology designs and plans entail?

CHAPTER ▪ 12

The Network Development Life Cycle

Concepts Reinforced

Top-Down Model
Cost–Benefit Analysis
Business Reengineering

Concepts Introduced

Network Development Life Cycle
Network Analysis and Design Methodology
Comprehensive Systems and Networking Budget Models
Integrated Computer-Assisted Network Engineering

OBJECTIVES

Having mastered the material in this chapter, you should be able to:

1. Understand how the network development life cycle relates to other systems development architectures and life cycles and, consequently, how the network analyst/designer must interact with analysts/designers involved in these related processes.

2. Understand the network development life cycle including: overall issues, process structure, detailed activities for each step of the process, as well as coping with the reality of today's multiprotocol, multivendor environments.

3. Understand how one remains focused with a business perspective throughout the network development life cycle (planning, implementation, evaluation).

4. Understand what automated tools are available to assist in the NDLC process as well as the cost justification necessary for the acquisition of such tools.

5. Understand the current shortcomings of these automated tools as well as possible proposals for solutions to these shortcomings.

6. Understand the role of vendors at various stages of the NDLC and how to maximize the effectiveness of these vendors.

☐ INTRODUCTION

This chapter is perhaps the most important chapter in the entire book. Although a process-orientation and top-down approach have been taken throughout the entire text as data communications concepts and technology have been introduced, the focus of this chapter is solely on the data communications process known as the **network development life cycle.** All of the concepts and technology mastered in previous chapters will serve as available resources for the actual network development process outlined in this chapter.

Simply stated, this chapter should tie together much of the material covered to this point in the text about data communications by explaining how to do data communications.

AN EMPHASIS ON THE PRACTICAL

As has been the intention throughout the text, the emphasis in this chapter will be on the practical aspects of network development. For example, case studies and practical examples will be interwoven with conceptual material throughout the chapter rather than being presented only at the end of the chapter. Many of the case studies used in this chapter are based on firsthand experience. The material presentation will have a strong reality orientation rather than the more theoretical approach to network analysis and design often included in data communications textbooks.

This chapter will not include instruction in network traffic engineering. Whereas this is an introductory text, an appropriate level of complexity will be presented for the more technical aspects of network design. Reemphasizing the practical aspect of this chapter, techniques for effective interaction with consultants and vendors who possess the technical expertise to perform network traffic engineering are stressed.

WHERE DOES NETWORK DESIGN FIT IN THE OVERALL SCHEME OF THINGS?

In order to fully understand the importance of a properly designed network to a smoothly operating information system, one must first understand how the network design process relates to other information system development processes. The top-down model, which has been a constant strategic framework throughout the text, serves as an appropriate means for portraying the relationship between the network development process and other information systems-related development processes. This relationship is illustrated in Figure 12-1.

As can be seen in Figure 12-1, the network development life cycle depends upon previously completed development processes such as strategic business

Top-Down Model	Information Systems Development Process
Business	Strategic business planning
Application	Business process reengineering
	Systems development life cycle
	Systems analysis and design
Data	Application development life cycle
	Database analysis and design
Network	Database distribution analysis
	Network Development Life Cycle
	Network analysis and design
Technology	Logical network design
	Physical network design
	Network implementation
	Technology analysis

Figure 12-1 The top-down model and the network development life cycle.

planning, applications development life cycle, and data distribution analysis. If an implemented network is to effectively deliver the information systems which will, in turn, fulfill strategic business goals, then a top-down approach to the network development life cycle must be taken.

Although the previous statement may seem obvious or self-evident, it is by no means a given in the information systems development community. Network analysts who begin their analysis by asking about strategic business plans are likely to be asked: "What does that have to do with networking?"

Detailed explanations of the system development processes involved at the business, application, and data layers are beyond the scope of this text. However, in order to understand the network development life cycle in its overall context, it is important to recognize these prerequisite processes.

UNDERSTANDING SYSTEMS DEVELOPMENT: PROCESS AND PRODUCT

Two key components to any systems development effort are the **process** and the **product** of each stage of that development life cycle. Simply stated, the process describes activities that should be taking place at any point during the development cycle, and the product is the outcome or deliverable from a particular stage of the overall cycle.

A focus on the process allows one to visualize what they will be or should be *doing* at any point in the development life cycle. The product, meanwhile, could be interpreted as a **milestone** indicating completion of one stage of the development cycle and a readiness to proceed with subsequent stages.

A focus on product and process will facilitate the understanding of any systems development life cycle, not only the network development life cycle. Identification of process and product can be beneficial on high-level or summarized development cycles as well as more detailed methodologies. Figure 12-2 takes the high-level processes identified in Figure12-1 and lists possible products, or outcomes, from each of the corresponding processes.

Figure 12-2 clearly points out the need for significant analysis and design, and associated products or deliverables, prior to the commencement of any network analysis and design activities. As has been stated many times previously in this text, network analysis and design cannot be successfully performed in a vacuum. Rather, network analysis and design is but one step in an overall comprehensive information systems development cycle, commencing with business layer analysis and concluding with an analysis of the technology currently available to implement the system as designed.

A similar process/product analysis will be performed on the more detailed network design-related development life cycles and methodologies as these models are introduced.

THE NETWORK DEVELOPMENT LIFE CYCLE

Although several models or frameworks will be used in this chapter to organize the presentation of material, the key model behind the network design process is known as the network development life cycle (NDLC). Figure 12-3 is a simple or summarized illustration of the NDLC which will be explained further in the following paragraphs.

The word "cycle" is a key descriptive term of the network development life

	Information Systems Development Process	Product or Milestone
Business	{ Strategic business planning Business process reengineering	Strategic business plan Long range business goals Business process models, methods, or rules
Application	{ Systems development life-cycle Systems analysis and design Application development life cycle	Information systems design Application programs design
Data	{ Database analysis and design Database distribution analysis	Database design Database distribution design
Network	{ Network development life cycle Network analysis and design Logical network design	Network requirements document Network design proposal
Technology	{ Physical network design Network implementation Technology analysis	Detailed network diagram Network product specifications Network circuit diagrams

Figure 12-2 Understanding systems development: process and product.

cycle as illustrated in Figure 12-3. It clearly illustrates the continuous nature of network development. A network designed "from scratch" clearly has to start somewhere, namely with an analysis phase.

Existing networks, however, are constantly progressing from one phase to another within the network development life cycle. For instance, the monitoring of existing networks produces management and performance statistics perhaps using a network management protocol such as SNMP. These performance statistics of this existing network are then analyzed by qualified network analysts. Design changes may or may not be implemented based on the analysis of these performance statistics. Many times, proposed network design changes are first simulated using sophisticated network simulation software packages or proto-

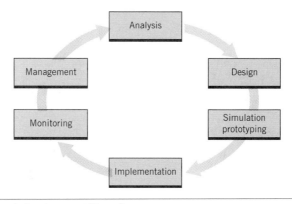

Figure12-3 Network development life cycle.

typed in a test environment, safely removed from a company's production network, before being deployed or implemented.

This cycle of monitoring, management, analysis, design, simulation, and implementation is on-going. Just as demands on a network are in a constant state of change due to changes in business, application, or data requirements, so must the network design itself be of a dynamic nature in order to successfully support these changing requirements. The network development life cycle describes the environment in which this dynamic network design is able to thrive.

☐ NETWORK ANALYSIS AND DESIGN METHODOLOGY

Although the network development life cycle is useful as a logical model of the overall processes involved in network development, it is not at all specific as to how the various stages within the life cycle are to be accomplished. What is required is a more detailed step-by-step methodology, which compliments the overall logical framework as outlined by the network development life cycle.

The **network analysis and design methodology** is a practical, step-by-step approach to network analysis and design and is illustrated in a summarized fashion in Figure 12-4.

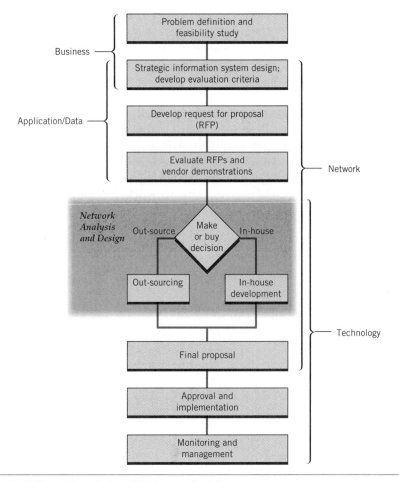

Figure 12-4 Network analysis and design methodology summary.

Overall Characteristics

Each of the major categories of the methodology as illustrated in Figure 12-4 is comprised of numerous activities which will be described in much greater detail. A few important characteristics of the overall methodology are worth noting, however.

First, the network analysis and design methodology is consistent with previous information systems development models in that business, application, and data requirements definition are prerequisites to network design activities.

Secondly, this methodology treats both in-house personnel as well as outside consultants as potential service providers by clearly documenting requirements in a formalized RFP (request for proposal) and expecting compliance with those requirements by whomever may be eventually chosen to perform network development duties.

Finally, although any diagram of a systems development methodology would indicate that activities are of a serial nature, occurring one after another, with discrete starting and ending points, such is very often not the case. In fact, as will be described in the more detailed explanations of each stage of the network analysis and design methodology, activities from various stages of the methodology often take place simultaneously. In addition, network analysts must often backtrack to previous activities when new or contradictory information is uncovered as the development process progresses.

Thus, the network analysis and design methodology as illustrated in Figure 12-4 should be looked upon as an overall guideline to the network development process rather than a step-by-step cookbook-style set of instructions.

Critical Success Factors of the Network Development Life Cycle

Also associated with the overall network development process, rather than with any specific step of the process, are several key behaviors or things to remember which can be of critical importance to the overall successful outcome of the network development life cycle. These **critical success factors** are summarized in Figure 12-5 and explained below.

Identification of All Potential Customers   The best source of information about system performance requirements are the people who must use the system most frequently. However, all user groups and levels of management must be consulted during the analysis and design phase in order to assure that no individuals or groups feel left out of the development process. Although one would like to think it isn't true, the best designed systems can be doomed to failure due to the effective internal sabotage of disenchanted users.

Political Awareness   At the very least, it is imperative to be aware of the so-called corporate culture of an organization. Corporate culture is sometimes described in terms related to network design. For instance, corporate cultures can be described as "hierarchical" or "distributed" or "open." If the corporate culture of the organization in which a network analyst is working is hierarchical, then it would be a mistake to make an appointment to interview an end-user without first interviewing and seeking approval of the required levels of management. On the other hand, "open-door" corporate cultures are less concerned with hierarchies of authority thereby allowing quicker and simpler access to end-users.

Unfortunately, so-called "back room" politics can play an important role in systems design as well. The best researched and planned network design may go

Success Factor	Explanation
Identification of all potential customers and constituencies	No one likes to feel left out or that their input does not matter. It is better to include too many as representative user groups than to inadvertently exclude anyone.
Political awareness	Awareness of the corporate political environment as well as the overall corporate culture can have a large impact on a project's success.
Buy-in	As each stage is concluded, buy-in or agreement as to conclusions from all affected customer groups is of critical importance.
Communication	Do not assume others know what is going on with the project. Write memos, newsletters, send E-mail, or communicate with key people in person.
Detailed project documentation	Document every phone call and every meeting. Keep the project well organized from day one with copies of all correspondence.
Process/product awareness	As a simple means of staying focused and on-track, keep in mind what is the process and product for each step in the network analysis and design methodology.
Be honest with yourself	Be your own harshest critic. Identify weak points in your proposal and address them accordingly. Play "devil's advocate" with your proposal and prepare for possible objections.

Figure 12-5 Critical success factors of the network development life cycle.

unimplemented if the company president's brother-in-law is in the computer business and has a different idea. Sad, but true. The best way to defend against such situations is first to be aware of any such possible political situations. Specific strategies for assuring the objectivity of the analysis and design process will be highlighted as the overall network analysis and design methodology is described further.

Buy-In All of the critical success factors listed in Figure 12-5 are important. However, one of the most important yet easiest to accomplish is **buy-in.** After having identified all potential customers and constituencies, it is imperative to gain buy-in from each of these groups for the deliverable or product of each stage of the overall network analysis and design methodology.

By reaching consensus on the acceptability of the results or deliverables of each and every stage, one avoids having initial assumptions or work on earlier stages brought into question during the presentation of the final proposal. In other words, the approved results of one stage become the foundation or starting point for the next stage. If buy-in from all affected parties is assured at each stage, the presentation of the final proposal should be much smoother with a minimum of back-tracking or rework required.

Communication Many of the other critical success factors listed in Figure 12-5 depend on effective communication, both verbal and written. Often in network or systems development projects, it is assumed that because network analysts and designers are aware of the project status, everyone must be fully informed as well. Unfortunately, this is not the case. As previously pointed out, no one likes to feel left out. More important, networks often cross the "territory" or authority of numerous individuals. In order to keep these people supportive of the project, it is imperative to keep them informed and to make them feel that they are an important part of the process.

Communication can take many forms. Newsletters, project status reports, and E-mail are all suitable means of keeping people informed and up-to-date. More ambitious communications schemes such as videoconferencing or the production of a VCR tape might be appropriate for critical tasks, public relations, or training opportunities.

Detailed Project Documentation   As a project manager, it is required to not only manage the overall network analysis and design project effectively with task schedules, project lists, and to-do lists, but also to document every aspect of the project. Every conversation, by phone or in person, should have notes entered into a log book indicating such things as date, time, persons involved, topics of conversation, and required followup. E-mail messages should be printed and filed. Meetings should be documented in a similar fashion with agendas and action item assignments included in a project binder as well as being sent to responsible parties and key managers.

Organization of this project documentation is of equal importance. A large binder with several sections for different portions of the project can be a very effective way to be able to quickly access any piece of project documentation required.

This documentation is of particular importance in the latter stages of the project when consultants and vendors become a part of the project. Document everything in writing and take no action on any agreement until it has been presented in writing. More specifics about effectively managing consultants and vendors will be presented later in the chapter.

Process/Product Awareness   As a facilitator in meetings of end-users trying to define system requirements, it is the network analyst's job to keep the participants focused and the meeting on track. In order to accomplish this, it is important for the network analyst to have a clear understanding of the appropriate topics of discussion associated with each point in the overall network analysis and design methodology (the process), as well as an awareness of the required outcomes or deliverables (the product) of each stage of that process.

Meetings can easily get off on tangents and aggressive participants can easily sway meetings toward personal agendas. By remaining focused on the proper topics of discussion and a clear visualization of the product of that discussion, a facilitator can maximize the effectiveness of the analysis and design process. As the leader of the meeting, it is important, however, not to go overboard on controlling the discussion of the meeting. With practice and patience, experienced facilitators can direct meetings which foster imaginative solutions and proposals without either stifling creativity or allowing discussion to wander ineffectively.

Be Honest with Yourself   One of the greatest advantages of being totally honest with oneself is that no one else knows the potential weaknesses or areas for improvement in a proposal better than the person who wrote it. The difficulty comes in forcing oneself to be totally honest and acknowledge the potential weaknesses in a proposal in order to either correct them or be prepared to defend them.

Peer review and egoless programming are other systems-development techniques employed to identify potential weaknesses in programs or proposals prior to implementation. Not all weaknesses can necessarily be corrected. Financial or time constraints may have restricted potential solutions. If that is the case, an honest self-review of the proposal will give one the opportunity to have an objective explanation to such weaknesses prepared in advance.

Critical Success Factors Are Learned Behaviors   Although many of the critical success factors listed in Figure 12-5 may seem to be nothing more than common sense, it has been the author's experience that more network analysis and design projects suffer from difficulties caused by a failure to address one or more of these critical success factors than from any other cause of failure. These critical success factors must be applied throughout the entire life of the network development project and are therefore best seen as habits or behaviors, rather than discrete events to be scheduled or planned.

☐ NETWORK ANALYSIS AND DESIGN METHODOLOGY

Start with a Clearly Defined Problem

A network cannot very well provide effective solutions to problems that have not been clearly defined in objective terms. To attempt to implement networks before everyone agrees to (buy-in) exactly what is the problem is somewhat akin to hitting a moving target. The network will never satisfy all constituencies' needs because no one has agreed what those needs are in the first place.

All network development efforts start with a problem as perceived by someone, be they management or end-users. At some point, management agrees that a problem exists which is worth expending resources to at least investigate. The responsibility for conducting the investigation may be given to in-house personnel or to an outside consultant or facilitator.

The first job of the facilitator is to identify all parties potentially affected by the perceived problem. Next, representatives of each of these constituencies are selected and convened for brainstorming sessions to determine the nature of the problem and, perhaps, the requirements of a solution. In order to make these problem definition sessions as productive as possible it is important that representatives do their "homework" prior to the meetings. Figure 12-6 shows an excerpt of a letter the author has sent to user group representatives prior to problem definition brainstorming sessions.

Understand Strategic Business Objectives

Once the group has been assembled, it is time to remember the top-down model. In order to keep the problem definition session and the subsequent solution proposal session on track it is vital to start with the strategic business goals of the organization as articulated by senior management. It is advisable to have either the chief executive officer or chief financial officer (or both) present at the initial meeting to explain the importance of the user group's work and the strategic direction of the corporate business goals. In addition, if strategic corporate goals have been prepared in writing, it is helpful to share these with the group, as allowed by company policy. In this way, the whole group starts off with the same focus, and strategic business direction and the proper attitude about the overall process.

Importance of Baseline Data

In order to measure the eventual impact, hopefully positive, of the installed network, one has to have **baseline data,** or the current status of the system and net-

Goldman Consulting and Development
101 Hickory Drive
Goodsville, ME 11321

Unautomated Materials Corporation
213 Old Way Avenue
Pastview, FL 32911

Nathan Investigator:

When we meet in November, we will *not* be talking about computers. We will be talking about your job, the decisions you have to make in your job, and the information you need to make those decisions.

Some questions that we might address to which you might want to give some thought:

1. If you had to break down your job into major functions or categories, what would they be?
2. When are you most buried in paperwork?
3. When do you find yourself saying, "A computer ought to be able to do this"?
4. What questions from customers or supervisors involve long searches through files or stacks of paper?
5. Where in your operation do you see possible increases in productivity if a computer could keep track of something that is tracked manually now?
6. Where in your operation do you see opportunities for improved customer service or improved bottom-line contribution?

I am looking forward to working with you. If you have any questions in the meantime please feel free to call me.

Sincerely,

James E. Goldman

Figure 12-6 Productive problem definition sessions require advance preparation.

work, from which to measure the network. This baseline data can often be collected from the various customer groups or constituencies of the information system and network who are chosen to attend the problem definition sessions. Depending on the extent, in terms of both geography and sophistication, to which current systems have been implemented, a structured framework may be required to record this systems information in a standardized manner. Fortunately, the top-down model is an excellent example of such a framework.

Top-Down Model Organizes Baseline Data

Using the top-down model as a framework for organizing the baseline data in order to reflect the current system and network status does not necessarily imply that a separate top-down model must be completed for every corporate location attached to the network or that every layer of the top-down model must be filled in for every location. Remember the current process (problem definition) and the current intended product (baseline data) describing the current status in objective measurable terms.

Therefore, just enough data should be collected at this point in the network analysis and design methodology in order to clearly define the problem in measurable terms. More extensive surveys of the current and/or proposed systems and network environment will be required as part of the **requirements gathering** phase of the next major step of the network analysis and design methodology: **strategic information system design.**

Information gathered in the top-down models at this stage should relate directly to the problems perceived by the user groups. Hopefully, the problems have some business layer impact, otherwise this whole process may be a waste of time. In other words, although the source of the problem may be in the application, data, network, or technology layers, if it has no impact on the business layer, why should time be spent studying it?

Notice how most of the questions in Figure 12-6 deal with *business problems* or situations. Once these business problems are identified, the sources of these business problems within the lower layers of top-down model should be subsequently investigated as part of the problem definition process. Conversely, these same lower layers of the top-down model will be redesigned to become the source of *business solutions* as delivered by the new network.

Figure 12-7 illustrates the relationship of the top-down model to business problems and solutions as investigated in the network analysis and design methodology.

Feasibility Studies and Buy-in

Once sufficient information has been gathered to document the current status of the systems and networks in objective, measurable terms in the form of a problem definition, the required product for this process has been completed and it is time to assure buy-in. The problem definition and its associated recommendations for further study are sometimes referred to as a **feasibility study.**

The need for buy-in on a problem definition or feasibility study will vary from one case to another. Much of the need for management buy-in and the associated

---

Problem Definition Phase

Business	Business Problems
Application Data Network Technology	Investigate lower layers of the top-down model as possible sources of the perceived business problems in an effort to define those problems in objective, measurable terms

Strategic Information System Design Phase

Business	Business Solutions and Opportunities
Application Data Network Technology	Redesign the lower layers of the top-down model as necessary to have the overall strategic information system design produce business solutions and opportunities rather than problems

Figure 12-7 Business problems and solutions and the top-down model.

approval to proceed will depend on the nature of the original charge from management.

In other words, if management's initial charge is, "Look into this problem and get back to me," then a feasibility study with management buy-in and approval before further study is clearly appropriate. However, if management's charge is, "Figure out what's wrong and fix it," then a formalized feasibility report with formal presentation is probably not called for. However, remember one of the key critical success factors—communications. Even if a formal feasibility report is not required, timely management reports should be completed and submitted on a regular basis in order to keep management abreast of progress and in tune with overall project strategic direction.

Figure 12-8 summarizes the key points of the Process and Product of the Problem Definition Phase.

Strategic Information System Design

The primary mission of a network is the *delivery* of the right information at the right time to the right decision maker in the right place. The determination as to what or who is the right information, time, decision-maker, or place, is the responsibility of the strategic information system (application and data layers, which lie above the network layer in the top-down model). Although this textbook cannot and should not give a comprehensive coverage of the applications development and database development methodologies, it is still important to understand the *process* of strategic information systems design as it relates to the network analysis and design methodology.

The *product* of this entire phase of the network analysis and design methodology, in addition to the **strategic information system design** itself, is the **evaluation criteria** by which the proposed new system, and its underlying network will be judged.

The Importance of Establishing Evaluation Criteria   The problem definition phase provides a starting point of baseline data for the new system while the strategic information systems design provides the operational goals for the new

Process

1. Problem is perceived.
2. Management perceives problem as worth investigating.
3. Management delegates responsibility for problem definition.
4. User/constituency groups are identified and representatives selected.
5. Representative groups are convened.
6. Senior management commitment and priorities are conveyed to representative group.
7. Representative groups produce baseline data of current status.
8. Depending on the extent of current system and network implementation, the top-down model may be used to organize this baseline data into a standardized format.
9. Buy-in.

Product

1. Baseline data describing current status in objective, measurable terms. Can be organized into multiple top-down models
2. A formalized feasibility study may be required depending on initial direction/charge from management

Figure 12-8 Key points of problem definition and feasibility study.

system to reach. Just as the baseline data has to be objective and measurable, so must the evaluation criteria of these operational goals. Exactly how these objective evaluation criteria are produced in the context of the strategic information systems design will be explored further in the coming paragraphs.

These goals may have a direct impact on network design when defined in terms such as maximum response time or transactions per second. By producing objective, measurable goals or performance evaluation criteria, and getting subsequent management buy-in on these goals, one helps to assure the objectivity of the entire network analysis and design process. For example, should a substandard system be suggested due solely to "backroom" politics, it is simply evaluated against the evaluation criteria as previously agreed upon by all appropriate levels of management.

Figure 12-9 summarizes the key points of the strategic information system design phase in terms of both process and product.

☐ STRATEGIC INFORMATION SYSTEM DESIGN FOSTERS BUSINESS PROCESS REENGINEERING

Identify Overall System Characteristics

The word "strategic" is used in the context of information systems design in order to portray the top-down, strategic business goal orientation of the entire information design process. As can be seen in Figure 12-9, the strategic information systems design process starts with a review of the strategic business goals as articulated by senior management.

With these strategic business goals in mind, the next step in the process is to describe the *overall characteristics* of an information system that could fulfill these strategic business goals. Examples for a corporation's strategic business goals might require a information system to:

1. Enable delivery of improved customer service.
2. Enable improved inventory control.
3. Allow for more flexible pricing.

Process

1. Review strategic corporate objectives.
2. Define the overall characteristics of an information system that can successfully support/achieve these objectives.
3. Break the overall business down into major functional areas.
4. List the business processes performed under each functional area.
5. Highlight the decision points in the listed business processes and list information required to make informed decisions at each decision point.
6. Highlight the opportunities for improvement in listed business processes and list information required to take advantage of these opportunities for improvement.
7. Prepare performance evaluation criteria.
8. Prioritize the various aspects of the strategic information system as designed.
9. Buy-in.

Product

1. Strategic information systems design
2. Performance evaluation criteria in objective, measurable terms

Figure 12-9 Key points of strategic information system design.

4. Enable shorter shelf re-stocking cycles.
5. Allow for more efficient use of labor.

Many other examples easily could be included. The point of these overall characteristics, in terms of the top-down model, is to assure and specify that the application layer solutions will deliver on the business layer requirements. As can be seen from Figure 12-9, one of the key products of this strategic information system design phase is the *performance evaluation criteria*. The overall required system characteristics as listed above serve as one set of evaluation criteria for proposed information systems designs. Other more objective evaluation criteria will be developed further along in the overall design process. However, the importance of the strategic system performance evaluation criteria lies in their ability to measure the extent to which proposed information systems designs deliver on strategic business goals.

Identify Major Business Functional Areas

Once overall system performance characteristics have been established, the overall business can be broken down into large functional areas. These functional areas may correspond to corporate departments or divisions. Examples might include manufacturing, inventory control, project management, customer service, accounting and payroll, human resources, etc.

In practice, each of these identified major **business functional areas** can be written on a separate large sheet of flip-chart paper and taped on the walls of the room in which the user groups meet. It is not important to argue about which functional areas deserve their own sheet of paper at this point. Consolidation and editing take place at a later time in the process.

Identify Business Processes Associated with Each Business Functional Area

Once the major functional areas of the business have been established, the **business processes** that take place in each major functional area are listed. This presents a wonderful opportunity for **business process reengineering.** Often user groups are made up of individuals from various business units who have not had the time to really understand each other's jobs and responsibilities. As business processes are described, brainstorming quickly takes over and problems that seemed deeply imbedded in current systems are solved as new or modified business processes are defined for the new strategic information system design. This process is repeated for every major business functional area identified in the previous step.

It is important for the facilitator of this process to keep the discussions on a fairly strategic level to avoid lower-level implementation issues such as screen design, report layouts, etc. Each major business area should have its own flip chart(s) with detailed business processes described for each large business functional area.

Identify Decision Points and Opportunities for Improvement

Recalling that one of the primary goals of a well-designed strategic information system is to deliver the right information to the right *decision-maker*, the next logical step in the design process is to identify the key **decision points,** in all of the documented business processes where decision makers must make decisions.

Once identified, each decision point is then analyzed as to what information (the "right" information) is required for the decision-maker to make an informed decision. This analysis process often brings out the fact that decision-makers are getting much more information than they need to make informed decisions. Entire reports hundreds of pages long may contain one or two figures of critical importance to a decision-maker at any given decision point.

Figure 12-6 highlighted some of the "homework" analysis questions to which user group representatives were to have given some thought. One of the key areas in which user group members can contribute is in the identification of *opportunities for improvement* which can be enabled by this strategic information system design. **Opportunity points** may imply improvement in any one of a number of areas: financial, productivity, inventory control, accounts receivable collections, customer service, customer satisfaction, repeat customers, employee retention, etc.

The important thing to remember is that if these opportunities for improvement support the strategic business goals of the corporation then they should be identified along with the information required to turn these opportunities into reality. Figure 12-10 illustrates the relationship of the various processes described thus far in the strategic information system design.

Develop Specific Evaluation Criteria

Once the strategic information system has been designed as described above, more *specific evaluation criteria* can be created from the business process descriptions, decision points, and opportunity points and their associated information requirements. This is not a difficult process. In reality, a checklist or report card is being

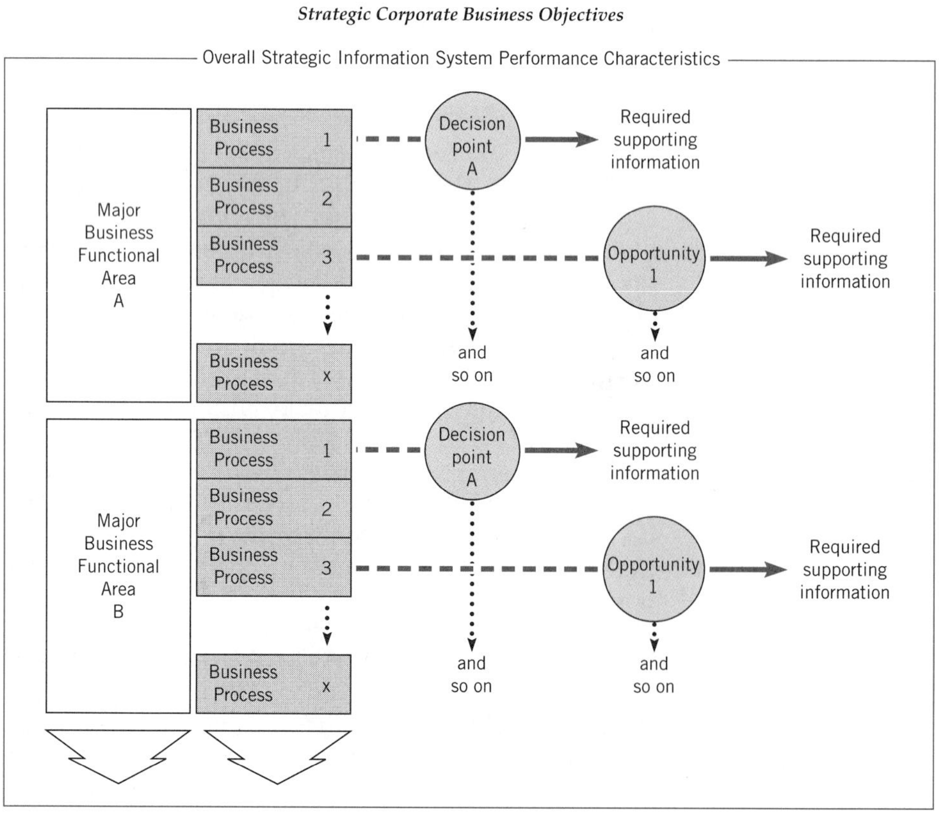

Figure 12-10 Process relationship of strategic information system design.

prepared consisting of all the system requirements (e.g., automated business processes, decision points, opportunity points) as defined in the strategic information systems design process. These specific evaluation criteria are then combined with the overall required performance characteristics to produce an unbiased, objective evaluation mechanism with which to judge prospective systems.

Prioritization

Priorities can then be assigned to each of the major functional areas, business processes, decision points, and opportunities. These priorities may assist in the evaluation process by identifying those systems which exhibit the most *important* elements of the strategic information systems design. A simple yet effective approach to systems design prioritization is known as the **three-pile approach.** In this prioritization scheme, there are only three priorities, defined as follows:

Priority One items are so important that the system is simply not worth implementing without them.

Priority Two items can be done without or "worked around," but need to be implemented as soon as possible.

Priority Three items would be nice to have, but can be done without.

One important point to remember is that these priorities should be considered in terms of *business impact.*

At this point, a *strategic,* or high-level, system design has been completed. Many details need to be added to this requirements document before proposals can accurately reflect their ability to meet not only the business and application layer system requirements, but the data and networking requirements which must support this strategic information system as well.

Producing the Request for Proposal (RFP)

By organizing the strategic information system design information into an understandable format and by adding detailed information concerning performance evaluation criteria for the data and network layers, a document known as an **RFP** (request for proposal) is produced. It is important to understand the benefits of an RFP in order to be able to justify the work which goes into it.

By taking the time to prepare a detailed RFP, a company assures that its priorities and unique business processes and requirements are fulfilled by the information system and network which is eventually installed. All vendor proposals are measured against the users' predefined requirements regardless of whom the vendor may be related to. If a vendor's proposal does not meet minimum standards for meeting the requirements of the RFP, it is dropped from further consideration regardless of how nice the screens look or how colorful the brochures are.

The RFP assures that the delivered system, whether developed in-house or purchased from an outside vendor, will be flexible enough to change as business needs and requirements change. Unfortunately, the alternative is all too often the case, in which businesses are forced to mold their business practices according to the constraints of the purchased information system and network.

Figure 12-11 summarizes both the processes and products involved in the RFP preparation phase of the network analysis and design methodology.

Examine Each Corporate Location

Now that the strategic information system design has been completed, the next step is to carefully examine each corporate location at which the information sys-

Process

Using the strategic information design as completed in the last phase:

1. Examine each corporate location.
2. Produce evaluation criteria for application and data layer considerations as required.
3. Survey all existing system resources:
   people
   hardware–software–media
   data
   physical plant
4. Prepare preliminary overall project schedule.
5. Determine information required from vendor.
6. Determine potential vendors—request for literature.
7. Determine percent-of-fit goal.
8. Compile and distribute RFP to selected vendors.

Product

1. Formalized request for proposal
2. Percent-of-fit goal

Figure 12-11 Preparing the request for proposal.

tem will be eventually deployed. The purpose of gathering this data about each of the corporate locations is to compile an accurate representation of the scope and requirements of the network over which this strategic information system will be implemented.

As each location is examined, the information gathered will help determine the unique data and processing requirements for those locations. This detailed location-specific information is distinct from the high-level information gathered in top-down model format as part of the problem definition phase.

Some corporate locations may be regional offices, concentrating data or transactions from several branch offices. These, along with many other facts must be recorded in order to accurately define data and network layer requirements for the overall information system. Although each company may differ in what location-specific statistics are important in terms of strategic network design, many of the following may warrant consideration:

People

Total number of employees
Number of employees performing each business function as listed in the
   strategic information system design
Feelings about the "new" system
Key political situations
Number of network-oriented/technically-oriented employees
Training needs

Hardware–Software–Media

Current level of computerization
Current applications software
Current networking status
Local phone company
Availability of data services from local phone company

Software performance requirements
   Maximum time for customer lookup
   Maximum Time for part number or pricing lookup
   Maximum Time for order entry
How "mission-critical" is each application?
Must backup systems be ready at a moment's notice?

Data

Number of customers
Number of inventory items
Number of open orders
Need for sharing data with other locations, regional offices, corporate head-
   quarters
Special security needs for data or transmission

Physical Plant

What is the condition of each remote site?
Will additional electrical, heating, data wiring, space, or security systems be
   required at any sights in order to accommodate the new systems?

The information gathered in such location-by-location surveys adds to the evaluation criteria of any potential system proposal. Any need identified must be met by a proposed system solution in accordance with the determined priority of each of these requirements. It is of critical importance that this survey is done as accurately as possible since this is the data upon which the initial network design will largely be based. Buy-off by all affected groups at this stage is especially important as outside vendors and in-house staffs will be using this data to prepare detailed application, database, and network designs.

Final RFP Preparation

The two major components of the RFP that should have been completed at this point are:

   Strategic information systems design
   Corporate location survey results

In order to put the finishing touches on the request for proposal, a few more pieces of information must be either supplied to or requested from potential system and network suppliers. This additional information is often included in a section of the RFP known as the **management abstract.** Figure 12-12 illustrates a sample table of contents from an RFP including the items that might be included in a Management Abstract.

Information Supplied to Vendors

Among the information included in the Management Abstract that should be supplied to potential vendors in order to give them as accurate a description as possible are the following items:

Company Profile. A brief description of the company issuing the request for proposal. Number of corporate locations, approximate yearly sales, anticipated growth rate, and a brief statement concerning the current state of computerization or networking could all be elements of this section.

Statement of the Problem. From a business perspective, what was the source of the initiation of the problem definition process and what did the problem definition team conclude?

MANAGEMENT ABSTRACT
   Company Profile
   Statement of the Problem
   Overall System Characteristics
   Project Phase Prioritization
   Proposed Project Schedule Summary
   Information Requested from Vendor
      System development experience
      Hardware, software, networking experience
      References
      Pricing
      Support
      Training and documentation
      Vendor background

SYSTEM DESIGN
   Summary Review
   Details of Geographic Locations
   System Requirements of Each Software Module

Figure 12-12 Sample RFP table of contents.

Overall System Characteristics. It is important to include overall system characteristics at the beginning of the RFP as some of these requirements may be beyond the capabilities of possible vendors and their systems. In this way, these vendors won't waste their time or yours in submitting a proposal that can't meet these basic overall requirements. Figure 12-13 lists some possible overall system characteristics that might be included in an RFP. Although some of the requirements listed in Figure 12-13 may seem obvious or unnecessary, it is important not to assume anything when shopping for information systems.

Project Phase Prioritization. If some modules (business area computerization plans) of the overall strategic information systems design are more critical than others, this prioritization should be conveyed to potential vendors. Often, a vendor may be able to supply some, but not all, of the information systems modules. If the vendors have a sense of which modules are most important, they will be better able to know whether or not to submit a proposal.

Proposed Project Schedule Summary. Figure 12-14 illustrates a sample proposed project schedule with key events which may be of concern to potential vendors listed. Before taking the time to prepare detailed proposals, many vendors appreciate knowing the implementation timetable of the proposed project. If the vendor already has projects underway or anticipated, they may lack a sufficient labor force to meet this RFP's proposed implementation schedule.

Information Requested from Vendors

At least as important as the information supplied *to* potential vendors is the information required *from* potential vendors. In order to avoid being sent standard proposals with preprinted product literature and brochures, it is advantageous to list specific information required from vendors and to evaluate only those proposals which supply the requested information.

Figure 12-15 lists some of the information that may be requested of vendors

In addition to controlling those areas identified in the statement of the problem section, this system must also conform to the following characteristics:

1. Source code must be owned by the client company.
2. The system must be easy to use and must contain on-line help as well as extensive input editing and verification to help prevent errors.
3. The system must require a minimum of training.
4. The system must be easy to install (hardware and software) in order to expedite installation throughout all corporate locations.
5. The system must allow multiple users simultaneous access to information. The system must have the capability to assure information integrity through record locking and must have adequate security to insure against unauthorized access to information.
6. The system must have windowing capabilities allowing drop-down menus and screens to allow simultaneous access to multiple files and/or modules.
7. The system must be easily transportable to numerous hardware and operating system platforms on both minicomputers and microcomputers.
8. The system must have the ability to output and input ASCII data files in order to assure necessary informational ties to regional centers.
9. The system must have database/file rollback capabilities to assure data integrity in the event of a system failure or power outage.

Figure 12-13 Overall system characteristics/requirements.

although the list is by no means authoritative or exhaustive. Information requested should satisfy corporate policies as well as business layer concerns from initial problem definition analysis. The overall purpose of this section is to assure that:

1. The vendor has significant experience in developing and implementing systems of a similar nature to the one described in the RFP.
2. The vendor has a sufficiently large organization to support the smooth and successful implementation of such a system.
3. The vendor is financially solvent so as not to be likely to declare bankruptcy in the middle of the project implementation.

Percent of Fit Goal

The RFP should now be fairly complete and ready to send to prospective system vendors. In addition to the RFP itself, one other important product of this phase of the overall network analysis and design methodology is known as the **percent-of-fit goal.** This is an especially important element if in-house development of the system and network is a possibility. The percent of fit goal is a rather arbitrary percent-

Event	Proposed Completion Date
Requests for proposals sent to selected vendors	07/29/93
Proposals due to consultant from vendors	08/29/93
Selection and notification of vendor finalists	09/14/93
Presentation/demonstration by vendor finalists	09/21/93–10/07/93
Make or buy decision	10/14/93
Pilot test	12/14/93
Projected system implementation date	04/01/94

Figure 12-14 Proposed project schedule summary.

In an effort to produce a vendor screening procedure as fair and equitable as possible, please address the following issues as specifically as possible in your proposal:

1. System Development
   a. Vendor's experience in the manufacturing area
   b. Number of installed systems
   c. Date of first installation
   d. Integration with related manufacturing and financial modules
   e. Scope of installed systems
2. Hardware, Operating Systems, Software
   a. Which hardware platforms does system run on?
   b. Multiuser?
   c. Operating systems
   d. Programming languages
   e. 4GL/ DBMS experience
   f. Ease of / availability of customization
   g. Source code availability
3. References
   a. Names, addresses, and phone numbers of three customers with manufacturing systems implemented
4. Pricing
   Hardware
   a. See Hardware/networking section of system design for guidelines and alternatives
   b. If vendor will supply hardware, please list cost by component including manufacturer and model number
   Software
   a. Please list cost per module
   b. Please list additional per user license costs, if any
   c. Please list source code costs
   d. Please list cost for software customization
   e. Please list cost for maintenance/support agreements
   f. If vendor will supply operating or run-time systems, please include these costs
5. Training
   a. Facilities
   b. Courses
   c. Materials
   d. Instructors available
   e. Schedule
   f. Media used
   g. Cost
6. Support
   a. Hours—hotline available?
   b. Cost—800 number?
   c. Experience of support personnel
   d. Software guarantees
   e. Bug fixes—turnaround time
   f. Software updates—maintenance
7. Vendor Background
   a. Number of employees
   b. Yearly sales (approximate)
   c. Growth pattern
   d. Strategic direction
   e. Research and development

Figure 12-15 Information requested from vendor.

age determined by the user representative group preparing the RFP and is subject to the same overall buy-in as the RFP itself.

The purpose of the percent of fit goal is to set a minimum threshold of compliance for vendor proposals in order to warrant further consideration and invitations for demonstrations. As an example, perhaps the users group feels that any proposal which meets at least 50 percent of the priority 1 features deserves further consideration.

This percent of fit goal offers an element of objectivity to the proposal evaluation process. The percent of fit goal combined with the specific descriptions of required features in the RFP, constitute an objective, comprehensive evaluation mechanism for evaluating proposals according to what is important to the corporation. By clearly defining this evaluation mechanism before receipt of the first proposal, evaluators are less likely to be swayed by fancy brochures or systems' "bells and whistles."

If an in-house systems development group feels that they should rightfully be developing and/or implementing this system, they must submit a proposal in compliance with the requirements outlined in the RFP. Their proposal will be evaluated along with all of the outside vendors' proposals.

The percent of fit of a particular proposal can be easily calculated. Recalling that all features or requirements of the RFP were given a priority of 1, 2, or 3, by merely counting how many features of each priority are present in a given proposal, an overall objective "score" can be determined for each proposal. The process is fair, objective, and, to a large extent, eliminates politics from the proposal evaluation process.

Proposal Evaluation and the Make or Buy Decision

Having determined a percent of fit score for each proposal as well as a percent of fit goal for proposals to warrant further consideration, invitations to selected vendors are the next logical step. However, before selected vendors are invited for demonstrations, it is important once again to gain buy-in from all affected parties, especially management, on not only the selected vendors, but perhaps more importantly, the vendor selection process. Only when all groups agree that the vendor screening and proposal process has been fair and objective should the overall process move forward to the vendor demonstration stage.

At vendor demonstrations, it is important once again for the users, rather than the vendors, to be in charge. Have a copy of the vendor's proposal at the demonstration and ask to see each and every feature demonstrated that was described as included or supported in the vendor's initial proposal. Score should be kept on those features successfully demonstrated and this score should be compared to the score received based on the proposal evaluation.

Following all of the vendor demonstrations comes time for the **make-or-buy decision.** Were any of the vendor's systems worth considering further or should the system be developed in-house? Once again, before proceeding, buy-in of the vendor demonstration evaluation and the make or buy decision should be assured.

Network Analysis and Design

Although it may seem as if a great deal of analysis and design has been done already, it is important to note that the network layer requirements are now ready to be addressed, having designed satisfactory solutions for business, application, and data requirements. As stated several times before, a network cannot be designed in a vacuum, but rather must be designed to deliver solutions and performance in response to specific, well-defined, data, application, and business layer requirements.

The overall network analysis and design summary process diagram as illustrated in Figure 12-4 shows both in-house as well as outsourcing options for the network analysis and design phase of the project based on the make or buy decision. Although both of these options will be explored in further detail, in-house design and development of corporate networks that deliver effective business solutions are the primary focus of this section.

In-House Network Analysis and Design

The term "network analysis and design" really refers to *wide area* network analysis and design to be more specific. LAN design considerations and internetworking (LAN-to-LAN) connectivity issues were covered in their respective chapters. In this chapter, a more corporate-wide view of networking will be taken by designing a network which will effectively support the strategic information system design across geographically dispersed corporate locations.

Figure 12-16 illustrates the key points, both process and product, of the in-house network analysis and design phase. Each of these steps will be explained in detail.

The overall network analysis and design process can be broken down into three major steps: data traffic analysis, circuit analysis and configuration alternatives, and network hardware analysis and configuration alternatives.

Data traffic analysis examines all aspects and characteristics of the traffic that will be passed between corporate locations over the proposed network. Since this data traffic is what the network must carry effectively, it is important to start with a thorough analysis of the data traffic in order to design an effective network. As an analogy, it would be equally wise to understand the driving patterns and transportation needs of an urban area before designing a new highway system.

Once the nature of the data traffic is thoroughly understood, **circuit analysis and configuration alternatives** explore the possibilities for delivering that data traffic in a reliable and effective manner. Whereas there are often alternative ways to transport data from point A to point B, it is important to document alternative network configurations along with an understanding of the advantages and disadvantages of each alternative.

Process

1. Data traffic analysis
   - Payload type analysis
   - Transaction analysis
   - Protocol stack analysis
   - Time studies
   - Mission-critical analysis
   - Traffic volume analysis
2. Circuit analysis and configuration alternatives
3. Network hardware analysis and configuration alternatives

Product

1. Data traffic analysis report for each geographic location
2. Alternative network configuration diagrams including circuit and network hardware details

Figure 12-16 In-house network analysis and design.

Finally, given the nature of the data traffic, especially its protocol-related characteristics, and the possible circuit configurations over which that data may be transported, **network hardware analysis and configuration alternatives** explore the possible data communications hardware devices that may be required to tie the various circuit configurations together into a reliable, manageable network.

Data Traffic Analysis

The exact types of analysis performed in the major step known as data traffic analysis may vary from one networking design to another. Figure 12-17 details some of the possible types of data traffic analysis. The required outcome from this step is a data traffic analysis report which will form the basis for circuit and networking hardware selection. It is the network analyst's obligation to perform whatever types of data traffic analysis are necessary in order to assure that the data traffic analysis report is as complete as possible while forming the foundation on which to build a network design.

Payload Type Analysis   Data traffic and the networks which transport that traffic should not be designed ignoring other payload types. For the most cost-effective network design, voice as well as data requirements should be considered during the network analysis and design phase. Videoconferencing, imaging, and multimedia requirements should also be considered due to their bandwidth-intensive transport demands. Digitized video and voice represent **streaming** data and often require **isochronous** transmission, while inter-LAN data tends to be of a more **bursty** nature. These data characteristics may have a major impact on network design decisions.

Data Traffic Analysis Type	Data Traffic Analysis Description
Payload type analysis	Most locations will require at least voice and data service. Videoconferencing and multimedia also may need to be supported. All payload types should be considered and documented prior to circuit and networking hardware selection.
Transaction analysis	Use process flow analysis or document flow analysis to identify each type of transaction. Analyze detailed data requirements for each transaction type.
Time studies	Once all transaction types have been identified, analyze when and how often each transaction type occurs.
Traffic volume analysis	By combining all types of transactions with the results of the time study, a time-sensitive traffic volume requirements profile can be produced. This is a starting point for mapping bandwidth requirements to circuit capacity.
Mission-critical analysis	Results of this analysis may dictate the need for special data security procedures such as encryption, or special network design considerations such as redundant links.
Protocol stack analysis	Each corporate location's data traffic is analyzed as to protocols which must be transported across the corporate-wide area network. Many alternatives for the transport of numerous protocols exist, but first these protocols must be identified.

Figure 12-17 Data traffic analysis.

Transaction Analysis   In order to determine the actual data traffic requirements from a given corporate location, the network analyst has to examine the source of that data: transactions of one type or another. Examples include customer entry or inquiry, order entry, inventory receipt, order fulfillment, part number or pricing lookup, and so on.

Each of these different transaction types should be identified from the business process definitions of the strategic information systems design. **Process flow analysis** and **document flow analysis** are also ways to identify and analyze transaction types.

Once each transaction type has been identified, the amount of data required to complete that transaction is calculated and documented. Some transactions such as credit card verifications or ATM machine transactions are comprised of short bursts of data which must be handled quickly and accurately. Some nightly backup or file transfer applications may not require the same type of high-speed, high-priority transmission. The difference in the characteristics of these transactions may warrant a difference in the network design in each case. Perhaps one type of transaction is better suited to a packet-switched approach, while the other may require a leased line.

Time Studies   Once all transaction types have been identified, the next step is to analyze when and how often these transactions are executed. One method of determining both the frequency as well as time distribution of these transactions is through a **time study.** Simply stated, a time study counts how often and at what time of day, week, or month a given transaction or process is executed.

For instance, a retail store's daily close-out procedure is executed once per day. However, is it the same time each day and are all stores executing the same process at the same time each day? What are the network implications of month-end closing procedures? The answers to these types of questions can have a major bearing on bandwidth requirements and the resultant network design.

Traffic Volume Analysis   Traffic volume analysis can be looked upon as the product of transaction analysis and time studies. By knowing the data and network requirements of every transaction type and by further knowing the frequency and time distribution of the execution of a given transaction type, a time-sensitive **traffic volume requirements profile** should be able to be constructed. Such a profile shows average network bandwidth requirements as well as peak or maximum requirements.

Seasonality of transaction volume should not be overlooked. The transaction frequency of retail businesses can easily double or even triple during the holiday shopping season. An undersized network must not be the cause of poor customer service during important periods of increased customer activity. As another example, power companies must design voice and data networks that can easily accommodate higher than normal demand in order to provide adequate customer service during power outages or other emergencies.

Mission-Critical Analysis   Although all data can be considered important, some transactions are so important to a business that they are known as **mission critical.** Electronics funds transfer is a good example of a mission critical transaction. The mission critical nature of some transactions can spawn further analysis and design in two other areas. Data security may require investigation. **Encryption**

of data transmitted over wide area networks may be a requirement. If so, this fact should be stated as part of the overall data traffic analysis report.

Secondly, it is a fact of life that data circuits fail from time to time. If certain mission-critical transactions cannot tolerate an occasional faulty data circuit, then **redundant links** may need to be designed into the initial network design configuration.

Protocol Stack Analysis   As has been seen in both the LAN and internetworking design processes, protocol stack analysis is of critical importance. Some protocols, such as SNA, are extremely time sensitive. Some protocols are routable while others are not. Others, such as SNA and some LAN protocols are very "chatty," sending constant status-checking and keep-alive messages onto the network and occupying precious bandwidth. As each corporate location's data traffic is analyzed, special attention must be paid to the various protocol stacks of that data.

Will the wide area network be required to support more than one protocol? What are the bandwidth and network hardware implications of a multiprotocol WAN? Is TCP/IP encapsulation an option or is SDLC conversion a more appealing alternative? Before reaching any conclusions as to how various protocols are to be transported over the corporate network, those protocols must be accurately identified and documented. This is the role of the protocol stack analysis.

Circuit Analysis and Configuration Alternatives

A thorough data traffic analysis should produce sufficient information to configure various network design alternatives that will effectively support the strategic information system design to all corporate locations. Evaluating alternative network configurations and computing circuit capacity are beyond the expectations of a person using this textbook in a first course in data communications. Upper-level courses in wide area networking or network analysis and design will better prepare a person to perform such tasks.

Wide area network design software has greatly simplified the design process but is relatively expensive. In most cases, even using the software requires a great deal of network design expertise. As a result, only companies that can afford to have full-time network analysts and designers on staff are likely to own copies of network design software. The various categories of network design software will be explored in greater detail later in this chapter.

A second alternative for circuit analysis and network configuration is to hire a data communications/networking consultant. This too may be a very expensive alternative. Furthermore, there is little or no regulation as to the level of expertise required to call oneself a telecommunications consultant.

Thirdly, telecommunications companies, both local carriers as well as interexchange carriers, have the ability to design networks according to customer data requirements. The network design process is part of preparing a quote and is done at no charge. Therefore, it may be advisable for the small company or novice data communications person to let the experts design the network. Talk to several carriers and get a network design proposal with associated costs from each. By allowing the carriers to design the network and quote a price, they can be held accountable for delivering service at the quoted price in accordance with the data traffic analysis and performance evaluation criteria.

Consideration of Network Alternatives

It is important to consider more than just the data traffic analysis when considering network configuration alternatives. The detailed survey of existing system resources should also be considered. For instance, local carriers servicing some remote corporate locations may be limited in their ability to offer certain data transmission services. This should be documented in the survey of existing system resources.

Regardless of who actually designs the network configuration alternatives, it is important to assure that sufficient bandwidth has been allocated to handle sudden increases in demand. More gradual increases in bandwidth demand due to expanding business opportunities can usually be accommodated with upgrades to higher capacity lines and their associated data communications equipment.

A second performance evaluation criterion for network configurations has to do with *reliability*. Based on the data traffic analysis study, sufficient redundancy should be implemented in the network to properly support mission-critical applications. Third, is the data transmission provided by these circuits sufficiently *secure?* Truthfully, the goal is to find a network configuration that has sufficient bandwidth to deliver reliably the data as described in the data traffic analysis report in a secure manner at a reasonable cost.

Alternative configurations must be understood in terms of both performance and costs. Comprehensive methodologies for project budgeting will be presented shortly. However, the point remains that the choice of a given network configuration may come down to a business decision. That decision may be that a given network configuration is all a company can afford and, as a result, that company will have to live with the associated performance. Conversely, the business decision may be that the business requires optimum network performance, regardless of the cost.

In any case, it is not the network analyst's role to dismiss network design alternatives on the basis of cost. The network analyst's job is to deliver network design alternatives capable of delivering required network functionality. Only senior management will determine the feasibility of any particular network design in terms of its affordability.

In any case, the person presenting the various network configurations to senior management for buy-in must know the pros and cons of each configuration. The ability of each configuration to handle expansion or business growth should be anticipated. This **what-if network analysis** looks at various network configurations and their ability to respond to various business scenarios. Again, specialized *network simulation* software has been developed to fulfill this role and will be explored further in a later section of this chapter.

Network Hardware Analysis and Configuration Alternatives

Before describing the process of network hardware analysis, it is important to first reiterate the information gathered thus far which will assist in the decision-making process. Two key products of earlier analysis efforts form the basis of the supporting material for selection of the particular networking devices which will be placed throughout the corporate-wide area network. These two key products are:

1. Alternative circuit configuration diagrams
2. Detailed data traffic analysis reports for each corporate location

Recall briefly the process involved in producing each of these products. The data traffic analysis report was based upon a detailed study of numerous aspects of the data traveling to or from each corporate location. The circuit configuration alternatives were designed, in turn, based on a careful study of the required bandwidth and delay-sensitivity of the transactions performed at each corporate location as identified in the data traffic analysis study. If the results of these two analysis efforts are valid, then the networking devices chosen to tie the network together based on these results should be valid as well.

User of the I-P-O Model

The actual decision-making process for network device selection utilizes a model of data communications which was first introduced very early in the text. By compiling the results of the data traffic analysis report and the circuit configuration diagram in an **I-P-O diagram,** the required processing ability of the sought-after device can be documented. Having identified performance characteristics of the required network device, product specifications can be reviewed and vendor presentations scheduled to find the proper networking device for each location.

Just as the data traffic analysis and circuit analysis were done on a location-by-location basis, so must the network device analysis be done. Figure 12-18 shows a sample of an I-P-O diagram as a tool for network device analysis.

Figure 12-18 is not meant to be all-inclusive. What Figure 12-18 attempts to portray is that by knowing the data characteristics of the local data, with particular attention paid to the protocol stack, and by knowing the circuit alternatives available for carrying that data over the wide area network, the choices among network devices that can join the two are relatively limited.

Careful analysis of the available alternatives that can join the *input* and *output* characteristics can then be further analyzed from a business or strategic planning objective. Additional information to assist in this evaluation may come from the detailed reports of each corporate location which were prepared as part of the RFP.

The Effect of Business Issues on Network Design

For example, one of the major concerns of building an expansive wide area network is the availability of employees qualified to manage these sophisticated wide area internetworking devices. Such support is especially rare, and least cost-effective, at corporate remote sights or branches. Personnel or business constraints can

I (Input)	P (Processing)	O (Output)
Local Data Characteristics	**Required Network Device Characteristics**	**Wide Area Network Circuit Characteristics**
Possibilities:	Possibilities:	Possibilities:
Terminal oriented data (leased)	Cluster controllers	Circuit-switched
IBM 3270	STDMs	DDS
Asynchronous (VT-100)	Modems	T-1
	T-1 muxes	T-3
Transport protocols	Bridges	
TCP/IP	Routers	Packet-switched
SNA/SDLC	Inverse muxes	X.25
IPX/SPX	Multiprotocol routers	Frame relay
others	Protocol independent routers	Switched services
Payload types	Boundary routers	Dial-up
LAN data		Switched 56k
Terminal data		ISDN
Voice		
Video		
Imaging		

Figure 12-18 I-P-O diagram as a tool for network design analysis.

● HUB with full function router (central location)
□ Spoke with boundary router (remote branch)

Figure 12-19 Boundary routing: WAN response to business need.

have just as much an impact on network device choice and WAN design as data transport protocols or circuit bandwidth. As an example of a wide area network design's response to such business constraint, 3Com Corporation has introduced a wide area networking architecture known as **boundary routing.**

Boundary routing recognizes the need for simple, affordable wide area network devices at remote offices while providing full routing capabilities throughout the wide area network. Figure 12-19 illustrates a possible physical topology of a boundary routing wide area network. This particular physical topology is sometimes referred to as a **hub and spoke** topology due to the fact that all remote branches are connected to a hub office via a single WAN spoke. If redundant spokes are a business requirement of a particular node, then it must be a full-function hub in this topology.

Full-function routers are placed at each hub node, while less sophisticated "boundary routers" are placed at each remote or spoke node. Since they are only connected to a single WAN link, these boundary routers make only one decision when examining each piece of data; that is, "If this data is not addressed to a local destination, then it should be forwarded." This "forward-if-not-local" logic should suggest that in fact, these boundary routers are acting as bridges. This allows them to be less complicated as well as less expensive, thereby meeting the business requirements of this network hardware analysis and configuration alternatives process.

Review of Overall Network Analysis and Design Process

Having completed the network hardware analysis, the circuit analysis, and the data analysis, the finishing touches can be put on the final proposal. Before doing so, a brief review of the network analysis and design process may be in order.

Notice that the network design process did not start with a discussion of network hardware device alternatives. To do so would have been to ignore the importance of the top-down model, a central theme of this book. Many so-called data communications experts still start with their favorite hardware alternative and adjust data and circuit characteristics to match the chosen network hardware.

In this case, just the opposite approach was taken to:

1. Determine data characteristics based upon a thorough examination of the transactions which generate the data.
2. Determine circuits based upon required bandwidth and delay-sensitivity as determined by the data analysis study.
3. Determine the networking hardware devices capable of transporting this data over these circuits while remaining responsive to business and location specific influences.

Preparing the Final Proposal

Figure 12-20 summarizes the key points of wrapping up the network analysis and design methodology. After preparing and presenting the final proposal, buy-in is

Final Proposal

Process

1. Prepare a detailed, comprehensive budget.
2. Prepare detailed implementation timetable.
3. Prepare project task detail.
4. Prepare formal presentation.
5. SELL!

Product

1. Comprehensive systems and networking budget model.
2. Project management details.
3. Presentation graphics.

Approval

Process

1. Final buy-in by all affected parties.
2. Contract negotiation—outsourcing only.
3. Executive approval.

Implementation

Process

1. Pilot test.
1a. In-house trial—outsourcing only.
2 Performance evaluation.
3. Prepare deployment schedule.
4. Roll-out.

Product

1. Detailed list of tasks and responsible parties with due dates.
2. Identify and satisfy needs for management, support, and training on new system/network.

Figure 12-20 Final proposal, approval, and implementation.

sought from all affected constituencies, hopefully followed by final approval and funding by senior management. One element of the final proposal process deserves further explanation: the comprehensive budget.

Preparing a Comprehensive Budget

It has been the author's experience that senior management can accept well-organized, comprehensive budgets representing large sums of money. What has been unacceptable are the so-called hidden or forgotten costs of network and systems implementation often left out of budgets.

As a result, a comprehensive budget format needed to be developed to help identify as many elements of potential implementation and operation costs as possible. Figure 12-21 illustrates a sample budget page from the **comprehensive systems and networking budget model.** Along the vertical axis, major budget categories are listed including: hardware/equipment, software, personnel, communications (carrier services), and facilities. There is nothing sacred about these categories. Change them to whatever best reflects your situation. The important point is to organize the budget grid in such a way that all possible costs are identified in advance.

The horizontal axis has three columns representing the major categories of costs with respect to time. Networking and systems budgets typically focus only on the **acquisition costs** of the new system. Even within the acquisition category,

Proposal #: _____ Description:

	Acquisition	Operation	Incremental Change/ Anticipated Growth	Total
Hardware/equipment	DC: NO: AD:	DC: NO: AD:	DC: NO: AD:	DC: NO: AD:
Software	DC: NO: AD:	DC: NO: AD:	DC: NO: AD:	DC: NO: AD:
Personnel	DC: NO: AD:	DC: NO: AD:	DC: NO: AD:	DC: NO: AD:
Communications	DC: NO: AD:	DC: NO: AD:	DC: NO: AD:	DC: NO: AD:
Facilities	DC: NO: AD:	DC: NO: AD:	DC: NO: AD:	DC: NO: AD:

Totals

DC: Data Center
NO: Network Operations
AD: Application Development

Figure 12-21 Comprehensive systems and networking budget model.

costs associated with personnel additions, changes, and training have been often omitted. Likewise, costs involved with facilities upgrades or changes such as electrical wiring, cabinets, wiring closets, or security systems have also likely been overlooked or unanticipated. Preventing surprises such as these takes a two-step approach:

1. Required or anticipated facilities upgrades and personnel needs are identified during the location-by-location survey as part of the final preparation of the RFP.
2. Any legitimate need identified in the location-by-location survey should be budgeted for in the comprehensive systems and networking budget model.

Even a budget which identifies all acquisition costs is still neither complete nor accurate. Two other major cost categories must be accounted for:

1. Operations
2. Incremental change/anticipated growth

Operation costs include estimated monthly costs for leased line or dial-up line usage as well as the estimated cost for the additional electricity required to run new equipment. If additional cooling, heating, or environmental control will be required as a result of system implementation, these costs should be included as well. Service contracts, maintenance agreements, or budgeted time and materials for repairs should also be considered as operation costs.

Anticipating Network Growth

Another aspect of project budgeting often overlooked at proposal time is the **anticipated growth costs** of the system during the first five or so years after implementation. These costs may be significant if certain elements of the system or network design are not expandable or are only moderately expandable. As an example, perhaps a remote sight starts with a four-port STDM as its networking device. To add four more users, an upgrade kit could be installed for $1300. However, for a ninth user to be added would require replacing the entire STDM with a higher capacity unit at a cost of $5000. Although the costs in this example may not be precise, the point of the example remains: Anticipated growth should be budgeted. In some cases, this budgeting of the anticipated growth may cause changes in the equipment choices at acquisition time.

In order to accurately budget for anticipated systems and network growth, the network analyst must have access to strategic business plans which outline the anticipated growth of the business. After all, the implemented system and network are a direct result of the business requirements, including the required ability to respond to changing business conditions, in accordance with the overall business vision as articulated in a strategic business plan. Depending on the corporate culture, network analysts may not be allowed access to such strategic business planning information.

As shown in Figure 12-21, each budget category which is formed by an intersection of a column and row can be further subdivided if such department budgeting is required within the overall project budget. In Figure 12-21, the three abbreviated categories shown stand for three typical departments within an overall MIS operation: DC (data center), NO (network operations), and AD (application development). Make this budget grid fit your business. If departmental or cost center budgeting is not required for your business, ignore these subcategories. If other departmental designations are more appropriate, substitute them.

The Implementation Process

Although specific details of an implementation process will vary from one project to the next, there are a few general points worth making. Perhaps most importantly, regardless of how well designed an information system or network may be, it is still essential to test that design in as safe a manner as possible. "Safe" in this case can be defined as the least likely to have a tragic effect on production systems or networks.

Pilot tests are a popular way to safely roll out new systems or networks. For example, bring one retail store on-line and monitor performance, fix unanticipated problems, and gain management experience, before deploying the system on a wider scale. Honest feedback and performance evaluation are essential to smooth system implementations. User groups can be a helpful feedback mechanism if managed skillfully to prevent degeneration into nothing more than gripe sessions.

Project Management

Another important skill to a smooth implementation process is effective **project management.** Detailed task lists including task description, scheduled start and finish dates, actual start and finish dates, and responsible parties are at the heart of good project management. Some systems and network professionals use Project Management Software. The author has used project management software on occasion, but found in general that loading and maintaining all of the project details in the project management software was more work than managing the project manually. Although perhaps overly simplistic, the general rule of thumb as to when to use project management software goes something like this: When a project is too complicated to manage manually, then you may benefit from the use of project management software.

People Are Important

Despite this book's focus on networking hardware and software, *people* are the most important element of any systems implementation. Buy-in at every stage by all affected parties has been stressed throughout the network analysis and design process in order to assure that everyone involved gets behind the new system and network and feels they have had an opportunity to make their thoughts known. The best designed network will fail miserably without the support of people.

Therefore, a key element of system and network implementation is to assure that people-related needs such as management, support, and training have been thoroughly researched and appropriately addressed.

☐ AUTOMATING THE NETWORK DEVELOPMENT LIFE CYCLE

Sophisticated software packages now exist to assist network analysts in the analysis and design of large and complicated networks. These software tools can vary greatly in sophistication, functionality, scope, and price. Figure 12-22 lists the major categories of network development tools. Differences between these categories as well as details of examples of software within each category will be explained further. In some cases, as will be seen, a given software package may deliver more than one category of functionality.

Notice in Figure 12-22 how the categories of network development software parallel the major phases of the **network development life cycle** as illustrated in Figure 12-3. The only categories of tools not specifically mentioned are prototyping and implementation. In the case of the network development life cycle, prototyping refers to the process of actually testing the interaction of key networking com-

	Analysis	Design	Simulation	Monitoring	Management
Examples					

Figure 12-22 Automating the network development life cycle.

ponents in a hands-on testing environment safely removed from production networks. Although software may exist to assist in the organization of network prototyping and implementation, these tools do not offer the level of functionality offered by the categories of tools listed in Figure 12-22.

The entire network development life cycle is sometimes referred to as network engineering. The use of software tools of one type or another to assist in this process is known as **computer assisted network engineering (CANE).** More highly developed tools are used in the areas of systems analysis, design and applications development and are collectively referred to as **CASE** (computer assisted software engineering) tools. The relationship between these two development platforms will be explored in the section entitled "The Future of the Automated Network Development Life Cycle."

The Business Case for Computer Assisted Network Engineering
Companies must be able to make a strong business case for the payback of this computer assisted network engineering software when the prices for the software generally range from $10,000 to $30,000 per copy. Besides the obvious use of the software for designing new networks "from scratch," several other uses of computer-assisted network engineering software can offer significant paybacks.

By using analysis and design software to model their current network, companies are able to run **optimization** routines to reconfigure circuits and/or network hardware to deliver data more efficiently. In the case of optimization software, "efficiently" can mean maximized performance, minimized price, or a combination of both.

When current networks have grown over time in a somewhat helter-skelter manner without any major redesigns, network optimization software can *redesign* networks that can save anywhere from thousands of dollars per month to millions of dollars per year depending on the size of the network.

Another important use of analysis and design software on a corporation's current network is for **billing verification.** Most analysis and design packages have up-to-date tariff information from multiple regional and long-distance carriers. By inputting a company's current network design in the analysis and design software and by using the tariff tables to price individual circuits within that network, prices generated from the tariff tables can be compared to recent phone bills. Such verification often uncovers discrepancies in billing amounts, some of which can be significant.

Either of these two uses of computer assisted network engineering software could pay back the cost of that software within six months to a year. Another very common use of this type of software with a less tangible short-term financial payback but significant future benefits is **proactive performance assurance.** For the rapidly growing network, the ability of this software to *simulate* different possible future combinations of traffic usage, circuits, and networking equipment can avoid costly future network congestion problems or failures.

Figure 12-23 illustrates the various categories of computer assisted network engineering software along with a few examples of each type. There are many other software packages available in each category offering a range of features at a range of prices. The important features of each category of CANE software will be explained further.

Analysis and Design Tools

Following is a listing of some of the important features to look for when considering network analysis and design tools:

Tariff Databases. How current are they? How many carriers and types of circuits are included? How often are the tariff databases updated? Is there an additional charge for tariff database updates? Tariff structures have become very complicated and are calculated in a variety of different ways. Confirm

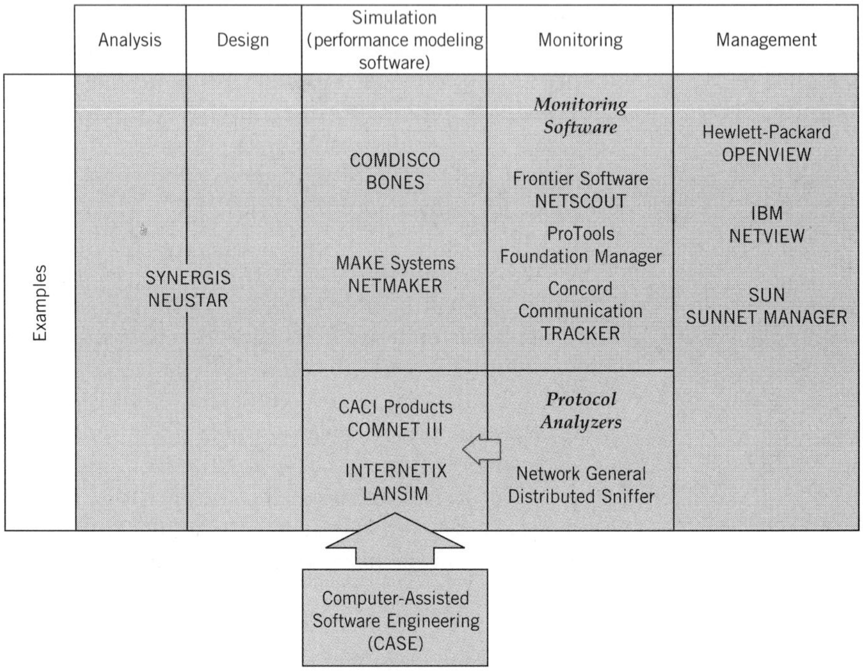

Figure 12-23 Automating the network development life cycle.

that the tariff database in the analysis and design software includes all necessary tariffs.

Response Time Calculation. Does the software take into consideration the processing time of the particular host computer which may be a part of the network? Can user-defined elements be taken into account in the response time calculation? For example: applications programs of various types, different types of networking equipment.

Multiple Transport Protocols. Can the software take into consideration the effect of various transport protocols on response time? How many protocols are included: SNA, DECNET, ISDN, TCP/IP, X.25?

Multiple Topologies. How many different topologies can the software model? Examples: hierarchical, hub and spoke, mesh, point-to-point, multipoint, concentrated, packet-switched, multiple host.

Circuit Design. Can the software configure circuits for a combination of simultaneous voice and data traffic or must voice and data circuits be designed separately? Can multiplexers be cascaded? Are tail circuits allowed?

Financial. Can the software roll up costs for network equipment as well as for circuits? Can costs as well as performance be optimized simultaneously? Can costs be compared across multiple carriers for comparison shopping?

Input/Output. Can protocol analyzers or network monitoring or management systems be interfaced directly to the analysis and design software for automatic input of current system performance data? Can analysis and design results be output directly to spreadsheet, database, and word-processing packages?

Simulation Tools

Simulation software tools are also sometimes known as **performance engineering software tools.** All simulation systems share a similar trait in that the overall network performance that they are able to model is a result of the net effect of a series of mathematical formulae. These mathematical formulae represent and are derived from the actual performance of the circuits and networking equipment which comprise the final network design.

The value of a simulation system is in its ability to predict the performance of various networking scenarios otherwise known as **what-if network analysis.**

The key characteristics which distinguish simulation software are:

Network Types. Which different types of networks can be simulated? Circuit-switched, packet-switched, store-and-forward, packet-radio, VSAT, microwave?

Network Scope. How many of the following can the simulation software model either individually or in combination with one another? Modems & Multiplexers, LANs, Netware only?, Internetworks, WANs, MANs

Network Services. How many of the following advanced services can be modeled? Frame Relay, ISDN (BRI & PRI), SMDS, X.25

Network Devices. Some simulation systems have developed performance profiles of individual networking devices to the point where they can model particular networking devices (bridges, routers, muxes) made by particular manufacturers.

Network Protocols. In addition to the network transport protocols listed in the analysis and design section, different router-to-router protocols can have a dramatic impact on network performance. Examples: RIP, OSPF, PPP

Different Data Traffic Attributes. As studied in previous chapters, all data traffic does not have identical transmission needs or characteristics. Can the software simulate data with different traits? For example: bursty LAN data, streaming digitized voice or video, real-time transaction-oriented data, batch-oriented file transfer data.

Traffic Data Entry. Any simulation needs traffic statistics in order to run. How these traffic statistics may be entered can make a major difference in the ease of use of the simulation system. Possibilities include: manual entry by users of traffic data collected elsewhere, traffic data entered "live" through a direct interface to a protocol analyzer, a traffic generator which generates simulated traffic according to the user's parameters.

User Interface. Many simulation software tools now offer easy to use graphical user interfaces with point-and-click network design capability for flexible "what-if" analysis. Some, but not all, produce graphical maps which can be output to printers or plotters. Others require users to learn a procedure-oriented programming language.

Simulation Presentation. Some simulation tools have the ability to animate the performance of the simulated network in real time, while others perform all mathematical calculations and then playback the simulation when those calculations are complete.

Object Oriented Technology Meets Network Engineering

As network simulation software has shifted its intended audience from network engineers well versed in the intricacies of network performance optimization to network analysts most familiar with networking requirements, the designers of that software have had to make some fairly radical changes in the ease of use as well as the sophistication of the software.

The previously mentioned graphical user interface allows point-and-click network design. But what are these users pointing and clicking on? Recall in the brief discussion of object oriented technology in Chapter 9 that an *object* is made up of data, methods and attributes. This combination of elements is a perfect way to represent networking devices and circuits in a network simulation package.

The mathematical formulae representing the performance characteristics of individual networking elements become the *methods* of the network objects, while the *attributes* describe the details such as manufacturer, model, price, capacity, and so on.

By merely clicking on one of these network objects representing a particular network device or circuit, the user automatically adds all of the associated methods and attributes of that network object to the network simulation. Particular applications programs or transport protocols can also be represented as network objects and be clicked upon in order to be added to the overall network simulation. In this way, all seven layers of the OSI model can be included in the final simulation run.

Management: Proactive LAN Management

Sophisticated proactive LAN management software is now beginning to appear with the ability to *monitor* network performance on an ongoing basis and to report unusual network conditions or activities to a network management workstation. The term "unusual network conditions" is really user definable. **Thresholds** or desired limits of certain performance characteristics are set by the user. In some cases the user may have no idea what to set these thresholds at. To aid in such a situation, some management systems can record "normal" performance characteristics over an extended period of time in order to gather valid **baseline performance statistics.**

Some management software systems even have the ability to feed this "alarm data" back to certain simulation systems which can simulate the "threshold crossing" and allow what-if analysis to be performed in order to diagnose the cause of the problem and propose a solution.

☐ THE FUTURE OF THE AUTOMATED NETWORK DEVELOPMENT LIFE CYCLE

Computer-assisted network engineering software tools continue to evolve and mature. The key word in terms of the future of these various tools which comprise the automated network development life cycle is *integration.* The real potential of network engineering software integration has just barely scratched the surface and only in a few vendor specific cases.

For instance, as can be seen in Figure 12-23, certain protocol analyzers such as Network General's distributed sniffer have the ability to interface directly into certain network simulation systems such as Comnet III and LANSim. In such a scenario, actual traffic statistics from the current network configuration are fed directly into the mathematical engines underlying the simulation software. Such vendor specific, product specific integration is significant. However, in order to have true transparent integration of all the computer assisted network engineering tools, a more open and standardized approach must be undertaken.

Horizontal Integration

Figure 12-24 illustrates, on a conceptual level, how such a standardized open architecture offering seamless **horizontal integration** might be constructed. Rather than having to know the intricacies, and, in some cases, the trade secrets of how each other's products work, vendors of computer-assisted network engineering software merely pass the output from their particular software product to a "neutral" data platform known as **CNIP (common network information platform).** Any

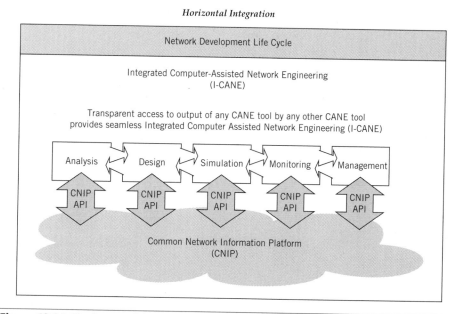

Figure 12-24 The future of the automated network development life cycle: horizontal integration.

other CANE tool which could use that output to provide transparent integration with other CANE tools would import the standardized, formatted data from the CNIP. The end result of the use of such a standardized platform for CANE tool data output and retrieval is the seamless integration of a variety of CANE tools spanning all phases of the network development life cycle.

The Final Frontier: Vertical Integration

Integration implies not only horizontal integration with software from other categories of the CANE family but also **vertical integration** with applications development platforms such as the CASE tools mentioned previously. Integrated CASE **(I-CASE)** tools could generate code for a new corporate-wide client–server application and could download key information concerning that new application to the CANE suite of software products in order to predict network impact of the new proposed application.

Proactive network management is the result when the network implications of the deployment of new network-intensive applications are known before the actual release of the software.

As can be seen in Figure 12-25, the actual gateway between the I-CASE and **I-CANE** tools may not be a simple API as we have seen in so may previous cases of vertical integration of distinct software layers such as middleware. Due to the sophistication of the interface between these two platforms, expert systems may be required to dynamically model the relationships between the objects underlying the CASE tools and those underlying the CANE tools.

Extending the vertical integration above the CASE tools and the strategic

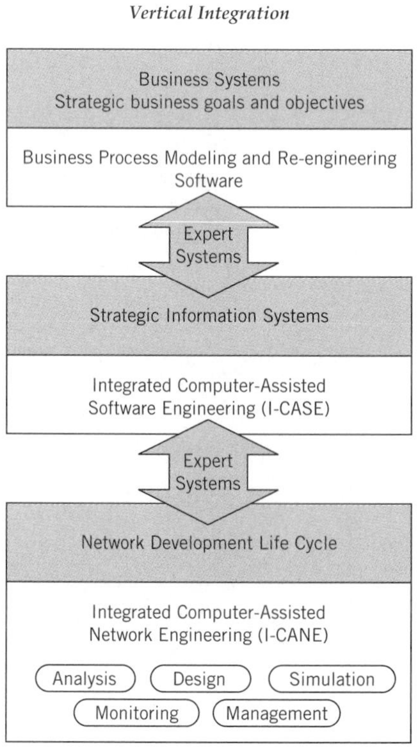

Vertical Integration

Figure 12-25 The future of the automated network development life cycle: vertical integration.

information systems that they produce, expert systems could again maintain the relationships between major software platforms. Applications layer objects used by the CASE tools could be dynamically linked via expert systems to the objects representing the business rules and processes which, in turn, support strategic business goals and objectives.

Thus, although current technology may not possess the capability, the business information system of the future may interface to the strategic business planning person who amends strategic business goals and objects via a graphical user interface and point-and-click manipulation of business process objects. The changes caused by this business process reengineering are immediately forwarded via an expert system interface to the strategic information systems design which supports these business processes. Applications program changes are automatically generated by integrated CASE tools.

Resultant changes in the applications programs produced by the CASE tools are immediately forwarded via expert systems to the integrated computer assisted network engineering platform. Finally, network objects, circuits, and networking devices, are amended as necessary due to the impact of the new applications programs. Network simulation programs are automatically run to assess network impact while network design optimization programs automatically reconfigure the network design to adjust most appropriately to the new network impacts. The amazing part of this whole process is that it was initiated originally by a change in *strategic business objectives*. The future of computer assisted network engineering software represents one of the most exciting opportunities in data communications and networking.

CHAPTER SUMMARY

In keeping with the overall theme of the text, this chapter took a practical approach to network analysis and design. To begin with, network design can no longer be performed in a vacuum. Effective network designs will only result from adherence to the top-down model by beginning with business objectives rather than networking hardware. A short discussion of strategic information systems design as well as application development analysis was offered in order to stress the importance of information systems design that responded to strategic business objectives. The importance of the strategic information systems design lies not only in its delivery of business objectives but also in its role as a template for network design.

The detailed step-by-step process of network analysis and design was outlined. Data traffic analysis, circuit analysis, and network hardware analysis were discussed in detail. Computer-assisted network engineering was introduced as an overall platform for a variety of software packages which supported various phases of the network development life cycle. The future of integrated computer-assisted network engineering was described as offering both horizontal integration across various CANE tools as well as vertical integration with CASE and business process modeling platforms.

KEY TERMS

acquisition costs	billing verification	business processes	CNIP
anticipated growth costs	boundary routing	buy-in	common network
backroom politics	bursty	CANE	information platform
baseline data	business functional areas	CASE	comprehensive systems
baseline performance	business process	circuit analysis and	and networking budget
statistics	reengineering	configuration	model

computer-assisted
  network engineering
critical success factors
data traffic analysis
decision points
document flow analysis
encryption
evaluation criteria
feasibility study
horizontal integration
hub and spoke
I-CANE
I-P-O diagram

isochronous streaming
make-or-buy decision
management abstract
milestone
mission critical
network analysis and
  design methodology
network development
  life cycle
network hardware
  analysis and
  configuration
operation costs

optimization
opportunity points
payload type analysis
percent-of-fit goal
performance engineering
pilot tests
proactive performance
  assurance
process
process flow analysis
product
project management
protocol stack analysis

redundant links
requirements gathering
RFP
strategic information
  systems design
three-pile approach
thresholds
time studies
traffic volume
  requirements profile
transaction analysis
vertical integration
what-if network analysis

REVIEW QUESTIONS

1. Where does the network development life cycle fit into the overall systems development life cycle?
2. How can one ensure that a network design will meet strategic business requirements?
3. How can a company cost-justify the expense of network analysis and design software?
4. What does optimization accomplish in network design software?
5. What are the two major characteristics on which networks are optimized?
6. Can these two optimization characteristics conflict with each other?
7. How is horizontal integration of CANE tools likely to be enabled?
8. How is vertical integration of CANE tools likely to be enabled?
9. What is so significant about the comprehensive systems and networking budget model?
10. What is meant by a critical success factor? Discuss three.
11. What is the significance of process and product in the network analysis and design methodology?
12. What are the important elements of data traffic analysis?
13. Explain the relationship of data traffic analysis, circuit analysis, and network hardware analysis.
14. Explain the importance of evaluation criteria and percent of fit goals to the overall network design process.
15. What is the purpose of an RFP?
16. What are the major components of an RFP?
17. How can the RFP process be kept as objective and nonpolitical as possible?
18. What kind of information must be gathered about each corporate location?
19. How can a network analyst assure widespread support of new systems or network implementations?

20. What is cyclic about the network development life cycle?
21. How can computer-assisted network engineering software products exhibit this same cyclic nature?
22. Why are seasonal or occasional differences in transaction volumes or processes so important to network design?
23. What are some of the potential advantages and disadvantages of outsourcing network analysis and design functions?
24. How can so-called "backroom politics" affect network development and how can a network analyst minimize such effects?
25. What does corporate culture have to do with the method in which a network development project is carried out?
26. What does buy-in imply beyond simple agreement and why is it important to the network development life cycle?
27. How can responses to RFPs be objectively evaluated to determine those vendors worthy of further consideration?
28. What is the role of protocol analyzers in the network development life cycle and in the functionality of network optimization tools?
29. How do network analysts assure that they have a clear understanding of a business problem before proceeding to networking solutions?
30. What is the importance of baseline data to the ability to articulate the eventual success or failure of a network development effort?
31. How can too much information be as detrimental as too little information for decision makers? What effect on network design might this have?
32. What is the danger in not starting the network development life cycle with an examination of business

layer issues but merely networking business operations as they currently exist?

33. How can the amount of work invested in the development of the RFP be justified?

34. Why is the customer's proposed project schedule important to potential vendors?

35. What is the importance of the corporate location-by-location survey?

36. Although specific questions asked of vendors in an RFP may vary, what are the overall objectives in asking for this information?

37. How can a network analysis project leader assure that vendor demonstrations are objective and useful and don't revert to "dog and pony" shows?

38. What are some of the difficulties of transporting

voice and data simultaneously? of transporting video and data simultaneously?

39. What are some of the promising network technologies for simultaneous transmission of video and data on both the LAN and WAN?

40. How can an I-P-O diagram be used to assist in the proper selection of networking hardware devices?

41. Describe those items beyond acquisition costs which should be included in a networking budget as well as the importance of those items.

42. What impact has object-oriented programming had on networking design and simulation tools?

43. What is so proactive about proactive LAN management? What is the likely business impact of proactive LAN management?

ACTIVITIES

1. You have been asked to design a network for a state lottery commission connecting between 1500 and 2000 outlets to lottery headquarters. Without knowing any further details, what might some of the strategic requirements for such a network be? In other words, from a business perspective, if the state lottery is to prosper as a business, what characteristics must the networking supporting this business venture exhibit?

2. Concerning the state lottery example, how important are seasonality or peak transaction periods to network design and performance? What network design characteristics might reflect this level of importance?

3. You have been asked to be project leader of a network design team. Rumor has it that the company president's golf partner already has been hired to install the network and that this network design project is to give the appearance of an objective process. Prepare a detailed outline of your approach including long-range project plan, detailed task list, meetings to schedule, and alternative courses of action based on the results of those scheduled meetings.

4. You are in charge of a nationwide voice and data network that has grown in piecemeal fashion and may benefit from design optimization using automated software. It is essential to demonstrate a relatively short payback period for the software investment. The software must contain current tarriff information from a number of different carriers so that actual installation and operating costs are generated along with various network design scenarios. Contact any of the following vendors for product literature and pricing information. Determine which packages might best meet your needs and write a memo to the company president outlining your recommendation.

Vendor	Phone
Comdisco	(415) 574-5800
CACI	(619) 457-9681
Make Systems, Inc.	(800) 545-6253
Concord Communications, Inc.	(508) 460-4646
Synergis Neustar	(312) 644-9299

5. Modify the requirements in question 4 to include a need for the ability to model all seven layers of the OSI Model rather than the more typical ability of network simulation packages to model only layers 1–3. By modeling all seven layers, you should be able to model the impact of a given application (layer 7) or transport protocol (layer 4). This package must allow you to define your own objects for any layer of the OSI model.

6. Modify the requirements in question 4 to include a need for the ability to model the performance of network devices from a particular manufacturer. It should be obvious that the performance of network devices have a great deal to do with the overall performance of the network. Network device performance can vary widely between manufacturers. As an example, it may be a requirement in this question to be able to differentiate between the performance of routers manufactured by Cisco, Wellfleet, and 3Com.

7. Prices for network design and simulation packages range from less than $1000 to nearly $40,000 per copy. Delineate the key characteristics that distinguish between the variously priced packages.

8. Investigate an opportunity to perform a network analysis and design project within your department or business. By dividing the entire project into sections performed by various teams, more can be accomplished in a shorter time. Perhaps your instructor, supervisor, or department chairperson

has such an opportunity in mind. If not, consider one of the following scenarios:

a. Develop a network to deliver local and remote E-mail interoperability.

b. Develop a network to deliver transparent database distribution.

c. Develop a network to deliver CAD/CAM engineering drawings to a manufacturing environment or shop floor.

d. Develop a network that can handle electronic funds transfers between banks on an international basis.

The outcome of such studies may not be a physical network design. A great deal of meaningful learning can take place on the way to a physical design. Take a top-down approach by starting with strategic business layer concerns. Try to get through the development of the RFP and the Data Traffic Analysis stages.

9. Choose a networked application for your department or business.

a. Gather baseline data on this process.

b. What is the nature of the transactions involved?

c. How much data is transmitted per transaction?

d. Perform a time study in order to produce a traffic volume requirements profile.

e. What networking resources are currently involved?

10. Describe how a network analyst might cope with a "Because that's the way we've always done it!" attitude during the business process analysis phase of the network development life cycle.

11. Develop a corporate location survey covering people, hardware, software, media, data, physical plant, and networking resources. Use this survey on at least five corporate locations or academic departments. Reevaluate the survey and modify and/or improve it as necessary.

12. Prepare a data traffic analysis report on the data transmitted between these 5 locations by performing as many of the different types of data traffic analysis as possible from the types listed in the chapter (payload, transaction, time study, etc.). Protocol stack analysis must be completed for each location.

13. Contact your local or long-distance phone company to determine how one gets a quote for various types of data services. Are there different contacts for:

a. Analogy leased lines

b. Digital leased lines

c. Digital switched services such as switched 56K

d. Packet services such as X.25

e. Advanced packet services such as SMDS or frame relay

14. One of the vendors who responded favorably to the RFP has been in business less than three years. What are your concerns and how should these concerns be addressed?

15. Invite a local vendor of data communications or networking equipment to present a guest lecture or demonstration. Notice how the vendor responds to questions.

16. Prepare a comprehensive budget proposal for one of the networks proposed in question 8 above.

Featured References

Network Management

Aaron, Stuart, Marvin Chartoff, and Bob Reinhold. "Net Management Platforms: Buyers Guide," *Network World*, vol. 10, no. 27 (July 5, 1993), p. 35.

Network Planning

Black, Ulysses. *Data Networks: Concepts, Theory, and Practice*, (Englewood Cliffs: Prentice Hall, 1989).

Kuo, F. F., ed. *Protocols and Techniques for Data Communications Networks*, (Englewood Cliffs: Prentice Hall, 1981).

Schwartz, M. *Telecommunications Networks: Protocols, Modeling and Analysis*, (Reading, MA: Addison-Wesley, 1987).

Spragins et al. *Telecommunications Protocols and Design*, (Reading, MA: Addison-Wesley, 1991).

Brown, Bob. "Siemens Nixdorf Sets up New Integration Business," *Network World*, vol. 9, no. 23 (June 8, 1992), p. 27.

Dortch, Michael. "Transitions to Tomorrow," *Communications Week*, no. 428 (November 9, 1992), p.61.

Woek, Paul, and Joseph LeBlanc. "Taking the Guesswork out of Network Design," *Data Communications*, vol. 21, no. 18 (December 1992), p. 95.

Network Troubleshooting

Hayes, Stephen. "Analyzing Network Performance Management," *IEEE Communications*, vol. 31, no. 5 (May 1993), p. 52.

Serre, Jean-Marc. "Implementing OSI-Based Interfaces for Network Management," *IEEE Communications*, vol. 31, no. 5 (May 1993), p. 76.

Nassar, Daniel. "Steps to Becoming a Protocol Analysis Pro," *LAN Times*, vol. 9, no. 13 (July 20, 1992), p. 36.

Jander, Mary. "Proactive LAN Management," *Data Communications*, vol. 22, no. 5 (March 21, 1993), p. 49.

Homer, Blaine. "Low-End Software-Only Analyzers," *LAN Times*, vol. 10, no. 5 (March 8, 1993), p. 65.

Network Design and Simulation

Mierop, John. "Service Interaction in an Object-Oriented Environment," *IEEE Communications*, vol. 31, no. 8 (August 1993), p. 46.

Bean, Angelo. "Specifying Goal-Oriented Network Management Systems," *IEEE Communications,* vol. 31, no. 5 (May 1993), p. 30.

Marchisio, Lucia. "Modeling the User Interface," *IEEE Communications,* vol. 31, no. 5 (May 1993), p. 68.

Jander, Mary. "Network Design Gets Real," *Data Communications,* vol. 21, no. 16 (November 1992), p. 53.

Jander, Mary. "Simulation Made Simpler," *Data Communications,* vol. 21, no. 11 (August 1992), p. 69.

Cope, Patricia. "Buyers Guide: Design and Optimization Packages; Building a Better Network," *Network World,* vol. 10, no. 1 (January 4, 1993), p. 34.

Liebing, Edward. "Network Simulation: Look before You Leap," *LAN Times,* vol. 9, no. 8 (May 11, 1992), p. 37.

CASE STUDY

A Textbook Example of Network Expansion

PORTLAND, Maine—The network and internetworking efforts of Maine Medical Center, a 598-bed facility and the largest nonprofit teaching hospital in the Pine Tree State, provides a textbook example of one mid-sized user's successful strategy for expanding the size and scope of its networks.

Like most health-care facilities in major cities, Maine Medical Center (MMC)—which opened its doors as the 40-bed Maine General Hospital in 1874—must keep abreast of the latest advances in medical technology *and* computer networking to give its patients the best possible care and to help its staff operate at peak efficiency.

While MMC doesn't have the high profile of a Johns Hopkins, it is a top-notch facility and the third-largest private employer in Maine. It may also be the busiest hospital north of Boston, providing in- and outpatient care to more than 40,000 people annually. In addition, it is a teaching hospital affiliated with the University of Vermont, Southern Maine University, and Westbrook College.

Also bringing MMC into the spotlight these days is the recent election of Dr. Robert McAfee, an attending physician at the hospital who specializes in vascular surgery, as president-elect of the American Medical Association. McAfee will assume the presidency in 1994.

First Networks

Like many industries, MMC began installing 4Mbps token-ring networks running Novell NetWare in the mid-1980s as an adjunct to its existing mainframe/dumb-terminal setup.

At that time, recalls Jeffrey Drumm, MMC's manager of microcomputer systems, only about 30 percent of the health-care facility's personnel—about 70 people—had access to the network. But things began changing rapidly after Drumm joined the hospital almost four years ago.

"At that time, we had five servers all running NetWare 2.x. These servers were used by the emergency room, medical records, and data management for general-purpose use," Drumm said. One of the first things he did was hire a microcomputer-support specialist, which freed him to concentrate on more network-specific tasks.

Challenges

The requirements of MMC's physicians and administrative staff presented Drumm with two immediate challenges. The first was to install a centralized multiuser calendar/scheduling system to keep track of the many daily meetings of both hospital administrators and the doctors. The second entailed installing an initial E-mail system.

"Hospital administrators and doctors must schedule and attend an incredible number of meetings," Drumm said. "An average of eight to 12 meetings a day is common around here—and some days there are as many as 15."

MMC spent six months evaluating products before settling on two: WordPerfect Corp.'s WordPerfect Office for E-mail and MicroSystems Software Inc.'s Calendar for scheduling. Drumm chose Calendar because it fit MMC's specialized requirements.

"We needed to be able to schedule by proxy easily—to access multiple users' calendars from a central schedular—and we needed a high-performance scheduling system that let us quickly select a meeting time or set up meetings at the last minute," Drumm said.

The Calendar scheduling software provides MMC with a variety of reporting capabilities, including a daily organizer. It supports links to Sharp Electronics Corp.'s Wizard palmtop organizer, which many staff members carry with them "so they're never out of touch," Drumm said.

"Linking Calendar and Wizard was a real godsend," Drumm said. "It allows us to enter appointments in either Calendar or Wizard, search schedules on both lists, determine if there are scheduling conflicts, and override if necessary—accepting or declining any appointment on the list. And since the Wizards are portable, it gives people few excuses to miss meetings."

While these days E-mail is the most popular and ubiquitous network application, it wasn't always that way. MMC only got WordPerfect Office in 1989. As Drumm explained, it was a totally new concept for most of the hospital's staff, and just getting them to overcome their initial computer phobia and use the mail system was a challenge.

"Once they started using E-mail, keeping up with an ever-increasing number of requests for access became an even bigger challenge," Drumm said. "That's because we didn't have enough servers to facilitate all the users who needed access."

Between 1989 and 1990, MMC's NetWare file servers doubled from five to the present complement of 10. In the short term, Drumm said, MMC will install two additional file servers: IBM PS/2 Model 95s running NetWare 3.11.

Netware 4.0 Plans

"We do need NetWare 4.0," Drumm said. "We could use the directory-services feature right now because it's difficult to manage even 10 file servers when local departmental users on one LAN need to access data across multiple remote LANs."

According to Drumm, MMC's networks have "incredibly complex login scripts." So when one department wants to access an application on another group's file server, it requires complicated and time-consuming setups.

Like many budget-conscious users, MMC bought NetWare 4.0 at the introductory discount price that came with the NetWare Premium upgrade package.

"We definitely need a global management system," Drumm said. "We've already bought 4.0, but we're not going to install it until a lot more users have taken the plunge ahead of us. Until then, I'm monitoring NetWare and waiting until Novell's got all the kinks worked out."

Internetworking

With their network plans firmly in place, Drumm and his colleagues are concentrating on several internetworking projects, Including:

- installing communications servers so MMC's affiliated physicians can dial in from their offices;
- replacing dumb MAUs with intelligent hubs and routers;
- connecting to the Internet; and
- installing 56Kbps and T-1 leased lines to connect LANs in new facilities a half-mile away.

No one is more enthusiastic about the networks and the ongoing internetworking efforts than Dr. Nathaniel James, who is director of ambulatory medicine in MMC's outpatient clinic and who runs a clinic serving the region's immigrant and refugee population.

"The networks let me spend more time being a doctor," James said. "I do everything on the network except set bones. We've got networked PCs in two of our 10 examination rooms, and it's great.

It enables us to display patients' medical histories onscreen to review their problems and medication lists. We can also check off which prescriptions we want to refill."

Internetworking Variety

MMC has a wide range of internetworking equipment, much of it from New England vendors, such as Cabletron Systems Inc. and CrossComm Corp. The health-care facility is running TCP/IP in limited applications right now, via CrossComm's ILANs, to provide LAN users with access to Hewlett-Packard Co. (HP) 3000 series minicomputers.

MMC is in the process of replacing its 8228 IBM MAUs with Cabletron's intelligent MMAC hubs "because they offer a much higher level of stability," Drumm said. "The 8228 MAUs just aren't reliable enough for us. If you have one workstation where the plug is slightly out of its socket, the ring beacons; it goes into error condition and doesn't recover until the faulty lobe is located and manually fixed.

"We can't afford to have a couple hundred users on a patient-care network out of commission," Drumm said.

The Cabletron hubs have a fault-isolation feature that automatically isolates faulty lobes and disconnects them from the token ring without disrupting service to the other users on the network.

Life Blood

MMC made its internetworking purchasing decisions after visiting Cabletron and CrossComm.

"We have a 24-hour computer-maintenance staff, and Cabletron's and CrossComm's support has been very good," Drumm said.

The ILANs provide MMC with transparent bridging from an Ethernet segment that houses the

HP 3000 system. The minicomputer is used by several different departments, including the medical-records department to house the master patient index and the radiology department to store X-rays and scans.

The health-care facility is also using a bidirectional print gateway—Quest Software Inc.'s NBSpool—to route print jobs between the NetWare and HP 3000 environments.

This setup allows departmental LAN users to employ system printers attached to the HP 3000 as network printers. For massive jobs, the hospital has a Xerox 4050 printer in the computer room, and users access it from network-based applications. The radiology department, for instance, prints reports all day long, Drumm said.

"We've also got a number of systems, including accounting and human resources, that are attached to the HP mini," Drumm said. "Now with the bidirectional gateway, we can deliver reports directly to the appropriate department automatically. It's a big time-saver."

The advantages provided by MMC's networks have not gone unnoticed by high-level hospital administrators, Drumm said.

"We don't have to plead the case that networks are necessary anymore," he said. "People are well aware that data communications are a vital resource. Networked and internetworked microcomputers are the strategic way we do business."

Source: Laura Didio, "A Textbook Example of Network Expansion," *LAN Times,* vol. 10, no. 15 (August 9, 1993), p. 35. Reprinted with permission of McGraw-Hill, *LAN Times.*

Business Case Study Questions

To Do

1. After reading the article describing this business analysis case, prepare a top-down model by organizing pertinent facts into their proper layers within the top-down model. Use the following questions as a guideline to build the top-down model.

Business

1. What were some of the strategic business objectives or perspectives that made the hospital's networks a high-priority initiative?
2. What were the two more specific business processes that required automating?

Application

1. What specific network applications were evaluated to directly satisfy the high-priority business processes identified above?
2. How was application software chosen?
3. What specific criteria determined the actual application software chosen?
4. Which applications ran on PCs and which ran on the minicomputer?
5. Do you think that the choice of platforms for the different applications was deliberate? Could applications have been deployed differently?

Data

1. To what other platforms were the scheduling data to be distributed?
2. What effect did this have on actual application software and/or technology chosen?
3. How did this link support business layer objectives?
4. What kinds of demands for sharing of data between departments existed?

Network

1. What kinds of network functionality were required to link the scheduling platforms mentioned above?
2. What was the limitation of the current network operating system in its ability to deliver on data layer requirements?
3. What solution to this shortcoming was proposed in the case?
4. What alternative proposals could you suggest?
5. How could these problems have been avoided in the first place?
6. What kinds of internetworking functionality are currently being considered?
7. For each internetworking initiative, attempt to identify a particular business process or objective supported by the initiative.
8. Are there any network plans that don't seem to correspond to any business initiative?
9. What were the network requirements for connectivity to minicomputers?

Technology

1. What issues concerning servers were encountered as network demand grew?
2. How was this issue resolved for both the short and the long term?
3. What was the network operating system of choice?
4. How did this choice affect the network's ability to deliver on business, application, and data-layer requirements?
5. What was the company's philosophy on the installation of new software releases?
6. What kinds of reliability features do the newer hubs offer that the older MAUs do not? Could this have a direct effect on business layer issues?

CHAPTER 13

Where Do We Go from Here?
Trends to Watch

Concepts Reinforced

Top-Down Model
Data Communications Industry Model
Regulatory Issues
Standards-Making Process and Organizations

Concepts Introduced

Future Trends of These Key Aspects of the Data Comm Industry

Business	Standards
User perspective	Research and Technology
Regulatory, Legislative and Carrier	

Future Views of the Following Technology Categories:

Local area networks	Voice networks
Internetworking	Enterprise networks
Metropolitan area networks	Wide area networks

Having mastered the material in this chapter, you should be able to:

1. Understand the relationship between business trends and data communications/networking trends.

2. Understand the changing roles and influence of various players in the data communications industry.

3. Understand the enabling technology that will support the networking trends of the future.

4. Understand the various models introduced in this textbook sufficiently to be able to predict with some assurance the impact of yet unknown business trends/needs and/or enabling technologies on the data communications and networking industry of the future.

5. Understand the importance of your role as informed participants in the data communications/networking industry.

6. Understand the educational and career implications of business and data communications trends.

☐ INTRODUCTION

This final chapter will be guided primarily by two of the fundamental models that have structured the approach of the entire text:

> Top-Down Model
> Systems Diagram of the Data Communications Industry

The importance of the **top-down model** is reinforced once again in this final chapter as the relationship between business trends and the resultant data communications trends are explored. This top-down approach to the analysis of possible future trends in the data communications industry will start with emerging business trends and will conclude with an examination of the trends in various categories of data communications and networking technology which may meet those future business needs.

In order to more fully understand trends in data communications however, one must refer to the **systems diagram of the data communications industry** (Figure 1-1). Only after exploring trends in each of the elements of influence illustrated in that diagram can the total impact of the sum of those influences on the data communications industry be predicted. Figure 1-1 is reprinted here as Figure 13-1.

Once the regulatory, business, and standards-making trends, on both a domestic as well as international scope, are understood, emerging data communications technology can be explored with a clearer understanding of the significance of these technology trends. Separate sections will be devoted to the exploration of possible trends in each of the major areas of technology explored in the text: LANs, internetworking, voice networking, enterprise networking and MANs, and finally WANs.

Finally, issues of more immediate concern to students will be addressed. The educational and career implications of the trends detailed previously in the chapter will be discussed, followed by some thoughts on the important role that savvy data communications and networking professionals can play in the exciting data communications industry of tomorrow.

☐ BUSINESS

No Guarantees

Although long-term projections of economic trends are extremely difficult at best, certain business trends during uncertain economic times have emerged which

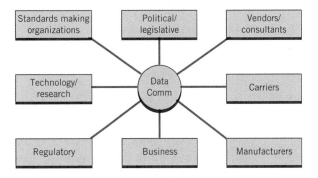

Figure 13-1 Tomorrow's data communications environment.

may have an impact on the use of technology in general, and data communications in particular.

Technology, however, should not be viewed as a quick fix to economic woes. As stated previously, applying technology to a badly designed business system will only produce a more expensive, technologically advanced, badly designed business system.

For example, for every imaging success story in which a company has eliminated warehouses full of paper and trimmed paperwork processing cycle times by more than 10 times, thanks to imaging technology and automated workflow software, there are at least an equal number of companies that have abandoned such efforts after considerable monetary and human investments.

Business Process Re-engineering

Likewise, technological advances that meet success in a certain business or situation, offer no guarantee to the portability of that technological solution to any other business situation. For instance, one of the most popular business-layer trends of late, mentioned in the network development life cycle discussion, is known as **business process reengineering.** Among the expected benefits from this fresh-look approach to how a corporation does business are:

> Improved customer service
> Increased productivity
> Improved quality
> Reduced costs
> Increased sales

Although some companies actually derive many of these benefits from the business reengineering process, many others actually receive fewer benefits than expected.

Outsourcing

Another popular business trend related to data communications and networking which has met with a fair amount of success as well as failure is **outsourcing.** Outsourcing, sometimes also known as external facilities management, is a process by which a corporation's networks and/or information systems are managed by a third-party organization rather than by corporate employees. Outsourcing is expected to represent a $27.7 billion-a-year industry by 1997.

Computer Industry Woes

Another important trend in the business sector is the *major downturn of the computer industry* overall and of the larger computer manufacturers such as IBM and DEC in particular. This could have a major impact on the data communications industry and on those individuals properly trained to compete in the data communications industry.

To be more specific, as proprietary mainframe and minicomputer platforms continue to be either abandoned or relegated to roles as servers on distributed computing networks, the demand for highly dependable, robust, networks which are able to connect numerous clients and servers transparently, thereby offering scalable computing power, will increase exponentially. The types of hardware, software, networks, and middleware products required to build these networks and described in Chapter 9, "Enterprise Networking and Client/Server

Architectures," will be at the heart of the data communications environment of the near future.

Internetworking hardware such as bridges and routers will continue to develop in terms of power and sophistication as classical mainframe to terminal traffic is integrated with inter-LAN traffic over a single wide area network.

Corporate Downsizing   The shrinking, or near elimination, of layers of middle management in corporations of all sizes has been enabled to a great extent by the increasingly more extensive and more powerful networks within, and extending from, those corporations. This process is commonly referred to as **corporate downsizing** and is not to be confused with computer downsizing, which refers to the phenomena in which mainframe-based systems are being replaced by client–server architectures. Widespread corporate downsizing has produced an overall "flattening" of corporate hierarchy in many companies, meaning fewer layers of management between frontline operations people and senior management. For instance, multi-billion-dollar communications carrier MCI with over 30,000 employees has only five or six layers of management.

Corporate Downsizing Presents Technology Openings   This corporate downsizing has created a technological opening for one of the most time-consuming of all corporate functions, the committee meeting. Meetings, and the administrators responsible for arranging, conducting, and consequently reporting on meetings, can be eliminated with the introduction of effective E-mail and groupware systems running over well-designed networks. A well-designed network implies transparent access by corporate workers regardless of their location. Integration of mobile computing with corporate headquarters-based networks will become increasingly important in order to offer hassle-free communications between corporate workgroup members.

As bandwidth-on-demand becomes a reality, meetings will be scheduled via group scheduling software and run via multipoint desktop or laptop videoconferencing regardless of the geographic location of the meeting participants. Less time will be spent traveling between meetings, allowing more time to be spent in scheduled or impromptu meetings of a more productive nature.

☐ USER PERSPECTIVE

From a user's standpoint, what demands or pressures are likely to be placed on the data communications and networking industry? In other words, in order to be as productive as possible, and hopefully keep one's job, what must the data communications and networking environment of the future deliver in terms of functionality?

Based upon some of the business/technology interactions mentioned previously, here are a few possibilities:

Declaration of the Network User of the 1990s

Network Access from a Single Device—As opposed to carrying a laptop computer, cellular phone, personal communicator, several types of beepers, short-range radio transceiver, etc.

Easy, Transparent Access—Users don't want to have to worry about LAN operating systems, WAN protocols, or whether a protocol is routable or not. They only want to be able to connect to required network services easily and quickly.

Access to People or Knowledge Resources—Users want to get in touch with people regardless of where that person may be. Playing "telephone tag" and speaking to someone's voice mail are becoming unacceptable alternatives to immediate, transparent access. Users may want to access expert systems, artificial intelligence systems, decision support systems, or knowledge agents which travel through multilocation corporate databases located anywhere in the world seeking answers to complex questions.

Access Regardless of Location—Perhaps implied by the term "transparent" above, users do not wish to write special codes or maintain special tables manually in order to locate the person or knowledge resource that they wish to access.

Access with Sufficient Bandwidth—If high-quality video is required in order to support a business decision or answer a question, then the network must not be a limiting factor in its ability to offer sufficient bandwidth to support any required application.

Access at a Reasonable Cost—Businesses must make a profit. This will not change. Corporate information highways must become a reasonable cost of doing business for the average company, rather than a luxury afforded by only a privileged few. It will not matter that "knowledge workers" are more productive thanks to the sophistication of the network if the cost of the network is excessive or prohibitive.

Access to Support Business and Decision Making Processes—The network of a corporation will increasingly become the nervous system or information highway of that corporation as all intra- and inter-company communication, meetings, business processing, and decision support activities travel in a transparent, integrated fashion over this key corporate infrastructure.

Users Demand Sufficient Bandwidth

Of all these previously mentioned phrases, perhaps none has more potential impact on network analysis and design than *"with sufficient bandwidth."* Sufficient bandwidth makes no distinction between local area or wide area architectures. The transparency demanded by users will no longer allow WAN links to be the overall network transmission bottleneck. If 100Mbps is to be delivered to the desktop, then users will expect, and perhaps demand, 100Mbps over wide area networks connecting those desktops, at an affordable price.

In order to understand the source of this demand for ever increasing amounts of bandwidth, one must examine the types of applications which users wish to run over tomorrow's local area and wide area networks. Most of these applications, including approximate bandwidth consumption, were explained in detail, in previous chapters.

Among the bandwidth-hungry applications of the future are the following:

Imaging. The dream of a paperless office will not die. As imaging and storage technology improves and becomes more affordable, imaging will become more of a mainstream application. Paperless offices also save trees and reduce trash. Workflow software working in conjunction with imaging systems can have significant positive impacts on productivity.

Multimedia. Some feel the jury is still out on multimedia. In some cases, side-by-side pictures, text, and video can't be beat for effective presentation or distance learning. In any case, should multimedia use become widespread, image- and video-linked objects require large amounts of both bandwidth and storage, not to mention special transport protocols.

Videoconferencing. Video compression techniques have significantly reduced bandwidth requirements while lowering the overall cost of entry into this technology. As videoconferencing costs continue to drop, and travel costs increase in terms of both expense and lost productivity while traveling, deployment of this bandwidth-hungry application will increase. Don't forget the isochronous or streaming nature of video transmission. Desktop videoconferencing will be as common tomorrow as desktop teleconferencing (voice) is today.

Fax. As fax servers and Windows-based fax software allow faxes to be sent transparently from within Windows applications, network integrated fax transmission will become increasingly popular. Faxes will be printed out on networked laser printers rather than on dedicated fax machines.

E-mail. E-mail servers and X.400 Universal backbones will help make E-mail interoperability transparent and more of a viable communication medium over wide areas. As a result, E-mail with attached documentation will become more common, perhaps replacing the phone call followed by a fax.

EDI. As pressures continue on business to cut costs while increasing productivity, EDI usage will increase. Standards will emerge as industries define common electronic forms and terms. Industry leaders will force trading partners into the EDI arena by giving promises of doing business strictly electronically.

CAD/CAM. Three dimensional modeling programs require enormous computing power as well as bandwidth. In the name of productivity and cooperative engineering, wide area CAD/CAM sessions will become more common, creating a significant demand on local as well as wide area networks.

Distributed computing. Finally, the architecture which is to deliver all of these distributed applications makes some significant demands on the network itself. Distributed management of not just internetworking devices, but also database servers, and applications or object servers, will require significant amounts of management traffic to be transmitted. Routers must be constantly communicating to keep routing tables up to date.

Although router-to-router protocols may change and become more efficient over time, the network impact of discovery, keep-alive, and polling messages cannot be ignored.

Applications Are Bandwidth Drivers

In order to predict bandwidth requirements for a given location, one must be able to predict what applications, or **bandwidth drivers,** will be executed at that particular location. By referring once again to the top-down model, it should be obvious that strategic business objectives and detailed business process analysis or reengineering will reveal which of these bandwidth-hungry applications might be required.

Figure 13-2 summarizes significant business trends and user demands that may have an impact on the data communications environment of the near future. Those technological trends that are enabling strategic changes on the business layer of the top-down model are mentioned as well.

☐ REGULATORY, LEGISLATIVE AND CARRIER TRENDS

Regulatory trends have a great deal to do with the overall complexion of the data communications environment of the future. The carriers, including RBOCs and

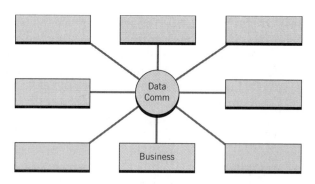

Trend	Explanation/Implication
Increased desire for less paper shuffling (customer-oriented re-engineering)	By automating document flow through a combination of imaging technology and work flow software, drastic increases in productivity and improved customer service can be achieved
Business process re-engineering	Integrated computer-assisted software engineering tools that support business process re-engineering can be linked directly to computer assisted network engineering software. Technology applied to inefficient business processes will not eliminate the inefficiency of the process
Outsourcing	By no means a guaranteed success story for all companies, outsourcing does make sense and saves money under certain circumstances. Best situations require close scrutiny, monitoring, and management by user organization
Demise of the mainframe and computer industry downturn	Emphasis on distributed or client/server computing has focused more attention than ever on networking. Multivendor, multiplatform, multiprotocol networks are becoming the norm as enterprise networks grow in both scope and importance
Corporate downsizing	Sometimes referred to as the flattening of corporate America, downsizing has created opportunity for networking, E-mail, groupware, and videoconferencing to increase productivity while reducing time spent in meetings
User demands	Bandwidth on demand Universal access/service Usage-based billing Transparent interoperability and any-to-any networking Better decision support/artificial intelligence software

Figure 13-2 Business trends and the data communications environment.

inter-exchange carriers, which provide wide area network services, are all subject to regulatory constraint as to which services may be offered as well as the rates that may be charged for those services.

Modified Final Judgment

The legal instrument that continues to control divestiture and the operation of AT&T and the RBOCs is known as the **modified final judgment,** or MFJ, and is administered by Federal Justice Harold H. Greene. Although the Justice Department's control of the American telecommunications industry originated in the late 1970s, rulings and interpretations have been issued on an ongoing basis since. A recent ruling with the potentially greatest impact on the data communications environment was the ruling which allowed RBOCs to offer value-added services, such as news, information, and video services, over their own networks. Field trials of video-dialtone by various carriers are underway.

Cable TV Regulation

Also in the same relative timeframe, Congress passed the Cable Regulation Act which, among other things, gives local government agencies more authority over the regulation of rates for local cable companies. Cable TV is currently a one-way, broadcast service. However, cable TV companies are conducting field trials in order to gain experience and a market toe-hold in the video-on-demand market. Video-on-demand requires the ability within the network to handle two-way communication, one for requests for video services from users and the other for the delivery of those requested video services.

In some cases, RBOCs and local cable companies have entered into cooperative field trials drawing on each other's respective strengths and experience. NYNEX and Liberty Cable have entered into such a field trial in New York City. Figure 13-3 illustrates the potential for competition between carriers and cable companies for the potentially lucrative video-on-demand market.

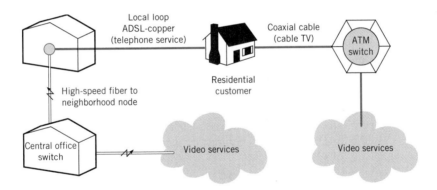

Telephone Companies	Comparative Characteristics	Cable TV Companies
Local carrier	Service provider	Local cable TV
Voice	Classic market	Cable TV
Voice Video-on-demand Bandwidth-on-demand?	Expanded market	Cable TV Video-on-demand Voice?
July 1992: carriers allowed to deliver video services	Regulatory status	Cable Bill 1992 regulated by local authorities
Underway	Trials	Underway
Must add sufficient bandwidth for video at a reasonable cost	Technological challenges	Must add two-way transmission and switching

Figure 13-3 Competing for your video-on-demand dollar: Telcos and cable companies.

An important technological aspect of this competitive environment is that it is the establishment of the digital data highway to people's homes that is most important in the eyes of both the carriers and the cable TV companies. The specific services delivered to homes can be decided upon at a later date, once the digital pipeline has been established. From a technological standpoint, if cable companies can establish the digital residential connection more quickly and effectively, then there is no *technological* reason that they could not transport digitized voice over that network as well.

However, without central offices for switching calls and handling billing and administrative tasks, the cable companies will be hard-pressed to offer voice services over a widespread area even if regulatory authorities allow such services. Perhaps the most likely scenario is an eventual cooperative effort on the parts of the cable industry and the carriers to work together for the delivery of voice, data, and video services to residential and business customers. Figure 13-3 summarizes some of the issues concerning competing interests in the video-on-demand market.

Spectrum Allocation

Another federal regulatory issue with the potential for significant impact on the data communications environment is the allocation of sufficient frequency spectrum to support the demand for wide area *wireless* voice and data services. In fact, if wireless services are to reach their full potential, this allocated spectrum is not just a federal issue but an *international* issue as spectrum will have to be allocated around the world for such wireless services. The problem in the United States is: Where will this needed spectrum come from?

There are only two possible answers: from the current holders of rights to certain frequency ranges or from the reserve of spectrum which the federal government has kept for itself. In fact, this is both a *legislative* as well as a regulatory process as Congress must first pass legislation in order to allocate the bandwidth while the FCC will subsequently enact the legislation.

Increased Competition

State regulatory authorities, generally known as Public Utilities Commissions, are also facing some interesting trends. In many states, **intra-LATA competition** is now allowed. In this scenario, carriers other than the local RBOC—possibly interexchange carriers such as AT&T, MCI, or Sprint, or even another RBOC—would sell intra-LATA local and long-distance services, often over the RBOC's network. These alternate carriers pay an **access charge** to the local RBOCs for the privilege of using their network. The state regulatory authorities assure that alternate carriers are able to compete for the intra-LATA traffic by restricting these access charges to a sufficiently low level.

Related to intra-LATA competition is a concept known as **colocation.** When colocation is mandated by state regulatory commissions, RBOCs must allow other carriers or even customers to locate their own switching equipment inside the RBOCs central office. From a regulatory standpoint, the idea behind colocation is to assure that the RBOCs as well as their competitors are able to offer the same level of service and convenience to their customers.

Alternative Regulatory Scenarios

Another important state regulatory trend is known as **incentive regulation.** With traditional or earnings-based regulation, a carrier is allowed to make a certain amount of profit or earnings during the time period of a regulatory agreement. Any profit generated above and beyond this earnings ceiling is most often returned to customers in the form of rebates.

One of the weaknesses with earnings-based regulation is that there is no real incentive on the part of the carrier to operate more efficiently or cost-effectively from either a technical or operations standpoint. Therefore, many states are now adopting some form or another of incentive regulation in which the earnings cap is removed in exchange for rate guarantees and/or promises of technological improvements, such as a commitment to upgrade all central offices to fully digital technology.

The Intelligent Network

From a carrier's standpoint, competition in both inter- and intra-LATA arenas has created a need to design services based primarily on users' needs and demands rather than on carriers' desires. In general, this has fostered an "opening up" of the once sealed realm of the carrier's network. Bundled loosely as **intelligent network services,** these service offerings allow users to look and sometimes touch inside the carrier network. For instance, wide area network performance statistics are output from some carriers and captured by users' network management stations. In this way, users can monitor and control not just local area but also wide area network resources from a single location.

Configuration options include private **SDN**s (software defined networks) in which users can reroute calls dynamically to alternate locations in the event of a need for load balancing or disaster recovery. Network reconfiguration services allow users to allocate traffic over additional facilities. However, at this time, users can only allocate traffic over facilities which have already been provisioned, or installed, for their own use. Although not quite there yet, all of these *user empowerment* services are ever closer to the goal of *bandwidth-on-demand*.

Bypass

A final issue or trend facing RBOCs which bears mentioning is **bypass.** Bypass entails the transmission of data or voice without employing the service of the local carrier. Bypassing the local phone company means lost revenue to the local phone company. Bypass transmission may be between two user locations or between a user location and the nearest POP of a long-distance carrier. Bypass always resurfaces as an issue whenever some type of transmission-related disaster strikes.

For instance, in May 1989, a fire in a central office in Hinsdale, Illinois left many suburban Chicago businesses without long-distance service for several days. Some companies had had the foresight to install bypass systems directly to POPs of long-distances carriers. Other businesses were less fortunate and, in many cases, suffered great financial losses or even closure as a result of this telecommunications tragedy. Although bypass transmission may be a negative circumstance for local carriers and RBOCs, it is the lifeblood of an entirely new telecommunications market niche known as bypass or **alternative access carriers.**

International Issues

From an international perspective, in many cases the relationship between governmental regulatory agencies and the telecommunications carriers seem to be following trends similar to the United States. For instance, in Canada, Japan, and much of Europe, *deregulation* either has been enacted or is under consideration in order to introduce competition into the telecommunications infrastructure of these countries. In many cases, this transition may be even more difficult than the break-up of AT&T, as many of the telecommunications companies around the world are totally government owned.

As telecommunications deregulation continues around the world, the concept of **global carriers** will emerge as regulatory constraints to such multinational corporations are gradually eliminated. MCI's partnership with British Telecom is an example of such a global presence. From a user's perspective, global carriers will probably mean a more coordinated, one-stop-shopping approach to global networking offering improved services at more reasonable prices.

Figure 13-4 summarizes many of the regulatory and carrier-related trends which could affect the future data communications environment.

☐ STANDARDS-MAKING ORGANIZATIONS

Implications of Ad Hoc Standards Making Organizations

In Chapter 1, a relatively few standards making organizations such as ANSI, CCITT, and ISO were mentioned. Figure 1-9 illustrated the possible lag time between technological development and the final issuance of official standards by one of these recognized standards-making organizations. Perhaps in response to this lag time, or perhaps in response to the ever-broadening scope of data communications-related technology, many **ad hoc standards-making organizations** have formed. Known by a variety of terms including task forces, user groups, interest groups, consortium, forum, alliances, or institutes, these groups have taken it upon themselves to develop standards for specific areas of the data communications industry.

Although able to produce standards faster, in most cases, than "official" standards making organizations, the existence and operation of these ad hoc standards-making organizations pose a few potential problems. Vendor-initiated ad hoc standards-making organizations are occasionally organized into opposing camps, with users left victims between multiple standards for a single operation. These vendor-driven consortia do not necessarily have the best interests of end-users as their highest priority. For example, in the area of multiprotocol packet drivers for network adapter cards, NDIS and ODI are both standards with a significant following.

Likewise, in the area of E-mail APIs, MAPI and VMI are both viable alternatives. In some cases, users have successfully demanded that a single standard be set from multiple possibilities. In the case of E-mail APIs, an organization known as XAPIA (X.400 API Association) has been formed to recommend a single universal E-mail API.

Interim standards proposals are also occasionally the result of the relatively slow official standards-making process. For example, due to the length of time expected to get a V.Fast (V.34) modem standard proposed and ratified, an interim standard known as *V.32ter* delivering 19.2Kbps transmission speed has been proposed by vendors. This interim standard has run into some difficulty due to conflicting technical implementations of the standard from various vendors. In this case, "ter" refers to the third version of the V.32 standard, and is popularly incorporated into the standard as V.32terbo.

Occasionally, different ad hoc standards-making organizations may even share the same name, thereby adding to the confusion they were formed to eliminate. For example, the *SMDS Interest Group* based in the United States has a distinct mission from a similarly named European organization. While the U.S. SMDS

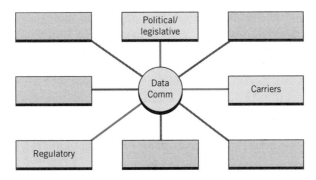

Trend	Explanation/implication
Competition between carriers and cable TV industry for video-on-demand services	Both carriers and cable TV operators want to be the dominant market force in the lucrative video-on-demand market. Field trials are underway. Cooperation between carriers and cable TV operators may be the ultimate solution
Spectrum allocation for wireless services	Without adequate frequency allocation on an international basis, the vision of transparent data and voice access from anywhere in the world may never become a reality
Intra-LATA competition	Deregulation of the local loop. Access charges to local network which are charged to alternative carriers must be low enough to allow alternate carriers to remain competitive
CO-location	Alternative carriers, as well as large end-users, are allowed to locate their transmission and switching equipment within local carrier's central office
Incentive regulation	As opposed to traditional earnings—cap regulation—incentive regulation encourages carriers to operate more efficiently and invest in new technology
Intelligent network services, SDNs	Opening up the carrier network to the user. Performance statistics, rerouting of calls, and reconfiguration of provisioned circuits are among the possibilities
ByPass	Can be between user locations or from user location to POP of long-distance carrier. Microwave often employed. Used effectively as disaster recovery technique
Global carriers	As international telecommunications become further deregulated, opportunities will arise for a new class of telecommunications companies known as global carriers

Figure 13-4 Regulatory, legislative, and carrier trends and the data communications environment.

group has been focusing its attention on access-line technology to SMDS networks, the European organization has been advocating the universal adoption of the IEEE 802.6 MAN standard for SMDS also known as DQDB (distributed queue dual bus).

Research Priorities
Rather than continuing in this pattern of forming new standards making organizations as needed and proposing new protocols for every new data communications opportunity, perhaps it is time to step back and take a broader view of protocol development, proposal, and interaction. This recommendation to *investigate the*

theoretical foundations of protocol design and engineering is one of the major conclusions of a National Science Foundation study entitled *Research Priorities in Networking and Communication.* The desired end result of such research is the ability to produce protocols with such qualities as "reusability, portability, efficiency, correctness, modifiability, and maintainability."

Figure 13-5 lists additional standards-making organizations and their purpose or general area of interest. The list is by no means exhaustive, but nonetheless serves as an indication of the sheer enormity of the protocol standardization process as it relates to data communications and networking.

Standards Developed in Response to Business Demand

ISO 9000   Certainly one of the most prevalent business trends of the last few years has to be *TQM* (total quality management). One of the major frustrations of data communications professionals attempting to implement total quality networks (TQN?) has been the dependence on technology which was developed and manufactured by organizations over whose quality these same data communications professionals had no control.

Perhaps in response to this situation, the International Standards Organization has established a rigorous certification program to assure quality in the development, design, manufacture, testing, inspection, and installation of data communications and networking equipment. *ISO 9000* is a certification which signifies that a given company has documented in detail the procedures in place to assure quality throughout a product's development life cycle. The implementation of these quality principles is then verified by on-site, independent auditors before the official ISO certification is granted. Continuing inspections by auditors help to assure continued compliance with established quality-control procedures.

It is important to note that ISO 9000 certification assures that the product was developed in a quality manner, but does not necessarily assure its suitability to perform in a given networking situation. In other words, an ISO 9000 certified device will perform according to its product specifications, but that does not necessarily mean it will solve a given networking problem.

The ISO 9000 certification does not preclude the need for network analysts to ask detailed questions and pay unwavering attention to technical details in order to assure that the proper networking device is employed to solve each unique networking situation.

☐ RESEARCH AND TECHNOLOGY—GENERAL TRENDS

Before exploring technological trends and advances which apply to a specific area of data communications and networking such as LANs, WANs, or internetworking, it may be helpful to first explore some general data communications trends. General data communications trends should be related in some way to the general business trends discussed earlier. It should be clear by now that the achievement of future business objectives will be delivered via the data communications network of the future.

Chip Development

Whereas most data communications transmissions are digital in nature, it should come as no surprise that at the heart of most data communications devices is a *DSP* (digital signal processor). Referring back to the generalized business user demands of data communications as outlined earlier in this chapter, one can see easy, trans-

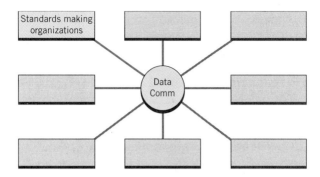

Organization Name and Abbreviation	Purpose/Area of Interest
European Telecommunications Standards Institute	Standardized ISDN Application Program Interface
ATM Forum	All issues of standardization regarding deployment of asynchronous transfer mode technology
INTERNET Engineering Task Force—IETF	1. PPP (Point to Point Protocol) for serial access to INTERNET 2. E-mail security 3. HUB/Repeater MIB (Management Information Base) definition
INTERNET Engineering Steering Group	SNMP2 and Secure SNMP
INTERNET Architecture Board	Dealing with impending INTERNET address crisis. Given the current address scheme, available addresses may be exhausted as soon as 1995
National Institute of Standards & Technology	Producing its own E-mail security recommendation in conflict with IETF proposal
IEEE 802.x groups	Working on a variety of LAN-related issues including specification for voice/data LAN (802.9) and an enhanced parallel port which operated at 1.5Mbps
AppleTalk Networking Forum	Working to make AppleTalk more easily integrated with other networking protocols
Global Service Providers Group	Developing standards for international high bandwidth digital switched services based on ISDN B channels
Multimedia and Hypermedia Information Coding Expert Group	Developing standards for WAN communication of multimedia files containing multiple linked objects
FAX Bios Association	Developing standards for integrating FAX capabilities into personal application software such as word processing, spreadsheets, and database

Figure 13-5 Trends in standards making organizatons.

parent access as key aspects of any future networking device or service. The speed, ease of use, and transparency of any future data communications device will depend largely on the speed and sophistication of the DSPs contained within that device.

Recent advances in chip technology make the prospect of significantly faster and more sophisticated data communications devices a real possibility. To be specific, AT&T Bell Laboratories scientists have been able to produce computer chips that can send and receive data via packets of light rather than by pulses of electricity as is the case with today's computer chips and integrated circuits. When fully developed, this technology will enable faster DSPs and other processing chips which will be incorporated into devices delivering such things as faster signal switching and image processing. As production increases, prices of these sophisticated chips will fall enabling their inclusion in still more data communications and networking devices.

The Electronic Superhighway

Given the aforementioned as well as other technological improvements, what is the network of the future likely to resemble from the user perspective? The terms *information backbone* and **electronic superhighway** are often used to refer to the network of the future. Not unlike the services offered by carrier and cable operator pilot tests, these information superhighways will offer voice, data, and video services of all types through a single interface to business and residential users. Home shopping, banking, and video programming will all be as close as a TV remote control device. Menu-driven application programs will allow subscribers to select only those services they desire.

How will such video-on-demand, or video dialtone, services differ from pay-per-view services currently available on many cable TV systems? The answer is: In at least two important ways. First, the video service will be available whenever consumers wish rather than at predetermined starting times decided upon by the cable service. Specially developed video jukeboxes will be employed to offer video services to multiple customers simultaneously.

Secondly, the service will be ordered via a "back-channel" on the copper local loop currently carrying phone service to most residences. The new video transmission and current voice transmission can co-exist on existing copper local loops. A new transmission protocol known as **ADSL** (asymmetrical digital subscriber line) will be employed to enable this two-way transmission. Current pay-per-view services are ordered via a separate phone call to the cable operator.

NREN

In addition to the field trials of carriers and cable TV operators in this area, the U.S. government is also sponsoring research in the area of super-networks and super-computing with the launching of its **NREN** (National Research and Education Network) project. Sometimes seen as a multi-gigabit upgrade to the Internet backbone, NREN researchers are exploring the details of what it takes to deliver a wide variety of services at multi-gigabit speeds. "What it takes" can be divided into several major areas of important research. Key among these are the network architectures that can cost-effectively deliver required bandwidth up to the multi-gigabit range, the protocols which will assure the reliability of the delivered payloads, and the applications with which users will interface to this electronic superhighway.

Interim steps are planned on the road to the multi-gigabit backbone with initial plans calling for the Internet backbone to be upgraded from T-3 (45Mbps) speeds to 155Mbps (OC-3 SONET). From an architectural standpoint, both *transmission* as well as *switching* technologies will be researched. SONET at OC-12 (622Mbps) and ATM are the current transmission and switching testing platforms, respectively.

Connectivity to this multi-gigabit superhighway by high-speed workstations or LANs is another area being investigated. Using an analogy to the construction of the interstate highway system, the design of safe and reliable access from smaller roads was as important as the construction of the multilane high-speed highways themselves. Many of the protocols necessary to effectively control bandwidth management and congestion control at multi-gigabit speeds have yet to be developed. High-bandwidth applications for such an information superhighway include many variants of medical imaging including MRI and CAT scans.

HPCC

NREN is actually only part of a larger initiative known as **HPCC** (high performance computing and communications initiative). Additional areas of research to be funded under HPCC that could have a bearing on the electronic superhighway or the future state of data communications include investigations of optical computing, and optical switching. Optical transmission is currently a reality with the use of fiber optic media and such transmission methodologies as SONET. When optical computing and optical switching become a reality, we will have closed the loop on optical processing and be truly processing and transporting information at speeds up to the speed of light.

Recommendations of the National Science Foundation

In a document entitled *Research Priorities in Networking and Communication*, the National Science Foundation outlines recommendations for research in several other areas of data communications as well. Among the most interesting conclusions of the report was the fact that, where data communications and networking research are concerned, "funding levels are still well short of the needs of the field relative to its national importance."

Calls for increased support of not only research, but also advanced education in networking and communications were key among the recommendations of the report. The report outlined 17 priorities for basic research in data communications and networking. Among these were:

Coding and coded modulation
Data compression
Communications signal processing
Radio systems and networks
Mobile network management
Protocol theory, design, and engineering
Network interface architectures
Dynamic network control
Internetworking
Lightwave network architectures
Network security and survivability
Switching systems
Fundamental limits of networking
Networking of applications

Many of these recommended topics of research are extensions of topics introduced earlier in this text and illustrate additional, fundamental trends in data communications which could influence the field of networking and its impact on business for many years to come.

Figure 13-6 summarizes some of the important research and technology trends which may have a major impact on the future data communications environment.

☐ EMERGING TECHNOLOGY

From a manufacturer's standpoint, technology is brought to market which will hopefully meet with significant demand and generate a reasonable profit. Market demand is largely a product of users' outlook on networking requirements as

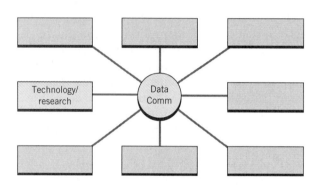

Trend	Explanation/implication
Computer chips with integrated optical transmission	Each chip contains multiple communication switching elements. Future versions of these photonic chips will contain thousands of switching elements allowing higher processing speeds than current chip technology. These extremely powerful computer chips will be used as signal processors in data communications devices
Electronic Superhighway	Also known as information backbone. From a consumer viewpoint the electronic superhighway will be the single source for all voice and video-on-demand services. Multi-billion-dollar market that is being contended for by phone and cable TV companies
NREN (National Research and Education Network)	A vision of a multi-gigabit information backbone upgrade to the current INTERNET. Current activity centers around research into architectures, protocols, and applications that will be used to implement this information backbone
National Science Foundation Research priorities	Today's research priorities indicate tomorrow's technology trends. Some important conclusions: Need for advanced educational opportunities in networking and communication; need for greater funding levels for research in networking and communications. Some significant research topic priorities:

Coding and coded modulation	Data compression
Communications signal processing	Radio systems and networks
Mobile network management	Dynamic network control
Protocol theory, design, and engineering	Network interface architectures
Internetworking	Lightwave network architectures
Network security and survivability	Switching systems
Fundamental limits of networking	Networking of applications

Figure 13-6 Research and technology trends and the future data communications environment.

viewed through the frame of reference of strategic business objectives. Reviewing the **declaration of the network user of the 1990s** stated previously:

From a single device; easy, transparent access to people or knowledge resources, regardless of location, with sufficient bandwidth at a reasonable cost to support business and decision-making processes.

This single statement of user demands cuts across networking platforms from LANs, through internetworking and MANs, and ultimately to WANs. Because emerging technology is brought to market in anticipation of immediate or near immediate demand and acceptance, it is difficult to predict networking trends far into the future based on currently emerging networking technology.

Nonetheless, a survey of emerging technology across LAN, internetworking, and WAN platforms does reveal trends that tend to support the vision described in the declaration of the network user of the 90s. The analysis of this emerging networking technology will be divided into four sections: LANs, internetworking, MANs and WANs, and finally wireless technology.

LANs

An analysis of emerging LAN technology can be categorically segmented into hardware and software trends. In the hardware category, trends in servers and workstations will be discussed; while on the software side, trends in network architectures, network operating systems, graphical user interfaces, and networking applications will be reviewed.

Factory Installed Networking   The heart of any network architecture such as Ethernet or Token Ring is the network interface card (NIC), and the heart of the interface card is the computer chip which processes the Ethernet or Token Ring frames. The prices of these chips continue to drop allowing PC makers to include built-in network connectivity. This network-readiness may be either in the form of an additional card known as a daughter board or as chips installed directly on the main processing board, known as the mother board.

According to the Gartner Group, the majority of PCs will ship network-ready beginning around 1994. One potential pitfall to this grand scheme is the question of which network architecture should be installed. Among the choices are Ethernet, Token Ring, Fast Ethernet, FDDI, CDDI, or perhaps even ATM.

By choosing *wireless* network interface adapters for factory installation in workstations and servers, manufacturers can eliminate any need for, or possible confusion over, network wiring. By also installing self-configuring peer-to-peer networking software such as Windows for Workgroups, manufacturers can offer networks which are fully operational after merely being unpacked and plugged in.

The LAN Superbox   Also known as a Superserver, GODBox, or numerous other superlatives, this modular server packs local area, wide area, and internetworking components into a single chassis with sufficient fault tolerance and disaster-recovery capabilities to overcome its obvious single-point-of-failure stigma.

By combining the functions of hubs, bridges, and multiprotocol routers, all over a common switching platform such as ATM, a superbox offers the opportunity for all network traffic to travel through a single device. This presents a perfect opportunity for inclusion of protocol analyzers and monitoring tools as well as network management modules and the SNMP agents required to deliver performance data. By having all components integrated in a single chassis by a single manufacturer, subtle inter-device incompatibilities which can negatively effect performance—as well as the subsequent, inevitable, finger-pointing—can be avoided.

More Bandwidth to the Desktop   It should come as no surprise that a likely trend in LANs will be more bandwidth to the desktop with numbers such as 100Mbps often suggested. The question becomes, Which network architecture will likely deliver the 100 Mbps? FDDI and CDDI are certainly viable alternatives. ATM, which has the potential for transmission speeds far greater than 100Mbps, is also a possibility.

The type of media required to be run to each desktop will have a lot to do with which network architecture becomes widely deployed. UTP, unshielded twisted pair, is inexpensive and easy to work with. In addition, UTP is currently installed in many networks due to the popularity of Ethernet's 10BaseT standard, thereby precluding the need to rewire for higher network performance. Recall, however, that there are multiple types of UTP. Voice-grade UTP, the least expensive, is perfectly suitable for 10Mbps Ethernet, but not necessarily of sufficient quality for 100Mbps network architecture alternatives.

CDDI specifies running 100 Mbps over data-grade UTP, although products such as network interface cards have been relatively slow to market and rather pricey ($900–$1500) when compared with current Ethernet NIC prices ($150–$200). The possibility of running a *slowed-down ATM* at 25Mbps is being investigated by the ATM Forum while proposals for **fast Ethernet** at 100 Mbps have also been proposed.

Fast Ethernet   Part of the appeal of fast Ethernet centers around its ability to run over the same voice-grade UTP employed in current 10BaseT Ethernet networks. One of the potential stumbling blocks to the acceptance of a fast Ethernet standard is that there are conflicting proposals on the exact protocol details of the fast Ethernet network architecture.

Much of the controversy of the standards-making process centers around the MAC (media access control) protocol to be used. 10Mbps Ethernet employs CSMA/CD, while at least one of the fast Ethernet proposals, known as 100Base-VG, advocates replacing CSMA/CD with an access methodology known as **demand priority protocol.** Detractors argue that Ethernet without CSMA/CD is not Ethernet, while proponents point out that DPP will allow transmission of delay-sensitive payloads such as voice and video due to its ability to prioritize transmissions. CSMA/CD offers no process for prioritization.

Unfortunately, the IEEE 802 committee responsible for choosing a Fast Ethernet standard was unable to choose between the alternative proposals. As a result, 100Base-VG, also known as 100VG-AnyLAN, was given the designator IEEE 802.12 while the 100 Mbps Ethernet with CSMA/CD will either be given its own standard number in the future or may be designated as an update to IEEE 802.3. The real losers in this situation are the data communications users. Choices between rival standards will be difficult as vendors lobby conflicting claims as to which standard is the best user choice.

LAN Switches   Another method of delivering increased bandwidth to each LAN-attached workstation creates a separate LAN segment for each workstation. Ethernet switches, as well as emerging FDDI switches, deliver the full bandwidth of a given network architecture to each attached workstation rather than sharing that bandwidth among all attached workstations. Network switches may also turn out to be the wave of the future in the quest for the delivery of increased bandwidth to the desktop.

The Evolution of LAN Network Operating Systems Just as LAN network architectures are evolving, the network operating systems which run over these network architectures continue to evolve in response to changing user demands. As businesses have evolved into enterprises, the standalone departmental LAN has evolved into a highly distributed enterprise-wide network operating system.

Perhaps no LAN network operating system illustrates this evolution better than *Novell Netware.* With the release of Netware 4.0, Novell introduced named directory services which offer transparent enterprise-wide directory services for locating users and sharing resources up to over 1000 nodes. Such enterprise-wide directory services are not new, Banyan Vines has featured its StreetTalk global naming services for some time.

One of the keys to a successful distributed computing implementation is the ability to manage those distributed computing resources from a central location. Netware 4.0 offers that capability.

An architectural characteristic of Netware maintained in version 4.0 will continue to ensure the abundance of compatible enhancements to the basic network operating systems, NLMs (netware loadable modules) offer users the ability to tightly integrate features such as imaging or full-motion video into the basic network operating system.

AT&T and Novell are jointly developing a **telephony services NLM** which will integrate PBX functionality such as conference calls, call forwarding, and speed dialing with desktop PC features such as E-mail and faxing. In this manner, a user's telephone can be looked upon as just another workstation-attached input device, whose services are controlled from the users workstation offering well coordinated voice and data network functionality. The possibility may exist that third-party applications will bring **computer integrated telephony** applications to the LAN platform. In the past, CIT applications have run primarily in the minicomputer and mainframe environments.

Client Operating Systems As client–server architectures and distributed computing have begun to take hold, the designs of operating systems for the client and server components of the network have begun to diverge. Servers have gravitated towards high-performance operating system "engines" such as the previously mentioned Netware 4.0, while clients have concentrated on graphical user interfaces (GUI) and client-based tools which enhance the productivity of end-user computing.

Microsoft Windows has crossed the line from client operating system, or graphical user interface, into the networking arena with two recent product introductions: **Windows for Workgroups** and **Windows NT.**

Windows for Workgroups delivers on the "easy-to-use" demand of the declaration of the network users of the 90s. In addition to Windows, Windows for Workgroups includes E-mail, group scheduling software, and a peer-to-peer network operating system. Automatic detection and configuration of NICs also delivers on the "easy-to-use" requirement. The ease of setup and use of Windows for Workgroups does not imply a closed, or nonexpandable architecture, however. Users can easily attach to Netware or LAN Manager LANs or to other Windows for Workgroups LANs as well.

Windows NT (New Technology) is a 32-bit client operating system designed to support powerful client applications easily and transparently in a distributed computing environment. Built-in support for TCP/IP and SNMP management are indications of NT's ability to integrate easily into an enterprise-wide network. Local networking capabilities include built-in file sharing and printer sharing functionality. Available APIs (application program interface) and RPCs (remote procedure calls) constitute a quasi-middleware layer for transparent interfacing to distributed applications. The multitasking, multiprocessing nature of Windows NT allows it to be deployed as a server operating system as well in a separate product known as Windows NT Advanced Server. The truth is that most of the Microsoft LAN Manager network operating system has been built into Windows NT.

Microsoft and Novell are clearly the two current giants in the LAN operating system market. It is difficult to predict whether one will dominate in the near future with either Windows NT or Netware 4.0, respectively. Users must keep their own best interests in mind by applying only that technology which meets specific networking and business needs and by avoiding purchasing the latest technology as a result of market-hype and slick advertisements.

Figure 13-7 summarizes emerging trends in LAN hardware and software, as well as the possible implication of those trends.

Internetworks

Just as the LAN environment has emerging technological trends in both hardware and software categories, the realm of internetworking has important emerging trends in both areas as well.

Trend	Explanation/implication
Factory installed network	Falling chip prices allow vendors to ship PCs network ready. The question is, Which network architecture should be installed? Some vendors include wireless network adapters and pre-install networking software for true plug and play networking.
The SUPERBOX	The SUPERBOX not only combines hub, bridge, and router components over a common switching architecture, but also includes protocol analysis and network monitoring components in order to take full advantage of all network traffic passing through a single point—the SUPERBOX.
More bandwidth to the desktop	Speeds of 100 Mbps to the desktop are a definite possibility. The key question is which standard will dominate? Price may be the ultimate determining factor as FDDI, CDDI, ATM, and fast Ethernet are all possibilities. Competing proposals for fast Ethernet standards may delay standards making process.
Netware 4.0	More focused on distributed computing as named directory services supports up to 1000 nodes. NLMs continue to be developed for cutting-edge technologies such as imaging, video, and computer integrated telephony.
Windows for Workgroups	Includes auto-configuring network operating system, E-mail, group scheduling software, and, of course, Windows. All have links to Netware and LAN Manager.
Windows NT	32-bit client/server operating system GUI with built-in TCP/IP and SNMP management capabilities. A powerful distributed computing front-end environment.

Figure 13-7 Emerging trends in LAN hardware and software.

Routers, the key hardware component of any internetwork, continue to evolve in terms of both processing power and sophistication. On the software side, middleware of various types offers the transparency between clients and servers demanded by users as stated in the declaration of the network user of the 90s.

Routers Router performance is most often measured in packets per second (PPS) for both filtering and forwarding rates. Filtering brings packets into the router, examines the network layer protocol information, consults routing tables, and decides on the best path for this packet to reach its destination. Forwarding involves physically placing the examined packet on the proper outbound interface card and appended circuit.

Maximum filtering and forwarding rates of 5000 to 10,000 were commonplace in the early 1990s. High-end centralized routers are now capable of forwarding hundreds of thousands of packets per second! Wellfleet Communications, whose Backbone Concentrator Node boasts forwarding rates of nearly 500,000 pps, has also formed an alliance with Novell to produce a more modestly performing software version router to run on Novell servers.

The concept of boundary routing, also known as peripheral routing, access routing, or bridged routing, was discussed in a previous chapter. In this routing scenario, lower cost, easier-to-use, less sophisticated routers are placed in remote offices. These remote "boundary" routers converse with high-powered central routers at corporate or regional headquarters buildings. The central routers are maintained by more technically adept network personnel, who keep routing and filter tables up to date. No such maintenance is required at the boundary routers since they draw all their routing information from the centralized routers. Boundary routing is an excellent example of an adaptation in networking technology in response to business-layer characteristics and was illustrated in Figure 12-19.

Middleware Middleware was first examined in Chapter 9. Middleware that offered transparency on the operating system and transport protocol level, as well as on the database level, was examined.

Pipes from Peerlogic, Inc. is perhaps the best example of operating system middleware. A component of Pipes known as a Pipes kernel runs on each client and server. Current operating environments supported include Windows, OS/2, UNIX, and MVS. These Pipes kernels keep in constant contact with each other creating a truly distributed operating system and providing total transparency to differences in transport protocols and operating systems for the user.

Glue from Oracle Corporation does much more than just provide simple database transparency. It provides transparency between numerous database front-end tools even including pen computers running Pen Windows or Pen Point. Data can be transparently retrieved from not only nearly every popular database but also from mail servers of various types, and even from personal digital assistants (PDAs) such as the Sharp Wizard.

Figure 13-8 summarizes emerging trends in internetworking hardware and software as well as their possible implications.

MANs and WANs

MANs Metropolitan area networks (MANs) are delivering on one of the key components of the declaration of the network users of the 90s; namely, transparency. More specifically, *transparent LAN interconnection* via MAN services offered by alternative carriers overcomes the tradition bottleneck imposed by WANs in

Trend	Explanation/Implication
Routers	Routers will continue to develop in terms of processing power and sophistication, offering increased performance and transparency in complicated multiprotocol environments. Lower-cost, less sophisticated, easy-to-use "boundary" routers will be deployed at remote LAN-attached sights.
Middleware– Operating System Network Transport Protocols	Offering transparency to differences in client and server operating systems and network transport protocols, *middleware* is at the very heart of distributed computing.
Middleware– Database	Distributed databases are part of the reality of distributed computing. Transparent access from multiple client-based front-end tools to multiple types of database, E-mail, and file servers is the job of database middleware. Oracle GLUE is one of the first examples of this category of middleware.

Figure 13-8 Internetworking hardware and software trends.

typical LAN to LAN interconnection. A variety of implementation architectures for MANs were introduced in Chapter 8 and summarized in Figure 8-1.

IEEE 802.6 DQDB (distributed queue dual bus) and FDDI are among the most popular MAN architectures, while SMDS (switched multimegabit data service) is probably the most popular MAN service.

Metropolitan Fiber Service (MFS) is the dominant player in the U.S. MAN market. Among the numerous competitors entering this market are several cable TV operators seeking to find alternate sources of revenue for established infrastructure. Spare capacity on cable TV systems seems like an ideal means of providing transparent LAN-to-LAN connectivity within a metropolitan area. The MAN market is also appealing to alternative carriers due to the projected financial growth of the market in the next few years. Estimates range anywhere from $500 million to $1 billion per year in potential revenue by the mid- to later 1990s.

Many corporations, however, need transparent inter-LAN connectivity not just within the metropolitan area covered by a cable TV system, but also *between* metropolitan areas as well. This is where an established alternative carrier such as MFS has an advantage over local or metropolitan cable operators. MFS has constructed a nationwide fiber optic network anchored by ATM switching technology. This nationwide capability will allow *switched inter-MAN* traffic to be carried over the MFS network. Initial inter-MAN offerings by MFS will carry traffic between New York, Chicago, and Washington, D.C., to be followed by coverage for all cities on the MFS network.

The logistics behind the installation and operation of the local loop portion of MANs has been simplified thanks to a recent regulatory trend, mentioned previously, known as colocation. With colocation, alternative carriers can conveniently gather LAN traffic from several local customers at an RBOC's central office (CO) and forward the conglomerated traffic onto their own metropolitan area network.

MAN activity is not confined solely to the United States. Australia offers MAN service in several cities, while MANs in Germany offer inter-LAN service transporting of not just data, but voice and video as well. In order for the delivery of true inter-LAN transparency, MAN, inter-MAN, and WAN traffic will have to be merged into a single, global service. Differences in services, architectures, and protocols will require resolution prior to the actualization of such a global vision.

WANs   The wide area network architecture of the future was first introduced in Figure 8-22, reprinted here as Figure 13-9. Perhaps the greatest value of such a diagram is not in the predicted services and protocols, but in the framework itself. Much like the value of the OSI Model, this wide area network architecture model can serve as a means of organizing and reconciling the relationships of the constituent parts of multiple future wide-area networking scenarios.

As new elements are offered, they can be placed in such an architecture for further analysis of their impact on other elements of the overall wide area network architecture. As possible future scenarios are described in the following section, consider their implication on the overall WAN architecture through the use of this WAN architecture framework. Based upon these concluded WAN architecture implications, what might be the comparative probability of the deployment of any proposed future WAN scenario?

A Changing Wide Area Network Architecture   Two important elements have been added to the wide area network architecture framework in Figure 13-9. The **access line** element was added to indicate the importance of the final leg of WAN service delivery to the customer. For instance, SMDS may be just what the customer ordered, and really needed, in terms of a data transport service. However, if a leased T-1 access line is required to access the SMDS service, and a user's data traffic is insufficient to justify the cost of the T-1, then the utility of the SMDS service becomes irrelevant.

The **network-to-network interface specification** element brings up another potential trap for the wide area network services customer. When contracting with

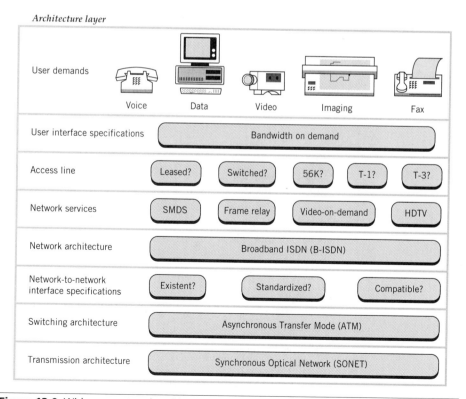

Figure 13-9 Wide area network architecture of the future.

a single carrier to deliver WAN data services of one type or another, network-to-network interface specification is usually not an issue because most carriers install architectures in a consistent manner across their service area. However, when requested long-distance WAN services require multiple carriers to coordinate the delivery of a customer's WAN traffic, interface specifications between multivendor networks are not necessarily compatible or even existent. The presence of this block in the overall WAN architecture forces a network analyst to consider this network-to-network interface specification.

Globalization Impact on Networks In order to consider possible future scenarios for wide area networking, one must really refer back to the top of the top-down model and reconsider wide area implications of the business layer. The key word in any such consideration is **globalization.** The effects of globalization can be felt through all layers of the top-down model. Globalization of business leads to:

> *Globalization of applications:* Multilingual, multicultural applications will be enabled in a distributed environment using object-oriented technology. By clicking on an icon representing a language, culture, or country, application level software will automatically reconfigure to the user's chosen environment. Global videoconferencing will save tremendously on international travel and will put increased demands on the global network. Such global applications will lead to:
>
> *Globalization of data:* The object-oriented multicultural applications previously mentioned will be implemented thanks to the methods and rules associated with the globalized data stored in multiple object servers, distributed around the world. This global distribution of data will lead to:
>
> *Globalization of networks:* Although international data networks are nothing new, the opportunity exists for a massive expansion of private global networks. One must, however, bear in mind a key element of the declaration of the network user of the 90s: *at a reasonable cost.* The news on the cost of global networks may be encouraging as international deregulation has led to increased international competition and the beginnings of an industrial phenomenon known as global carriers.

Is Desktop-to-WAN ATM in the Future?

Depending on which networking futurist one listens to, it is possible to hear varying opinions on the extent to which ATM will be deployed. ATM is a cell relay switching technology or architecture. Cell switches are currently being manufactured and deployed. Some conform to the 53-byte, cell-length ATM standard while others do not. These cell switches can be used to build private WAN networks.

The real questions concerning ATM are:

> When will carriers replace their existing switches with cell relay switches?
> and
> What percentage of all carrier switches will be replaced with ATM switches?

Until these questions are answered, it is difficult to make any solid predictions about the universal availability of WAN ATM services for global WAN data networking.

To add to the confusion, in terms of the WAN network architecture, ATM is an underlying switching architecture. The WAN services which are offered to users transparently employ ATM as an underlying switching fabric. Standards must be developed for the interface which connects these WAN services to the ATM switching fabric. Such *interface specifications* are currently being developed by the ATM Forum in order to allow SMDS and frame relay to run over ATM switching.

From a carrier's perspective, there is good reason to proceed with caution on replacing all of one's switching equipment. Unfortunately, ISDN has illustrated all too clearly the chicken-and-egg nature of this dilemma. Carriers do not want to commit to purchasing and installing expensive new equipment until sufficient user demand warrants such purchases. Conversely, users do not want to commit to purchasing cutting-edge WAN services until such services are available universally for all corporate locations. The outcome of such a situation will probably be a mixture of network services offered by a variety of different carriers for a period of time until a dominant technology prevails in the minds of both users and carriers. ATM may or may not be that technology.

ATM's Multiplatform Reputation

A large part of the appeal of ATM is that this same technology can be employed from a desktop workstation, through hubs, routers, and onto WANs. The implementation of ATM on the workstation, LAN, and inter-LAN is not nearly as complicated as on the WAN. If a user wants ATM in the LAN, all they have to do is purchase and install ATM network interface cards for their workstations, and upgrade their chassis-based, hub-concentrators with a new slide-in ATM module.

Hub-based ATM router modules will convert Ethernet or Token Ring frames to ATM cells prior to routing them to the nearest ATM switch. Using an ATM switch at the heart of a LAN rather than a hub or MAU will change a basic architectural characteristic of most of today's LANs. Rather than supporting a typical shared media LAN, an ATM switch supports a switched LAN architecture, much in the same way that an Ethernet switch offers the full 10Mbps to *each* attached workstation rather than having all workstations share the 10Mbps LAN media. Instead of Ethernet NICs building variable length Ethernet frames, the ATM card will build fixed length, 53-byte cells.

ATM's Efficiency

This brings up one of the frequently mentioned negatives concerning ATM: high overhead percentage. Five bytes of the 53-byte cells are actually header information. Header information is nothing new. Ethernet frames have headers. However, Ethernet frames can carry up to 1500 bytes of data for each header and ATM cells can only carry 48 bytes of data for each header. Is this seemingly high overhead percentage really an issue, however?

ATM's Dependence on Transmission Capacity

That really depends on the bandwidth of the circuit over which the ATM cells will be traveling. Recall that ATM is a switching architecture in the wide area network architecture model. The switching architecture must work cooperatively with the transmission architecture to deliver higher level WAN services. When it comes to transmission architectures, ATM is ideally suited for SONET which will be deployed initially at the OC-3 level of 155Mbps. With 155Mbps of bandwidth to play with, a 10 to 15 percent overhead percentage is not a large issue.

If this overhead proves to be excessive at lower bandwidth levels, such as T-1 or T-3, this may provide an opportunity for other WAN services such as SMDS or frame relay to fill that niche. Another WAN service that has really benefited from the demand of applications such as videoconferencing and LAN-interconnection accompanied by a lack of high-speed, reasonably priced services that can support video as well as data, is the switched 56K market.

Switched 56K Market   Prices for the **switched 56K** service range from $30 to $100 per month flat fee plus 3 to 14 cents per minute usage charges. Through the use of specialized CSU/DSUs and inverse multiplexers, users are able to dial-up bandwidth as needed on a *switched* basis, allowing for flexible reconfiguration of source and destination points. Fortunately, switched 56K is a standardized service among all of the RBOCS removing the worry concerning that key network-to-network interface introduced in the wide area network architecture model.

ATM—A Data-only Service?   A second current shortcoming of ATM which could be overcome with additional protocol and standards development is its current inability to transfer cell-switched voice and video as well as data. It would seem that as voice and video become increasingly integrated on the LAN, the need for WAN switching/transmission services to support this same payload integration transparently will increase as well. Currently available non-ATM cell switches from PBX vendors such as Northern Telecom can concurrently support voice, video, and data.

The isochronous or delay-sensitive nature of voice and video requires a different type of transmission than typical packetized LAN data. Some network architectures, such as the IEEE 802.6 metropolitan area network standard known as DQDB (distributed queue dual bus), are trying to offer the best of both worlds by offering circuit-switched isochronous transmission for voice and video while offering connectionless packet transmission for data.

Other ATM standards development needs include flow control and congestion control protocols. The ATM Forum, a vendor consortium, is working to develop proposals for necessary standards as quickly as possible for submission to official standards-making organizations such as ANSI and CCITT. The combination of the current lack of ATM standards, other previously mentioned shortcomings of ATM, as well as an understandable caution on the part of carriers in terms of wholesale investment in the technology, probably means a period of WAN architecture transition in which a multitude of services will be available from a variety of carriers. Figure 13-10 summarizes some of the issues surrounding WAN architectures of the future.

Wireless

In order to fully deliver on the "regardless of location" requirement of the declaration of the network user of the 1990s, both LANs and WANs will have to incorporate wireless technology. An analysis of currently available LAN and WAN tech-

Trend	Explanation/Implication
Globalization	Globalization of business has a ripple effect on all lower layers of the top-down model. Global networks must be designed in such a way as to support global business objectives. International deregulation and emergence of global carriers could reduce the operating expenses of global networks.
ATM (Asynchronous Transfer Mode)	Although seamless ATM communication from the workstation, through the LAN, to the WAN, is not beyond the realm of possibility, significant work, especially in the area of standards development remains to be done. ATM is a switching architecture or fabric that supports the WAN services to which users subscribe. With properly defined interfaces, SMDS, and frame relay or as yet unknown user services, can run over ATM.

Figure 13-10 Wide area networking trends and implications.

nology will reveal, however, that an overall lack of standardization and lack of allocated frequency spectrum are two key limiting factors to the "transparent" and "easy-to-use" requirements of the declaration.

LANs   Wireless LANs, including currently available technology alternatives, were explored in Chapter 5. Spread-spectrum, narrowband radio (otherwise known as microwave), and infra-red are the three wireless LAN transmission methodologies currently available. As stated in Chapter 5, wireless LANs have not turned out to be the *wire replacement* solution as they were first marketed. Rather, the application of wireless LANs as dictated by business needs and objectives has been to deploy wireless technology where wired LANs don't make sense. (For example, in older buildings in which data wiring would be excessively expensive, or in situations where LANs are to be set up in a temporary location for a limited amount of time.) Applications include outside auditing, stock inventories, seasonal customer service surges, or standby disaster recovery sights.

As a network analyst comparing wireless LAN alternatives, it is important to analyze which LAN components are being replaced with wireless technology. For instance, Motorola's Altair Wireless LAN consists of a user module and a central module. The user module is attached to the PC's *normal* Ethernet adapter card. Ethernet traffic is transmitted wirelessly to the Altair central unit which attaches to a wired hub or building backbone.

In contrast, NCR's Wavelan Wireless LAN requires a specialized Wavelan adapter card with an attached antenna. All PCs with Wavelan cards installed become a wireless LAN. In order to bridge to a wired backbone, two alternatives are possible. In the "homegrown" bridge scenario, one PC must be outfitted with both a Wavelan card as well as a wired Ethernet card. In the second scenario, a specialized NCR WavePOINT bridge can be employed.

Every NIC card, wired or wireless, requires drivers. If specialized cards such as the Wavelan card are to be used, make sure that the drivers that will be compatible with installed operating systems and network operating systems are included. Figure 13-11 illustrates the differences between these two popular wireless LANs.

Ethernet Means 10Mbps, Right?   Although wireless LANs are in fact transmitting Ethernet frames, they are not transmitting those frames at "native" Ethernet speeds of 10 Mbps. Most wireless Ethernet LANs have actual throughput of between 2.5Mbps and 5.7Mbps with some as little as 242Kbps. The truth is that even wired Ethernet has considerable overhead and delivers closer to 5.7Mbps than to the often quoted 10Mbps. The distance ranges between wireless Ethernet LAN stations are dependent on the LAN technology more than Ethernet distance limitations. Depending on the amount and nature of obstructions between wireless workstations, maximum distances can be as little as 40 feet.

Portable Computing + Wireless Networking = CWWA   The size of wireless LAN technology is shrinking along with the shrinking size of computers. PCMCIA-based wireless LAN adapters are now available for notebook and laptop size computers. This combination of portable computing and wireless LAN technology may be the critical mass required to really ignite the wireless LAN chain reaction. Workers or students could carry notebook computers with them throughout the day. In order to access corporate network facilities or computing resources, the worker or student would only need to get within range of one of the

Motorola Altair

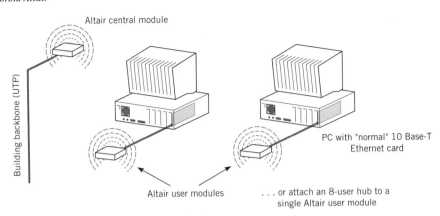

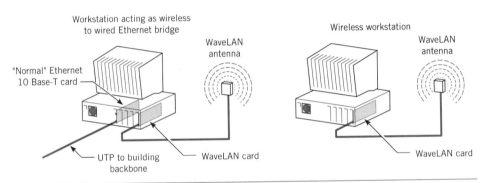

Figure 13-11 Wireless LANs are *not* all the same.

many wireless LAN hubs dispersed throughout the corporate or college campus. The combination of portable computing and wireless networking will yield a new paradigm in information systems—computing while wandering around **(CWWA).**

Wireless Technology   Nearly all emerging technologies analyzed in this chapter have suffered from a current lack of standardization. Wireless LANs are no exception. The various wireless LAN technologies employed by different manufacturers are all proprietary in nature and do not interoperate with each other. Help is on the way, however. The **IEEE 802.11** committee has set about the task of defining a new MAC (media access control) layer protocol which will be common to all wireless LANs regardless of the underlying wireless transmission methodology employed.

In addition, the internet engineering task force is in the process of defining a new **mobile IP** protocol which will allow network nodes (user's workstations) to change physical locations without changing IP addresses. This work is particularly important to the CWWA scenario depicted above. Finally, as part of the overall PCS (personal communications systems) frequency allocation proposal, a portion of frequency may be allocated to *wireless office networks* thereby adding to the standardization of the wireless LAN technology.

WANs   Many of the same issues surrounding wireless LANs apply to wireless WANs as well. For example, wireless WANs will only be successful if two key requirements can be met:

1. Significant demand for such services must be generated by business layer trends and objectives which require large numbers of mobile professionals to be in touch with customers and corporate headquarters via wireless WAN services regardless of location.

2. Equally as important as demand, without sufficient frequency allocation to support wireless WAN services, such services as PCS and wide area wireless data services will not become a reality.

In the meantime, wireless WAN service alternatives are available. However, these services, in general, fall short on the universal coverage and sufficient bandwidth requirements of the most demanding wireless WAN users.

Most such services are known as **packet radio nets.** The largest examples of such networks are ARDIS, which is a partnership of IBM and Motorola; and RAM Mobile Data. In order to access such services for data transmission, users must purchase a specialized *radio packet modem,* sometimes known as a **mobidem.** Among the shortcomings for such applications as wireless LAN interconnection over the wide area are the relatively slow speed of these services (4.8Kbps) and the proprietary nature of the transport and error control protocols within the network.

As a possible solution to some of these shortcomings, Motorola's Iridium Project is in the process of launching 77 low earth orbit **(LEO)** satellites which will eventually offer global coverage of wide area wireless data transmission. Still, significant work remains to be done in the area of standardization, especially for internetwork transmission. Another wireless WAN alternative is the use of the cellular network and a proposed standard known as **CDPD** (Cellular Digital Packet Data) to transmit data at 19.2 Kbps. Even with these present obstacles, the wireless WAN industry is forecasted to be supporting 5 million users and producing $175 million in annual revenue by the mid-to late 1990s.

PEOPLE IMPACT

From a network manager's perspective, the real value in examining emerging technology trends lies in being able to better anticipate the impact of such trends on business and network planning activities. Even as technology rapidly changes, the application of the changing technology to models or frameworks such as the top-down model and the wide area network architecture framework will assist in uncovering its potential.

The combination of paradigm shifts such as the trend to distributed computing and client–server architectures, combined with an increasingly competitive business climate, and rapidly changing technology can put an enormous strain on corporate networks and the people who must manage and operate those networks. It is important to examine both the current pressures and factors with which networking personnel must cope, as well as the opportunities that exist for individuals properly trained in the realm of enterprise networking, distributed computing, and client server architectures.

Pressures and Trends

Among the pressures and trends faced by today's networking professionals are increased demands on networks and the information systems they support, accompanied by decreased networking budgets and staffs as a result of corporate downsizing. Networks are growing in terms of numbers of workstations attached as well as complexity in the number of protocols which must be simultaneously supported. Mobile professionals must be transparently incorporated into corporate networks despite incompatible technologies and an overall lack of standards. Distributed computing and client–server architectures are forcing a need for software tools to accomplish centralized management of distributed networks. The only problem is that such standards based tools are virtually nonexistent.

Strategic planning of businesses as well as networks has become absolutely essential. However, given the speed with which networking technology is changing, it is virtually impossible to perform any meaningful strategic network planning beyond much more than a two-year horizon.

Coping with a Changing Networking Landscape

Given this seemingly impossible scenario as a backdrop, what can a network manager do to cope? Recall a few of the key points from chapter 12 on the network development life cycle. In such difficult situations as described above, it is more essential than ever to assure that network planning initiatives are closely tied to overall corporate business objectives as articulated by senior management. Verbal and written communication skills are essential in securing buy-in from all affected parties, in particular senior management. Reengineered network designs should be based on reengineered business processes.

From a network analyst's perspective, the best way to cope with such a situation is to stay informed. Read trade journals religiously, paying particular attention to the deployment plans and actions of carriers when it comes to new technology. Attend trade shows or professional conferences as often as possible, but at least once a year, to hear from industry leaders what's really going on at the cutting edge of networking technology.

Finally, evaluate technology from a top-down perspective. What functionality is actually being delivered and at what price? What does the cost/benefit analysis look like? In this way, one can avoid being swept up by the bandwagon effect and the media hype which all too often accompanies data communications technology.

Opportunities Created by Paradigm Shift to Client–Server

As more and more companies are addressing the shift from mainframe-based systems to distributed or client–server architectures, the consensus of opinion seems to be that the people issues of such a shift are more challenging than the technical issues. In many cases, people have spent more than 20 years in a mainframe/terminal environment and are being asked to completely shift their outlook on the design and delivery of corporate computing resources. The truth is that some of these people will not be able to make such a shift. It is estimated that between 10 and 30 percent of computer personnel will leave their present position rather than be retrained in the new client–server paradigm.

In order to make this transition between paradigms as smooth as possible, communication is once again the key. Overall strategic direction on both a corporate and information systems level should be shared and reinforced with personnel as often as possible. More specific implementation plans, schedules, and issues should be discussed as far in advance as possible. Surprises and sudden changes should be avoided whenever possible as people tend to focus more on job security when faced with significant change in their work environment. Change should be seen as an opportunity to update one's skills and increase one's value and marketability. It has been said that in business (and the same holds true for networking), there's no such thing as standing still or maintaining the status quo. If you're not moving forward, then you're losing ground to someone who is.

A shift of this magnitude in the basic architectural framework of information systems creates an enormous opportunity in the education and training sectors of the information systems and networking industry. Training requirements include not only operational level training on the new tools of the trade, but also strategic and tactical level training on planning and designing the shift to the new distributed computing paradigm. As stated frequently before, distributed computing has brought more attention than ever before to the key role that networks play in the overall information systems architecture. Without well-designed, intelligently deployed, and efficiently-managed distributed enterprise networks underlying the emerging client–server information systems, corporations are courting potential disaster.

As a result, those individuals who are fortunate enough to understand data communications and networking from a top-down, enterprise-wide perspective are in high demand and well compensated. The importance of the enterprise network in the client–server architecture has resulted in shifting job responsibilities and new job titles and descriptions. Increasingly, corporate networking resources for voice, data, and video are becoming the focus of centralized management, whereas in the past it was the shared processing power of the corporate mainframe which was the focus of centralized management attention. The real opportunities in this time of rapid technological change are for people who understand the "big picture" when it comes to data communications and networking.

By understanding that networking decisions are first and foremost business decisions, and by further understanding the importance of designing networks that meet business objectives through a thorough analysis of the distributed applications and data which must be delivered via this distributed enterprise network, networking professionals can truly distinguish themselves while enjoying a career that is most rewarding both professionally and financially.

CHAPTER SUMMARY

This final chapter reiterated a key initial premise of the book, introduced in Chapter 1. In order to understand emerging trends in networking and data communications, one must understand the trends in those business, technological, and regulatory arenas which have a direct effect on the data communications industry.

Both the systems model of the data communications industry and the top-down model were employed in the analysis of currently emerging trends of data communications and networking. Perhaps more importantly, it was pointed out how these models, as well as the wide area networking architecture framework, can be used in the future for analysis of the impact of business, regulatory, or technological trends on the data communications industry.

As this massive paradigm shift from mainframe/terminal-based systems to distributed computing systems unfolds, the impact on the people involved is enormous. Some people will not be able to handle the change and will leave their present positions while others will retool and retrain for the future. Tremendous opportunities exist for networking professionals properly trained in distributed systems and enterprise networking, as well as for people qualified to offer training and education in those areas.

KEY TERMS

access charge
access line
ad hoc standards-making
   organizations
ADSL
alternative carriers
bandwidth drivers
business process
   reengineering
bypass
CDPD
colocation

corporate downsizing
CWWA
declaration of the network
   user of the 1990s
demand priority protocol
electronic superhighway
fast Ethernet
global carriers
globalization
HPCC
incentive regulation
IEEE 802.11

intelligent network
   services
intra-LATA competition
LEO
mobidem
mobile IP
mobile professional
modified final judgment
network-to-network
   interface specification
NREN
outsourcing

packet radio nets
SDNs
switched 56K
systems diagram of the
   data communications
   industry
telephony services NLM
top-down model
Windows for Workgroups
Windows NT

REVIEW QUESTIONS

1. How can the top-down model and systems diagram of the data communications industry be used to organize and analyze trends that may affect the future of data communications and networking?

2. What are the present business trends which have the greatest potential impact on the data communications industry?

3. What are the present trends concerning regulation and the carriers which have the greatest potential impact on the data communications industry?

4. What are the expectations of users of the network of the 1990s?

5. What are the major bandwidth drivers affecting the future of networking?

6. What trends are currently evident in the standards-making arena and what is the potential impact of these trends?

7. What are the general trends in research and technology and what potential impact might these research priorities have?

8. What is NREN and how might that affect the data communications and networking industry?

9. For each category listed, state emerging technological trends and the potential impact of those trends:

   LAN
   Internetworking
   MAN/WAN
   Wireless

10. Given the paradigm shift from mainframes to client–server architectures, what are the potential impacts on the people affected by such a shift?

11. What are the opportunities created during a paradigm shift of such proportion?

12. What are the skills and/or perspectives required of networking professionals who will be designing and building the enterprise networks which will support distributed computing architectures?

13. What are the role and the effect of business process reengineering on network analysis and design?

14. What are some of the impacts on networking directly attributable to corporate downsizing?

15. What types of networking technology are likely to be demanded as a result of corporate downsizing?

16. How does the modified final judgement continue to affect the telecommunications industry?

17. What are some possible scenarios for the future role of the cable tv industry in telecommunications?

18. If intra-LATA competition becomes widespread, what will be the RBOC's major sources of revenue?

19. What are some of the difficulties with spectrum allocation for PCS?

20. What are the advantages of incentive regulation to the RBOCs?

21. What are the advantages of incentive regulation to states and consumers?

22. What are the advantages to large network users of intelligent network services?

23. What is the underlying enabling technology of the intelligent network?

24. What are the advantages and disadvantages of a bypass network?

25. What circumstances have enabled the formation of global carriers and what is their potential benefit?

26. What are some of the positive and negative effects of ad hoc standards-making organizations?

27. What are the role and limitations of the local loop in any electronic superhighway scenario?

28. What are some of the possibilities for the local loop of the future?

29. Which proposal for the local loop of the future do you believe is the most likely to be implemented and why?

30. What is the role of wireless technology in delivering requirements outlined in the declaration of the network user of the 90s?

31. What are some of the current negative characteristics of wireless technology?
32. What are some of the network architecture alternatives for high-capacity LAN bandwidth?
33. Which do you feel is the most likely LAN network architecture to be widely implemented and why?
34. Why do some data communications people feel that fast Ethernet is not Ethernet?
35. How has Netware allowed close integration of phone and computer usage?
36. What is the difference in terms of application, features, and sophistication between Windows NT and Windows for Workgroups?
37. What is the key negative attribute of wide area wireless networks?
38. What solutions have been proposed to this negative attribute? .
39. What two elements were added to the wide area network architecture in this chapter, and what is their significance?

40. Which areas of standardization of ATM are either underway or undeveloped?
41. Why is ATM considered a relatively inefficient switching/transmission architecture?
42. How can this inefficiency be minimized?
43. What user demands underlie the growing popularity of switched 56K services?
44. When does the installation of a wireless LAN make the most sense?
45. What are the attributes of a person who could survive the paradigm shift from mainframe/terminal to client/server?
46. What skills or actions might a network analyst exhibit to better cope with the rapid changes in the field of data communications?
47. What approach or frame of reference is most valuable to network analysts in times of rapid change?

ACTIVITIES

1. Contact your state Public Utilities Commission to investigate current issues being considered by the commission.
2. Request biographies of the people serving on the state Public Utilities Commission. What is the extent of their telecommunications background?
3. Contact the House of Representatives Committee on Telecommunications and ask about current members and pending legislation.
4. Contact the U.S. Senate Committee on Telecommunications and ask about current members and pending legislation.
5. Contact the White House and ask about administration initiatives and directions in the area of telecommunications in general and regarding the NREN (National Research and Education Network) in particular.
6. Contact your local RBOC and ask about the status of field trials in the areas of video dialtone or advanced packet services such as frame relay or SMDS.
7. Investigate and report on globalization efforts by AT&T and MCI.
8. Contact the ATM Forum, (415) 962-2593, and inquire about current and pending standards and operational issues being deliberated by that organization.
9. Dial into *Network World*'s Networking Careers On-Line, (508) 620-1178, (up to 9600bps, 8-N-1). Survey the career opportunities and note the kinds of skills required. What percentage of the positions require excellent verbal and written communications skills?

10. Contact Bellcore regarding their role in the assignment of the the 500 area code phone numbers for Personal Communications Systems (PCS).
11. Discuss Figure 13-1. How would you suggest changing the diagram, if at all? Are influences missing? Are some included influences unimportant enough to be removed? Develop your own model or diagram illustrating the current state of the data communications industry.
12. Using a reference such as *Business Week,* investigate and report on the efforts and relative success of business process reengineering by various companies. Can nonprofit organizations such as colleges or universities perform business process reengineering? Give examples of processes in your department which you believe deserve reengineering.
13. Debate the relative merits of PCS and/or video dialtone. Will these revolutionary new services be in high demand? Are they over-marketed hype on the part of the telecommunications industry? Or are they something in between?
14. Investigate why the Justice Department (Judge Harold Greene specifically), rather than the Federal Communications Commission, is overseeing the AT&T divestiture. What would have to happen for the authority to be transferred?
15. What were the major provisions of the Cable Regulation Bill of 1992? What effects, if any, have you seen in your local cable company? Contact your local cable company to inquire about their feelings about the legislation.

16. Conduct a survey of a student or business population of a generalized background (not all of them Data Comm students). Ask them what "ATM" stands for. Graph your results. What do your results tell you?

17. Contact your local cable TV company regarding any plans to transport anything other than cable TV (e.g., video-on-demand, LAN interconnection, voice, etc.).

Featured References

Alternate Access/Bypass

Messmer, Ellen. "Alternative Services Mart to Undergo Metamorphosis," *Network World*, vol. 9, no. 25 (June 22, 1992), p. 43.

Lindstrom, Ann. "MFS Launches Nationwide, Speedy LAN Link," *Telephony*, vol. 223, no. 15 (October 12, 1992), p. 8.

Future Competitive Environment

Mason, Charles. "What Does Cable Bill Mean for Telcos?," *Telephony*, vol. 223, no. 15 (October 12, 1992), p. 6.

Future Network Planning

Dortch, Michael. "Transitions to Tomorrow," *Communications Week*, no. 428 (November 9, 1992), p. 61.

General Business Trends

Cummings, Joanne. "Reengineering Falls Short of Expectations, Study Finds," *Network World*, vol. 10, no. 12 (March 22, 1993), p. 27.

Verity, John. "Deconstructing the Computer Industry," *Business Week*, no. 3294 (November 23, 1992), p. 90.

Micossi, Anita. "Facing the Future, Technology: How Will It Shape Your Organization?," *Enterprise*, vol. 6, no. 4 (April 1993), p. 20.

General Data Communications Trends

Brust, Lauren, and Mean-Sea Tsay. "Mixing Signals on Chip," *IEEE Spectrum*, vol. 30, no. 8 (August 1993), p. 40.

Kujuro, Akihito. "Systems Evolutions in Intelligent Buildings," *IEEE Communications*, vol. 31, no. 10 (October 1993), p. 22.

Kishimoto, Tomio. "Virtual Offices," *IEEE Communications*, vol. 31, no. 10 (October 1993), p. 36.

Huston, Dryver. "Intelligent Materials for Intelligent Structures," *IEEE Communications*, vol. 31, no. 10 (October 1993), p. 40.

Douligeris, Christos. "Intelligent Home Systems," *IEEE Communications*, vol. 31, no. 10 (October 1993), p. 52.

Anderson, Howard. "Networking: A View from the Next Century," *Data Communications*, vol. 21, no. 12 (September 1992), p. 129.

Rebello, Kathy, and Catherine Arnst. "The Great Digital Hope Could Be a Heartbreaker," *Business Week*, (November 30, 1992), p. 94.

Elmer-Dewitt, Philip. "Electronic Superhighway," *Time*, vol. 141, no. 15 (April 12, 1993), p. 50.

Walker, Robyn. "Bankers Say Networks Best Way to Improve Productivity," *LAN Times*, vol. 9, no. 8 (May 11, 1992), p. 49.

National Science Foundation. *Research Priorities in Networking and Communications*, National Science Foundation, Washington, D.C. (April 1992).

Yang, Dori, and Kathy Rebello. "Microsoft's Other Boss Jumps into Multimedia," *Business Week*, (November 30, 1992), p. 106.

Herman, James. "Superworkstations Will Change Networking Irrevocably," *Network World*, vol. 9, no. 27 (July 6, 1992), p. 35.

International Trends/ Standards

Mossotto, Cesare. "Pathways for Telecommunications: A European Outlook," *IEEE Communications*, vol. 31, no. 8 (August 1993), p. 52.

Siding, Wan. "An Overview of Telecommunications Planning in China," *IEEE Communications*, vol. 31, no. 7 (July 1993), p. 18.

Motiwalla, Juzar. "Building the Intelligent Island," *IEEE Communications*, vol. 31, no. 10 (October 1993), p. 28.

Zandleven, Ids. "A Leading Light in Pan-European Networking," *Data Communications*, vol. 21, no. 12 (September 1992), p. 113.

Cureton, Tim. "An Eastern Approach to Global Networking," *Data Communications*, vol. 21, no. 12 (September 1992), p. 119.

Heywood, Peter. "Global Carriers: Fresh Air for Cross-Border Networking," *Data Communications*, vol. 22, no. 6 (April 1993), p. 83.

Roussel, Anne-Marie. "ISO 9000: A Measure of the Measurement," *Data Communications*, vol. 22, no. 14 (October 1993), p. 55.

Internetworking

Jessup, Toby. "LAN-Speed Links Available Now," *LAN Times*, vol. 10, no. 5 (March 8, 1993), p. 32.

Dolgicer, Max, and Larry DeBoever. "Taking Middleware One Step Beyond," *Data Communications*, vol. 22, no. 6 (April 1993), p. 35.

Salamone, Salvatore. "Router Runs Faster by Getting off the Bus," *Data Communications*, vol. 22, no. 6 (April 1993), p. 35.

Lippis, Nick. "Crossover Dreams for Networking Vendors," *Data Communications*, vol. 22, no. 6 (April 1993), p. 31.

Salamone, Salvatore. "This Router's Ready for Remote Offices," *Data Communications*, vol. 22, no. 1 (January 1993), p. 64.

LANs

Didio, Laura. "Novell Makes Good on 4.0 Promises," *LAN Times*, vol. 10, no. 5 (May 10, 1993), p. 55.

Brown, Jim, and Stephen Mattin. "Looking into Windows for Workgroups," *Network World*, vol. 10, no. 5 (February 1, 1993), p. 55.

Saunders, Stephen. "Wireless LAN Users: Take a Hike," *Data Communications*, vol. 22, no. 10 (July, 1993), p. 49.

Layland, Robin. "The Superbox: A Cure for This Old LAN," *Data Communications*, vol. 21, no. 12 (September 1992), p. 103.

Brandel, William. "Novell, AT&T to Develop New Telephony Services," *LAN Times*, vol. 10, no. 2 (January 25, 1993), p. 1.

Linnell, Dennis. "Windows NT: Can Microsoft Make the Jump from the Desktop to Distributed Computing?" *Data Communications*, vol. 22, no. 6 (April 1993), p. 68.

Saunders, Stephen. "Wireless LANs: Closer to Cutting the Cord," *Data Communications*, vol. 22, no. 5 (March 21, 1993), p. 59.

Saunders, Stephen. "Ethernet Gears up for 100 Mbits/s," *Data Communications*, vol. 22, no. 2 (January 21, 1993), p. 35.

Chernicoff, David. "Wired for the Future," *PC Week*, (March 15, 1993), p. 49.

Brandel, William. "Low-Cost Chips Spur Network Ready PCs," *LAN Times*, vol. 10, no. 7 (April 5, 1993), p. 1.

Clegg, Peter. "Instant Networking: AST Builds Ready-to-Go System," *LAN Times*, vol. 10, no. 6 (March 22, 1993), p. 1.

Brandel, William. "Netware 4.0 Branches Out with Objects," *LAN Times*, vol. 10, no. 5 (March 8, 1993), p.1.

Brandel, William. "Netware 4.0 Is Ready to Roll," *LAN Times*, vol. 10, no. 3 (February 8, 1993), p. 1.

Brandel, William. "Fluent NLM Incorporates Video into Netware," *LAN Times*, vol. 10, no. 4 (February 22, 1993), p. 13.

Saunders, Stephen. "Choosing High Speed LANs," *Data Communications*, vol. 22, no. 13 (September 21, 1993), p. 58.

Management/People Issues

Eckerson, Wayne. "Net Managers Trim Costs, Keep Workers," *Network World*, vol. 9, no. 33 (June 8, 1992), p. 33.

Brown, Bob. "Client–Server Nets Spark Need for Computing Skills," *Network World*, vol. 10, no. 9 (March 1, 1993), p. 25.

Walker, Robyn. "Service, Education, Training Market Grows," *LAN Times*, vol. 9, no. 8 (May 11, 1992), p. 49.

Eckerson, Wayne. "People Management Skills Vital to Downsizing Effort," *Network World*, vol. 9, no. 33 (June 8, 1992), p. 33.

Network Management

Herman, James. "Distributed Network Management: Time Runs out for Mainframe-Based Systems," *Data Communications*, vol. 21, no. 9 (June 1992), p. 74.

Outsourcing

Verity, John. "They Make a Killing Minding Other People's Business," *Business Week*, (November 30, 1992), p. 96.

Therrien, Lois. "Consultant, Reengineer Thyself," *Business Week*, no. 3314 (April 12, 1993), p. 86.

Llana, Andy. "The Ups and Downs of Outsourcing," *Data Communications*, vol. 22, no. 2 (January 21, 1993), p. 69.

Regulatory Impact

Higgins, Steve. "Wireless Nets Still Facing Obstacles," *PC Week*, (March 22, 1993), p. 129.

WANS/Enterprise Networking

Johnson, Johna. "NREN: Turning the Clock Ahead on Tomorrow's Networks," *Data Communications*, vol. 21, no. 12 (September 1992), p. 43.

Sinnreich, Henry, and John Bottomley. "Any-to-Any Networking: Getting There from Here," *Data Communications*, vol. 21, no. 12 (September 1992), p.69.

Johnson, Johna. "Telecom Giant Gives Cell Relay a Big Boost," *Data Communications*, vol. 22, no. 6 (April 1993), p.43.

Herman, James, and Christopher Serjak. "ATM Switches and Hubs Lead the Way to a New Era of Switched Internetwork," *Data Communications*, vol. 22, no. 4 (March 1993), p. 68.

Layland, Robin. "Unfinished Business: A Theory of Evolution for ATM Technology," *Data Communications*, vol. 22, no. 4 (March 1993), p. 89.

Goldenberg, Barton, and Walter Sonnenfeldt. "The Sky's the Limit for Wireless WANs," *Data Communications*, vol. 22, no. 3 (February 1993), p. 101.

Langer, Mark. "The Network Graduates," *Network World*, vol. 9, no. 31 (August 3, 1992), p. 34.

Johnson, Johna. "Switched 56 Service Takes Off," *Data Communications*, vol. 22, no. 6 (April 1993), p. 93.

Johnson, Johna. "The ATM Circus Gets a Ringmaster," *Data Communications*, vol. 22, no. 5 (March 21 1993), p. 43.

Appendix A

GOLDMAN'S LAWS OF DATA COMMUNICATIONS

Law 1: You will never know all there is to know about Data Communications.

Law 2: Be honest with yourself concerning what you don't know.

Law 3: There are no Data Communications police.

Law 4: If the network doesn't make good business sense, it probably makes no sense.

Law 5: Technical details are important, technical details are important, technical details are important.

Law 6: There is no such thing as a data communications failure, only networking solutions as yet unfound.

Law 7: Beware of self-proclaimed data communications experts.

Law 8: It is more important to be able to ask data communications questions than it is to be able to supply data communications answers.

Law 9: If you're not moving forward, then you're losing ground to someone who is.

Appendix B

TOP 10 REASONS TO BE IN DATA COMMUNICATIONS

10. It's a great way to meet Star Trek fans.
9. You get to meet other interesting networking type people.
8. You get to carry a beeper, walkie-talkie, cellular phone, mobile fax, and a bunch of other really cool gadgets.
7. You always have an excuse to miss important family events due to "networking emergencies."
6. You get to work long hours doing interesting things for sorta-OK money. (Sorta-OK means you don't get rich!)
5. You get interesting calls in the middle of the night.
4. You get to work on weekends and holidays so you don't interfere with *normal* working people.
3. You can speak entire sentences in acronyms and not use a single English word.
2. Bloodshot eyes from late-night troubleshooting are so attractive.
1. Having a predictable workday is no fun at all!

Index